I0762949

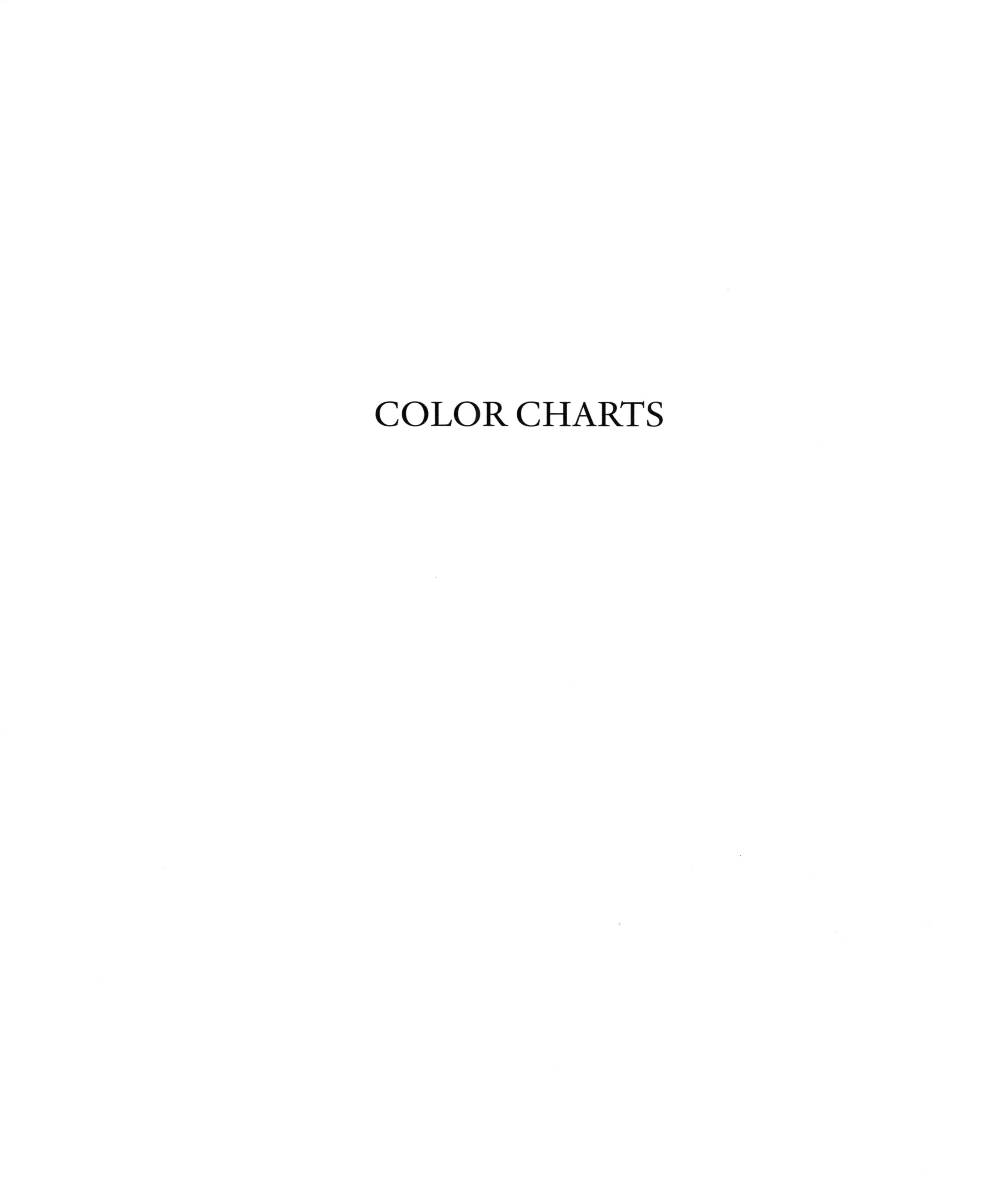

COLOR CHARTS

ANNE VARICHON

TRANSLATED BY KATE DEIMLING

COLOR CHARTS

— A HISTORY —

PRINCETON UNIVERSITY PRESS
PRINCETON AND OXFORD

First published in the French language by Editions du Seuil, Paris, under the title: *Nuanciers* by Anne Varichon

Published by Princeton University Press, 41 William Street, Princeton, New Jersey 08540
In the United Kingdom: Princeton University Press, 99 Banbury Road, Oxford OX2 6JX

press.princeton.edu

Cover design by Katie Osborne
Cover art: *Inks for Printing*, Gebr. Jänecke & Fr. Schneemann, Hanover, Germany, late 1880s, paper, approximately 20 × 26 cm, Bibliothèque Forney, Paris, call number RES ICO 8104

Photographs by Philippe Durand Gerzaguet, except pages 12–26, 33, 36–37, 40, 45, 57, 70, 85, 107 (left), 191, 209, 230 (top), 231, 240 (top), 254, and 256–267.

ISBN 9780691255170
ISBN (ebook) 9780691255187

Library of Congress Control Number: 2023943772

British Library Cataloging-in-Publication Data is available

This book has been composed in JJanon and Plain

Printed on acid-free paper. ∞

Printed in Spain

3 5 7 9 10 8 6 4 2

To Viaggio, to Armand,
For your sharp sense of humor,
your freedom of thought,
your courage,
your radiant humanity.

INTRODUCTION

Together we will explore some of the trails of culture, the trains of thought, the footpaths of feeling. . . . Feeling is everything. Without feelings motivating a thought, it risks being abstract and the knowledge it imparts will not affect one's whole being. . . . We may also see what is happening elsewhere, meet other cultures and, who knows, discover unsuspected echoes there.

Kenneth White, *L'Atelier du Héron*, 1994, p. 67

For centuries, people have preserved documents containing color samples, creating a treasure trove for future generations of researchers. This book is a tribute to them, and to those who, by studying and publishing color charts, began to trace the rich past of these documents.

The history of what we today call "color charts" is a field that is still being discovered. In this book, I offer almost two hundred examples, the majority of which are previously unpublished, in the hopes of contributing to our understanding of this area of study. Ranging from modest to splendid, these charts illustrate the evolution of color sampling from the fifteenth century to the present day.

This book is a sample of an extensive corpus, over several thousand charts in total, that I was able to examine due to the trust of both private collectors and public institutions. This corpus is very diverse, including a watercolor teaching manual from the seventeenth century, a nineteenth-century exercise book with notes written by an apprentice dyer, flyers distributed by department stores in the 1870s, thick volumes published by the chemical industry in the 1920s, color scales for determining the ripeness of an apricot, and leaflets to help choose the right color for a tractor or blush for the cheeks.

Each of these charts embodies a small piece of the larger story. But to be understood, each must be placed in its original context, asking when, where, and why it was produced, who produced it, and for whom. It was necessary to establish timelines and chronology, identify long-lost materials, research the traces of forgotten skills, and sketch a picture of the women and men who once worked with these materials.

This archaeological and anthropological research became something of a balancing act. I had to find links between the few archives that have come down to us across the ages and the profusion of charts that emerged starting in the early twentieth century. It was also necessary to find the right balance between the desire to include as many details as possible to help future researchers and the impulse to produce a book that would be accessible to all.

I would have loved to reveal all these splendid examples in their immense variety! But there came a point when I had to make choices. After selecting the best examples for outlining the rich history of the color chart, I chose to emphasize a few categories (such as garment manufacture and artists' supplies) to be able to convey the genre's evolution and variety more accurately. I then identified within these categories the chart that would best provide the key information and, finally, its most relevant page or plate.

This book is rather like a color chart of color charts.

The term "color chart" did not appear in France until the 1930s and corresponds to a specific color presentation tool. Its logic and design came about over centuries, coexisted with other color sampling methods, and only really became established in the late nineteenth century. The topics covered here go far beyond the current generic term "color chart" to include referencing systems, sample collections, formula and laboratory notebooks, and teaching manuals.

This book is written for all those with a passion for color, so that everyone can explore the multiplicity, ingenuity, poetry, and beauty of the methods that were developed over centuries in very diverse contexts to present color selections and to communicate their chromatic richness with accuracy. It has been designed for all those who wish to discover the world of color charts. Readers can browse at will: each chart is accompanied by a short text highlighting its characteristics and placing it in the broader context of a particular category of use, which is situated within its historical period. Readers can also dive in deeply: notes at the end of the book provide additional information and indicate the sources used.

This book also aims to highlight how color tools have functioned as active interfaces between scholars, artists, artisans, industrialists, merchants, and society. They brought about key changes in the way color is conceptualized, which we have inherited today. This research also reveals that from its beginnings color sampling has held a powerful fascination that transcended functionality. Color charts have long provided fertile ground for the imagination, and in recent decades they have even abandoned the very functions that inspired their existence, as they have increasingly become images themselves.

Perhaps this is ultimately their most lasting influence.

der verf konst 35

GRASPING COLOR

FIFTEENTH TO SEVENTEENTH CENTURIES

From the fifteenth through the seventeenth centuries, European civilization underwent radical transformations of all kinds—political, economic, social, scientific, and philosophical. These had significant effects on the approach to color. Several documents illustrate the fertile ground in which the history of color sampling took root.

AN AGE-OLD INTEREST IN COLOR

I pray you, My Lord, that the red be as red as possible; likewise the white and the yellow must be exquisite. . . . The siglaton dress[1] *is of the greatest beauty, but it is not exactly what I wanted, because it is white and blue, whereas I would have wanted . . . an onion color, an open color. The lead-colored dress is superb, it is the most beautiful of all.*

Letter ordering fabrics,
Cairo, early twelfth century

These words published by Dominique Cardon and taken from a document in the genizah (an archive of sacred documents) in the Ben Ezra Synagogue in Cairo indicate that people have been interested in color throughout human history.[2]

While many physical traces of colors have deteriorated or been lost over the centuries, numerous texts evoke this sensitivity to shades and the pleasure the subtlety of their harmony or the power of their contrast provides. For instance, in fourteenth-century Europe, documents list the colors of woolen fabrics using the following terms: blood, vermilion, crimson, peony, columbine, peach blossom, or heather reds; clove or gladiolus purples; yellows associated with marigold, saffron, and lion fur; cheerful or meadow greens; heavenly sky blue; and leaden or donkey-back gray.[3]

These archives demonstrate that in the world of textiles, customers expressed very precise expectations to their suppliers. But the names of such specific shades were probably understood only within the context of close interactions between a manufacturer and a buyer at a specific time, because words describing color quickly become insufficient. When we approach the subtlety of shades, color "causes the failure of language . . . , [as] no evidence can describe it with certainty."[4] Even with a great deal of practice, it is very difficult for a human being to describe and remember shades of colors.

Color is a characteristic that evades language as well as memory and can only be grasped by example. A precise approach to color, both for those producing it and those receiving it, could only be accomplished with reference tools. These tools made it possible to closely associate a term such as *mulberry* with a dyed fabric. This was especially important as the names given to shades were connected to specific practices (painters did not use the same terms as dyers), which were linked to local terminology and could come in and out of fashion.

THE SAMPLE, A TINY WORLD

——— The primary reference tool was the color sample.[5] It was used in the textile trade beginning in the fourteenth century and probably earlier.[6] It is also likely that selections of pigments were circulating among artists.[7] These samples offered the opportunity of accurately identifying such an elusive element as color, and their benefits were perceived very early on. The philosopher Nelson Goodman, however, pointed out their limits: "A sample is a sample of—or exemplifies—only some of its properties; and the properties with which it has this relationship of exemplification vary according to the circumstances."[8] For Goodman, the very act of sampling alters the information that is communicated. Although the sample's reduced dimensions are part of its appeal, they also mean that it cannot replicate the drape of a fabric or the effect of a larger pattern. Its format can also generate a distortion of perception: the color often appears less light and more vivid.

Yet, over the centuries, the sample has remained the most relevant tool for remembering or communicating color. Doctors, artists, dyers, and naturalists included fragments or swatches (product samples) or attempted to replicate as accurately as possible the color of a substance that they could not preserve (reproduction samples).

The need to identify color more precisely than allowed by standard terms such as *white*, *black*, *purple*, *pink*, and such, while conveying its physical and material existence as much as possible, was at the center of a wide range of endeavors and gave rise to a variety of tools, including the color chart.[9]

OPPOSITE

The *Rotae Urinarum*: Identifying Shades of Urine

The quality of fluids excreted from the body after circulating within it has been a factor in treating disease since ancient times, as these fluids have been perceived as conveying valuable information about the patient's health.[10] This is especially true of urine. Beginning in the thirteenth century, some medical manuscripts presented a circular classification called the *rota urinarum*, showing the range of colors urine can present, so that they could be identified by name and used to determine a diagnosis.[11] A physical sample of urine would not be functional, as its color would quickly change or fade. Something perishable therefore had to be made permanent, which could be done by reproducing the characteristics of the sample on paper using a longer-lasting medium such as ink or paint. Johannes de Cuba, a doctor practicing in Frankfurt in the second half of the fifteenth century, made use of this technique in his essay on herbalism, "The Garden of Health." Before the eighteenth century, shades of color were often illustrated, as in this example, by a series of *matulae*, spherical containers of clear glass.[12] While their number varied, they were always classified in a logical order based on Hippocrates's theory of humors, which associated color tones with the four temperaments: red for sanguine, white for phlegmatic, black for melancholic, and yellow for choleric. Since these reference documents were intended for teaching, the subtle differences in color were accentuated to make them easier to distinguish and commit to memory.

The *rotae urinarum* are some of the few surviving signs of how medieval Europeans relied on the accuracy of the sample in order to identify subtle shades of color and to learn to distinguish them from one another. They are also a very early example of how samples were arranged and presented. Finally, they reveal that the color of a sample was imitated by artistic means as early as the thirteenth century, a transformation that would be very significant in the history of color sampling.

Urine wheel, *Hortus sanitatis* (*The Health Garden*), Johannes de Cuba, Germany, fifteenth century, Bibliothèque Nationale, Paris, MS lat. 11229, folio 19v

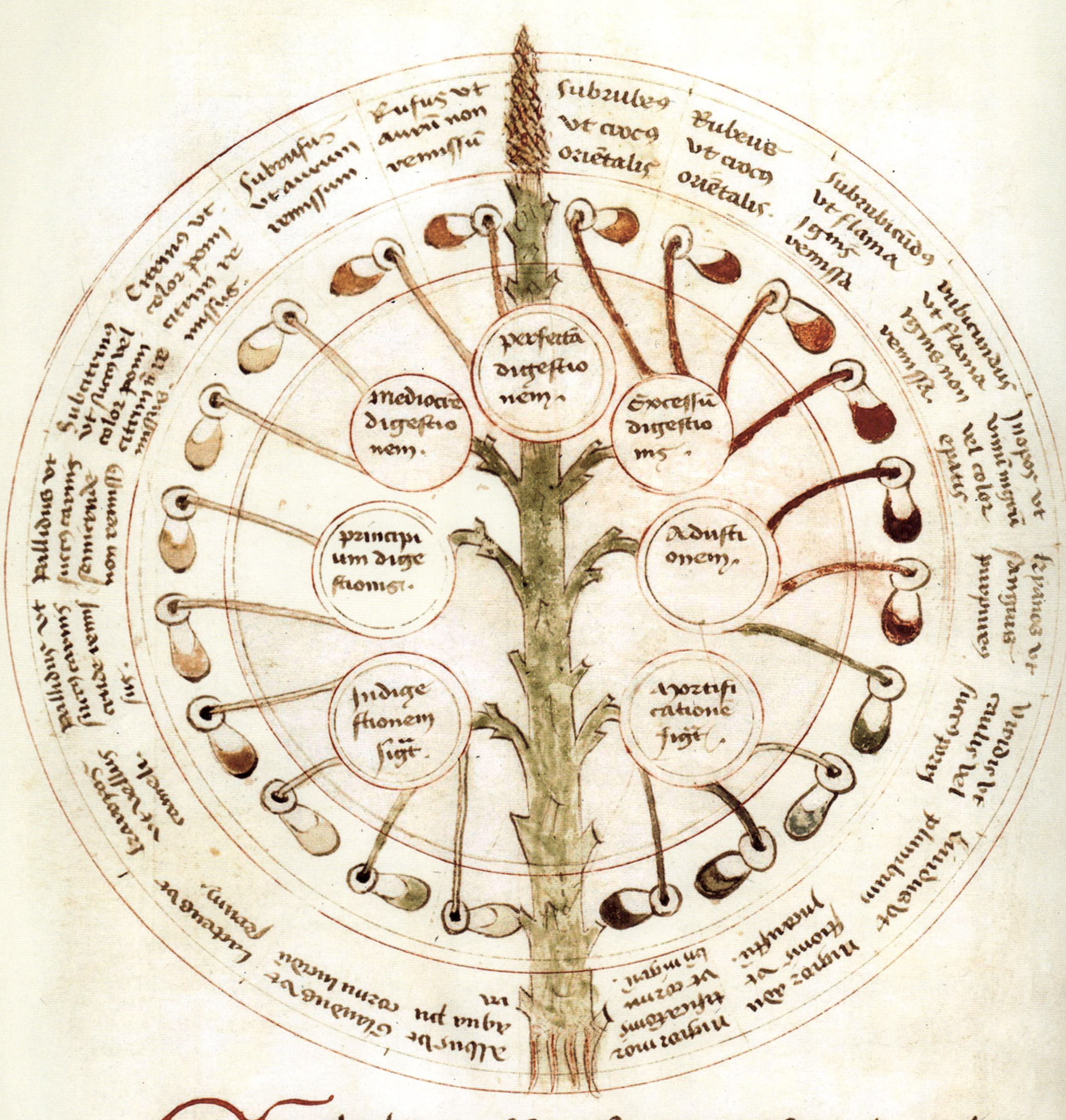

Ex coloribus urine sunt quedam citrinitatis sicut subalbaris citrinus
postea flavus deinde rufus postea citrangularis postea igneus qui tin
cture crocee assimulatur. Et ipse quidem est vehementer citrinus quia
croceus assimilatur capillis safiram. Et iste est quem vocant

IN THE SEVENTEENTH CENTURY, A GROWING RANGE OF TOOLS

In this era, science began to be organized as a discipline based on experimentation, measurement, and the publication of results. As naturalists studied the world, color also became a subject of research and was better understood.[13] In this new order of things, color became one of the most immediately accessible parameters for distinguishing or bringing together elements in a set and communicating these differences or similarities.[14] The need to consider color according to increasingly precise observation protocols required developing accurate and suitable techniques for its representation. This would be the naturalists' great endeavor.

Science also became increasingly focused on the application of its discoveries, and the materials with which colors were produced benefited from this. New pigments and dyes were developed, drawing on the fabulous natural resources imported from the New World. These products supplied the workshops and then the factories, which took off during the second half of the seventeenth century, responding to a high demand for colorful products brought about by the improvement of living standards in European countries.

Demonstrating or Teaching Artistic Practices

The Renaissance saw profound changes in artistic techniques, and watercolor and oil painting became a pastime for the wealthy. In the seventeenth century, artists still had to make their own colors by combining crushed pigments with a binding agent. Practical manuals for teaching artistic techniques to amateur artists had proliferated since the sixteenth century.[15] They sometimes listed the names of pigments and explained how to recognize imitations. Indeed, these products, which were expensive whether imported (lapis lazuli blue) or manufactured (vermilion red made with sulfur and mercury, orpiment yellow from sulfur and arsenic), were sometimes replaced by others offering similar colors of lower quality.

Among these collections of artistic practices, two stand out in particular because their authors included color samples as early as the seventeenth century.

OPPOSITE

Experimenting with the Manufacture of Color Inks

Théodore de Mayerne was a French Protestant doctor with a curious mind who was passionate about alchemy and wrote a variety of books ranging from travel guides to treatises on medicine or cooking.[16] He recorded various practices, especially related to artistic techniques, which he found in written works and through his contacts with a vast network of informants all across Europe. His notes were later gathered in an eclectic collection, *Pictoria, Sculptoria et quae Subalternarum Artium*.

This manuscript contains 170 folios, and four of them, dated 1634, concern colored inks made by mixing pigments, water, and various binding agents.[17] The information was collected from those who used these inks, including not only artists but also printers, leather curriers, botanists, and even cooks. The author transmitted this knowledge using a true sampling approach. He recorded the list of pigments in both Latin and a Flemish-German dialect, organized his remarks according to the different binding agents (such as egg white, egg yolk, or bile) or additives (such as wine vinegar or honey), and tested the formulas. For instance, he recommended "egg white for lead white, lime, cinnabar and all light colors." Most importantly, he accompanied his remarks with circular-shaped samples made with the ink described (292 in all). He also sorted them by shade. Readers could thus easily perceive within the same color the different shades that could be made depending on the process used.

By establishing a direct relationship between the materials, the formula, and the color they produced, Théodore de Mayerne took a prescientific approach that was resolutely rational and empirical. But his goal was also to enable precise

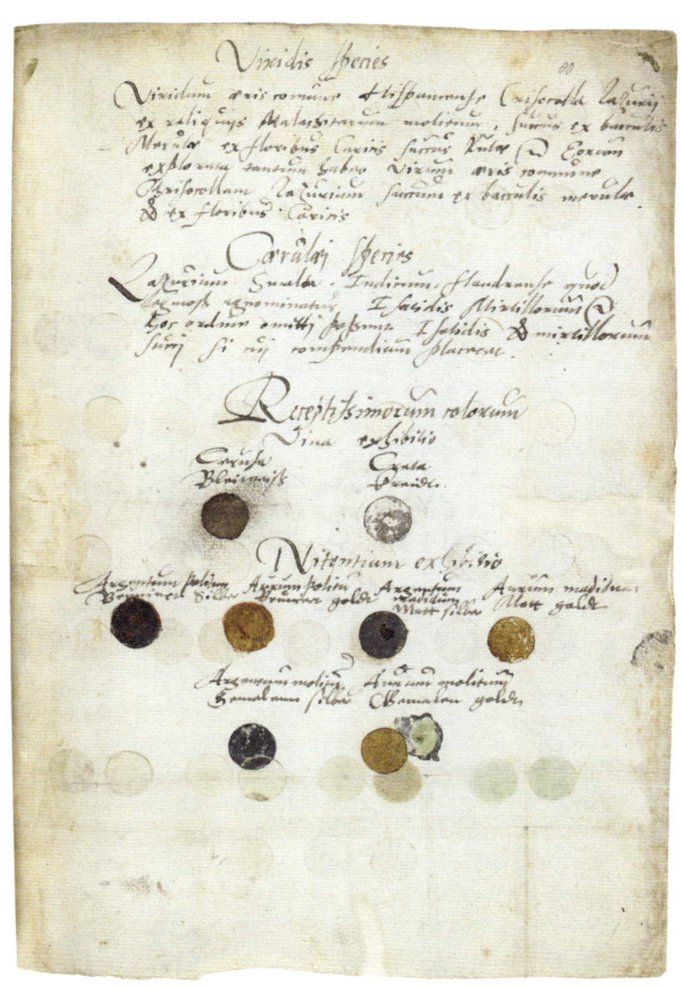
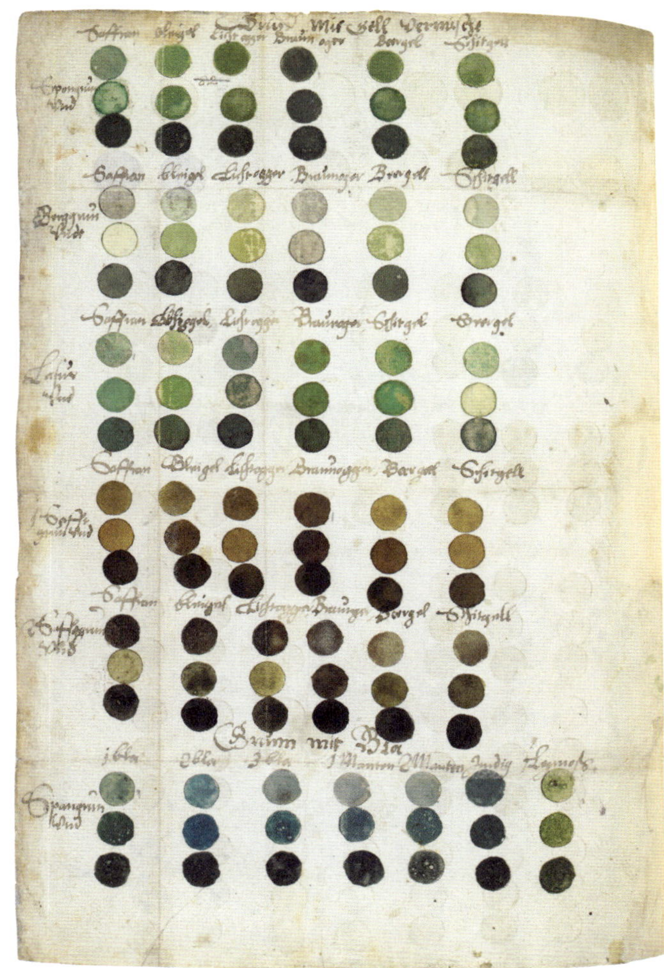
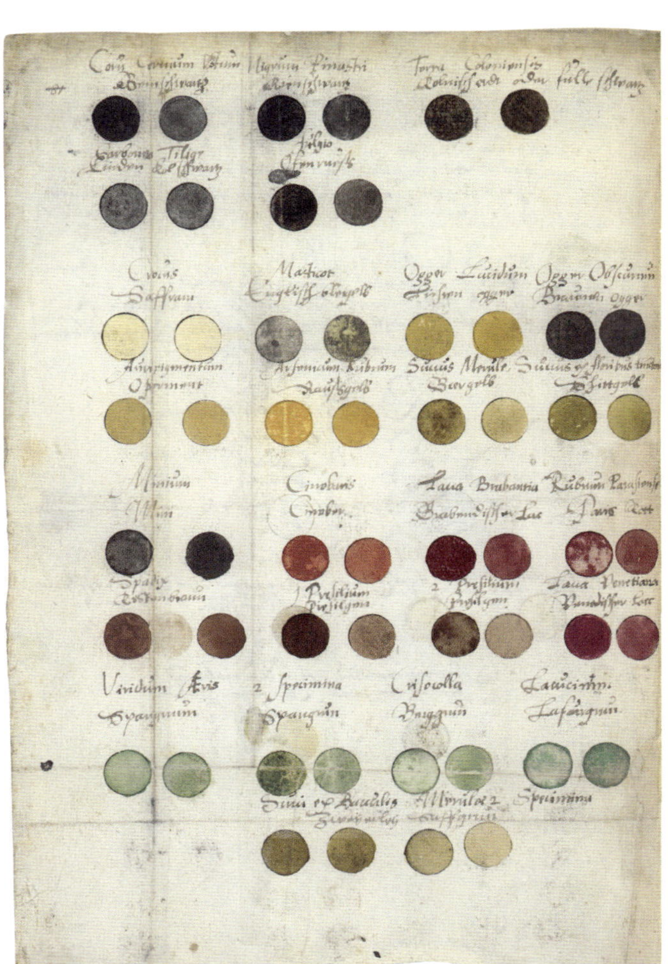
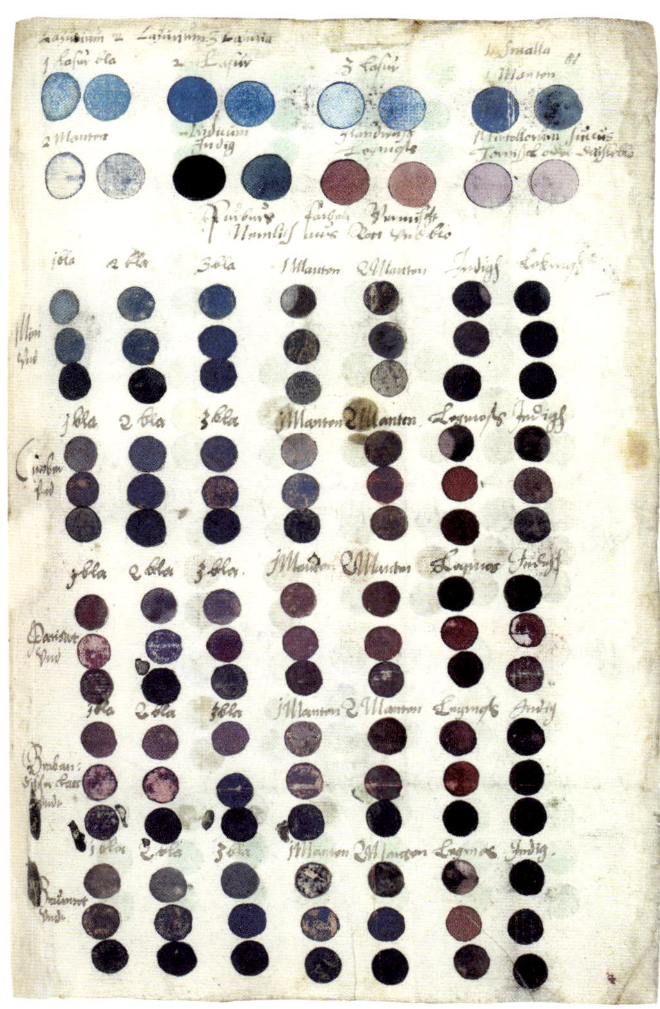

communication with the many artists of his circle, including the Flemish painter Van Dyck. Without samples, conveying such information would have been almost impossible, and Mayerne understood this very early on.

Pictoria, Sculptoria et quae Subalternarum Artium (Painting, sculpture, and minor arts), Théodore de Mayerne, 1620–1640, British Library, London, Sloane MS 2052, folios 80r to 81v

OPPOSITE AND FOLLOWING PAGE SPREAD

An Enchanting Treatise on Watercolor

Rectangle, square, line: the garden is at the center of a geometry in which the greens frequent each other, complement each other, play with all the degrees of mixture between yellow and blue, in plates fringed with the blue glow of the lark's feet, the limited heliotropism of the white daisies, the pink-flowered odorless verbena, or this thin, flowering saxifrage that we call "the painter's despair" because its color is so fine and vivid.

Marie Rouanet, *Every Garden is Eden*, 2010

This manuscript by the Dutch painter A. Boogert opens with a discussion of the use of color in painting and the manufacture of watercolor paints. Whereas this information was common in artist manuals of the time, the rest of this almost eight-hundred-page book is exceptional because it is entirely devoted to formulas explaining how to obtain specific shades, all of which are illustrated with color samples.

The book is made up of three main parts.[18] The first contains approximately forty folios of watercolors made with a single pigment, often illustrated in three different concentrations in gum arabic. The second part concerns the shades obtained by mixing these pigments with black and white. This perfectly accomplished structure is already complex, but Boogert creates an even more elaborate branching structure: in the third part, he presents five shades from a mixture of two pigments, obtained by varying the percentage of each color. And the grand finale is an index of thirty-three tables, each with two columns and six rows next to a corresponding shade (388 in all). Each is identified by a number, making it possible to refer to the page in the first or second part of the manuscript where the pigment or combination of pigments is presented.

Boogert thus classified, named, and described nearly seven hundred pigments or mixtures of pigments. The structure of the book was perfect. Readers could leaf through the index to identify the desired shade and then refer to the technical instructions explaining how to make it, while taking note of the pigment's origin and the names used to describe it. However, there was at that time no technique that could accurately reproduce the approximately 2,100 watercolor samples that constituted the exceptional value of this work.[19] Even if the text had been printed, its publication would have required the painstaking task of applying colors with a brush to preserve the subtlety of water-based painting techniques.

Not only does this color chart have a particularly elaborate and complex structure for the late seventeenth century, but it also reveals an impressively designed layout. The architecture of each page evokes the gardens of medieval monasteries that were subdivided into square or rectangular plots.[20] In this simple design, separate garden beds (preventing any mixing of plant varieties) are framed by paths for tending to the plants. In the color chart, it is no longer the gardener's body that moves around, but the eye, passing from one sample to the next, each contained in its frame as if in a flower bed. But these gardens are also places of contemplation and meditation. They evoke both the lost paradise of Eden and the heavenly reward promised to the blessed. Boogert's manuscript possesses an aesthetic power and an ability to appeal to the imagination that would continue in later color charts, which would adopt this orderly arrangement interspersing areas that stimulate the eye with others that are left empty, so that the eye may rest.

We know virtually nothing about this manuscript and its author or about the examples that might have inspired his approach. It remains a unique phenomenon in the history of color sampling.

Treatise on Colors Used for Water-Based Paint, A. Boogert, Delft, Holland, 1692, Bibliothèque Méjanes, Aix-en-Provence, Ms 1389 (1228), folios 35, 264, 378, 387, 399

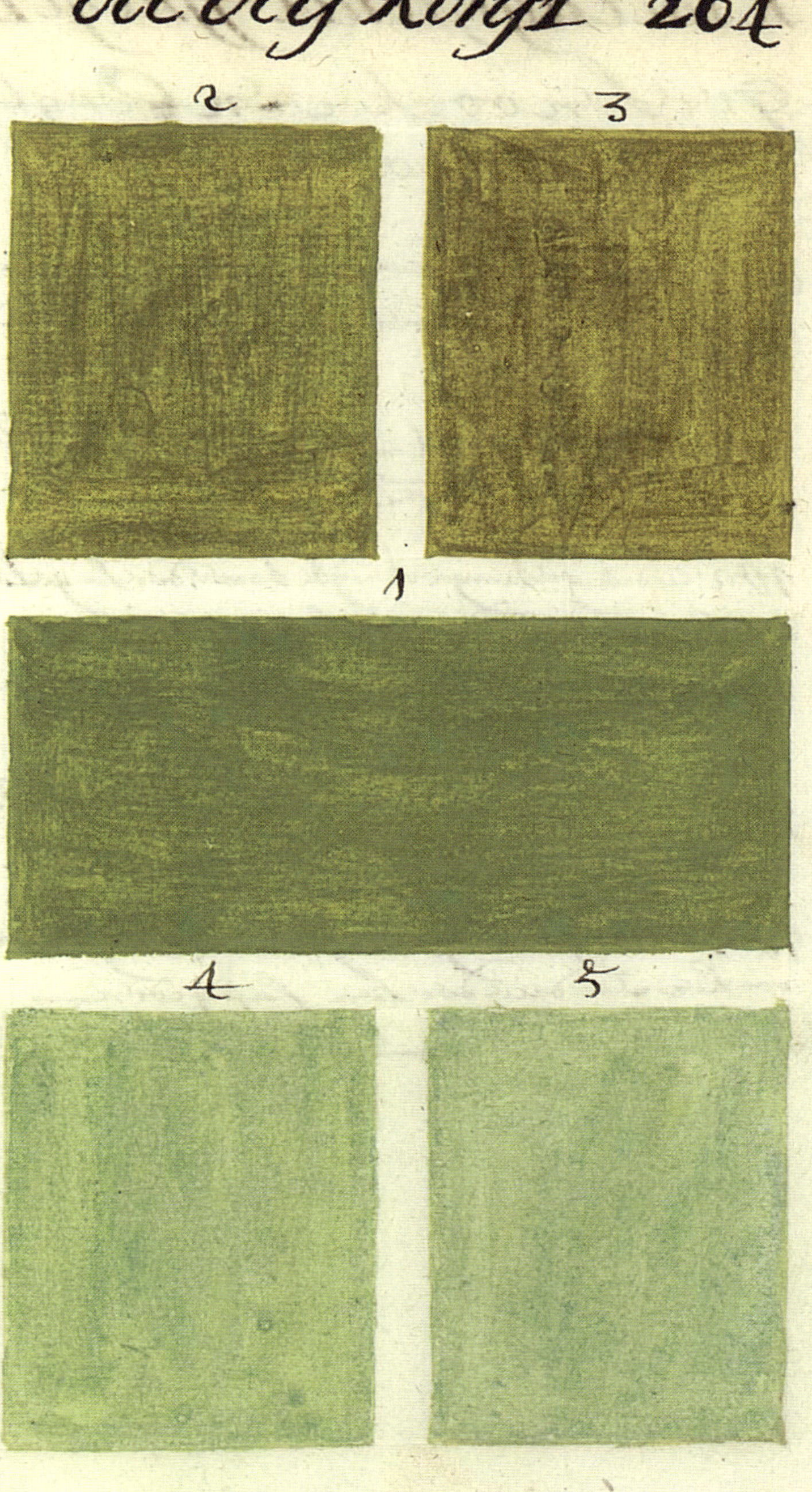
der verf konst 261
2
3
1
4
5

Register.

w1: Bij fol: 118:

w1: Bij fol: 119:

w1: Bij fol: 120:

w1: Bij fol: 121:

w1: Bij fol: 122:

w1: Bij fol: 123:

w1: Bij fol: 124:

w1: Bij fol: 125:

w1: Bij fol: 126:

vande kleuren
die door asschen
woorden getem
pert

w1: Bij fol: 127:

w1: Bij fol: 128:

Reg

w1: Bij fol: 221:

w1: Bij fol: 222:

w1: Bij fol: 223:

w1: Bij fol: 224:

w1: Bij fol: 225:

w1: Bij fol: 226:

...ster.

N1: Bij fol: 227

N1: Bij fol: 228

N1: Bij fol: 229

N1: Bij fol: 230

N1: Bij fol: 231

N1: Bij fol: 232

Register.

N1: Bij fol: 353:

N1: Bij fol: 354

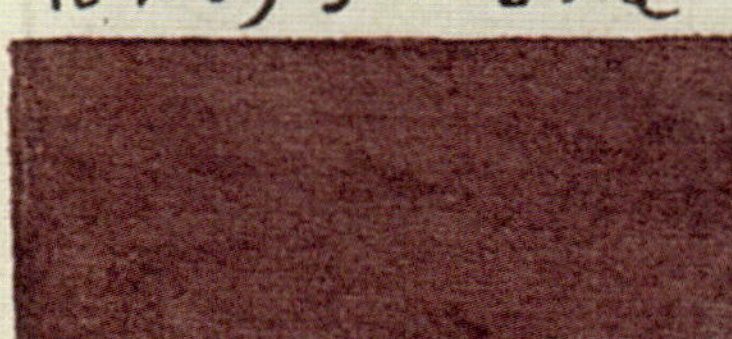

N1: Bij fol: 355:

N1: Bij fol: 356

N1: Bij fol: 357

Vande kleuren die door bedsijtje verf worden getempert

N1: Bij fol: 358:

N1: Bij fol: 359

N1: Bij fol: 360

Vande kleuren die door bedsijtje verf met potas worde getempert

N1: Bij fol: 361:

N1: Bij fol: 362:

Tabula Colorum Physiologica tam Mixtorum quam Simplicium, Quadrilinguis unà cum Speciminibus adjectis Regiæ Societati Londinensi humillime D.D.D. a Ric. Waller S.R.S.

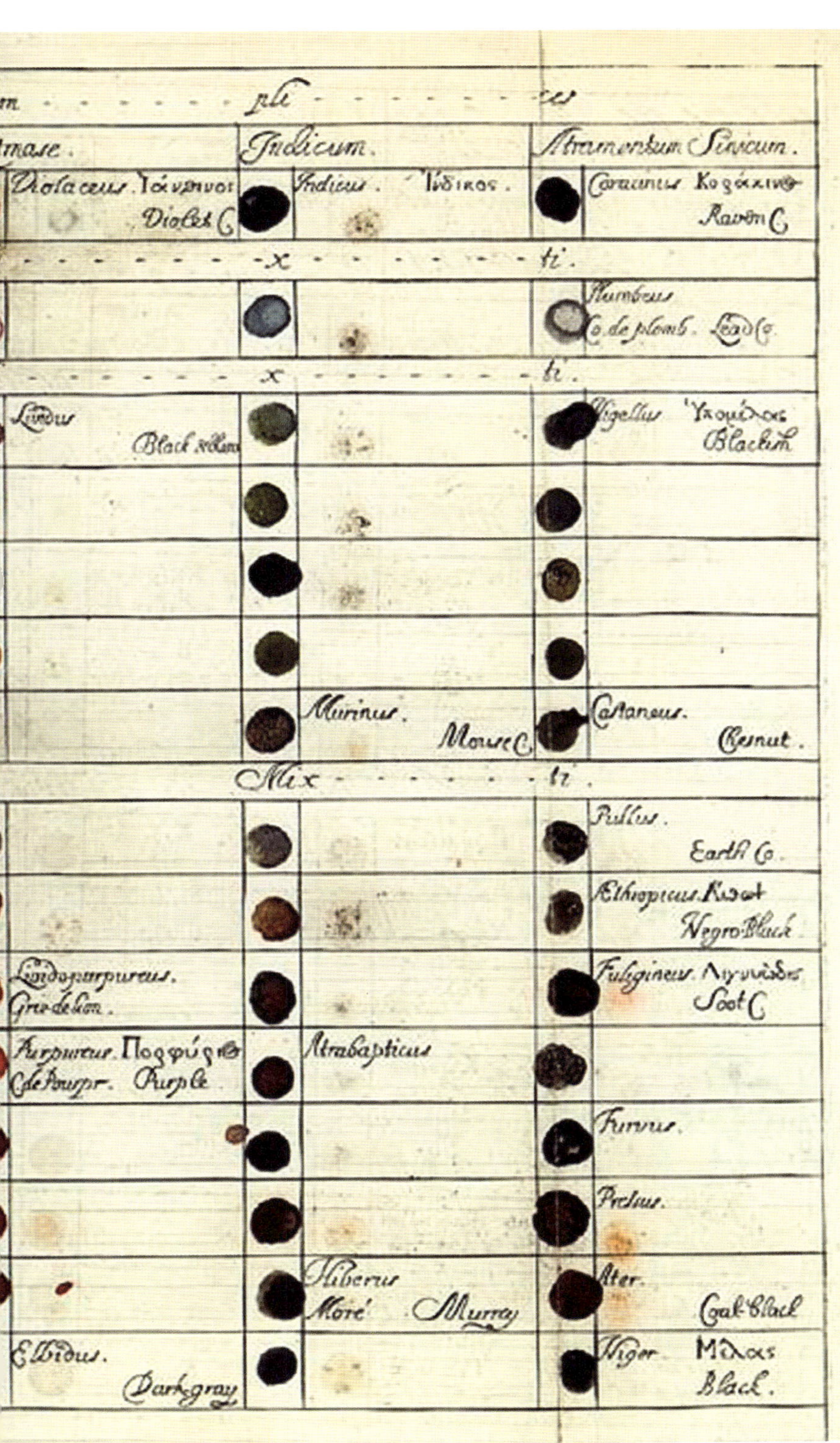

Naturalists Use Samples to Describe the World

The supremacy of appearance is a fact of daily life from which neither the laboratory technician nor the philosopher can shirk, which he must constantly find at the end of his experiments or his studies and which proves its strength by never being modified or influenced by what they have discovered by turning away from it.

Hannah Arendt, *The Life of the Mind*, 1981

———— At the end of the seventeenth century, naturalists worked to develop color references so that their taxonomic descriptions would match reality as closely as possible,[21] for observations that ranged from algae to feathers. These reference charts played a decisive role in mastering the subtlest shades of color, because they were simultaneously transcription techniques, methodological tables, and standards for an observational method whose conditions were constantly being refined in a struggle to eliminate persistent flaws.

OPPOSITE

Waller *Tabula Colorum Physiologica*

In the introduction to his *Tabula Colorum Physiologica*, English naturalist Richard Waller clearly stated his ambitions: readers should be able to use this work to describe living things, whether plants or animals, and to communicate this exact information to other readers provided with the same table, regardless of their language. For example, a naturalist could describe a bird with *Carmine* wings and a *Negrus* throat to a correspondent. This was an attempt to solve the problem posed by the ambiguity of terms used for colors by providing color samples. The field of exploration was vast and the objects to be described were perishable. Waller could not include petals, fur, or skins in his table. He therefore reproduced their colors, with each shade being painted on the paper. The aim of his *Tabula Colorum* was thus very different from that of Boogert's contemporaneous manuscript. It was more related to the *rotae urinarum* that had been in circulation since the thirteenth century.

Starting with a row of seven colors and a column of fourteen, Waller organized a table by color groups, moving from the lightest shades to the darkest. The origin of each was presented with varying degrees of accuracy. For instance, the naturalist associated the sample *Ultramarine* with lapis lazuli, but was unsure of the one named *Litmase* or *Litmose* ("I suppose the juice of a plant") and described indigo as "foam collected at the foot of reeds." By using single pigments or mixtures, Waller managed to present 119 shades and named them when possible in Latin, Greek, French, and English.

This grid arrangement for presenting color samples was quite advanced for its time and perfectly functional in more ways than one. It established a clear structure so that users could easily find their bearings, making the best use of the available space while leaving a margin around each sample. This prevented them from mixing during the application of the paint. When the tool was used, this also ensured that the samples were far enough apart so as not to be confused, while being close enough for comparison. The conditions for identifying a color were therefore optimal.

The layout of the table, which can be read vertically as well as horizontally, from right to left and from left to right, merits further examination. It seems to correspond to the way in which numbers are arranged, especially measurements. The structure of the *Tabula Colorum* makes a statement that color can be controlled, quantified, and measured.

But reading along the vertical axis also resembles what Umberto Eco calls in *The Infinity of Lists* a "list *et cætera*." Eco states that this type of list is used when "we do not know the limits of the things that we wish to represent, when we do not know how many there are and we presuppose a number that is, if not infinite, at least astronomically large, when we cannot give something a definition by essence and that, to make it understandable, more or less perceptible, we list its properties."[22]

Hence this chart may reveal the new ambition of cataloging the world, at a time when this goal was still in its infancy and everything was still to be discovered. The context of the *Tabula Colorum* may thus separate a relatively controlled internal world from an unlimited external world, that of colors and their combinations, which resembled the universe itself, both of them immensely appealing, yet overwhelming.

However, this first step toward arranging color samples to satisfy the imperatives of scientific description does not seem to have had the impact it deserved, and it was not until one hundred years later that another naturalist, Abraham Gottlob Werner, attempted this endeavor. But the potential power of the color chart was already present in the *Tabula Colorum*. ●

Tabula Colorum Physiologica, in "A Catalogue of Simple and Mixt Colours with a Sample of Each Colour Prefixt Its Properties," Richard Waller, *Philosophical Transactions of the Royal Society of London*, 1666, vol. 6 for the years 1686 and 1687, Smithsonian Libraries and Archives, Washington DC

Vert de chou

AN IDEAL SYSTEM

EIGHTEENTH CENTURY TO MID-NINETEENTH CENTURY

Enlightenment thought of eighteenth-century Europe led to fundamental advances in the understanding of the phenomenon of color, especially because of Newton's contributions.[1] It also established color as an essential subject in areas including science, philosophy, technology, materials, customs, and commerce. According to Sarah Lowengard's groundbreaking research on the creation of color in eighteenth-century Europe, hypotheses and experiments on color and the innovations that it inspired permeated all levels of society, in the shared hope for a more educated, more just, and more affluent civilization.[2]

The Scientific Revolution finally gave painters, ceramicists, and dyers the means to tame the wild beast of color. From the eighteenth century through the first half of the nineteenth century, pigments and dyes were generally obtained in nature. Color was unpredictable, like everything else—from the quality of the rock, plant, or animal used to make the pigment or dye to the conditions in which they were collected, transported, and preserved. Only through the craftsman's expertise could color be expressed consistently.

The economic development of which color was a part benefited merchants, the leading representatives of the rising bourgeoisie. They would soon bring about an industrial society that would be even more avid for colors. Under pressure to produce large quantities quickly, to ensure reproducibility, and to control processes and costs, several different industries attempted to standardize their practices.

In this context, the approach to color sampling was connected to a range of interrelated issues. It played a role in the quest for knowledge and was also part of improvements in production methods. Color thus contributed both to the growth of trade and to developments in aesthetics.

THE DYERS' DRIVE TO INNOVATE

Mastering color was a difficult art for all those who produced and used it, but dyeing a fabric was like balancing a multibranched mobile in a strong wind. Achieving beautiful, deep, long-lasting color was a feat reserved for only the most talented and experienced dyers.

Textiles were at the heart of the Western economy in the eighteenth century, and fortunes were at stake. The regulations and controls put in place by Colbert in the second half of the seventeenth century stimulated the textile industry in France, and the quality of its dyes was soon renowned throughout Europe and beyond.[3] The expertise and aesthetic sense of the dyers would encourage explorations in empirical chemistry, which in turn would soon give rise to scientific chemistry. There was a proliferation of documents recording the most effective processes, and some authors, in Germany, England, and as far away as Japan,[4] began to attach samples to their writings.[5]

The sample performed multiple functions: in workshops and factories, it revealed the progress of the dyeing or printing process, was a visual indicator for experiments, served to record methods, and contributed to sharing and transmitting skills. It helped traveling sales representatives make sales;[6] for merchants, it confirmed that the finished product corresponded to what had been ordered and provided a record of transactions.

Already, collectors were beginning to show interest in textile samples, which is fortunate, as almost all the notebooks and records of the dyers were destroyed when their companies ceased operations.[7] Indeed, historians have only recently begun to pay attention to technical and commercial archives; in the past, due to their small size, textile samples may have been discarded when the context that gave them meaning was no longer understood.

Therefore, very few dyers' notebooks have survived for us to examine. Those still existing can, however, provide us with a great deal of valuable information: the plants and animals used for dyeing, their origin, the quantities required, the necessary additives, the nature of the processes for turning woven fabric into dyed fabric, including their various stages, the intended recipients, the sales networks, control and customs procedures, and even the names given to the shades. These notebooks hold the memory of toils and tastes.

OPPOSITE

A Languedoc Dyer's Notebook

As of the late seventeenth century, the Languedoc cloth factories met the needs of a wealthy clientele from the Levant (Turkey, Syria, Egypt). They were responsive to changing fashions and provided the high quality required, both in terms of the brightness and the variety of colors. In the highly competitive context of the textile trade, they were able to maintain the loyalty of this clientele.

Dominique Cardon discovered the life and work of one of their master dyers, Antoine Janot (1700–1778), who worked from 1719 to 1778 in Saint-Chinian, which at that time was an important center for the production of woolen cloth mainly intended for this Middle Eastern market.[8] He played a significant role in the development of this center during half a century by dyeing colossal quantities of cloth in some of the subtlest and deepest shades imaginable due to his particularly astute mastery of the precious dyeing resources.

Antoine Janot wrote three essays between 1744 and 1747, all featuring a large number of organized and annotated samples.[9] The context in which the dyer came to write them is fascinating in and of itself. In 1741, a new inspector of factories was appointed. He turned out to be dishonest and accused Janot of using substances for dyeing that the regulatory bodies did not authorize. Almost three hundred years later, Dominique Cardon would demonstrate that the accusation was unfounded, but it led to the humiliation and ruin of Antoine Janot, who attempted to defend himself and prove his expertise. He wrote down the ingredients and processes used to achieve a large number of colors and attached cloth swatches in the margins (sixty-five of them in the first essay alone). This early group of samples thus came about due to unusual circumstances in which skill alone was no longer sufficient.

The first folios are part of a section of the notebook titled "Colors that the vat produces when it is at work." This is a nice way of expressing it, which does justice to the living environment inside a dye vat of pastel and indigo.[10]

Folios 8v and 9r concern formulas for obtaining reds, so-called fiery colors prized by the elites in the port cities of the Levant. All the samples featured in Antoine Janot's essays have names, such as *Parrot Green*, *Crimson*, *Musk*, *Tobacco*, *Cinnamon*, *Hazelnut*, *Autumn Leaf*, *Coffee*, *Yellow Wax*, *Cherry*, *Rose*, *Jujuba*, *Spiny Lobster*, *Orange*, *Mimosa*, and *Daffodil*.

This essay, handed over to the king's intendant for Languedoc in Montpellier, announced the following ones that Antoine Janot would write. It seems quite clear that his efforts inspired experts[11] and encouraged other dyers to use samples in their writings.[12] However, the combination of written texts and samples that makes Janot's manuscripts so valuable also prevented them from being distributed more widely. This would have required too many swatches of expensive cloth. For this reason, they sank into oblivion until Dominique Cardon rediscovered them.

Like Boogert fifty years earlier, but in a very different context, Janot developed a specific arrangement for presenting

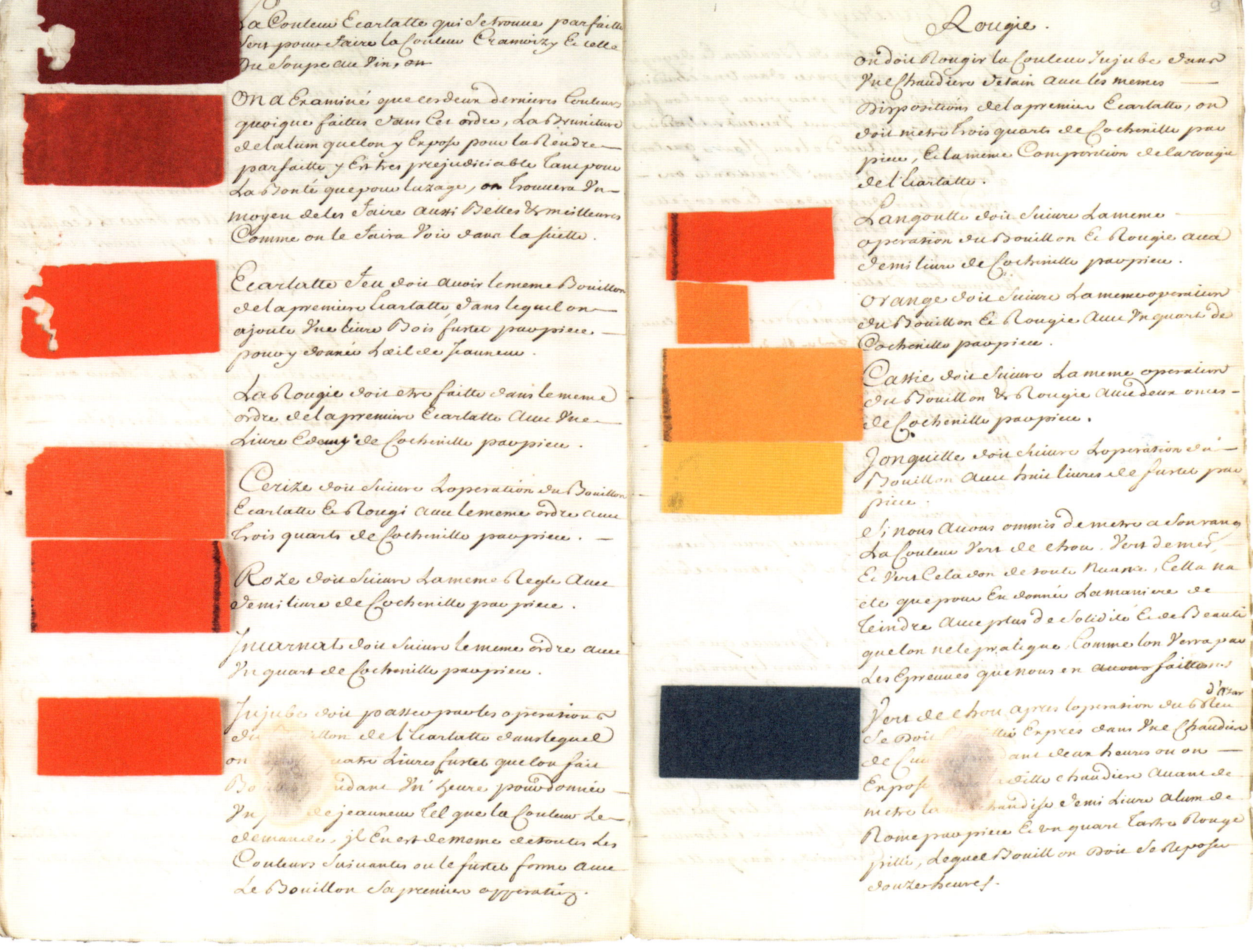

La Couleur Ecarlatte qui se trouve parfaitte sert pour faire la Couleur Cramoizy Et celle De Soupe au Vin, on

On a Examiné que ces deux dernieres Couleurs quoique faittes dans Cet ordre, La Bruniture de l'alum que l'on y Expose pour la Rendre parfaitte y Est tres prejudiciable tant pour La Bonté que pour luzage, on trouvera Un moyen de les faire aussi Belles Et meilleures Comme on le faira Voir dans la suitte.

Ecarlatte Feu doit avoir le meme Bouillon de la premiere Ecarlatte dans lequel on ajoute Une livre Bois fustet par piece, pour y donner l'œil de Jauneur.

La Rougie doit etre faitte dans le meme ordre de la premiere Ecarlatte avec Une Livre Et demy de Cochenille par piece.

Cerize doit suivre L'operation du Bouillon Ecarlatte Et Rougi avec le meme ordre avec trois quarts de Cochenille par piece.

Roze doit suivre La meme Regle avec demi livre de Cochenille par piece.

Incarnat doit suivre le meme ordre avec Un quart de Cochenille par piece.

Jujube doit passer par les operations du Bouillon de l'Ecarlatte dans lequel on … quatre Livres fustet que l'on faie Bo… dant Un heure, pour donner Un … de jauneur tel que la Couleur Le demande, il En est de meme de toutes les Couleurs suivantes ou le fustet forme avec Le Bouillon sa premiere operation.

9

Rougie.

On doit Rougir la Couleur Jujube dans Une Chaudiere detain avec les memes Dispositions de la premiere Ecarlatte, on doit mettre trois quarts de Cochenille par piece, Et la meme Composition de la Rougie de l'Ecarlatte.

Langoutte doit suivre La meme operation du Bouillon Et Rougie avec demi livre de Cochenille par piece.

Orange doit suivre La meme operation du Bouillon Et Rougie avec Un quart de Cochenille par piece.

Cattie doit suivre La meme operation du Bouillon Et Rougie avec deux onces de Cochenille par piece.

Jonquille doit suivre L'operation du Bouillon avec huit livres de fustet par piece.

Si nous avons ommis de mettre a son rang La Couleur Vert de Chou, Vert de mer, Et Vert Celadon de toute Nuance, Cella na été que pour En donner La maniere de teindre avec plus de solidité Et de Beauté que l'on ne le pratique, Comme l'on Verra par Les Epreuves que nous en avons faittes.

Vert de Chou apres l'operation du bleu … se doit … Expres dans Une Chaudiere de … pendant deux heures ou on Expose … dans ladite Chaudiere avant de mettre … demi Livre alum de Rome par piece Et un quart Tartre Rouge pillé, lequel Bouillon doit se Reposer douze heures.

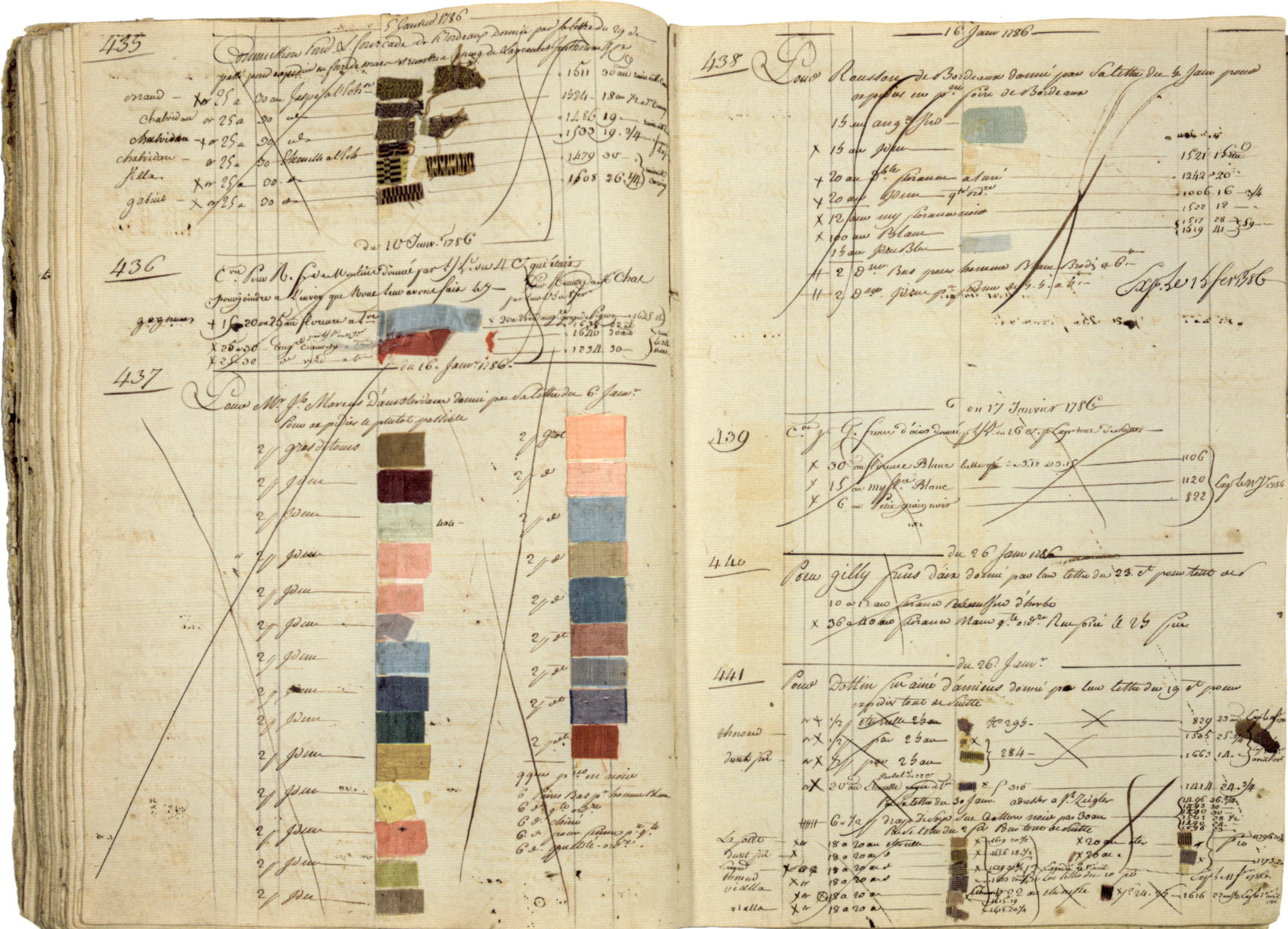

colors. This was not a completely novel idea.[13] But while Janot's essay was structured according to the substances used for dyeing, the arrangement of the colors (the samples' only distinguishing feature) served to allow them to be easily identified within a consistent visual space. Color was thus brought to the fore.

Essay—One will find the operations of dyeing in the great and good shade of the colors that are used in the Levant with the quantity and quality of the drugs that compose them, Antoine Janot, Saint-Chinian, 1744, archives of the Hérault department, call number C5569, folios 8v and 9r

OPPOSITE

The Role of the Sample in the Fabric Trade

The sample was used quite differently in sales records such as those of textile merchants in Nîmes in the late eighteenth century.[14] For three centuries, Nîmes merchants had been weaving and dyeing Cévennes silk, which they exported throughout the region, across Europe, and as far away as Latin America. The merchants—including Monsieur Bonnaud, whose register is seen here—recorded day after day the orders they fulfilled, attaching narrow strips of the fabrics that were delivered. In this case, therefore, the sample is not artfully presented. Its main function is to allow the same fabric to be reordered if necessary. The fabrics requested were generally quite varied. Here, the left page is an order for the same fabric in different colors (23?). This page is exceptional in that it forms a color chart that may have existed only in this record book.

Documents of this type preserved at the Vieux Nîmes Museum offer precise and priceless information about where the clients were located, how often they placed orders, and the type and quantity of their chosen fabrics.

Sales register, M. J. L. Bonnaud, Nîmes, October 4, 1784–April 26, 1787, record book, 41.5 × 28.5 cm, 190 pages, Musée du Vieux Nîmes, Nîmes, inv. 975.3.10, pages from January 5 to 26, 1786

THE WERNER-SYME NOMENCLATURE, A COLOR CHART FOR UNDERSTANDING THE WORLD

——— Color sampling raised the issue of how to use visual appearance for classification, and this continued to haunt the framing of theoretical writings about color from the seventeenth century onward. In the following century, the work of examining and understanding the world continued to gain momentum. Carl Linnaeus's publications encouraged scientists throughout Europe in this undertaking, especially naturalists, who sought to catalog all minerals, animals, and plants. More than ever, they needed a color referencing system that would suit the practical applications on which they were focused.

However, the first truly operational system did not come about until the beginning of the nineteenth century, almost 150 years after Waller, and it occurred in two stages. The first phase was achieved by Abraham Gottlob Werner, a mineralogist of Saxon origin. When he wrote *A Treatise on the External Characters of Fossils*, published in 1774, he based his classification of rocks and minerals on a sensory approach considering first and foremost their color and surface attributes (transparent, shiny, dull, and so on).[15] Like Waller, Werner found this aspect not only the most immediate but also the most reliable.[16]

The list that Werner proposed included eight colors divided into fifty-four shades.[17] This reduced number made it possible to attach a color chart to the document, especially since the printing of color plates was now possible. Essays explaining how to produce color catalogs were being published, and classification systems advanced the science of color and its understanding.[18] Werner was familiar with these various works but was still wary of color charts

WHITES.

No.	Names.	Colours.	ANIMAL.	VEGETABLE.	MINERAL.
1	Snow White.		Breast of the black headed Gull.	Snow-Drop.	Carara Marble and Calc Sinter.
2	Reddish White.		Egg of Grey Linnet.	Back of the Christmas Rose.	Porcelain Earth.
3	Purplish White.		Junction of the Neck and Back of the Kittiwake Gull.	White Geranium or Storks Bill.	Arragonite.
4	Yellowish White.		Egret.	Hawthorn Blossom.	Chalk and Tripoli.
5	Orange coloured White.		Breast of White or Screech Owl.	Large Wild Convolvulus.	French Porcelain Clay.
6	Greenish White.		Vent Coverts of Golden crested Wren.	Polyanthus Narcissus.	Calc Sinter.
7	Skimmed milk White.		White of the Human Eyeballs.	Back of the Petals of Blue Hepatica.	Common Opal.
8	Greyish White.		Inside Quill-feathers of the Kittiwake.	White Hamburgh Grapes.	Granular Limestone.

GREENS.

Nº	Names	Colours	Animal	Vegitable	Mineral
46	*Celandine Green.*		*Phalæna. Margaritaria.*	*Back of Tussilago Leaves.*	*Beryl.*
47	*Moun-tain Green.*		*Phalæna Viridaria.*	*Thick-leaved Cudweed. Silver-leaved Almond.*	*Actynolite Beryl.*
48	*Leek Green.*			*Sea Kale. Leaves of Leeks in Winter.*	*Actynolite Prase.*
49	*Blackish Green.*		*Elytra of Meloe Violaceus.*	*Dark Streaks on Leaves of Cayenne Pepper.*	*Serpentine.*
50	*Verdigris Green.*		*Tail of small Long-tailed Green Parrot.*		*Copper Green.*
51	*Bluish Green.*		*Egg of Thrush.*	*Under Disk of Wild Rose Leaves.*	*Beryl.*
52	*Apple Green.*		*Under Side of Wings of Green Broom Moth.*		*Crysoprase.*
53	*Emerald Green.*	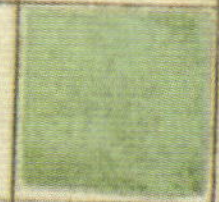	*Beauty Spot on Wing of Teal Drake.*		*Emerald.*

on paper, which he considered too fragile to guarantee color stability. Heat-based processes (such as ceramics, stained glass, and such) offered color that was much more permanent but raised other problems, including that of transport to observation sites. It would take forty years before Werner's color list included samples.

During these forty years, progress of all kinds did indeed make the task achievable, with new advances in the understanding, classification, and referencing of color.[19] Werner's students tried to associate colors with his list while adding to it, but ran into practical or methodological problems.[20] In short, naturalists still lacked a complete and convenient tool that could be used in a wide variety of disciplines. Robert Jameson, a student of Werner, refined the specifications: the nomenclature could not be too expensive to produce and replicate; it had to be transported easily (paper was therefore the best medium); and, above all, its colors had to be stable and durable. He recruited Patrick Syme, an artist specialized in botanical illustration, who would bring the project to its conclusion in 1814.

PREVIOUS PAGE SPREAD

Syme's Nomenclature of Colors

To the fifty-four colors already listed by Werner, Patrick Syme added an additional fifty-four hues in order to meet the needs of a wider range of disciplines. He arranged these 108 colors into tables according to color range[21] that were organized into four columns. The first one provides the color, a square of paper cut out of painted sheets and then glued into the preprinted table. Each shade is identified by a number and one or more familiar terms, with instructions for reproducing it provided in another section of the book. The following three columns propose an equivalent drawn from the plant, animal, or mineral world, if identifiable. For example, color no. 31, named *Berlin Blue* (the pure pigment according to Werner) is associated with the feathers of the jay, the hepatica flower (from the *Ranunculaceae* or buttercup family), and the blue sapphire. Color no. 78, *Orpiment Orange*, is compared to the collar of the golden pheasant and to a type of salamander, then to a variety of nasturtium, and so on.[22] Clearly an effort was made to ensure that this catalog of reference colors would be relevant to all the naturalist disciplines.

The nomenclature would, at long last, provide fitting conditions for several generations of English-speaking European scientists to carry out their scientific descriptions. Indeed, it constituted a shared foundation, removing any ambiguity about the visual appearance of their objects of study. In addition, it fulfilled Werner's hope of training the eyes of these scientists in their approach to color by offering a precise method for observation, referencing, and replicating. Even colors with special surfaces, later qualified as pearly (or pearl) or iridescent (resembling the plumage of the pigeon's throat), were covered. Darwin took a copy of the 1821 edition with him on his trip to the Madeira Islands. It was used to record the colors of the species he collected on his explorations (*primrose yellow* sea slugs, a *vermilion red* spider) before storing them in alcohol.[23] The wise precaution of noting their colors would later allow him to reproduce the original color of his samples, which had faded in the high concentration of ethanol.[24]

The success of the Werner-Syme nomenclature was perhaps also due to the spirit in which this reference work was designed. Once it became possible to print multiple copies of a catalog of a hundred colors selected for their variety and their stability when exposed to light, with each one numbered, was it still essential to give them names and link them to references? In theory, no. However, when Syme mentions *Campanula purple*, *Wine yellow*, or *Asparagus green*, he is facilitating their identification and the possibility of calling them to mind without a sample. Above all, when he lists the names of plants, animals, or minerals, most of which would only be familiar to a handful of scholars,[25] he conjures up the immense abundance of nature.[26] Like Boogert and Waller before him, Syme understood that the color chart could evoke wonder. He knew how to turn this nomenclature into something sublime, a landscape of color and an epic in praise of Creation.

Werner's nomenclature of colours, arranged so as to render it highly useful to the arts and sciences, particularly zoology, botany, chemistry, mineralogy, and morbid anatomy, annexed to which are examples selected from well-known objects in the animal, plant, and mineral kingdoms, Abraham Gottlob Werner, Patrick Syme, edition of 1821, 1821, Getty Research Institute, Los Angeles

IN THE EARLY NINETEENTH CENTURY, CHEMISTS WORK WITH TEXTILE SAMPLES

——— The sample also became a decisive element in the increasingly scientific world of textile color production, which was subject to standards of productivity and reproducibility that were becoming more and more demanding. Academic interest in systematizing the dyeing process continued to grow.[27] The chemistry of dyes was beginning to be understood more thoroughly, and samples were evidence of explorations in this scientific field.

Laboratory Notes of a Chemist from Alsace

——— European demand now turned to cotton fabrics, which were less easy to dye than protein fibers, such as wool and silk, but lightweight, cheaper than silk, and easy to print. Particularly popular were the patterned fabrics known as *indiennes*, which were dyed a deep red called *Turkish red* or *Andrinople red*. The dyeing plant used was madder, a long-established dye. But fixing it on cotton required a process that had remained secret for a long time and was only revealed by Greek dyers in the middle of the eighteenth century.[28] Madder plantations then became numerous, and the first signs of mass production in industrial history emerged in Rouen, Jouy-en-Josas, and Mulhouse where, in 1746, Samuel Koechlin founded the first factory in Alsace to make *indiennes*. Others followed, and for a century they would export tons of handkerchiefs and shawls and kilometers of fabrics for clothing and furnishings all over the world.

These major Alsatian entrepreneurs were also passionate about the emerging science of chemistry. They studied the subject, circulated their findings, and set about manufacturing the chemical products they required for their Mulhouse factories. In 1822, they even founded the oldest school of chemistry in France.

From the beginning of the nineteenth century, these leaders paved the way for dye innovations by closely combining theoretical knowledge, practical applications, and an artistic sense within the textile industry. The person who embodied this triple proficiency was the chemist-colorist,[29] a key part of these companies.

NEXT PAGE

Schwartz's Diary

This document is taken from the laboratory journal (referred to as "notes"[30]) of one such colorist, Léonard Schwartz (1802–1885), a chemist trained in Paris. When he joined the Isaac Schlumberger & Cie *indienne* factory, he endeavored, like his predecessors, to perfect the dyeing processes. To this end, he conducted numerous experiments, the steps of which he methodically recorded in notebooks, with samples attached.[31] The aim was to preserve and communicate the results while protecting their secrecy in a context of ruthless commercial competition. Hence, such laboratory notes often contain abbreviations and codes understandable only to insiders, which makes it more complicated for us to understand how these very first industrial colorists developed their skills.[32]

The two folios dated October 1838 explain various experiments involving mordants[33] and combinations of dyes on dry or wet fibers. Schwartz notes extremely subtle differences in hue between the samples, an indication of his perfectly trained eye. The texture of the color is carefully examined, a "powdery appearance" being undesirable. The chemist also mentions a yellowish tint immediately after printing, which "becomes stronger in an extraordinary way" after a few weeks. This means that the maturing time of the color is taken into consideration.

The wording is precise, and the carefully specified formulas refer to substances and processes whose properties and effectiveness had in some cases been known for a long time, while others had been discovered only recently.

Whether describing new or old dyes, Schwartz was a pioneer in the use of samples. He explored a new world and found his bearings. This is the major difference with Antoine Janot's use

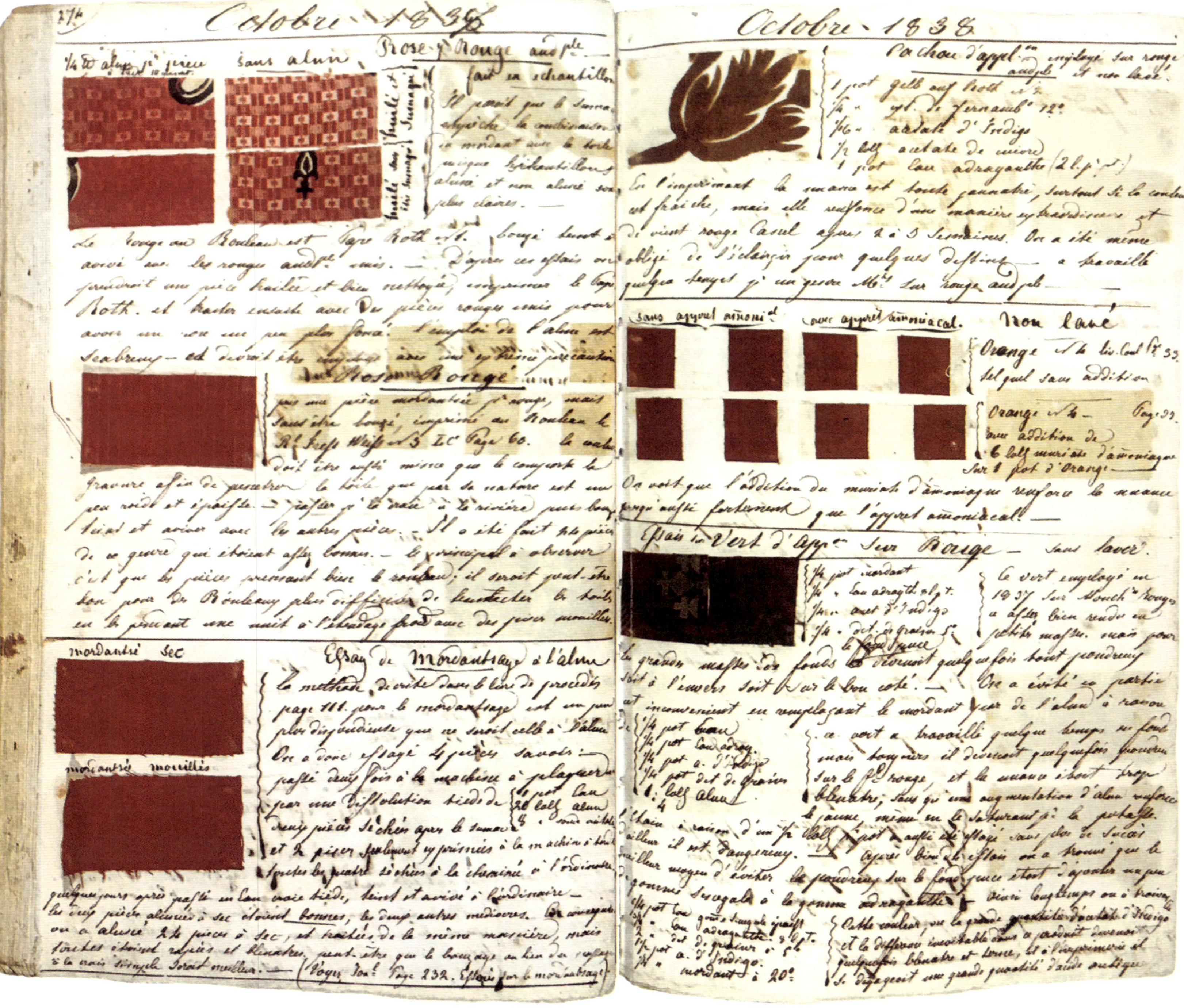
274

Octobre 1838

sans alun

Rose & Rouge

mordancé sec

mordancé mouillés

Essay de Mordançage à l'alun

Octobre 1838

sans apprêt ammoniacal

avec apprêt ammoniacal

Non lavé

Orange

Essais de Vert d'apprêt sur Rouge — sans laver

of the sample in his essays. It is not an issue of the quantity of dyed fabric, which, for Janot, could already be described as industrial. Nor does the difference lie in the skill of Alsatian chemists to obtain the precisely desired shade. One century earlier, the Languedoc master dyers already represented this combination of technical and color skills, and with a much more extensive palette.

Once again, Umberto Eco's reflection[34] can shed light on how the approaches of Janot and Schwartz differed. Like Waller, Schwartz was dealing with a new realm, in this case, chemistry, which was still in its infancy. But both approaches are expressions of "cultures . . . that still have an imprecise image of the universe, which do not know the limits of the things they intend to represent." However, in Antoine Janot's world, "everything was there, which is characteristic of cultures . . . that know the world around them, whose order they have recognized and defined." This is clearly due to the fact that Janot's color chart was intended to demonstrate this very expertise. Yet Janot owed his abilities to a context in which skills had been accumulated and refined for decades, without any major changes to the ingredients and processes used. In this sense, the samples and their presentation in Boogert's manuscript came from a comparable world because they were evidence of a similar mastery: that of an ability to reproduce color. While Schwartz's color charts also demonstrated expertise, this now meant the ability to discover a world in which dyes and their additives were constantly changing, being supplemented by others, and contributing to innovative processes. In other words, Janot's logic was that of a farmer, who sows and knows what he will reap and how he will use it. Léonard Schwartz, on the other hand, reflected the approach of the hunter-gatherer, taking a sample from his environment that may be interesting, testing it, and, in some cases, keeping it. At the time, this was the process used by scientists, who were focused on experiments of all kinds (botanical, chemical, mechanical, and such). Their approach was to search for an explanation, no longer motivated by its usefulness alone, but by an urge to understand and a desire to move forward from one innovation to the next.[35] This was particularly the case of chemists who attempted until the middle of the nineteenth century to unravel the mystery of natural dyes. While Antoine Janot was part of a continuity, the aim now was to be always one step ahead.

Laboratory journal of Léonard Schwartz at Isaac Schlumberger & Cie, Mulhouse, 1837–1838, Musée de l'Impression sur Etoffes (MISE), Mulhouse, inv. 667 KB 39 V, pp. 274–275. © Musée de l'Impression sur étoffes de Mulhouse (MISE)

The Manuals of Textile Chemists Now Approach the Ideal Form of the Color Chart

——— Since the middle of the eighteenth century, the knowledge acquired by chemists had begun to emerge from the secrecy of the workshops. Industrial development required more and more professionals to be trained to manufacture color. A growing number of publications were aimed at the textile industry to communicate the latest theoretical and practical advances, which continued apace. Dyeing was now taught in many schools in cities such as Paris, Lyon, Mulhouse, and Rouen. At the Gobelins Manufacture, a major center of tapestry dyeing, a new director was appointed in 1824: Michel-Eugène Chevreul. He immediately set about systematizing the processes used and gradually expanded his field of study to develop a scientific approach to color that would be widely circulated in various fields of application as of the 1830s.

This context of intense competition in textiles led the authors of treatises on dyeing to rely on the sample as a way of supporting their approaches. This was indeed a perfectly effective method to express the intimate joining of a color and a fabric, whose numerous qualities of texture and surface fully participated in the hue (such as shine or dullness, or luminous qualities).

The textile teaching manuals dealt mainly with printing on cotton, the most popular fabric at the time. Textile printing added value to fabrics at a low cost, and the patterns could be varied with ease. But in this context, color was no longer an end in itself, and there was no question of associating the finest color with the finest fabric. Rather, color was a useful variable to expand decorative options seemingly infinitely.

mordant, des dessins noirs avec le second, et des dessins puces avec le troisième.

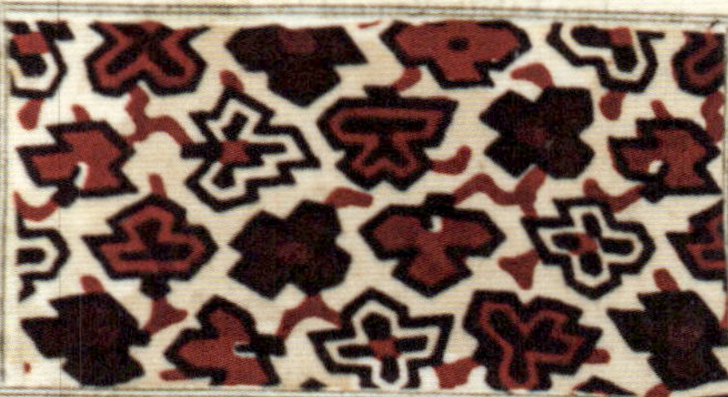

De même, en passant dans un bain de quercitron une toile chargée, par places, de mordant d'alumine, puis de mordant de fer, puis d'un mordant mixte des deux premiers, on a des dessins jaunes, fauves-verdâtres et olives.

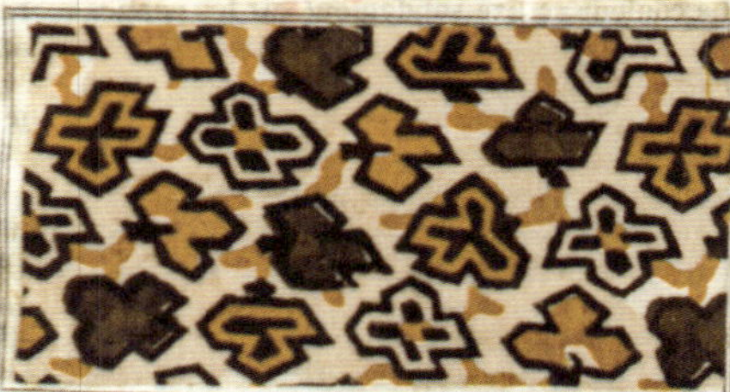

Pour avoir une indienne fond blanc chargée de dessins noirs,

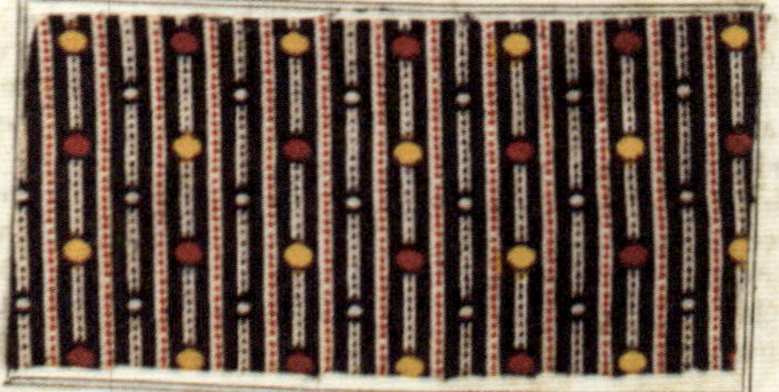

rouges et jaunes, on imprime d'abord le mordant de fer; on *rentre* le mordant d'alumine, puis on passe dans un bain de garance qui donne les deux premières nuances; on blanchit le fond blanc, et on rentre le jaune au moyen d'une décoction de quercitron, additionnée de dissolution d'étain et épaissie à la gomme; on lave à l'eau courante et on sèche, ou bien on rentre un mordant d'alumine, et on teint dans un bain de quercitron.

Pour les dessins bleus, on rentre sur l'indienne, déjà garancée,

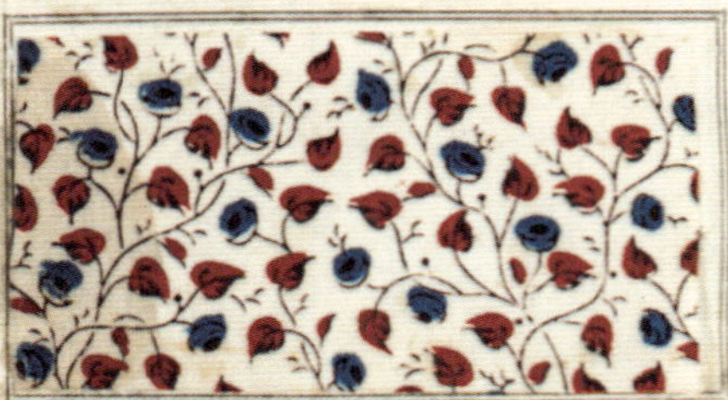

un mélange d'indigo, de soude caustique et de chlorure d'étain, convenablement épaissi, puis on passe dans une solution légère de potasse ou de soude, ou dans une eau de chaux saturée.

Pour les dessins chamois et rouille, on rentre avec un mordant d'acétate de fer plus ou moins concentré et épaissi; on passe dans une eau de savon, puis on rince. C'est alors du peroxide de fer qui est fixé sur la toile.

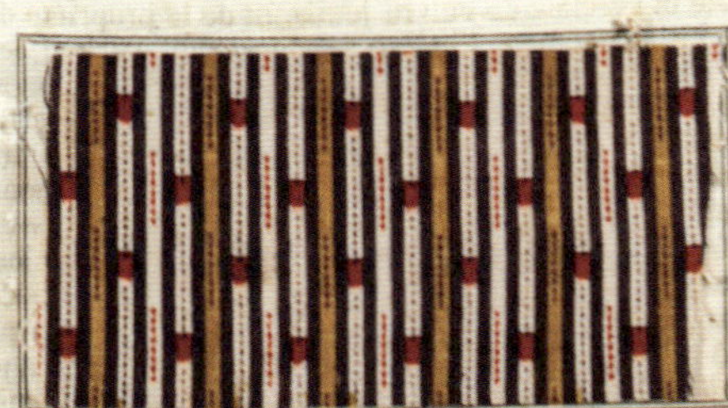

Pour les dessins solitaire ou bronze, on rentre avec une solution de sulfate ou de chlorure de manganèse, puis on passe dans

OPPOSITE

Girardin's *Lessons in Elementary Chemistry*

When Jean Girardin, professor of industrial chemistry in Rouen, dedicated his publication to the workers of Rouen in 1839, he expressed his desire "to compensate, through the clarity of the lessons, for the little time that the working class can devote to study." His description of the history of dyeing[36] gives an idea of the long road that Western society would need to travel in order to accept the surge of colors on the horizon: "Among the most barbaric peoples, we find this taste for colors; thus, savages rub their bodies with colored earth or plant juices; they dye their hair, color their teeth; and this practice common to all peoples of antiquity has continued today among the Oriental nations."

When the book was printed, frames were arranged to accommodate seventeen samples of printed fabrics[37] to closely illustrate the subjects to which they were related. No captions were necessary.

Color itself was not the central issue, but rather its application in patterns of several shades (in an extremely precise choreography of mordants, dyes, additives, and printing arrangements). Girardin was able to make use of the sample as early as 1839 as a teaching aid, sparing both the author and the reader tedious descriptions. Indeed, the colors are often named very succinctly (*white*, *orange*), although mention is sometimes made of specific shades, such as *puce*, *greenish-fawn*, *chamois*, *Carmelite*, or *wood tint*. The color lexicon of the master dyers of the past was not yet forgotten.

The author concludes his *Lessons* by welcoming the advances made in mechanics and chemistry. These were indeed important, but it was due to advances in publishing and the use of samples that this art could exert a wide-ranging influence through educational treatises, allowing the ideal device of the color chart to reach its full potential.[38]

Lessons in elementary chemistry on Sundays at the municipal school in Rouen, Jean Girardin, Rouen, 2nd edition, 770 pages, 1839, pp. 542–543, Bernard Guineau collection, Ôkhra-Ecomuseum of Ocher, Roussillon

PAGE 45

Gonfreville's *Art of Dyeing*

One book indicates that this full potential was reached before the middle of the nineteenth century. Unlike Girardin's *Lessons*, the treatise published in 1848 by M. D. Gonfreville, a student of both the Gobelins Manufacture and the Conservatoire des Arts, dealt exclusively with dyeing and not printing and concerned a single fiber: wool.

The author included eight plates of sixteen samples accompanied by "Formulas giving the composition of the colors."[39] Each plate treated a category of fibers (wool fleece,[40] wool yarn, woven wool), and only once this structure based on the nature of the material has been established are the colors presented. They are then classified according to the type of process producing them,[41] so that in each set, the samples are all identical except for their color or shade of color.

The consistency underlying this sequencing is strengthened by a uniform presentation: the samples have a consistent format and occur on each plate in identical number.
The primary role attributed to color is also evident in the identification of each sample with a color name (often a poetic one), which serves as the title for each formula. This plate includes *Poppy*, *Amaranth*, *Dragon Green*, *Field of Refuge*, *Corinth Grape*, *Anna's Purple*, *Dove*, and *Isère River Water*.

In these plates, the samples appear within a circumscribed and consistent space, according to a thoughtfully balanced presentation defined by a rhythmic order that would be jeopardized by the addition or removal of any individual sample. They are intimately connected with each other and only fully come into their own in relation to their neighbors. The color chart is therefore much more than a collection of samples. It is the complete summary of a closed list, as in Umberto Eco's "everything was there."

One of the major characteristics of the color chart can be found in this complete form, which is designed to have a beginning and an end.[42]

In *The Order of Things*, Michel Foucault describes how reading a text by Jorge Luis Borges made him feel uncomfortable.[43] "There is no worse disorder than that . . . which makes the fragments of a large number of possible orders sparkle in the dimension, without law or geometry, of the *disparate*; . . . things are 'set down,' 'posed,' 'arranged' in sites so different that it is impossible to find a welcoming space for them, to define above them all a common place."

The color chart provides this shared and welcoming space. It preexists in the *rotae urinarum*, the Boogert manual, and Janot's essay, but the form that it will finally take was crystallized at this precise moment in the history of color, just before the middle of the nineteenth century.

Art of Dyeing Wools in Fleece, Yarn, and Fabrics, M. D. Gonfreville, Librairie Scientifique, Industrielle et Agricole Lacroix et Baudry, Paris, 1848, 873 pages, Bibliothèque nationale de France, Paris

——— For a long time, the need to refer to examples of color had involved doctors and naturalists, but the interest in color that motivated society starting in the eighteenth century seemed finally to herald the origin of the true color chart. In particular, it led dyers to make the most of the possibilities offered by natural dyes in order to extract the most beautiful hues. They placed the sample at the heart of their craft, as a record of one step in the dyeing process, a reference to reproduce, or even, as in Janot's essay, as proof of an ability to create a color repeatedly.

An era was coming to an end, one in which practitioners knew how to adapt to the infinitely complex rules governing the emergence of color. Their expertise resulted from a careful and creative observation of what nature offered, from dyeing plants to minerals, from river water to mine veins, from the work of bacteria in dyeing tanks to the patient act of grinding a pigment in its binding agent.

A world of scholarship was arriving, and the considerable progress made by science at the beginning of the nineteenth century led to an unprecedented profusion of colors requiring constant use of samples. Precise and reproducible color became a necessity.

In the eighteenth century, experimental thinking had established color systems, formula workbooks, and then laboratory journals, but these tools no longer sufficed when the time came to share and teach the manufacturing processes of color. This abundance had to be classified, and a method of presentation had to be invented to highlight the subtlest differences. This was the color chart.

This priority given to distinguishing colors was accompanied by new formal constraints. Color charts had to be standardized—and clearly so. When these conditions were met, the small scraps of color that marked the history of the emerging Industrial Revolution in Europe would finally be used to the fullest. The color chart would exponentially increase the significance already present in the sample. ●

COULEURS BINAIRES.

Laines en fil.

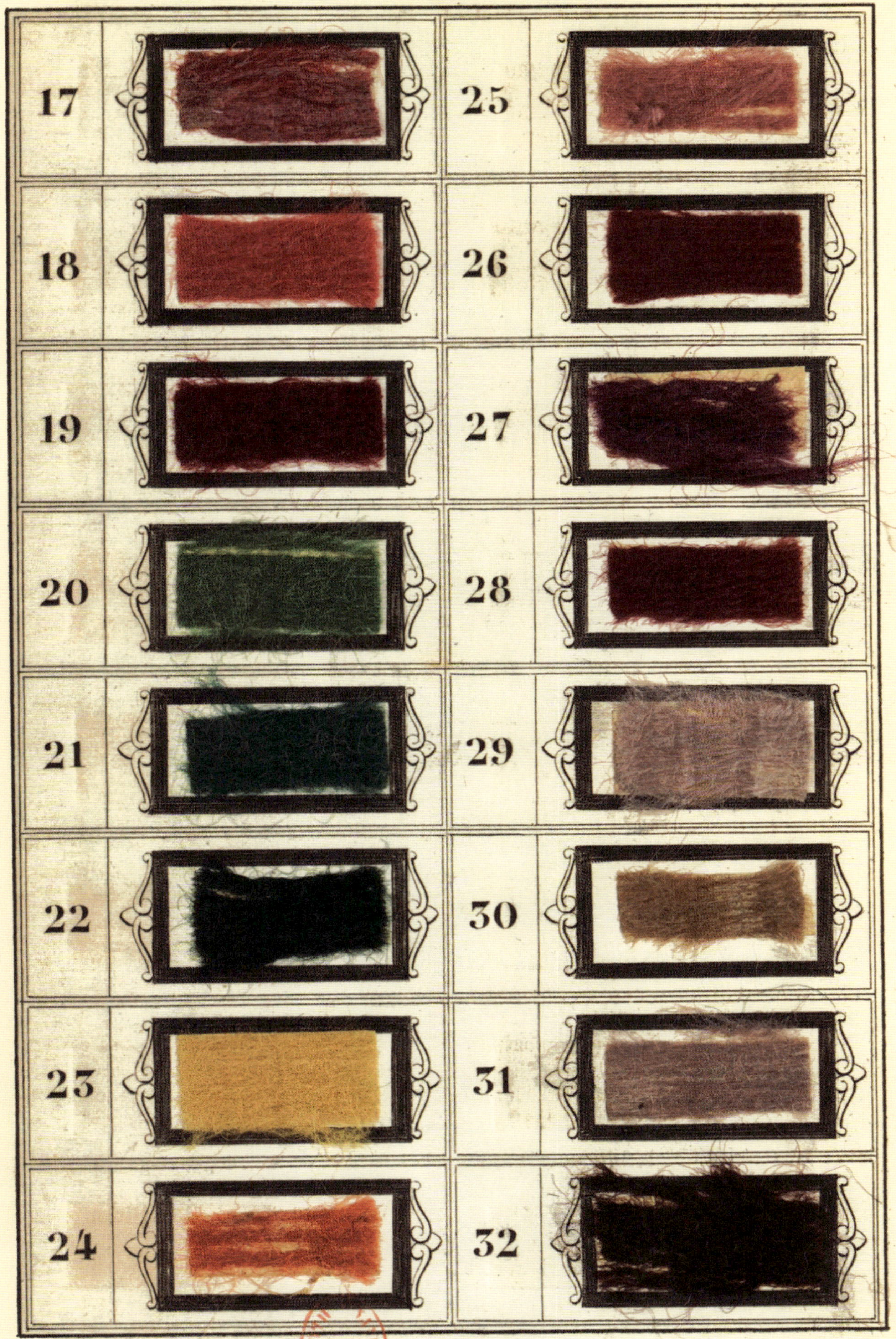

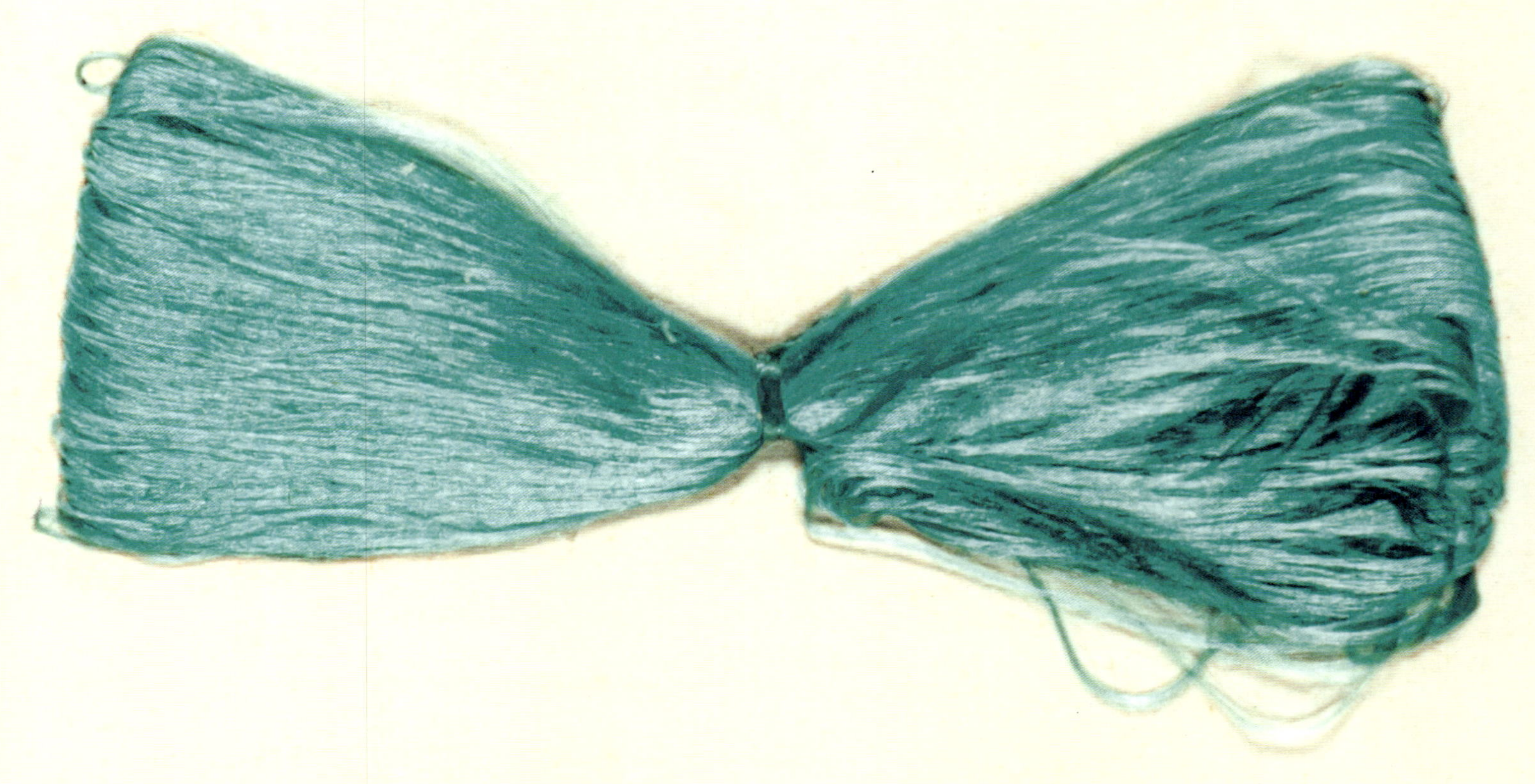

N° 130. — **Vert brillant** sur soie (*1.5 0/0*).

THE CHAOS OF SYNTHETIC COLOR

— MID- TO LATE NINETEENTH CENTURY —

By the middle of the nineteenth century, significant discoveries had already been made through applied research, and the functional properties of dyes and pigments had been identified and described. The making of color from natural products was in the process of being mastered down to its smallest details when in 1856, at the Royal College of Chemistry of London, a young chemist named William Perkin obtained a purple precipitate during an experiment with aniline, a derivative of coal tar. In less than a year, Perkin confirmed its dyeing properties on silk and then wool, filed a patent for the first synthetic dye, mauveine, and launched its industrial production.

Mauveine proved disappointing, but Perkin's discovery triggered intense competition among European chemists. They applied many different reagents to coal tar, quickly expanding the ability to create synthetic color. The Germans very soon became frontrunners in this new color market because, unlike the French or the English, they developed products specifically suited to the needs of manufacturers, protected their techniques effectively, and relied on the latest and most effective scientific innovations.

Perkin's discovery was therefore a turning point, but the momentum had begun much earlier and the discoveries of the emerging field of chemistry had already become part of color production. Similarly, synthetic color did not abruptly end the use of natural dyes or earlier color practices, which coexisted for some time alongside these innovations. However, within a few decades, the cultivation of dye plants in Europe and in the colonies subsided and the importation of dye wood and cochineal from Asia and America, as well as pigments, came to a halt. Above all, the arrival of synthetic color led to the disappearance of the rich chromatic variations nature-based dyes provided.[1]

While the circulation of dye materials decreased, the world economy entered an unprecedented phase of growth in the movement and intense trading of goods among European countries, the United States, and the colonies of the various powers. Indeed, the second half of the nineteenth century saw the development of consumer products. They were displayed at international exhibitions, and growing urban populations discovered them in the new department stores in major cities, especially Paris. Printing techniques were diversifying as the rise of the press and publishing allowed mass culture to flourish. In industrialized nations, synthetic color made an extensive selection available to everyone at attractive prices. Color, increasingly accessible, would soon become a necessity.

The phenomenon of color was also more thoroughly studied and better understood. In 1810, Goethe had made the perception of color a central concern in his *Theory of Colors*. At the Gobelins Manufacture, research had already been carried out, but unfortunately the results were not shared.[2] The chemist Michel-Eugène Chevreul published several key works within just a few decades, including his *Essay on a Way to Define and Name Colors* published in 1860 and, in 1864, *Colors and Their Applications in the Industrial Arts with the Help of Color Wheels*, which listed 14,420 shades.[3]

Widely circulated and translated, Chevreul's writings guided and inspired most of the later work on color. While the influence of these publications on the history of color charts may be difficult to define precisely, it is undeniable. By taking on the material challenge of a faithful reproduction of colors and developing rational systems for classifying shades that were suitable for many applications, Chevreul contributed to demystifying color and provided the basis for a methodical approach to representing it. Manufacturers and merchants of colored substances and products would draw on this approach when they began distributing commercial color charts.

But, first, the discovery of synthetic pigments and dyes, which interrupted the continuum of the mastery of natural color, caused real chaos in the teaching manuals for dyeing. The optimal form for presenting colored samples as achieved by someone like Gonfreville in the middle of the nineteenth century was no longer current. Yet it did not disappear and was still found in reference documents.

TEACHING MANUALS IN CHEMISTRY REFLECT THE TRANSFORMATION

The authors of teaching manuals on dyeing had presented samples supporting their lessons in the form of color charts, and this specific display of color could only have been the result of a mastery of processes.

As soon as it was perfected, this form of teaching was discarded. Color charts disappeared and were replaced by collections of samples, an early system of color sampling.[4] For about fifty years, teaching manuals revealed the disarray of chemists as traditional dyes and pigments began to become obsolete, while also expressing their excitement at the new possibilities of synthetic color. These manuals would also illustrate the aesthetic opportunities that this array of new dyes and pigments offered for color sampling.

OPPOSITE

Piéquet's *Chemistry of Dyers*

Oscar Piéquet was a chemical engineer, the director of a dyeing factory, and a member of the Industrial Society of Mulhouse. In his book on dyeing various fibers, he included nine sample plates (118 samples in total), specifying that they had been redesigned up until the very last moment in order to present the reader with the most recently discovered products: color had entered a cycle of rapid and constant change.[5]

His approach remained technical. However, when we examine the logic governing the presentation of the samples, we see that they are grouped first by colorant, and only then by color. In this way, samples of the same shade are scattered throughout. Above all, each dye was tested on several fabrics (wool, silk, cotton, linen, hemp, ramie, and so on), and this variety was further increased by the condition of the fibers (raw, carded, spun, combed, felted, woven, and such) and their finish (velvet, satin, woolen cloth, damask, either solid or printed). Finally, rectangular cutouts alternate with small bundles of yarn.

The variety of type and presentation of the samples overshadows the feature of color to such an extent that it is impossible to make any meaningful comparison between the shades themselves. The intention here is not to offer a range of colors to capture their subtlety, but to demonstrate the performance of a large number of dyes on varied fabrics. The 118 samples thus represent an inventory of dyes, not a color chart.

In other words, Gonfreville used the sample in a pragmatic approach while Piéquet exclaimed: "Look what magnificent colors all these dyes give to so many materials!"

The Chemistry of Dyers, New Theoretical and Practical Treatise on the Art of Dyeing and Printing Fabrics, Oscar Piéquet, 402 pages, Paris, 1892, Bernard Guineau collection, Ôkhra-Ecomuseum of Ocher, Roussillon

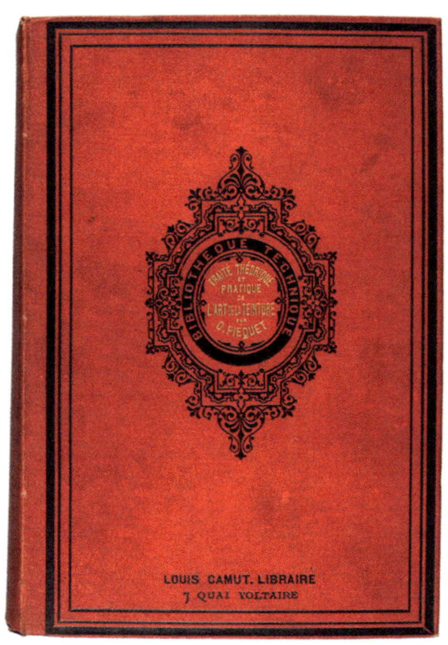
BIBLIOTHEQUE TECHNIQUE
TRAITÉ THÉORIQUE ET PRATIQUE DE L'ART DE LA TEINTURE PAR C. PIEQUET
LOUIS CAMUT, LIBRAIRE
7 QUAI VOLTAIRE
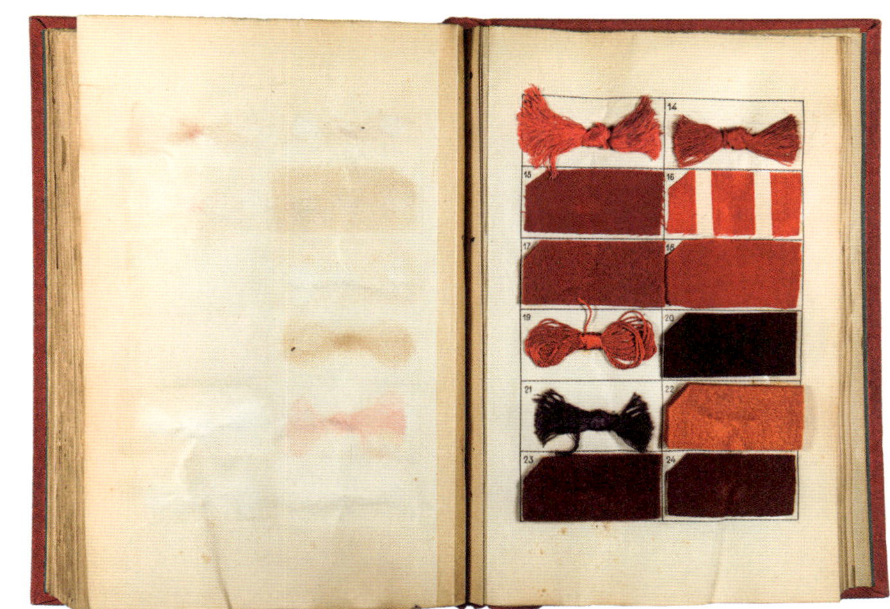
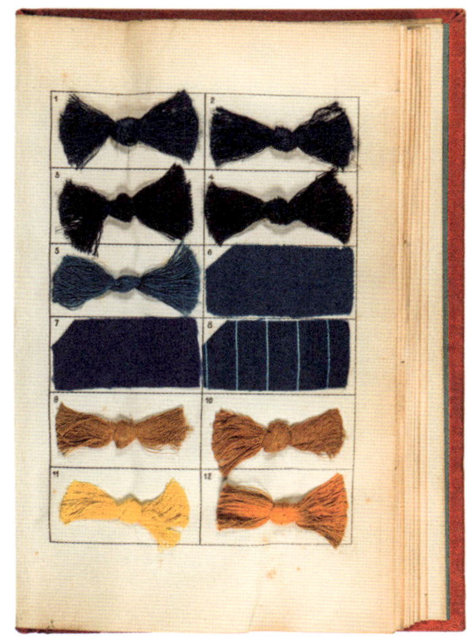
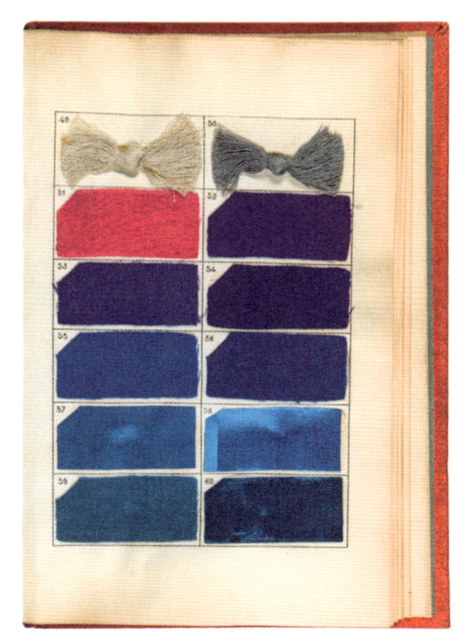
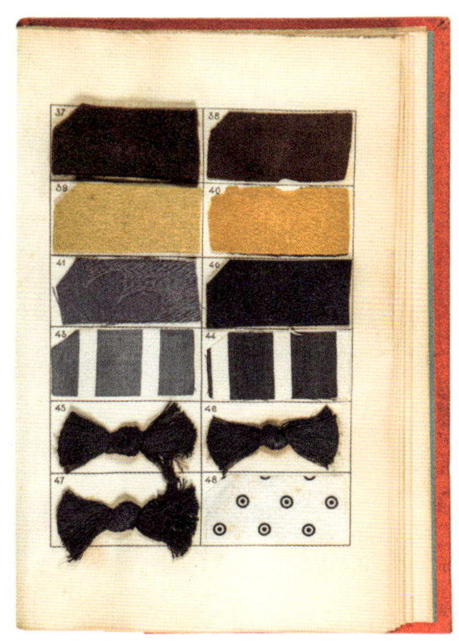
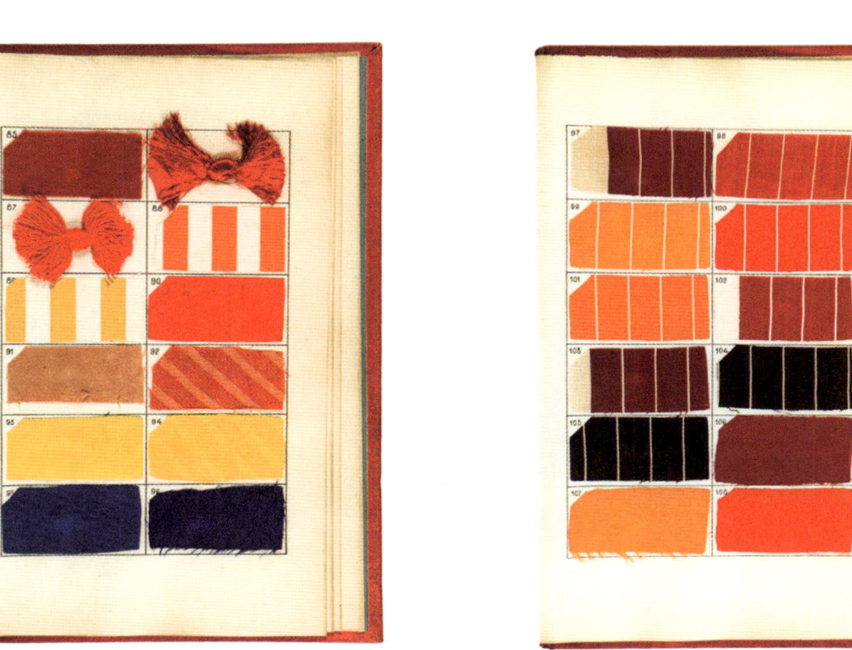
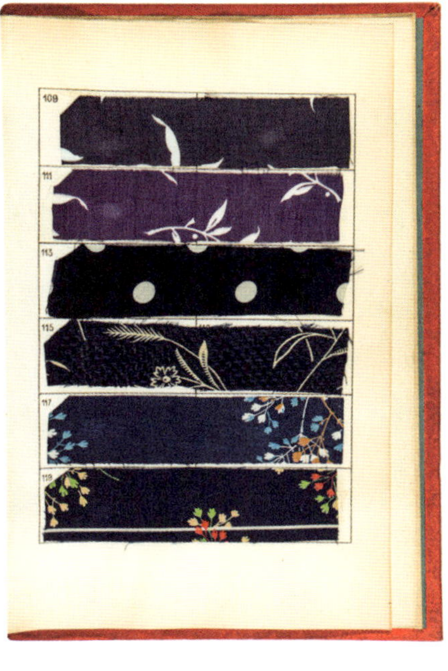

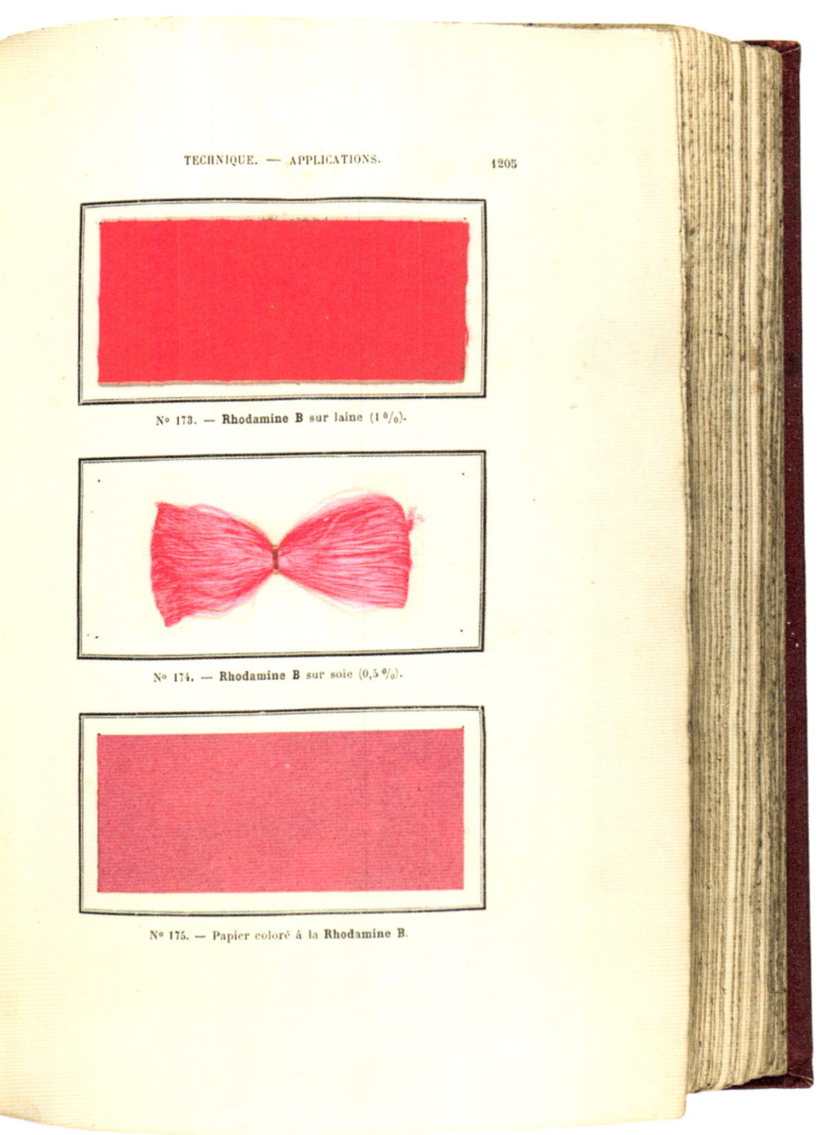

TECHNIQUE. — APPLICATIONS. 1205

N° 173. — Rhodamine B sur laine (1 %).

N° 174. — Rhodamine B sur soie (0,5 %).

N° 175. — Papier coloré à la Rhodamine B.

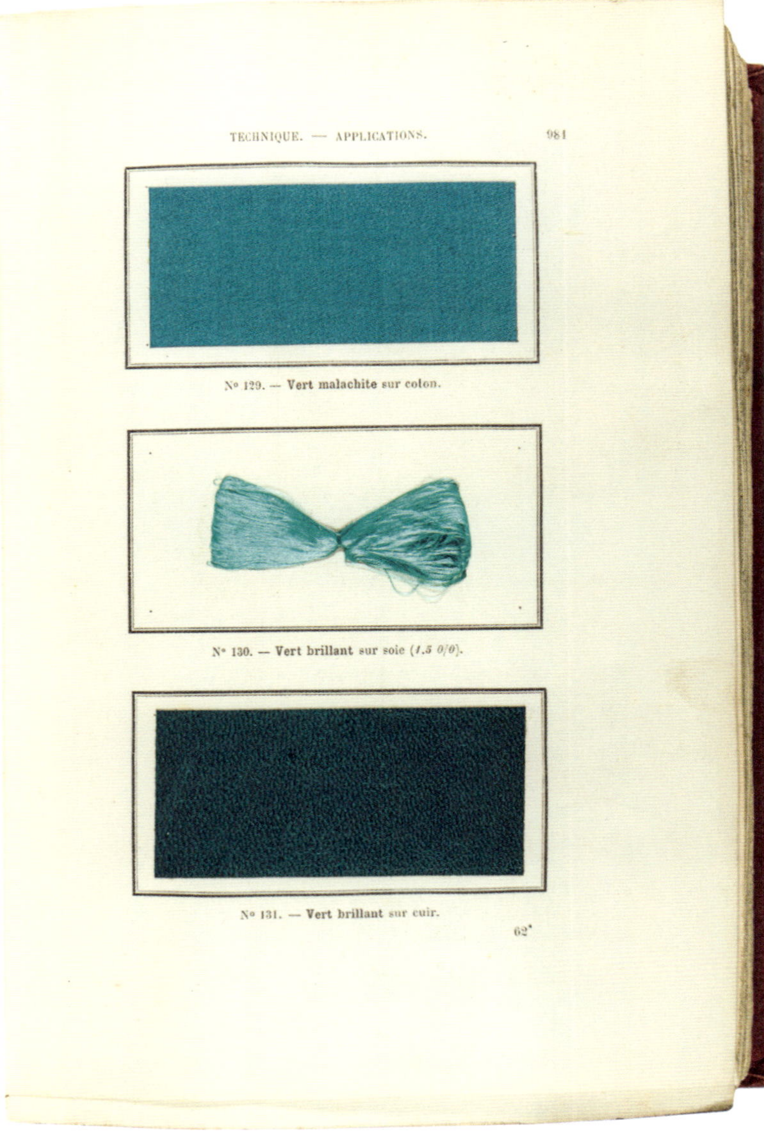

TECHNIQUE. — APPLICATIONS. 981

N° 129. — Vert malachite sur coton.

N° 130. — Vert brillant sur soie (1.5 0/0).

N° 131. — Vert brillant sur cuir.

62*

ABOVE

Lefèvre's Essay on Colorants

The content is similar, and the same observations apply to this treatise published in 1896 by Léon Lefèvre, an engineering assistant at the École Polytechnique. His 261 samples are interspersed with the text, as Girardin had done in 1839.

As seen in the pages above, Lefèvre took an all-inclusive approach to his collection of samples, even displaying the properties of dyes on surfaces such as leather and paper. Like Piéquet's work, Lefèvre's study was extremely thorough but did not make it easy to compare shades; he also presented the samples in creative formats.

Scientific explorations of synthetic chemistry thus brought about three fragmentations. The first was that of the methods for manufacturing color, which now depended on identifying and combining molecular structures. The second was that of color itself, which gave rise to infinite versions and was defined according to the exact percentage of its components. The last fragmentation was that of the presentation of color, which at this time could no longer be achieved in an orderly framework.

Essay on Organic and Artificial Colorants, Their Industrial Preparation, and Their Applications, volume two, Léon Lefèvre, Paris, 1896, private collection, Paris

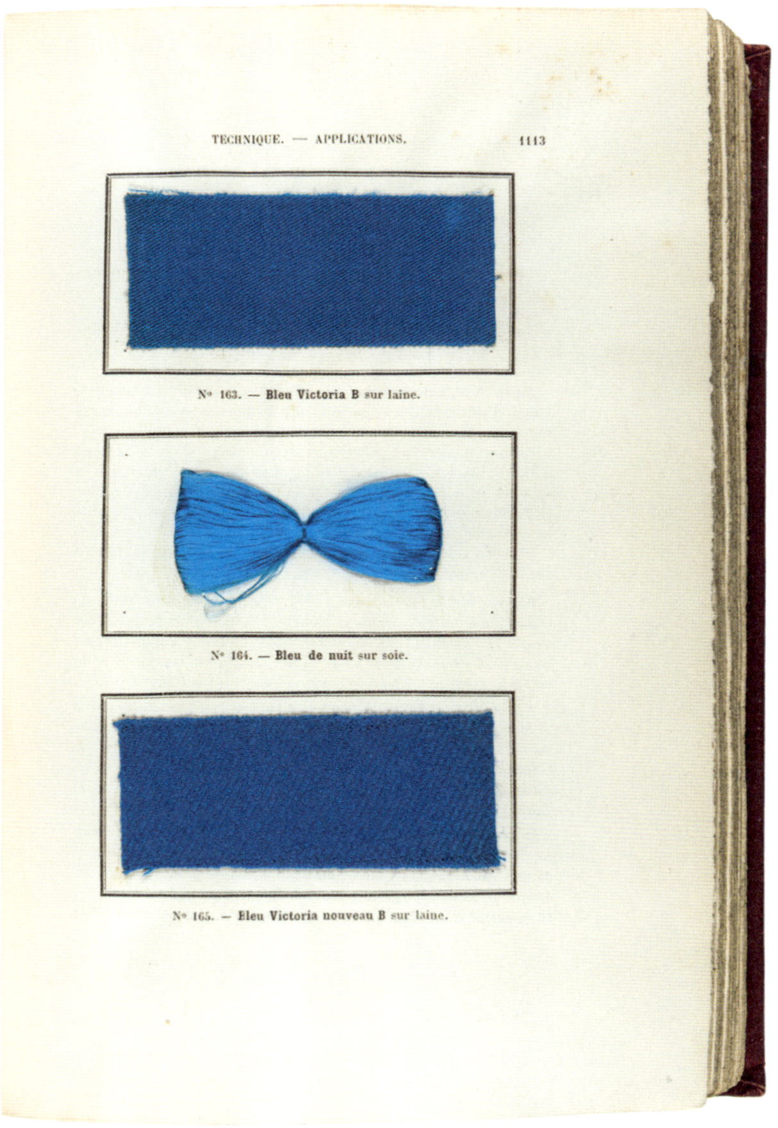

TECHNIQUE. — APPLICATIONS. 1113

N° 163. — Bleu Victoria B sur laine.

N° 164. — Bleu de nuit sur soie.

N° 165. — Bleu Victoria nouveau B sur laine.

NEXT PAGE SPREAD

Van Laer's *Mordant Dyeing Process*

This work by Van Laer appears to be a counterexample since it is contemporary with the previous ones and focuses on the same subject of fabric dyeing, even though the author, a chemistry assistant at the Verviers Vocational School in Belgium, humbly presents it as a practical study tool for the dyer.

However, the 206 samples that appear in this book form a "true color chart." Color and its shades determine the structure of the whole, not the dyes; grouping by material is respected. Color in this case comes first.

Van Laer's text provides an explanation: here we find the same substances as in Gonfreville's treatise, including aniline. The formulas for his reds use cochineal or madder, with yellows from weld, dyer's sumach, or quercitron, and his blues are taken from bluewood or fermentation tanks. The authors cited (Girardin in particular) all published their works before 1856. In short, Van Laer has adopted the perspective of a world that, after Perkin, had become outdated. He had access to the color chart because he had not experienced the chaos caused by the intrusion of synthetic dyes, but continued the pursuit of previous dyeing practices. Technical mastery seems to be necessary—or even essential—to the color chart. The color chart would therefore be incompatible with the struggles and excitement of experimentation.

Collection of the Principal Mordant Dyeing Processes for the Use of Dyers, third part, G. Van Laer, Imp. Vinche, Verviers, 1874, 200 pp., Musée du Vieux Nîmes, Nîmes, inv.

——— Like the seventeenth-century naturalists or Léonard Schwartz in his laboratory in Alsace, chemists in the second half of the nineteenth century who used synthetic dyes broke with the practices developed by their predecessors. They explored a new land and approached color in the same way that botanists of the seventeenth and eighteenth centuries examined unknown plants to see if their fruits were edible and to determine how to cook them. They returned to an explorer's logic, researching effects of color. There was no place here for the color chart, which resembled the tame orderliness of a vegetable garden, whereas new thinkers wanted to explore the wilds of nature.

PROCÉDÉS DE TEINTURES A MORDANT.

ÉCHANTILLONS.

123	130	137	144
124	131	138	145
125	132	139	146
126	133	140	147
127	134	141	148
128	135	142	149
129	136	143	150

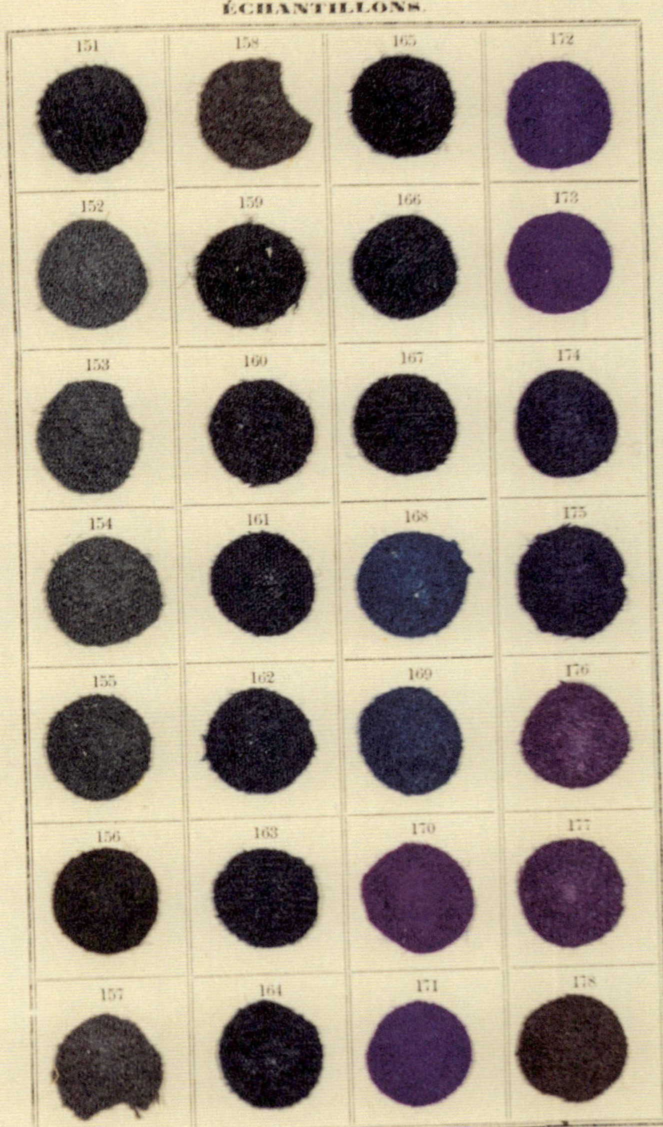

PROCÉDÉS DE TEINTURES A MORDANT.

ÉCHANTILLONS.

151	158	165	172
152	159	166	173
153	160	167	174
154	161	168	175
155	162	169	176
156	163	170	177
157	164	171	178

G. VAN LAER. 3e partie.

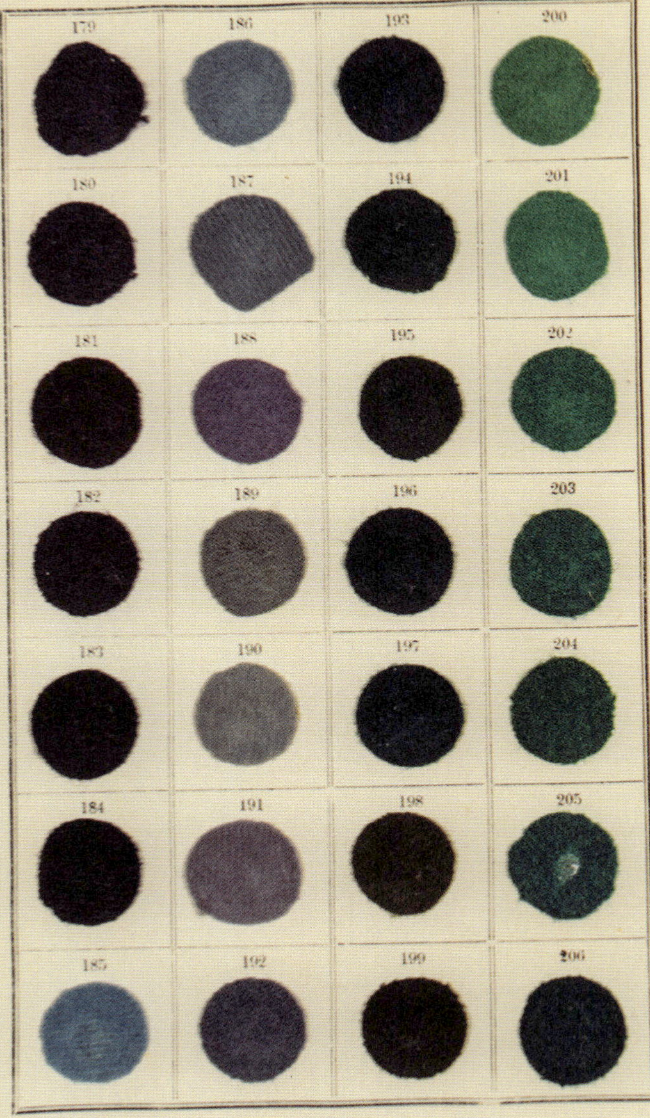
PROCÉDÉS DE TEINTURES A MORDANT.
ÉCHANTILLONS.
179 186 193 200
180 187 194 201
181 188 195 202
182 189 196 203
183 190 197 204
184 191 198 205
185 192 199 206
3e partie.
G. VAN LAER.

MÉMOIRES DE LA SOCIÉTÉ D'ANTHROPOLOGIE. T.II. PL.V.

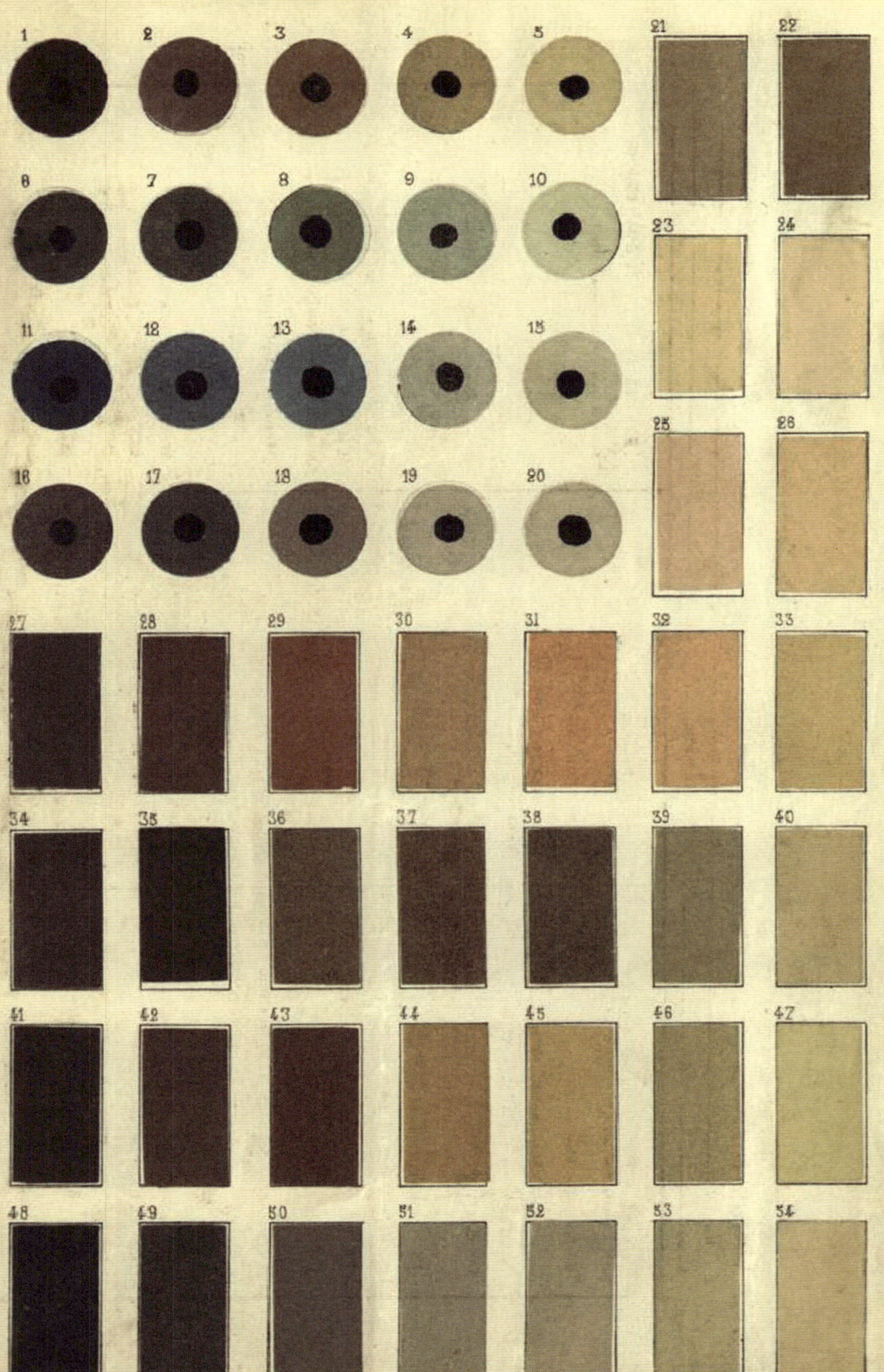

CONTINUING THE UNDERTAKING OF CREATING ORDER IN THE SCIENCES AND THE ARTS

——— The authors of didactic treatises used samples to educate color manufacturing professionals during the time their field experienced a revolution; the situation, meanwhile, was different for those who did not produce color but focused instead on establishing standards.[6] These professionals remained, as always, concerned with how to achieve adequate reproduction of the short-lived colors that they often encountered in their observations. Synthetic color now gave them access to a wide variety of stable inks and paints, and at a cost often lower than that of previous formulations. These synthetic colors would help them in their diverse projects. Thus, color references appeared for chemical precipitates, cartography, precious stones, urine as always, sugar, and honey. Color references were even applied to humans, an undertaking that carried the seeds of infamy.

OPPOSITE

Broca's Description . . . to the Point of Offensiveness?

Paul Broca, a medical doctor and a pioneer of physical anthropology, was one of the first to develop a color reference system for describing the human body.[7] His *General Instructions* set out various methods for taking measurements. Broca included in his book a plate with twenty colors of iris and thirty-four colors for hair and skin, recommending that for the skin, color analysis should be carried out on areas of the body not exposed to the sun. Broca would have liked to make a color scale for eyes using enamel paint to express their transparency and shimmer.[8] Instead, he had to rely on watercolor samples, making sure that they came from large strips that were painted and then cut and glued, so that his color chart would be identical in all copies of the work.

In a fascinating article on this unusual type of color chart, André Karliczek and Andreas Schwarz traced its development: in the late nineteenth century, reference charts such as this one began to support efforts to categorize races of people and arrange them hierarchically. This area of research grew markedly in the three decades before World War II.[9] Thus, these color charts paved the way for the Nazi racial classification system.

General Instructions for Anthropological Research to Be Done on Living Things, Paul Broca, 1864, volume 2, plate V, Bibliothèque nationale de France, Paris

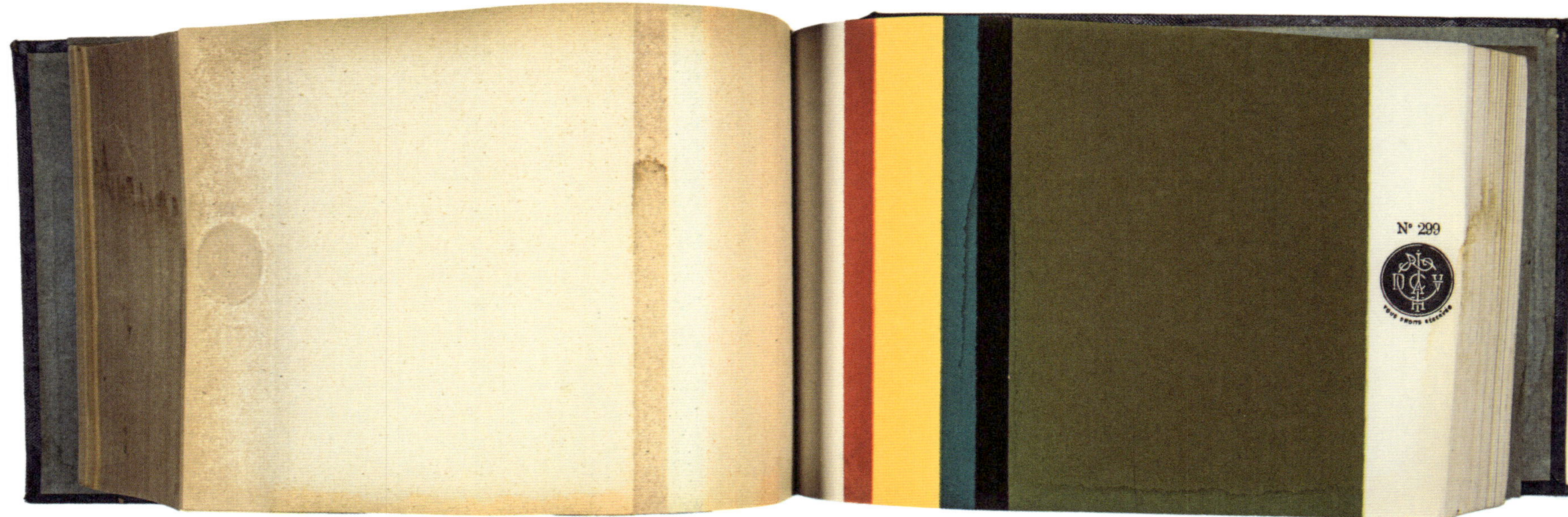

ABOVE

Guichard's *Grammar of Color*

Among the many textbooks for teaching about color that appeared during the second half of the nineteenth century, one work stands out: that of Édouard Guichard, an architect, decorator, and designer of textile patterns.[10] In the mid-1870s, Guichard embarked on an ambitious project. He was president of the Union Centrale des Beaux-Arts Appliqués à l'Industrie (Central Union of Fine Arts Applied to Industry), and he was convinced that the various trades working with color needed a manual with a wide range of examples and instructions for reproducing them easily.[11] Ultimately, Guichard published two books: *The Harmony of Colors* in 1880 on the study of color ranges and, two years later, the *Grammar of Color*.

In the foreword to his second book, Guichard explains the method he has developed: the foundation of his work is a standard of six colors that he describes as "pure" and defines as "those usually used in wallpaper": red, yellow, blue, orange, green, and violet, formulated especially for this publication. Guichard then mixed these pure colors with each other, "lifting" or "lowering" them by adding white or black. The widest strip on each book plate is the result of mixing the tones that appear to its left, the width of each component color being proportional (in volume) to the quantity used.

The book includes 765 numbered silk-screened plates. The tables and forms of the combinations list in French, German, and English the mathematical proportions of each color obtained. It is difficult to gauge the success of this *Grammar* with the artisans for whom it was intended, but we do know that it was used by the Gobelins Manufacture.

In addition to its technical data, the resulting study, with page after page of color references and plates classified by color family, forms a splendid and captivating collection.

The Grammar of Color, Seven Hundred and Sixty-Five Colored Plates Reproducing the Principal Shades Obtained by Mixing the Pure Colors with Each Other, Édouard Guichard, H. Gagnon Publisher, Paris, 1882, 3 volumes, 15 × 24.5 cm, Albi Couleurs, Association Mémoire des Industries de la Couleur, Albi

NEXT PAGE SPREAD

Promoting Department Stores

One site proved crucial in the development of society's approach to color: department stores, where customers discovered an array of colored items at low prices thanks to synthetic color. When customers could not go to a department store in person, they could peruse items that brands advertised featuring countless numbers of samples.

After the establishment of the Grands Magasins du Louvre in 1863, other department stores became popular in Paris.[12] The stores soon began distributing leaflets and booklets in the capital, then in the provinces, and even to the colonies. These materials were often widely circulated: in 1874, 360,000 copies of the Catalog of the General Exhibition of the spring season items of the Magasins du Louvre were produced.

In his novel *The Ladies' Delight*, published in 1883, Émile Zola explains how the booklets are made: "The sampling room . . . was a large square room. . . . In one corner were the large mechanical knives, to cut the samples. Whole rolls passed through, more than sixty thousand francs' worth of fabrics were shipped a year, torn like this in strips. From morning to evening, the knives chopped the silk, the wool, the canvas, with a scythe-like noise. Then notebooks had to be assembled, and either glued or sewn. There was even . . . a small printing house, for labels."[13]

Such documents often had the appearance of sample books insofar as they brought together different fabrics. Others were organized as color charts of a single fabric type, often with a large sample for assessing fabric quality and a series of smaller ones illustrating the color range.

By entering countless homes in the capital and the provinces, or even in distant lands, these pamphlets and promotional catalogs, which were often viewed by everyone in the household, instilled the image of a new reality: the wide range of colors now available for many fabrics. However, while the colors were shown, they were not named. Consumers soon had an even more thorough familiarity with this wide range of choices when the first color charts entered retail stores. They were then able to associate the colors with their names.

Printemps Department Stores advertisements, late nineteenth century, Bibliothèque Forney, Paris, 13 × 10 cm, RES ICO 5555 ½ Plano

——— The logic of the color chart was put into place before the second half of the nineteenth century, as evidenced by Gonfreville's educational treatise. In theory, nothing prevented Girardin in 1861, Piéquet in 1892, or Lefèvre in 1896 from inserting synthetic dyes into the logic of the color chart, since these authors referenced them in their formulas. However, even if they were gradually becoming comfortable with synthetic color, it was clearly too early for these chemists to fully understand this new world. They needed to start with a clean slate in order to embark on the promised dream of this opportunity for radically new colors.

However, they retained the sample because it had proven its pedagogical usefulness. Preserving it may also have had a different function. With synthetic chemistry, scientists were exploring a world of pure speculation where things were no longer self-evident. No more familiar smells escaped from their test tubes, and their new transparent formulas gave no sign of the intense colors they would transfer to fabrics and other materials. Perhaps samples allowed these men of the laboratory to return to the real world, the stability of common sense. The wealth of knowledge they offered would guarantee the survival of a world woven from tangible phenomena, obsolete but reassuring.

For merchants, synthetic chemistry offered the opportunity to have access to colors that were now strictly homogeneous and less expensive. For them, this step was easy to take.

The same was true for scientists working to produce reference documents because, by definition, they were concerned primarily with representing color. But these reference documents also announced the moment when professionals, ever more numerous and coming from very diverse backgrounds, would seek to define a color precisely, to describe it, identify it, communicate it. They thus implicitly hinted at an impossible challenge: to produce *the* color chart, the one that would succeed at last in capturing the rainbow. ●

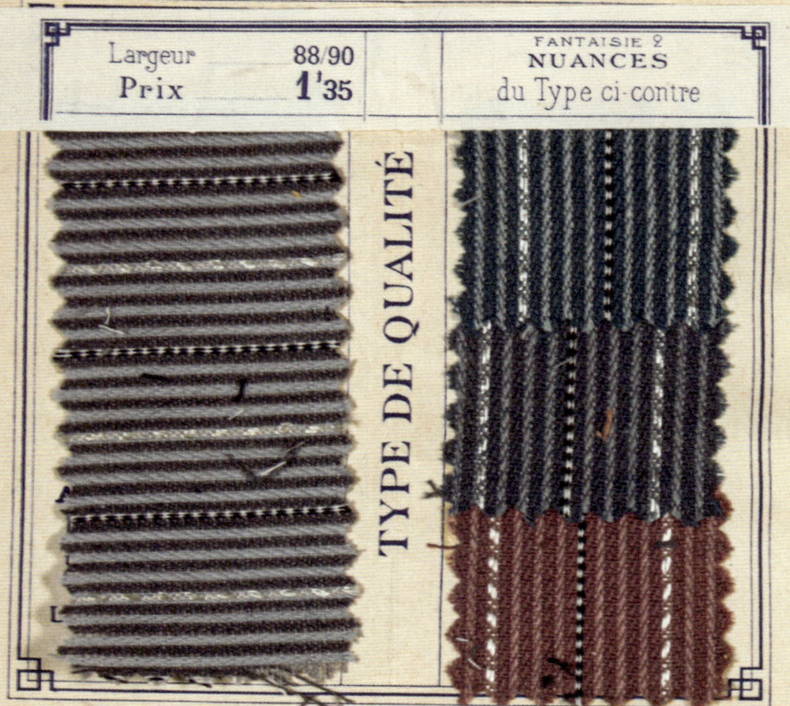
Grands Magasins du Printemps
PARIS LAGUIONIE & Cie PARIS
COMPTOIR DE FANTAISIE _ 2
Largeur 88/90
Prix 1f35
FANTAISIE 2
NUANCES
du Type ci-contre
TYPE DE QUALITÉ
NOTA: Afin d'éviter tout retard nous engageons nos clientes à designer un second échantillon pour le cas ou celui choisi serait épuisé.

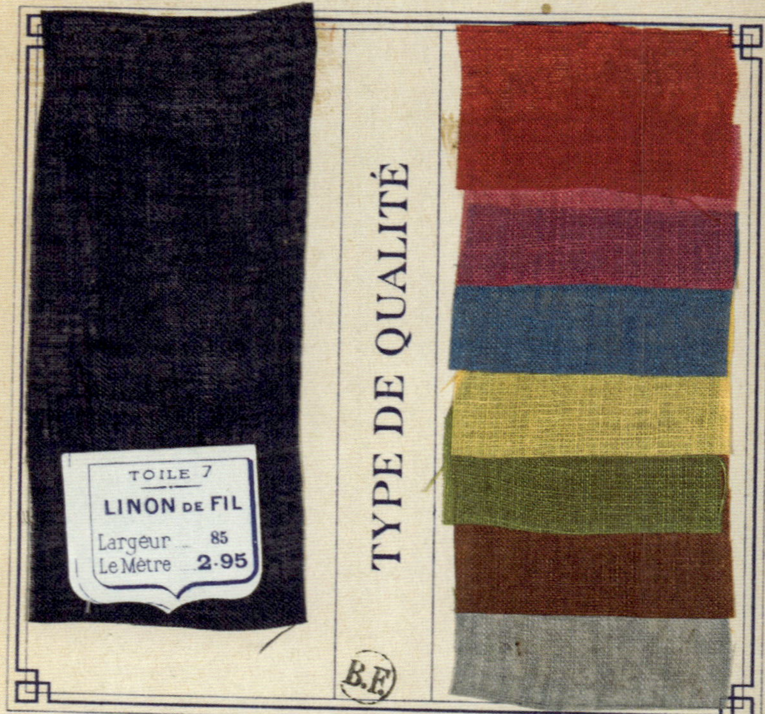
Grands Magasins du Printemps
PARIS LAGUIONIE & Cie PARIS
COMPTOIR DE TOILE _ 7
TOILE 7
LINON DE FIL
Largeur 85
Le Mètre 2·95
TYPE DE QUALITÉ
B.F.
NOTA: Afin d'éviter tout retard nous engageons nos clientes à designer un second échantillon pour le cas ou celui choisi serait épuisé.

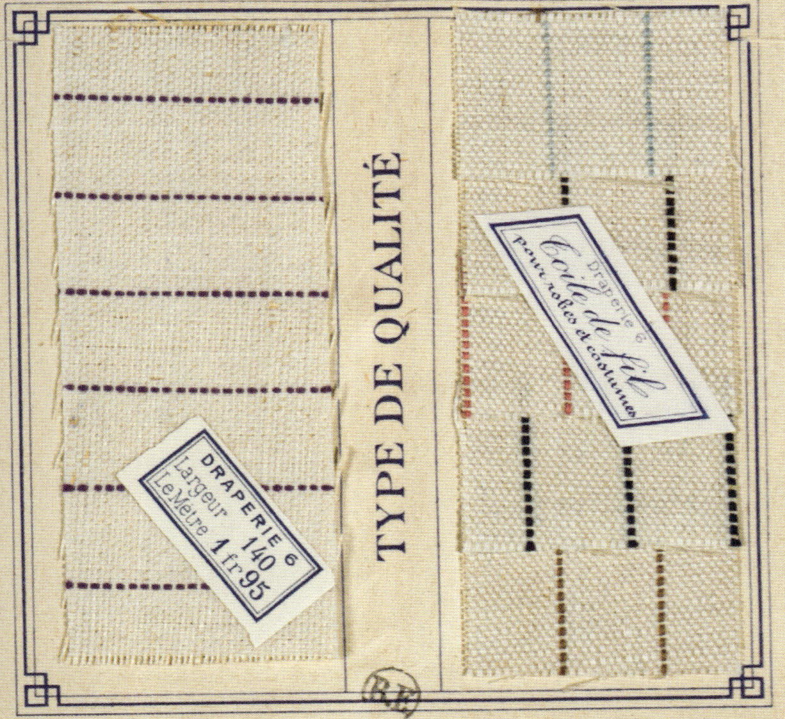

Grands Magasins du Printemps
PARIS LAGUIONIE & Cie PARIS
COMPTOIR DE DRAPERIE _6
TYPE DE QUALITÉ
Draperie 6
Toile de fil
pour robes et costumes
DRAPERIE 6
Largeur 140
Le Mètre 1 fr 95
NOTA: Afin d'éviter tout retard nous engageons nos clientes à designer un second échantillon pour le cas ou celui choisi serait épuisé.

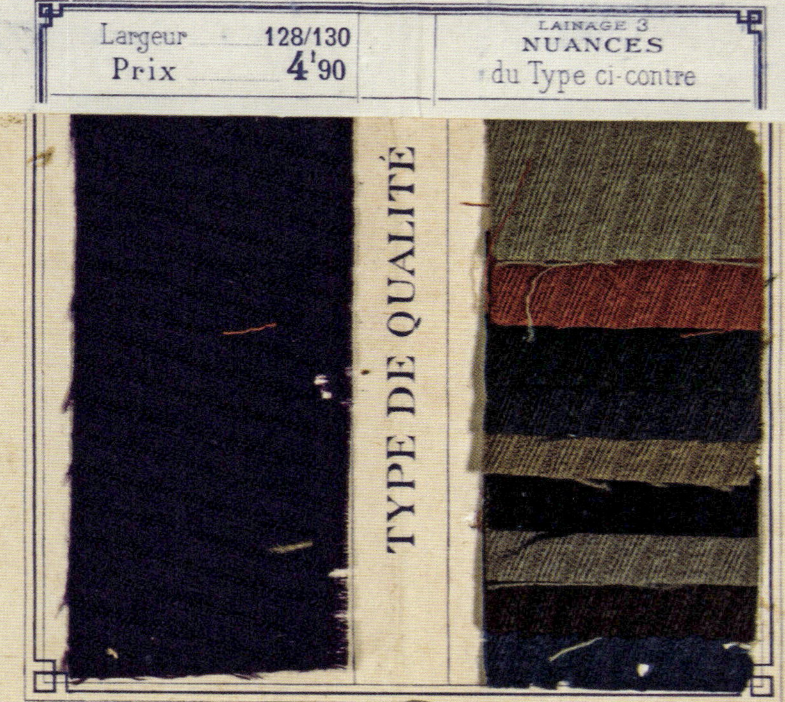

Grands Magasins du Printemps
PARIS LAGUIONIE & Cie PARIS
COMPTOIR DES LAINAGES UNIS _3
Largeur 128/130
Prix 4f90
LAINAGE 3
NUANCES
du Type ci-contre
TYPE DE QUALITÉ
NOTA: Afin d'éviter tout retard engageons nos clientes à designer un second échantillon pour le cas ou celui choisi serait épuisé.

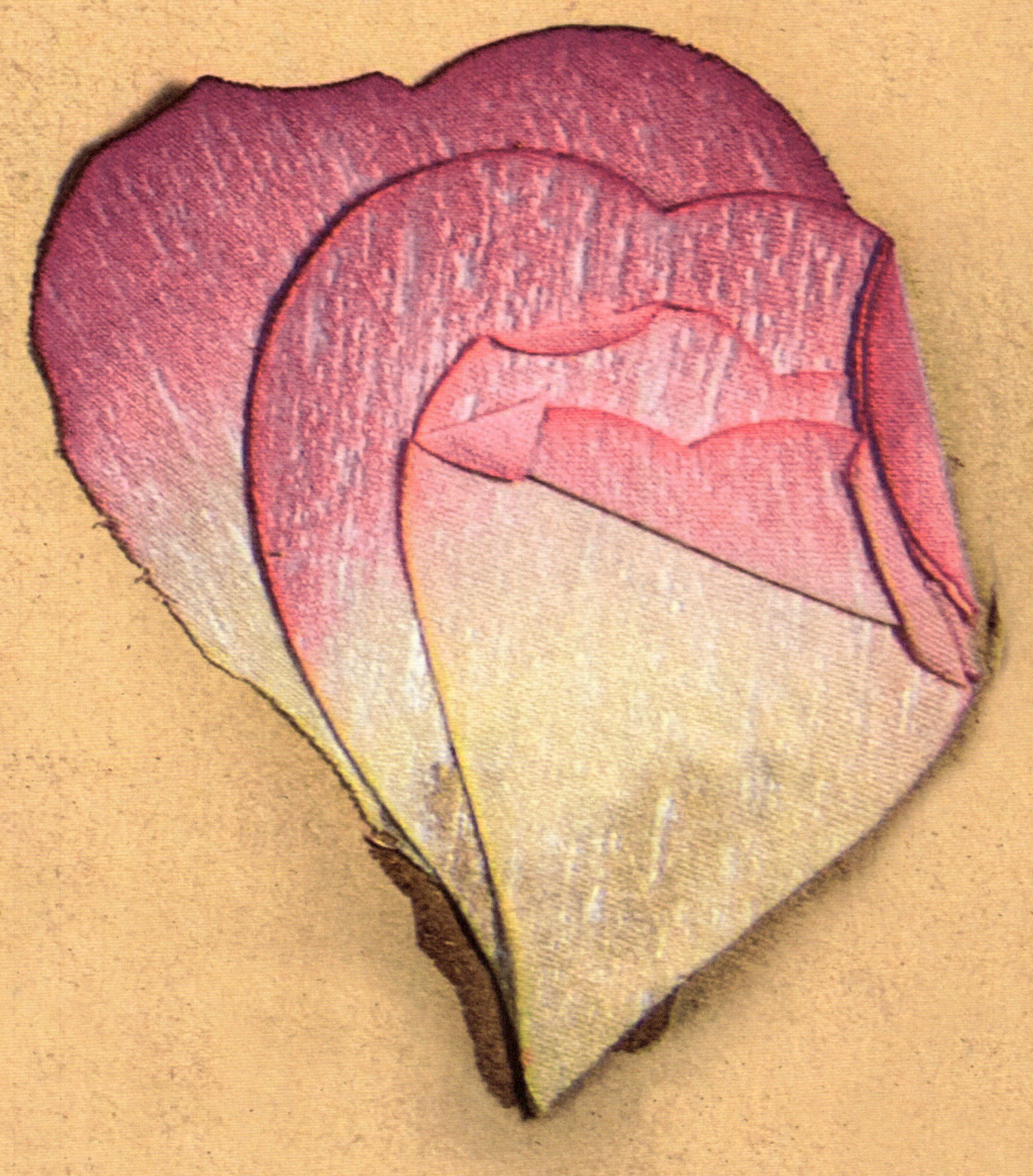

Saul Safran

A REVOLUTION IN COLOR

LATE NINETEENTH CENTURY TO WORLD WAR I

——— Commercial color charts, the products of a rapidly expanding industrial culture, spread throughout society and were no longer pertinent to only a few individuals.

When the period of social, economic, technological, and political progress called "la Belle Époque" began, the Western economy was dominated by four powers: Great Britain, closely followed by the German Empire, whose economic power was rapidly rising, the United States, where large-scale retail was taking shape, and France, in fourth place.

In the field of chemistry, the opportunities synthetic color offered had already led to industrial production. With this material aspect of color now mastered, the issue of its perception and the organization of its presentation became central. In laboratories, factories, and stores, the color sample circulated more every day. The results of the research conducted by Goethe, Chevreul, and others had encouraged the color education of new generations, in Europe and across the Atlantic and beyond, while progress in literacy and printing techniques accelerated the reach of a shared culture. The fauves, Matisse, the cubists, Kandinsky, Mondrian, Kupka, and Sonia and Robert Delaunay radically modernized color and opened new paths of exploration. Designers of haute couture wanted to liberate the female body from its constraints and offered bold palettes, which the public came across in fashion magazines.[1] Diaghilev's Ballets Russes familiarized audiences with exotic, saturated hues from the Slavic and Eastern worlds. This trend even influenced interior design, as varied, multicolored palettes began to be used for home decor, made possible by new production processes and materials.

In this context, color charts expressed the scientific, technical, and artistic energy of the era. They would become the instrument—and a very effective one—serving the manufacturers' ambitions to attract customers in France, Europe, and even the colonies, which had become more accessible due to steam navigation. The task of classification that had motivated Western thought for two centuries continued to crystallize in the logic of the color chart. The design of the color chart was refined at a time when the world of manufactured color was shaken up by the sudden appearance of new pigments and dyes. In the late nineteenth century, chemists seized this color chart tool to demonstrate their skills to manufacturers, who themselves were beginning to distribute color charts in wholesale trade and soon in retail, as stores began to produce documents showing the variety of colors available for a given item.

In these shops, consumers became familiar with this new opulence, and color charts would stimulate an appetite for color that would soon be fully expressed.

The selling power of color charts would also echo the issues that shook up society in this era: hygienic concerns were combined with wariness of new products, the fascination with versatility and abundance was hemmed in by financial constraints, and the liberation of women caused both hope and fear.

The Western world began to become colorful, and, finally, to be colorful for everyone. Soon, color would no longer be a luxury reserved for the privileged few. But the path would be long, especially as social constraints were still onerous, and for a long time color would be considered futile, feminine, or childish. It would also be viewed as a sign of the suspect morality of people of the night and, as always, the troubling extravagance of non-Western cultures.[2]

THE CHEMICAL INDUSTRY USES THE COLOR CHART TO PROMOTE THE DYEING OF RAW MATERIALS

The field of chemistry in Europe led Western societies and then the entire globe toward a world of abundant colors, available on many different materials and accessible even to those of little means. It opened the door to the standardization of color. Chemical manufacturers took advantage of this movement because dyes and pigments were at the heart of their process, and the future of their companies depended on the sale of these products.

Considerable funds and efforts were invested in applied research, not only to increase the brightness and ease of application of synthetic dyes but also to develop durable compounds. Several of them had already turned out to be unstable.

By 1900, industrial producers of synthetic colors were established, and many smaller factories also supplied the trade on a more modest scale.[3] Germany led the race to create dyes for the textile market, which was stimulated by the strong economic growth of the second half of the nineteenth century.

Facing fierce competition, chemical manufacturers were the first to use the color chart to promote sales. While we do not know the specific context in which these charts were created, it is likely that they were developed for manufacturers who wished to add color to the items they produced. But chemical manufacturers did not simply imitate the logic of the color chart; they offered versions of this tool in various forms and formats and structured it to suit their goals. The sample embodied their expertise, and they would transform its material appearance. Color charts had to be precise and informative for international users, and recognizing different types of dyes had to be routine. Additionally, space in the chart was reserved for instructions for using the products.

Despite this restrictive framework, and while maintaining scientific rigor, chemists managed to preserve and sometimes enhance the aesthetics of their documents and even introduce creative touches.

Exploring Various Modes of Presentation in Color Charts for Textile Dyes

OPPOSITE AND NEXT PAGE SPREAD

BASF's *Instructions for Silk*

In 1865, a group of companies established a factory in Mannheim to synthesize dyes, particularly aniline and its derivatives, which could produce a wide variety of shades. The name of the alliance included that of the dye: the Badische Anilin & Soda-Fabrik (BASF). Before the century was over, German chemical manufacturers mastered two dyes of major economic importance, alizarin and synthetic indigo. Less than two decades after Perkin's discovery, the BASF was able to market approximately sixty dyes for dyeing silk.[4] In order to promote the dyes, it adopted the leporello, or concertina, a very old system of attaching and folding pages that had been used in Mesoamerican codices. The fact that the leporello unfolded like an accordion made it perfectly suitable, and it allowed for a synoptic view, even with a very large number of samples. Moreover, since it was folded up, it protected the colors in the darkness of its folds and could be easily transported. The leporello became the ideal form for extensive color charts.

In the *Instructions for Silk*, the dyes determined the structure of the color chart. There are four groups of three rows of dyed threads rolled onto a strip of cardboard, with each one illustrating a degree of concentration (unsaturated, saturated,

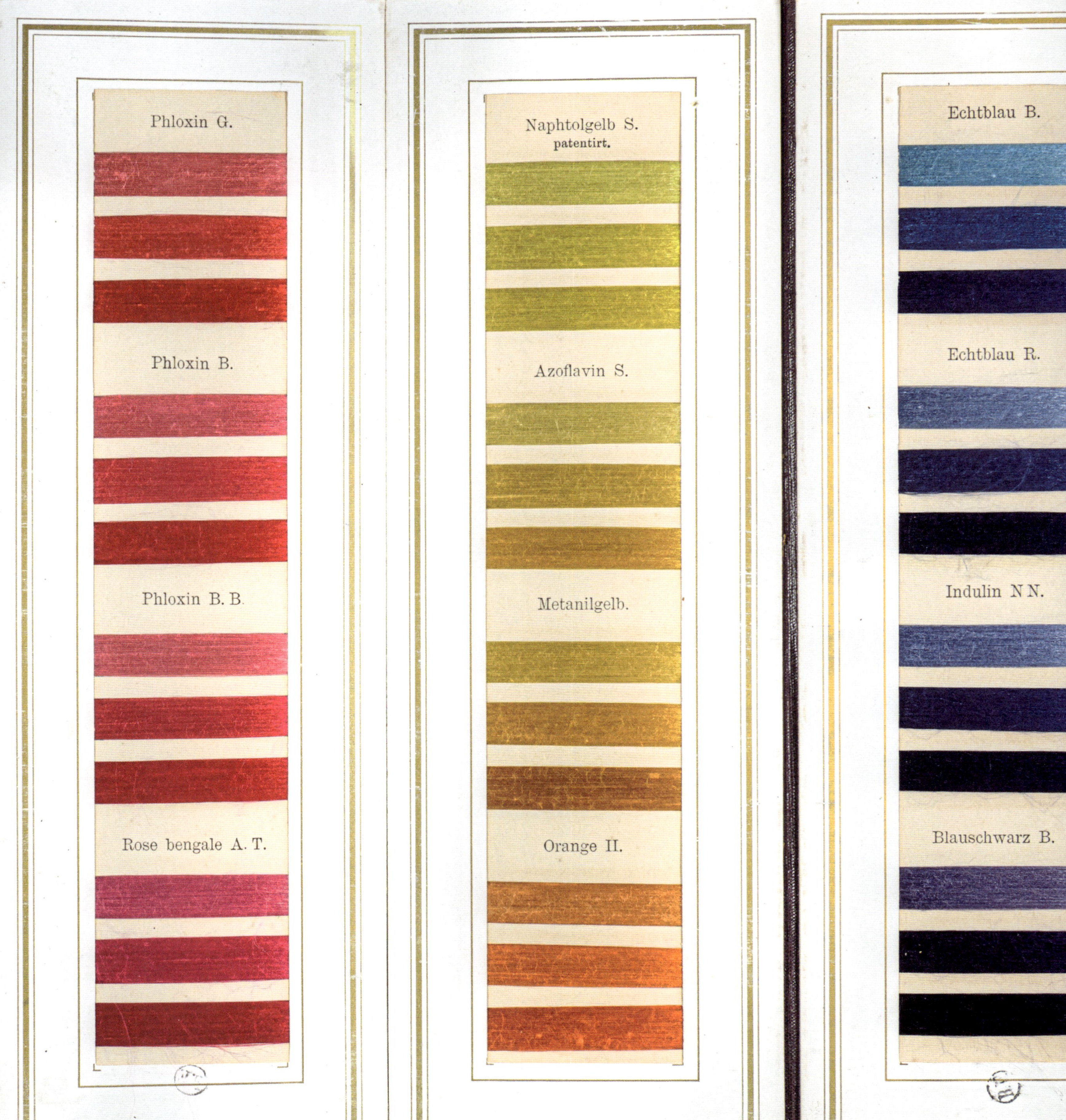
Phloxin G.
Phloxin B.
Phloxin B. B.
Rose bengale A. T.
Naphtolgelb S.
patentirt.
Azoflavin S.
Metanilgelb.
Orange II.
Echtblau B.
Echtblau R.
Indulin N N.
Blauschwarz B.

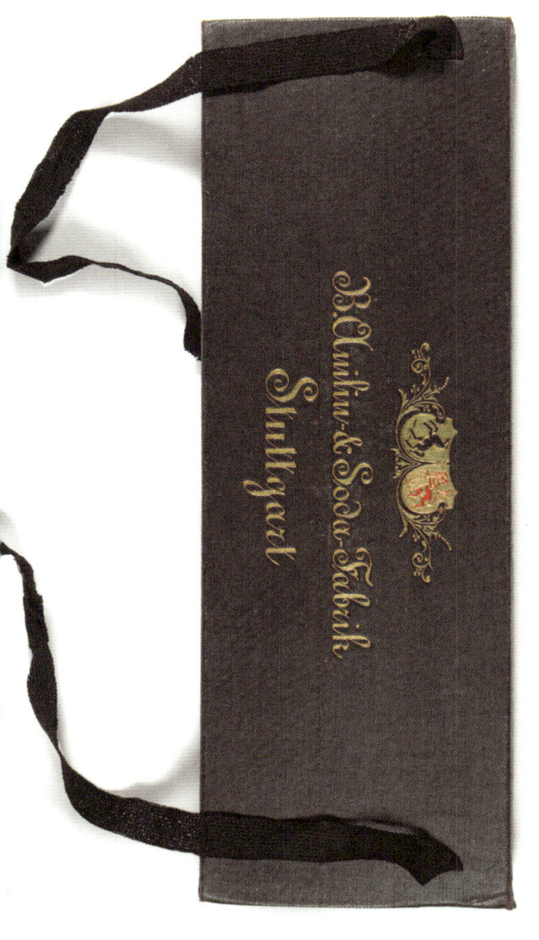

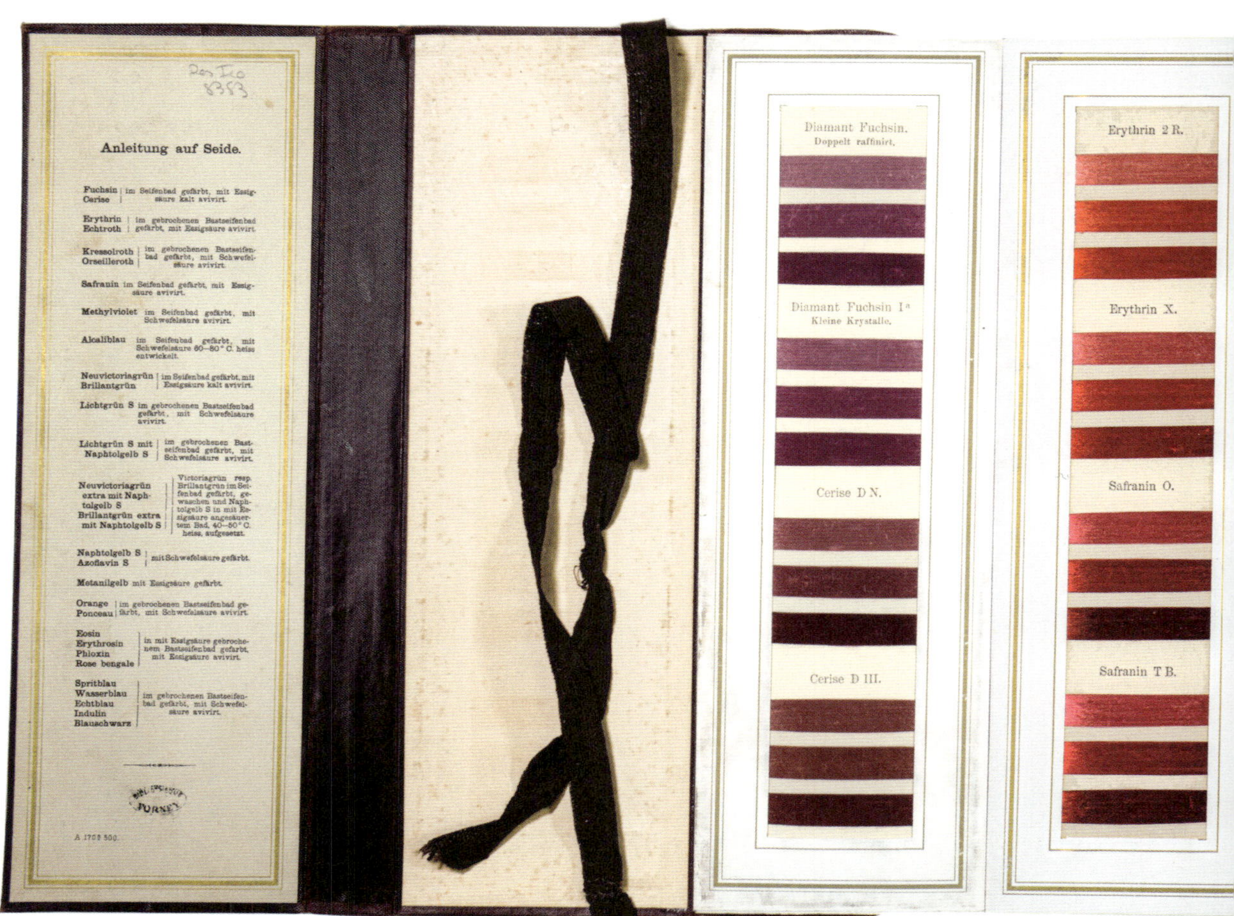

Anleitung auf Seide.

Fuchsin Cerise	im Seifenbad gefärbt, mit Essigsäure kalt avivirt.
Erythrin Echtroth	im gebrochenen Bastseifenbad gefärbt, mit Essigsäure avivirt.
Kressolroth Orseilleroth	im gebrochenen Bastseifenbad gefärbt, mit Schwefelsäure avivirt.
Safranin	im Seifenbad gefärbt, mit Essigsäure avivirt.
Methylviolet	im Seifenbad gefärbt, mit Schwefelsäure avivirt.
Alcaliblau	im Seifenbad gefärbt, mit Schwefelsäure 60–80° C. heiss entwickelt.
Neuvictoriagrün Brillantgrün	im Seifenbad gefärbt, mit Essigsäure kalt avivirt.
Lichtgrün S	im gebrochenen Bastseifenbad gefärbt, mit Schwefelsäure avivirt.
Lichtgrün S mit Naphtolgelb S	im gebrochenen Bastseifenbad gefärbt, mit Schwefelsäure avivirt.
Neuvictoriagrün extra mit Naphtolgelb S Brillantgrün extra mit Naphtolgelb S	Victoriagrün resp. Brillantgrün im Seifenbad gefärbt, gewaschen und Naphtolgelb S in mit Essigsäure angesäuertem Bad, 40–50° C. heiss, aufgesetzt.
Naphtolgelb S Azoflavin S	mit Schwefelsäure gefärbt.
Metanilgelb	mit Essigsäure gefärbt.
Orange Ponceau	im gebrochenen Bastseifenbad gefärbt, mit Schwefelsäure avivirt.
Eosin Erythrosin Phloxin Rose bengale	in mit Essigsäure gebrochenem Bastseifenbad gefärbt, mit Essigsäure avivirt.
Spritblau Wasserblau Echtblau Indulin Blauschwarz	im gebrochenen Bastseifenbad gefärbt, mit Schwefelsäure avivirt.

A 1708 500.

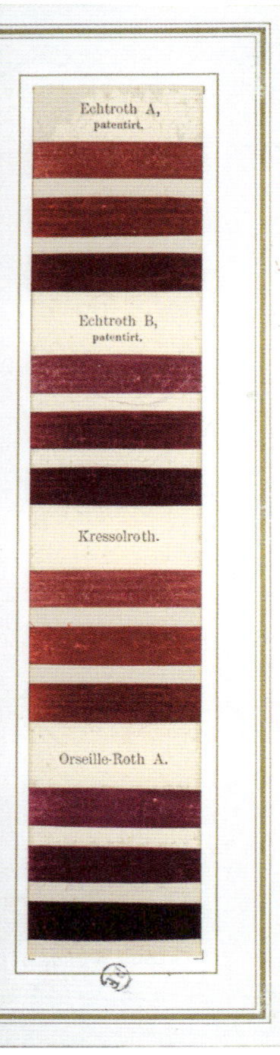
Echtroth A,
patentirt.
Echtroth B,
patentirt.
Kressolroth.
Orseille-Roth A.

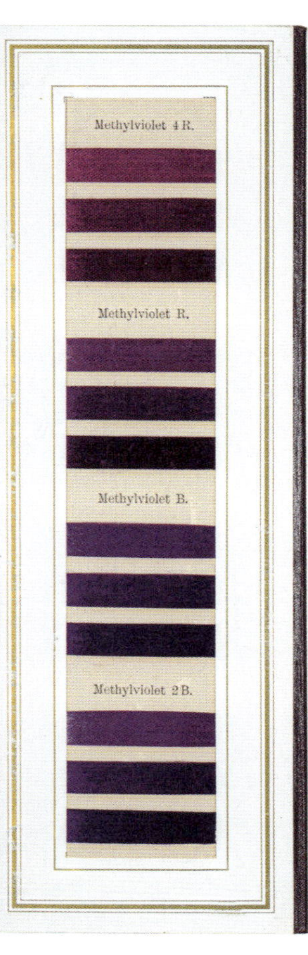
Methylviolet 4 R.
Methylviolet R.
Methylviolet B.
Methylviolet 2 B.

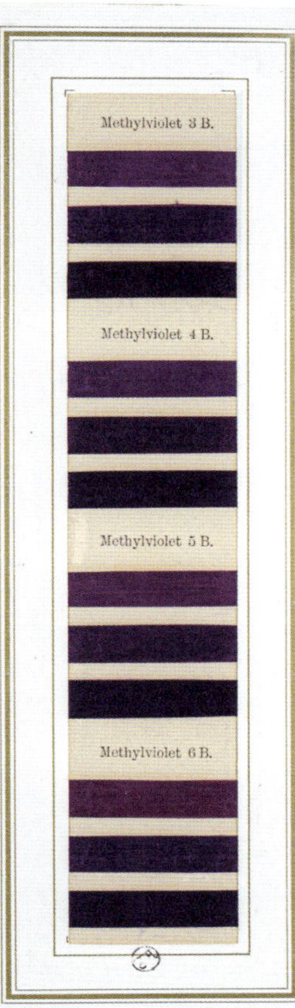
Methylviolet 3 B.
Methylviolet 4 B.
Methylviolet 5 B.
Methylviolet 6 B.

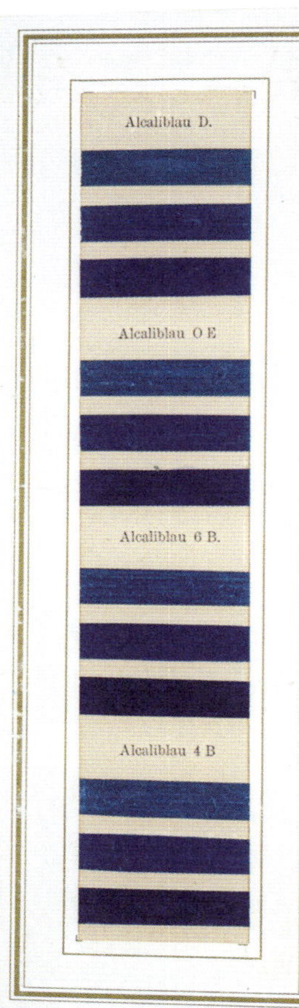
Alcaliblau D.
Alcaliblau O E
Alcaliblau 6 B.
Alcaliblau 4 B

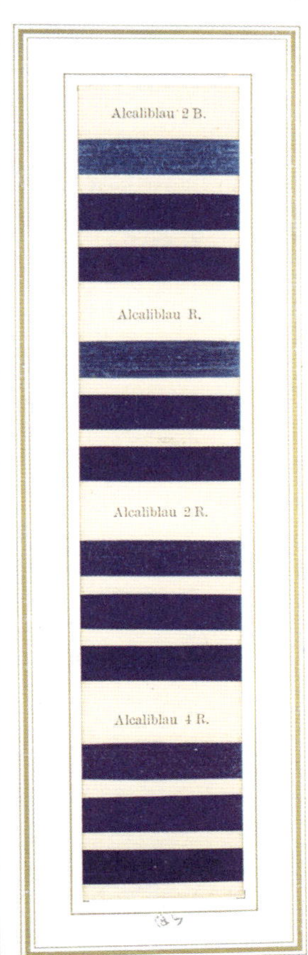
Alcaliblau 2 B.
Alcaliblau R.
Alcaliblau 2 R.
Alcaliblau 4 R.

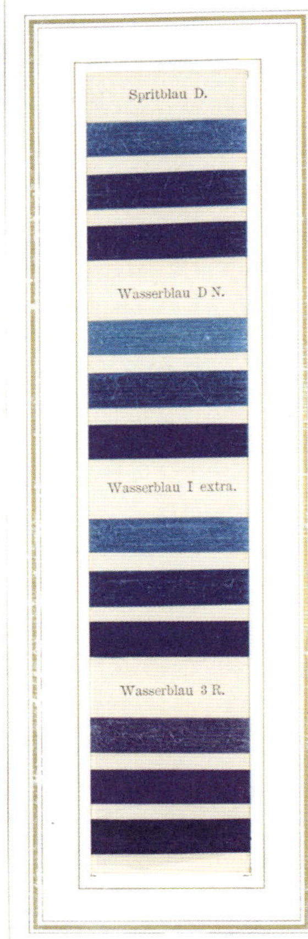
Spritblau D.
Wasserblau D N.
Wasserblau I extra.
Wasserblau 3 R.

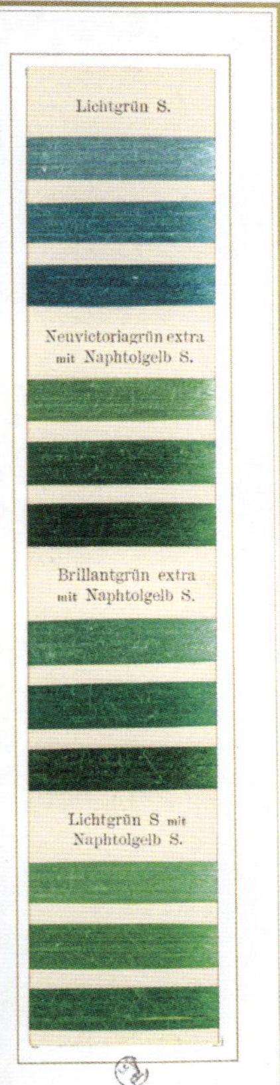
Lichtgrün S.
Neuvictoriagrün extra
mit Naphtolgelb S.
Brillantgrün extra
mit Naphtolgelb S.
Lichtgrün S mit
Naphtolgelb S.

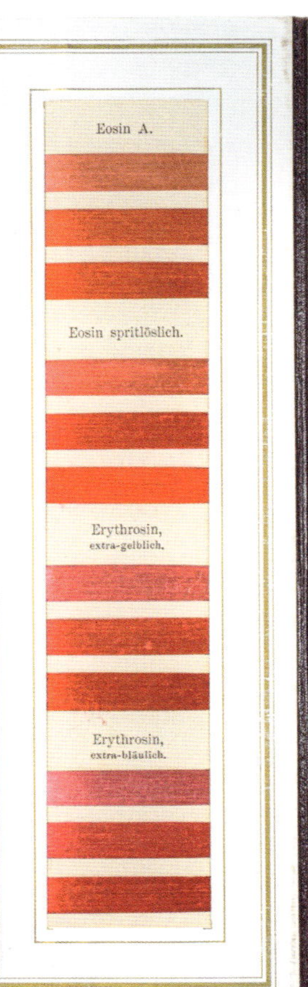
Eosin A.
Eosin spritlöslich.
Erythrosin,
extra-gelblich.
Erythrosin,
extra-bläulich.

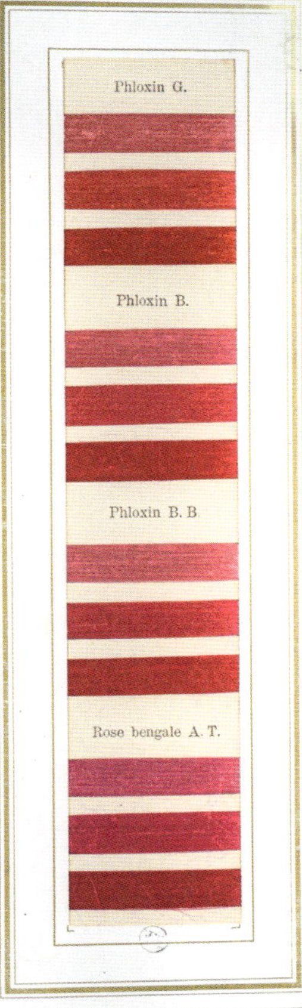
Phloxin G.
Phloxin B.
Phloxin B. B
Rose bengale A. T.

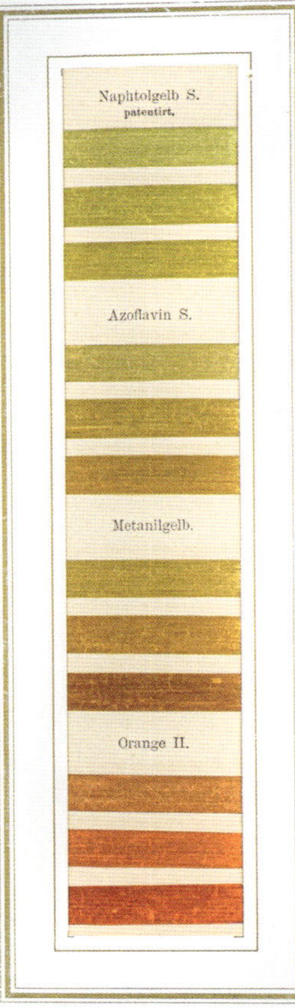
Naphtolgelb S.
patentirt.
Azoflavin S.
Metanilgelb.
Orange II.

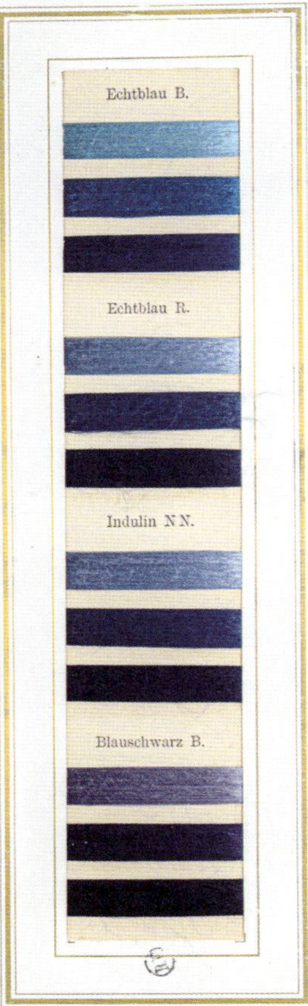
Echtblau B.
Echtblau R.
Indulin N N.
Blauschwarz B.

and very saturated shades). The primary role attributed to the dye means that a single shade can be found on different panels. This strategy also determined the identification of the colors, which were all designated (in German) by the name of the dye. Adding a formula of a few lines was the final touch.

This color chart could only be used by professional dyers. Carefully developed for their use, it would prove to be completely effective. The adventure of the commercial color chart for the chemical industry was underway.

Instructions for Silk (Anteilung auf Seide), Badische Anilin & Soda-Fabrik, Germany, c. 1880, leporello, 26 × 9 cm, 15 panels, Bibliothèque Forney, Paris, number RES ICO 8383 1

OPPOSITE, TOP

Société Anonyme Saint-Denis's *Colors from Sulfur*

A. Poirrier and G. Dalsace merged their companies in 1881 to become the Société Anonyme des Matières Colorantes et Produits Chimiques de Saint-Denis, so this color chart is probably one of their very oldest.

The company presented its sulfur dyes in a box and adopted a structure based on the dyes, with their names appearing on the eight double pages printed with views of the factory in Saint-Denis. The interior pages included on the left a summary of the properties of the dyes and instructions to dye 100 kilograms of cotton. The right-hand side of the page held the samples, which were bundles of cotton yarn held in place using an ingenious system of perforations. They displayed the shades that could be obtained depending on the concentration of the dye.

The sober shades of these dyes created a color chart that was less flamboyant than other charts distributed by the chemical industry at the same time. However, this color chart reveals the various approaches that were adopted to present a clear, complete, durable, and enjoyable demonstration of the qualities of various products.

Colors from Sulfur, Société Anonyme des Matières Colorantes et Produits Chimiques de Saint-Denis, Établissements A. Poirrier et G. Dalsace, Saint-Denis, c. 1885 (?), cardboard box, 25 × 17.5 × 18 cm containing 8 double plates, Albi Couleurs, Association Mémoire des Industries de la Couleur, Albi

OPPOSITE, BOTTOM

BASF Aniline Colors

As confirmed by this other document distributed by the BASF, the German chemical industry already offered various versions of color charts and established a particular aesthetic. This example is part of a teaching manual for dyeing devoted to the famous aniline dyes, the basis of synthetic color. One chapter discussed various dyeing processes on different fibers.[5]

The twenty plates of samples accompanying the text were presented by fiber category; it was only after this initial structure was set up that the grouping into plates of samples took place. The 669 samples were thus divided into several color charts, with the goal of covering the entire color spectrum for each type of fiber.

Nine years after the publication of Oscar Piéquet's treatise, *The Chemistry of Dyers, New Theoretical and Practical Treatise on the Art of Dyeing and Printing Fabrics*, this handbook presented the same subject—synthetic dyes for various textile fibers—and the same educational purpose. But in this work, the samples in a given plate differed only in their hue, making color clearly apparent. The samples of the BASF were there to indicate that the firm knew which dyes to use in order to obtain a certain shade on a certain fiber and that it was able to sell the required dye.

In these early years of the twentieth century, research gave way to winning over customers. This approach was already established enough that aesthetic pleasure could be associated with scientific and technical excellence. While the previous BASF color chart offered a very plain presentation, this one showed a desire to use the artistic opportunities of fiber sampling. The twenty plates feature rows or sets of fabric swatches and bunches of thread, with tufts of fabric, known as *mouchets*, tied in bows, fanned out, or formed into rosettes.[6] These tufts allowed for judging the effects of the color (which could be very different depending on whether the eye sees the fiber in the form of a tassel or tied), with the loose part available for touching in order to appreciate the texture of the material. This kind of sampling, perfectly suited for textile fibers, would remain the preferred method for a long time.

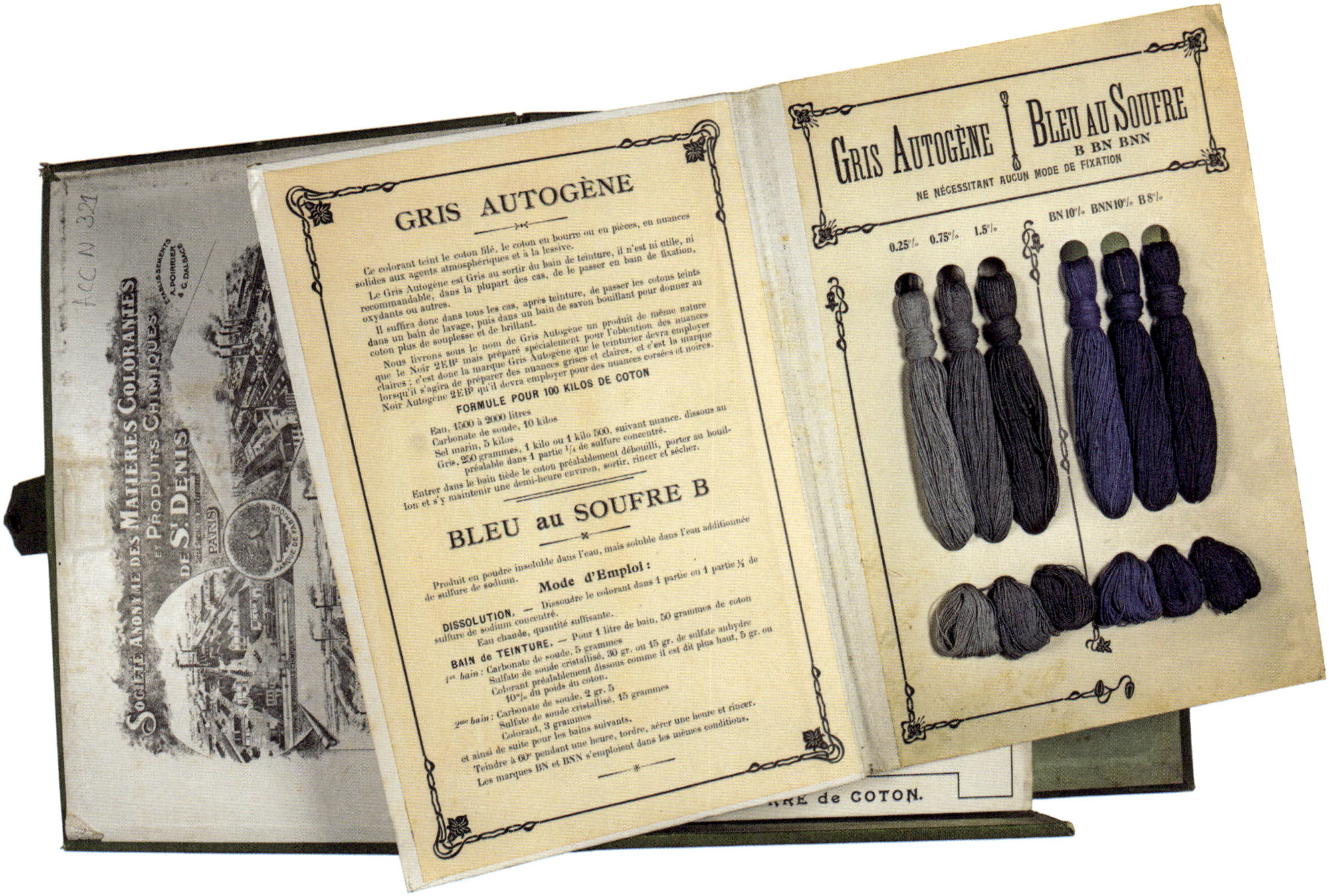

Société Anonyme des Matières Colorantes et Produits Chimiques de St. Denis

GRIS AUTOGÈNE

Ce colorant teint le coton filé, le coton en bourre ou en pièces, en nuances solides aux agents atmosphériques et à la lessive.

Le Gris Autogène est Gris au sortir du bain de teinture, il n'est ni utile, ni recommandable, dans la plupart des cas, de le passer en bain de fixation, oxydants ou autres.

Il suffira donc dans tous les cas, après teinture, de passer les cotons teints dans un bain de lavage, puis dans un bain de savon bouillant pour donner au coton plus de souplesse et de brillant.

Nous livrons sous le nom de Gris Autogène un produit de même nature que le Noir 2EB² mais préparé spécialement pour l'obtention des nuances claires ; c'est donc la marque Gris Autogène que le teinturier devra employer lorsqu'il s'agira de préparer des nuances grises et claires, et c'est la marque Noir Autogène 2EB² qu'il devra employer pour des nuances corsées et noires.

FORMULE POUR 100 KILOS DE COTON

Eau, 1500 à 2000 litres
Carbonate de soude, 10 kilos
Sel marin, 5 kilos
Gris, 250 grammes, 1 kilo ou 1 kilo 500, suivant nuance, dissous au préalable dans 1 partie 1/4 de sulfure concentré.

Entrer dans le bain tiède le coton préalablement débouilli, porter au bouillon et s'y maintenir une demi-heure environ, sortir, rincer et sécher.

BLEU au SOUFRE B

Produit en poudre insoluble dans l'eau, mais soluble dans l'eau additionnée de sulfure de sodium.

Mode d'Emploi :

DISSOLUTION. — Dissoudre le colorant dans 1 partie ou 1 partie ½ de sulfure de sodium concentré.
Eau chaude, quantité suffisante.

BAIN de TEINTURE. — Pour 1 litre de bain, 50 grammes de coton

1er bain : Carbonate de soude, 5 grammes
Sulfate de soude cristallisé, 30 gr. ou 15 gr. de sulfate anhydre
Colorant préalablement dissous comme il est dit plus haut, 5 gr. ou 10% du poids du coton.

2me bain : Carbonate de soude, 2 gr. 5
Sulfate de soude cristallisé, 15 grammes
Colorant, 3 grammes

et ainsi de suite pour les bains suivants.
Teindre à 60° pendant une heure, tordre, aérer une heure et rincer.
Les marques BN et BNN s'emploient dans les mêmes conditions.

GRIS AUTOGÈNE | BLEU AU SOUFRE B BN BNN

NE NÉCESSITANT AUCUN MODE DE FIXATION

0.25% 0.75% 1.5% | BN 10% BNN 10% B 8%

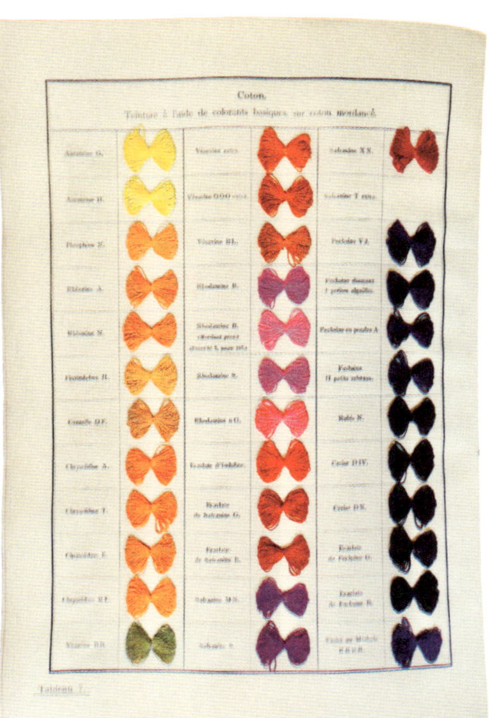

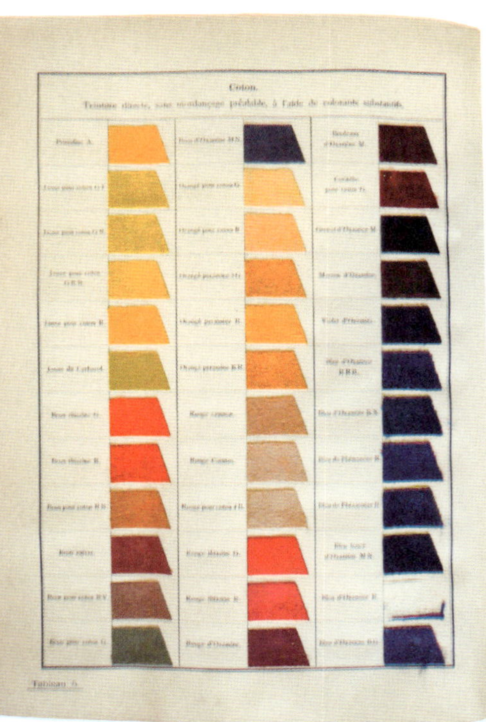

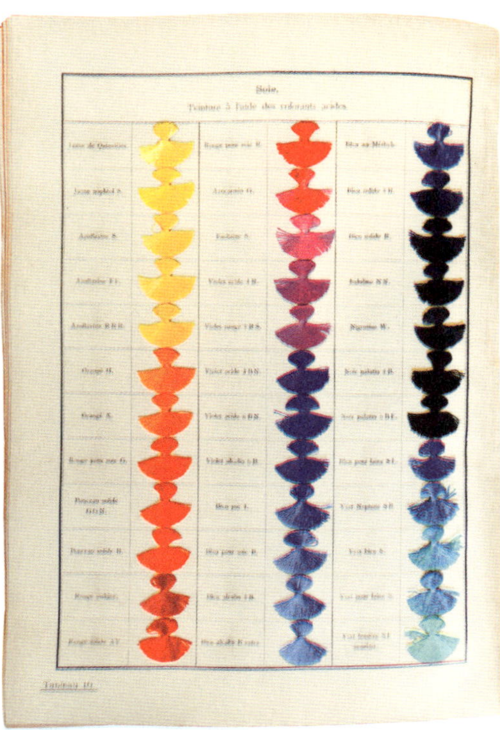

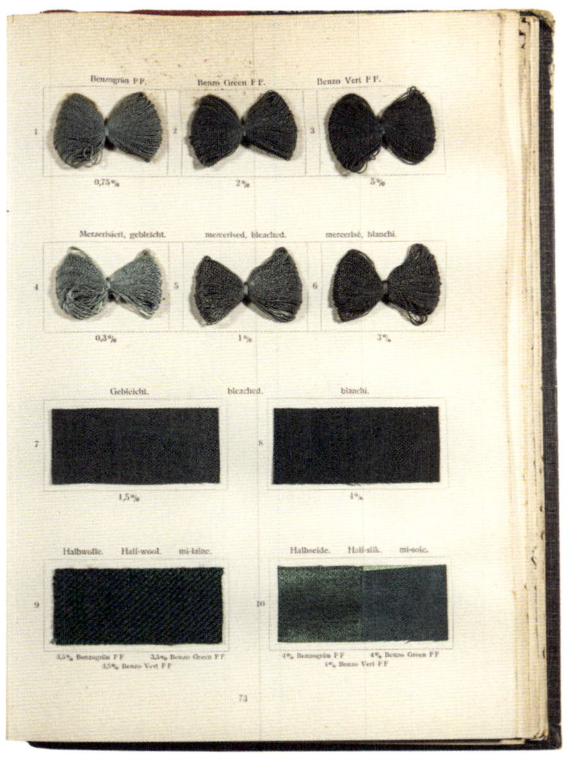

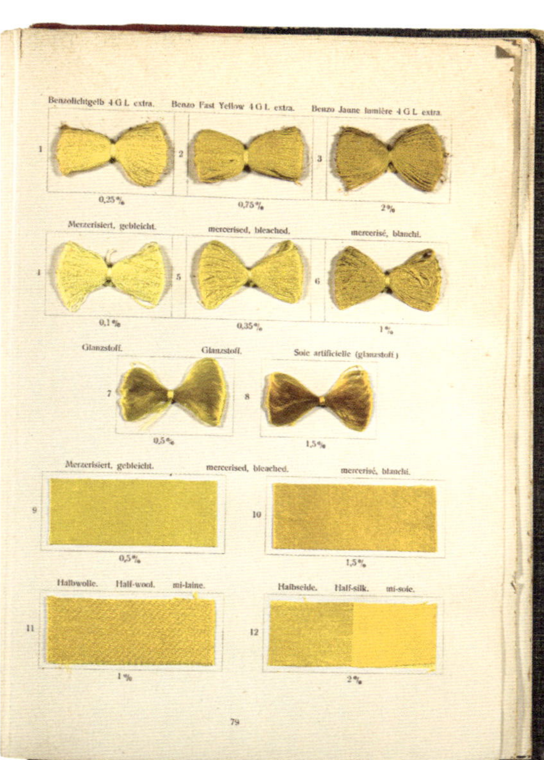

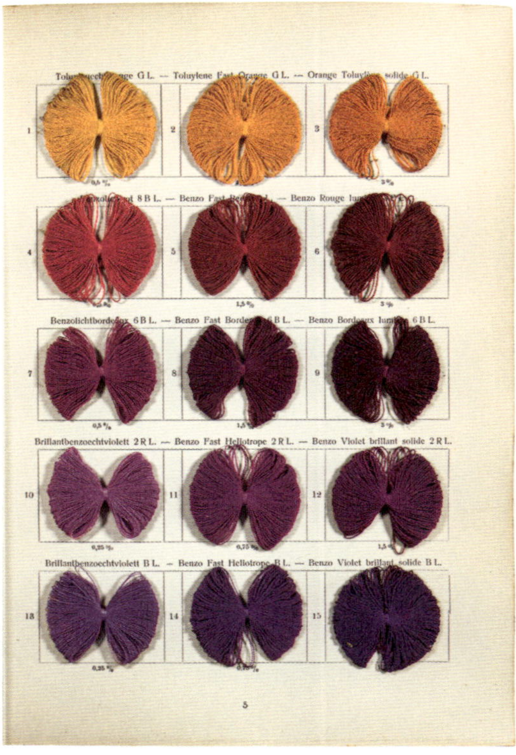

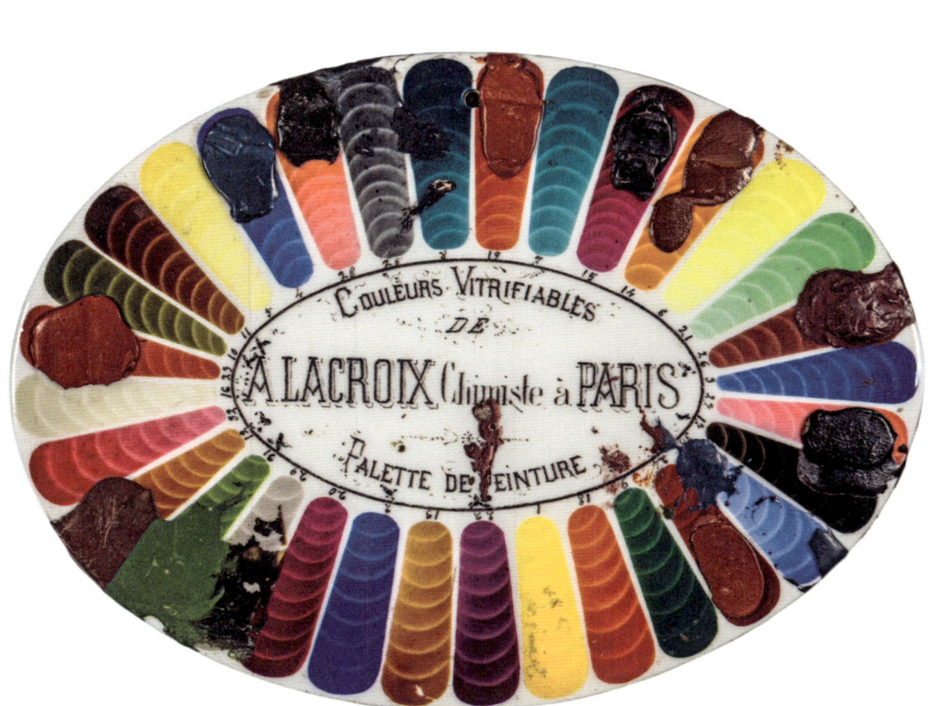

Couleurs Vitrifiables
de
A. LACROIX Chimiste à PARIS
Palette de Peinture

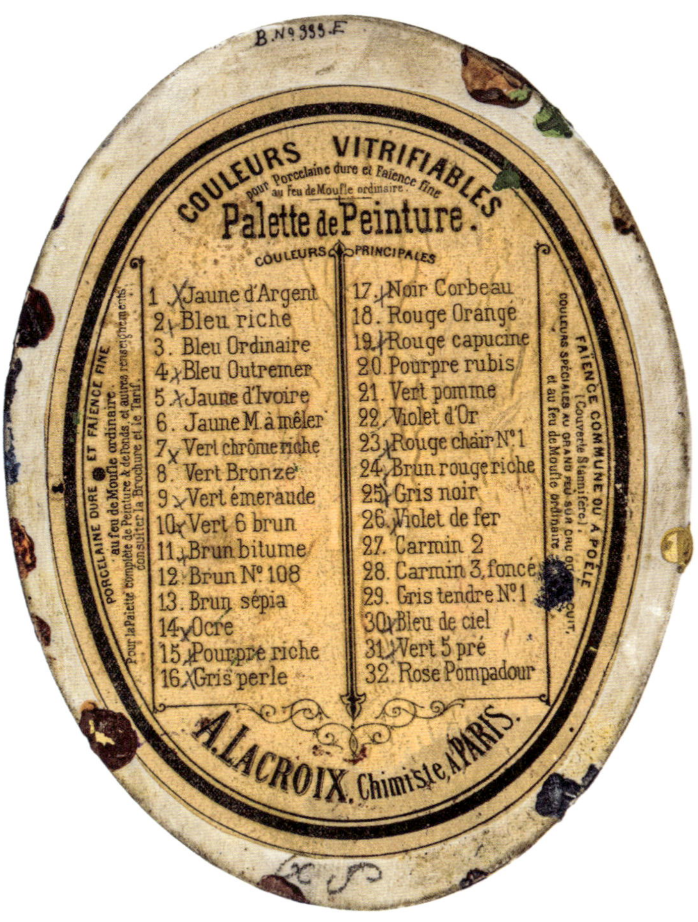

B. N° 333 E
COULEURS VITRIFIABLES
pour Porcelaine dure et Faïence fine
au feu de Moufle ordinaire
Palette de Peinture.
COULEURS PRINCIPALES
1. Jaune d'Argent
2. Bleu riche
3. Bleu Ordinaire
4. Bleu Outremer
5. Jaune d'Ivoire
6. Jaune M. à mêler
7. Vert chrôme riche
8. Vert Bronze
9. Vert émeraude
10. Vert 6 brun
11. Brun bitume
12. Brun N° 108
13. Brun sépia
14. Ocre
15. Pourpre riche
16. Gris perle
17. Noir Corbeau
18. Rouge Orange
19. Rouge capucine
20. Pourpre rubis
21. Vert pomme
22. Violet d'Or
23. Rouge chair N° 1
24. Brun rouge riche
25. Gris noir
26. Violet de fer
27. Carmin 2
28. Carmin 3, foncé
29. Gris tendre N° 1
30. Bleu de ciel
31. Vert 5 pré
32. Rose Pompadour
A. LACROIX, Chimiste, à PARIS.

With some exceptions (including *Cinnamon*, *Jet-Black*, *Salmon Red*, *Iris Violet*, *Copper Brown*), the names of the samples were, as in the previous color chart, and as would be the rule in all those distributed by the chemical industry, codes using the names of the dyes with or without an indication of tone (*Red Violet 5R extra*, *Nigrosin WH*, and so on). Developed to demonstrate scientific expertise to manufacturers, these documents required precision. Synthetic chemistry revived only a few terms referring to the rich history of natural dyeing (*Safranin Scarlet B*, *Solid Poppy G.*). Names such as *Vesuvine BB*, *Neptune Green SB*, *Ruby N.*, *Alcohol Mauve*, *Bengal Pink NT*, or *New Bordeaux L* illustrated the inventive efforts of finding a name for each individual color given an unprecedented profusion of shades. This was an old question that had been inherent to the thematics of color since the very first classification attempts, but it became increasingly complex and remained a thorny issue in the world of color charts.

The Aniline Colors of the Badische Anilin & Soda-Fabrik, and Their Applications on Wool, Cotton, Silk, and Other Textile Fibers (*Die Anilinfarben der Badischen Anilin-& Soda-Fabrik und ihre Anwendung auf Wolle, Baumwolle, Seide und sonstigen Textilfasern*), BASF, Ludwigshafen am Rhein, 1900, book, 16.5 × 18.5 cm, 270 pp., 20 charts, Albi Couleurs, Association Mémoire des Industries de la Couleur, Albi

OPPOSITE, TOP

Bayer Cotton Dyes

When Bayer presented its recently developed dyes in 1909, the company clearly shared the same ambition of offering the entire color spectrum. Page 5 thus displays colors from yellow to violet that can be achieved on mercerized cotton using different concentrations of various dyes. However, the book is structured around the dyes: the plates are dedicated to a single dye and show its effect on various types of fibers at the same time (cotton, artificial silk, wool-silk blends). However, the firm alternated tufts and swatches of fabric and designated the samples by the name of the molecules that were already noted in previous documents.

The desire to show the textile industry the opportunities offered by the latest dyes explains the structure used in this document. With text in German, English, and French, the company planned to circulate this document to an international clientele.

Dyes for Cotton for 1909, Société Anonyme des Produits Fréd. Bayer & Cie, Flers par Croix, 1909, book, 27 × 19 cm, 87 pp., 24 plates, private collection, Paris

Similar Research for Other Applications

OPPOSITE, BOTTOM

Lacroix Vitrifiable Colors

Although ceramics were much less important economically than textiles, chemistry did devote attention to ceramics. This sector required specific materials and techniques that led to early use of the color chart. Of particular importance is the fact that glazes reveal their colors only after being fired in the kiln.[7] Of course, the ceramicist's experience allowed him to predict the future appearance of his creations. In fact, in the mid-eighteenth century, color charts were developed by applying strokes of enamel identified by a name or number to pieces of earthenware or ceramic. This type of object was sometimes called by the name *palette aveugle* ("blind palette").[8]

The end products ceramicists produced became more complex when synthetic pigments became available, transforming and expanding the palette of available oxides.[9] In 1863, the chemist Adolphe Lacroix founded a company specializing in the production and commercialization of colors for ceramics. Starting in the 1880s, he attempted to eliminate the role of chance in firing colors by circulating a whole series of these blind palettes.[10] They would guide craftspeople, whether at the Manufacture de Sèvres, in the factories of Limoges, or in artisanal workshops.

No systematic order seemed to determine the presentation of the colors, except for avoiding showing the various shades of the same color next to each other. Each of the thirty-two samples was featured in eight different tones, depending on the concentration of oxide and the thickness of the glaze that was applied. On the back of the palette, the list of colors combined common names (*Apple Green*, *Orange-Red*, *Crow Black*, *Ultramarine Blue*, *Pompadour Pink*, and so on) with some that were more specific to ceramics (*Silver Yellow*, *Rich Blue*) or that mentioned the oxide used (*Rich Chromium Green*, *Iron Violet*).

Vitrifiable Colors for Hard Porcelain and Fine Earthenware, Adolphe Lacroix et Compagnie, Paris, 1870s, porcelain disc, 12.5 × 17 cm, Albi Couleurs, Association Mémoire des Industries de la Couleur, Albi

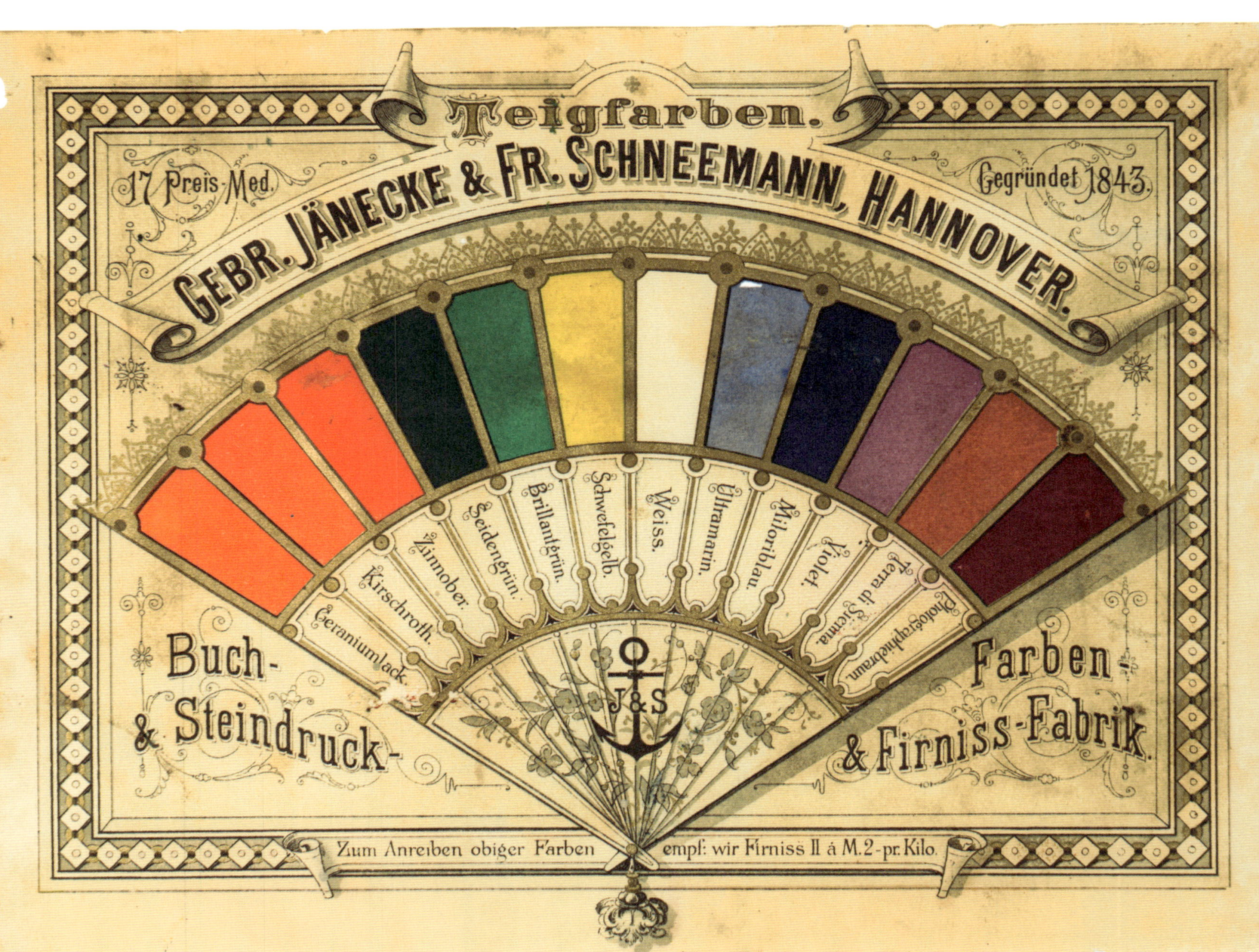
Teigfarben.
17 Preis-Med.
Gegründet 1843.
GEBR. JÄNECKE & FR. SCHNEEMANN, HANNOVER.
Geraniumlack.
Kirschroth.
Zinnober.
Seidengrün.
Brillantgrün.
Schwefelgelb.
Weiss.
Ultramarin.
Miloriblau.
Violet.
Terra di Sienna.
Photographiebraun.
J&S
Buch-
& Steindruck-
Farben-
& Firniss-Fabrik.
Zum Anreiben obiger Farben empf: wir Firniss II á M. 2-pr. Kilo.

OPPOSITE

Jänecke & Schneemann
Inks for Printing

The chemical industry was also interested in printing inks. Over the course of the nineteenth century, lithography, silkscreen printing, and chromolithography had opened up a wide range of possibilities for color printing.[11] By the century's end, the need for colored ink increased considerably for publishing illustrated books, textbooks, cards, images, and also for commercial printing purposes (product labeling and packaging, advertising, sales catalogs), and for printing color charts.

The Jänecke & Schneemann company, founded in 1843, was one of the first factories to produce black typographic inks in Germany, to which it added lithographic color inks in tubes in the late nineteenth century. The fan arrangement, which was rare at this time, was perhaps inspired by the blind palettes of ceramicists or Harris's color wheels, which had been reproduced from 1766 onward in many books on color (including those by Chevreul).

Of the twelve inks shown, the three shades of red now look almost identical. This is most likely because of deterioration due to the age of the document. On the segments of the fan, the names of the colors appear in beautiful calligraphy: *Geranium Lacquer*, *Cherry Red*, *Vermilion*, *Silk Green*, *Brilliant Green*, *Sulfur Yellow*, *White*, *Lapis-Lazuli*, *Milori Blue*,[12] *Mauve*, *Sienna Earth*, and *Photographic Brown*.[13]

This color chart was intended for artisans, not manufacturers. Using more familiar color names, instead of the molecules used as names in the contemporary chemistry color charts, expressed the manufacturer's desire to avoid intimidating his clients. These efforts increased when the color chart entered retail stores and it became necessary to attract individual consumers.

In an irony of history, color charts of printing inks promoted the very products that allowed colors to be reproduced, thus leading a few decades later to the elimination of samples, the fragments of fabric, paper, wood, and other colorful materials.

Inks for Printing, Gebr. Jänecke & Fr. Schneemann, Hanover, Germany, late 1880s, paper, approximately 20 × 26 cm, Bibliothèque Forney, Paris, call number RES ICO 8104

The chemical industry, aware of the potential for pleasure offered by a physical color that is attractively presented, even in the technical context of deals between manufacturers, explored all the artistic, aesthetic, and sensory opportunities the color chart offered. And this was only the beginning of the epic tale of materials that were dyed by synthetic chemistry. Many of the materials would come about after World War I.

SILK THREAD DYERS ORIENT THEIR COLOR CHARTS TOWARD CREATIVITY

Synthetic dyes transformed the practices of dyers of textile fibers, and also the way in which the dyers promoted their products: color charts of dyed threads began to multiply in the late nineteenth century in the major centers for spinning.[14] Chemistry color charts and dyers' color charts influenced each other reciprocally. The chemical industry had financial, technical, and human resources at its disposal that were far beyond those of the dyers' workshops or factories, but the textile world had a long history of color sampling, even if it had thus far only occasionally used the tool of the color chart. Chemical manufacturers and the dyeing industry both used the leporello format, but, as their clients had different expectations, they developed their tools in different ways.

The oldest color charts from the dyeing industry that have come down to us are devoted to silk thread and silk ribbons. Silk is a luxury fiber that reaped colossal profits, especially through exports.[15] The companies that made and sold it were able to devote significant budgets and time to producing color charts. They also felt obliged to do so because, on the threshold of the twentieth century, the silk market had become very competitive. Moreover, the appeal of cotton and man-made silk-like fabrics threatened their business. Finally, the fast pace of the rhythm of the fashion industry required anticipating production in advance of design. Using color charts, dyers could inform the marketplace about their art of color. Once again, the presence of the sample was critical. The beauty glimpsed by the eyes was inseparable from the pleasure felt by the fingertips. The tactile experience of the sample was essential in the world of textiles and would ensure the presence of fabric swatches or bundles of thread for quite some time.

The color charts presented here are from two major centers where the production of French silk had been well established since the seventeenth century: Nîmes and the regions of Lyon and Saint-Étienne.

Molecules Meet Fabric in the Color Chart of a Nîmes Dyer

OPPOSITE AND BELOW

Rouvière Frères Silk Threads

Did the Rouvière Frères company dye silk thread itself or did it simply sell it? Historical documentation is missing. In any case, its color chart appears to link those distributed by the contemporary German chemical industry and the color cards that were beginning to be developed by the silk dyers and ribbon makers of Lyon and Saint-Étienne.[16]

Each of the 360 thread samples, stretched over a cardboard sheet attached to the panels of the leporello, is identified by a number written in pen, with a vertical reading order. Fully extended, this color chart measures 2.16 m, with the colors organized by tones, from the lightest to the most saturated. The Rouvière Frères color chart is as exhaustive and comprehensive as the chemistry color chart. However, the complete absence of information about the dyes used confirms that the goal here is to promote silk thread that has already been dyed to weaving or dressmaking companies.

This color chart is not only evidence of its early use for the dyed silk market, but also of the circulation of color charts from the chemical industry among the dyers, who adopted the leporello despite its limitations and its cost. Indeed, the leporello was difficult to produce: the thread had to be dyed in several colors, and then it had to be offered in multiple shades, and finally the whole had to be organized with a clear and elegant presentation that was sturdy enough to allow handling with minimum damage.

Color chart of silk threads, Rouvière Frères, Nîmes, c. 1890, leporello, 27.5 × 9 cm, 24 panels, Musée du Vieux Nîmes, Nîmes, inv. 922.37.2

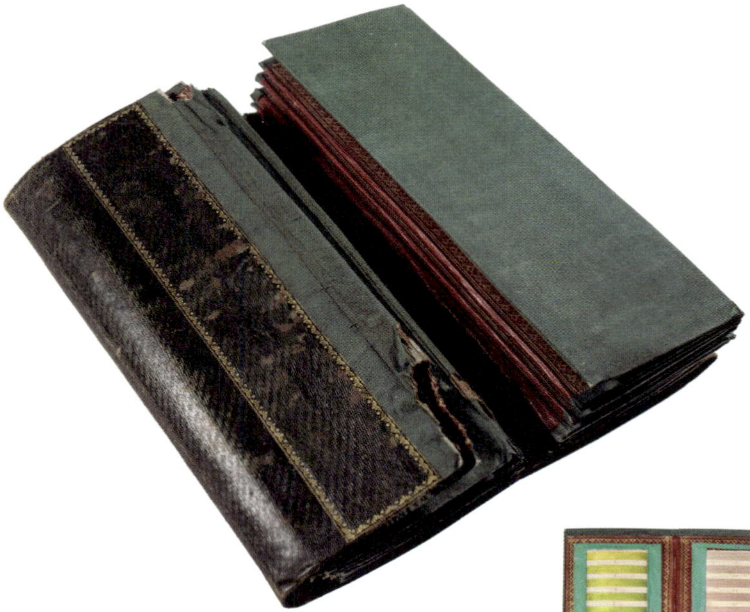

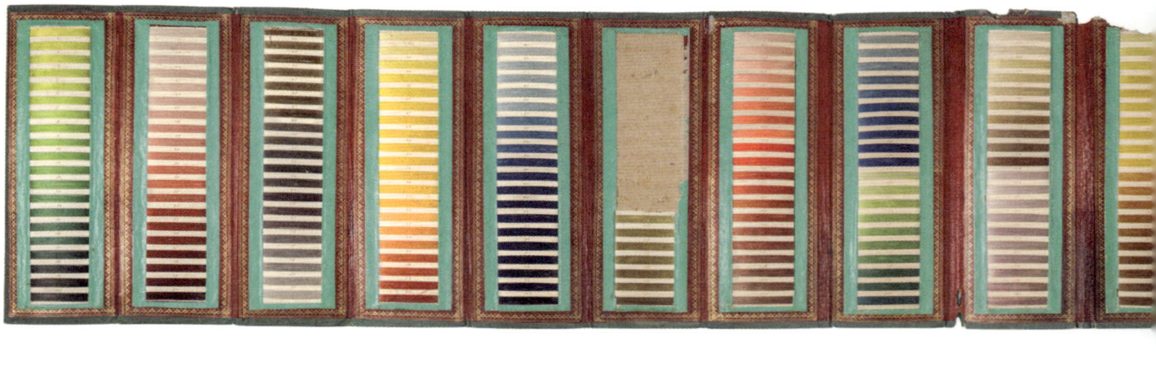

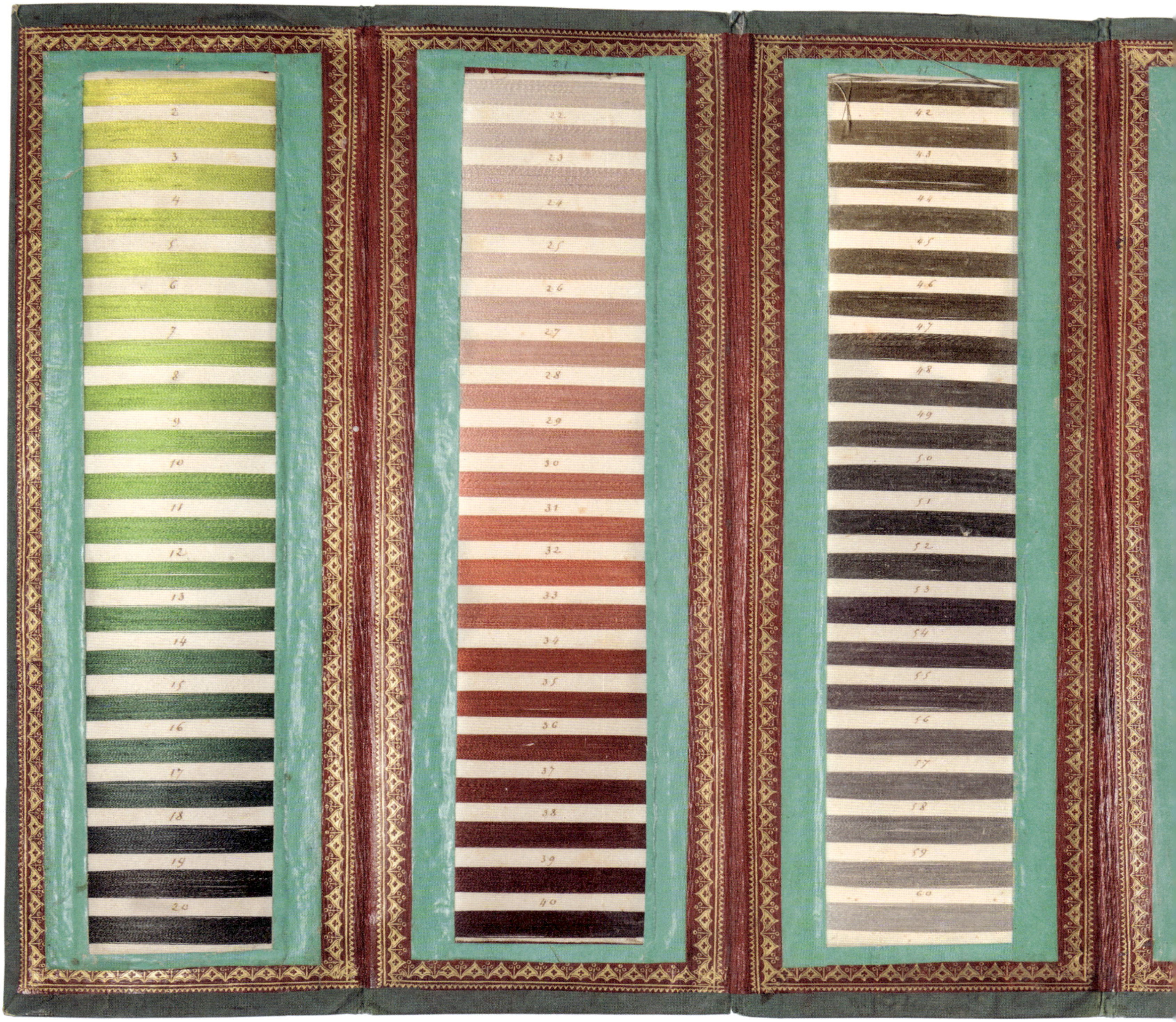

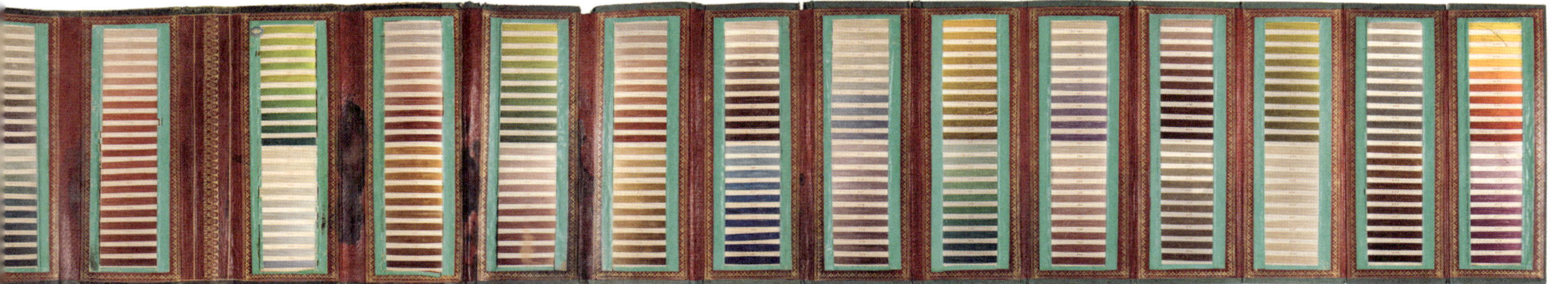

In Lyon and Saint-Étienne, the Silk Dyers Showcase Their Skills

The silk dyers of the Lyon and Saint-Étienne regions also invested in the color chart in the late nineteenth century.[17] While the unpredictability of the fashion market made production challenging, the silk manufacturers of "la Grande Fabrique" knew that unpredictability was also a powerful driver of consumerism.[18]

Synthetic compounds had been incorporated into the dyeing process, and some of them were developed by scientists trained in Lyon itself, either in schools of chemistry applied to silk dyeing or in the laboratories of major dyers. The three charts below were produced for the managers of weaving factories so that they could choose colors according to the intended fabrics. These charts illustrated the dyers' skill, but most of all they demonstrated dyers' ability to select a group of dyes to create a range of colors that would appeal to fabric manufacturers. Quite aware that the color chart was the ideal tool to showcase their expertise, the dyers featured them in the exhibitions they attended, and if they won awards, they added the accolades to their marketing material.

OPPOSITE

Corron and Vignat Silk Tufts

Enterprising dyers C. Corron and M. Vignat filed several patents from 1858 to 1880 to improve dyeing processes.[19] This color chart apparently dates to the 1880s. It presents sixteen rows of six tufts that are attached at the top with numbered labels that are sequenced for a horizontal reading from one end of the leporello to the other. There seems to be no logic in the order of the colors. However, the groups of six tufts are systematically arranged in a single tone with increasing saturation. For a long time, this would remain the rule for silk color charts.

While it was logical for the dyers to offer a smaller number of samples than the chemical industry offered, the absence of greens, bright blues, blacks, and true pinks on this color chart suggests that perhaps this chart was part of a larger set. There is also another noticeable difference that represents an early innovation: each group of tufts is designated by a fanciful name evoking the natural world (*Bulrush*, *Waves*, *Pomegranate Tree*, and even *Gnat*) or exotic locales (*Egypt*, *Bella Ombra*, *Marabou*, and so on).[20] This effort to describe colors using poetic terms indicated a real break with the color charts the chemical industry circulated, such as that of Rouvière Frères, which labeled them with numbers. These color charts were designed to seduce manufacturers to use the most beautifully colored silks. Creativity was essential. Adding expressive words to the description of colors was a smart strategy. However, it was not until the late 1900s that this practice became widespread.

Color chart with tufts of silk, Corron & Vignat, Saint-Étienne, 1880s, leporello, 32 × 16 cm, 10 panels, Bibliothèque Forney, Paris, inv. RES ICO 5884

NEXT PAGE SPREAD

Rolland and Cie Silk Tufts

The following years brought few changes in format, except for an increasing number of samples. However, the goal of the color charts became more clearly defined.

On the first panel of this color chart from the company E. Rolland & Cie, a handwritten note reads "spring season 1902." This indicates that the silk manufacturers now saw themselves as setting color trends for each season.

This color chart arrays 450 samples, but, as in the previous document, the groups of tufts seem to be arranged with no rhyme or reason. A client seeking a blue shade would need to consult almost every panel to find one. Therefore, it was necessary to unfold the entire color chart, especially if several hues had to be selected and compared with one another. This was no easy task since it required a space of 3.6 meters!

At the turn of the century, the color chart thus became an essential marketing tool to inform the public about the range and quality of a company's offerings twice a year, like the color charts of ribbons that the Union des Syndicats had circulated since the 1880s. Comparing the colors

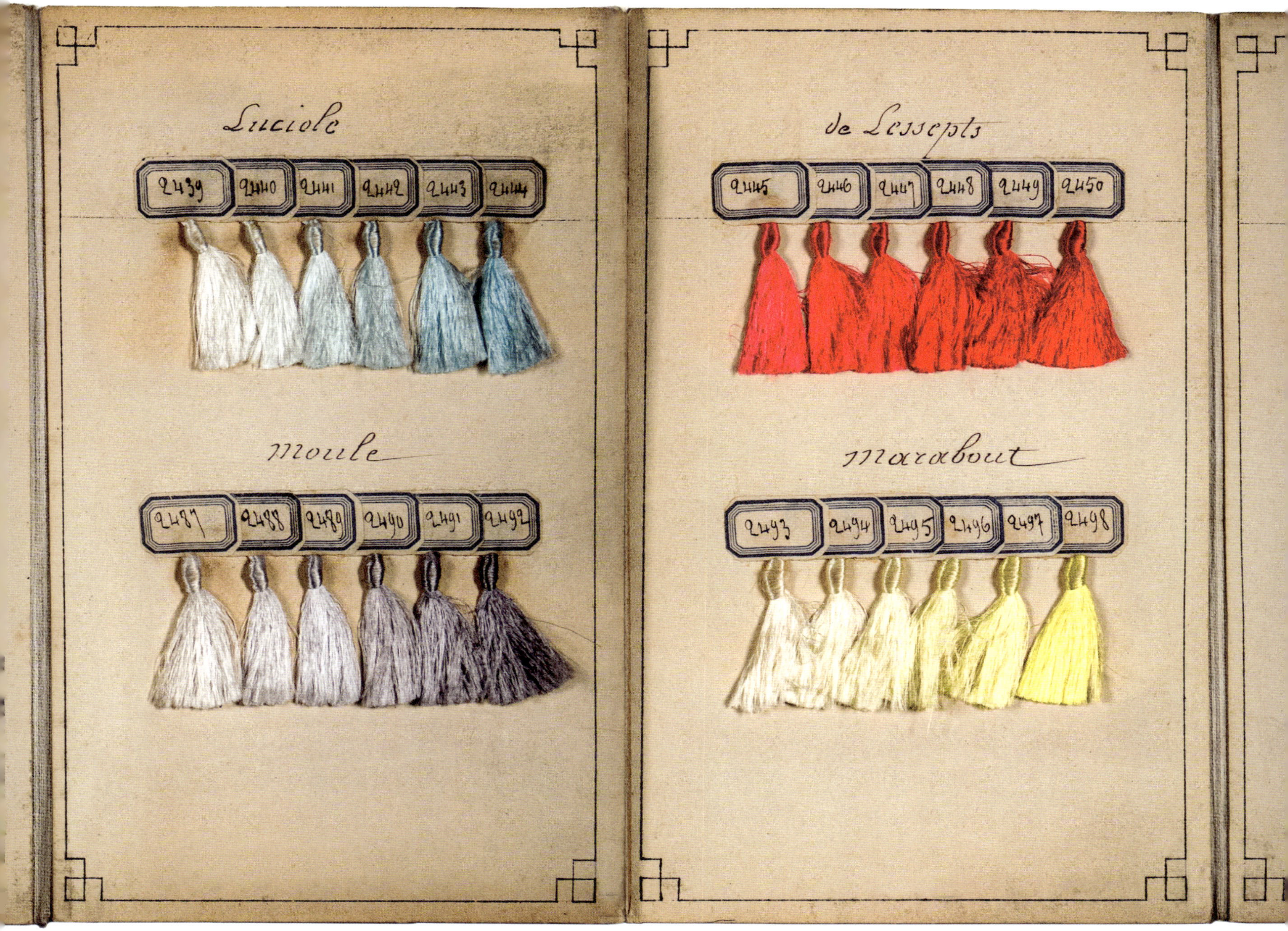

Luciole
2439 2440 2441 2442 2443 2444
de Lessepts
2445 2446 2447 2448 2449 2450
moule
2487 2488 2489 2490 2491 2492
marabout
2493 2494 2495 2496 2497 2498

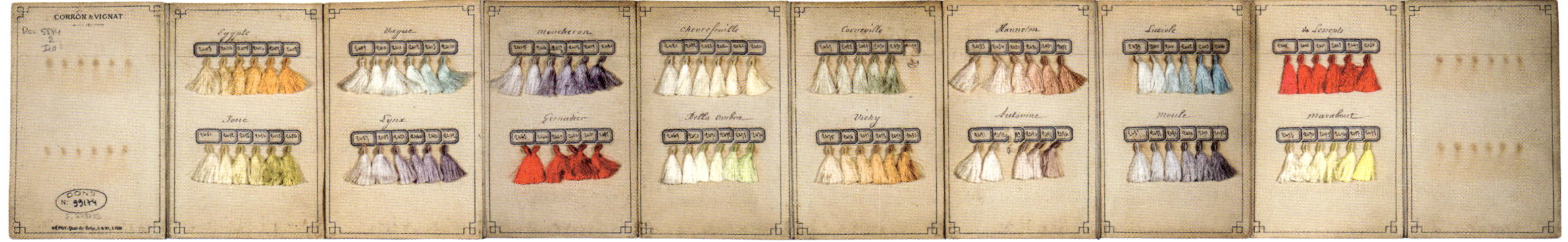

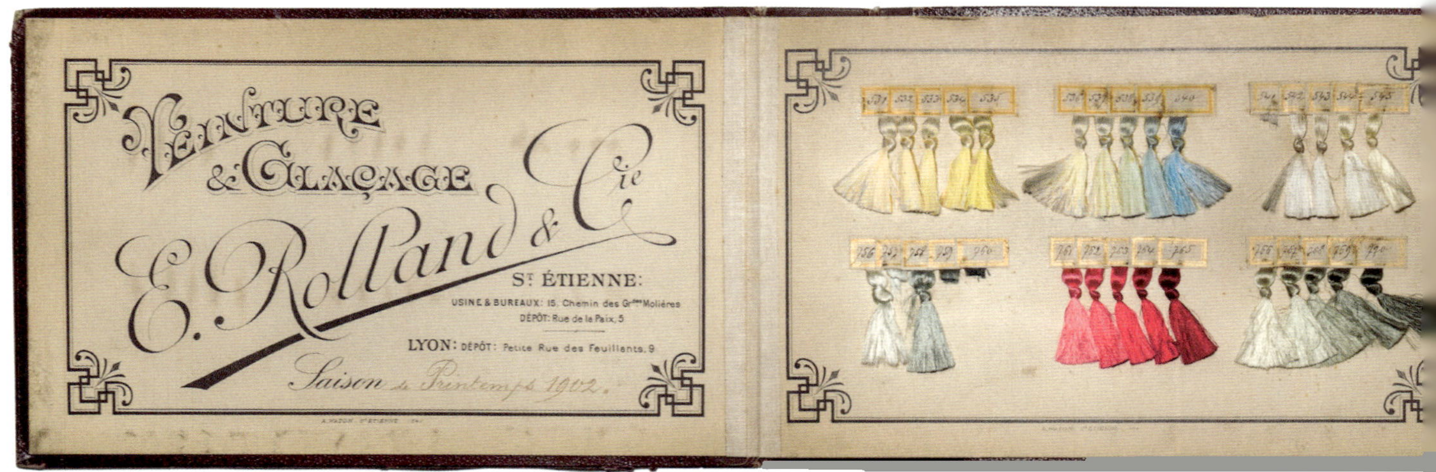
Teinture & Glaçage
E. Rolland & Cie
St ÉTIENNE:
USINE & BUREAUX: 15, Chemin des Grdes Molières
DÉPÔT: Rue de la Paix, 5
LYON: DÉPÔT: Petite Rue des Feuillants, 9
Saison de Printemps 1902.
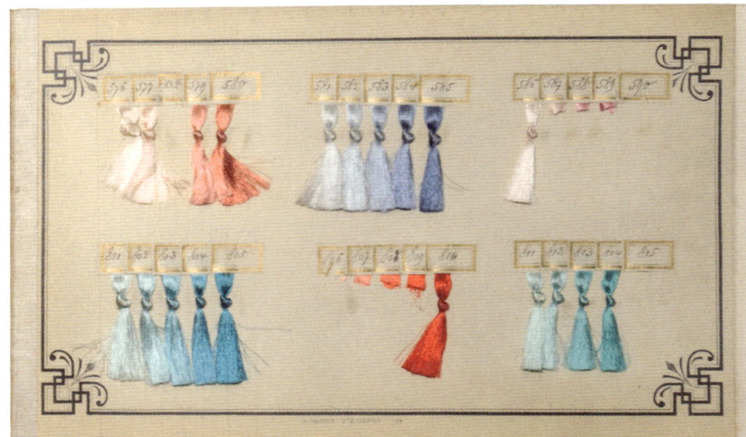
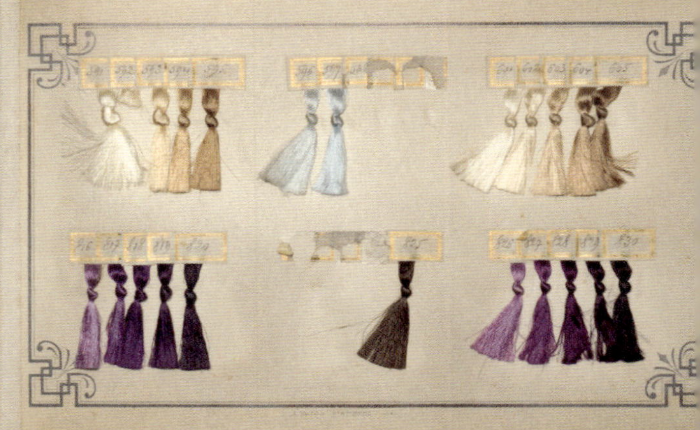
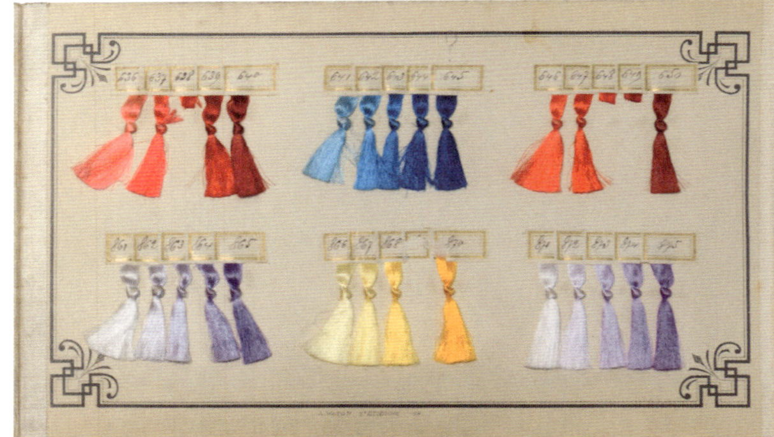
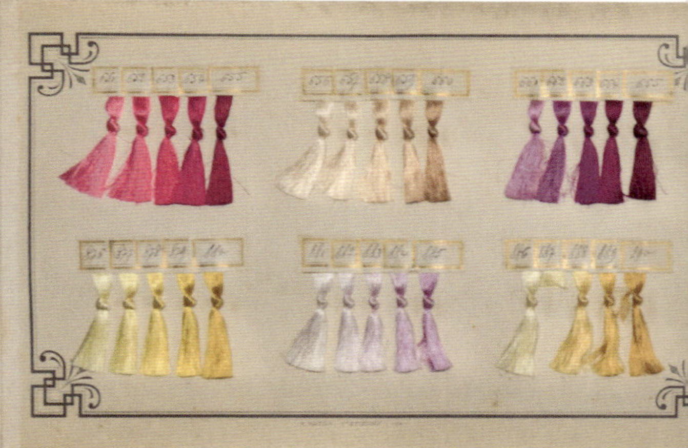
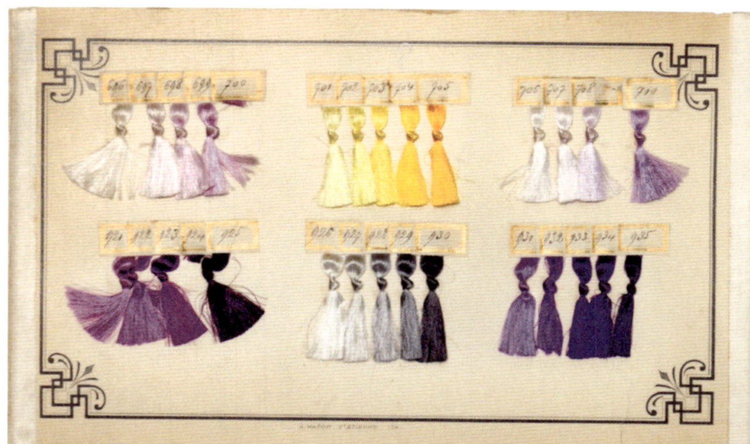
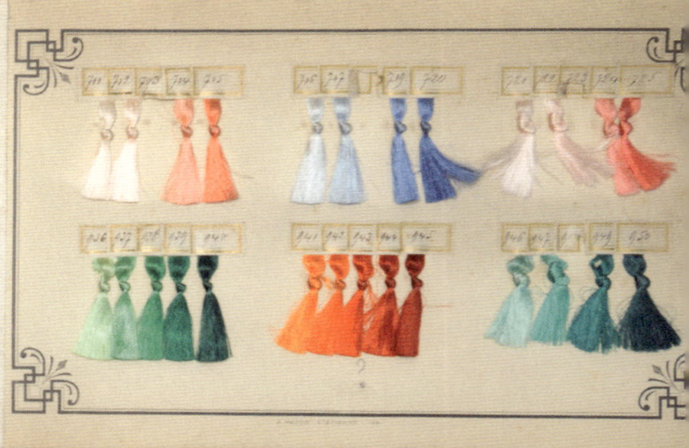

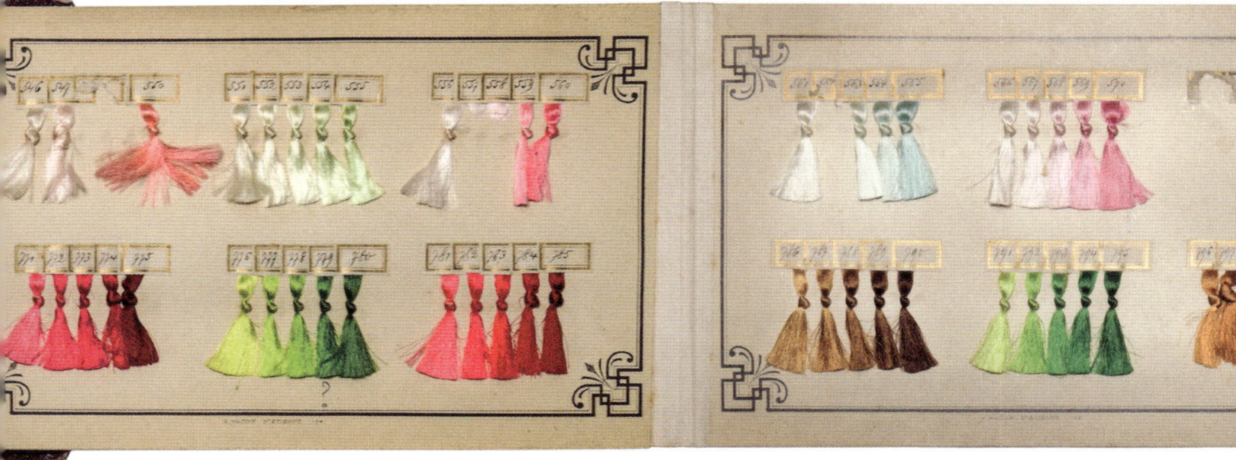
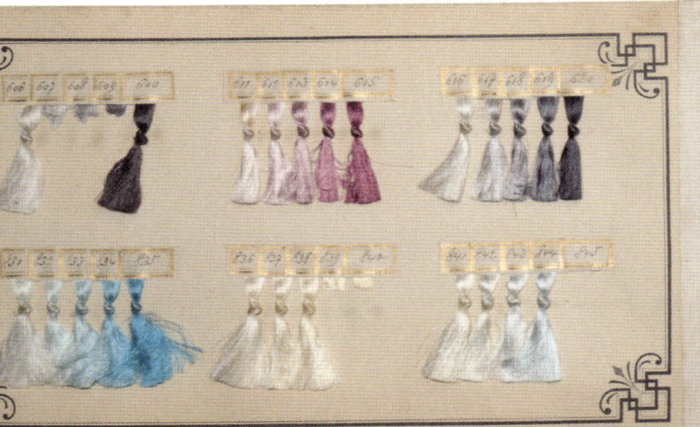
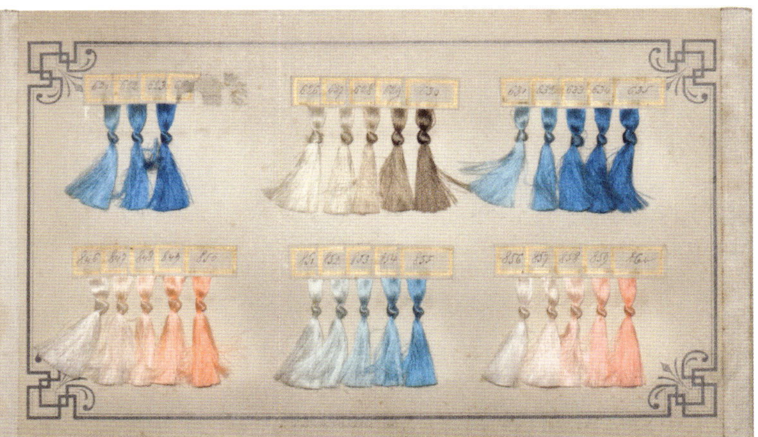
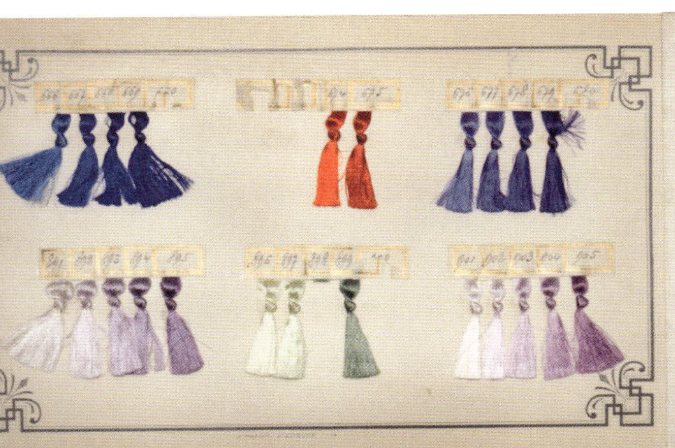
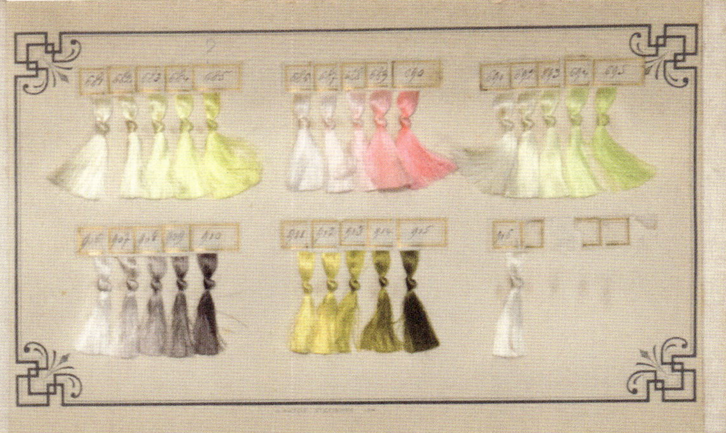
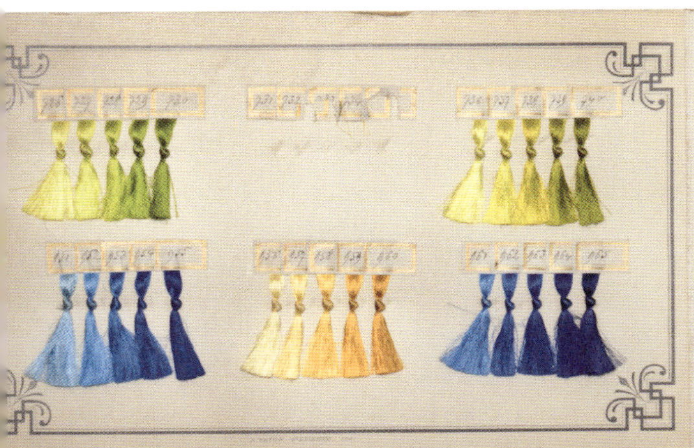
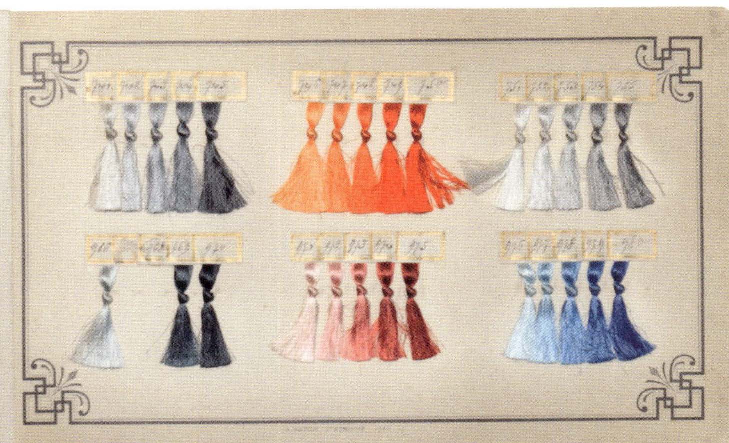

presented in two adjoining years for autumn and spring confirms, unsurprisingly, the choice of specific ranges.[21] Traditionally, since the cold weather required thicker fabrics that are difficult to dry, darker shades were emphasized in order to hide spots. Conversely, in the spring and summer, lightweight fabrics allowed for lighter tones and bright colors echoing the plethora of colorful plants and flowers.

Color chart with tufts of silk, E. Rolland & Cie, Saint-Étienne-Lyon, spring season, 1902, leporello, 15 × 24 cm, 15 panels, private collection, Paris

OPPOSITE

The Dyers of Saint-Étienne

The noticeable changes seen in this chart from five years after the previously illustrated chart indicate that several dyers were now collectively producing color charts and bearing the expense together. This one presents the silk dyes produced by eleven companies.

When the leporello was turned, the tufts could be displayed vertically. In this orientation the space the color chart took up was more economical: when unfolded, it measured only 145 cm. Most of all, the samples were now classified by intensity, with pale colors on the first four panels followed by bright colors. Despite a high number of colors (480), finding one's way in the range of shades became easier, even if it was still awkward to compare all the grays, yellows, pinks, and so on. Additionally, each group of tufts had its own name. As in the Corron & Vignat color chart, some names refer to the natural world, while others—after all, this was the golden age of the ocean liners—evoke exotic Mediterranean and Far Eastern locales, such as *Napoli*, *Rigoletto*, *Byzantine*, *Bosphorus*, *Nanking*, *Sisowath*, *Venice*, *Tanagra*, *Mousmé*.[22] It is interesting to note that the name *Electricity* was attributed to a series of bluish-gray shades. Silk color charts now seemed to rely on creative naming as a marketing strategy.

In many ways, the ribbon makers had been precursors for developments at the turn of the century. Already in the 1880s, their color charts had been developed collectively and poetic names had been given to the colors.[23] These names seem to have constituted a kind of lexical storehouse that was explored by dyers of threads. Names that were previously used for ribbons then appeared in the names that dyers gave to their colors. But their use was unpredictable, because the same term could be associated with very different colors.[24]

Color Card of the Dyers of Saint-Étienne, Saint-Étienne, spring season, 1907, leporello, 24 × 14.5 cm, 10 panels, private collection, Paris

——— At the turn of the twentieth century, the color chart was established in the silk industry, and its design would develop further in the following years. From the 1880s to the dawn of World War I, the chemical industry color chart guided the choice of dyes as dyers traced the path from cocoon to fabric. In their hands, dyed thread acquired significant added value, for the color quality of French silk enjoyed a global reputation at this time. The dyers' color chart also informed the work of fabric designers by providing them with preselected harmonies to respond to the tastes of the time in the best way possible. In this regard, far from being merely a type of technical expertise, the silk dyers' skills prefigured those of the trend forecasters of the future. Finally, to some extent these color charts were samples of the prestigious Lyon silk industry. At international exhibitions, they accompanied the company's sales staff abroad. In this way, they publicized the aesthetic selections of the luxury silk industry. The color harmonies that they depicted—along with paint color charts, catalogs of samples from department stores, and all exported products—spread European taste to lands it had previously barely reached.

These color charts continued being used until World War II, although at that time the fashion industry moved away from silk fabrics. They would disappear along with the major silk manufacturers who had created them when competition from man-made silk and other synthetic fibers drove these companies into bankruptcy.

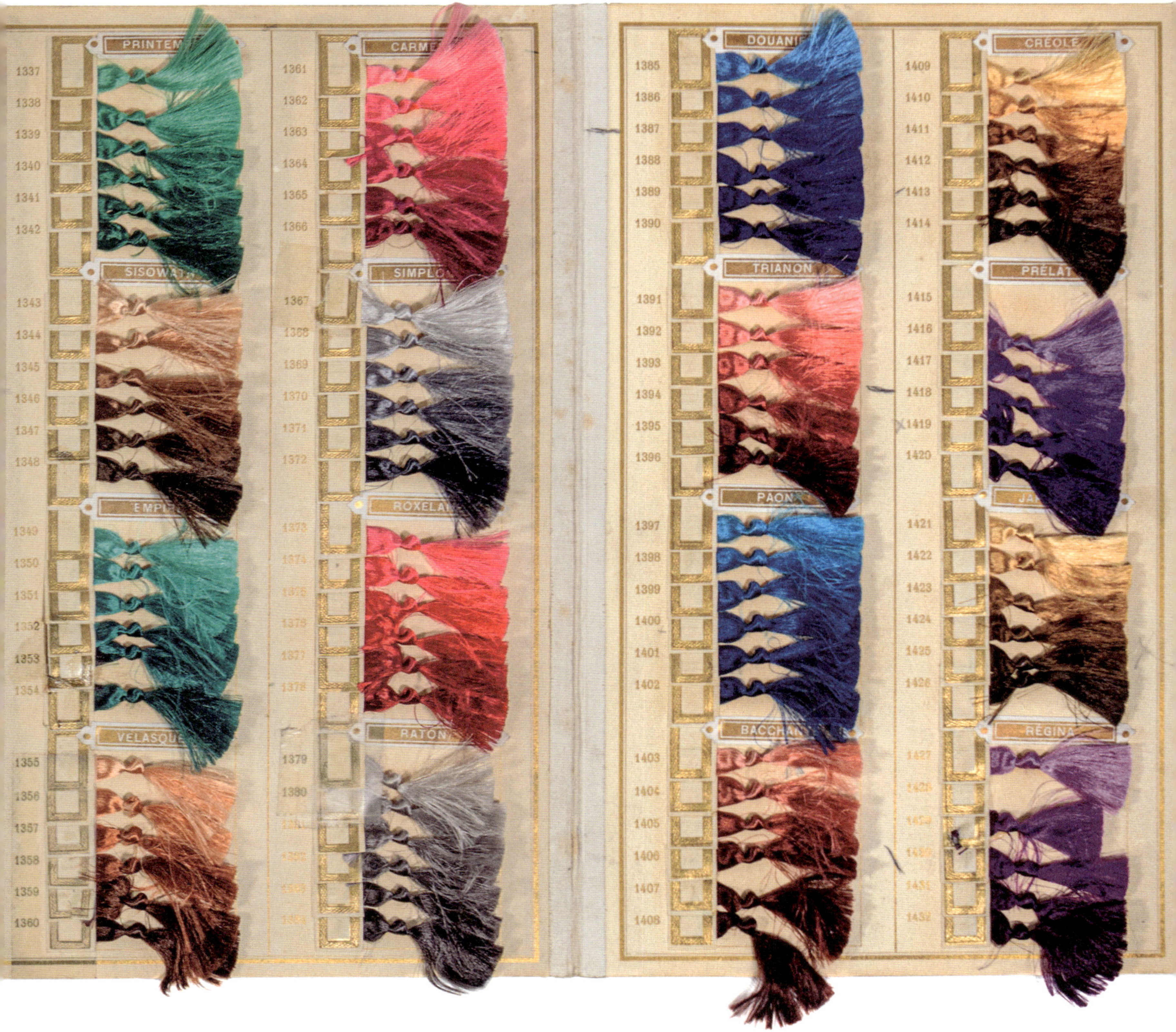

1337 1338 1339 1340 1341 1342
1343 1344 1345 1346 1347 1348
1349 1350 1351 1352 1353 1354
1355 1356 1357 1358 1359 1360
1361 1362 1363 1364 1365 1366
1367 1368 1369 1370 1371 1372
1373 1374 1375 1376 1377 1378
1379 1380
RATON
TRIANON
1385 1386 1387 1388 1389 1390
1391 1392 1393 1394 1395 1396
PAON
1397 1398 1399 1400 1401 1402
1403 1404 1405 1406 1407 1408
CRÉOLE
1409 1410 1411 1412 1413 1414
1415 1416 1417 1418 1419 1420
1421 1422 1423 1424 1425 1426
RÉGINA
1427 1432

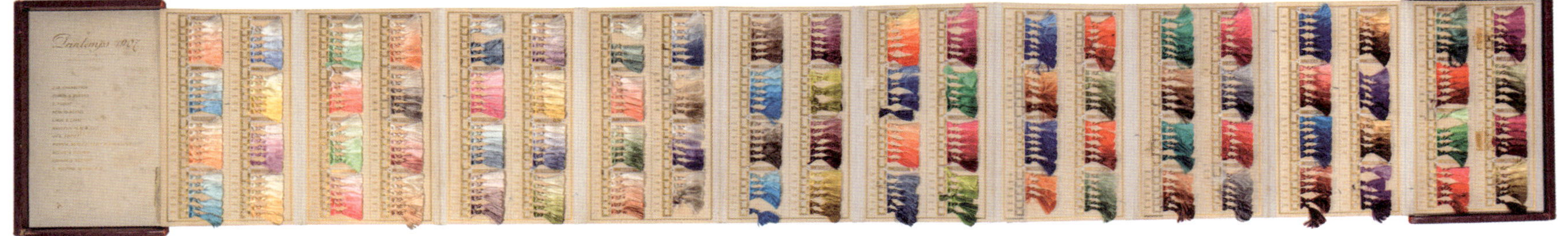

THE RETAIL COLOR CHART

The introduction of the color chart into retail stores in the late nineteenth century contributed slowly but radically to transforming Western societies' relationship to color. Until then, only scientists and manufacturers had seen color charts. By appearing in haberdasheries, hardware stores, and artists' supply stores, they added to the discovery of new colors, a phenomenon that had already begun when department stores in Western capitals distributed sales catalogs to the general populace.

In this way, color charts revealed ranges of colors that were not only extensive but also organized and able to be seen by artists, artisans, and ordinary consumers. The classification in which colors were presented was now designed so that anyone could easily understand it: the color chart also became educational. Because the colors were given poetic names (*Squire*, *French Blue*, and such), the color chart appealed to the imagination both visually and culturally. It embodied the color revolution. Color began to be an aspiration of an entire civilization.

In the World of Fashion

A haberdasher sells everything and makes nothing.
Encyclopédie, Diderot, D'Alembert, and Jaucourt (1751–1772), "Haberdashery" ("*Mercerie*")

Away from the capital cities and their department stores, there was a different shopping venue that was essential to any town or city until the development of ready-to-wear after World War II: the haberdashery. The Industrial Revolution had led many women to enter the factories, but the task of dressing the family and taking care of clothing still fell to them although they worked outside the home. While wealthy women hired seamstresses, they still embroidered. Thus women from all walks of life learned needlework from their elders or in convent schools, and they all needed to buy the necessary items for these pastimes, especially when the sewing machine entered the household and made it easier to make clothes.

The ribbon color charts start things off

Ribbons were present everywhere in women's outfits, whether they were humble strips of plain linen or cotton, narrow as a string and hardly more attractive, or splendid embroidered silk braids. They pulled back hairstyles, held up skirts, and tightened the corsets that shaped female bodies until the early twentieth century. They were also an inexpensive way of hiding the worn part of a sleeve or giving a new look to an old dress. Dangling or fluttering, charming and alluring, they appealed to the eye by their movement as well as their colors. Ribbons were also valuable items in men's wardrobes. Until the use of elastic became widespread between the two world wars, ribbons cinched suits or held stockings on the calf. Women and men also used ribbons for mourning rituals.

There were many factories producing ribbons in Belgium, Normandy, and around Saint-Étienne.[25] In fact, in the late nineteenth century, Saint-Étienne refocused its activity on producing plain ribbons. To promote this new industry, the Chambre Syndicale des Rubans et Soieries[26] distributed color charts two times per year, in significant quantities, judging by the large numbers of examples that we have today. During their travels, sales representatives gave these color charts to department stores, the workshops of seamstresses and milliners, and haberdasheries. In these locations, clients discovered the abundance of available colors, their constant replacement by new ones, and their accessible prices.

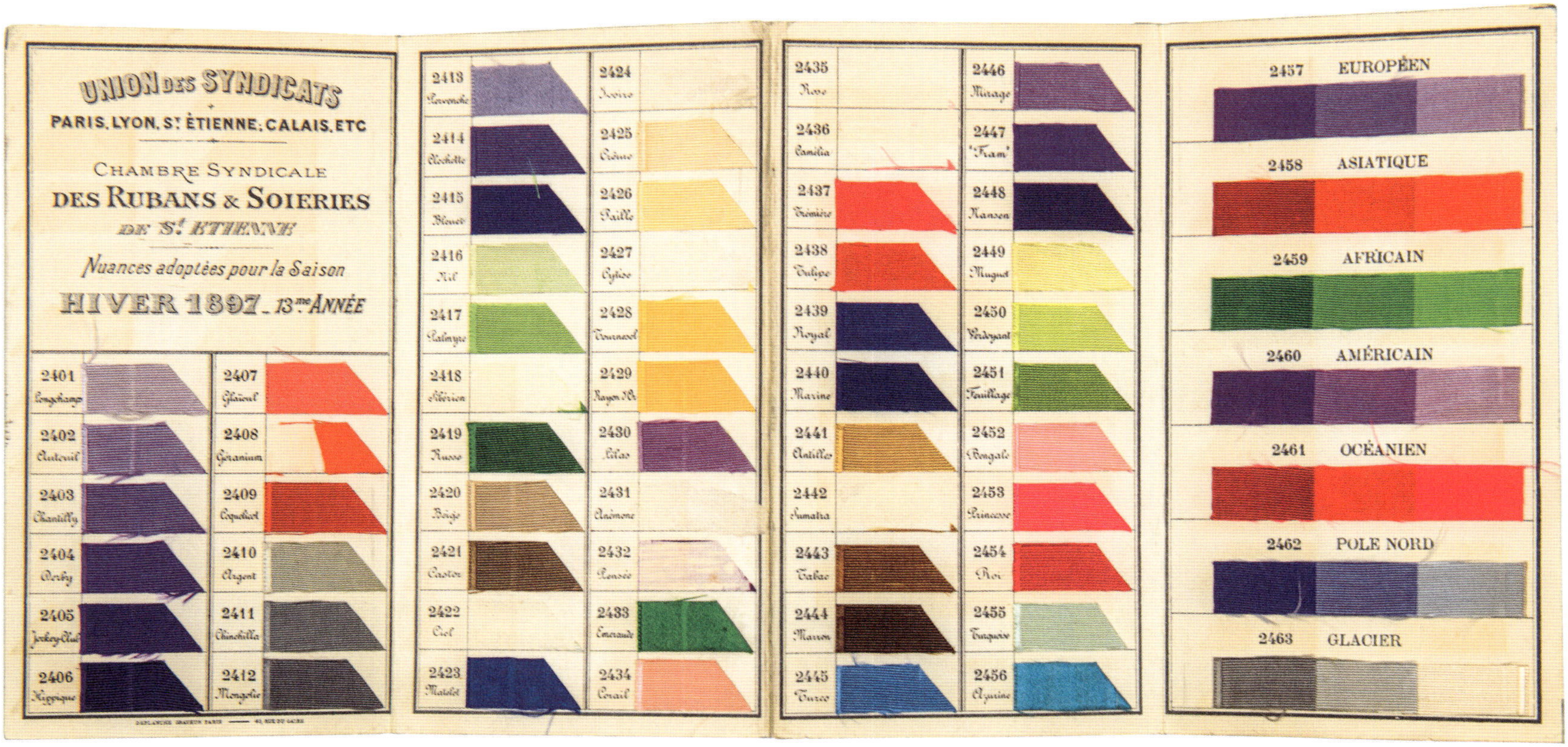

UNION DES SYNDICATS

PARIS, LYON, St ÉTIENNE, CALAIS, ETC

CHAMBRE SYNDICALE

DES RUBANS & SOIERIES

DE St ÉTIENNE

Nuances adoptées pour la Saison

HIVER 1897 – 13me ANNÉE

2401 Longchamp — 2402 Auteuil — 2403 Chantilly — 2404 Derby — 2405 Jockey-Club — 2406 Hippique

2407 Glaïeul — 2408 Géranium — 2409 Coquelicot — 2410 Argent — 2411 Chinchilla — 2412 Mongolie

2413 Pervenche — 2414 Clochette — 2415 Bleuet — 2416 Nil — 2417 Palmyre — 2418 Sibérien — 2419 Russe — 2420 Beige — 2421 Castor — 2422 Ciel — 2423 Matelot

2424 Ivoire — 2425 Crème — 2426 Paille — 2427 Cytise — 2428 Tournesol — 2429 Rayon d'Or — 2430 Lilas — 2431 Anémone — 2432 Pensée — 2433 Emeraude — 2434 Corail

2435 Rose — 2436 Camélia — 2437 Trémière — 2438 Tulipe — 2439 Royal — 2440 Marine — 2441 Antilles — 2442 Sumatra — 2443 Tabac — 2444 Marron — 2445 Turco

2446 Mirage — 2447 "Fram" — 2448 Nansen — 2449 Muguet — 2450 Verdoyant — 2451 Feuillage — 2452 Bengale — 2453 Princesse — 2454 Roi — 2455 Turquoise — 2456 Azurine

2457 EUROPÉEN

2458 ASIATIQUE

2459 AFRICAIN

2460 AMÉRICAIN

2461 OCÉANIEN

2462 POLE NORD

2463 GLACIER

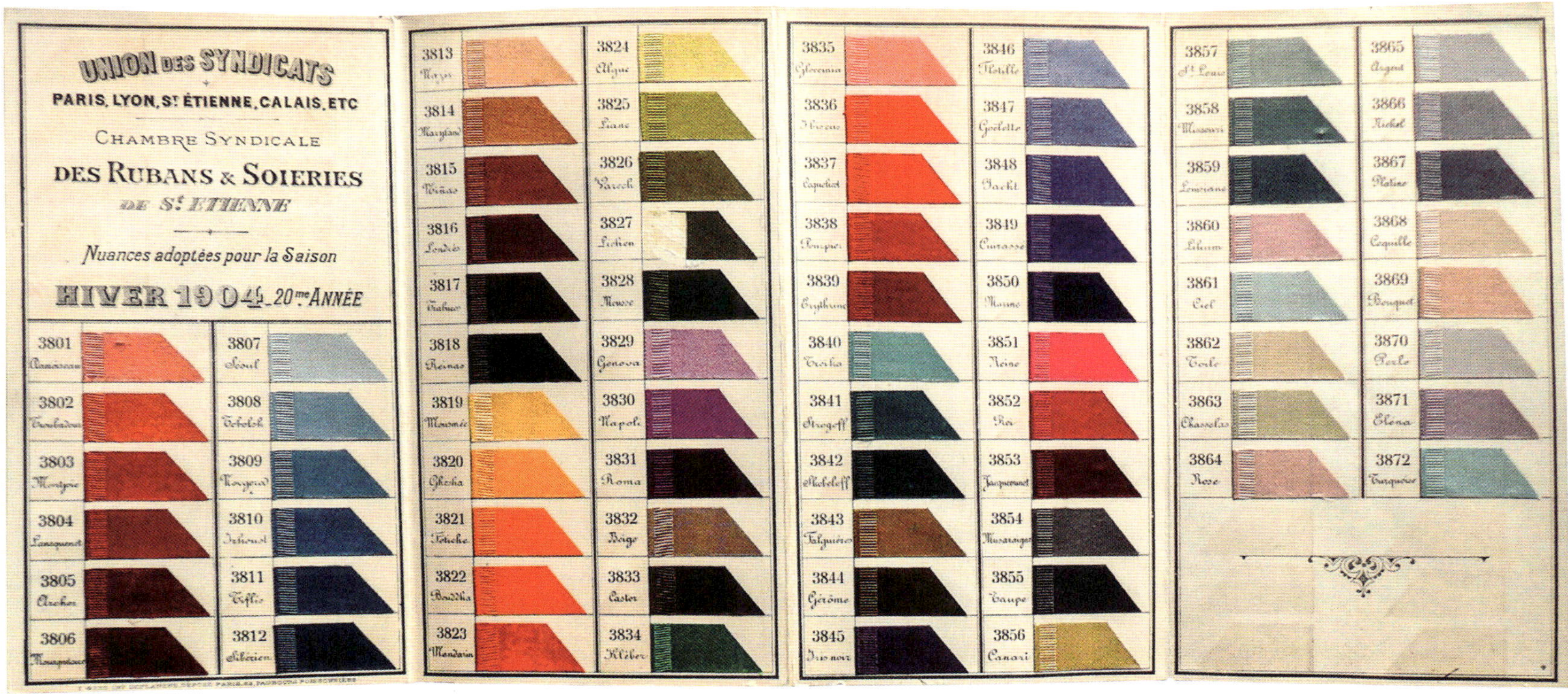

PREVIOUS PAGE

Colors Adopted for Winter 1897 and 1904

The 1897 chart features the words "13th year," suggesting that these color cards had circulated since 1884. The extensive experience of ribbon makers undoubtedly helped them to select quickly an optimum format and organization, because these color charts would change very little until the 1960s. The principal modifications were replacing the seasons of summer and winter by spring and autumn starting in 1925, and then by a double season (spring-summer and autumn-winter) after World War II.

The ribbon makers chose to use a leporello with seventy-one to seventy-seven ribbon samples completely attached to the backing, with one end cut at an angle. Classification was by colors, ranging from the lightest to the most saturated, but the order varied each year. The numbers suggest a reading from top to bottom of each column and a sequence planned to be uninterrupted throughout the seasons and years.

As of the 1880s—and thus before the silk dyers' color charts—a name was attributed to each color and carefully handwritten in ink. Those chosen for winter 1897 were taken from the world of flowers (*Poppy*, *Periwinkle*, *Lily of the Valley*, and such), from horse racing (*Auteuil*, *Jockey Club*, and such) and travel (*Nile*, *Russian*, *Sailor*, *Antilles*).[27] This interest in faraway places was indicated by the seven rows of ribbons named for the continents. The color names selected for winter 1904 featured the plant world, but also exotic names (*Geisha*, *Talisman*, *Genova*, *Troïka*, *St-Louis*, and such) and evoked historical roles (*Squire*, *Landsknecht*, *Musketeer*, and such).

Attributing a name to each color seems to have continued until World War I. The names were rarely repeated from one year to the next, which meant that twice a year, approximately one hundred terms were chosen from words evoking far-off places, nature, or even emotion, resulting in some six thousand names from 1884 to 1914![28]

The plethora of names helped ordinary people find their way through the vast field of color. Distinguishing the shades *Coral*, *Camellia*, *Hollyhock*, *Bengal*, or *Oceanians* trained the consumer's eye. Moreover, because the exotic color names encouraged remembering a shade by associating it with visual imagination (you could dream of being a *Princesse*, or fantasize about *Troubadour*), the names strengthened the attraction that the color chart already exerted. Additionally, they constructed an appetite for color that would become legitimate. However, the unpredictability of the vocabulary did not allow for reliable familiarity with the names of colors, because a strong yellow could be called *Golden Ray* in 1897, *Mousmée* in 1904, and *Nabob* the following year, and terms were also sometimes repeated (*Poppy*, *Navy*, *Beaver*, *King*) for colors that were completely different!

Colors Adopted for the Winter Season 1897, Union des Syndicats, Paris, Lyon, Saint-Étienne, Calais, etc., Chambre Syndicale des Rubans et Soieries de Saint-Étienne, 1897, leporello, 20 × 10.5 cm, 4 panels, private collection, Paris

Colors Adopted for the Winter Season 1904, Union des Syndicats, Paris, Lyon, Saint-Étienne, Calais, etc., Chambre Syndicale des Rubans et Soieries de Saint-Étienne, 1904, leporello, 20 × 10.5 cm, 4 panels, private collection, Paris

NEXT PAGE SPREAD

G.G. & Cie Silk Velvet Ribbons

Small companies also used color charts. Particularly impressive and refined, this one features 225 samples of velvet ribbons displayed over more than four meters, with each fold reinforced by a ribbon glued to the back.

It is organized with a tone attributed to each panel, ranging from the lightest shades at the top to the most saturated ones at the bottom, although this was not systematically applied, and variations of a given color did not always follow each other. For instance, the greens appear on panels 7, 13, 19, 26, and part of 28.

The ribbons are attached to the backing at one end by glue, and a thin strip of paper holds the other end of each ribbon in place, allowing for the possibility of examining its reverse side and feeling the material. A handwritten number is associated with each color, without any logical sequence. This color chart clearly brings together samples from previous series, from which certain colors were selected and then meticulously organized here in order to present a color range that is as complete and harmonious as possible.

This ambitious goal has been met. The density and luster of the velvet samples are enhanced by the splendor of each color; the panels, whether considered individually or in their alternating pattern, reveal a completely mastered aesthetic. Nothing shocks the eye, while it is stimulated by an abundance of delicate or intense shades.

This magnificent chart is the sole trace of a company of which we know nothing today.

Color chart of silk velvet ribbons, G.G. & Cie, France, leporello, 24 × 13 cm, 31 panels, late nineteenth century, Bibliothèque Forney, Paris, inv. RES ICO 8398

Specific color charts for workshops of decorative feathers and fabric flowers

——— It was not until the 1950s that women could leave their homes with their heads uncovered without being accused of impropriety or being associated with the working class. In large cities, hats were thus at the heart of an entire economy. Many workshops were devoted to supplying the necessary decorations. Their activity was intense and complex due to changing fashions and the combination of many different materials. While manufacturers provided hat-making artisans with color charts for selecting decorative elements, the workshops themselves developed their own color charts in order to standardize and inspire their practice while also allowing their customers to indicate the exact ribbons, feathers, or fabric flowers of their choosing.

Since the mid-nineteenth century, feather workers and makers of fabric flowers had been listed together as *plumassiers-fleuristes* in the record books of the Chambre Syndicale des Fleurs, Plumes et Modes.[29] Workshops often combined the two specialties, as they followed an unchanging rhythm and were carried out by the same female artisans, who worked at home: in winter, the fabric flowers for decorating summer hats were made, and summer was devoted to constructing feathered decorations for winter headgear.[30] The rules of propriety required these decorations to be divided in a nontechnical way: feathers, whose animality was apparently deemed too seductive, were reserved for married women, while young single women from good families had to be satisfied with fabric flowers.

At the turn of the twentieth century, the Parisian feather industry, accused of plundering hummingbirds, ptarmigans, marabous, and egrets, had to fall back on feathers from barnyard birds or game birds, whose color range was far less varied and shimmering. But they could take on an exotic appearance through dyeing. This was one of the many skills of feather makers, which all required precision and meticulous attention.[31] Synthetic dyes arrived at just the right time to imitate a rhea or bird of paradise with goose, turkey, or rooster feathers, and the chemical industry between the two world wars would be able to offer this significant market whatever it needed to perfect all the illusions it strove to create.[32]

The color charts published here come from the archives of three companies: the feather maker Lemarié, which was founded in the 1880s, when bird-inspired hats were fashionable, and the fabric flower producers Legeron (also founded in the 1880s) and Guillet (founded in 1896). The workers, knowledge, tools, and archives of Guillet and Legeron were preserved by the Maison Lemarié, which became Métiers d'Art at Chanel in 1996.

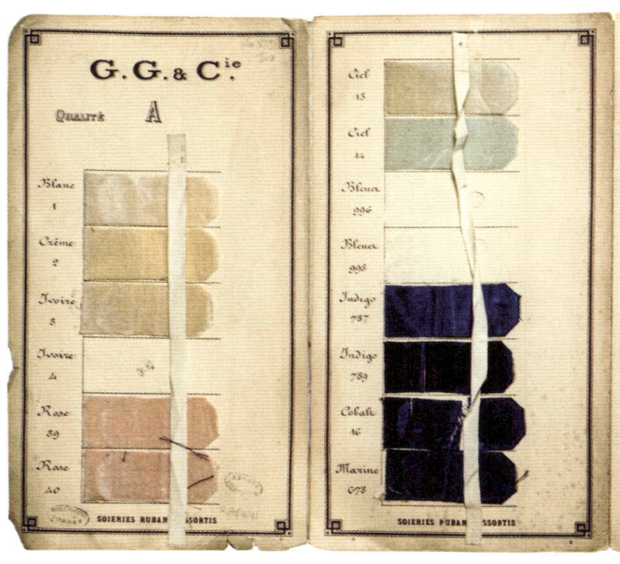
G.G. & Cie
Qualité A
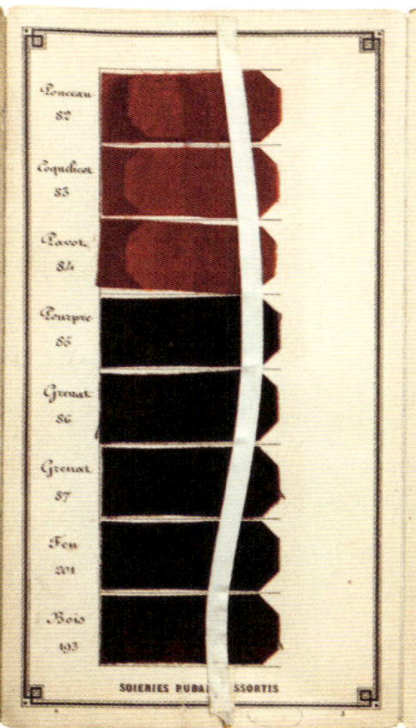
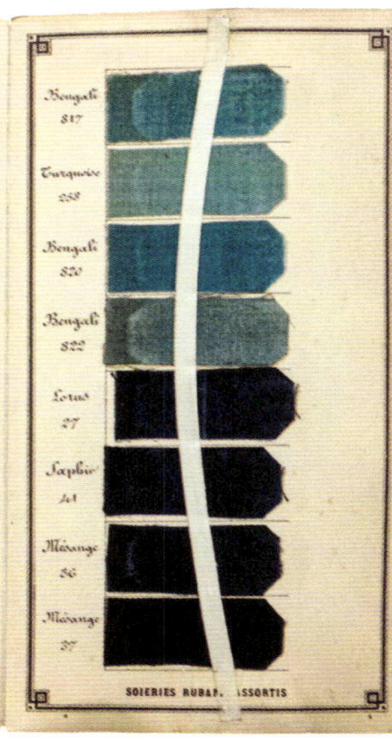
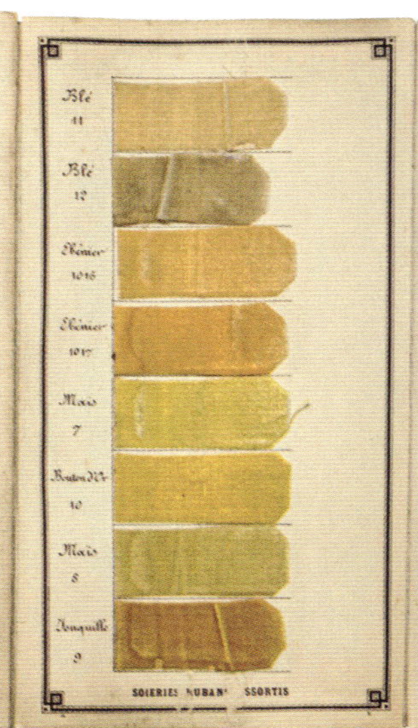
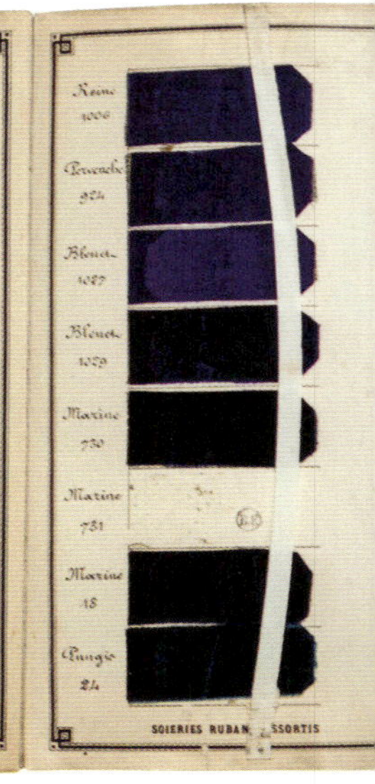
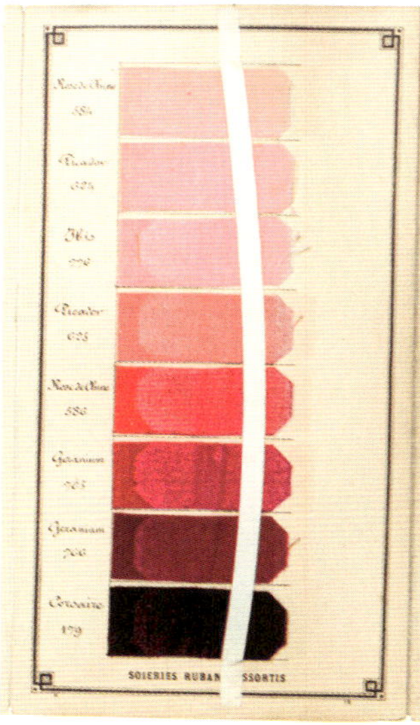
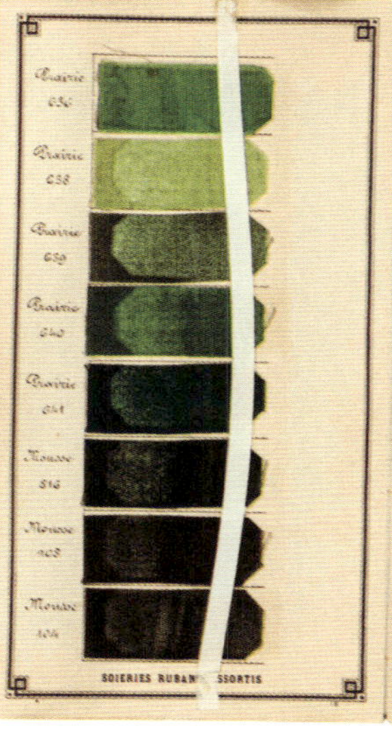
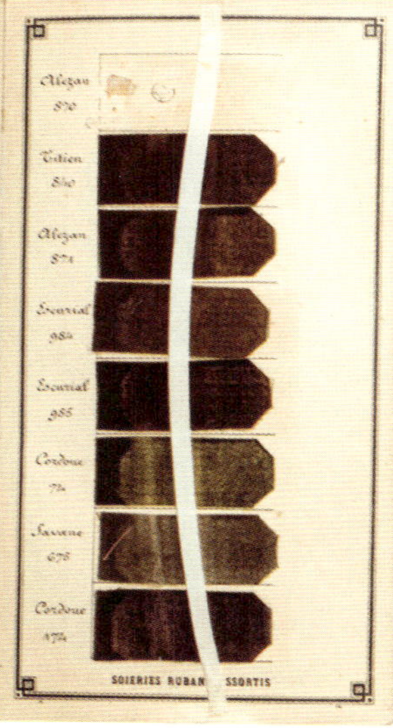
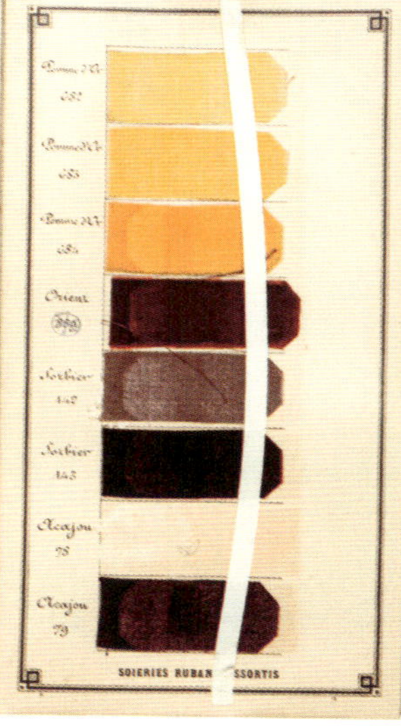
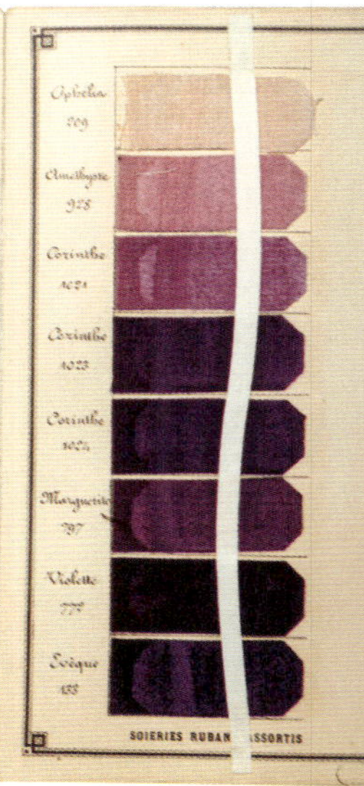
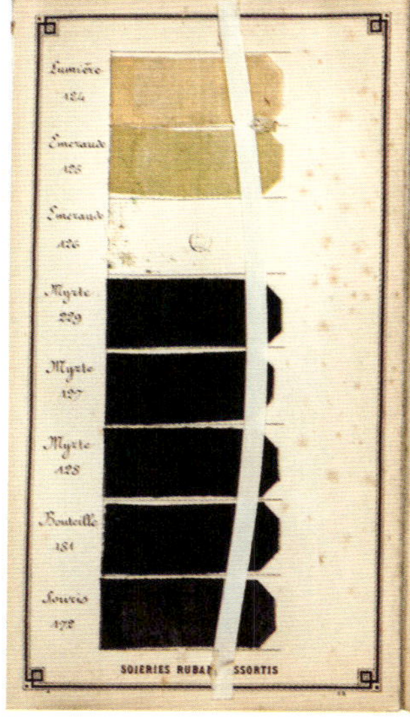
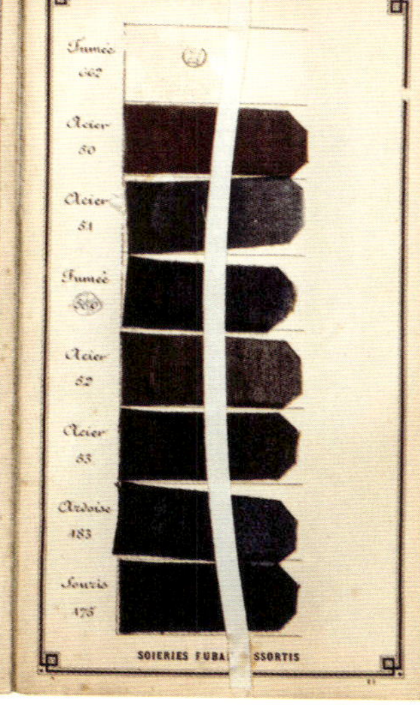
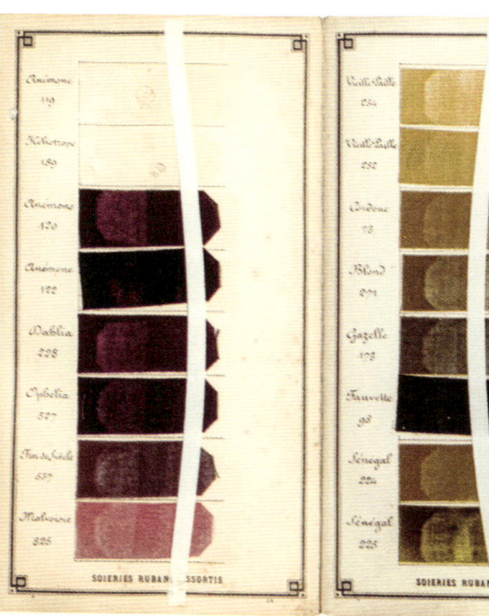

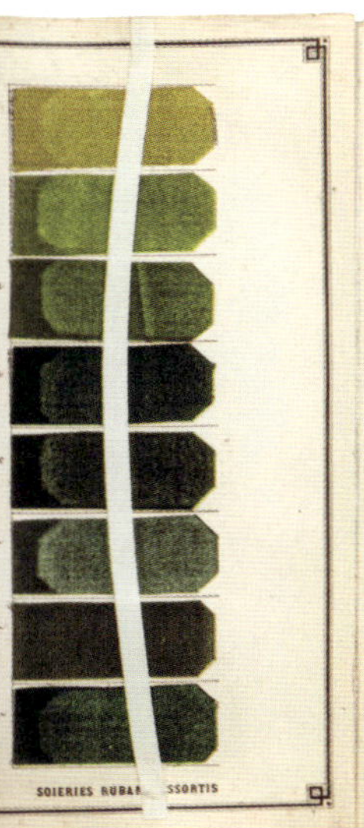
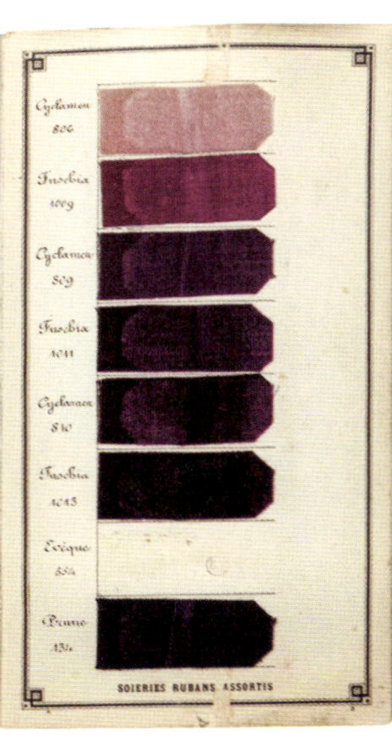
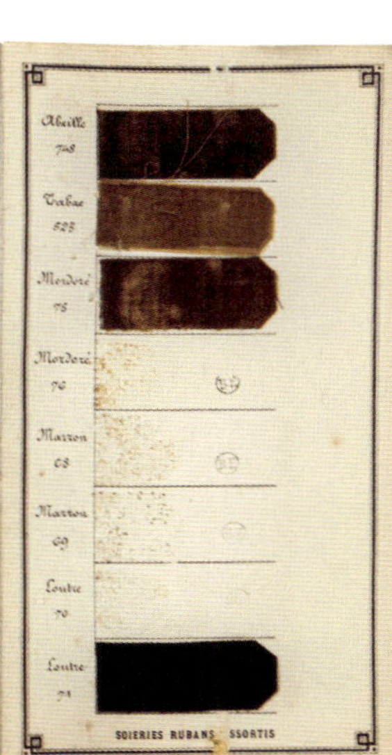
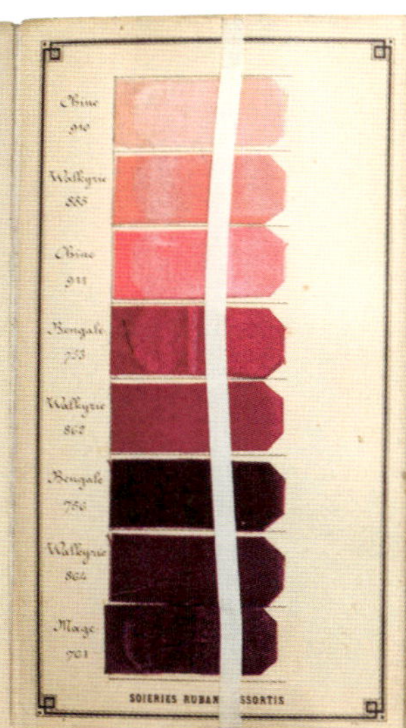
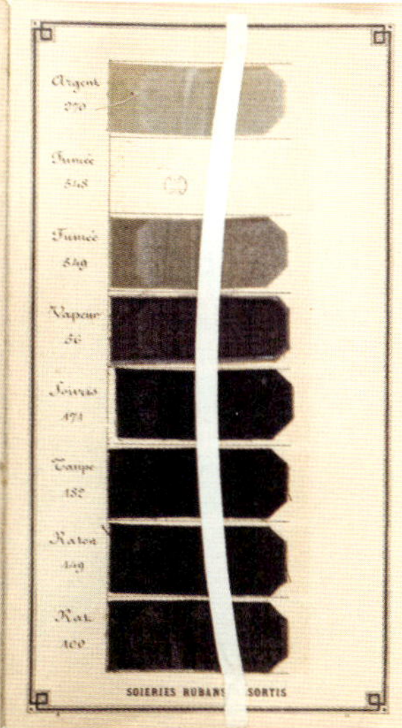
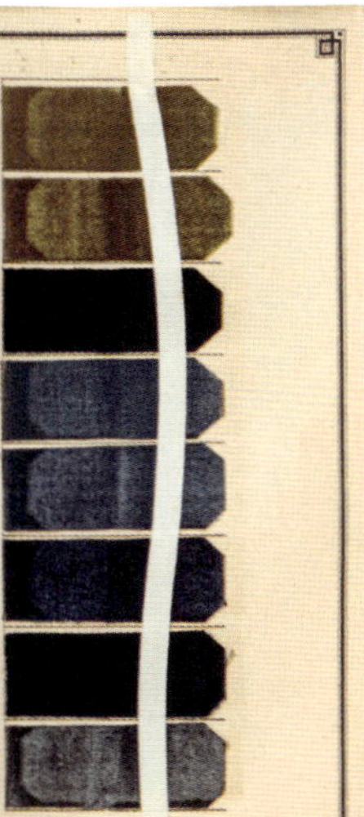
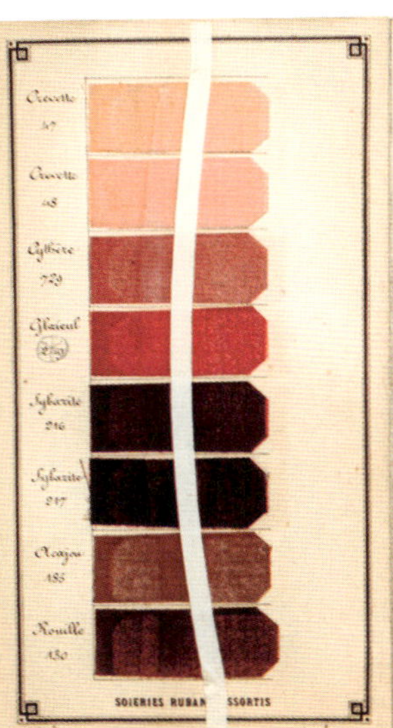
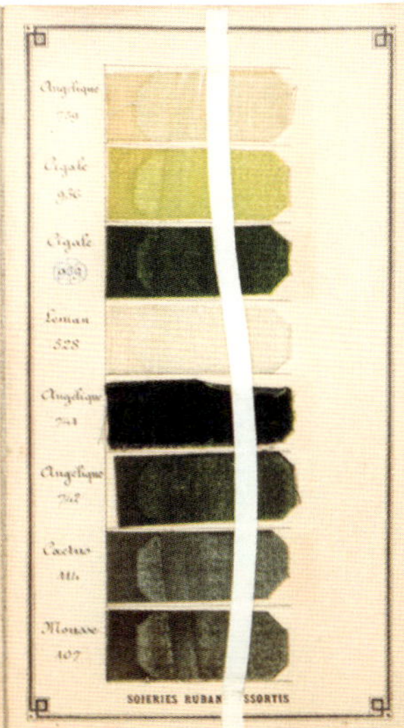
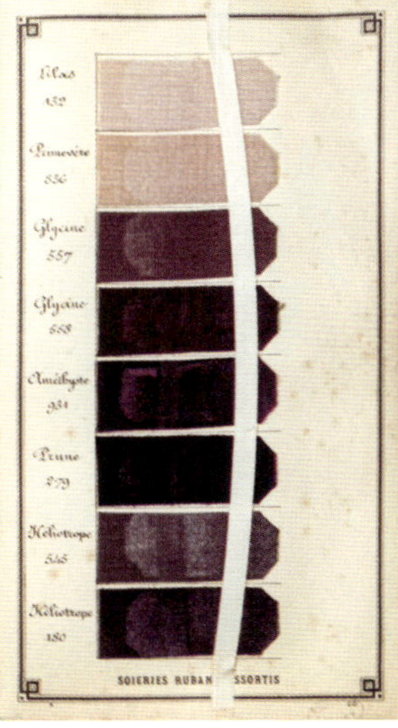
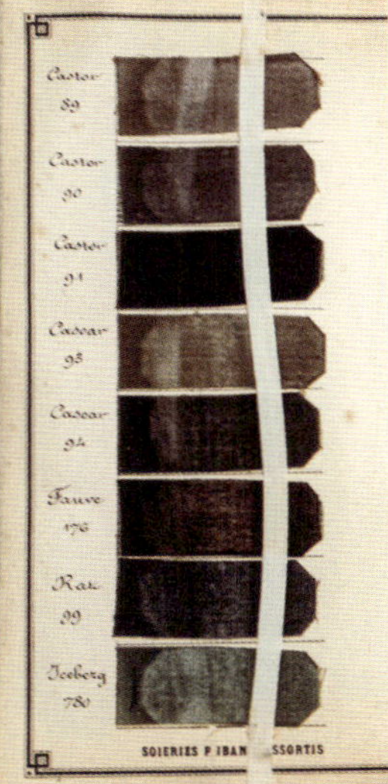
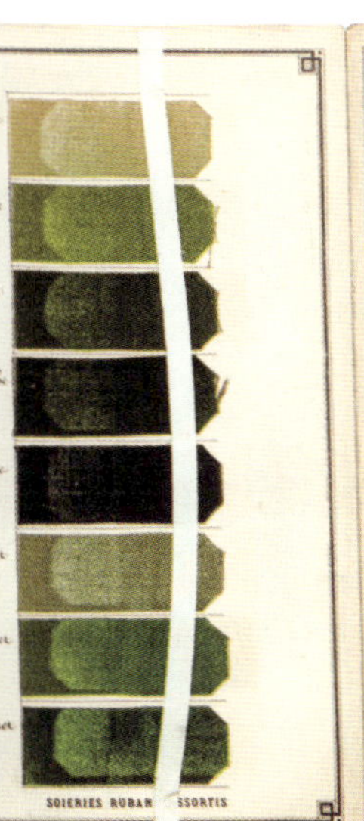
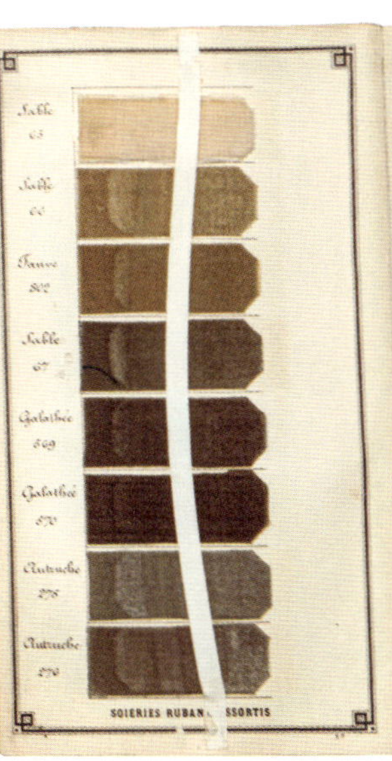
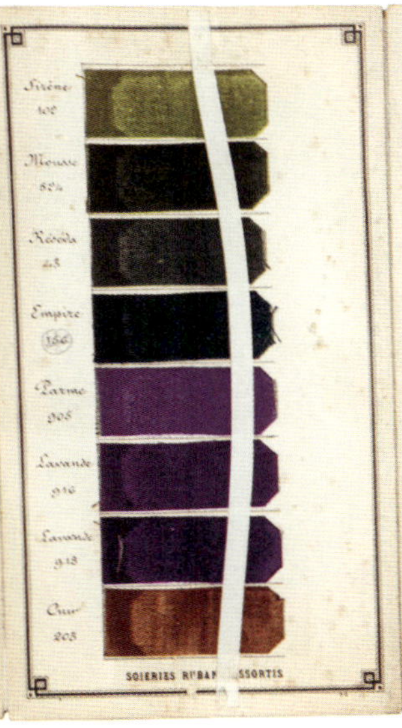
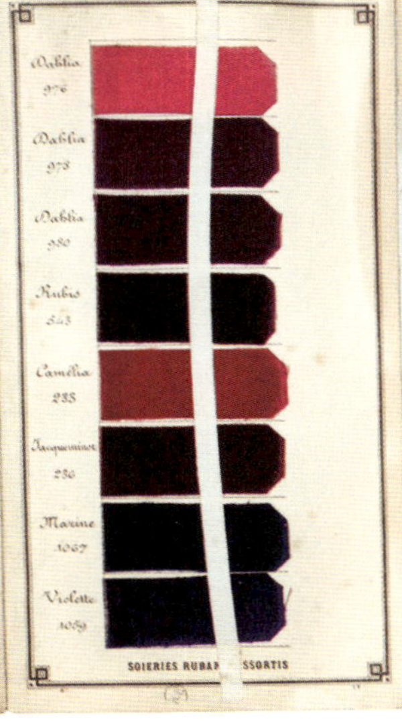
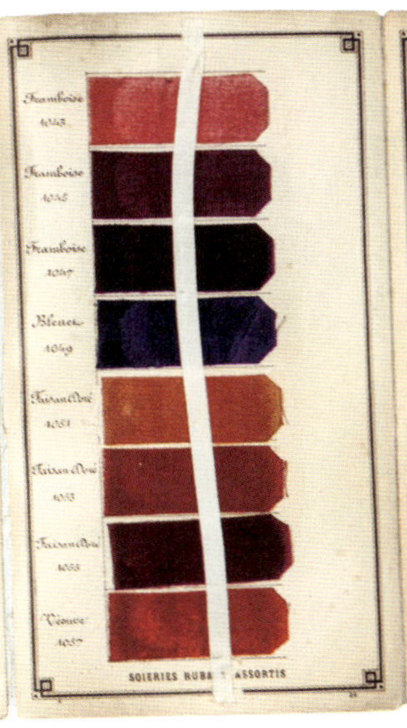
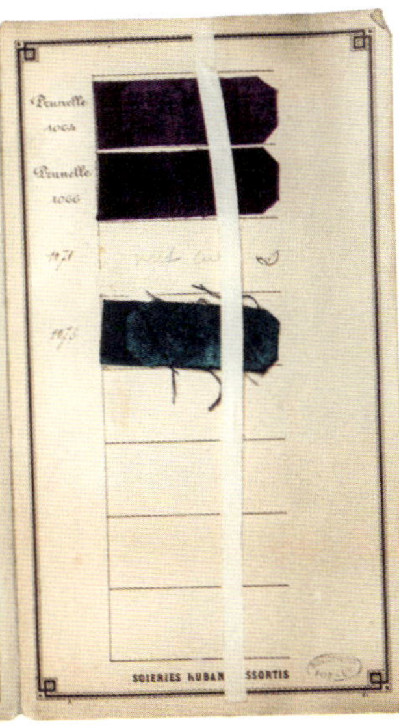

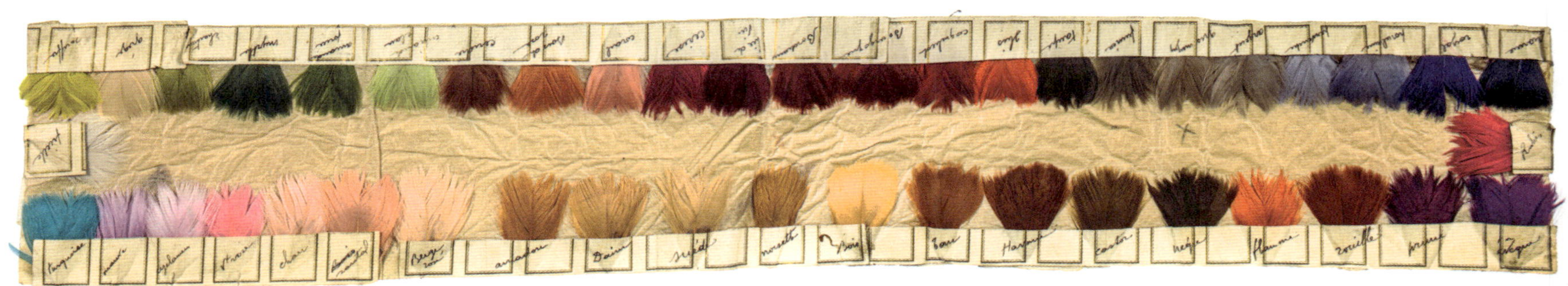

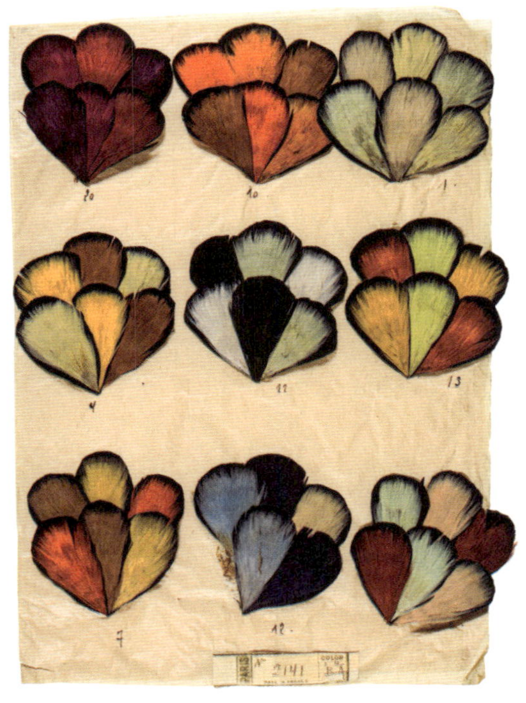

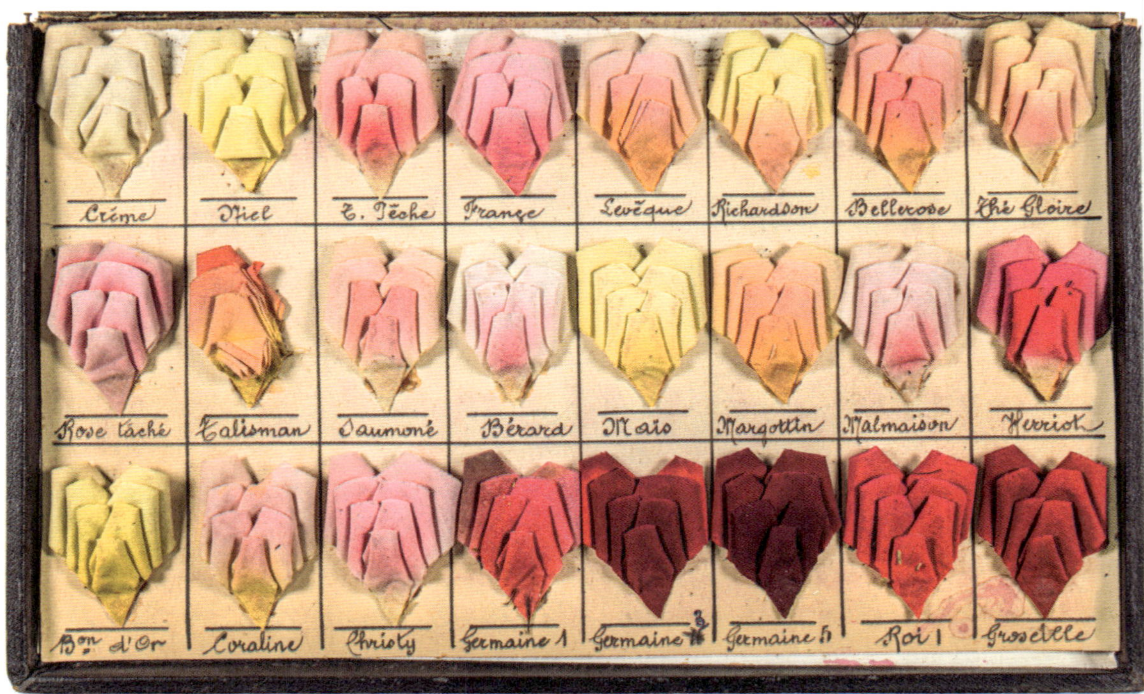
Crème
Niel
E. Pêche
France
Levêque
Richardson
Bellerose
Thé Gloire
Rose taché
Talisman
Saumoné
Bérard
Maïs
Margottin
Malmaison
Herriot
Bon d'Or
Coraline
Christy
Germaine 1
Germaine 3
Germaine 5
Roi 1
Groseille

OPPOSITE, TOP

Lemarié Goose Feathers

These forty-two feathers are generally organized by color group. Unlike all the previous color charts, the names this time are conventional (*Smoke*, *Coral*, *Wine Lees*, *Dark Almond*, *Havana Tobacco*, *Rosewood*, *Beaver*, *Dark Brown*, *Bishop's Purple*, *Flesh*), which tends to confirm that these color charts were also intended for customers' use.

Goose feather color chart, Maison Lemarié, Paris, late nineteenth century (?), strip of paper, 11 × 67.5 cm, Patrimoine Lemarié–Fonds Lemarié, Paris

OPPOSITE, BOTTOM LEFT

Lemarié Feather Flowers

In this color chart, dyed and cut feathers were arranged into nine flowers of feathers with distinct colors. The feather makers' vocabulary, which was extremely rich and precise, specified their shape.[33] The round shapes of these flowers were known as "fins."

Color chart of flowers of goose feathers, Maison Lemarié, Paris, late nineteenth century (?), sheet of paper, 34.5 × 23.5 cm, Patrimoine Lemarié–Fonds Lemarié, Paris

OPPOSITE, BOTTOM RIGHT

Legeron Cotton Roses

The handwritten inscriptions under each of the twenty-four samples in this box refer to a color reference (*Cream*, *Honey*, *Salmon*, *Corn*) combined with a naturalist's vocabulary. The plant terms come from different varieties of roses, without, once again, any systematic connection between the color and the flower.

The samples correspond to one of the last stages in producing an artificial rose, which is shown here partially, with the appearance of a half flower.[35] After the delicate work of fashioning, each of the seven petals was dyed by dipping it in dye baths of varying concentrations. The women who worked in these feather and fabric flower workshops mastered both form and color, as shown by these color charts. They could reproduce garden flowers or develop completely fantastical creations using real feathers.

Color chart of roses of cotton fabric, Maison Legeron, Paris, late nineteenth to early twentieth century (?), box, 23 × 36.5 cm, Patrimoine Lemarié—Fonds Legeron, Paris

NEXT PAGE SPREAD

Legeron Silk Fabric Petals

Evidence of the combined production of feather decorations and artificial flowers in the same workshops, the 123 samples of petals in dyed cotton fabric on this color chart are designated by the names of birds and then of flowers, either handwritten or applied with a stamp to the chart. The colors are conventionally organized on most of the panels into three rows of three samples of the same tone, in order of increasing saturation.

The first eight panels feature a colorful bird menagerie from the tropics or Western ponds and forests. However, the colors of the petals are not related to the bird that is mentioned: the petals of *Couroucou* (trogon or quetzal) do not offer the metallic blue, red, or bright orange of this bird, and in nature the feathers of the *Woodcock* are not azure. Instead, the names used on this color chart are related to the feather makers' habit of using exotic names for ordinary species. It was important to maintain the prestige of their wares and to perpetuate the dream of far-off lands through words, even when the material in question was fabric instead of feathers.[34]

The names on the six following panels, the majority of which refer to flowers, are just as capricious. The shape of the petals does not correspond to that of the flowers mentioned, and while there is a relationship between the color *Eminence* and the red of Roman Catholic cardinals, the primary function of these names was to stimulate the imagination, as also evidenced by references to literature, theater, and opera, such as *Frivolité*, *Fortunio*, *Mephisto*, and *Aramis*.

Despite the appearance of an ornithological and botanical catalog, this color chart is also a notebook of dye formulas, a tool where ingredients, proportions, and instructions are noted in several places. Some dyes appear under the names used by contemporary scientific nomenclature (*R. Violet*, for example), but most are indicated by direct association between the color and the product (*Saffron Foot*, *Raspberry*, or even *iridescent highlights* from the vocabulary of jewelers). We are not in the laboratories of scientists, but in the workshop of artisans, in a milieu where creating beauty is central. The color charts of the feather makers and flower makers were also designed so that their customers could construct delightful illusions, both in terms of the decorations on their hats and their evocative hues.

Color chart of petals of silk fabric, Maison Legeron, Paris, late nineteenth to early twentieth century, leporello, 21.5 × 17.2 cm, 14 panels, Patrimoine Lemarié–Fonds Legeron, Paris

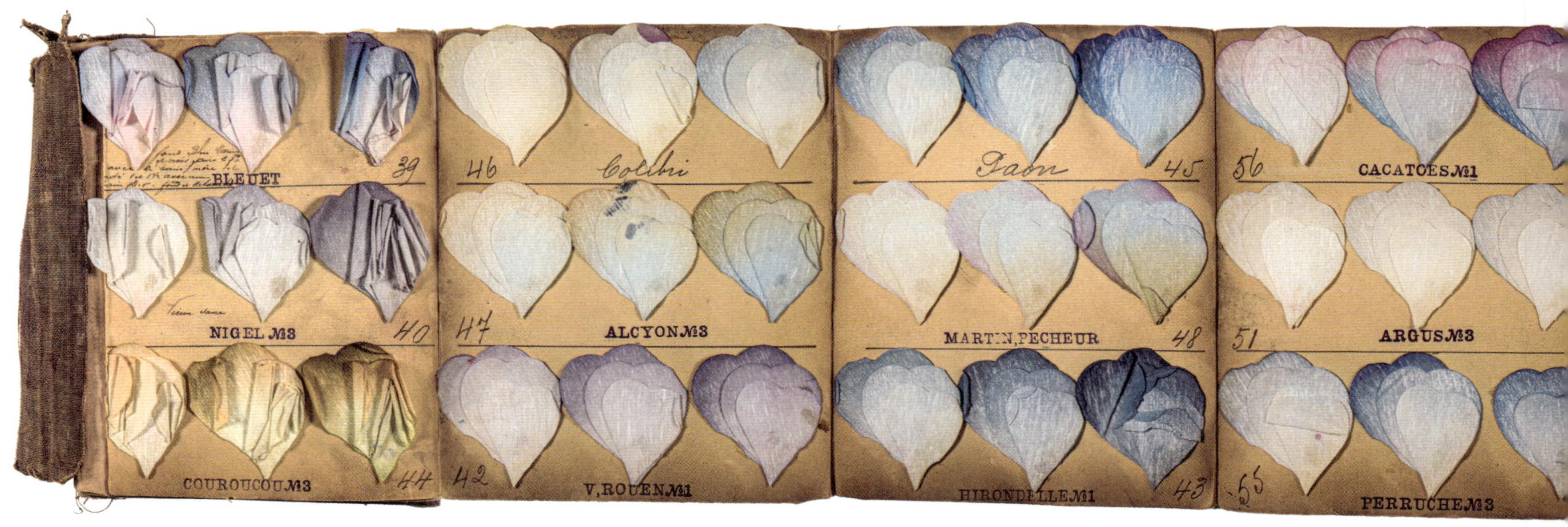
BLEUET
39
NIGEL №3
40
COUROUCOU №3
44
46
Colibri
47
ALCYON №3
42
V,ROUEN №1
Paon
45
MARTIN,PECHEUR
48
HIRONDELLE №1
43
56
CACATOES №1
51
ARGUS №3
55
PERRUCHE №3

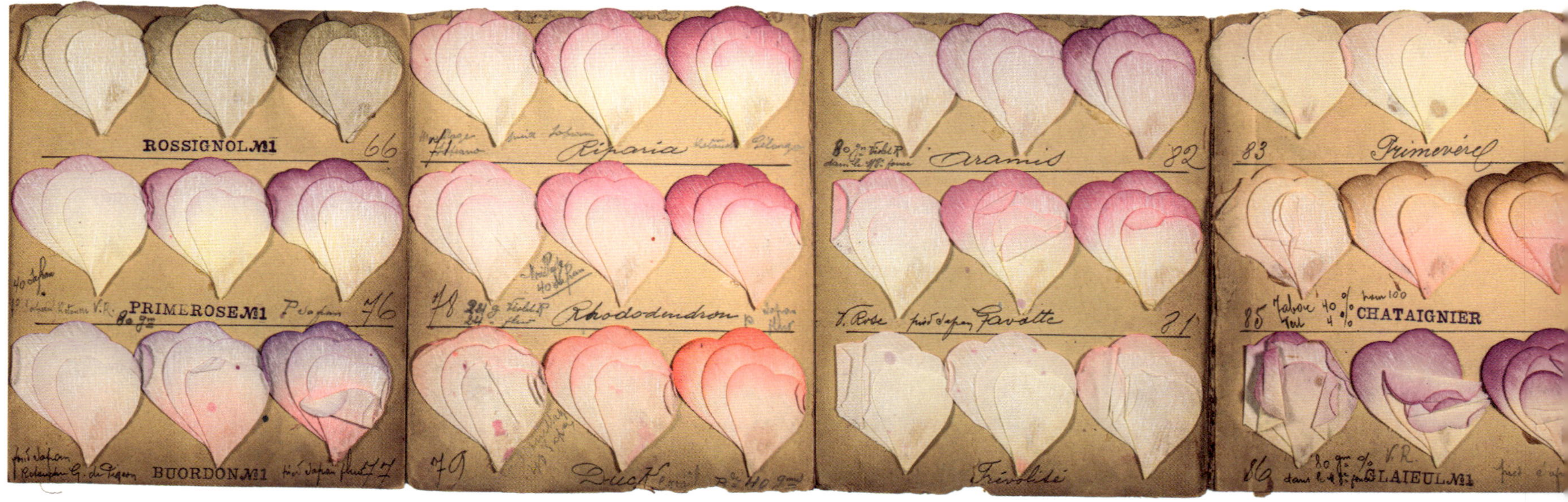
ROSSIGNOL №1
66
PRIMEROSE №1
76
BUORDON №1
77
Riparia
78
Rhododendron
79
Aramis
82
Gavotte
81
Frivolité
83
Primevère
85
CHATAIGNIER
86
GLAIEUL №1

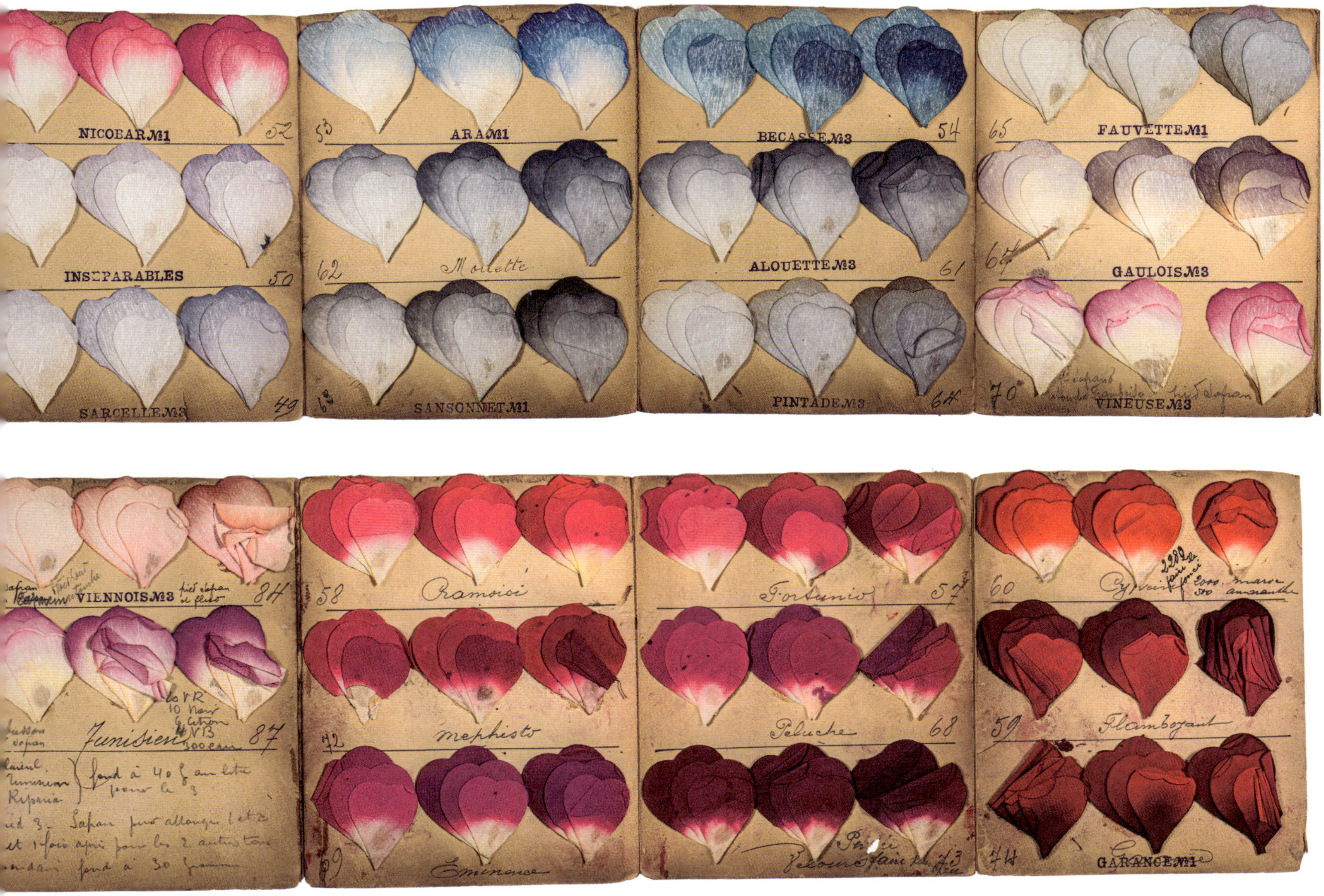

NICOBAR No1
INSEPARABLES
SARCELLE No3
ARA No1
Mouette
SANSONNET No1
BECASSE No3
ALOUETTE No3
PINTADE No3
FAUVETTE No1
GAULOIS No3
VINEUSE No3

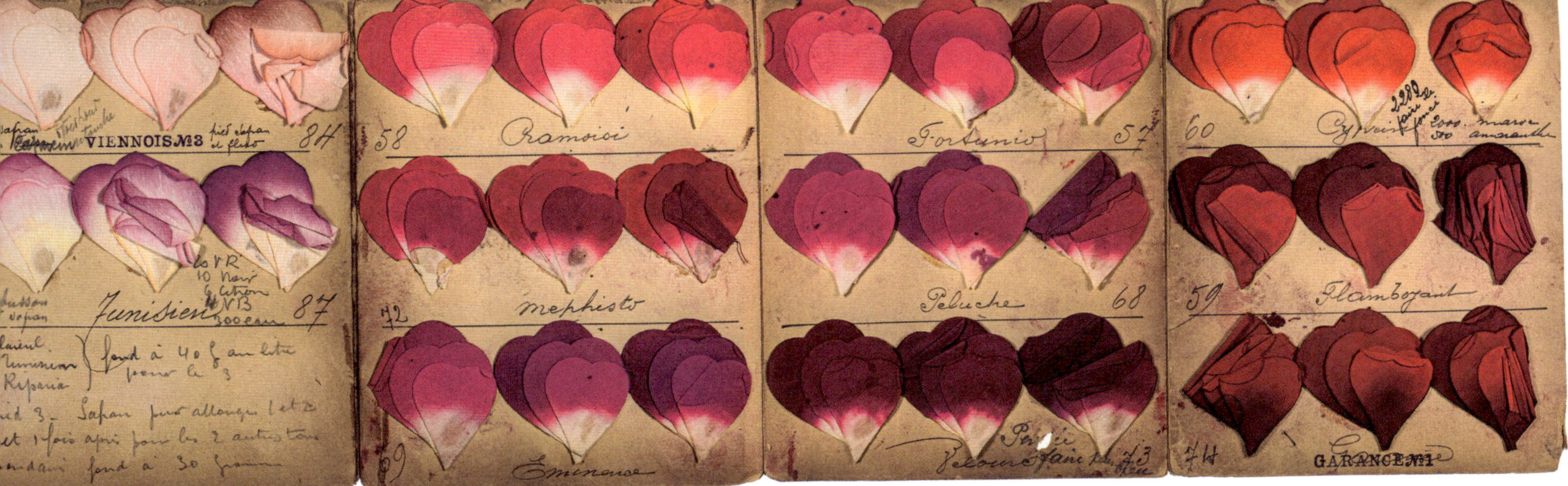

New types of samples for fabrics

To promote various fabrics for sewing, Parisian department stores came up with skillful advertising strategies. These fabrics were advertised and displayed as a mixed bag of samples. In the late nineteenth century, these samples became increasingly organized into color charts, with the same fabric available in several colors.

BELOW AND OPPOSITE, BOTTOM

Brauns Curtain Fabrics

Brauns, a Swiss producer of dyes for home use, began marketing its products in 1874. This was a promising market, because the possibility of changing or brightening up the color of a textile oneself allowed for significant savings. Brauns realized very early the usefulness of a color chart for presenting the available shades, but it also anticipated the difficulty of imagining, based on a sample, how the fabric would look spread over a large area. The company therefore designed a color chart where one sample was glued flat onto the backing, and a second one was slightly folded and attached as if over a small window frame. The arrangement was clever, but the range of colors was surprisingly limited at a time when, due to synthetic dyes, fabrics could take on an almost limitless choice of hues.[36]

Color chart for curtain fabrics, Brauns, Switzerland, late nineteenth century, folding card, 25 × 10 cm, 2 folds, Bibliothèque Forney, Paris, call number RES ICO 8609

OPPOSITE, TOP, AND BELOW

Brauns Footwear Dyes

Apparently produced a short time later, this color chart demonstrates the extent of the range of dyes that Brauns could furnish for a market of elegant footwear, from dainty ankle boots to silk slippers. On the back, an explanation in German explains how to choose the correct color depending on the existing color of silk that one wished to change. It warns users that colors may look different under artificial light,[37] alerts them of possible minor differences in shade between the sample card and the result depending on the nature of the fabric and its reaction to the dye, and even denies liability in case of staining! Moreover, the instructions specify that dye colors may be mixed to obtain the desired tone. However, there was little risk that that would be necessary, for the ninety-six shade samples (strips of silk glued to a cardboard sheet with rectangular openings) form a varied range of delicate or saturated tones arranged according to the color spectrum. Yet they are designated only by numbers, probably to facilitate international distribution.

Brauns Colovit dye for the surface of silk shoes, Brauns, Switzerland, 1910s, leporello, 23 × 11 cm, 4 panels, Bibliothèque Forney, Paris, call number RES ICO 8401

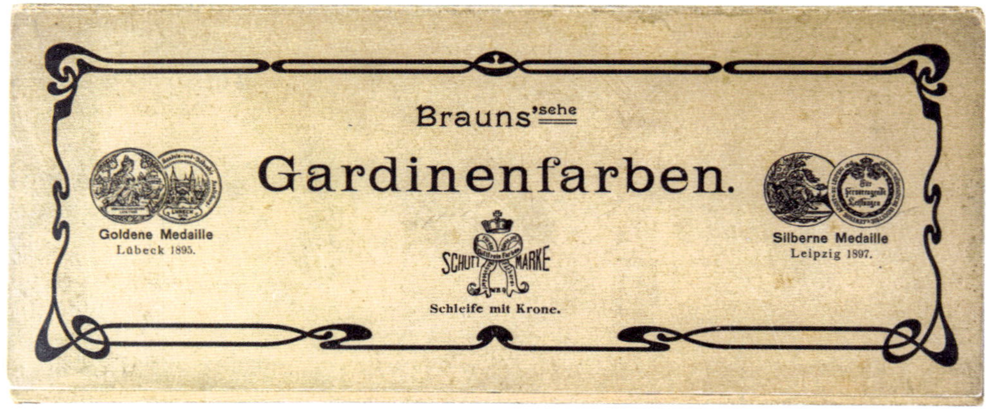

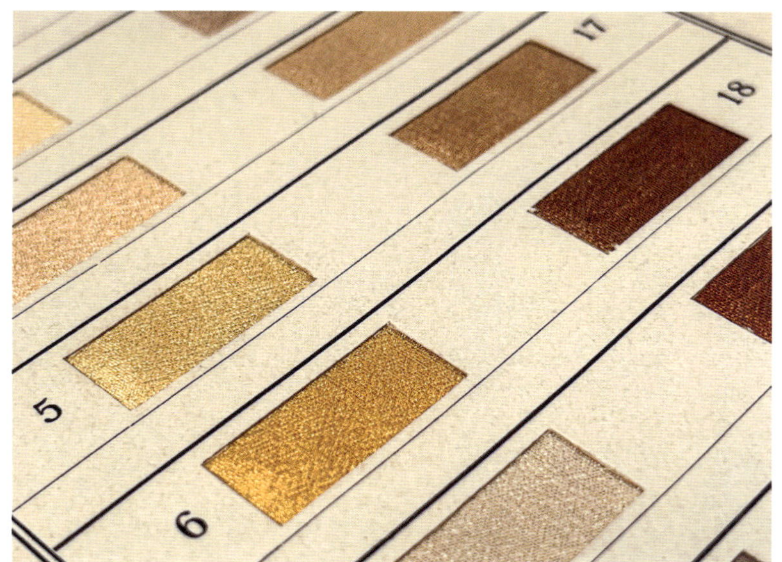

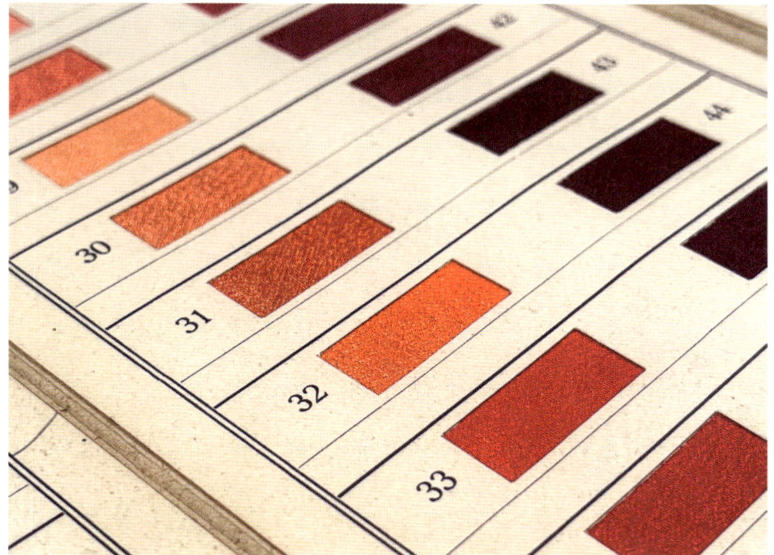

SCHUTZ MARKE

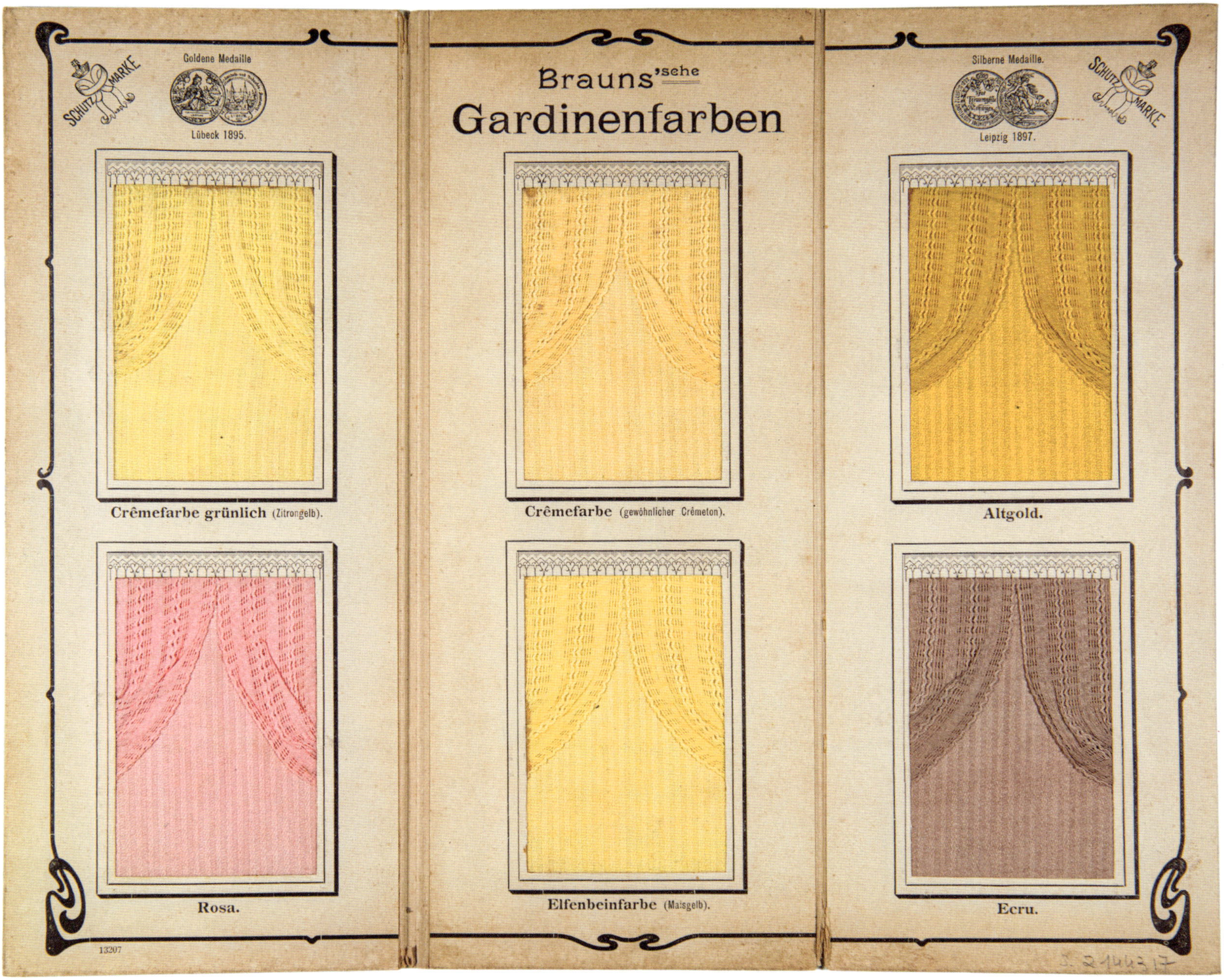

Goldene Medaille

Lübeck 1895.

Brauns'sche

Gardinenfarben

Silberne Medaille.

Leipzig 1897.

SCHUTZ MARKE

Crêmefarbe grünlich (Zitrongelb).

Crêmefarbe (gewöhnlicher Crêmeton).

Altgold.

Rosa.

Elfenbeinfarbe (Maisgelb).

Ecru.

13207

Planche nº 1 Saint-Hubert

Nuances des Bandes Molletières et Jambières moulées " BOB "
DRAP EXCLUSIF

Références 1 et 2 (18 nuances)

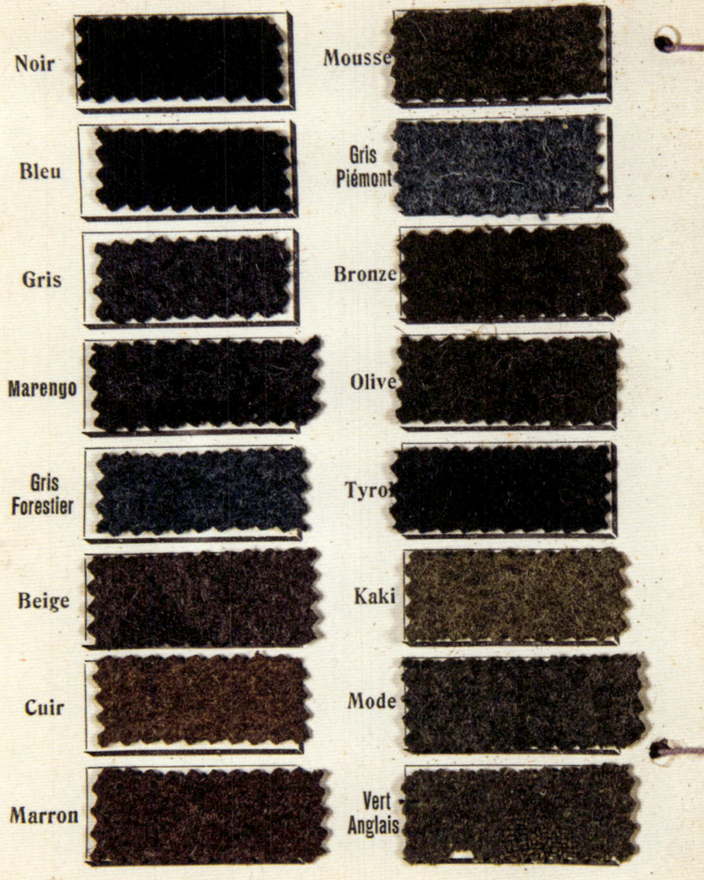

En ***gris clair, gris neigeux*** et ***gris capote*** réglementaire infanterie.

Planche nº 2 Saint-Hubert

Bandes Molletières drap fantaisie.

Nuances :
Noir, bleu, gris, marron, tyrol, kaki, olive, marengo.
Carreaux écossais tissés.

Référence 3

Type de qualité

Référence 4

La bande unie et l'extrémité en carreaux écossais formant bas cycliste.

Nuances : ***noir, gris, marron, kaki, tyrol, mode.***

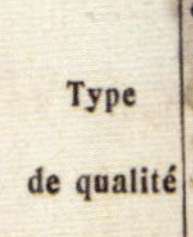

OPPOSITE

Tite Fabrics for Puttees and Gaiters

The Alexandre Tite company produced utilitarian goods but made them available in several shades of color. Its booklet of eleven plates and forty-four fabric swatches allowed customers to assess the quality of the fabrics and also to choose a color. The effort is noteworthy, even if it is difficult to perceive a significant difference between the colors *Marengo*, *Olive*, *Tyrol*, or *Bronze*. The choice of *Fashion* as the name of a color is somewhat perplexing. It is also difficult to distinguish among the samples on plate two, which features fabrics called "whimsical," as the plaids are barely visible. Three shades of gray, *Light*, *Snowy*, and *Greatcoat*, are described as "infantry regulation."

This color chart implies that at the beginning of World War I, the Western textile industry offered multiple colors as a sales strategy, even for purely functional items, whether in a civilian or military context, and even if the shades of color are more described than visible.

Color chart of fabrics for puttees and gaiters, Manufacture Générale de Bandes Molletières et Guêtres Alexandre Tite, Lyon, 1913–1914, booklet, 23 × 15.5 cm, 16 pages and 11 plates, Bibliothèque Forney, Paris, call number RES ICO 8599

Clearly, color charts helped consumers absorb the transformations that the world of fabric color was experiencing at the time. Expressing a new abundance, they also showed that a single color could be offered in variations on a scale from light to dark, and they began to create an aesthetic foundation—and also stimulate the imagination—through the names of the samples. However, these names were too varied (in the ribbon color charts, they changed almost completely every season) and too unstable or specialized to establish a true vocabulary of color.

For Decorative Painters, Illustrated Color Charts

The late nineteenth century also saw the appearance of decorative paint color charts. Even before the arrival of the color charts, decorative painters had protected and embellished facades, walls, door and window frames, or furniture by producing paint from raw materials according to the needs of their customers. Color had to be formulated for each project.

In the second half of the century, significant advances were made in binding agents and pigments.[38] Above all, various types of mixtures that were already formulated and could be applied immediately flooded the market. These innovations arrived at an opportune time, as a rising standard of living in industrialized countries led to a widespread interest in the aesthetics of the home. This trend was spurred by numerous home decor guides, especially in England, that clarified concepts such as good taste and provided instructions in how to use and harmonize various colors.

Decorative paints began to undergo a standardization process that encouraged the rise of color charts. Their multiplication accompanied the flourishing of a plethora of manufacturers, whose products traveled long distances over the railroads of Europe and the United States.[39] These color charts were the first ones to make occasional appearances inside homes, since the painter brought them to the client during the color selection process. Another difference was quite major: the colors were identified with names that were markedly less whimsical than in fabric color charts. These names were also more constant, often common to various brands, and they continued in use for long periods of time. Much like the color charts for artist supplies (with which they share some names), the paint color charts facilitated the formation of a fixed color vocabulary.[40] This lexicon would allow for naming—and thus for conceptualizing—color.

The design used for the decorative paint color charts conformed to the rules of the time and applied the same strategy of variations of tones in lines or columns. It should be noted that the French paint companies demonstrated superior ease in this exercise, perhaps because of Chevreul's influence. The samples were produced, with some exceptions, with paint applied directly to the color chart or to small pieces of paper that were then glued to the chart.

These charts were more serious than those of the fabric industry, with their tactile pleasures and flowery names. However, paint manufacturers found ways to add creative touches, such as giving new shapes to the samples or composing bold ranges with bright colors and shiny new enamel paints. Above all, an important role was reserved for illustrations where the artists' talent could have free rein. The illustrators would take full advantage of this.

BELOW AND OPPOSITE

Ripolin Paint Shades

The Ripolin color chart is to paint what the DMC color chart is to embroidery: the company's name became a synonym for a color chart.[41] These charts were distributed until World War II; they maintained many of their original characteristics. They were strong reference points, which became even better known in the 1910s when Ripolin introduced its iconic logo with the three painters.

The layout of the chart had already been established by the beginning of the twentieth century. Eighty-four colors grouped by tone were placed in columns over raised circles. Greens and browns dominated, probably because these colors were used on woodwork at the time. A few metallic colors allowed decorative painters to refurbish metal items. The designations were names of colors (*Pale rosy gray*), sometimes with the addition of references from the historical color lexicon (*Prussian Blue*, *Ultramarine Blue*, *Roman Green*, etc.), nature (*Salmon Pink*, *Sand Yellow*, *Ivory White*), or the industrial world (*Train Car Green*). The simplicity of color classification and the clarity of names formed a didactic whole whose recurrence through the years contributed to train those who spent time with these color charts.

All the space on the chart is used: promoting the brand's other products, instructions, application examples, awards won, and so on. The color chart also specifies: "As these dots are made with a thin layer of Ripolin itself, the colors are therefore identical to the delivered product." We are indeed dealing with paint specimens, and in fact this term is used in the French name of the document (*Spécimen des nuances*). This indication would recur throughout the development of paint color charts.

Ripolin, Color Samples, Société Anonyme Française de Peintures Laquées et d'Enduits Sous-Marins, France, c. 1902, pamphlet, 15.5 × 10 cm, 2 folds, Bibliothèque Forney, Paris, call number RES ICO 8104

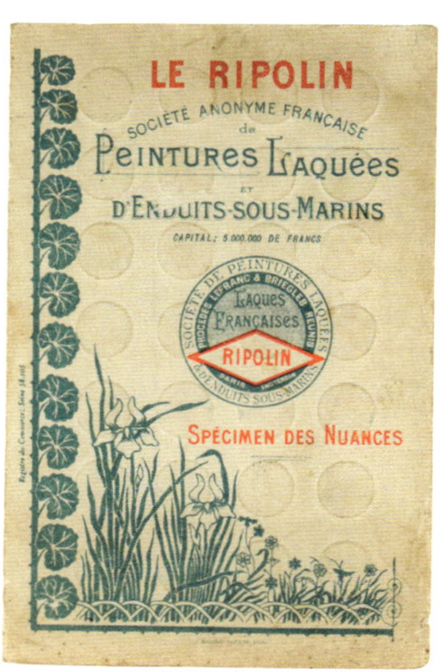

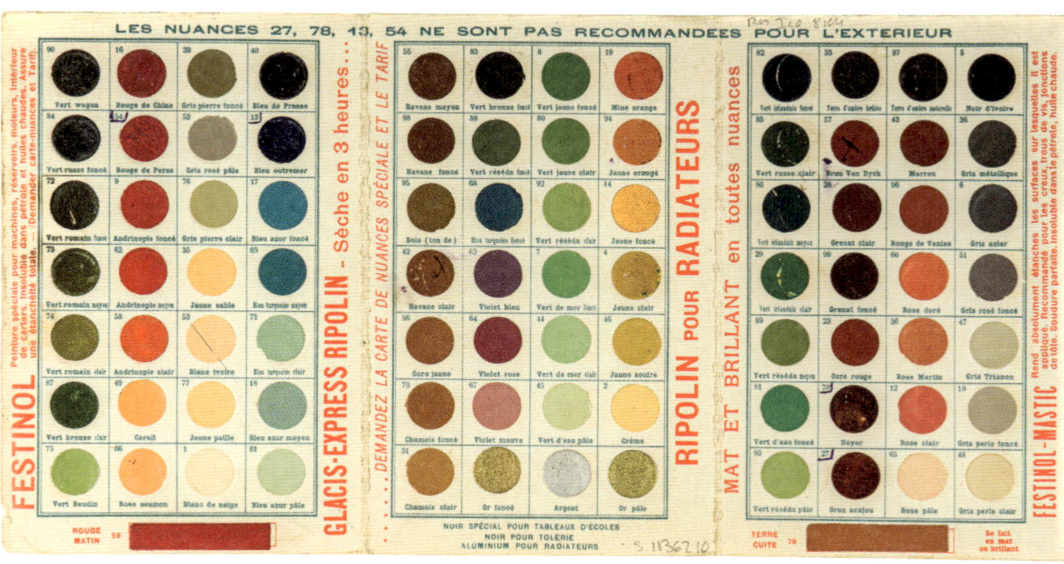

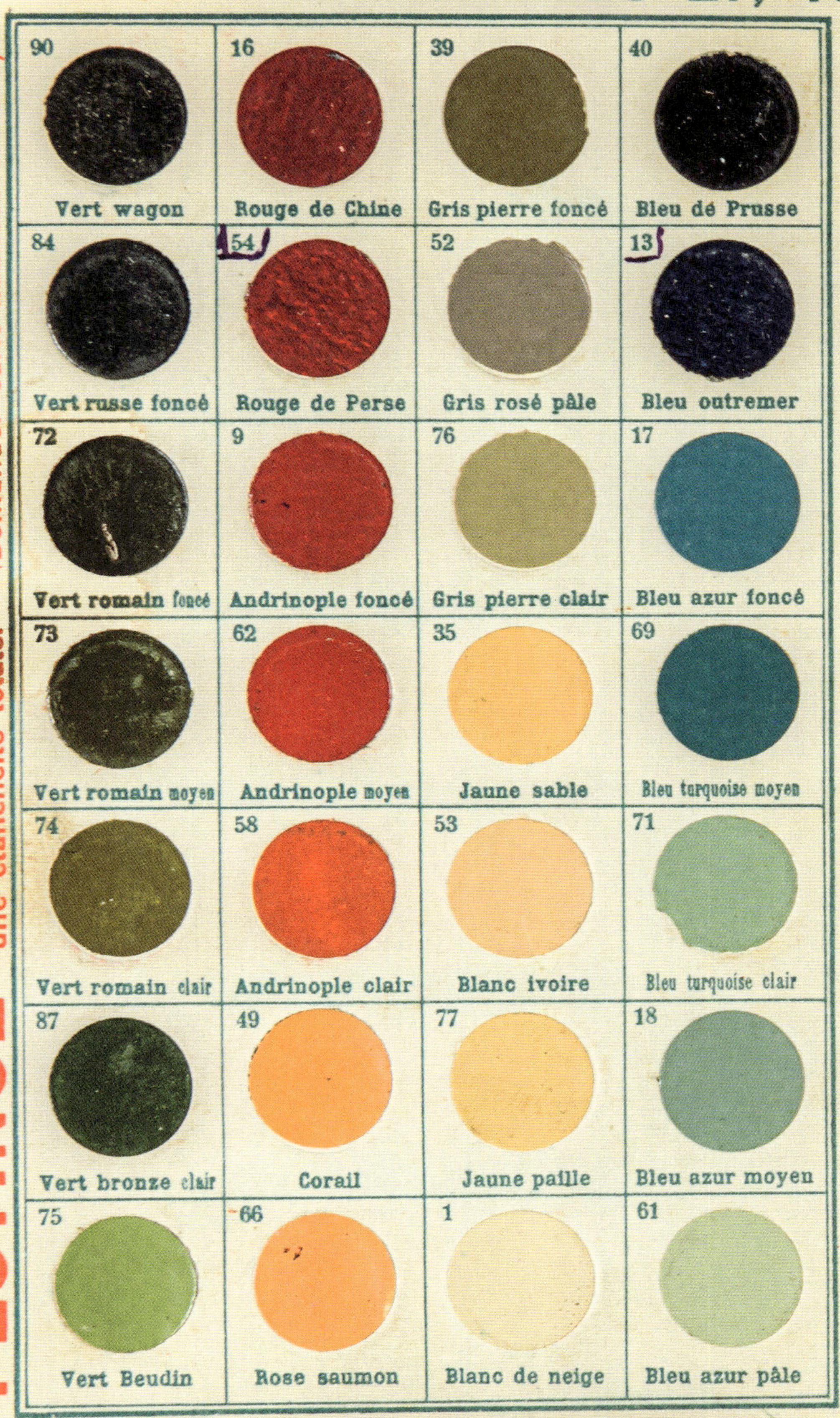
LES NUANCES 27, 78, 13, 54 NE SONT
FESTINOL
Peinture spéciale pour machines, réservoirs, moteurs, intérieur de carters. Insoluble dans pétrole et huiles chaudes. Assure une étanchéité totale. — (Demander carte-nuances et Tarif).
90 Vert wagon
16 Rouge de Chine
39 Gris pierre foncé
40 Bleu de Prusse
84 Vert russe foncé
54 Rouge de Perse
52 Gris rosé pâle
13 Bleu outremer
72 Vert romain foncé
9 Andrinople foncé
76 Gris pierre clair
17 Bleu azur foncé
73 Vert romain moyen
62 Andrinople moyen
35 Jaune sable
69 Bleu turquoise moyen
74 Vert romain clair
58 Andrinople clair
53 Blanc ivoire
71 Bleu turquoise clair
87 Vert bronze clair
49 Corail
77 Jaune paille
18 Bleu azur moyen
75 Vert Beudin
66 Rose saumon
1 Blanc de neige
61 Bleu azur pâle
ROUGE MATIN 59
GLACIS-EXPRESS RIPOLIN - Sèche en 3 heures...
...DEMANDEZ LA CARTE DE NUANCES SPÉCIALE ET LE TARIF
55 Havane moyen
83 Vert bronz
98 Havane foncé
88 Vert késé
95 Bois (ton de)
68 Bleu turquoise
42 Havane clair
63 Violet b
56 Ocre jaune
64 Violet r
70 Chamois foncé
67 Violet m
31 Chamois clair
Or fon
NOIR SPÉCIAL
NOIR
ALUMINIUM

OPPOSITE, TOP

La Pastorine Enamel Paints

As soon as paint manufacturers began using the color chart, some of them almost immediately inserted persuasive information related to health concerns of the era. This is true of Pastorine.[42] The indication "Contains no substance that is harmful to health" implicitly refers to a very old pigment, lead white.[43] Although this pigment was known to cause lead poisoning, it was inexpensive, luminous, and provided good coverage, and was thus hard to replace. Regulations limiting its use would not come into effect until 1902. This product's claim to be "the ultimate antiseptic and hygienic paint" and the company's name of "Pastorine" can both be linked to the fame of Louis Pasteur, whose discoveries excited a society that was afflicted by many scourges, including tuberculosis.

The range was limited, with only twenty-four samples, but with an attractive presentation of the samples in the shape of shields. Except for some (*Celestial Blue*, *Parma Violet*, *Geranium*), the names are simple (*Stone Tone*, *Wood Tone*, *Salmon*, *Vermilion*), as in other contemporary color charts.

Pastorine, Hygienic Enamel Paint, La Pastorine, Saint-Denis, 1900s, pamphlet, 16 × 9.5 cm, 1 fold, Bibliothèque Forney, Paris, call number RES ICO 8104

OPPOSITE, BOTTOM

Coaltarine

The fear of noxious fumes also fueled the sales approach of this color chart: the name of the product comes from *coal tar*, the oily residue of tar that made paint water repellent, while the presence of phenols was believed to destroy microbes and mildew. Customer testimonials and the iconography of frightening insects and monstrous parasites annihilated by Coaltarine were intended to win over any skeptics. The desire for a healthy home was one of the factors explaining the success of the new enamel paints. They were washable, which was not true of the whitewash-based paints that had dominated until then.

Alongside this disturbing background, the twenty-four samples were applied in the shape of delicate silkscreened pennants fluttering in the wind. A unique name appears here, *Beudin Green*, which remains mysterious.

Coaltarine, Enamel Paint, J. Lassailly & L. Bichebois, Issy-les-Moulineaux, 1913, pamphlet, 13 × 10 cm, 2 folds, Bibliothèque Forney, Paris, call number RES ICO 8104

NEXT PAGE SPREAD, LEFT

Astrolin

This color chart consists of seventy-two paint samples that seem to have been varnished. The darkening of the colors makes the range difficult to evaluate visually today, but the explicit names allow us to reconstruct the rich original palette. The recommended applications are once again very extensive (furniture, booths, train cars, streetcars, farming implements). Yet the instructions indicate that the task is accessible to novices. By opening up this practice to nonprofessionals, the next development in paint color charts is predicted; charts would soon be primarily intended for ordinary individuals.

Astrolin Color Card, Établissement Georget Fils Peintures Laquées et Vernis, Chantenay-Lès-Nantes, c. 1906, pamphlet, 16 × 9.5 cm, 2 folds, Bibliothèque Forney, Paris, call number RES ICO 8104

NEXT PAGE SPREAD, TOP RIGHT

Laquotine

A similarly wide range of applications is suggested for this enamel paint, which calls itself "Lacquer of Japan" and reinforces this pseudo-origin with an illustration. The manufacturer took advantage of Japonism, a trend that fostered many clichés that would become rooted in public perception. The design is delicate, as is the range, and the names of the forty-eight samples (applications of paint on sheets cut into colored dots that were then glued to the backing) remained very simple and quite French.

Laquotine, Permanent Enamel Paint, Établissements Julliot & Mouquet formerly Emile Sancy, Paris, 1900s, pamphlet, 15.5 × 11 cm, 2 folds, Bibliothèque Forney, Paris, call number RES ICO 8104

NEXT PAGE SPREAD, BOTTOM RIGHT

Bengaline

The world had become interconnected; cultures began to mingle and products traveled all over the globe. More and more Western companies entered foreign markets. The Société des Peintures Françaises, which supplied several ministries and large manufacturers and mining companies, had a sales agency at the Compagnie du Commerce Extérieur, which supported exports. The text makes the claims that Bengaline paint is "resistant to atmospheric influences, humidity, heat, the effects of sulfides, and seawater," that is, tropical conditions.[44] It is therefore possible that the product was intended for a clientele of colonists and expatriates, which would explain the flag shape of the samples and the rather unusual color names (*Gallic Green*, *French Green*, *Omnibus Red*), as if to remind those living in far-off places of their homeland.

Bengaline, French Enamel Paint, Société des Peintures Françaises, Paris, 1900s, pamphlet, 16 × 12 cm, 1 fold, Bibliothèque Forney, Paris, call number RES ICO 8104

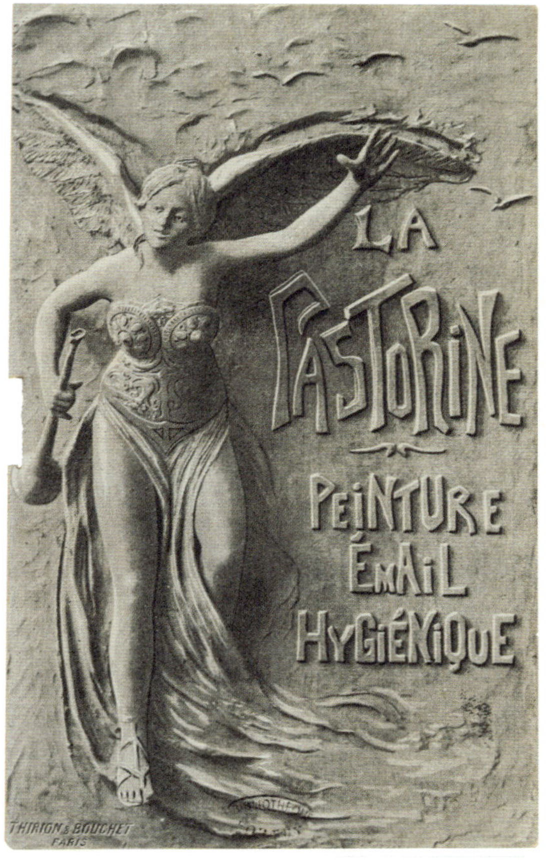

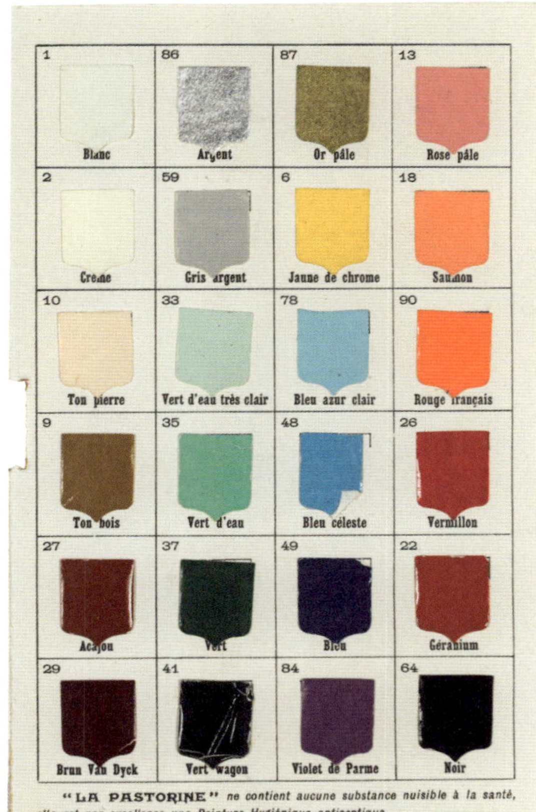

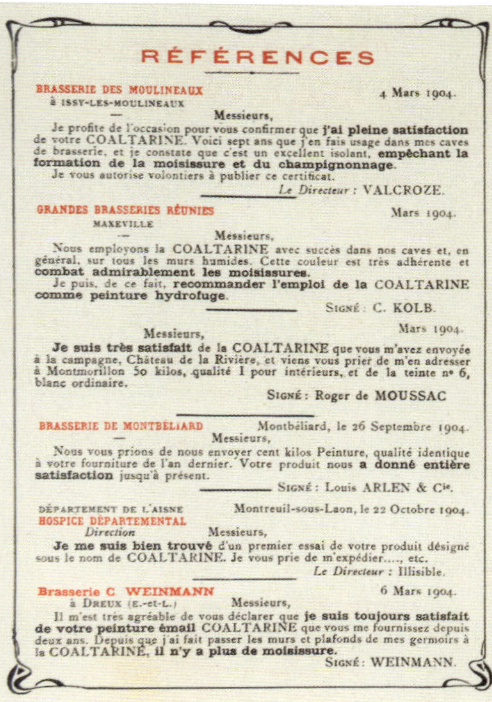

RÉFÉRENCES

BRASSERIE DES MOULINEAUX
à ISSY-LES-MOULINEAUX
4 Mars 1904.

Messieurs,

Je profite de l'occasion pour vous confirmer que **j'ai pleine satisfaction** de votre COALTARINE. Voici sept ans que j'en fais usage dans mes caves de brasserie, et je constate que c'est un excellent isolant, **empêchant la formation de la moisissure et du champignonnage**.

Je vous autorise volontiers à publier ce certificat.

Le Directeur : VALCROZE.

GRANDES BRASSERIES RÉUNIES
MAXEVILLE
Mars 1904.

Messieurs,

Nous employons la COALTARINE avec succès dans nos caves et, en général, sur tous les murs humides. Cette couleur est très adhérente et **combat admirablement les moisissures**.

Je puis, de ce fait, **recommander l'emploi de la** COALTARINE **comme peinture hydrofuge**.

SIGNÉ : C. KOLB.

Mars 1904.

Messieurs,

Je suis très satisfait de la COALTARINE que vous m'avez envoyée à la campagne, Château de la Rivière, et viens vous prier de m'en adresser à Montmorillon 50 kilos, qualité I pour intérieurs, et de la teinte n° 6, blanc ordinaire.

SIGNÉ : Roger de MOUSSAC

BRASSERIE DE MONTBÉLIARD
Montbéliard, le 26 Septembre 1904.

Messieurs,

Nous vous prions de nous envoyer cent kilos Peinture, qualité identique à votre fourniture de l'an dernier. Votre produit nous **a donné entière satisfaction** jusqu'à présent.

SIGNÉ : Louis ARLEN & Cie.

DÉPARTEMENT DE L'AISNE
HOSPICE DÉPARTEMENTAL
Direction
Montreuil-sous-Laon, le 22 Octobre 1904.

Messieurs,

Je me suis bien trouvé d'un premier essai de votre produit désigné sous le nom de COALTARINE. Je vous prie de m'expédier...., etc.

Le Directeur : Illisible.

Brasserie C. WEINMANN
à DREUX (E.-et-L.)
6 Mars 1904.

Messieurs,

Il m'est très agréable de vous déclarer que **je suis toujours satisfait de votre peinture émail** COALTARINE que vous me fournissez depuis deux ans. Depuis que j'ai fait passer les murs et plafonds de mes germoirs à la COALTARINE, **il n'y a plus de moisissure**.

SIGNÉ : WEINMANN.

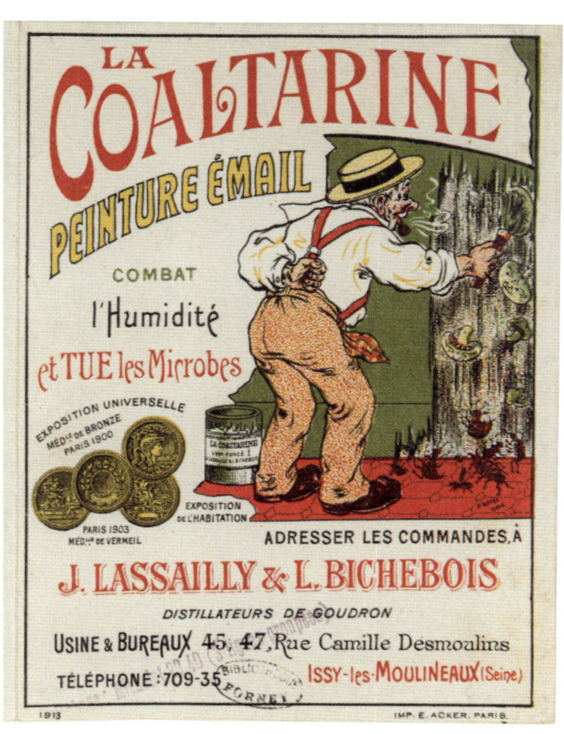

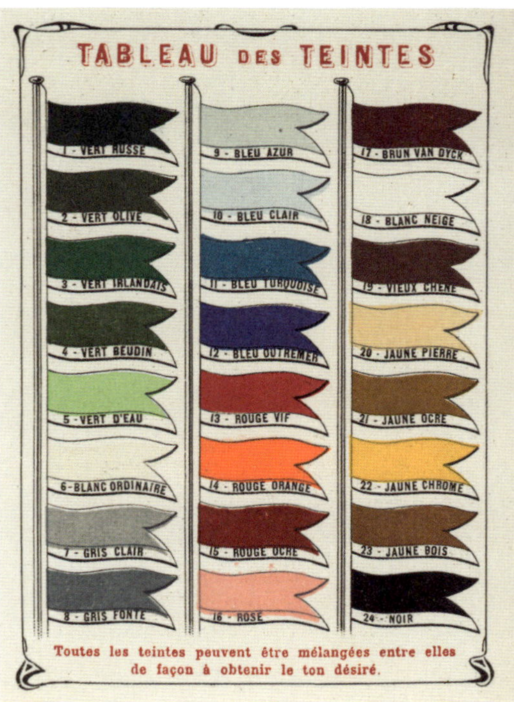

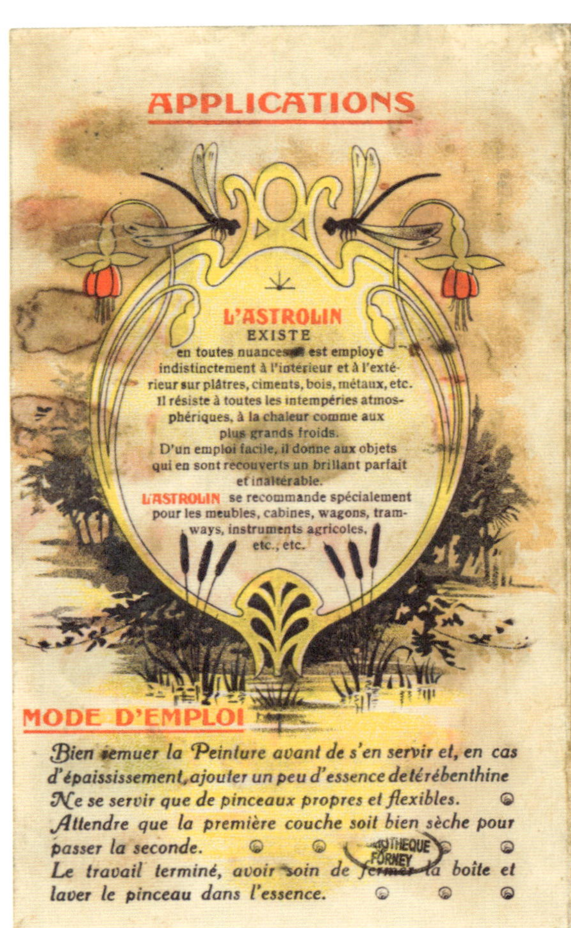
APPLICATIONS
L'ASTROLIN
EXISTE
en toutes nuances et est employé indistinctement à l'intérieur et à l'extérieur sur plâtres, ciments, bois, métaux, etc.
Il résiste à toutes les intempéries atmosphériques, à la chaleur comme aux plus grands froids.
D'un emploi facile, il donne aux objets qui en sont recouverts un brillant parfait et inaltérable.
L'ASTROLIN se recommande spécialement pour les meubles, cabines, wagons, tramways, instruments agricoles, etc., etc.
MODE D'EMPLOI
Bien remuer la Peinture avant de s'en servir et, en cas d'épaississement, ajouter un peu d'essence de térébenthine
Ne se servir que de pinceaux propres et flexibles.
Attendre que la première couche soit bien sèche pour passer la seconde.
Le travail terminé, avoir soin de fermer la boîte et laver le pinceau dans l'essence.

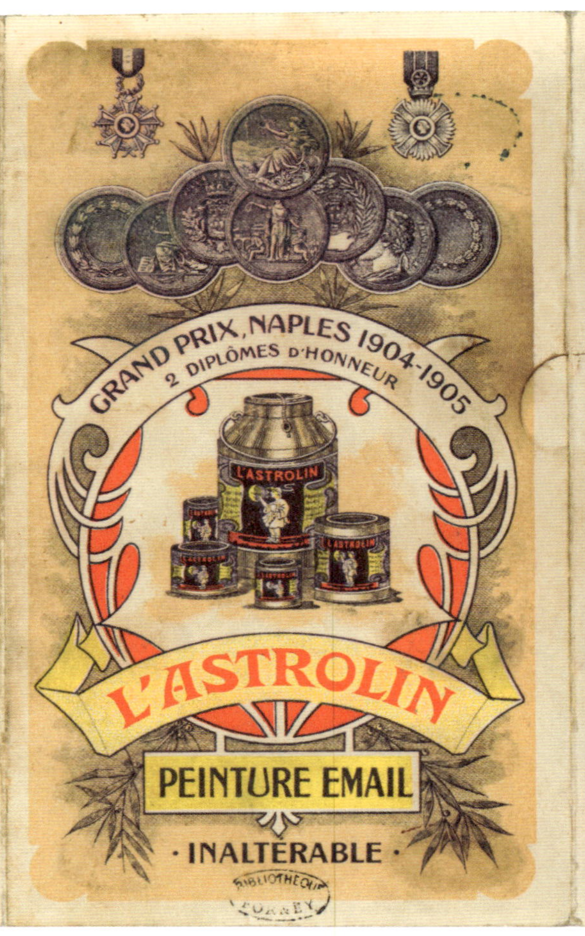
GRAND PRIX, NAPLES 1904-1905
2 DIPLÔMES D'HONNEUR
L'ASTROLIN
L'ASTROLIN
PEINTURE EMAIL
· INALTÉRABLE ·

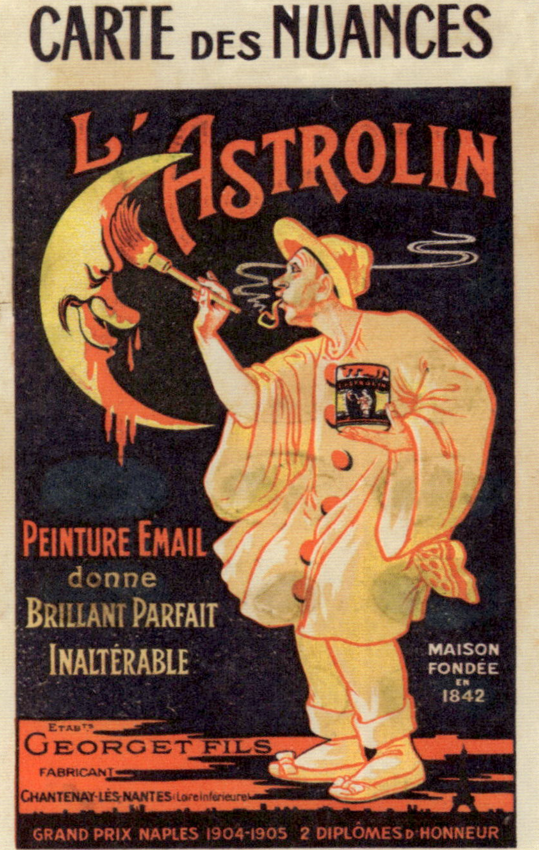
CARTE DES NUANCES
L'ASTROLIN
PEINTURE EMAIL
donne
BRILLANT PARFAIT
INALTÉRABLE
MAISON FONDÉE EN 1842
ETABts GEORGET FILS
FABRICANT
CHANTENAY-LES-NANTES (Loire Inférieure)
GRAND PRIX NAPLES 1904-1905 2 DIPLÔMES D'HONNEUR

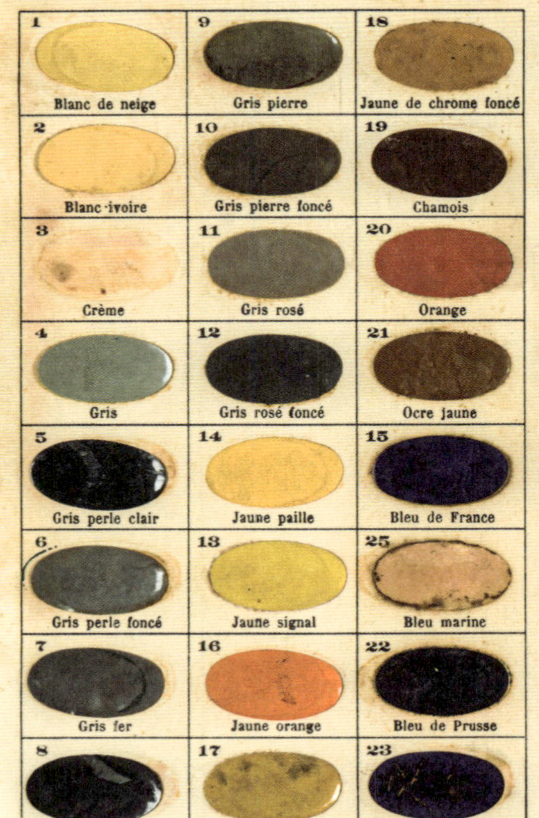
ETABLISSEMENTS GEORGET FILS - PEINTURES LAQUÉES & VERNIS
1 Blanc de neige
9 Gris pierre
18 Jaune de chrome foncé
2 Blanc ivoire
10 Gris pierre foncé
19 Chamois
3 Crème
11 Gris rosé
20 Orange
4 Gris
12 Gris rosé foncé
21 Ocre jaune
5 Gris perle clair
14 Jaune paille
15 Bleu de France
6 Gris perle foncé
13 Jaune signal
25 Bleu marine
7 Gris fer
16 Jaune orange
22 Bleu de Prusse
8 Gris fonte
17 Jaune de chrome
23 Bleu outremer

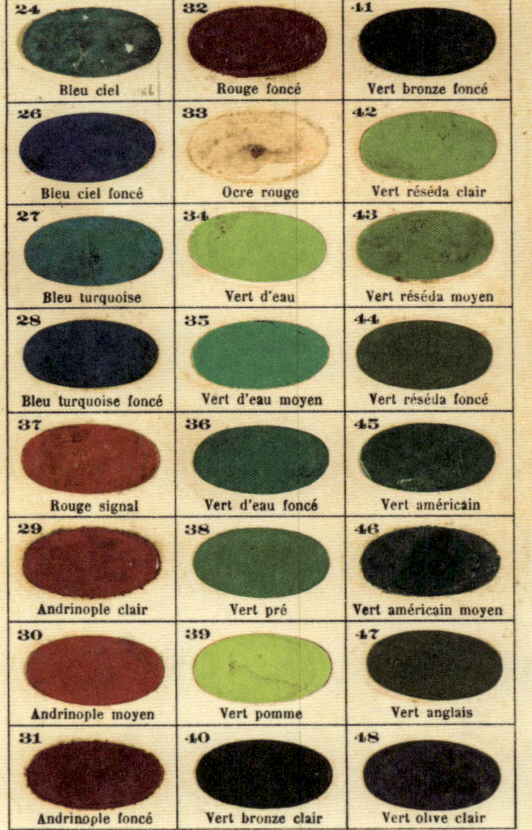
24 Bleu ciel
32 Rouge foncé
41 Vert bronze foncé
26 Bleu ciel foncé
33 Ocre rouge
42 Vert réséda clair
27 Bleu turquoise
34 Vert d'eau
43 Vert réséda moyen
28 Bleu turquoise foncé
35 Vert d'eau moyen
44 Vert réséda foncé
37 Rouge signal
36 Vert d'eau foncé
45 Vert américain
29 Andrinople clair
38 Vert pré
46 Vert américain moyen
30 Andrinople moyen
39 Vert pomme
47 Vert anglais
31 Andrinople foncé
40 Vert bronze clair
48 Vert olive clair

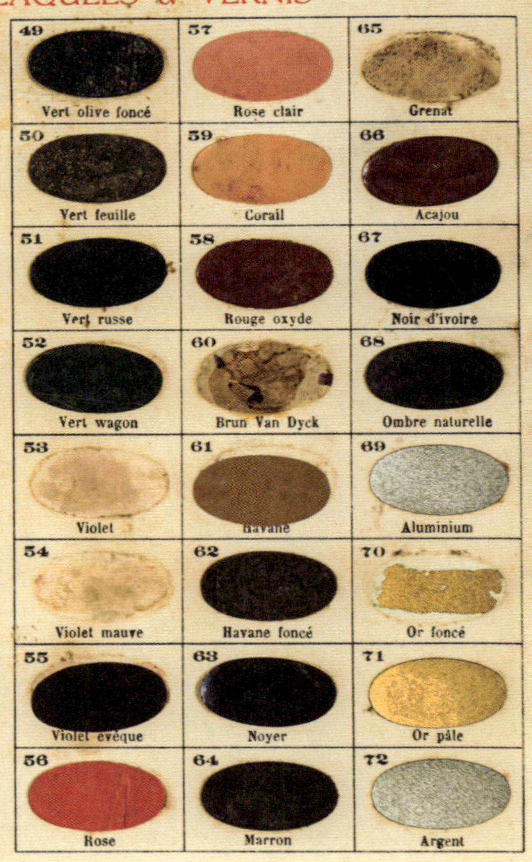
49 Vert olive foncé
57 Rose clair
65 Grenat
50 Vert feuille
59 Corail
66 Acajou
51 Vert russe
58 Rouge oxyde
67 Noir d'ivoire
52 Vert wagon
60 Brun Van Dyck
68 Ombre naturelle
53 Violet
61 Havane
69 Aluminium
54 Violet mauve
62 Havane foncé
70 Or foncé
55 Violet évêque
63 Noyer
71 Or pâle
56 Rose
64 Marron
72 Argent

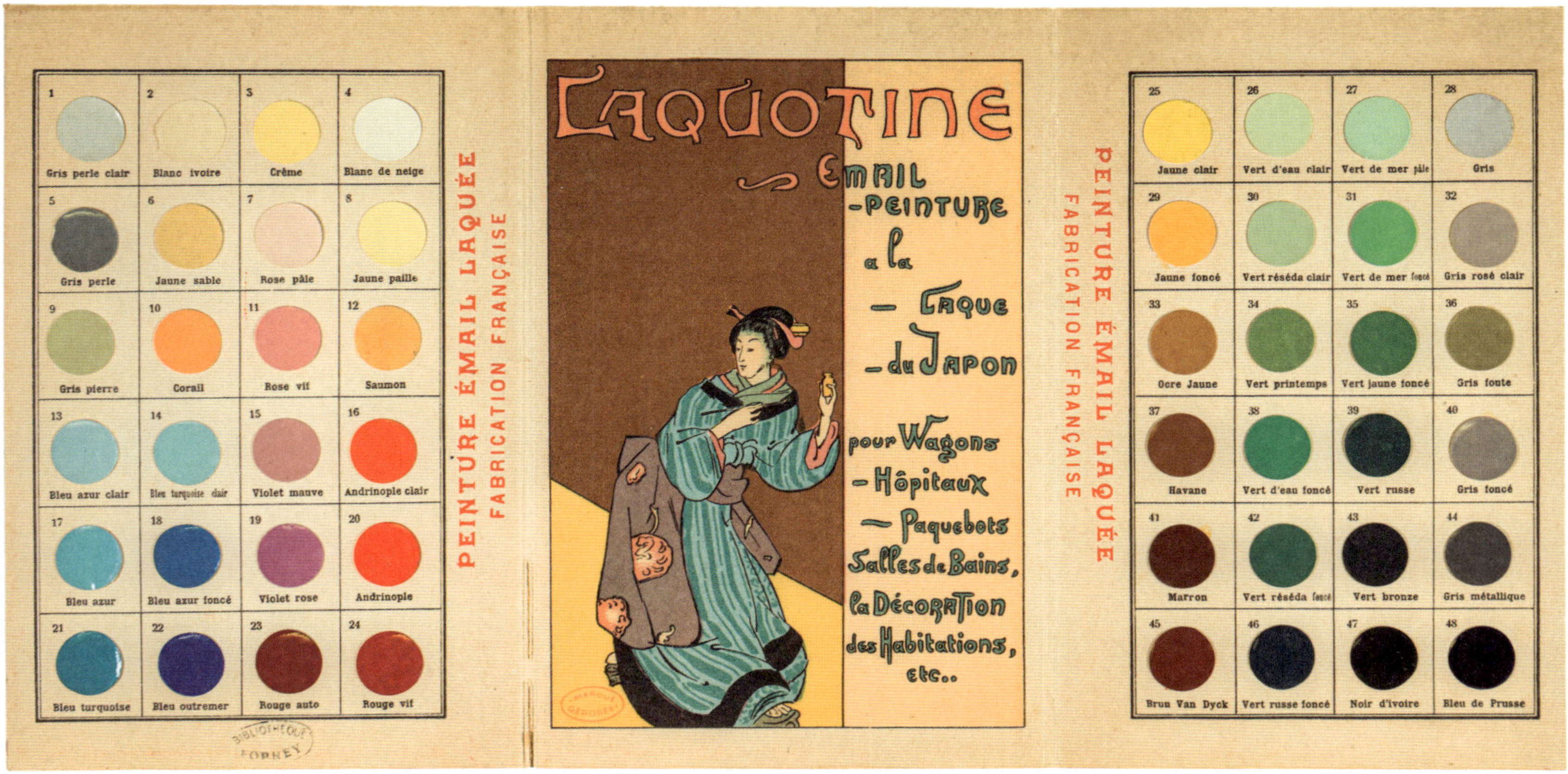

1 Gris perle clair	2 Blanc ivoire	3 Crème	4 Blanc de neige
5 Gris perle	6 Jaune sable	7 Rose pâle	8 Jaune paille
9 Gris pierre	10 Corail	11 Rose vif	12 Saumon
13 Bleu azur clair	14 Bleu turquoise clair	15 Violet mauve	16 Andrinople clair
17 Bleu azur	18 Bleu azur foncé	19 Violet rose	20 Andrinople
21 Bleu turquoise	22 Bleu outremer	23 Rouge auto	24 Rouge vif

PEINTURE ÉMAIL LAQUÉE
FABRICATION FRANÇAISE

LAQUOTINE

EMAIL
-PEINTURE
a la
– LAQUE
–du JAPON

pour Wagons
–Hôpitaux
–Paquebots
Salles de Bains,
la Décoration
des Habitations,
etc..

PEINTURE ÉMAIL LAQUÉE
FABRICATION FRANÇAISE

25 Jaune clair	26 Vert d'eau clair	27 Vert de mer pâle	28 Gris
29 Jaune foncé	30 Vert réséda clair	31 Vert de mer foncé	32 Gris rosé clair
33 Ocre Jaune	34 Vert printemps	35 Vert jaune foncé	36 Gris fonte
37 Havane	38 Vert d'eau foncé	39 Vert russe	40 Gris foncé
41 Marron	42 Vert réséda foncé	43 Vert bronze	44 Gris métallique
45 Brun Van Dyck	46 Vert russe foncé	47 Noir d'ivoire	48 Bleu de Prusse

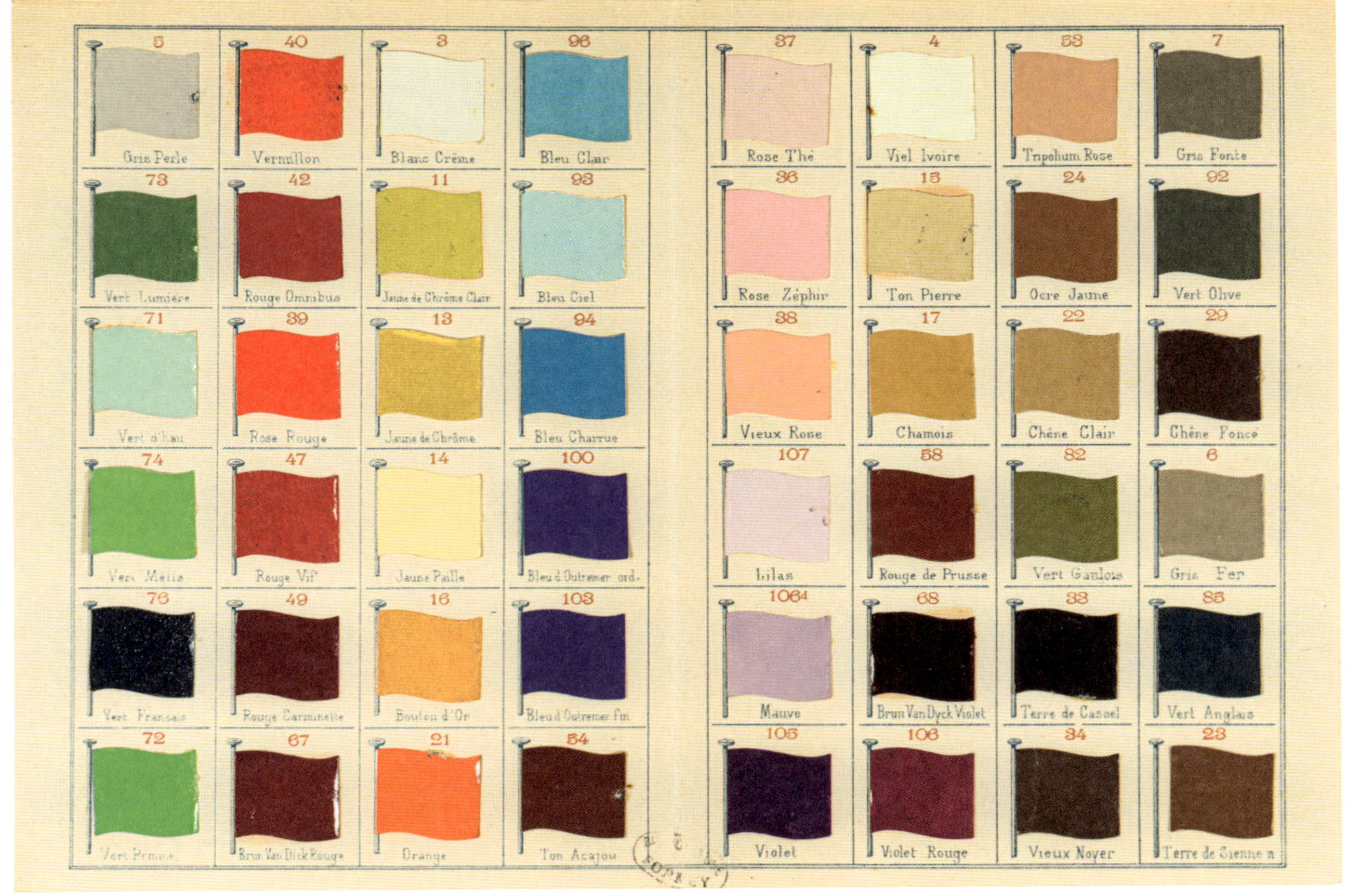

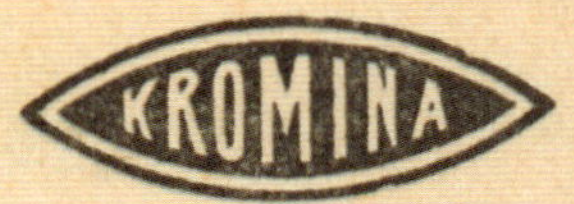

MODO DE EMPLEO

Colocar en un recipiente la KROMINA en polvo; **añadir agua por muy pequeñas cantidades**, remover con un palo hasta humedecer toda la masa, aplastar todos los terrones para que el agua penetre, se llega a formar así una pasta espesa que tiene la apariencia de la pasta del pan.

Dejar reposar media hora añadir agua **poco a poco** mezclando fuertemente con un palo hasta que todos los pequeños terrones hayan desaparecido y que se llegue a tener el espesor que se requiere para pintar.

Si la pintura es demasiado espesa añadir agua, si es demasiado liquida, si corre al pintar, **preparar aparte** en otro recipiente otra cantidad de pintura empleando **lo menos posible de agua** y mezclar esta pasta a la KROMINA que resulte demasiado clara.

La cantidad aproximada de agua que se debe de emplear es de un litro de agua por un kilo de Kromina en polvo.

Preparación de fondos

EN PAREDES DE YESO NUEVO.—Dar a estas paredes una mano de apresto de agua y cola, o bien de aceite de linaza cocido, o bien de agua y jabón; el agua de jabón debe de prepararse derritiendo en agua muy caliente jabón cortado en copos; la proporción es de medio kilo de jabón por 10 litros de agua. Impregnar perfectamente con esta solución fría las paredes de yeso nuevo.

PINTURAS AL ACEITE NUEVAS.—Pasar el cepillo para quitar el polvo y raspar todas las superficies que no sean sólidas.

PAREDES PINTADAS VARIAS VECES A LA CAL, BLANCO GELATINOSO O COLA.—Hacer desaparecer estas pinturas antiguas rascando y lavando con agua caliente.

PINTURAS VIEJAS U OTRAS MEZCLAS.—Tapar las grietas o hendiduras y limpiar bien con cepillo.

Preparar con agua para un solo día la pintura necesaria.
Utilizar con Kromina fresca la pintura vieja
Limpiar perfectamente en agua las brochas después de su uso.

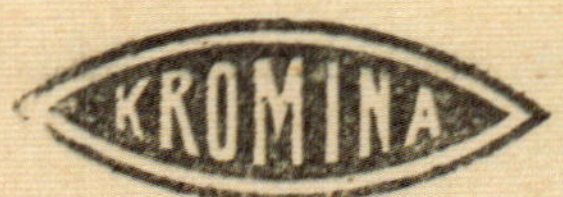

Pintura en polvo seco para ser preparada añadiendo agua fría solamente

El empleo es sencillo, cubre bien, resiste perfectamente sobre el CEMENTO
El color blanco da mucha claridad en locales oscuros.

Pedir la lista completa de los colores de KROMINA

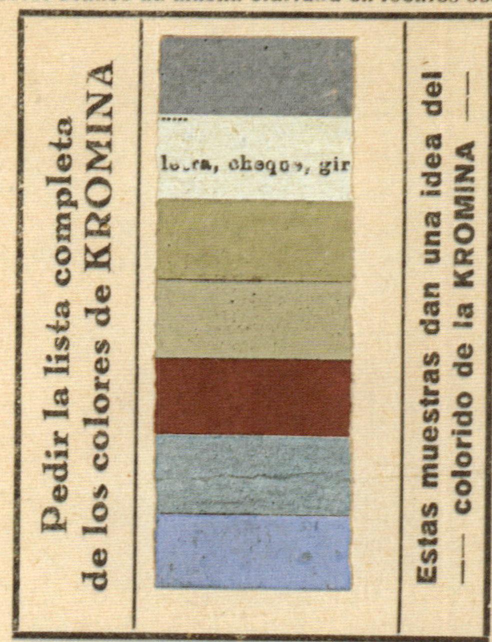

Estas muestras dan una idea del colorido de la KROMINA

La KROMINA se emplea simplemente mezclada con agua, es decir, que su preparación no ofrece ninguna dificultad.

JOSE SUPERVIELLE.-Fábrica de Productos Químicos
RENTERIA (Guipúzcoa)

OPPOSITE

Kromina

There were also color charts for traditional paints, such as these colored whitewashes ready to be diluted that were distributed by this company from the Basque region in Spain. Very economical, sterile, easy to prepare and apply, and benefiting from synthetic dyes that had recently come to market, whitewashes had many qualities but also, like distemper, a big disadvantage: they could not be washed.[45] Moreover, it was difficult to obtain saturated colors because whitewash considerably lightened the mixture. Therefore, new formulations of these "pebble solutions"[46] were developed in the second half of the nineteenth century, especially by emulsifying water and oil. Their colors could be a bit stronger but not enough to compete with the bright, luminous, and varied palettes of contemporary enamel paints. Distemper and whitewash would be limited to modest dwellings and rooms where hygiene was essential (kitchen, pantry, sanitary facilities, or children's rooms).

Kromina, Jose Supervielle, Renteria, Spain, c. 1910, pamphlet, 14 × 10 cm, 1 fold, Bibliothèque Forney, Paris, call number RES ICO 8104

——— The techniques for shaping a paint color chart were distinctly less onerous and expensive than for textiles, as it was easier to mechanize the application of a pigment than the cutting of a swatch of fabric. The chart cost less to produce and was more widely distributed, especially since at the turn of the twentieth century, paint manufacturers were required to advertise their wares. Manufacturers needed to stand out and attract attention, and thus there was a significant effort to embellish color charts with illustrations, which reveal a great deal about the aesthetic tastes of the era. Moreover, maintaining and beautifying one's home was an investment: color charts for decorative paints provided professional painters with technical information and instructions that sometimes took up an entire booklet before the color chart. While this information helps us to understand the products today, it also trained painters in the new paints and served as fertile ground that would soon allow ordinary consumers to pick up a brush themselves. The circles of paint on these color charts evoked the contemporary boxes of gouache and their little wells of paint, while the rectangular samples recalled boxes of watercolors. They both invited the user to dip in a brush and get started on a new project.

Fine Art Paints: From Traditional Colors to New Shades

——— No one experienced the profound changes in color theory and practice over the course of the nineteenth century more intimately than artists. The availability of color charts of oil paints, watercolor, gouache, or pastels transformed artists' approach to color starting in the final decades of the nineteenth century. Society's approach to color changed as well.

In the seventeenth century, establishing a connection between a formula and the final product had led to the presence of samples in the manuscripts of Théodore de Mayerne and Boogert.[47] The situation was quite different in the late nineteenth century. The color theories developed over the course of the century led painters to play with primary and complementary colors and to transform their palettes.[48] Manuals for teaching artistic practices multiplied. Due to research carried out by naturalists since Patrick Syme[49] who were trying to stabilize the colors in their works,[50] these manuals were illustrated with color samples, which made them the precursors of the color charts of painting materials that began to circulate in the late nineteenth century.

Over the course of the previous century, the methods for producing paints for use in the fine arts also transformed.[51] Merchants could now offer their customers prepared paint that contained a pigment and a binding agent. Starting in the middle of the century, packaging in cubes or tubes facilitated sales, storage, and transportation of paint. Painters stopped mixing their own paints and could now paint outdoors.[52] Finally, synthetic pigments and dyes[53] fulfilled the demand for very saturated, shiny colors and considerably increased their standardization.[54]

These innovations and the overall rise in standards of living and education enabled the increase in the numbers of painters, both experienced ones and amateurs. By the late nineteenth century, this growing market gave the color seller an important role in England and in most European countries.[55] Many of the manufacturers who supplied the artists understood that acquiring chemistry skills had become essential in order to master mixtures and their storage.

The makers of the "fine colors" that were distributed until World War I had already taken into account the fact that pigments could change or fade over time; this had become a crucial issue.[56] Indeed, when already prepared colors came to market, painters' expertise no longer applied, especially since the components of these paints were not specified. Above all, many bright paints from lacquers[57] or synthetic ingredients[58] turned out to be much less stable than their predecessors: the colors of many impressionist or fauve paintings today are drastically different from the colors the artist originally applied to the canvas.

This attentiveness to the endurance of colors is the first specific quality of these charts. The second is their naming vocabulary. It contains on the one hand traditional names for pigments still in use or their imitations and, on the other hand, names mentioning recently created pigments. Otherwise, the color charts for artists' supplies reveal, like other contemporary color charts, the same attempt to organize the color ranges and use product samples. Most often, the samples were an application of paint on strips of paper that were glued to the backing, either in gradations (various degrees of dilution of the medium) or full application (one single degree). The order of presentation of the colors, grouped by tone, emphasizes the comparison of complementary colors, most likely to facilitate making distinctions between shades. Unfortunately, they are rarely dated, requiring conjectures based on the history of the companies, the addresses of their headquarters, or the date of the appearance of the pigments.

OPPOSITE, LEFT

An Ideal Watercolor Palette

This card, from a company we know nothing of today, with its six cubes of paint, is a combination of a watercolor box and a chart of the colors the paint can produce.[59] A list of these colors appears on the back of the card, and it is specified which mixtures will produce them, the pigments all existing prior to synthetic chemistry. Their combinations are based mainly on the mixture of three primary colors, but the color chart is comprehensible only to connoisseurs, for the conditions are not present here to show the thirty possible colors, nor is it possible to perceive the color of the cubes, which will appear only once they are diluted. This card's function is somewhere between a painter's palette and a color chart, and also between colors that are ready to use and colors to be composed.

Ideal Palette for the Watercolor Artist, P. R., France, late nineteenth century, stiff cardboard, approx. 35 × 25 cm, Albi Couleurs, Association Mémoire des Industries de la Couleur, Albi

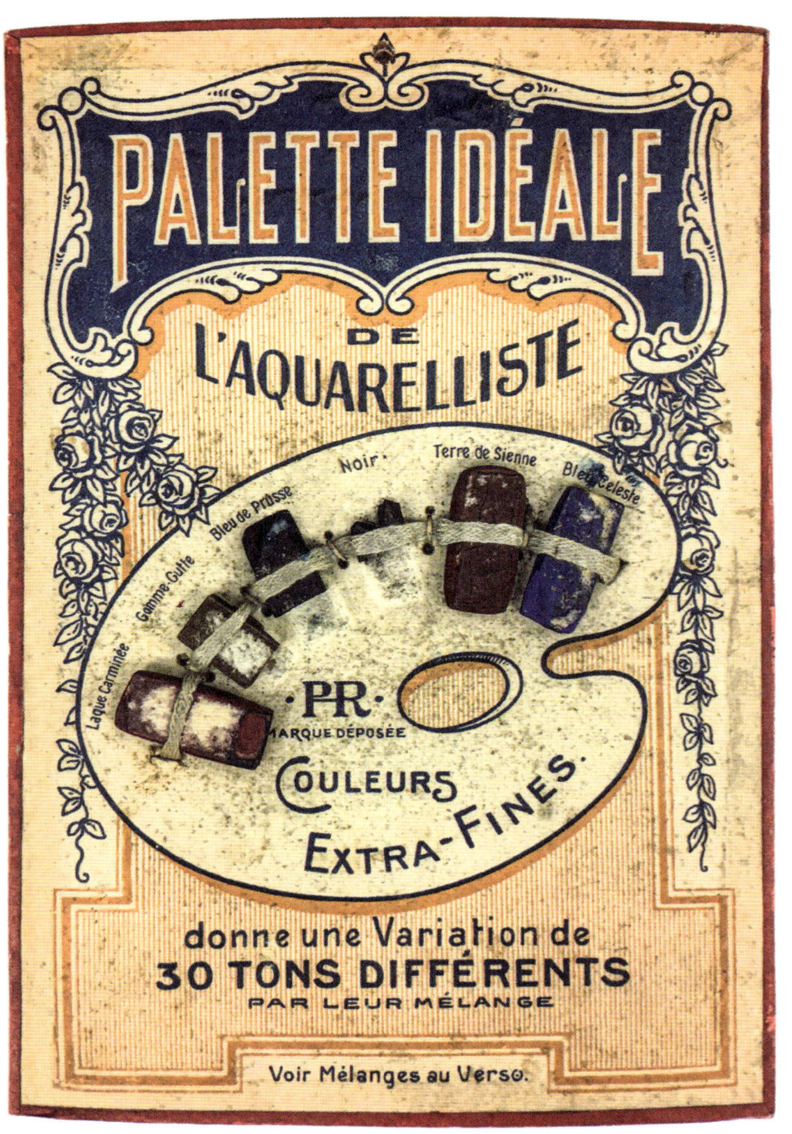

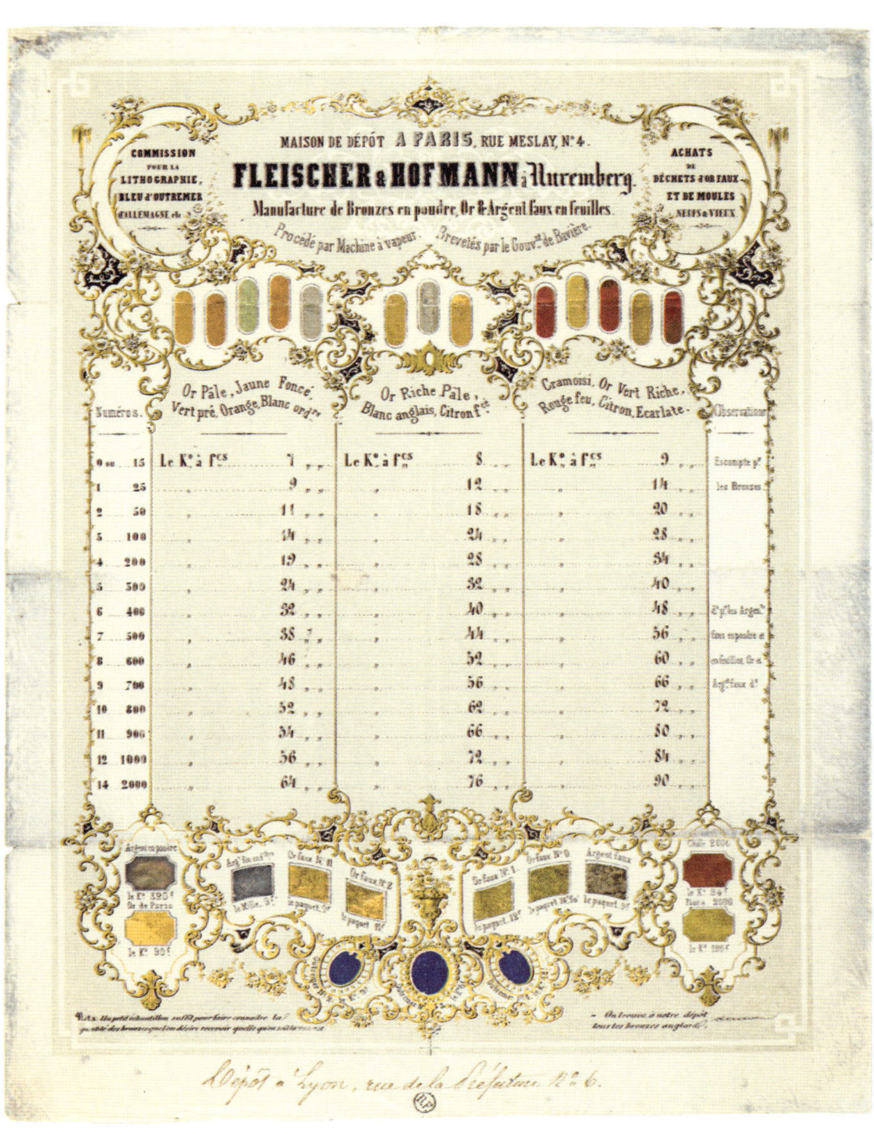

COMMISSION POUR LA LITHOGRAPHIE, BLEU d'OUTREMER d'ALLEMAGNE &c.

MAISON DE DÉPÔT A PARIS, RUE MESLAY, N° 4.

FLEISCHER & HOFMANN à Nuremberg.

Manufacture de Bronzes en poudre, Or & Argent faux en feuilles.

Procédé par Machine à vapeur. Brevetés par le Gouv.nt de Bavière.

ACHATS DE DÉCHETS d'OR FAUX ET DE MOULES NEUFS & VIEUX

Numéros.	Or Pâle, Jaune Foncé, Vert pré, Orange, Blanc ord.re	Or Riche Pâle, Blanc anglais, Citron f.cé	Cramoisi, Or Vert Riche, Rouge feu, Citron, Ecarlate.	Observations
0 ou 15	Le K.o à f.cs 7	Le K.o à f.cs 8	Le K.o à f.cs 9	Escompte p.r
1 25	9	12	14	les Bronzes
2 50	11	18	20	
3 100	14	24	28	
4 200	19	28	34	
5 300	24	32	40	
6 400	32	40	48	d.o p.r les Argen.ts
7 500	38	44	56	fins en poudre et
8 600	46	52	60	en feuilles, Or et
9 700	48	56	66	Arg.t faux d.o
10 800	52	62	72	
11 900	54	66	80	
12 1000	56	72	84	
14 2000	64	76	90	

Dépôt à Lyon, rue de la Préfecture N° 6.

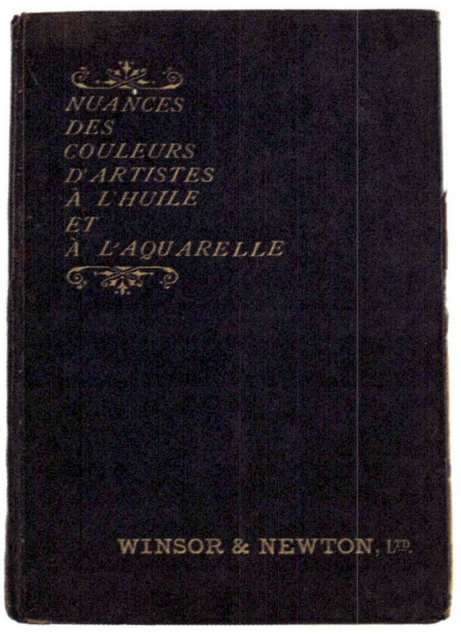
NUANCES
DES
COULEURS
D'ARTISTES
A L'HUILE
ET
A L'AQUARELLE
WINSOR & NEWTON, LTD.

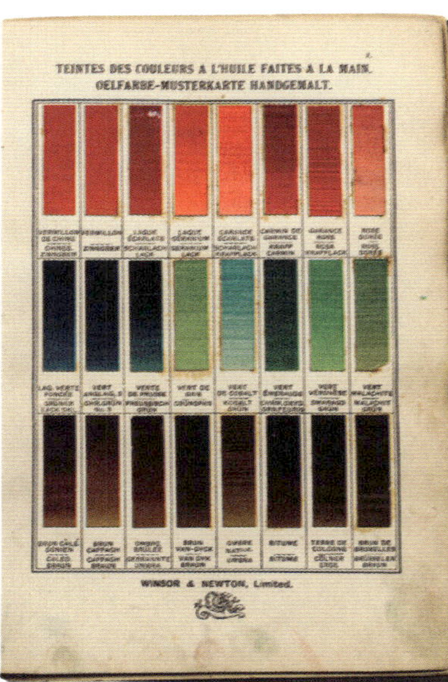
TEINTES DES COULEURS A L'HUILE FAITES A LA MAIN.
OELFARBE-MUSTERKARTE HANDGEMALT.
WINSOR & NEWTON, Limited.

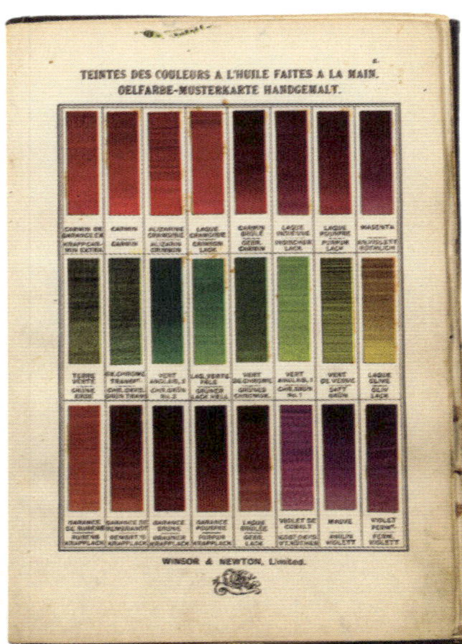
TEINTES DES COULEURS A L'HUILE FAITES A LA MAIN.
OELFARBE-MUSTERKARTE HANDGEMALT.
WINSOR & NEWTON, Limited.

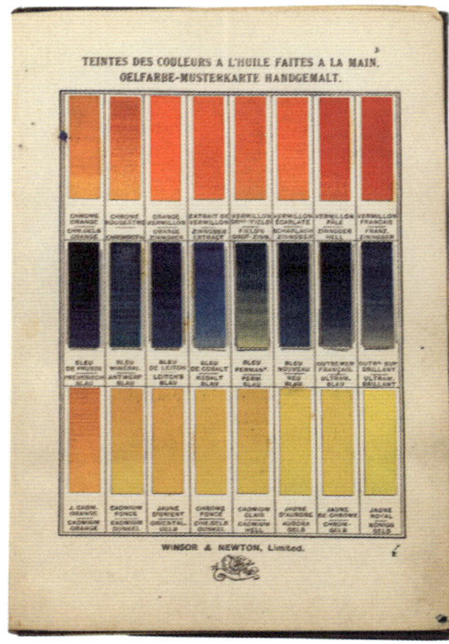
TEINTES DES COULEURS A L'HUILE FAITES A LA MAIN.
OELFARBE-MUSTERKARTE HANDGEMALT.
WINSOR & NEWTON, Limited.

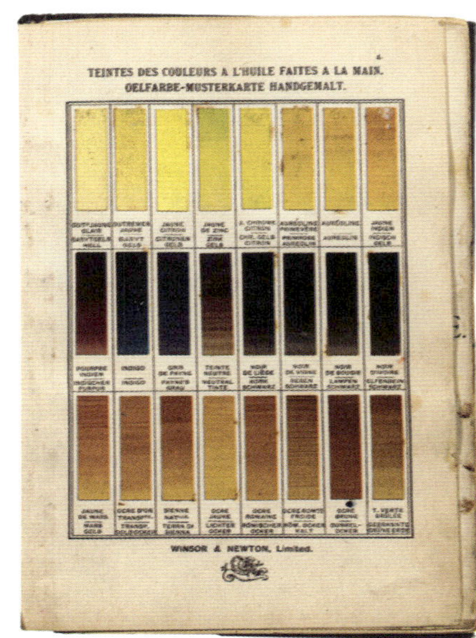
TEINTES DES COULEURS A L'HUILE FAITES A LA MAIN.
OELFARBE-MUSTERKARTE HANDGEMALT.
WINSOR & NEWTON, Limited.

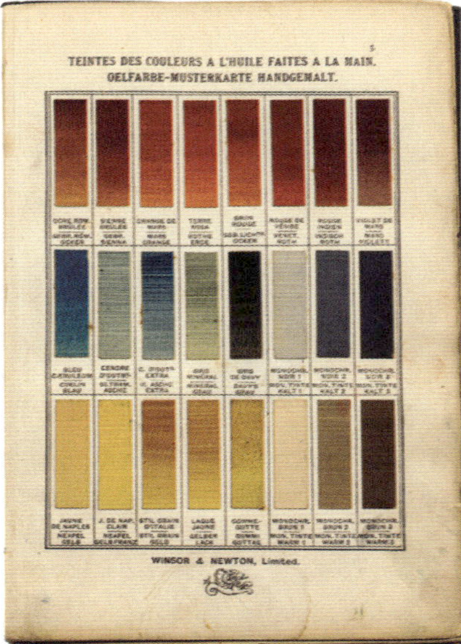
TEINTES DES COULEURS A L'HUILE FAITES A LA MAIN.
OELFARBE-MUSTERKARTE HANDGEMALT.
WINSOR & NEWTON, Limited.

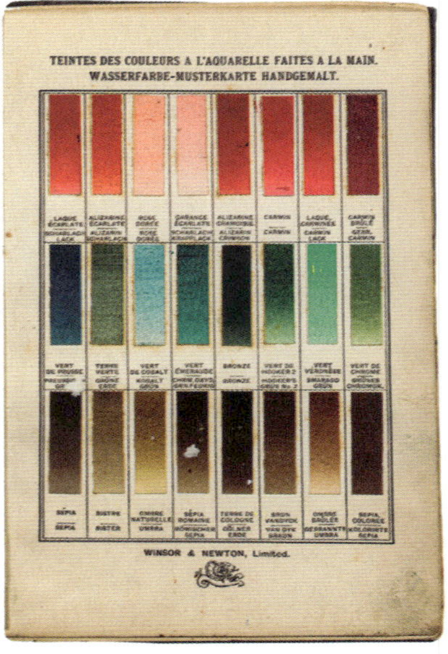
TEINTES DES COULEURS A L'AQUARELLE FAITES A LA MAIN.
WASSERFARBE-MUSTERKARTE HANDGEMALT.
WINSOR & NEWTON, Limited.

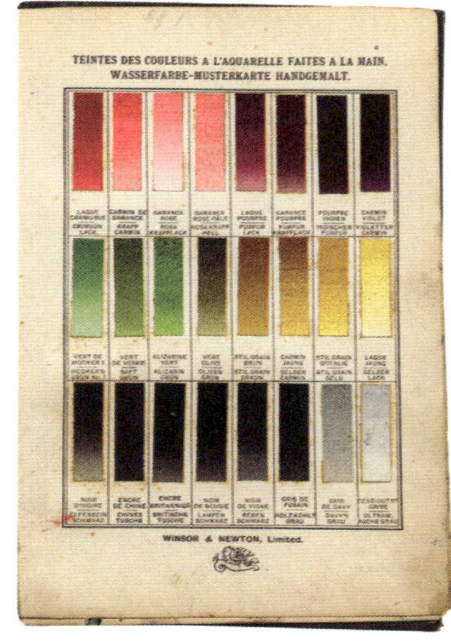
TEINTES DES COULEURS A L'AQUARELLE FAITES A LA MAIN.
WASSERFARBE-MUSTERKARTE HANDGEMALT.
WINSOR & NEWTON, Limited.

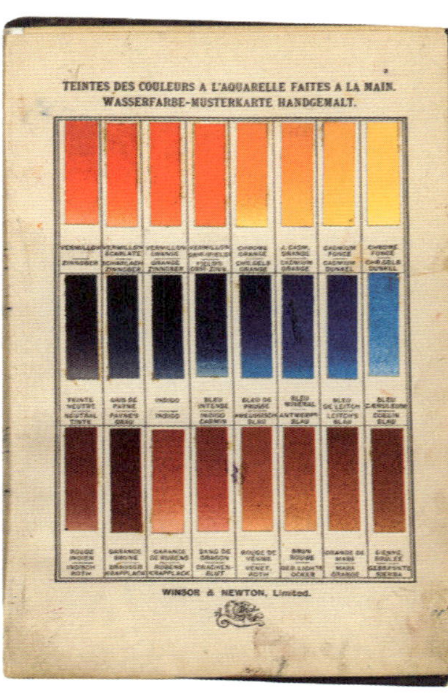
TEINTES DES COULEURS A L'AQUARELLE FAITES A LA MAIN.
WASSERFARBE-MUSTERKARTE HANDGEMALT.
WINSOR & NEWTON, Limited.

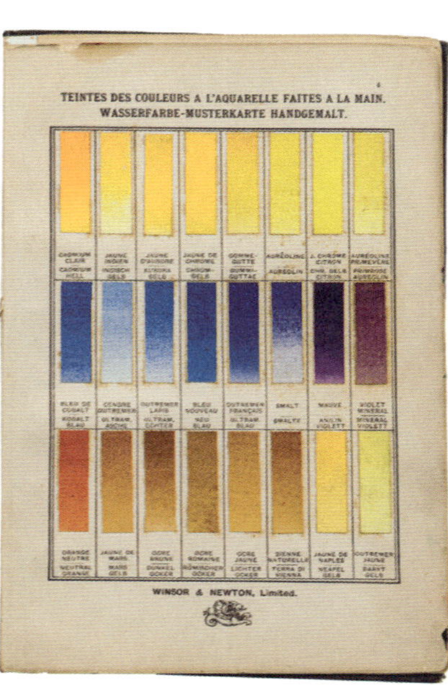
TEINTES DES COULEURS A L'AQUARELLE FAITES A LA MAIN.
WASSERFARBE-MUSTERKARTE HANDGEMALT.
WINSOR & NEWTON, Limited.

PREVIOUS PAGE, RIGHT

Fleischer & Hofmann Metallic Colors

During the nineteenth century, the making of metallic pigments was simplified through chemical processes that produced extremely fine powders, thus changing the age-old arts of gold calligraphy and decorative miniatures or illuminations.

The Fleischer & Hofmann company, which already produced these metallic pigments in Nuremberg in 1847, later specialized in powders and sheets intended for lithographs. This color chart seems to have been preprinted with this technique (frame, decorative scrollwork, and some of the information and samples), with the prices being filled in by hand as costs changed.

Nineteen gilded tones (including an astonishing *Meadow Green*), three silvered ones, one copper hue (*Flesh*), and three blue shades are presented. Their names clearly correspond to the specific customs of the professions using these media and are purely conventional. Real gold, silver, or ultramarine from true lapis lazuli could not be sold at these prices.

References on the document to warehouses in Paris and Lyon are evidence of the active distribution of artists' supplies between the countries of production (in the late nineteenth century, mainly England, France, and Germany) and of sales (large European cities).

Chart of Metallic Colors in Powder and Sheets, Fleischer & Hofmann, Nuremberg, Germany, late nineteenth century, sheet of paper, 32 × 24 cm, Bibliothèque Forney, Paris, call number RES ICO 7208 Plano PF

OPPOSITE

Winsor & Newton Oils and Watercolors

This color chart confirms this international distribution of products, but it is also an example of manufacturers' development of increasingly scientific skills. Winsor & Newton was one of the oldest color companies in England, founded in 1831 by a chemist, William Winsor, and an artist, Henry Newton. They soon made many innovations and grew alarmed at the instability of certain pigments.

This presentation book is divided into two parts: the first presents five plates of oil paints and the second, four watercolor plates. Each is preceded by a list of the colors in French and English, with the samples designated in French and German. Thus, this document was clearly designed to adapt to the mobility of artists in late nineteenth-century Europe.

We find the names of pigments that already existed in the fifteenth century (*Naples Yellow*, *Candle Black* or *Ivory Black*, *Ochers*, *Umber*, and *Sienna*), but *Orpiment*, a toxic arsenic trisulfide, was replaced by imitations produced using pigments discovered after the beginning of the century. Some names mention the chemical element (*Chromium Oxide* and *Chromium Green*, *Cadmium Yellow*). They show an effort to dispel the secrecy surrounding the composition of paints.

Despite its variety, this vocabulary of colors demonstrated a kind of stability, which was certainly connected to artists' attachment to the materials of their predecessors and to the loyalty that many of them felt toward colors of which they were especially fond. However, this consistency in terminology did not necessarily correspond to consistent formulas—quite the contrary.

While some of the lacquers on this color chart were already reputed to be short-lived, it is possible that their formulas were changed after initial warnings were issued, though there is no way to tell.[60] It took time and a great deal of research to gradually eliminate ephemeral colors from color charts, and the indication "Permanent" for some violets or blues on this color chart shows that stability was beginning to be taken into consideration.[61]

Shades of Artists' Colors in Oil and Watercolor, Winsor & Newton Ltd., London, England, late nineteenth century, book, 22.7 × 15.5 cm, Sennelier family collection, Paris

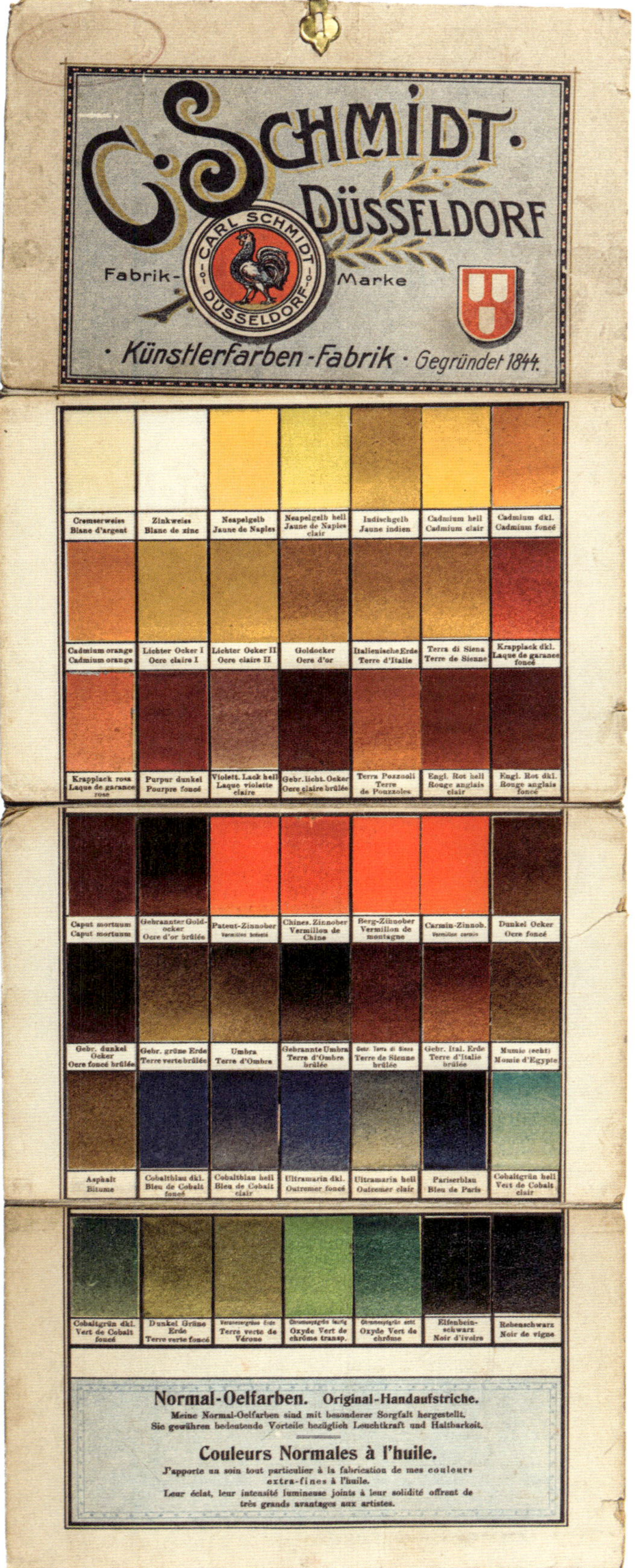

LEFT

Schmidt Oil Colors

Like other companies, the German paint producer Carl Schmidt adopted a folded format that allowed, when unfolded, for a synoptic view of the colors. As in other contemporary charts, its forty-nine oil paint colors are identified by bilingual names, in this case, German and French. Comparing this chart to samples on charts from the same era shows that the color terms were variable. Thus, the green obtained by chromium oxide, which is known by the German name *Chromoxydgrün Feurig* here and on the Winsor & Newton color chart, is translated on the first by *Transparent Chromium Oxide Green* (*Oxyde vert de chrome transparent*) and on the second by *Emerald Green* (*Vert émeraude*). Moreover, the colors are not at all identical. The same is true for *Naples Yellow* (French *Jaune de Naples* and German *Neapelgelb*), which refers, insofar as the state of preservation of the charts allows us to judge, to two distinct colors.

Standard Oil Colors, C. Schmidt, Düsseldorf, Germany, c. 1900, pamphlet, 12.3 × 19 cm, 3 folds, Sennelier family collection, Paris

OPPOSITE

Sennelier Oil Colors

Given the ongoing changes in formulating paints and the hazards of translations, the color chart was the only option for an artist to choose the desired color with certainty. As soon as Gustave Sennelier founded his company in 1887, he produced his own chart. Like most of the producers of this era, Sennelier had studied chemistry at the Conservatoire des Arts et Métiers. This background enabled him to formulate colors for oil paint, watercolor, and dry pastel. Moreover, in his 1895 catalog, he indicated the chemical composition of his paints—which was rare for the time—and pointed out colors of proven stability.[62]

While the range and its associated vocabulary are also found in contemporary color charts, this one, completely made by hand, offers a plate for each tone and presents up to twelve shades, with the thickness of the brushstroke allowing the viewer to visualize the effects of the paint when applied. This chart was a work in progress, both an effective tool of choice for artists who purchased supplies at the store on Quai Voltaire and an inventory for the manufacturer, designed to be updated. New colors were added to it. This was the case for *Cadmium Red* (plate six) (which quickly replaced the mercury-based vermilions, which were toxic) and also for *Helios Red*. This intense, luminous red was specific to the company and was much appreciated by the postimpressionists. Gustave Sennelier created *Helios Red* in 1912.[63]

That same year, he self-published a brochure, *The Chemistry of Colors*, a thorough manual on painting materials and tools, which he distributed to his customers free of charge. His wife Juliette perceived very early the interest of the middle class in the decorative arts and supplied the store with appropriate materials.

Color Chart of Extra-Fine Strokes of Oil Color, Gustave Sennelier, Paris, c. 1896, 24 plates of stiff cardboard, 23.8 × 21 cm, Sennelier family collection, Paris

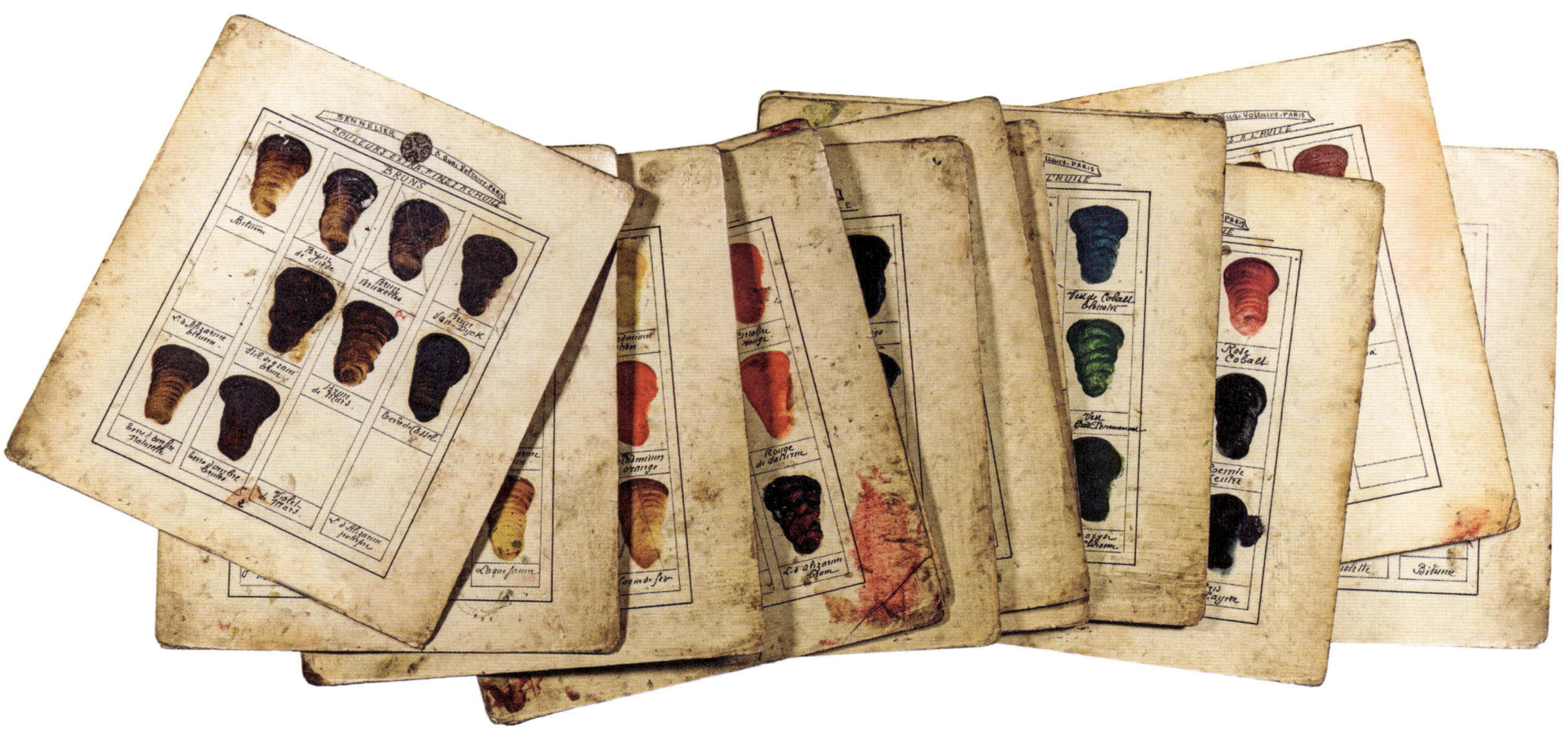

NEXT PAGE SPREAD

Macle Pastels

The Macle company, founded in 1720, was the precursor of the Maison du Pastel, makers of the colored paste shaped into sticks. Henri Roché, a chemist who was passionate about art, bought the firm in 1865 and increased the original range of pastels to more than a thousand different shades.

This color chart includes handwritten sheets titled "Color Names 1927," but comparison with an album dated 1908 and preserved in another collection revealed that the two copies were similar, and it was thus decided to feature this document in this chapter. The sheets dated 1927 appear to have been added later in order to update the prices. Indeed, color charts were used for many years, especially charts of this type with so many color samples.

In fact, the colors are so abundant that concordance tables listing the old and new references were provided to allow artists to find the colors to which they were accustomed. Nevertheless, the ability to create new shades was still offered: "Customers can send samples of fabric for color matching." The manufacturer established himself as an accomplished colorist, which he clearly was, considering this color chart.

It is read vertically, with the colors following each other in an order close to that of the color spectrum. The samples were applied by rubbing soft and medium pastels on a sheet of paper, which was then cut into rectangles and glued to the backing. Small labels identify the various shades (titled "Ranges") of pastel crayon (175 ranges). Each is available in several distinct degrees of lightness (with a maximum of nine, called "tones"), classified by increasing lightness and numbered with a stamp.

Many of the color names are shared by contemporary paint color charts. However, the profusion of the supply required the invention of many color names (especially for greens, which have forty-eight ranges). Distinctions are then made through specific naming such as *Reddish Green*, *Golden Red*, *Purplish-Blue Pink*, *Red Violet*, *Very Red Violet*, or by using references, usually taken from nature (*Cornflower Blue*, *Lichen Green*, *Fallen Leaf Green*, *Alfalfa Green*, *Turtledove Gray* . . . even including *Distant Violet* and *Storm Green*). These descriptions can be compared to those of the ribbon makers of the same era.

Plate ten is unusual, for under the title "Combined Colors," it shows how one color can almost imperceptibly be changed into another by mixing them in eight steps, but without giving any instructions. This therefore seems to be a tactful invitation to try the adventure on one's own.

Bundle of Pastels, S. Macle, Paris, c. 1910, album, 48 × 32 cm, 10 plates, Sennelier family collection, Paris

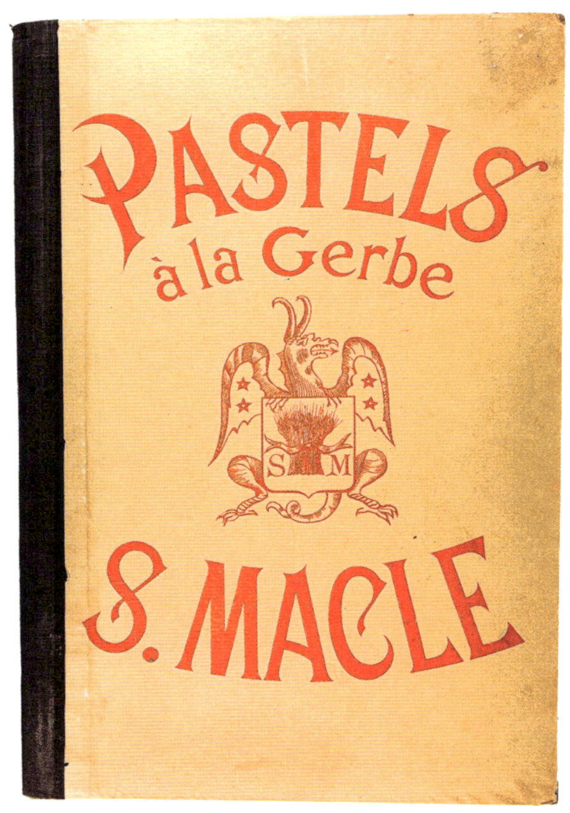
PASTELS
à la Gerbe
S M
S. MACLE

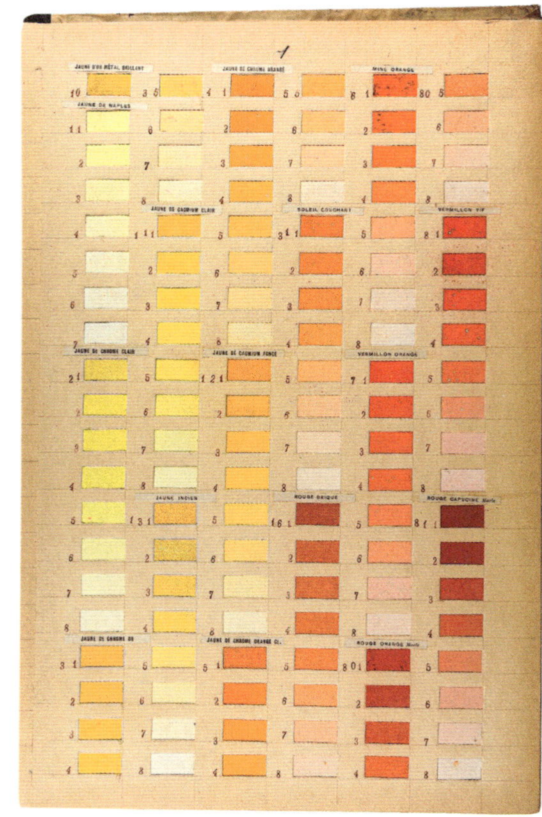

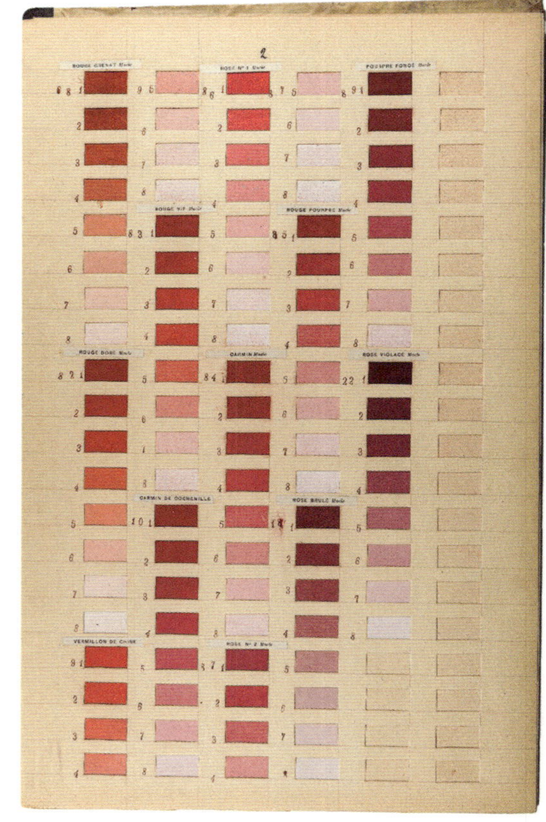

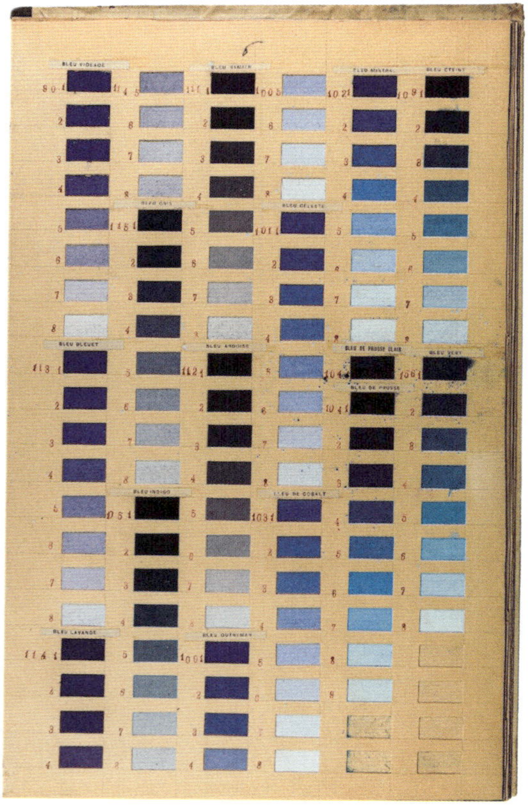

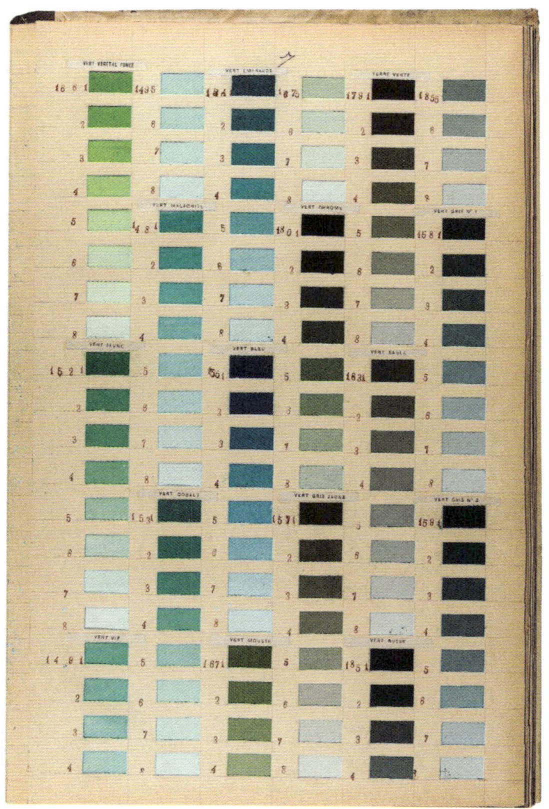

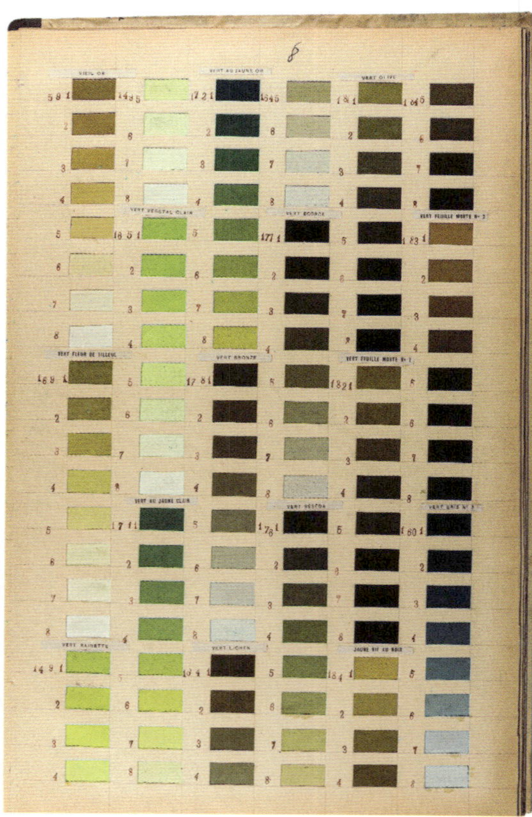

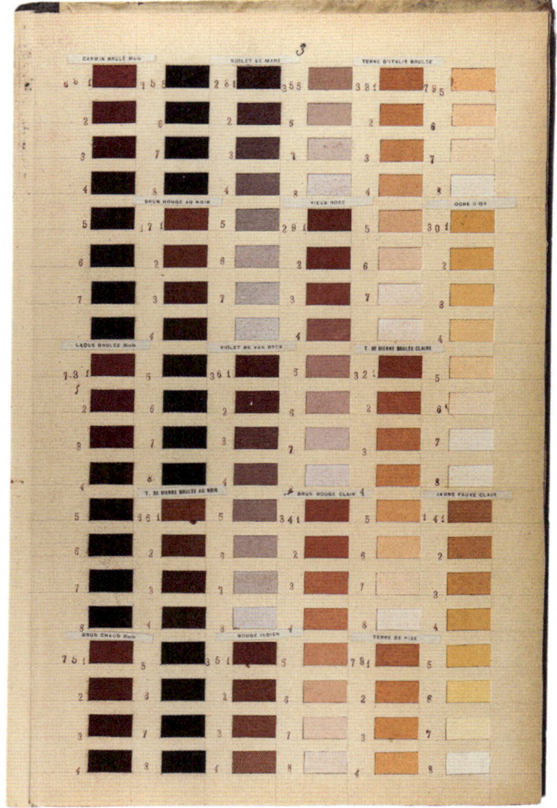

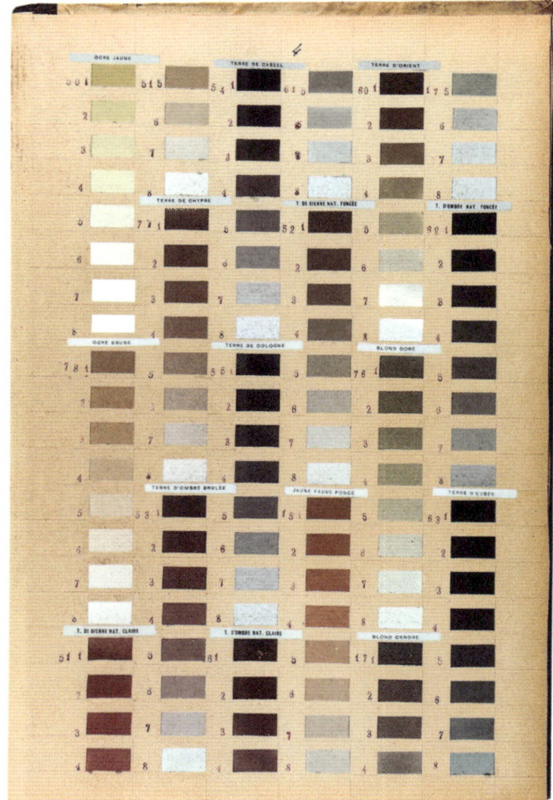

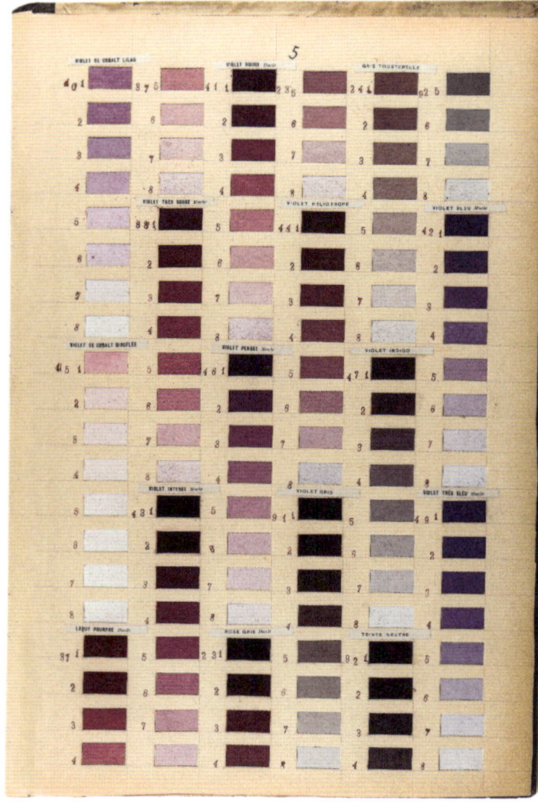

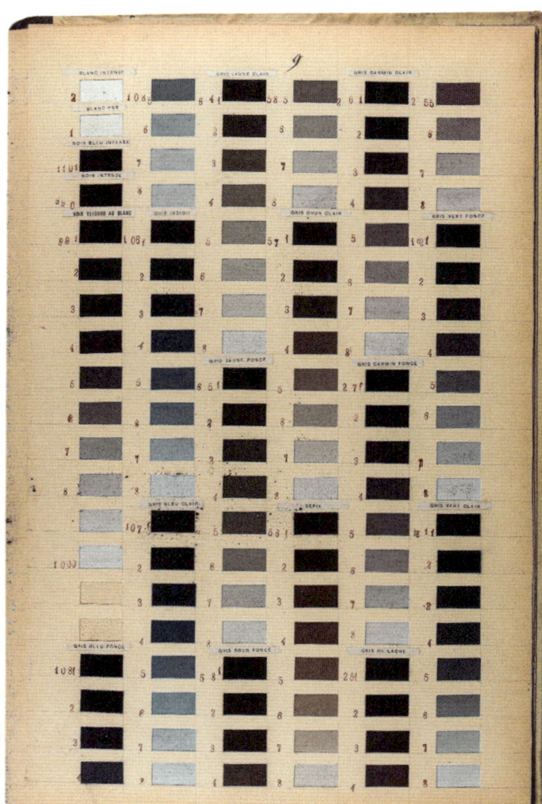

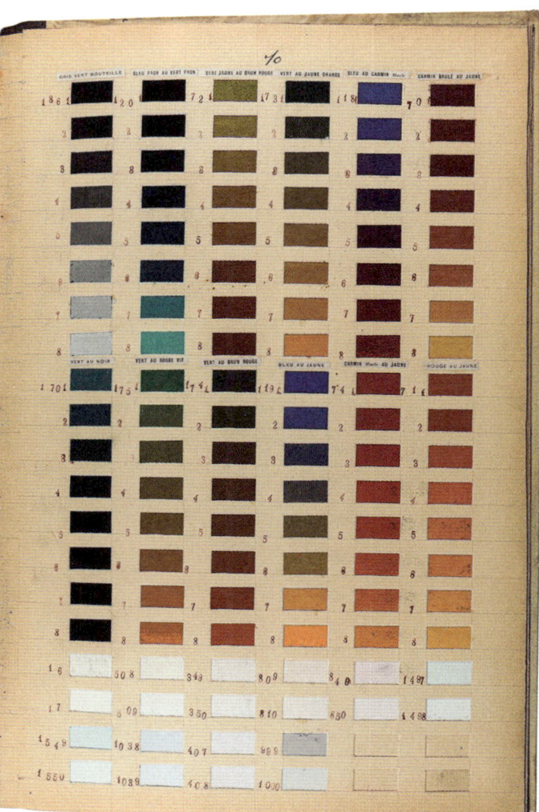

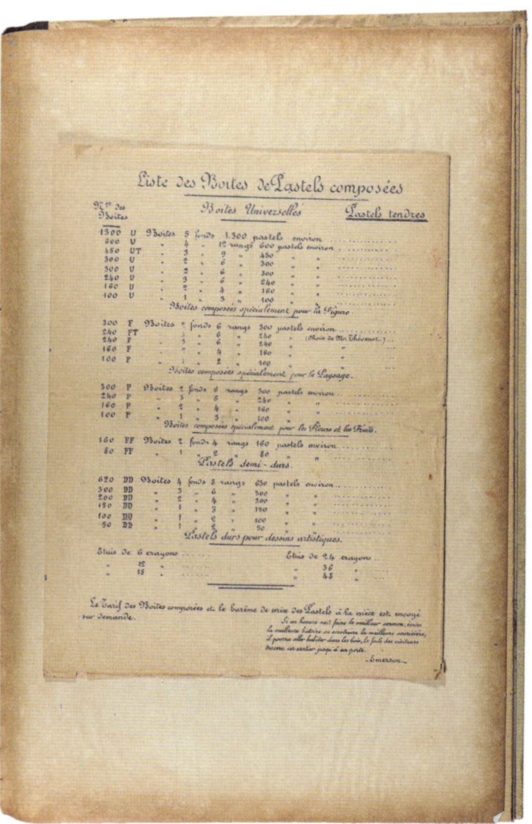

Liste des Boîtes de Pastels composées

Boîtes Universelles — *Pastels tendres*

N.os des Boîtes							
1300	U	Boîtes	5 fonds	1.300 pastels environ			
600	U	„	4 „	12 rangs	600 pastels environ	
450	UT	„	3 „	9 „	450	„ „
300	U	„	2 „	6 „	300	„ „
300	U	„	2 „	6 „	300	„ „
240	U	„	3 „	6 „	240	„ „
160	U	„	2 „	4 „	160	„ „
100	U	„	1 „	3 „	100	„ „

Boîtes composées spécialement pour la Figure

300	F	Boîtes 2 fonds	6 rangs	300 pastels environ		
240	FT	[illegible] „	6 „	240	„	(Choix de Mr. Thévenot)
240	F	3 „	6 „	240	„	„
160	F	2 „	4 „	160	„	„
100	F	1 „	2 „	100	„	„

Boîtes composées spécialement pour le Paysage.

300	P	Boîtes 2 fonds	6 rangs	300 pastels environ	
240	P	„ 3 „	6 „	240	„ „
160	P	„ 2 „	4 „	160	„ „
100	P	„ 1 „	3 „	100	„ „

Boîtes composées spécialement pour les Fleurs et les Fruits.

160	FF	Boîtes 2 fonds	4 rangs	160 pastels environ	
80	FF	„ 1 „	2 „	80	„ „

Pastels semi-durs.

620	DD	Boîtes 4 fonds	8 rangs	630 pastels environ	
300	DD	„ 3 „	6 „	300	„ „
200	DD	„ 2 „	4 „	200	„ „
150	DD	„ 1 „	3 „	150	„ „
100	DD	„ 1 „	2 „	100	„ „
50	DD	„ 1 „	2 „	50	„ „

Pastels durs pour dessins artistiques.

Étuis de 6 crayons	Étuis de 24 crayons
„ 12 „	„ 36 „
„ 18 „	„ 48 „

Le Tarif des Boîtes composées et le barème de prix des Pastels à la pièce est envoyé sur demande.

Si un homme sait faire le meilleur sermon, écrire la meilleure histoire ou construire la meilleure souricière, il pourra aller habiter dans les bois, la foule des visiteurs tracera un sentier jusqu'à sa porte.

— Emerson —

Color charts for artists' paints used a common vocabulary, but the formulas were often specific to each manufacturer and were frequently changed. This common vocabulary led to the illusion of a strict equivalence between a term and its color, although in fact this was far from the case.[64] This nomenclature helped to preserve terms from a vanishing history in the collective memory. This memory was widely shared, for translations helped establish an international community of artists who, before World War I, met and exhibited all over Europe. Furthermore, color charts for artists, unlike those for decorative painting or fabrics, were consulted by both men and women, since upper-class women engaged in art as a pastime. This is one of the few fields of knowledge that were shared by both sexes. These color charts were admired by women and men alike; they are indeed beautiful. Their relative scarcity also made them prized; they were conserved for a long time. The names of shades (even if these were ambiguous) were used over several generations. Through the care of attentive families—the Sennelier family in particular—these color charts today reveal a moment in history when palettes were gradually freed of toxic pigments (lead white, orpiment, minium, for example). But they also represent the standardized, ready-to-use products that would mark a shift in artists' development, eliminating the skills for mixing colors that previously had to be mastered during a period of study and apprenticeship.

Colors Make Inroads

Synthetic dyes and pigments opened up many new avenues for using color in areas where it may not have been expected previously. The color charts below evoke a period when color enhanced more or less everything, for everyone.

OPPOSITE

V. Vert Packaging

Located in the Drôme department of France, this manufacturer of cardboard and paper packaging apparently developed the items in this catalog for food vendors to give them approximately one hundred designs to choose from. The printed information suggests that these were samples from completed orders, with the album's string tie allowing new and different items to be added easily.

The catalog illustrates types of bags and available colors on sheets of blue packaging. This is glassine paper, which is very thin, resistant to humidity and oily substances, and has a neutral pH. Its translucence allows the contents of the bag to be seen, but glassine can also be made opaque or printed with a design. And, because of the availability of synthetic dyes, by the late nineteenth century it could be dyed in many colors.[65] The ranges, although limited in this example (a maximum of twelve), still offered grocery stores and hardware stores the possibility of associating a color with certain contents; in addition, colored bags could brighten up the transaction between merchant and customer.

Color chart of bags for packaging, Manufacture de Sacs en Papier V. Vert, Tain, late nineteenth century, album, 13 × 23 cm, 52 pages, Bibliothèque Forney, Paris, call number RES ICO 5250

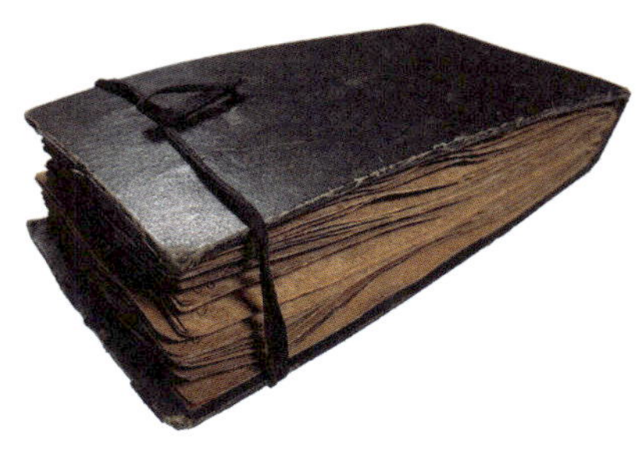

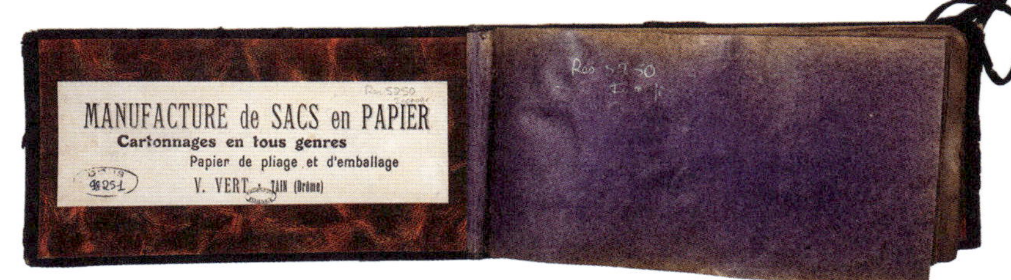
MANUFACTURE de SACS en PAPIER
Cartonnages en tous genres
Papier de pliage et d'emballage
V. VERT TAIN (Drôme)

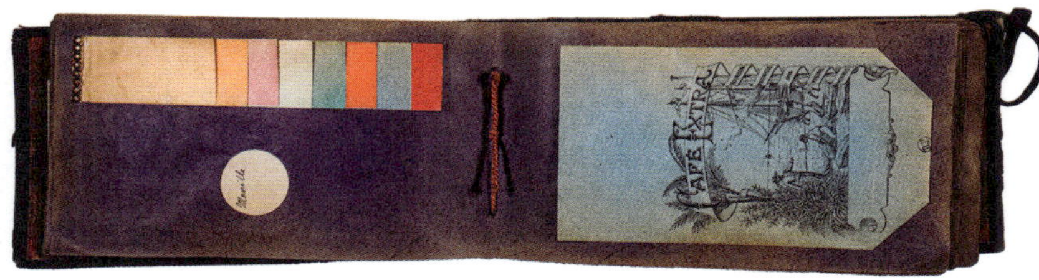

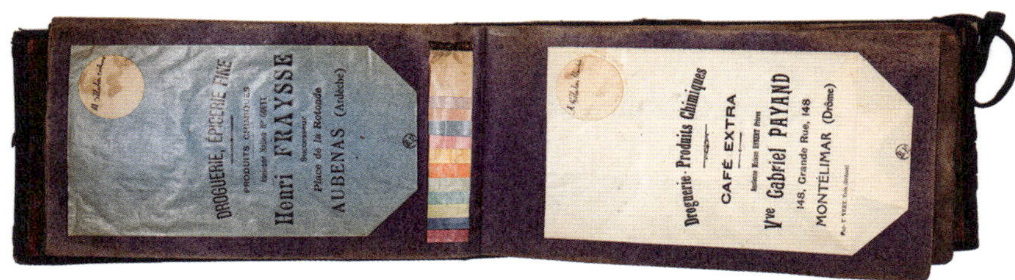
DROGUERIE, ÉPICERIE FINE
Henri FRAYSSE
AUBENAS (Ardèche)
Droguerie - Produits Chimiques
CAFÉ EXTRA
Vve Gabriel PAYAND
148, Grande Rue, 148
MONTELIMAR (Drôme)

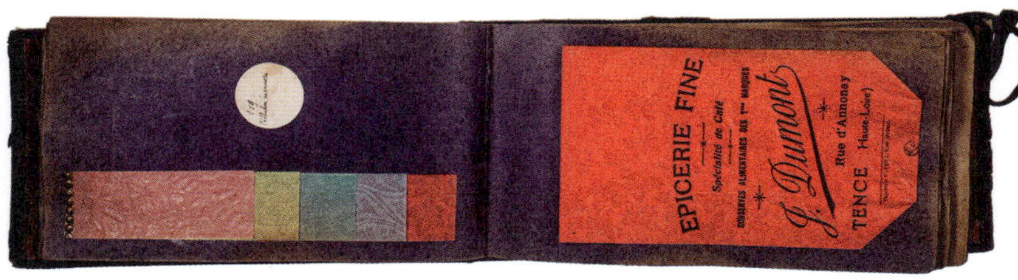
ÉPICERIE FINE
J. Dumont
Rue d'Annonay
TENCE

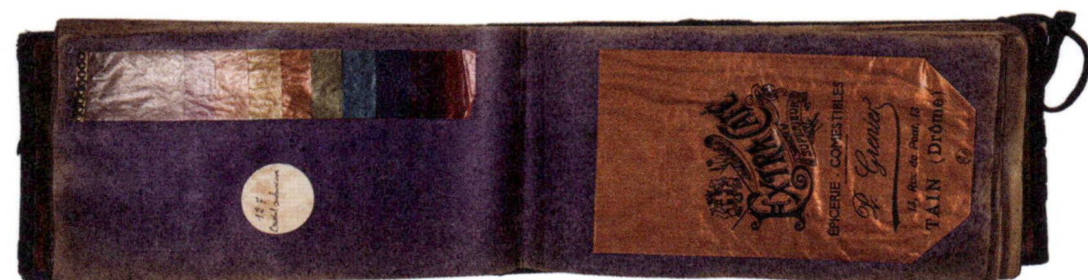
TAIN (Drôme)

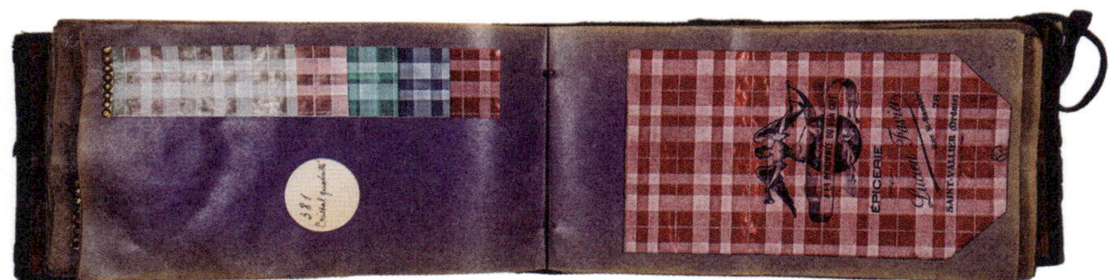

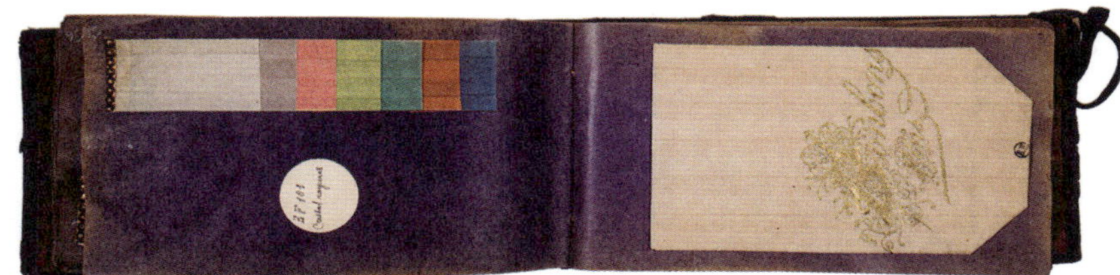

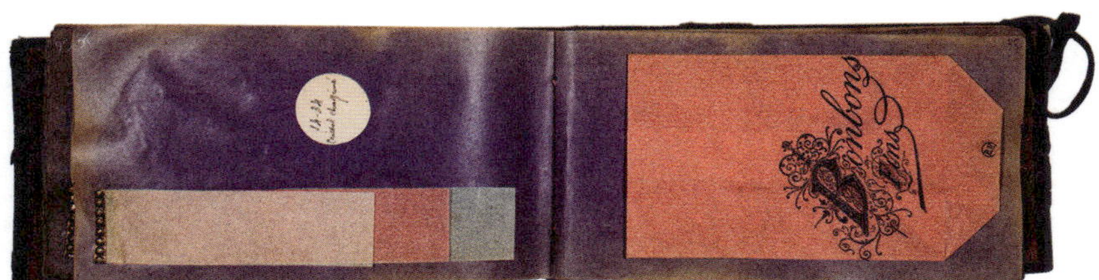
Bonbons Fins

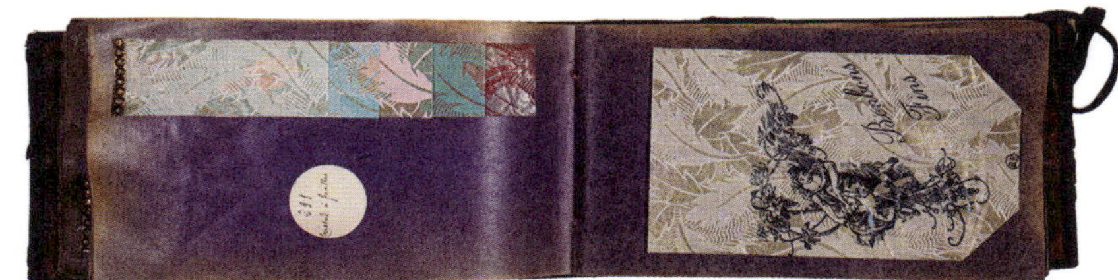

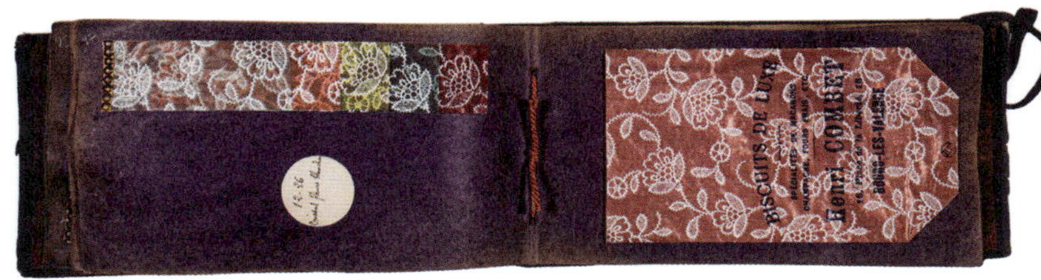

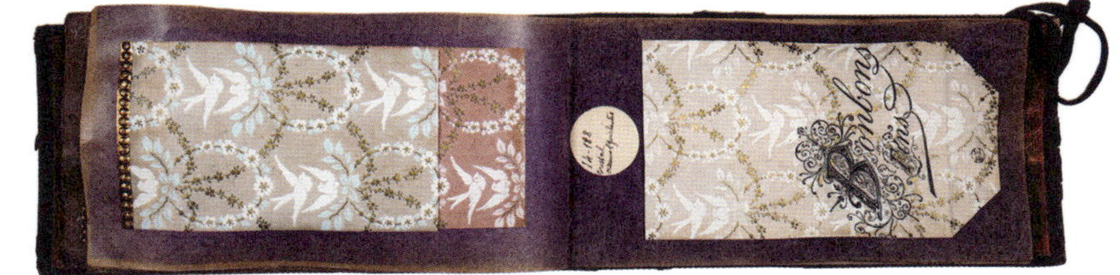

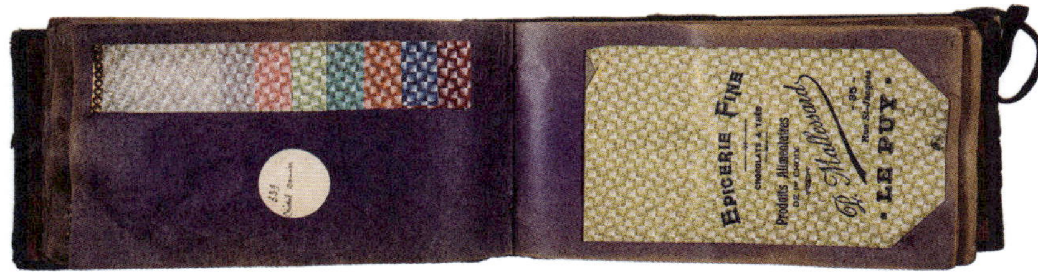
ÉPICERIE FINE
LE PUY

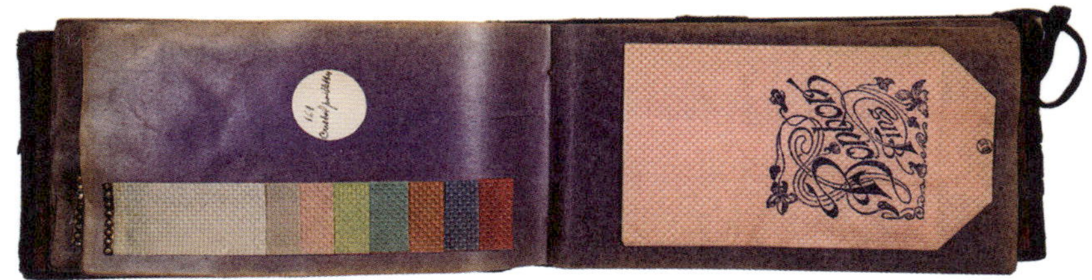

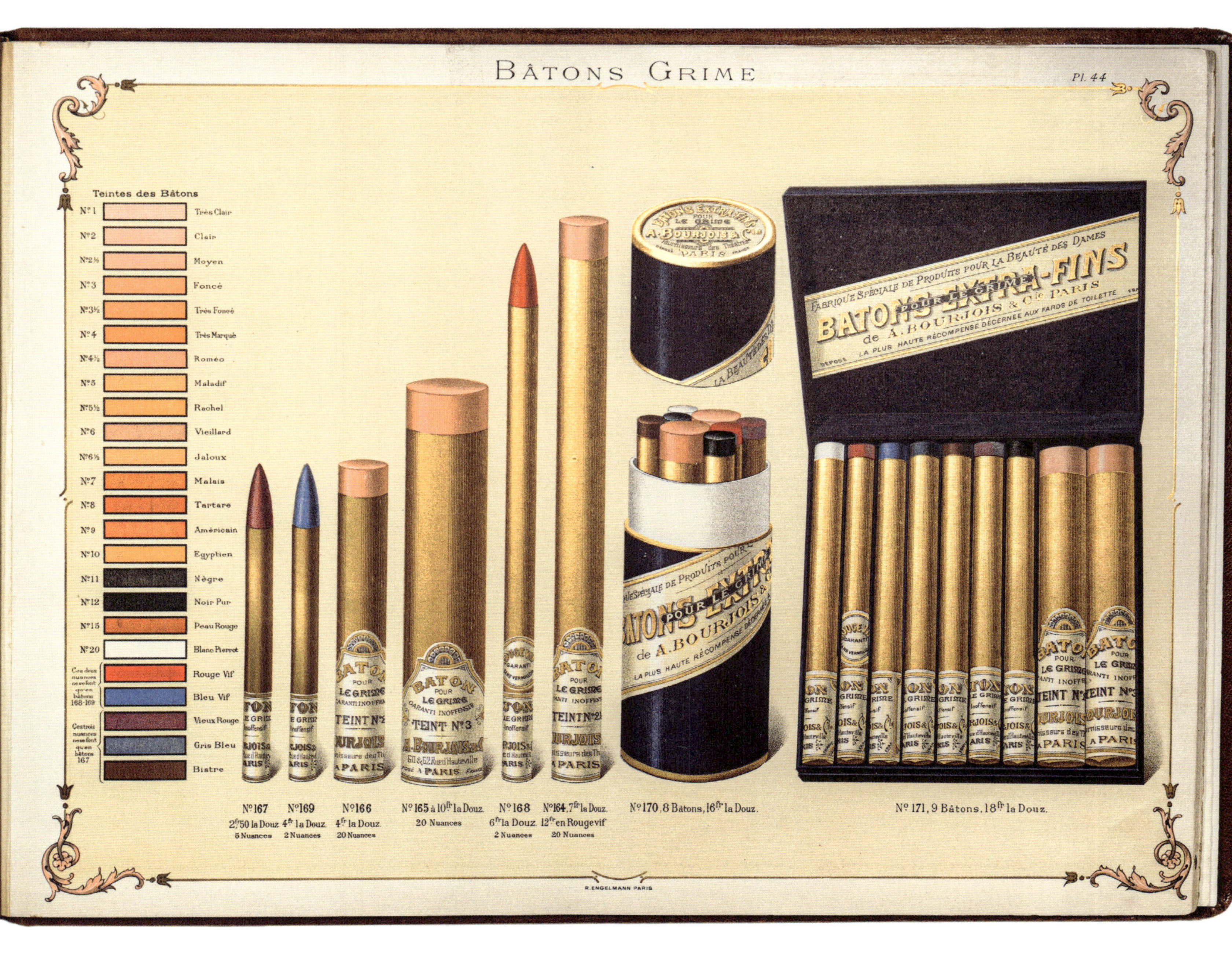

Bâtons Grime
Pl. 44
Teintes des Bâtons
N°1 Très Clair
N°2 Clair
N°2½ Moyen
N°3 Foncé
N°3½ Très Foncé
N°4 Très Marqué
N°4½ Roméo
N°5 Maladif
N°5½ Rachel
N°6 Vieillard
N°6½ Jaloux
N°7 Malais
N°8 Tartare
N°9 Américain
N°10 Egyptien
N°11 Nègre
N°12 Noir Pur
N°15 Peau Rouge
N°20 Blanc Pierrot
Ces deux nuances ne se font qu'en bâtons 168-169
Rouge Vif
Bleu Vif
Ces trois nuances ne se font qu'en bâtons 167
Vieux Rouge
Gris Bleu
Bistre
BATON POUR LE GRIME GARANTI INOFFENSIF TEINT N°3 A. BOURJOIS & Cie 60 & 62 Rue d'Hauteville PARIS
BÂTONS EXTRA-FINS POUR LE GRIME A. BOURJOIS & Cie PARIS
FABRIQUE SPÉCIALE DE PRODUITS POUR LA BEAUTÉ DES DAMES
BATONS POUR LE GRIME EXTRA-FINS de A. BOURJOIS & Cie PARIS
DÉPOSÉ LA PLUS HAUTE RÉCOMPENSE DÉCERNÉE AUX FARDS DE TOILETTE
N°167 2fr50 la Douz. 5 Nuances
N°169 4fr la Douz. 2 Nuances
N°166 4fr la Douz. 20 Nuances
N°165 à 10fr la Douz. 20 Nuances
N°168 6fr la Douz. 2 Nuances
N°164, 7fr la Douz. 12fr en Rouge vif 20 Nuances
N°170, 8 Bâtons, 16fr la Douz.
N° 171, 9 Bâtons, 18fr la Douz.
R. ENGELMANN PARIS

OPPOSITE

Bourjois Cosmetics

Starting in the 1860s, French perfumers[66] published sales catalogs[67] illustrating their various product lines. In 1863 the actor Joseph-Albert Ponsin founded his Parfumerie Théâtrale in Paris, where he sold makeup sticks. Two years later, it became the Société A. Bourjois & Cie, which developed what was called "city" makeup; the firm still supplied the theater world. This market could not be neglected. The widespread use of gas lighting and then electricity on theater stages exposed the actors to bright lights; makeup with a thick texture and good coverage was needed to highlight their expressions.

When Bourjois published this catalog in 1898, the vast majority of its silkscreen-printed plates were already devoted to hygiene products and cosmetics. As customs evolved in the second half of the nineteenth century, middle-class women began discreetly enhancing the color of their cheeks and lips with rouge and using makeup to emphasize their eyes. This was a revolution and would soon result in the cosmetics color chart. Like those of other perfumers, this catalog exhibits makeup products in open boxes, so that the color of the makeup, reproduced with inks, is visible. It is thus possible to perceive the difference between shades such as *City Pink* and *Plant Red of Java*. But only the face makeup has a color chart with twenty-four available shades. Some refer to stock characters (*Jealous Man*), to theater characters (*Sickly Man*, *Old Man*, *Rachel*,[68] *Romeo*, *White Pierrot*), or to contemporary ethnic stereotypes (*American*, *Redskin*, *Tartar*).

This color chart anticipates the constraints that cosmetics producers would have to overcome. When Bourjois published this catalog, it was already possible to reproduce the colors of "city" makeup. But it was not until the 1920s that color charts for cosmetics for ordinary consumers were produced. The reason is probably more cultural than technical. These color charts did not yet exist because the perfumers' female customers had barely stopped considering makeup to be a suspect trick that was forbidden to the virtuous, modest, and reserved wives they were required to be. And, among all the colorful products beginning to be produced and marketed, makeup was the one with which they had the most sensual and personal relationship. They bought or ordered it after having examined, touched, tested, and maybe even sniffed the product in shops. Tangible proof was essential. The time when women would accept the risk of choosing makeup for their skin based on a series of little printed rectangles had not yet arrived.

Color chart of makeup sticks, Parfumerie A. Bourjois, Paris, 1898, bound sales materials, 30 × 40.5 cm, 49 plates, Patrimoine de Chanel collection, Paris, plate 49

A STRUGGLE WITH THE LIMITATIONS OF THE COLOR CHART

NEXT PAGE SPREAD

Dauthenay Flowers, Leaves, and Fruits

Toward the end of the nineteenth century, manufacturers and merchants of colored materials or objects that were impossible to sample attempted to make faithful reproductions. This brochure is part reference guide and part commercial color chart: its objective is to provide a useful range of colors for the horticultural world.

Henri Dauthenay, the principal contributor to this list, explains the origin of his undertaking.[69] The project began in 1899. The Société Française des Chrysanthémistes wanted to establish a range of chrysanthemum colors to facilitate commerce between flower producers and buyers and avoid inconsistencies in catalog descriptions. René Oberthür, an enthusiastic amateur horticulturalist and head of the Oberthür Frères printing company in Rennes, funded the project. But the undertaking failed and was then entrusted to Henri Dauthenay, the editor of the *Revue Horticole*, who was passionate about terminology.[70] His mission was to catalog all the colors of chrysanthemums—classifying the shades according to a scientific system, establishing color names that would be appropriate for the plant world and understandable by all, and, finally, overseeing the printing of the brochure.

Rouge Géranium

Origine : Dénomination très usitée dans le commerce des couleurs. — Reproduction lithographique de la couleur à l'aquarelle « Géranium » de Bourgeois. — Les teinturiers emploient un dérivé complexe de la Houille, la Géranine G, que l'on précipite par l'acide chlorhydrique ou l'acide sulfurique, ce qui donne des nuances différentes.

Synonymes français : Laque de Garance cerise (nº 52, Lefranc) et tons foncés de Bourgeois. Laque anglaise (Bourgeois).

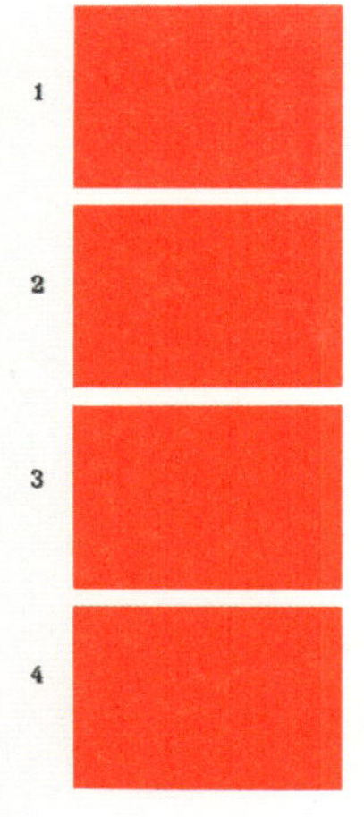

Synonymes étrangers :

All. : Geraniumrot.
Angl. : Geranium.
Esp. : Rojo Geraniom (nombre que dan los commerciantes de colores).
Ital. : Rosso Geranio.

Remarques :

Ton 1 : Revers des jeunes pétales du centre de la Rose *Comtesse Festalics Hamilton.*

Tons 1 à 4 : Nuances dominantes du pourtour des pièces périanthales, dans le *Masdevalia ignæa.* Le ton 4 s'étend sur les fleurs bien développées.

Ton 4 : Pélargonium zoné *Caroline Schmidt.*

Nuance très fréquente dans un grand nombre de Dahlias et de Pélargoniums zonés.

— 111 —

Jaune indien

Origine : Dénomination commerciale de cette couleur. Le Jaune indien vrai vient du Bengale. Il est le produit de la fermentation de l'urine de vache avec des feuilles de Mangoustan (*Garcinia Mangostana*). L'industriel est obtenu par un mélange de dérivés nitrés, ou par une solution d'acide euxanthique, sulfate de magnésie, alun et sel ammoniac.

Synonymes français : Jaune indien vrai : Purrey, Pioury. — Jaune indien industriel : Jaune azo, Azoflavine, Jaune nouveau, Curcumine.

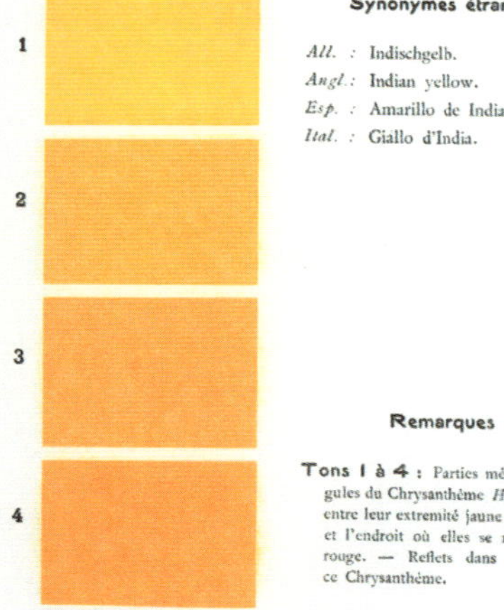

Synonymes étrangers :

All. : Indischgelb.
Angl. : Indian yellow.
Esp. : Amarillo de India.
Ital. : Giallo d'India.

Remarques :

Tons 1 à 4 : Parties médianes des ligules du Chrysanthème *Hortus tolosanus* entre leur extremité jaune gomme gutte et l'endroit où elles se recouvrent de rouge. — Reflets dans le cœur de ce Chrysanthème.

— 27 —

Carmin de Cochenille

Origine : Le modèle de cette planche a été obtenu par le délayage de la poudre de Carmin de Cochenille. En traitant ce produit par différents procédés, on obtient le Carmin fin, le Carmin extra, la Laque carminée et le Rouge Cardinal. — Il se fabrique aujourd'hui un Carmin d'Alizarine.

Synonymes français : Rouge de Perse (Lor.). Laque rose extra (Bourg.). Carmin fin. — Analogue : Laque carminée rose (Bourg.).

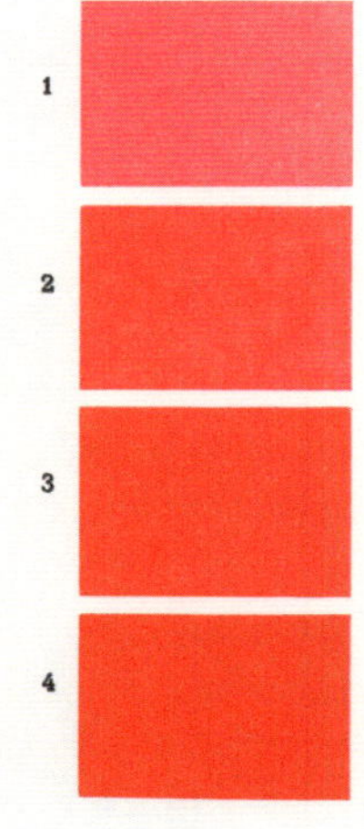

Synonymes étrangers :

All. : Carmin. Cochenillcarmin.
Angl. : Carmine. Cochineal carmine.
Esp. : Carmin. Carmin de Cochinilla.
Ital. : Carminio. Carminio di Cocciniglia.

Remarques :

Ton 1 : *Canna Iridiflora* (sauf le calice et le labelle).

Ton 2 : Ensemble des revers des pétales de la Rose *Madame de Vatry,* à leur base.

Tons 3 et 4 : Reflets intérieurs, macules, marges et panachures de la Rose *Marie d'Orléans.*

— 116 —

Chocolat

Origine : Couleur ordinaire du Chocolat en tablettes : tons 1 et 2 : intérieurement ; tons 3 et 4 : extérieurement.

Synonymes français : Teinte brune (nº 44, Lorilleux).

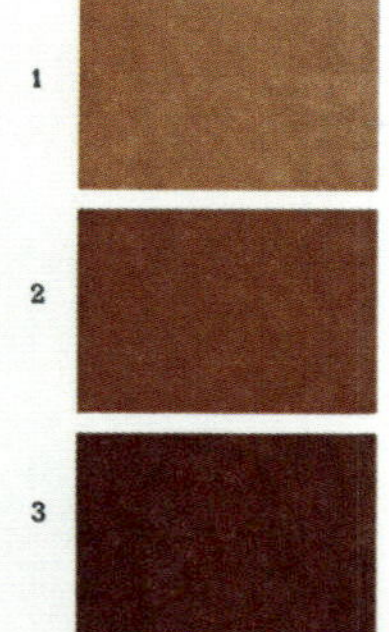

Synonymes étrangers :

All. : Chocolatfarbig.
Angl. : Chocolate.
Esp. : Chocolate.
Ital. : Cioccolato.

Remarques :

Tons 1 à 4 : Couleur d'ensemble des grains du Haricot *nain Emile (Perrier),* âgé d'un an, et sans considérer leur panachure.

Ton 4 : Couleur ordinaire du grain du Haricot *Rivoire,* âgé d'un an.

— 343 —

Vert Mousse passé

Origine : Mousse d'emballage non teinte, ayant beaucoup vieilli en magasin.

Synonymes français : néant.

Synonymes étrangers :

All. : Verbleicht Moosgrün.
Angl. : Old Moss green.
Esp. : Verde Musgo pasado.
Ital. : Verde Vellutello appasito.

Remarques :

Tons 1 à 4 : Tons observés sur la marge de feuilles âgées du *Coleus Verschaffelti,* et sur certaines feuilles, placées bas, de l'*Althernanthera paronychioides.*

Tons 3 et 4 : L'une des nuances sur sur le dessus du Champignon des vieilles souches *Polyporus versicolor.*

— 290 —

Mordoré

Origine : Dénomination de cette couleur dans les commerces des rubans, soieries et chaussures (de *morulus* « à peau noirâtre », d'où est sortie la désignation de *Maure* et « doré », à cause du reflet).

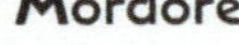

Synonymes français : néant.

Synonymes étrangers :

All. : Gold Braunrot.
Angl. : Golden reddish brown.
Esp. : Castaño dorado.
Ital. : Bruno rosato.

Remarques :

Nous paraît peu applicable au règne végétal, si ce n'est à la tonalité de certains Chrysanthèmes.

— 306 —

Bleu Capri

Origine : Bleu obtenu par la condensation de la nitrosométhylaniline et du diméthylmétaamidocrésol. Très employé pour teindre les cotons (mordancés) et les soies.

Synonymes français : Bleu Turquoise (Lor.). Bleu gendarme.

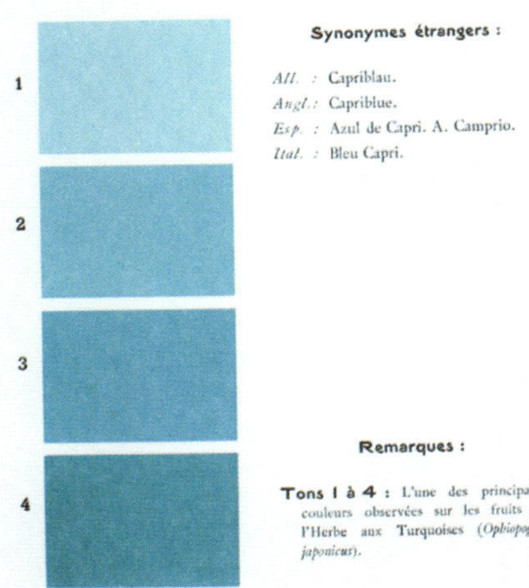

Synonymes étrangers :

All. : Capriblau.
Angl. : Capriblue.
Esp. : Azul de Capri. A. Camprio.
Ital. : Bleu Capri.

Remarques :

Tons 1 à 4 : L'une des principales couleurs observées sur les fruits de l'Herbe aux Turquoises (*Ophiopogon japonicus*).

— 226 —

Vert Pois

Origine : Tonalité générale du feuillage des Pois potagers vu de près, à la lumière diffuse.

Synonymes français : Vert grisâtre.

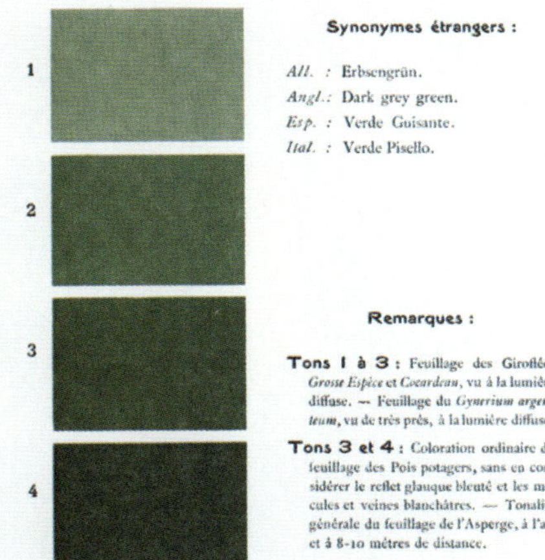

Synonymes étrangers :

All. : Erbsengrün.
Angl. : Dark grey green.
Esp. : Verde Guisante.
Ital. : Verde Pisello.

Remarques :

Tons 1 à 3 : Feuillage des Giroflées *Grosse Espèce* et *Cocardeau*, vu à la lumière diffuse. — Feuillage du *Gynerium argenteum*, vu de très près, à la lumière diffuse.

Tons 3 et 4 : Coloration ordinaire du feuillage des Pois potagers, sans en considérer le reflet glauque bleuté et les macules et veines blanchâtres. — Tonalité générale du feuillage de l'Asperge, à l'air et à 8-10 mètres de distance.

— 277 —

Rose de Nymphe

Origine : Désignation conventionnelle pour exprimer la délicatesse et la fraîcheur de cette teinte, par allusion à ce que pourrait être la couleur de la chair des Nymphes de la mythologie.

Synonymes français : néant.

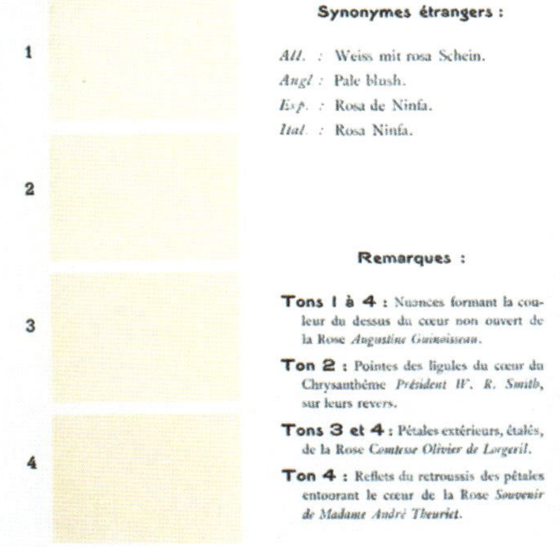

Synonymes étrangers :

All. : Weiss mit rosa Schein.
Angl : Pale blush.
Esp. : Rosa de Ninfa.
Ital. : Rosa Ninfa.

Remarques :

Tons 1 à 4 : Nuances formant la couleur du dessus du cœur non ouvert de la Rose *Augustine Guinoisseau*.

Ton 2 : Pointes des ligules du cœur du Chrysanthème *Président W. R. Smith*, sur leurs revers.

Tons 3 et 4 : Pétales extérieurs, étalés, de la Rose *Comtesse Olivier de Lorgeril*.

Ton 4 : Reflets du retroussis des pétales entourant le cœur de la Rose *Souvenir de Madame André Theuriet*.

— 137 —

Teinte neutre

Origine : Dénomination de cette couleur dans le commerce des couleurs à l'aquarelle[1]. — Reproduction de l'*Ater* du professeur Saccardo.

Synonymes français : Gris sombre. Gris ardoisé foncé.

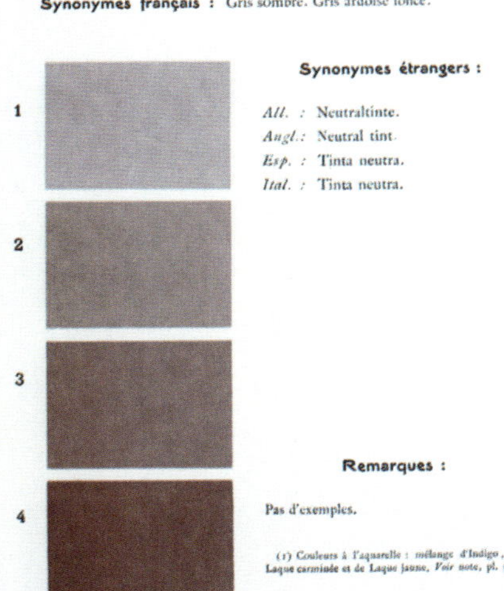

Synonymes étrangers :

All. : Neutraltinte.
Angl. : Neutral tint.
Esp. : Tinta neutra.
Ital. : Tinta neutra.

Remarques :

Pas d'exemples.

(1) Couleurs à l'aquarelle : mélange d'Indigo, de Laque carminée et de Laque jaune. *Voir* note, pl. 159.

— 361 —

Argent

Origine : Couleur la plus ordinaire des monnaies d'argent ayant environ cinq ans de circulation.

Synonymes français : Argent mat (des doreurs). Nickel.

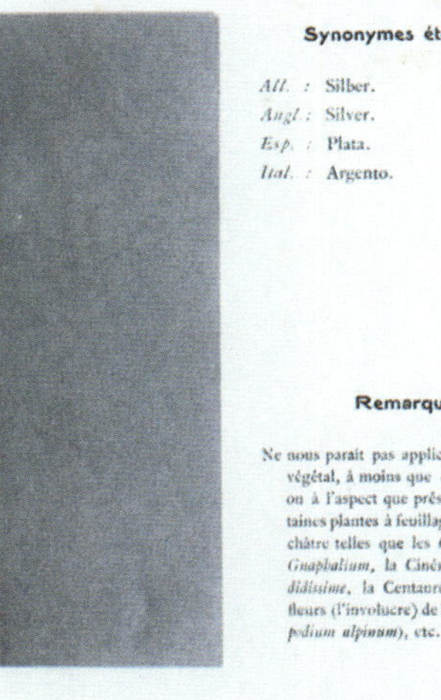

Synonymes étrangers :

All. : Silber.
Angl. : Silver.
Esp. : Plata.
Ital. : Argento.

Remarques :

Ne nous paraît pas applicable dans le règne végétal, à moins que ce ne soit au reflet ou à l'aspect que présentent de loin certaines plantes à feuillage tomenteux blanchâtre telles que les *Cerastium*, certains *Gnaphalium*, la Cinéraire *maritime candidissime*, la Centaurée *candidissime*, les fleurs (l'involucre) de l'*Edelweiss* (*Leontopodium alpinum*), etc.

— 365 —

Vert Eau-de-Javel

Origine : Couleur ordinaire de l'Eau de Javel telle qu'on la vend au commerce de détail, c'est-à-dire colorée par un peu de bichromate de potasse.

Synonymes français : Vert pomme.

1
2
3
4

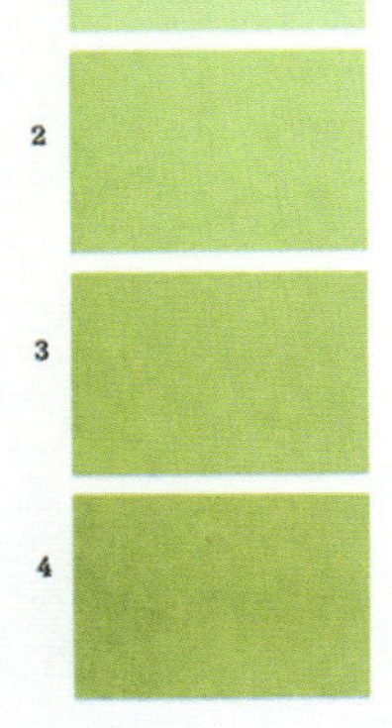

Synonymes étrangers :

All. : Javelwassergrün auch Lichtgrün.
Angl. : Yellowish sap green.
Esp. : Verde Agua de Javel.
Ital. : Verde cromo chiaro.

Remarques :

Tons 1 à 3 : Couleur d'ensemble des fleurs du Chrysanthème *Madame Edmond Roger*; ton 1 : tonalité générale; ton 2 : dessus de la fleur; ton 3 : cœur et reflets intérieurs.

Ton 1 : Couleur ordinaire de la Pomme *Amère de Berthecourt* du côté opposé à l'insolation.

— 265 —

Dauthenay adapted the classification method developed by Chevreul to organize his colors and thus arrived at 365 plates, each presenting four distinct tones with regular gradations (or almost 1,400 shades), divided into twelve series.[71] The removable sheets allowed the user to arrange them in any way desired.

Dauthenay summarized his approach to the task of researching names with a dose of humor. He observed that although synthetic chemistry had considerably increased the nomenclature of terms for colors, it overflowed with confusing synonyms. Moreover, using terms such as *trioxytriphénylcarbinoltricarboxylésodique* or, even worse, $C_20 H11 Az_2 O_7 Na_2$ to designate the color of a petal seemed unsuitable. His attempts to explore the vocabulary of silk manufacturers and producers of typo-lithographical inks also led him to a dead-end.[72] However, color manufacturers of decorative and artistic paints provided names of colors that were still associated with their origins, even if the pigments were now produced by synthetic chemistry. Moreover, these names were familiar because the products were often used for art or for the household. Finally, the color charts that had been circulating for some years merged these names and the colors they described. For these reasons, Dauthenay borrowed a great number of these existing names. Another terminological resource was identified in the vocabulary for cotton and wool, composed of names that were widespread in the public at large, and used, according to him, by "any housewife."[73] He drew the most meaningful names from this set. Two colors were especially challenging for the author: blues, which are rare in the floral world and have few equivalents among minerals, and greens, which are, on the contrary, extremely present and complex. He decided to name them using references to common plants as much as possible (*Ivy Green*, *Holly Green*, *Lavender Blue*). After radically abridging the available names, Dauthenay managed to give a name to each of his plates, with a short explanation of their origin, etymology, or meaning, and with their translation into German, English, Spanish, and Italian! Finally, the lithographical method was chosen for printing and the crucial problem of the stability of the colors was solved by the choice of good-quality inks, including metallic ones, which were essential for reproducing the shimmering color or coppery sheen of some flowers.

Dauthenay wrote up specific instructions for his color list. He indicated the ideal light and how to arrange the plates in order to avoid reflections, advised making sketches in fields using pastels rather than taking the list outdoors, warned of possible visual handicaps readers could have, and even provided a template for covering up some of the colors in order to compare two shades without interference from other hues.

The column "Remarks" on each plate demonstrates advanced knowledge of plants and extremely close attention to them, while also giving key information to the reader. Thus, tone 1 of *Bluish-Green* is that "of the color of an artichoke leaf seen from a man's height, about one meter away from the feet, with diffuse light (observation made during summer)"; tone 2 of *Carmine Lacquer* is compared to the "heart of a rose of the variety known as Souvenir de Madame André Theuriet, without considering the petals curling around it."

This document is astonishing for several reasons. While it is extremely rigorous, it also remains beautifully humble.[74] Perfectly practical, it is still filled with humanity and deeply attentive to the physiological limits of the eye as well as to the boundaries of the mind. Above all, it is radiant with poetry, both in the names attributed to the colors and in the explanations and remarks that accompany them. In the plate titled "Pure White," Dauthenay decided to leave the frame empty—a touch that seems to foreshadow surrealism. This list is a true source of contemplation.

List of Colors to Aid in the Determination of the Colors of Flowers, Leaves, and Fruits, Henri Dauthenay and René Oberthür for the Société Française des Chrysanthémistes Paris, 1905, 2 volumes, 23.8 × 15.9 cm, 82 pages and 365 plates, Anne Varichon collection, Sète

——— By the late nineteenth century, once the color chart was present in many shops in Europe and the United States, or sent by mail to various countries, the die was cast, and it prompted a chain reaction: the range of colors that manufacturers placed before the eyes of consumers caused a desire for color, which then fed a demand that manufacturers would meet with increasingly numerous and varied colorful items.

The color chart provided access to this new world of color; it took on new a physical form—booklet, pamphlet, or leporello—that led to new color harmonies. By creating ranges of shades or pairings of complementary colors, the color chart structured users' understanding of color. It offered a narrative with color names associated with samples, which allowed consumers to grasp shades in their new and vast diversity, to remember them, and, ultimately, to demand them. Above all, the color chart still provided tactility through the extensive use of product samples. Color remained intrinsically linked to a material or substance, to its physical presence, and to the multiplicity of sensory experiences it offered. In this sense, the color charts of the late nineteenth and early twentieth centuries belong to the Belle Époque.

At the heart of this revolutionary color dynamic that the color chart brought into print, the close contact of an entire society with colors also carried an inverse movement, which was quite well hidden. The quantitative obsession that mobilized the industry had already started to lead to standardization. The mastery of color and its classification into abstract systems thus led the relationship to color to be less sensual, and to become weakened. Moreover, the goal of selling products internationally would end the proliferation of poetic names, which were turned into a reduced color lexicon, or even into plain numbers. In this way, color began to be channeled into opaque tubes. Finally, in the late nineteenth and early twentieth centuries, the need to reduce the cost of color charts led to exploring possibilities of replacing product samples with reproductions. This would lead to a radical rethinking of color. And it would eventually end the heyday of the color chart.

Another harmful dynamic was at work, and its effects would be major: in the early twentieth century, entire communities were still subjected to the industrialized nations' need for colors, especially for the extraction of indigo from plants in British India. This use of raw materials for producing color was then accompanied and supplanted by the policy of exporting manufactured products, including synthetic colors, from industrialized countries to the colonies. The color chart contributed to this and, by doing so, helped promote a Western civilization that was still fully convinced of the universal virtues of progress. This promotion initiated the silent but irreversible process of wiping out the vast body of knowledge and skills regarding color that nonindustrial cultures had developed over centuries.[75] ●

5 % Tartrazine

BRINGING COLOR TO THE MASSES

BETWEEN THE WORLD WARS

——— After World War I, the color chart was part of the growth of manufacturing and consumption that swept industrialized nations, with the United States in the lead. In 1929, the Great Depression revealed the vulnerabilities of global economies and led to the bankruptcy of many businesses. Nevertheless, the two decades between the wars saw the color chart's importance increase for promoting and selling a variety of colorful goods and materials, the likes of which had never been seen before. Beneath the surface of these marketing tools, we can glimpse the development of professional practices, social customs, and even ideologies.

The chemical industries were once more the leaders of this evolution in a landscape that had been completely transformed by war. Their color charts demonstrated not only the ability of new dyes to be used on countless materials but also the attention paid to the aesthetics of these charts. As an economic instrument, the color chart reflected and supported the power of the Western chemical industry, and even became a political tool when in the 1920s synthetic dyes began to be sold in the marketplace of colonized countries. The color chart would then be used for the colonialist and expansionist ambitions of industrial societies.

At the same time, the growing force of industrialization was accompanied by an increasing need to characterize colors. This led to the publication of classification systems. In the United States, companies used Albert H. Munsell's very functional *Munsell Book of Color*, which was published in 1905 and included over one thousand colors.[1]

Industrialization also required standards. In the 1930s, first in England and then in France, organizations that set standards began to pay attention to color, starting with paints for the home.[2]

This dual movement of standardization and normalization of colors paved the way for the creation of trend forecasting after World War II, which would further standardize the world of color by recommending fashionable shades for many items from one season to the next. For example, "the color to wear in spring 1947 is aqua."

But color had already become central in consumer habits between the wars, especially in major cities in Europe, Japan, and the United States, where mass production had increasingly become a part of daily life. The desire for new and varied color ranges, which had been aroused by turn-of-the-century color charts, came back in force after the trauma of the Great War and the great wave of mourning it produced. Various movements seized on it.[3] The Exposition Internationale des Arts Décoratifs et Industriels Modernes of 1925 in Paris celebrated art deco with its contrasting, metallic palettes and established its worldwide influence. De Stijl and the Bauhaus gave color a central role in the creative process in architecture and applied arts, and the Bauhaus school even offered a course designed by Johannes Itten on color.

In this context of intense social, cultural, and artistic activity, the color chart created a link between stylistic explorations, innovative materials and technologies, new products, and consumers who were now informed and tempted by omnipresent media and advertising.

This period, which would later be named the "Roaring Twenties," also found women continuing to pursue the liberating activities they had begun during the war, when they were finally able to hold professional positions that had been previously reserved for men. They gained independence, transformed social conventions, and took charge of their appearance. Fashion evolved toward designs that liberated the body, but without any significant changes to textile color charts. However, a major shift took place in the cosmetics field. As demand grew, the cosmetics industry introduced women to new makeup products that they could choose using the very first cosmetics color charts. But these color charts used printed colors instead of product samples. Printing also spread to color charts for decorative paints. This was a decisive step, and society would now become accustomed to considering color separately from its material. The divorce was underway.

THE COLOR CHARTS OF A THRIVING CHEMICAL INDUSTRY

The Great War had undone the markets that ensured the Western world's access to materials for producing color, and this highlighted the crucial importance of chemistry and the Allies' dependence on Germany for obtaining pigments and dyes.[4] After the war, the Allies divided up the German color patents as war reparations.[5] During the 1920s, the chemical industries of Europe, the United States, and Japan reorganized themselves into cartels and became exporters.[6] New families of synthetic colors were introduced onto the market, particularly phthalocyanines, which still produce a large portion of blues and greens today. Synthetic fibers appeared in the textile industry, and resins and plastic materials found multiple applications. Chemistry became an even more powerful field, and the color chart was essential for emphasizing and advertising the skills of dye and pigment producers to manufacturers.

However, it seems that only the Société Anonyme des Matières Colorantes et Produits Chimiques de Saint-Denis, a major French chemical company, distributed color charts in great number.[7] Indeed, few charts from other European countries have been located for this study.[8] The dominance of color charts from the Société de Saint-Denis may partially be explained by the significant role of France in the 1920s and 1930s both on the national market and abroad, due to the development of a national dye industry that had previously been almost nonexistent. This may also represent a bias endemic to the archives consulted for this book. Indeed, an important collection of French chemical color charts was saved in the late 1980s by the organization Mémoire des Industries de la Couleur, and it is preserved and promoted by the organization Albi Couleurs.[9] The Société Anonyme's color charts are very present in this collection. However, this bias does not seem sufficient to explain such a significant imbalance. Between the two world wars, dye color charts seemed to be a French specialty at which the Société de Saint-Denis excelled.

These color charts show the use of new pigments, dyes, and materials. They also show that color was being used for materials that had long been available but had not previously been dyed—or at least not in such extensive and imaginative color ranges. Could it have been done previously? Perhaps no one had even considered it. Finally, the presentation of samples in many marketing tools shows that the very rigorous world of chemistry occasionally had a whimsical side. This humorous dimension was added to the requirement for elegance and harmony that its color charts had already displayed before the war.

The organization of colors by type of dye led to the presence of distinct color charts, with each illustrating different degrees of intensity, with the colors arranged according to the color wheel. The dyeing process was described in text ranging from a few lines to a complete booklet. Finally, the samples were identified by names taken from the chemical lexicon.

The leporello was the format usually used. The samples, arranged on a strip of cardboard that was attached to the backing, were protected by sheets of glassine. Product samples were consistently used, which is logical since these color charts were intended for highlighting dyeing properties on a given material, with the sensory quality of the result being key. More surprising was the configuration of the sample: it was shaped like a little soap when the dye was intended for saponification, or like a button when it was used for synthetic resins, and so on. Even in industrial applications, clear and visually appealing connections were made between a dye substance and its intended use. Once again, the color chart stimulated the conception of images and projects.

As shown by the charts below, the Société Anonyme des Matières Colorantes et Produits Chimiques de Saint-Denis had expert skill in developing color charts. As early as 1885, the company had already used this tool to present its *Sulfur Colors*.[10] Following three decades of silence, which have not yet been explained, it returned to distributing color charts in 1921.

Dyeing Traditional Fibers

NEXT PAGE SPREAD

Cotton

Synthetic dyes simplified the process of dyeing cotton. The Badische Anilin & Soda-Fabrik (BASF) had first seized on this opportunity in 1900.[11] The 217 small bundles of dyed cotton thread, held at both ends by a tie on a strip of cardboard attached to the backing, show that by the 1920s any color was possible.

Dyes for Cotton, nº 2, Société Anonyme des Matières Colorantes et Produits Chimiques de Saint-Denis, Saint-Denis, c. 1921, leporello, 22 × 14.5 cm, 13 panels, Anne Varichon collection, Sète

PAGE 130

Spun Wool

The dyes here have been selected to respond to a particular requirement: resisting salt water. The context is not given. If they were for clothing for sailors, the extent, variety, and brightness of the range (sixty-seven samples) could be considered a demonstration of the company's expertise—something like a stylistic flourish. Another hypothesis is that they were intended for bathing suits. In the 1930s, beach activities were booming, stimulated by the paid vacations the Front Populaire made mandatory by law. From the beginning of this decade, women's magazines advised their readers to use a combination of wool and cotton to create knit bathing suits that would not lose their shape. In 1934, an article signed "Frivoline" in the magazine *Marianne*[12] also recommended knitting swimwear: "If we once thought that knitting was only for socks, hats, and our children's gaiters, that time is clearly in the past. We can make all kinds of attire by knitting . . . from swim caps and bathing suits to beach robes and cover-ups, everything can be made by our own hands, and this will definitely be an elegant solution as well as a sure cost-saver."

Colors That Are Resistant to Saltwater on Spun Wool, Société Anonyme des Matières Colorantes et Produits Chimiques de Saint-Denis, Saint-Denis, 1936, booklet, 21.5 × 15 cm, 6 pages, Albi Couleurs, Association Mémoire des Industries de la Couleur, Albi

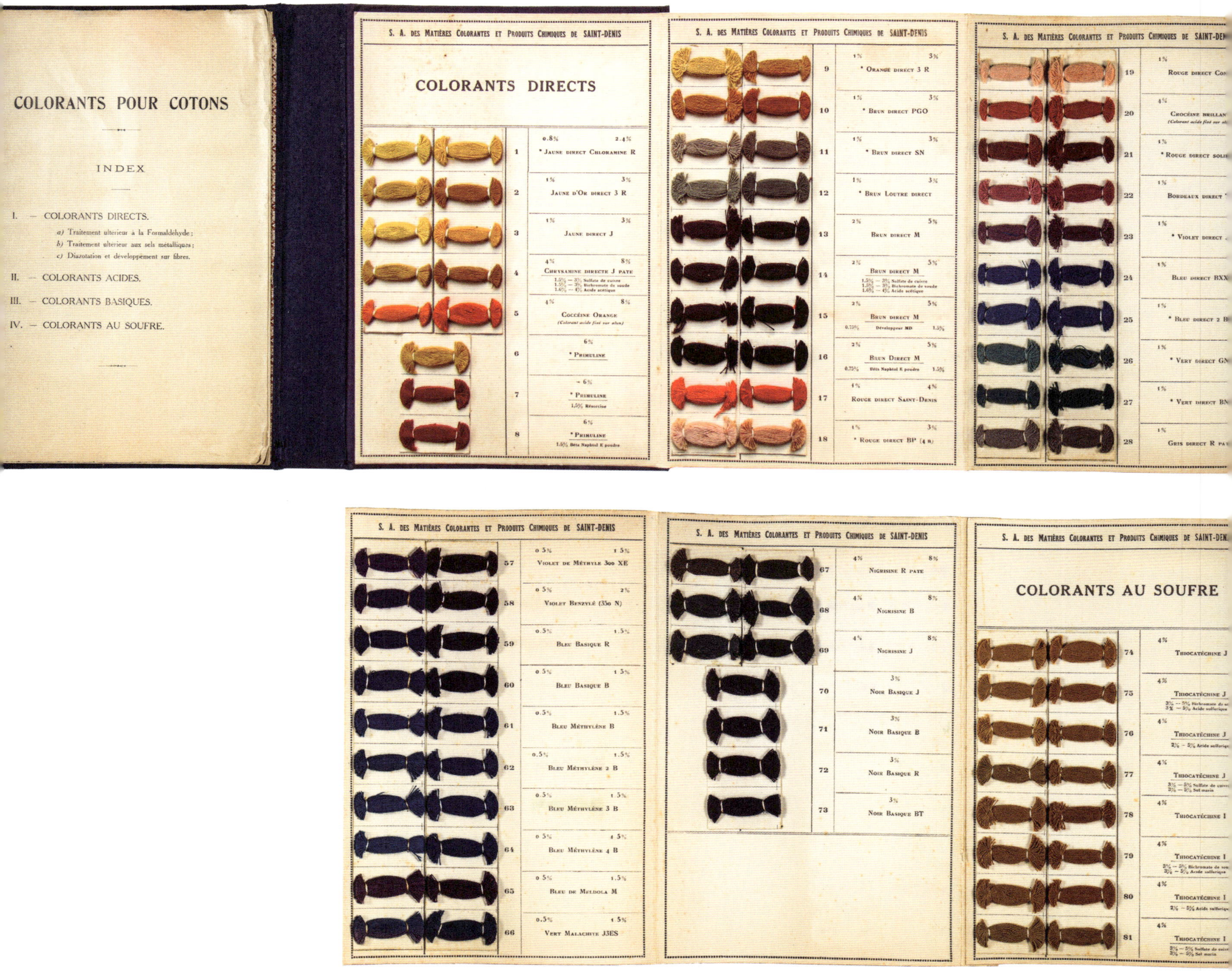

COLORANTS POUR COTONS

INDEX

S. A. des Matières Colorantes et Produits Chimiques de Saint-Denis

COLORANTS DIRECTS

No.		
1	0.8% — 2.4%	* Jaune direct Chloramine R
2	1% — 3%	Jaune d'Or direct 3 R
3	1% — 3%	Jaune direct J
4	4% — 8%	Chrysamine directe J pate 1.5% — 3% Sulfate de cuivre 1.5% — 3% Bichromate de soude 1.6% — 4% Acide acétique
5	4% — 8%	Coccéine Orange *(Colorant acide fixé sur alun)*
6	6%	* Primuline
7	6%	* Primuline 1,5% Résorcine
8	6%	* Primuline 1.5% Béta Naphtol E poudre

S. A. des Matières Colorantes et Produits Chimiques de Saint-Denis

No.		
9	1% — 3%	* Orange direct 3 R
10	1% — 3%	* Brun direct PGO
11	1% — 3%	* Brun direct SN
12	1% — 3%	* Brun Loutre direct
13	2% — 5%	Brun direct M
14	2% — 5%	Brun direct M 1.5% — 3% Sulfate de cuivre 1.5% — 3% Bichromate de soude 1.6% — 4% Acide acétique
15	2% — 5%	Brun direct M 0.75% Développeur MD 1.5%
16	2% — 5%	Brun Direct M 0.75% Béta Naphtol E poudre 1.5%
17	1% — 4%	Rouge direct Saint-Denis
18	1% — 3%	* Rouge direct BP (4 B)

S. A. des Matières Colorantes et Produits Chimiques de Saint-Den

No.		
19	1%	Rouge direct Con
20	4%	Crocéine brillan *(Colorant acide fixé sur al*
21	1%	* Rouge direct soli
22	1%	Bordeaux direct
23	1%	* Violet direct
24	1%	Bleu direct BXX
25	1%	* Bleu direct 2 B
26	1%	* Vert direct GN
27	1%	* Vert direct BN
28	1%	Gris direct R pa

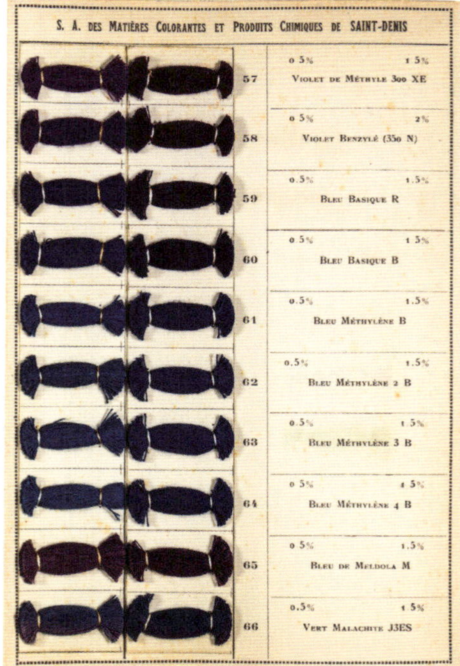

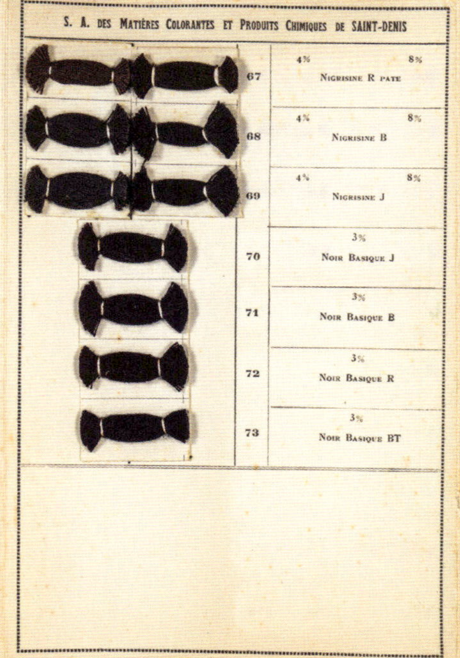

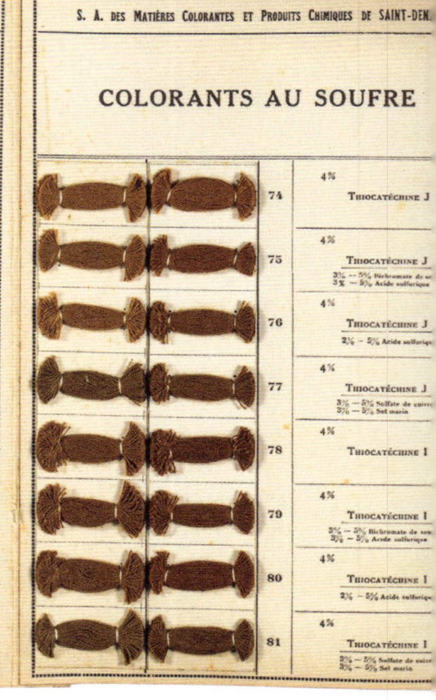

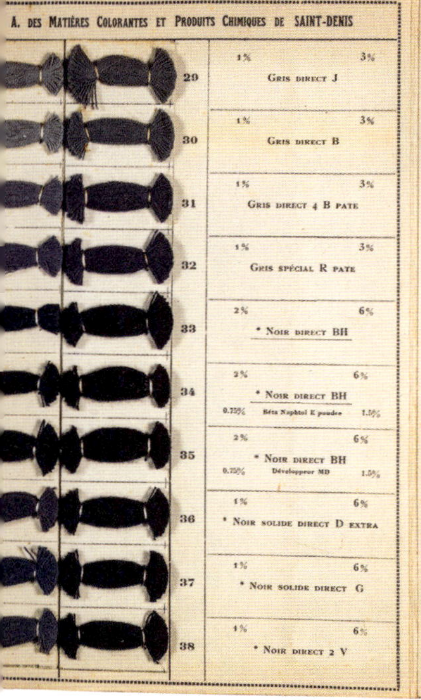

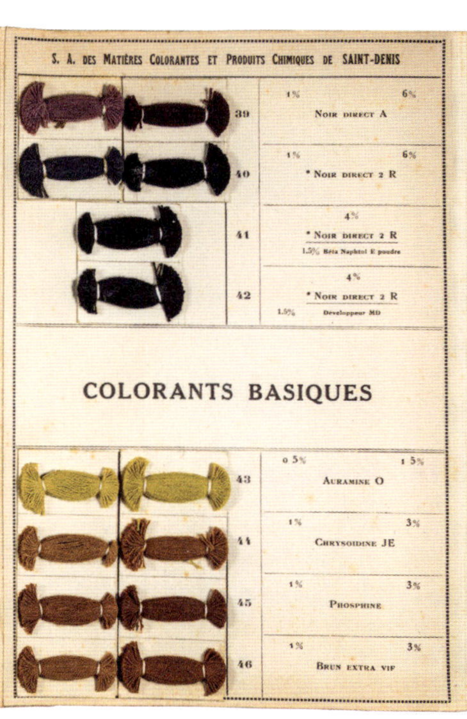

S. A. des Matières Colorantes et Produits Chimiques de Saint-Denis
47 1% 3% Brun de Phénylène C
48 1% 3% Brun de Phénylène S
49 0.5% 2% Brun NM
50 0.5% 1.5% Safranine A
51 0.5% 1.5% Safranine AB
52 0.5% 1.5% Grenadine R
53 0.5% 1.5% Fuschine A
54 0.5% 1.5% Cerise
55 0.5% 1.5% Violet de Methyle 90
56 0.5% 1.5% Violet de Methyle 170

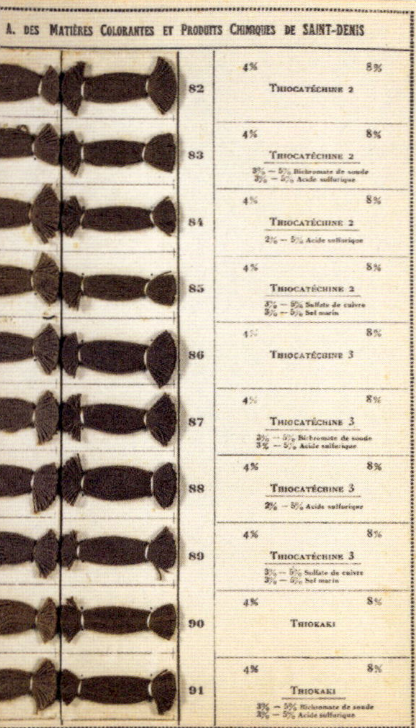

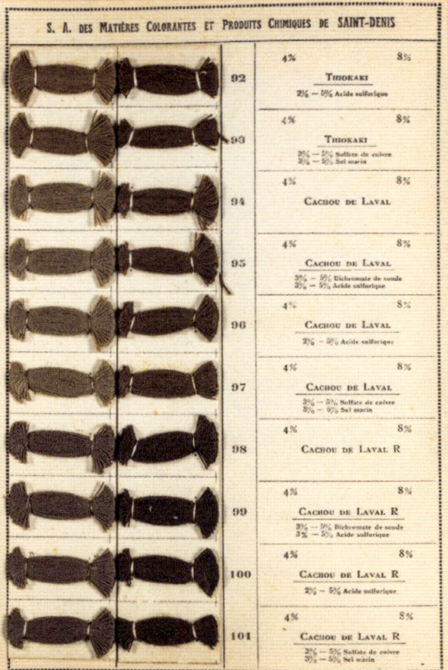

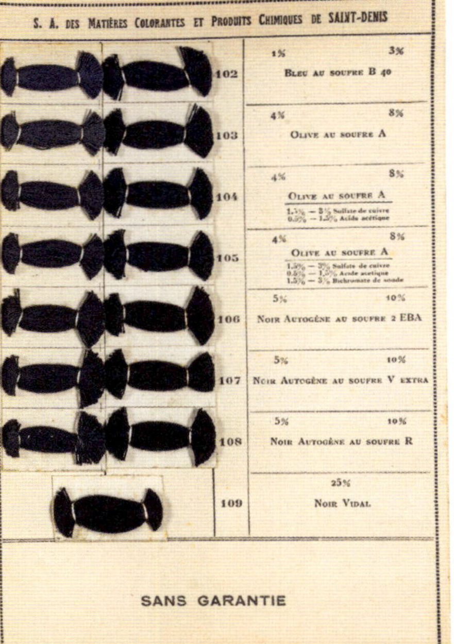

SOCIÉTÉ ANONYME DES MATIÈRES COLORANTES ET PRODUITS CHIMIQUES DE SAINT-DENIS

Colorants Acides

	Méthodes de Teinture		
1	S	2 %	Jaune supracide R
2	AS	2 %	Bleu acide brillant G
3	AS	0,1 % 0,07 %	Jaune neutre P2J Bleu acide brillant V
4	AS	2 %	Rouge foulon M
5	AS	1 % 1 %	Jaune neutre P2J Rouge neutre J
6	AS	1 % 0,5 %	Jaune neutre P2J Bleu acide brillant V
7	A	2 %	Rouge neutre B
8	AS	3 % 0,1 %	Rouge foulon M Bleu acide brillant 6B
9	AS	1,4 % 0,6 %	Jaune neutre P2J Rouge neutre J
10	AS	2 % 0,4 % 0,5 %	Jaune neutre P2J Ecarlate foulon R Cyanine foulon B

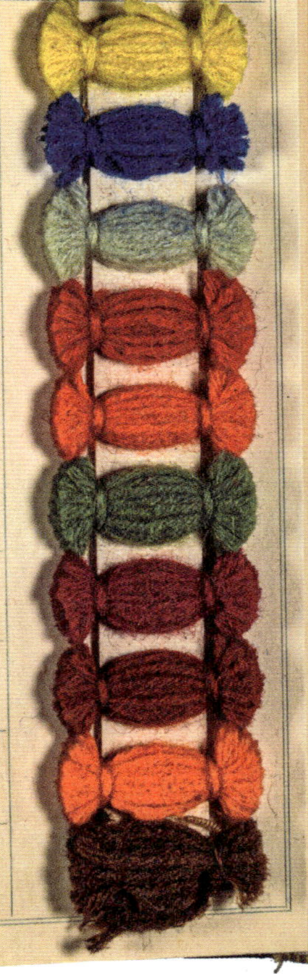

SOCIÉTÉ ANONYME DES MATIÈRES COLORANTES ET PRODUITS CHIMIQUES DE SAINT-DENIS

	Méthodes de Teinture		
11	AS	2 % 0,2 %	Jaune neutre P2J Bleu acide brillant V
12	AS	1 % 0,007 %	Jaune neutre P2J Bleu acide brillant V
13	AS	2 % 0,1 %	Jaune neutre P2J Cyanine foulon B
14	AS	0,1 % 0,03 % 0,03 %	Jaune neutre P2J Ecarlate foulon R Bleu acide brillant 6B
15	AS	1 % 0,2 % 0,2 %	Jaune neutre P2J Ecarlate foulon R Cyanine foulon B
16	AS	2 % 0,4 % 0,5 %	Jaune neutre P2J Ecarlate foulon R Bleu acide brillant V
17	AS	1 % 0,1 %	Jaune neutre P2J Bleu acide brillant V
18	AS	1 % 0,05 % 0,5 %	Jaune neutre P2J Ecarlate foulon R Bleu acide brillant V
19	AS	1 % 0,5 %	Jaune neutre P2J Cyanine foulon B
20	AL	2 %	Bleu alcalin 6B
21	AS	0,01 % 0,005 % 0,4 %	Jaune neutre P2J Rouge foulon M Bleu acide brillant V
22	AS	0,3 % 0,07 %	Ecarlate foulon R Bleu acide brillant B6

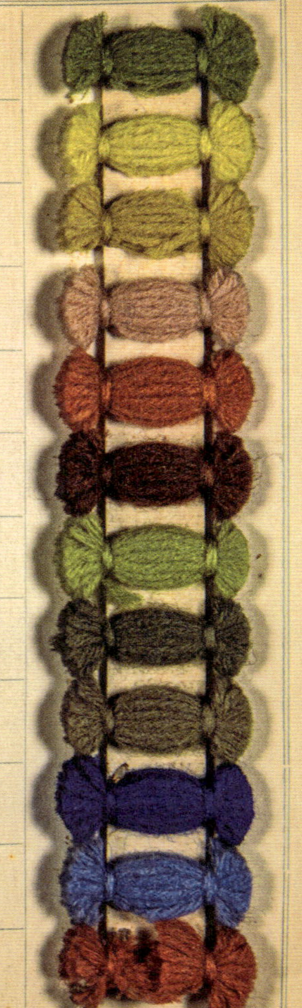

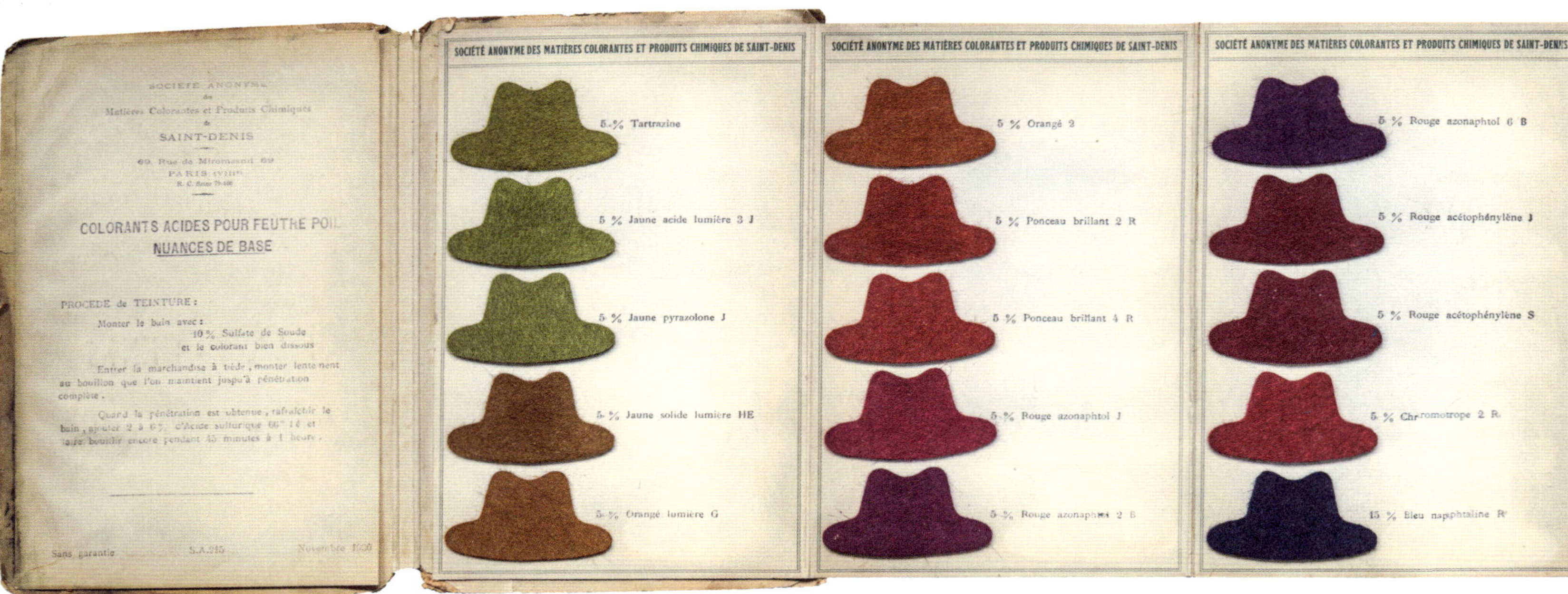

SAINT-DENIS
PARIS
COLORANTS ACIDES POUR FEUTRE POIL
NUANCES DE BASE
PROCEDE de TEINTURE :
Monter le bain avec :
10 % Sulfate de Soude
et le colorant bien dissous
Entrer la marchandise à tiède, monter lentement au bouillon que l'on maintient jusqu'à pénétration complète.
Sans garantie
S.A.215
SOCIÉTÉ ANONYME DES MATIÈRES COLORANTES ET PRODUITS CHIMIQUES DE SAINT-DENIS
5 % Tartrazine
5 % Jaune acide lumière 3 J
5 % Jaune pyrazolone J
5 % Jaune solide lumière HE
5 % Orangé lumière G
SOCIÉTÉ ANONYME DES MATIÈRES COLORANTES ET PRODUITS CHIMIQUES DE SAINT-DENIS
5 % Orangé 2
5 % Ponceau brillant 2 R
5 % Ponceau brillant 4 R
5 % Rouge azonaphtol J
SOCIÉTÉ ANONYME DES MATIÈRES COLORANTES ET PRODUITS CHIMIQUES DE SAINT-DENIS
5 % Rouge azonaphtol 6 B
5 % Rouge acétophénylène J
5 % Rouge acétophénylène S
5 % Chromotrope 2 R
15 % Bleu naphtaline R

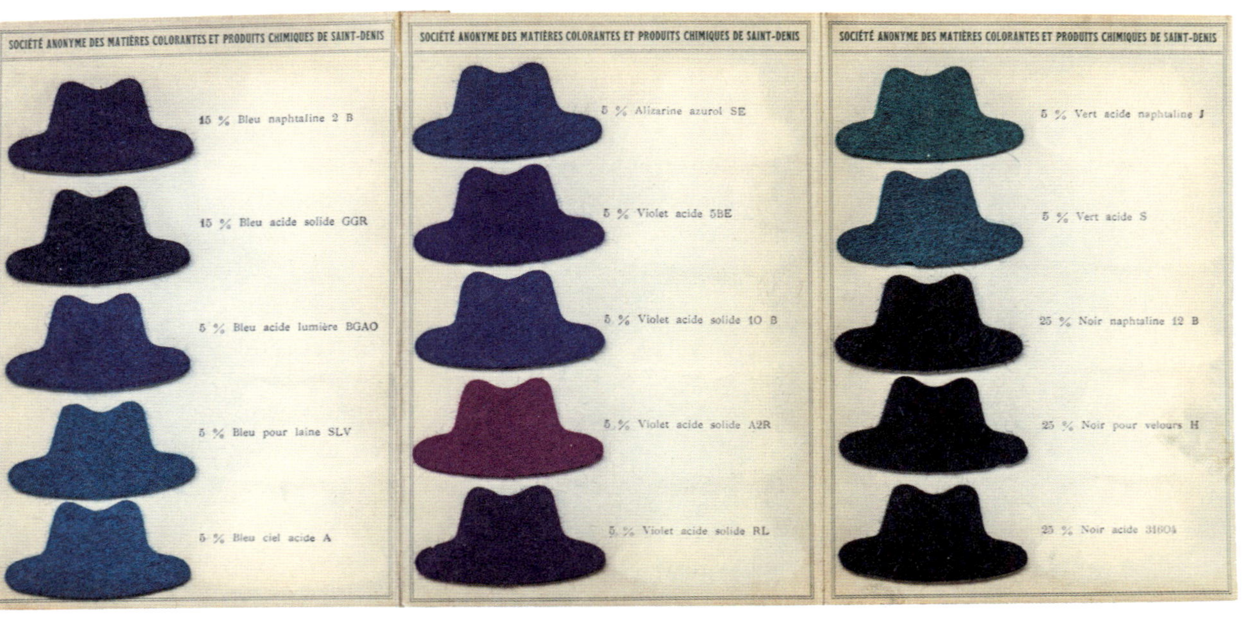

SOCIÉTÉ ANONYME DES MATIÈRES COLORANTES ET PRODUITS CHIMIQUES DE SAINT-DENIS
15 % Bleu naphtaline 2 B
15 % Bleu acide solide GGR
5 % Bleu acide lumière BGAO
5 % Bleu pour laine SLV
5 % Bleu ciel acide A
SOCIÉTÉ ANONYME DES MATIÈRES COLORANTES ET PRODUITS CHIMIQUES DE SAINT-DENIS
5 % Alizarine azurol SE
5 % Violet acide 5BE
5 % Violet acide solide 10 B
5 % Violet acide solide A2R
5 % Violet acide solide RL
SOCIÉTÉ ANONYME DES MATIÈRES COLORANTES ET PRODUITS CHIMIQUES DE SAINT-DENIS
5 % Vert acide naphtaline J
5 % Vert acide S
25 % Noir naphtaline 12 B
25 % Noir pour velours H
25 % Noir acide 31604

PREVIOUS PAGE

Felt

The chemical industry had already displayed its artistic presentation of color charts by the late nineteenth century, and after World War I it initiated other stylistic innovations. This color chart, with samples in the shape of fedoras, shows the contrast between the serious tone of the text and the playfulness of the presentation. Hat-making was an important market for felt. Shaped into various forms and sizes, it was then shaved for a consistent texture. The palette, which covers the entire spectrum of bright colors, demonstrates that this color chart was designed for headgear for both sexes.

Acid Dyes for Felt Pile, Base Colors, Société Anonyme des Matières Colorantes et Produits Chimiques de Saint-Denis, Saint-Denis, November 1930, leporello, 22 × 15 cm, 7 panels, Albi Couleurs, Association Mémoire des Industries de la Couleur, Albi

Experimenting with New Textile Fibers

OPPOSITE, TOP

Artificial and Synthetic Fibers

The introduction of artificial and synthetic fibers was a new challenge for the dyeing industry. One of the first of these fibers was viscose rayon, which was used as a replacement for expensive natural silk.[13] Its low cost and shiny appearance met with success, and in the 1920s, it was produced industrially for affordable clothing and lingerie, including stockings. This fiber also had the advantage of being easily colored using synthetic dyes. This can be seen here in this formula, reduced to the simplest expression: "Leave the product for a few minutes in a 60° bath containing 1 g of dye per liter. Wring and let dry." However, the tufts on this color chart were dyed in a process that required much more care: only the lower part is dyed, with the upper part of the fabric untouched.

Semipermanent Dyes for Artificial Silk, Société Anonyme des Matières Colorantes et Produits Chimiques de Saint-Denis, Saint-Denis, 1928, leporello, 22 × 15 cm, 5 panels, Albi Couleurs, Association Mémoire des Industries de la Couleur, Albi

Bold Color Ranges Appear on the Scene

OPPOSITE, BOTTOM

Graphic Inks

Since the beginning of the century, the growing need for color printing had led to improvements in ink quality and to ever wider ranges. The principle of a single image printed in multiple shades (this booklet contains seventy in all) is a classic approach on printers' color charts. As for the bust of Voltaire—which sometimes flirts with neon tones—it shows once again that the Société Anonyme des Matières Colorantes et Produits Chimiques de Saint-Denis added a touch of humor to its marketing tools.

Dyes for Graphic Inks, n° 19, Société Anonyme des Matières Colorantes et Produits Chimiques de Saint-Denis, Saint-Denis, 1926, booklet, 22 × 14 cm, 70 pages, Albi Couleurs, Association Mémoire des Industries de la Couleur, Albi

NEXT PAGE SPREAD

Paper

Paper was also dyed in large quantities, and this color chart offers seventy-two shades that can be applied at different stages in the manufacturing process: paper pulp (including paper for artists), printing (wallpaper), and production of dyed paper. The colors appear on rectangles of paper glued to the backing, like color charts of artists' paints, with each color shown in three different concentrations, totaling 218 samples that form a rich palette.

Dyes for Paper n° 5, Société Anonyme des Matières Colorantes et Produits Chimiques de Saint-Denis, Saint-Denis, 1922, leporello, 22 × 15 cm, 15 panels, Bibliothèque Forney, Paris, call number RES ICO 8406—5

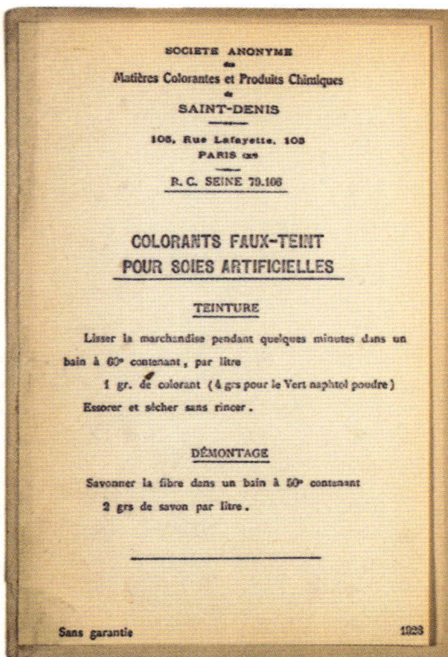
SOCIETE ANONYME
des
Matières Colorantes et Produits Chimiques
de
SAINT-DENIS
105, Rue Lafayette, 105
PARIS (9e)
R. C. SEINE 79.106
COLORANTS FAUX-TEINT
POUR SOIES ARTIFICIELLES
TEINTURE
Lisser la marchandise pendant quelques minutes dans un bain à 60° contenant, par litre
1 gr. de colorant (4 grs pour le Vert naphtol poudre)
Essorer et sécher sans rincer.
DÉMONTAGE
Savonner la fibre dans un bain à 50° contenant
2 grs de savon par litre.
Sans garantie
1928

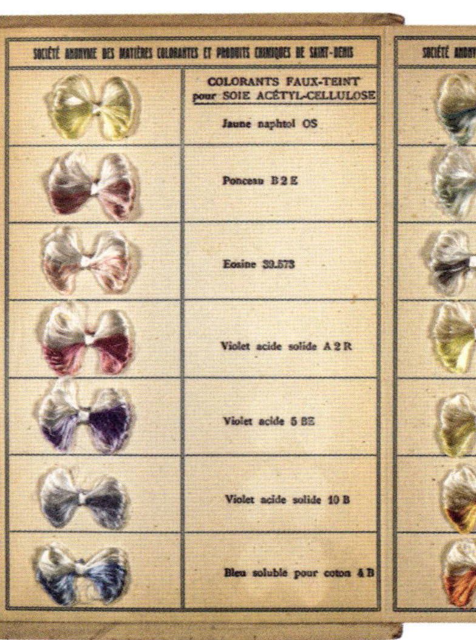
SOCIÉTÉ ANONYME DES MATIÈRES COLORANTES ET PRODUITS CHIMIQUES DE SAINT-DENIS
COLORANTS FAUX-TEINT
pour SOIE ACÉTYL-CELLULOSE
Jaune naphtol OS
Ponceau B 2 E
Eosine 39.573
Violet acide solide A 2 R
Violet acide 5 BZ
Violet acide solide 10 B
Bleu soluble pour coton 4 B

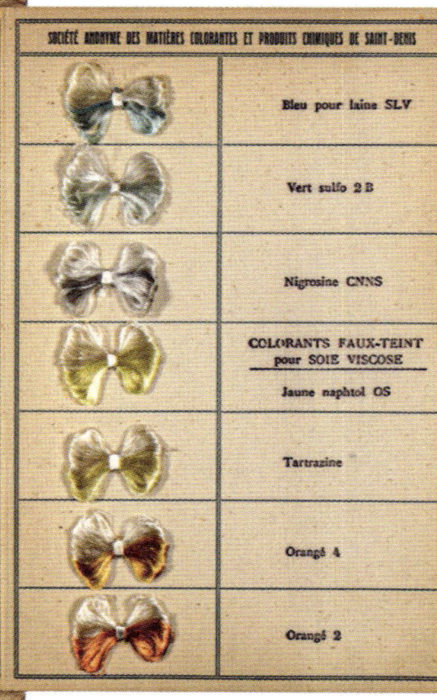
SOCIÉTÉ ANONYME DES MATIÈRES COLORANTES ET PRODUITS CHIMIQUES DE SAINT-DENIS
Bleu pour laine SLV
Vert sulfo 2 B
Nigrosine CNNS
COLORANTS FAUX-TEINT
pour SOIE VISCOSE
Jaune naphtol OS
Tartrazine
Orangé 4
Orangé 2
SOCIÉTÉ ANONYME DES MATIÈRES COLORANTES ET PRODUITS CHIMIQUES DE SAINT-DENIS
Nacarat
Chromotrope 2 R
Rouge azonaphtol 6 B
Eosine 39.573
Violet acide solide RL
Violet azoïque 4 BS
Bleu acide solide 2 GR
SOCIÉTÉ ANONYME DES MATIÈRES COLORANTES ET PRODUITS CHIMIQUES DE SAINT-DENIS
Bleu soluble pour coton 4 B
Sulfindigotine
Bleu pour laine SLV
Vert naphtol poudre
Vert acide naphtaline J
Nigrosine CNNS
Noir naphtaline 5 B

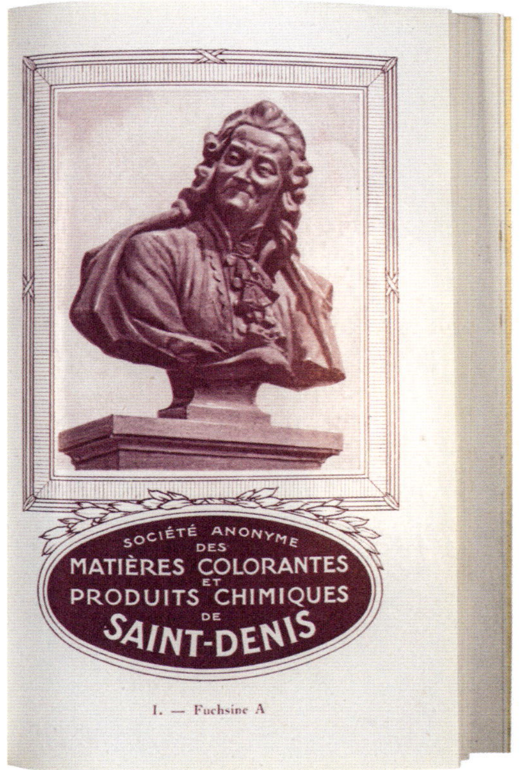
SOCIÉTÉ ANONYME
DES
MATIÈRES COLORANTES
ET
PRODUITS CHIMIQUES
DE
SAINT-DENIS
I. — Fuchsine A

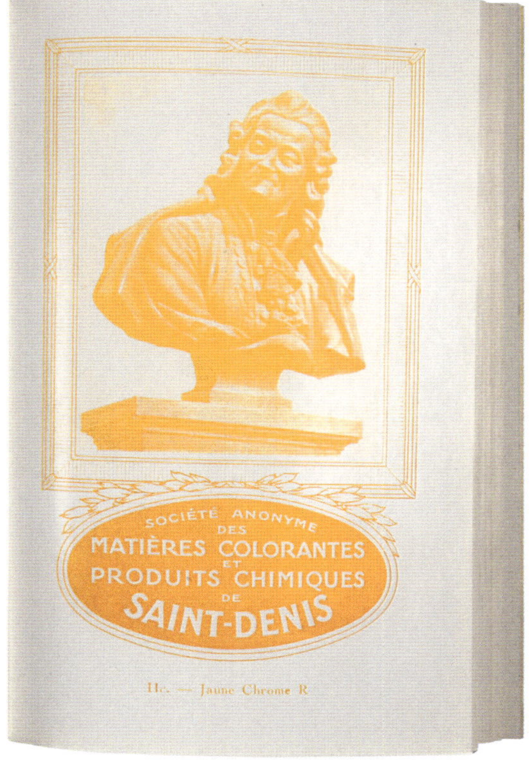
SOCIÉTÉ ANONYME
DES
MATIÈRES COLORANTES
ET
PRODUITS CHIMIQUES
DE
SAINT-DENIS
IIc. — Jaune Chrome R

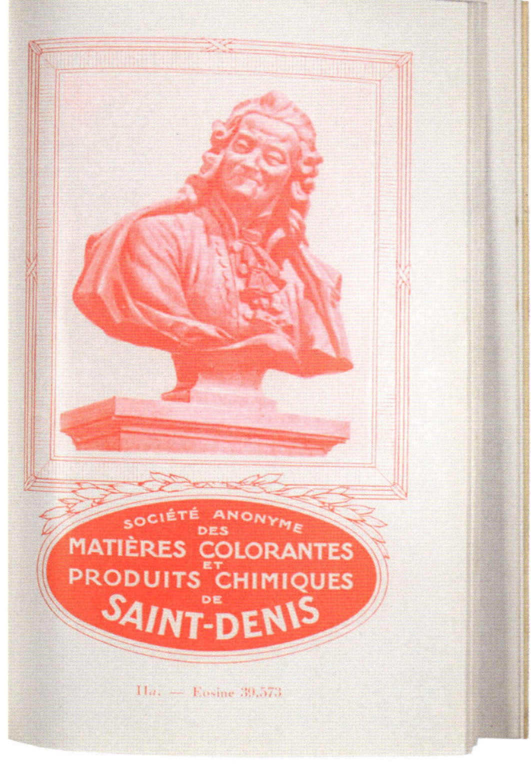
SOCIÉTÉ ANONYME
DES
MATIÈRES COLORANTES
ET
PRODUITS CHIMIQUES
DE
SAINT-DENIS
IIa. — Eosine 39.573

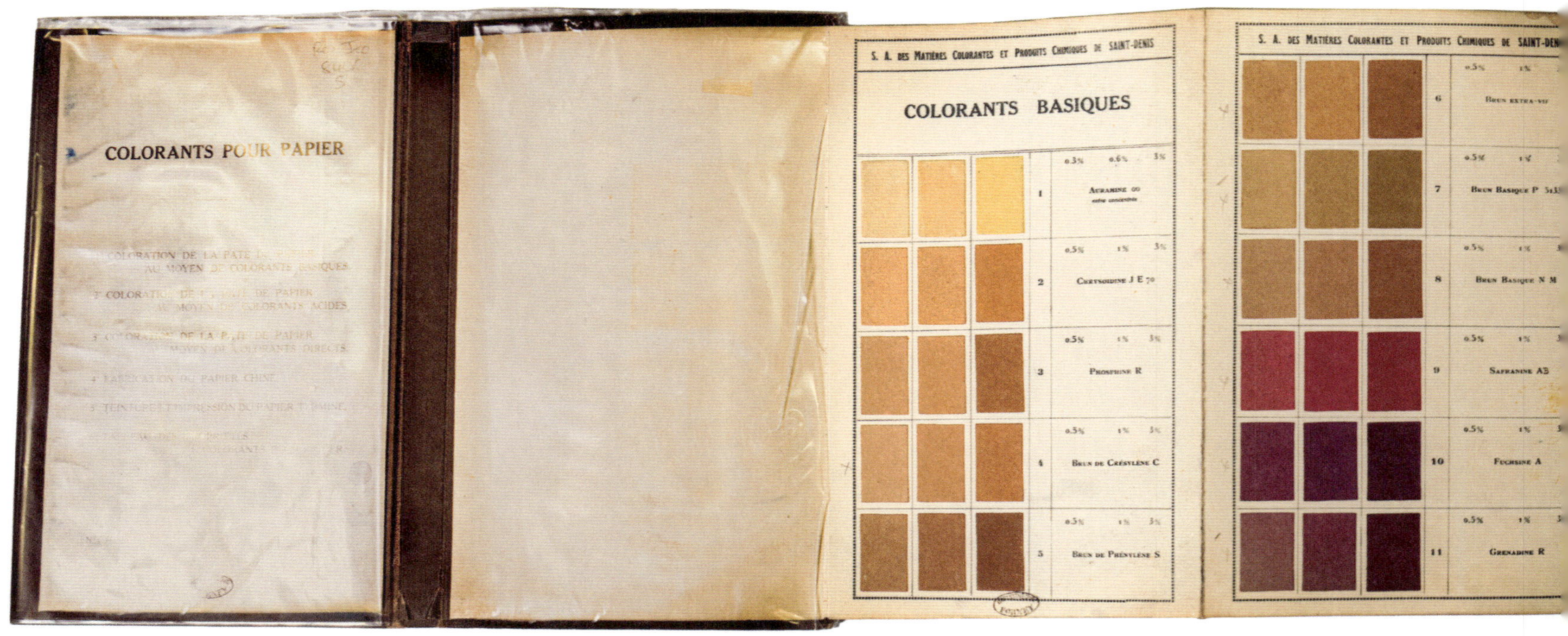

COLORANTS POUR PAPIER
S. A. des Matières Colorantes et Produits Chimiques de Saint-Denis
COLORANTS BASIQUES
1 Auramine OO
2 Chrysoïdine J E 70
3 Phosphine R
4 Brun de Crésylène C
5 Brun de Phénylène S
6 Brun extra-vu
7 Brun Basique P
8 Brun Basique N M
9 Safranine AS
10 Fuchsine A
11 Grenadine R

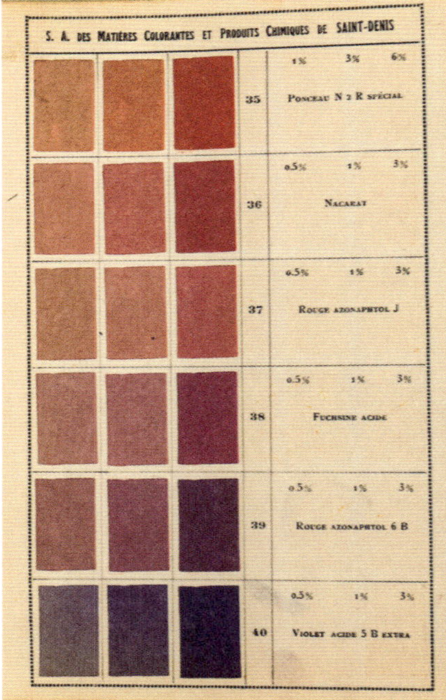

S. A. des Matières Colorantes et Produits Chimiques de Saint-Denis
35 Ponceau N 2 R spécial
36 Nacarat
37 Rouge azonaphtol J
38 Fuchsine acide
39 Rouge azonaphtol 6 B
40 Violet acide 5 B extra

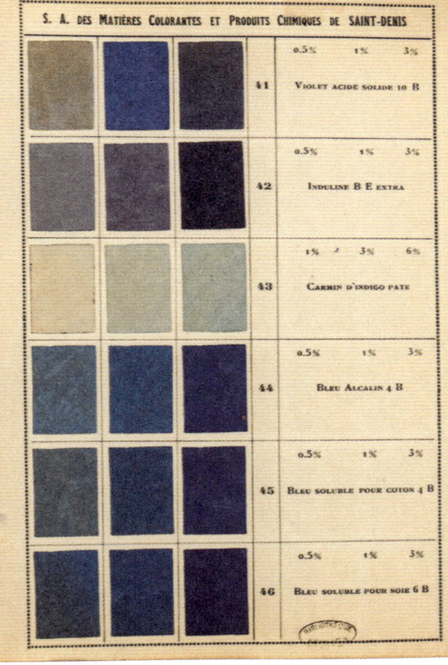

S. A. des Matières Colorantes et Produits Chimiques de Saint-Denis
41 Violet acide solide 10 B
42 Induline B E extra
43 Carmin d'indigo pate
44 Bleu Alcalin 4 B
45 Bleu soluble pour coton 4 B
46 Bleu soluble pour soie 6 B

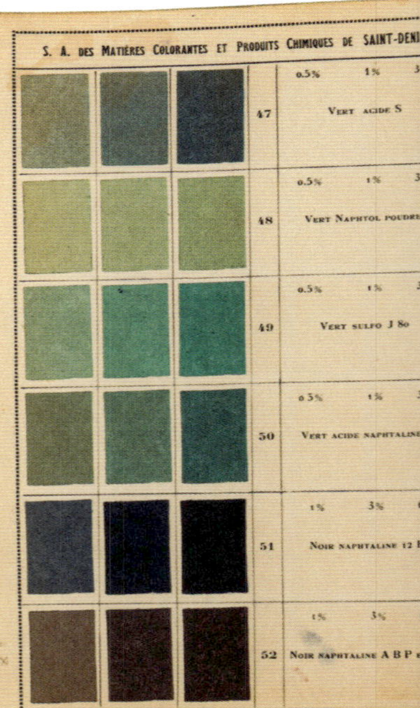

47 Vert acide S
48 Vert Naphtol poudre
49 Vert sulfo J 80
50 Vert acide naphtaline
51 Noir naphtaline 12 B
52 Noir naphtaline A B P

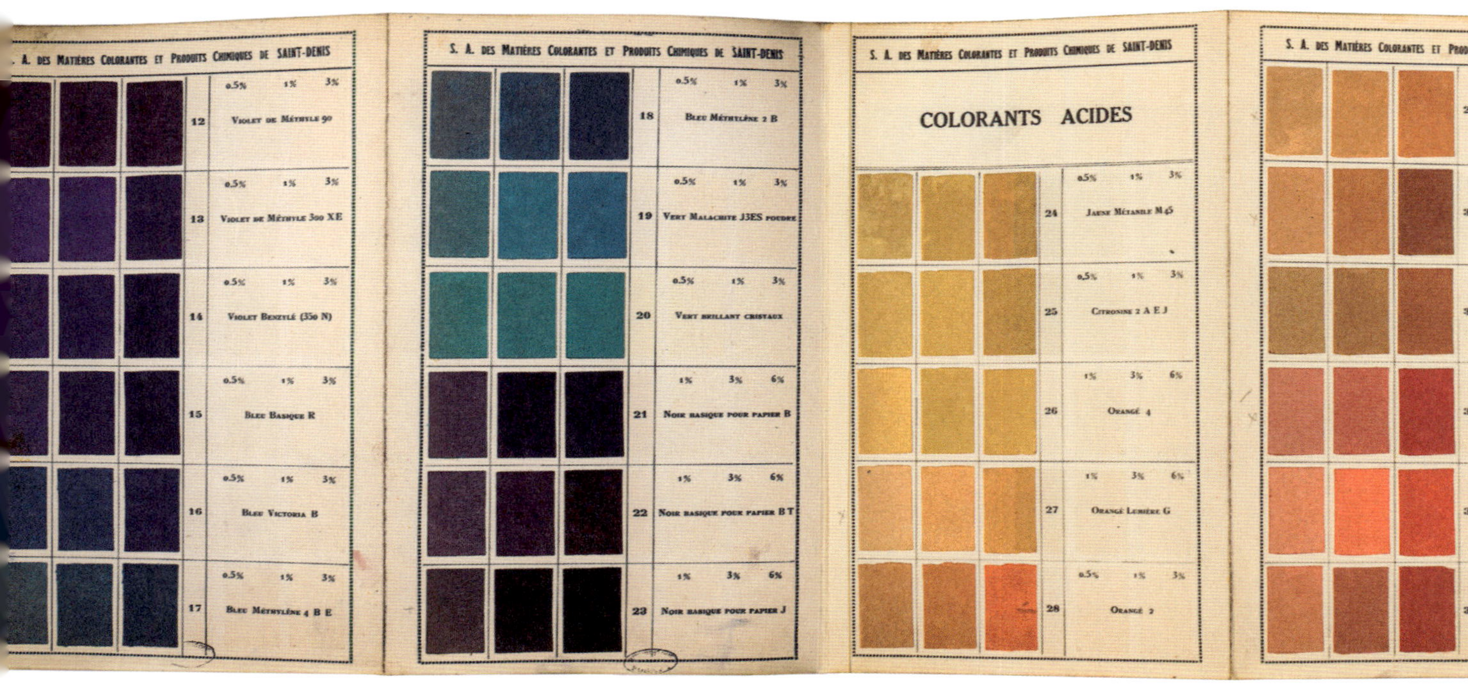

S. A. des Matières Colorantes et Produits Chimiques de Saint-Denis
0.5% 1% 3%
12 Violet de Méthyle 90
0.5% 1% 3%
13 Violet de Méthyle 300 XE
0.5% 1% 3%
14 Violet Benzylé (350 N)
0.5% 1% 3%
15 Bleu Basique R
0.5% 1% 3%
16 Bleu Victoria B
0.5% 1% 3%
17 Bleu Méthylène 4 B E
S. A. des Matières Colorantes et Produits Chimiques de Saint-Denis
0.5% 1% 3%
18 Bleu Méthylène 2 B
0.5% 1% 3%
19 Vert Malachite J3ES poudre
0.5% 1% 3%
20 Vert brillant cristaux
1% 3% 6%
21 Noir basique pour papier B
1% 3% 6%
22 Noir basique pour papier B T
1% 3% 6%
23 Noir basique pour papier J
S. A. des Matières Colorantes et Produits Chimiques de Saint-Denis
COLORANTS ACIDES
0.5% 1% 3%
24 Jaune Métanile M45
0.5% 1% 3%
25 Citronine 2 A E J
1% 3% 6%
26 Orangé 4
1% 3% 6%
27 Orangé Lumière G
0.5% 1% 3%
28 Orangé 2

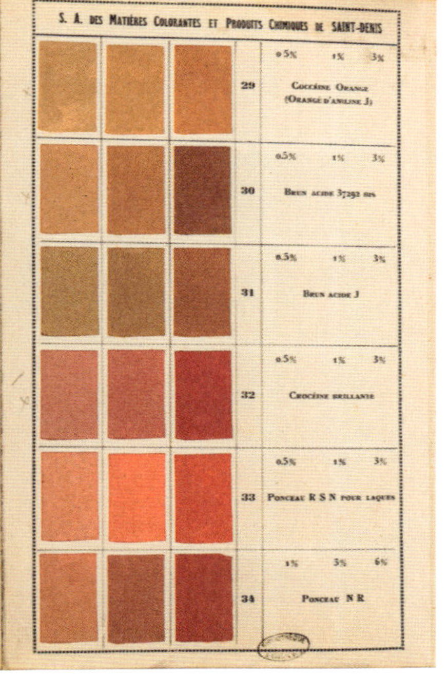

S. A. des Matières Colorantes et Produits Chimiques de Saint-Denis
0.5% 1% 3%
29 Coccéine Orange (Orangé d'aniline J)
0.5% 1% 3%
30 Brun acide 37292 bis
0.5% 1% 3%
31 Brun acide J
0.5% 1% 3%
32 Crocéine brillante
0.5% 1% 3%
33 Ponceau R S N pour laques
1% 3% 6%
34 Ponceau N R

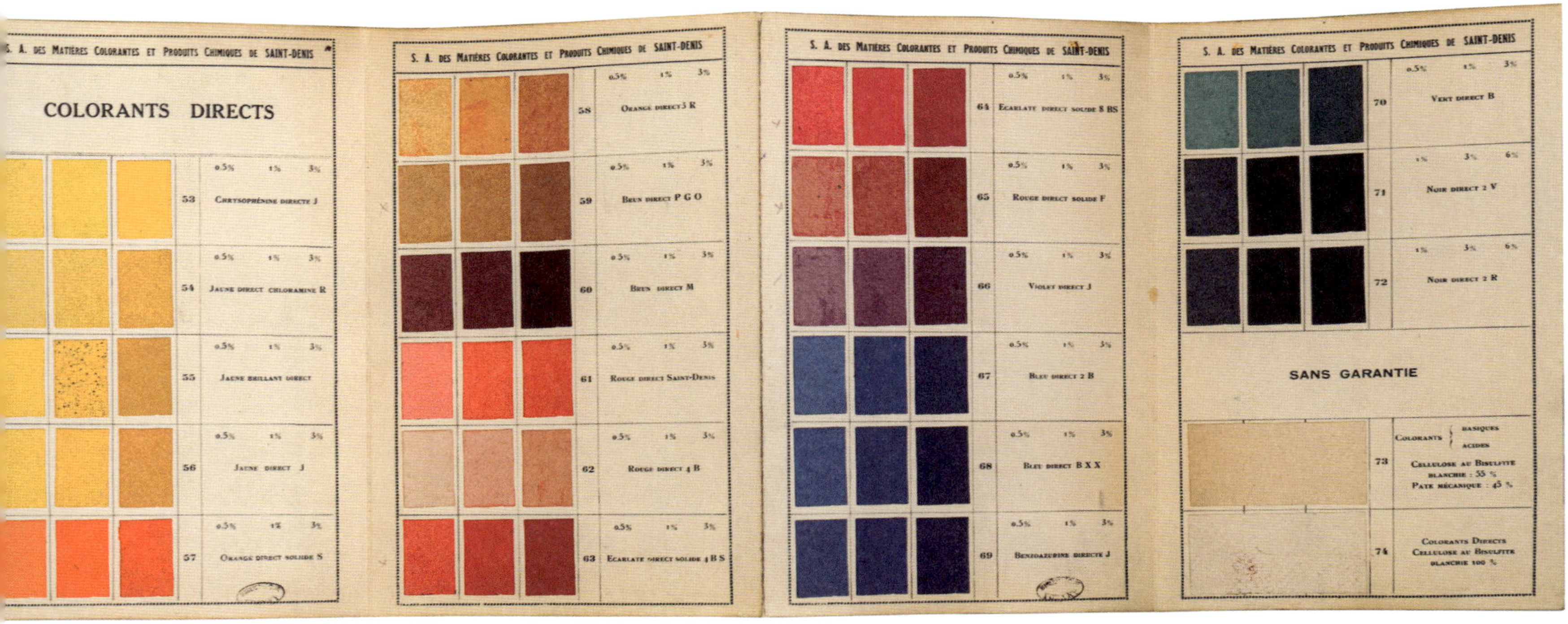

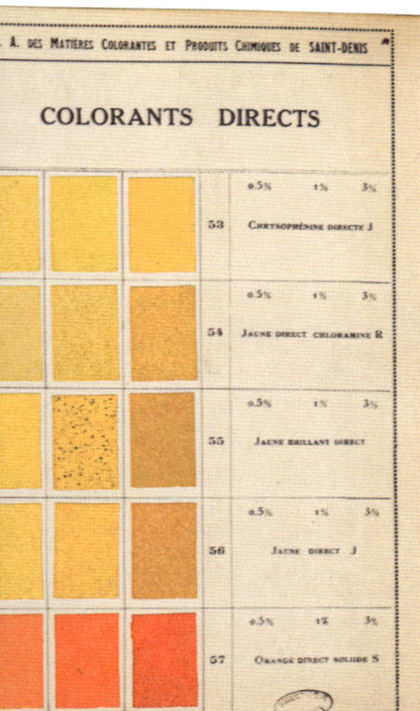

S. A. des Matières Colorantes et Produits Chimiques de Saint-Denis
COLORANTS DIRECTS
0.5% 1% 3%
53 Chrysophénine directe J
0.5% 1% 3%
54 Jaune direct chloramine R
0.5% 1% 3%
55 Jaune brillant direct
0.5% 1% 3%
56 Jaune direct J
0.5% 1% 3%
57 Orange direct solide S

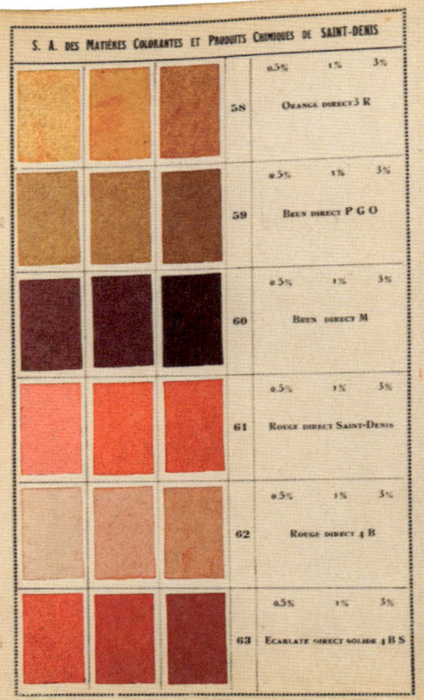

S. A. des Matières Colorantes et Produits Chimiques de Saint-Denis
0.5% 1% 3%
58 Orangé direct 3 R
0.5% 1% 3%
59 Brun direct P G O
0.5% 1% 3%
60 Brun direct M
0.5% 1% 3%
61 Rouge direct Saint-Denis
0.5% 1% 3%
62 Rouge direct 4 B
0.5% 1% 3%
63 Ecarlate direct solide 4 B S

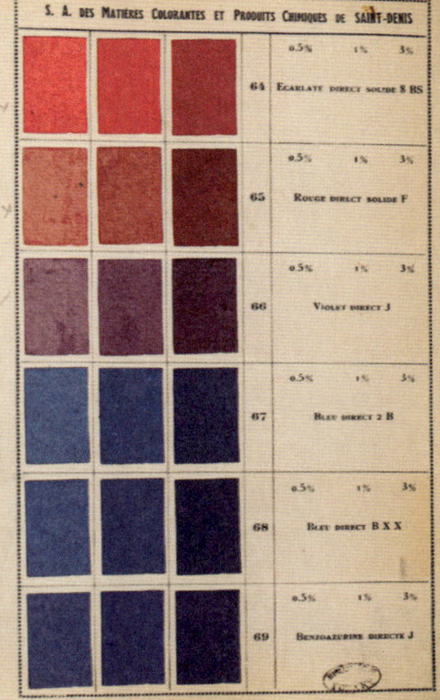

S. A. des Matières Colorantes et Produits Chimiques de Saint-Denis
0.5% 1% 3%
64 Ecarlate direct solide 8 BS
0.5% 1% 3%
65 Rouge direct solide F
0.5% 1% 3%
66 Violet direct J
0.5% 1% 3%
67 Bleu direct 2 B
0.5% 1% 3%
68 Bleu direct B X X
0.5% 1% 3%
69 Benzoazurine directe J
S. A. des Matières Colorantes et Produits Chimiques de Saint-Denis
0.5% 1% 3%
70 Vert direct B
1% 3% 6%
71 Noir direct 2 V
1% 3% 6%
72 Noir direct 2 R
SANS GARANTIE
73 Colorants basiques / acides
Cellulose au Bisulfite blanchie : 55 %
Pate mécanique : 45 %
74 Colorants Directs
Cellulose au Bisulfite blanchie 100 %

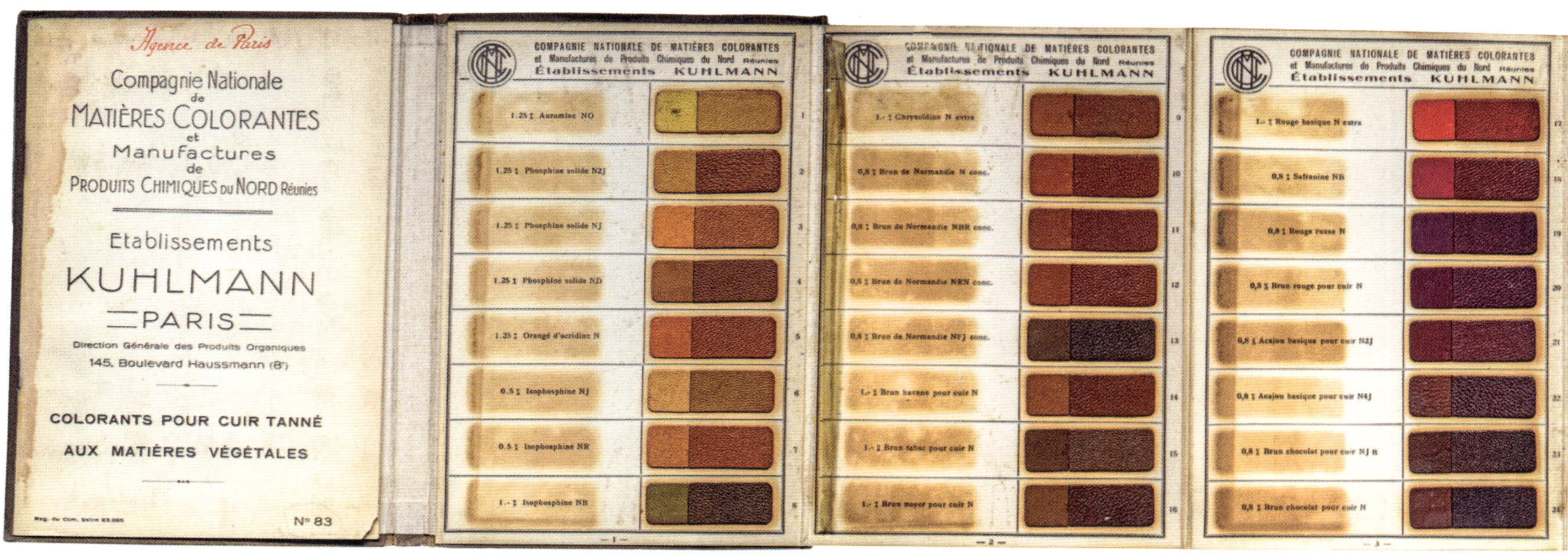
Agence de Paris
Compagnie Nationale de Matières Colorantes et Manufactures de Produits Chimiques du Nord Réunies
Etablissements KUHLMANN
PARIS
Direction Générale des Produits Organiques
145, Boulevard Haussmann (8e)
COLORANTS POUR CUIR TANNÉ AUX MATIÈRES VÉGÉTALES
N° 83
COMPAGNIE NATIONALE DE MATIÈRES COLORANTES et Manufactures de Produits Chimiques du Nord Réunies Établissements KUHLMANN
1.25 % Auramine NO 1
1.25 % Phosphine solide N2J 2
1.25 % Phosphine solide NJ 3
1.25 % Phosphine solide ND 4
1.25 % Orangé d'acridine N 5
0.5 % Isophosphine NJ 6
0.5 % Isophosphine NR 7
1.- % Isophosphine NB 8
— 1 —
1.- % Chrysoïdine N extra 9
0,8 % Brun de Normandie N conc. 10
0,8 % Brun de Normandie NBR conc. 11
0,8 % Brun de Normandie NRN conc. 12
0,8 % Brun de Normandie NFJ conc. 13
1.- % Brun havane pour cuir N 14
1.- % Brun tabac pour cuir N 15
1.- % Brun noyer pour cuir N 16
— 2 —
1.- % Rouge basique N extra 17
0,8 % Safranine NB 18
0,8 % Rouge russe N 19
0,5 % Brun rouge pour cuir N 20
0,8 % Acajou basique pour cuir N2J 21
0,8 % Acajou basique pour cuir N4J 22
0,8 % Brun chocolat pour cuir NJB 23
0,8 % Brun chocolat pour cuir N 24
— 3 —

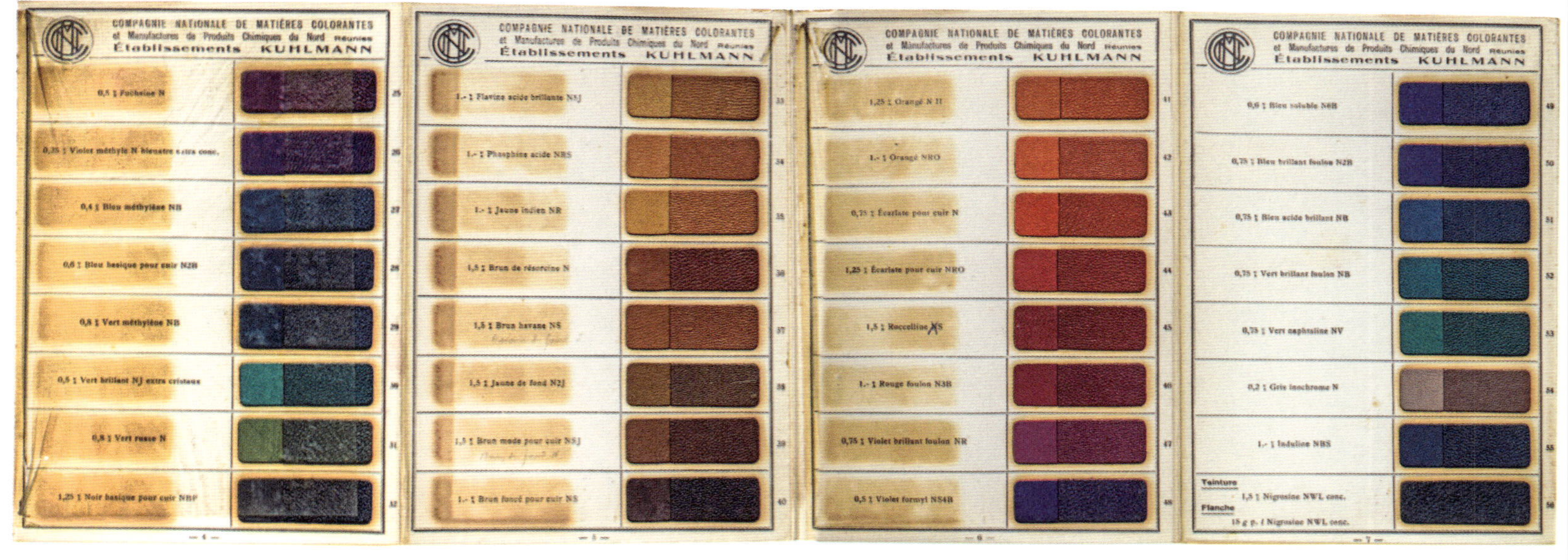
COMPAGNIE NATIONALE DE MATIÈRES COLORANTES et Manufactures de Produits Chimiques du Nord Réunies Établissements KUHLMANN
0,5 % Fuchsine N 25
0,35 % Violet méthyle N bleuâtre extra conc. 26
0,4 % Bleu méthylène NB 27
0,6 % Bleu basique pour cuir N2B 28
0,8 % Vert méthylène NB 29
0,5 % Vert brillant NJ extra cristaux 30
0,8 % Vert russe N 31
1,25 % Noir basique pour cuir NBP 32
— 4 —
1.- % Flavine acide brillante N5J 33
1.- % Phosphine acide NBS 34
1.- % Jaune indien NR 35
1,5 % Brun de résorcine N 36
1,5 % Brun havane NS 37
1,5 % Jaune de fond N2J 38
1,5 % Brun mode pour cuir NSJ 39
1.- % Brun foncé pour cuir NS 40
— 5 —
1,25 % Orangé N II 41
1.- % Orangé NRO 42
0,75 % Écarlate pour cuir N 43
1,25 % Écarlate pour cuir NRO 44
1,5 % Roccelline NS 45
1.- % Rouge foulon N3B 46
0,75 % Violet brillant foulon NR 47
0,5 % Violet formyl NS4B 48
— 6 —
0,6 % Bleu soluble N6B 49
0,75 % Bleu brillant foulon N2B 50
0,75 % Bleu acide brillant NB 51
0,75 % Vert brillant foulon NB 52
0,75 % Vert naphtaline NV 53
0,2 % Gris inochrome N 54
1.- % Induline NBS 55
Teinture
1,5 % Nigrosine NWL conc.
Flanche
15 g p. l Nigrosine NWL conc. 56
— 7 —

OPPOSITE

Tanned Leather

Long restricted to hues and shades of tan, leather became available in a variety of colors after World War I due, once again, to synthetic dyes. The fifty-six samples on this color chart have a dual appearance: on the left they show leather that has been merely dyed, and, on the right, leather after being smoothed and shagreened. Once again, we notice the attention to color embodied in a material, with its perceptible texture and relief. Of course, leather offers a wide range of sensory experiences (including smell), whether it is used for shoes, clothing, furnishings, or objects such as bindings.

Dyes for Tanned Leather with Plant Materials, Compagnie Nationale de Matières Colorantes et Manufactures de Produits Chimiques du Nord Réunies, Établissements Kuhlmann, Paris, 1930s, leporello, 20.5 × 14.5 cm, 9 panels, Albi Couleurs, Association Mémoire des Industries de la Couleur, Albi

NEXT PAGE SPREAD

Feathers

By the 1920s, the chemical industry could offer feather makers, now deprived by law of exotic birds, any shade they desired.[14] However, this color chart seems to have been created on an ad hoc basis; the text has been typewritten at a time when the other color charts by the Société de Saint-Denis were printed. The brief formula does not raise the possibility of mixing the dyes, but in any feather-making studio, a worker with a trained eye would be able to create new shades. Another color chart from the same source and era, which is not illustrated here, lines up elegant but sorrowful columns of black feathers with names that are just as depressing (*Naphthaline 5B Extra Black*, etc.). Mourning customs prevented wearing colors, especially bright ones, for a long period of time, but the hundreds of thousands of women who had lost a husband, son, or brother to war or to the Spanish flu could still decorate their hats.

Dyes for Feathers, Société Anonyme des Matières Colorantes et Produits Chimiques de Saint-Denis, Saint-Denis, April 1925, leporello, 22 × 15 cm, 5 panels, Albi Couleurs, Association Mémoire des Industries de la Couleur, Albi

PAGE 140, TOP

Wood Stain

Wood was traditionally protected by paint or wax. After World War I, it became possible to stain it, and in a variety of colors. The transparent stain allowed the wood grain to show through; the stain penetrated the wood. The company that published this color chart in the 1930s understood the decorative possibilities that the use of stain on wood enabled.[15] A book explains various types of staining in three languages (German, French, and English). The stain could be applied with a sponge to lightly graze the wood surface, or an entire tree trunk could be immersed into high-pressure vats so that the color could penetrate to the wood's heart.

The names of the ninety-four pieces of dyed wood indicate whether the dye is artificial or not. Some are compared to natural wood colors (*Rosewood*, *Water-Soluble Cedar*), while others (ranging from yellows to bright violets) are named for the dye used (*Quinoline Yellow*, *BB Brilliant Blue*). Two samples illustrate the natural color of a light wood, maple, and a darker one, oak.

While wood tones dominate, the range covers the entire spectrum, offering the home furnishings and interior decorating industries a choice between saturated tones or lighter ones that reveal the pattern of the wood grain underneath.

In the United States, Formica, a laminate made of sheets of paper or textile infused with melamine resins, had introduced a rich palette into the world of interior design. Formica would not reach Europe until after World War II, in 1946.

Stain on Wood, Gesellschaft für Chemische Industrie [Company for the Chemical Industry] Basel, Switzerland, 1930s, leporello, 25 × 17 cm, 13 panels, Bibliothèque Forney, Paris, call number CC 3736[1920] Plano—Théma PEIN

SOCIÉTÉ ANONYME
des
Matières Colorantes et Produits Chimiques
de
SAINT-DENIS

105, Rue Lafayette, 105
PARIS (Xe)

R. C. PARIS 79.106

COLORANTS POUR PLUMES

Nous présentons ci-contre ceux de nos colorants convenant le mieux pour la teinture des plumes.

Les quantités indiquées s'entendent pour 1 Kg de plumes.

1- 25 grs Jaune naphtol OS
2- 25 grs Jaune métanile ME
3- 25 grs Orangé lumière G
4- 25 grs Orangé 2
5- 35 grs Ponceau NR
6- 35 grs Ponceau N 2 R
7- 35 grs Ponceau N 3 R
• 8- 8 grs Eosine 30.573
• 9- 8 grs Rhodamine B
10- 35 grs Ponceau brillant 4 R
11- 25 grs Crocéine brillante
12- 25 grs Roccelline
13- 25 grs Cérasine
14- 25 grs Nacarat
15- 25 grs Rouge azonaphtol J
16- 25 grs Amaranthe acide
17- 25 grs Fuchsine acide
18- 25 grs Violet acide solide A 2 R
19- 18 grs Violet acide 5 BE
20- 25 grs Violet acide solide 10 B

T. SVP.

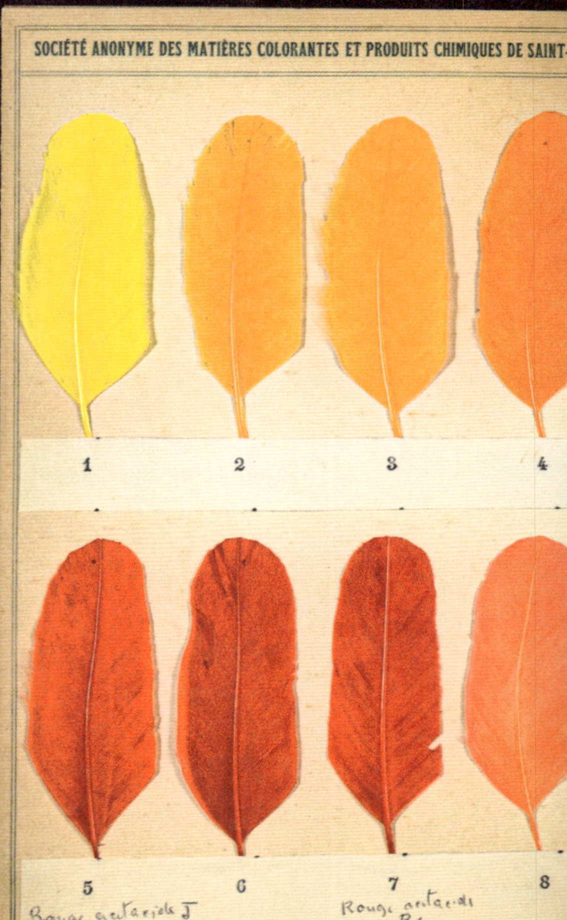

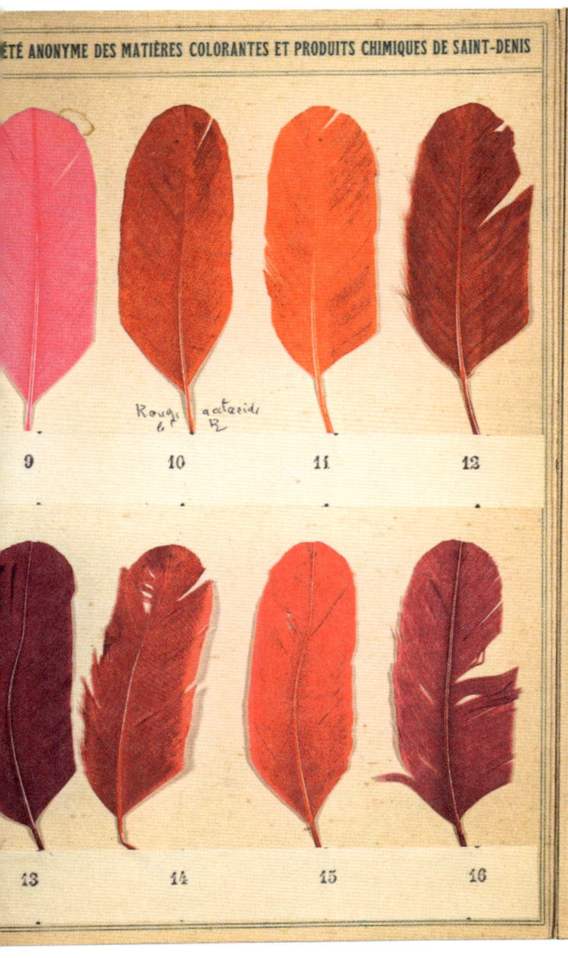
ANONYME DES MATIÈRES COLORANTES ET PRODUITS CHIMIQUES DE SAINT-DENIS
9
10
11
12
13
14
15
16

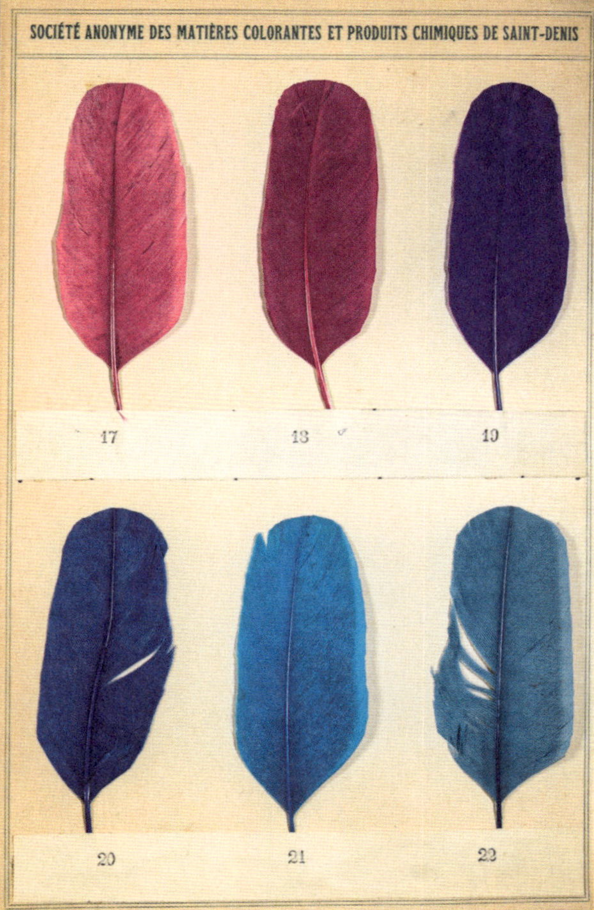
SOCIÉTÉ ANONYME DES MATIÈRES COLORANTES ET PRODUITS CHIMIQUES DE SAINT-DENIS
17
18
19
20
21
22

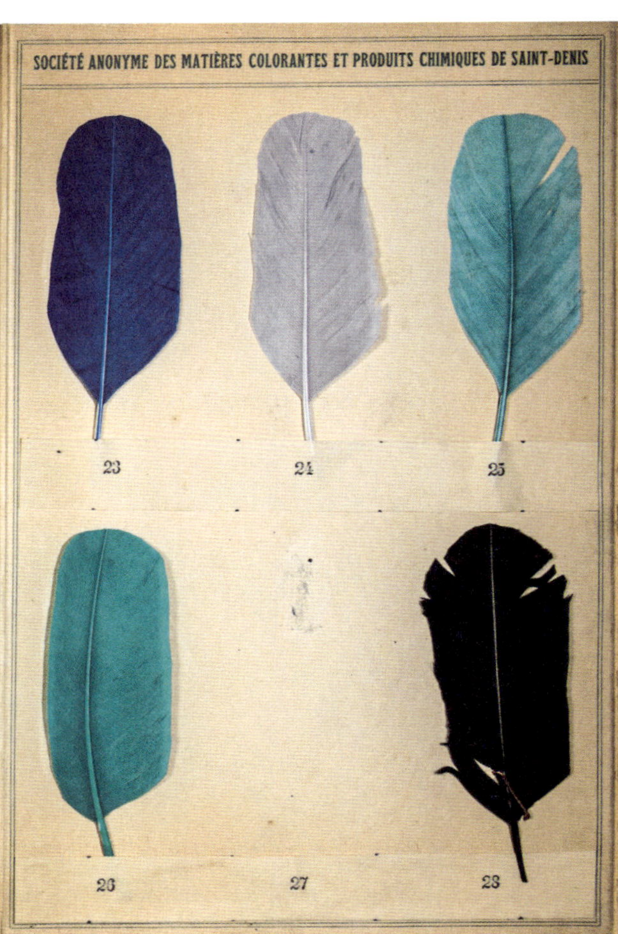
SOCIÉTÉ ANONYME DES MATIÈRES COLORANTES ET PRODUITS CHIMIQUES DE SAINT-DENIS
23
24
25
26
27
28

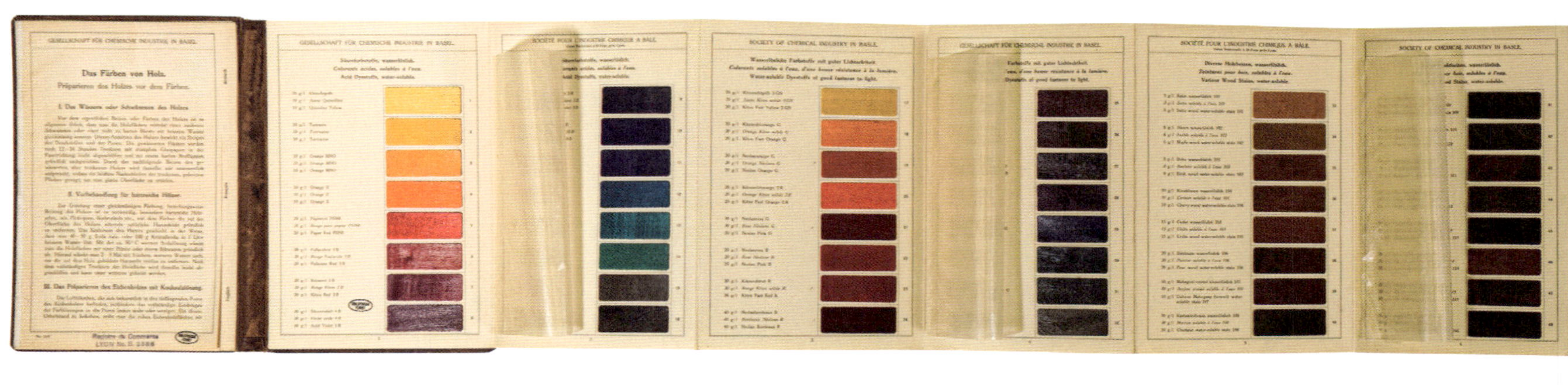
GESELLSCHAFT FÜR CHEMISCHE INDUSTRIE IN BASEL
Das Färben von Holz.
SOCIÉTÉ POUR L'INDUSTRIE CHIMIQUE A BÂLE
SOCIETY OF CHEMICAL INDUSTRY IN BASLE

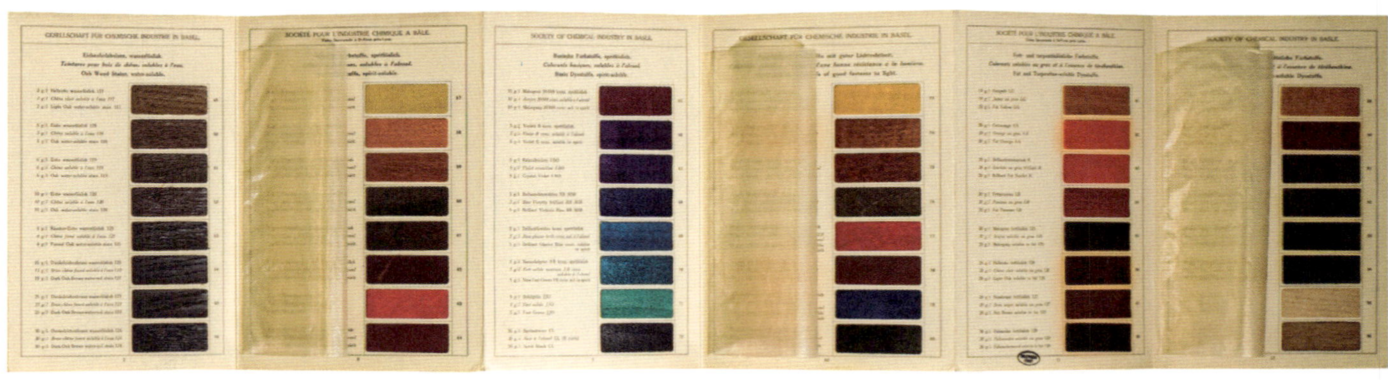
GESELLSCHAFT FÜR CHEMISCHE INDUSTRIE IN BASEL
SOCIÉTÉ POUR L'INDUSTRIE CHIMIQUE A BÂLE
SOCIETY OF CHEMICAL INDUSTRY IN BASLE

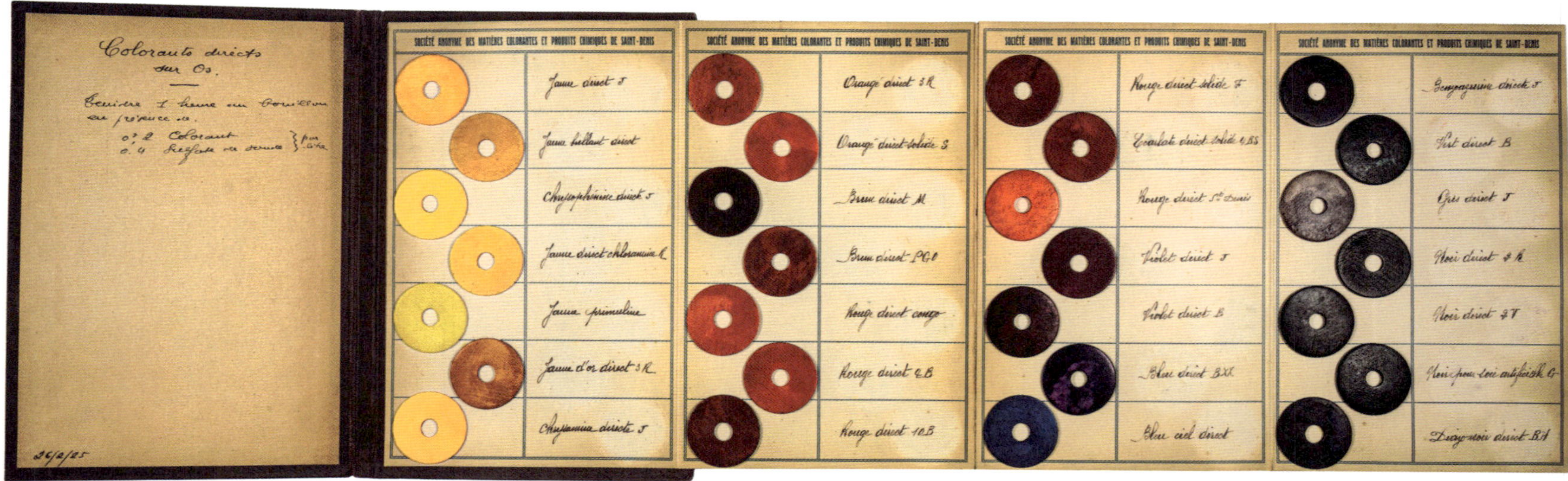
Colorants directs sur Os.
SOCIÉTÉ ANONYME DES MATIÈRES COLORANTES ET PRODUITS CHIMIQUES DE SAINT-DENIS
Jaune direct 5
Orange direct 3R
Brun direct M
Violet direct B
Gris direct 5

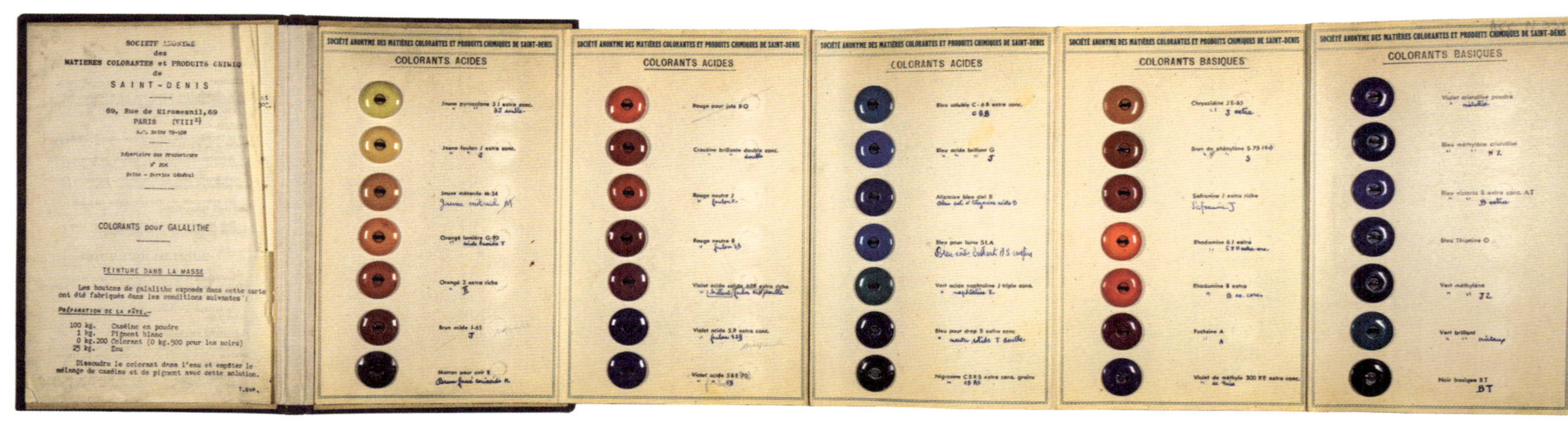
SAINT-DENIS
COLORANTS pour GALALITHE
TEINTURE DANS LA MASSE
SOCIÉTÉ ANONYME DES MATIÈRES COLORANTES ET PRODUITS CHIMIQUES DE SAINT-DENIS
COLORANTS ACIDES
COLORANTS BASIQUES

A Craze for Color

After World War I, the chemical industry used synthetic dyes on innovative materials that it had helped to produce. But it also applied these dyes to materials that had previously been available only in their natural colors. In this way, it established a new environment for color and produced hitherto unknown desires that would soon become needs.

OPPOSITE, MIDDLE

Bone

Bone was used for fashion accessories such as buttons, knobs for walking sticks, jewelry, and pins, or for objects in the home, including doorknobs and small boxes. It was less expensive than ivory but had a similar color—which was the main reason for its use. However, during the 1920s, the Société Anonyme de Saint-Denis colored bone using various dyes. These small bone disks are bright yellow, red, violet, or blue; in contrast, the green, gray, and black colors are all quite dark. The dark shades may have changed over time. A more likely possibility, as this color chart is handwritten, is that these were isolated tests conducted in the laboratories at client request. They showed the colors that had been mastered and those that still needed further work.

Direct Dyes on Bone, Société Anonyme des Matières Colorantes et Produits Chimiques de Saint-Denis, Saint-Denis, February 26, 1925, leporello, 22 × 15 cm, 5 panels, Albi Couleurs, Association Mémoire des Industries de la Couleur, Albi

OPPOSITE, BOTTOM

Galalith

As ivory was rare and expensive, chemists since the mid-nineteenth century had attempted to replace it, leading them to the discovery of the artificial polymers that would later be called plastics. In 1892, one chemist, Auguste Trillat, found a way of integrating casein (milk protein) with formaldehyde. His invention, which he named "milkstone," was improved in the following years and was called Galalith. This substance was harder than horn, shinier than bone, and smooth and silky to the touch, like ivory. It would be used for billiard balls, but especially for buttons, large quantities of which were needed in the clothing industry. Green shades seem to have been difficult to master. There are few of them (only three), and they appear dark.

Dyes for Galalith, Société Anonyme des Matières Colorantes et Produits Chimiques de Saint-Denis, Saint-Denis, c. 1928, leporello, 22 × 15 cm, 6 panels, Albi Couleurs, Association Mémoire des Industries de la Couleur, Albi

NEXT PAGE SPREAD

Fur

The development of dyes for fur, here called Fouramines, is especially astonishing considering that costly fur is less susceptible to trends than textile fibers or clothing accessories. However, several color charts show that dyes for fur were marketed starting in 1927. The dyes were initially used to obtain quite staid colors (grays and browns), but starting in 1928 the colors became bolder.

This innovative color chart was arranged in such a way that the samples were in columns according to the mordant used with the dye. More strikingly, amid a large majority of colors that were dark, beige, or fawn (125 samples out of 137), this 1928 color chart showed that very bright yellows and oranges, some true blues, and even a green were now available as well. Considering that these exact shades appear in a color chart from 1937, it is possible that they found a market among furriers, however narrow it may have been (perhaps for small pieces such as muffs, glove linings, or hat decorations). Once again, the product sample (chrome-tanned rabbit) was crucial, as it provided evidence that the dye did not compromise the softness of the fur. It should be noted that at this time, fur was reserved for married women, like feathers, and for the same reasons: the animality of the material was considered seductive.

Fouramines, Products for Dyeing Furs, n° 30, Société Anonyme des Matières Colorantes et Produits Chimiques de Saint-Denis, Saint-Denis, 1928, leporello, 21.5 × 14.5 cm, 13 panels, Albi Couleurs, Association Mémoire des Industries de la Couleur, Albi

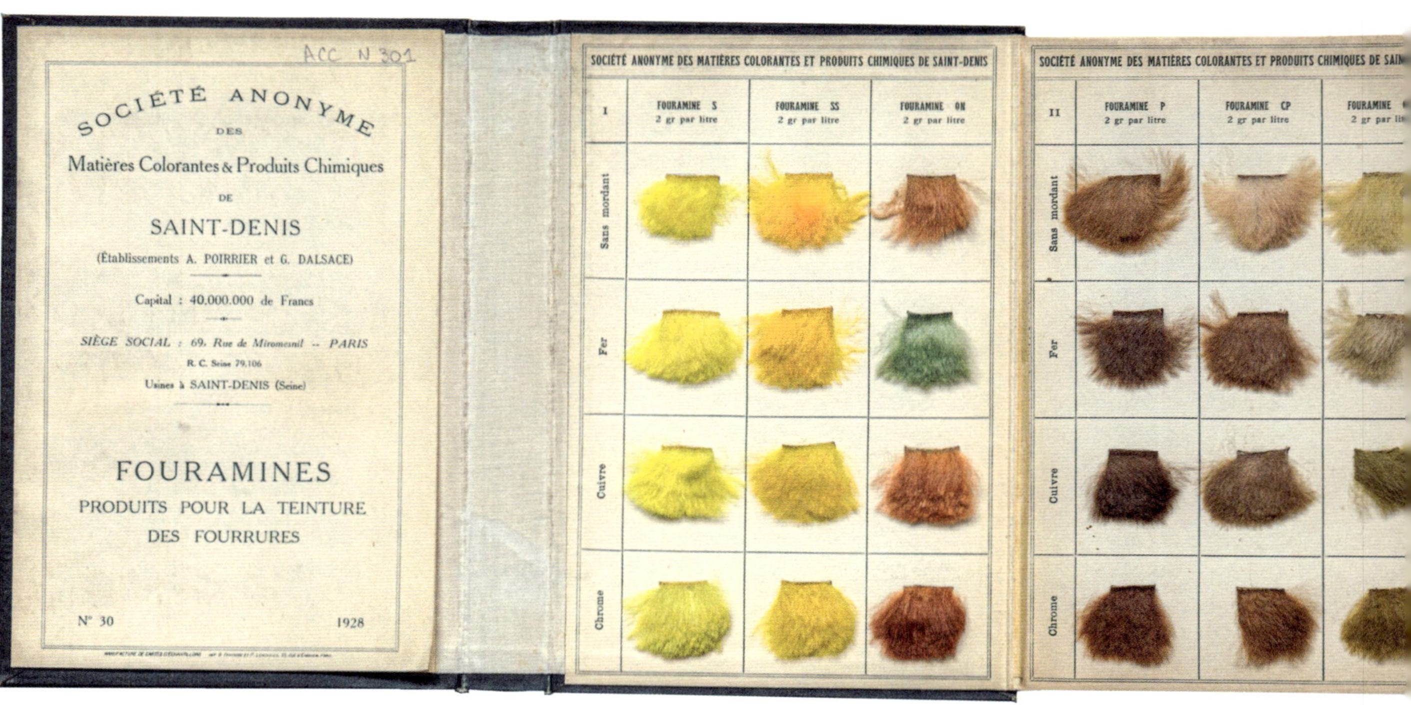
ACC N 301
SOCIÉTÉ ANONYME
DES
Matières Colorantes & Produits Chimiques
DE
SAINT-DENIS
(Établissements A. POIRRIER et G. DALSACE)
Capital : 40.000.000 de Francs
SIÈGE SOCIAL : 69, Rue de Miromesnil -- PARIS
R. C. Seine 79.106
Usines à SAINT-DENIS (Seine)
FOURAMINES
PRODUITS POUR LA TEINTURE
DES FOURRURES
N° 30
1928
SOCIÉTÉ ANONYME DES MATIÈRES COLORANTES ET PRODUITS CHIMIQUES DE SAINT-DENIS
I
FOURAMINE S
2 gr par litre
FOURAMINE SS
2 gr par litre
FOURAMINE ON
2 gr par litre
Sans mordant
Fer
Cuivre
Chrome
II
FOURAMINE P
2 gr par litre
FOURAMINE CP
2 gr par litre

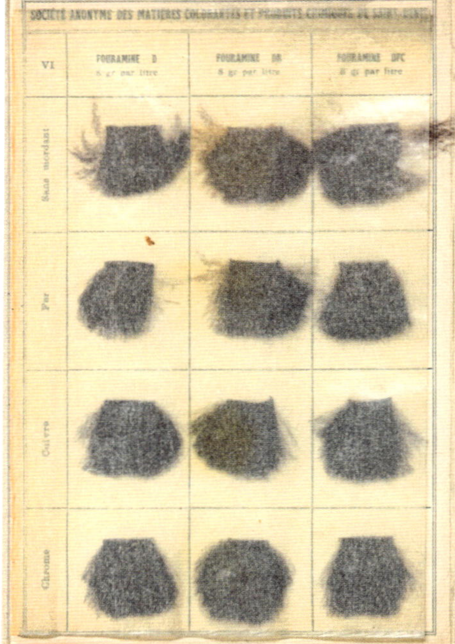
VI
Sans mordant
Fer
Cuivre
Chrome

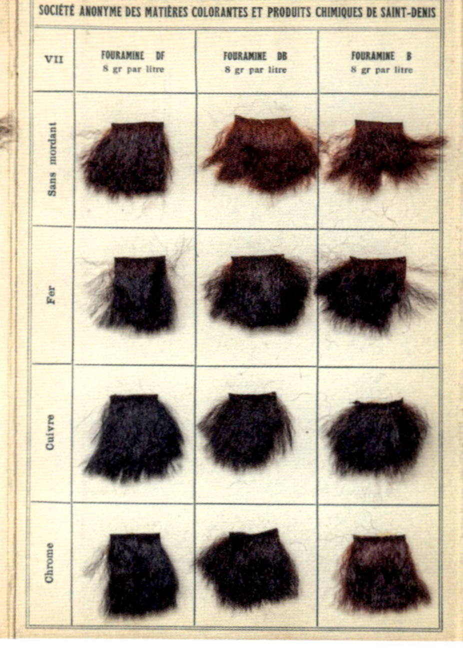
SOCIÉTÉ ANONYME DES MATIÈRES COLORANTES ET PRODUITS CHIMIQUES DE SAINT-DENIS
VII
FOURAMINE DF
8 gr par litre
FOURAMINE DB
8 gr par litre
FOURAMINE B
8 gr par litre
Sans mordant
Fer
Cuivre
Chrome

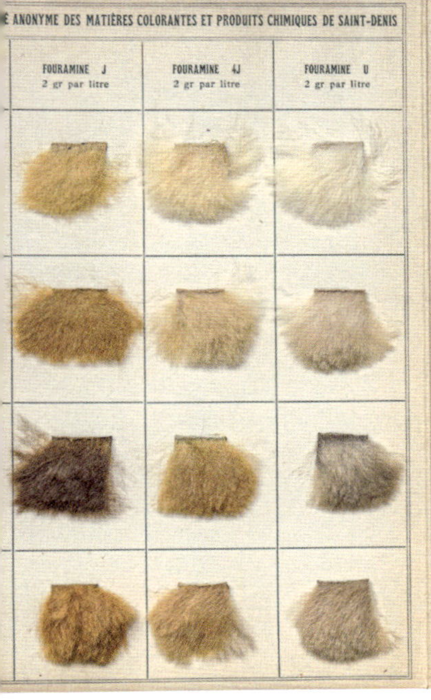

SOCIÉTÉ ANONYME DES MATIÈRES COLORANTES ET PRODUITS CHIMIQUES DE SAINT-DENIS

IV	BRUN FOURAMINE AP 2 gr par litre	FOURAMINE BA 2 gr par litre	FOURAMINE SA 2 gr par litre
Sans mordant			
Fer			
Cuivre			
Chrome			

SOCIÉTÉ ANONYME DES MATIÈRES COLORANTES ET PRODUITS CHIMIQUES DE SAINT-DENIS

V	FOURAMINE RS 2 gr par litre	FOURAMINE 4R 4 gr par litre	BRUN ROUGE FOURAMINE GR 2 gr par litre
Sans mordant			
Fer			
Cuivre			
Chrome			

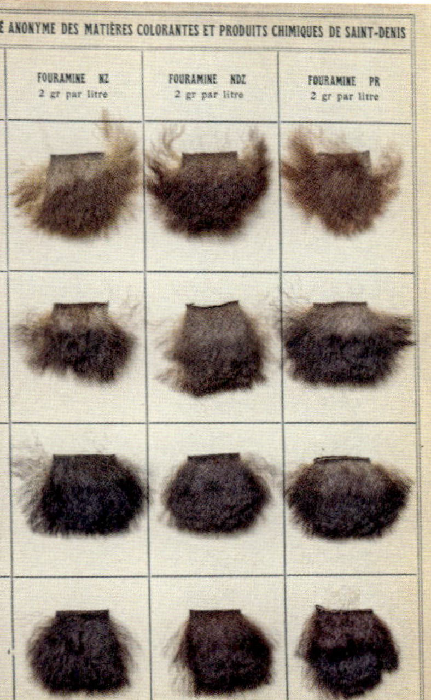

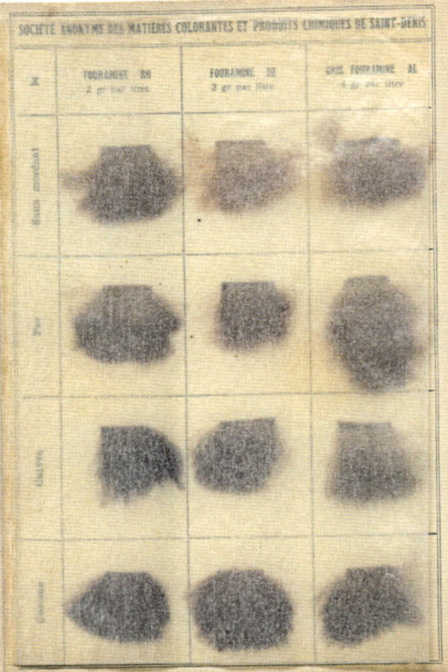

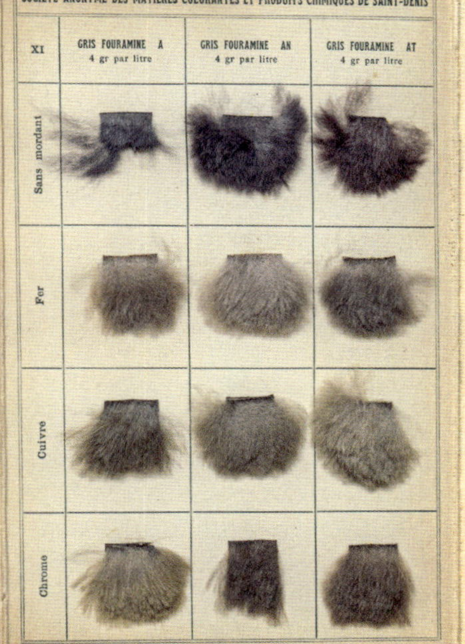

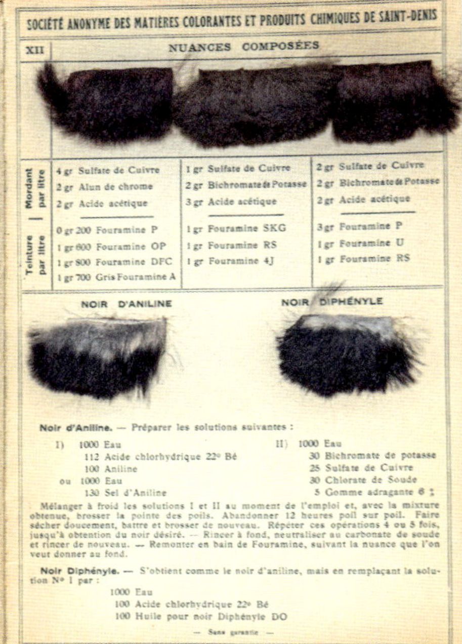
SOCIÉTÉ ANONYME DES MATIÈRES COLORANTES ET PRODUITS CHIMIQUES DE SAINT-DENIS

XII NUANCES COMPOSÉES

Mordant par litre	4 gr Sulfate de Cuivre 2 gr Alun de chrome 2 gr Acide acétique	1 gr Sulfate de Cuivre 2 gr Bichromate de Potasse 3 gr Acide acétique	2 gr Sulfate de Cuivre 2 gr Bichromate de Potasse 2 gr Acide acétique
Teinture par litre	0 gr 200 Fouramine P 1 gr 600 Fouramine OP 1 gr 800 Fouramine DFC 1 gr 700 Gris Fouramine A	1 gr Fouramine SKG 1 gr Fouramine RS 1 gr Fouramine 4J	3 gr Fouramine P 1 gr Fouramine U 1 gr Fouramine RS

NOIR D'ANILINE NOIR DIPHÉNYLE

Noir d'Aniline. — Préparer les solutions suivantes :

I) 1000 Eau
112 Acide chlorhydrique 22° Bé
100 Aniline
ou 1000 Eau
130 Sel d'Aniline

II) 1000 Eau
30 Bichromate de potasse
25 Sulfate de Cuivre
30 Chlorate de Soude
5 Gomme adragante 6 %

Mélanger à froid les solutions I et II au moment de l'emploi et, avec la mixture obtenue, brosser la pointe des poils. Abandonner 12 heures poil sur poil. Faire sécher doucement, battre et brosser de nouveau. Répéter ces opérations 4 ou 5 fois, jusqu'à obtention du noir désiré. — Rincer à fond, neutraliser au carbonate de soude et rincer de nouveau. — Remonter en bain de Fouramine, suivant la nuance que l'on veut donner au fond.

Noir Diphényle. — S'obtient comme le noir d'aniline, mais en remplaçant la solution N° 1 par :

1000 Eau
100 Acide chlorhydrique 22° Bé
100 Huile pour noir Diphényle DO

— Sans garantie —

OPPOSITE, TOP

Seasonal Colors, 1939

Color charts reflected the chemical industry's close attention to clients in order to meet—or even anticipate—their expectations. This special relationship, especially in the fashion industries, led the Société Anonyme des Matières Colorantes de Saint-Denis to offer seasonal colors in 1939, something that the silk producers and ribbon makers had been doing since the late nineteenth century.[16] This table in this color chart is technical, but the order of the twenty samples highlights each shade by featuring complementary colors. In addition, poetic names were added for the colors, which include a tempting *Orange Marmalade* and an intimate *Blue of Your Eyes*. However, choices such as *Vitriol Green* and *Grass Snake* are more puzzling. The new forecasting aspect of the color chart expanded after World War II in the predictions of trend forecasters.

Fashion Colors on Silk Fabric, 1939 Season, Société Anonyme des Matières Colorantes et Produits Chimiques de Saint-Denis, Saint-Denis, 1939, box, 21.5 × 15 cm, Albi Couleurs, Association Mémoire des Industries de la Couleur, Albi

Color Even in the Most Technological Applications

While the chemical industry provided color for the fashion and interior design worlds, it also offered color to industries that were decidedly less glamorous, as if no material should be excluded from the new chromatic world it was mapping out.

OPPOSITE, MIDDLE

Rubber

As indicated by the information on the inside of this color chart's cover, the Société Anonyme des Matières Colorantes had established a laboratory for exploring new opportunities, including coloring rubber.

The arrival of pliable materials was a revolution whose scope is difficult to perceive today.[17] The vulcanization of latex in the 1850s led to many applications in the clothing industry and especially in the mechanical industries, particularly automobiles.

The traditional orange color of rubber was a by-product of the necessity of adding a second substance to latex in order to make it more flexible. Ocher was perfect, and the rubber industry was one of the important outlets for ocher producers of the Vaucluse department of France in the nineteenth century, until ocher was replaced by lampblack.[18] Synthetic dyes made it possible to move away from these two colors, ocher and lampblack, to much more extensive color ranges. Here there are fourteen colors presented on disks attached to the backing by small rivets. The idea of coloring rubber was appealing, but, unfortunately, these "Vulcafixe" dyes seem to have left few traces.

Dyes for Rubber, n° 31, Société Anonyme des Matières Colorantes et Produits Chimiques de Saint-Denis, Saint-Denis, 1928, pamphlet, 21.5 × 15 cm, 3 folds, Albi Couleurs, Association Mémoire des Industries de la Couleur, Albi

NEXT PAGE SPREAD

Varnish

Transparency was another contribution of chemistry. Transparency was one of the advantages of cellophane, a film made from cellulose that was discovered by a Swiss engineer in 1908. In this color chart, the manufacturer used cellophane to create "windows" for viewing the forty-nine available varnish colors. As of 1917, cellophane, which created a barrier against microorganisms, was produced industrially for food packaging. But new outlets were soon found for this material in the theater, and before long in color photography and cinema as well: colored filters to alter light.

Dyes for Varnish, n° 23, Société Anonyme des Matières Colorantes et Produits Chimiques de Saint-Denis, Saint-Denis, 1927, leporello, 21.6 × 15 cm, Sennelier family collection, Paris

OPPOSITE, BOTTOM

Cellophane

Research sometimes leads to discovering strange objects. This box contains sixteen cubes with metal borders. Three sides have a film of colored cellophane, and the fourth features an engraved code. Apparently, each cube could be picked up and held in the light to assess the color of the film. The range consists only of yellows and oranges, but this is clearly a color chart, as confirmed by the name *Official Range* on the cover. It has not been possible to identify the company. The set preserves its mystery and beauty.

Official Range of Cellophanes, I.D.P., France (?), 1930s (?), box, 15 × 15 cm, 16 cubes, Albi Couleurs, Association Mémoire des Industries de la Couleur, Albi

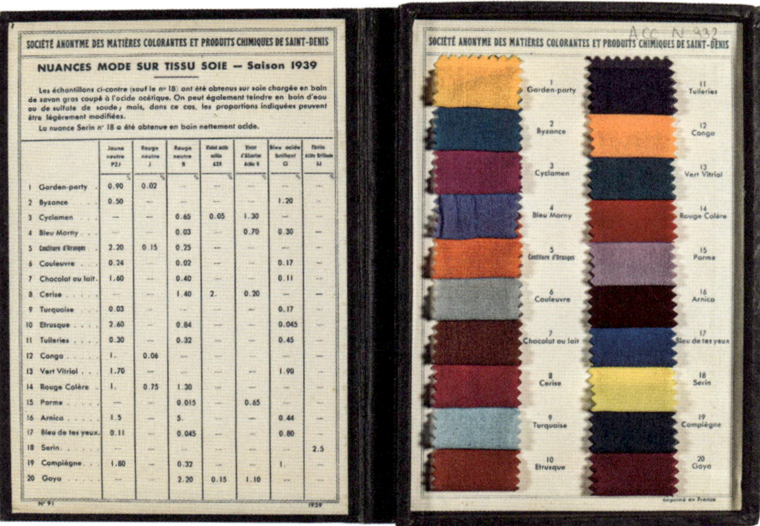
SOCIÉTÉ ANONYME DES MATIÈRES COLORANTES ET PRODUITS CHIMIQUES DE SAINT-DENIS
NUANCES MODE SUR TISSU SOIE — Saison 1939

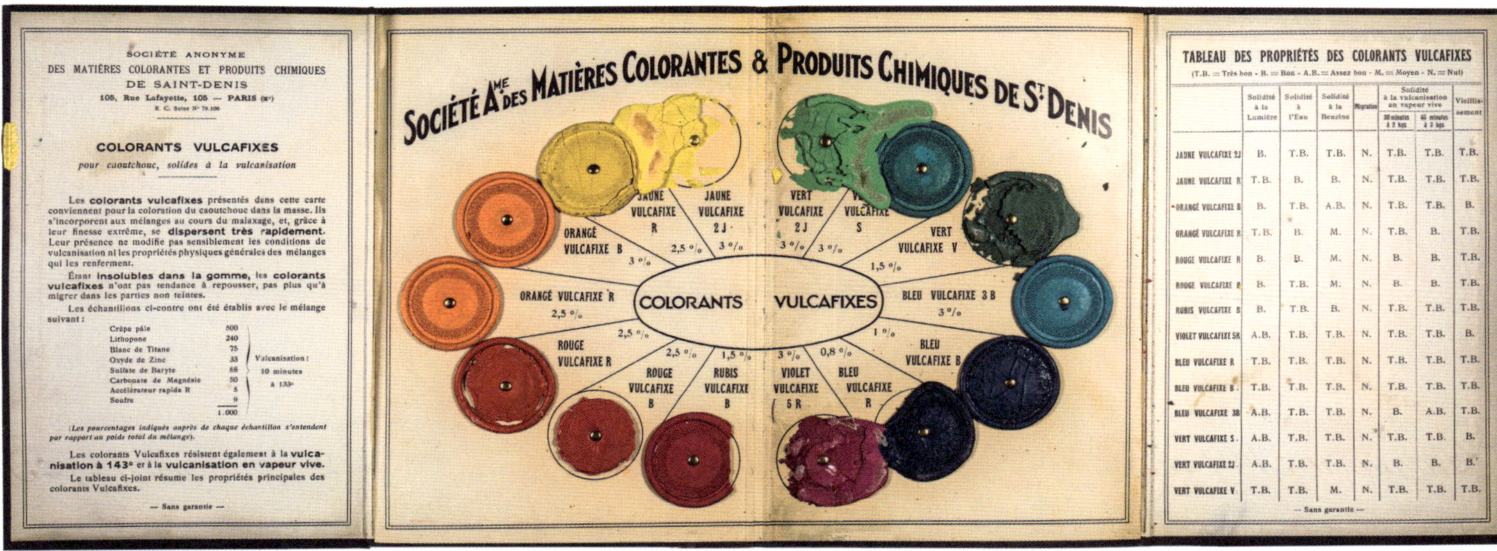
SOCIÉTÉ ANONYME
DES MATIÈRES COLORANTES ET PRODUITS CHIMIQUES
DE SAINT-DENIS
COLORANTS VULCAFIXES
pour caoutchouc, solides à la vulcanisation
SOCIÉTÉ Ame DES MATIÈRES COLORANTES & PRODUITS CHIMIQUES DE St DENIS
COLORANTS VULCAFIXES
TABLEAU DES PROPRIÉTÉS DES COLORANTS VULCAFIXES

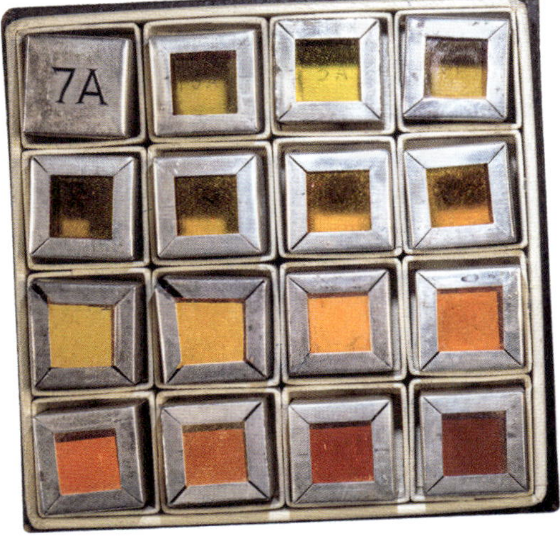
7A

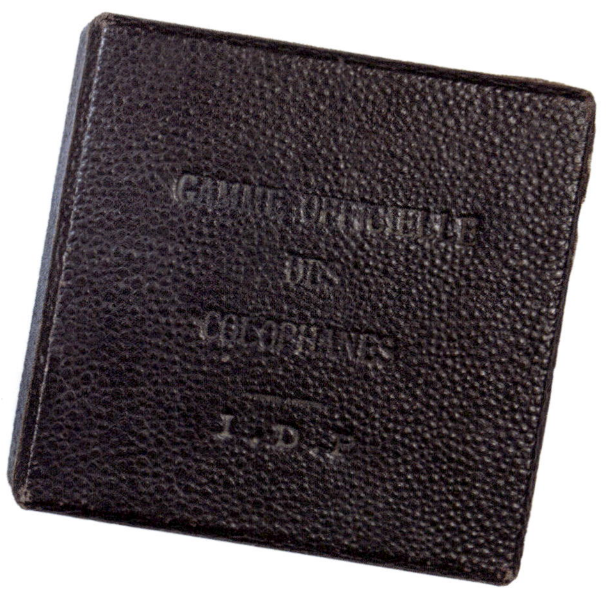

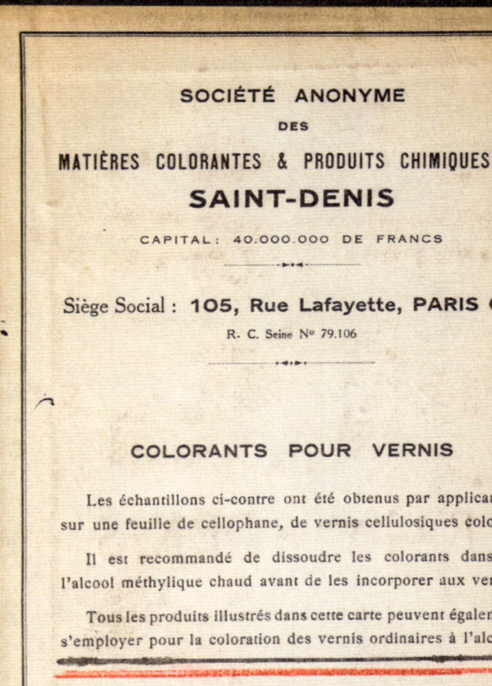

SOCIÉTÉ ANONYME
DES
MATIÈRES COLORANTES & PRODUITS CHIMIQUES DE
SAINT-DENIS

CAPITAL : 40.000.000 DE FRANCS

Siège Social : **105, Rue Lafayette, PARIS (x^e)**
R. C. Seine N° 79.106

COLORANTS POUR VERNIS

Les échantillons ci-contre ont été obtenus par application, sur une feuille de cellophane, de vernis cellulosiques colorés.

Il est recommandé de dissoudre les colorants dans de l'alcool méthylique chaud avant de les incorporer aux vernis.

Tous les produits illustrés dans cette carte peuvent également s'employer pour la coloration des vernis ordinaires à l'alcool.

N° 23 Sans Garantie 1927

SOCIÉTÉ ANONYME
DES MATIÈRES COLORANTES & PRODUITS CHIMIQUES
DE SAINT-DENIS

VUE DE L'USINE A. C.

SOCIÉTÉ ANONYME DES MATIÈRES COLORANTES & PRODUITS CHIMIQUES DE SAINT-DENIS

22	BLEU THIONINE G 1 o/oo
23	VERT MÉTHYLÈNE 1 o/oo
24	VERT MALACHITE J 3 E CRISTAUX 0,75 o/oo
25	VERT BRILLANT 1 o/oo

COLORANTS INSOLUBLES DANS L'EAU

26	BASE D'AURAMINE 2 o/oo
27	CHRYSOÏNE INSOLUBLE 2 o/oo
28	JAUNE AMIDO T 2 o/oo

4

SOCIÉTÉ ANONYME DES MATIÈRES COLORANTES & PRODUITS CHIMIQUES DE SAINT-DENIS

29	JAUNE B 2 o/oo
30	JAUNE AMIDO 7200 2 o/oo
31	ORANGÉ 2 INSOLUBLE 2 o/oo
32	ORANGÉ R INSOLUBLE 2 o/oo
33	ORANGÉ 2 R INSOLUBLE 2 o/oo
34	BASE DE CHRYSOÏDINE JE 2 o/oo
35	BASE DE CHRYSOÏDINE RE 2 o/oo

5

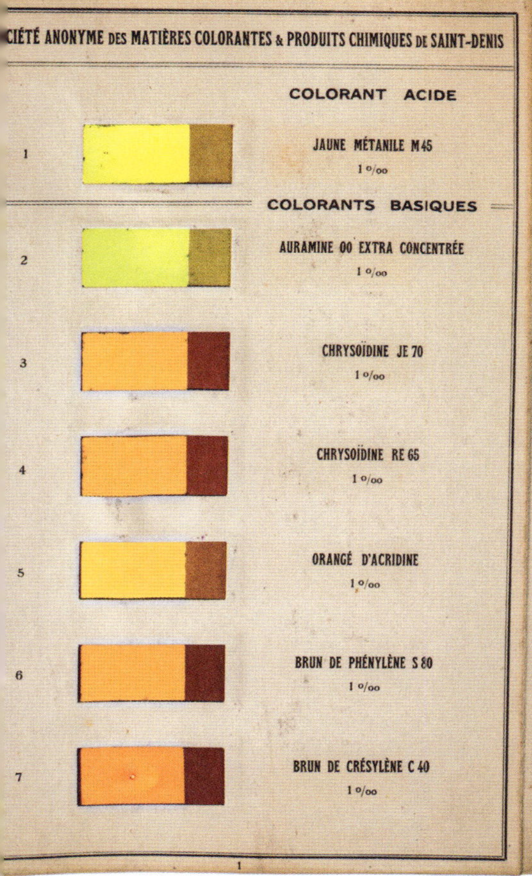
CIÉTÉ ANONYME DES MATIÈRES COLORANTES & PRODUITS CHIMIQUES DE SAINT-DENIS
COLORANT ACIDE
1 JAUNE MÉTANILE M45 1 ‰
COLORANTS BASIQUES
2 AURAMINE 00 EXTRA CONCENTRÉE 1 ‰
3 CHRYSOÏDINE JE 70 1 ‰
4 CHRYSOÏDINE RE 65 1 ‰
5 ORANGÉ D'ACRIDINE 1 ‰
6 BRUN DE PHÉNYLÈNE S 80 1 ‰
7 BRUN DE CRÉSYLÈNE C 40 1 ‰
1

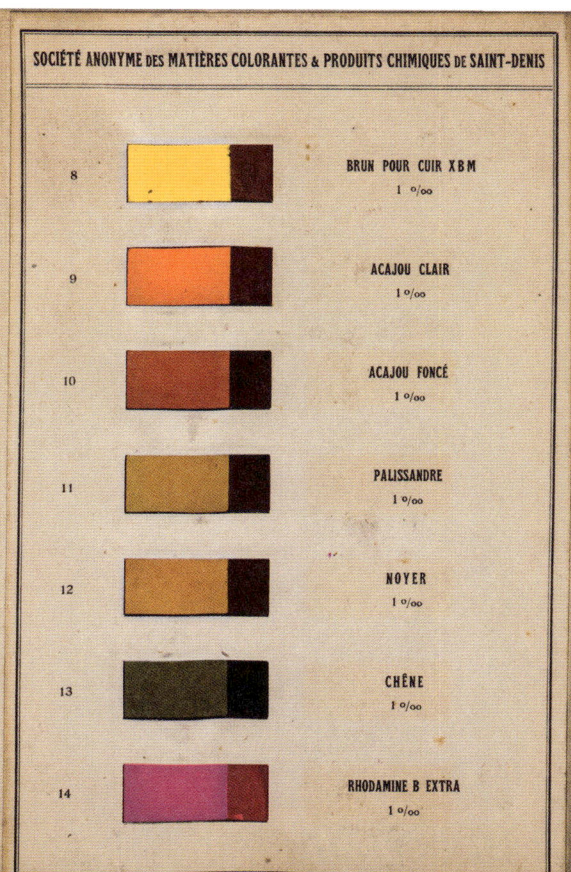
SOCIÉTÉ ANONYME DES MATIÈRES COLORANTES & PRODUITS CHIMIQUES DE SAINT-DENIS
8 BRUN POUR CUIR XBM 1 ‰
9 ACAJOU CLAIR 1 ‰
10 ACAJOU FONCÉ 1 ‰
11 PALISSANDRE 1 ‰
12 NOYER 1 ‰
13 CHÊNE 1 ‰
14 RHODAMINE B EXTRA 1 ‰
2

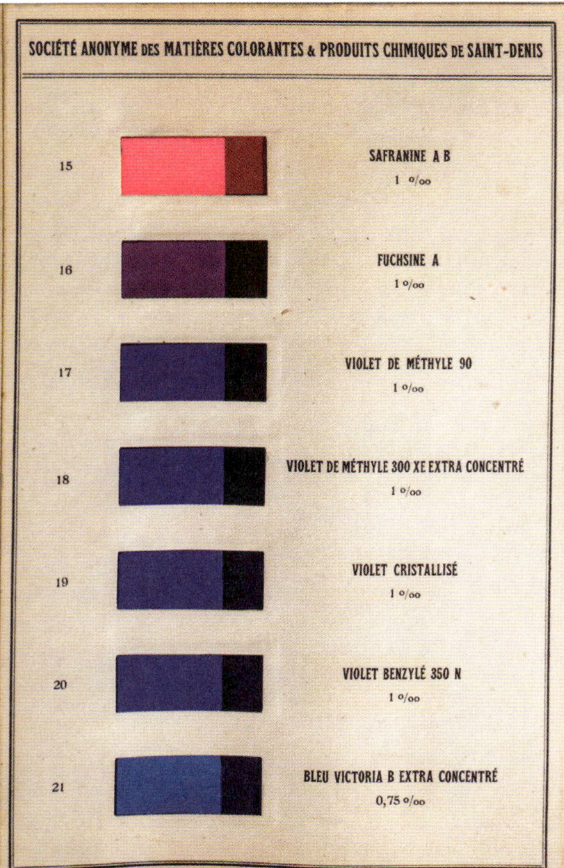
SOCIÉTÉ ANONYME DES MATIÈRES COLORANTES & PRODUITS CHIMIQUES DE SAINT-DENIS
15 SAFRANINE A B 1 ‰
16 FUCHSINE A 1 ‰
17 VIOLET DE MÉTHYLE 90 1 ‰
18 VIOLET DE MÉTHYLE 300 XE EXTRA CONCENTRÉ 1 ‰
19 VIOLET CRISTALLISÉ 1 ‰
20 VIOLET BENZYLÉ 350 N 1 ‰
21 BLEU VICTORIA B EXTRA CONCENTRÉ 0,75 ‰
3

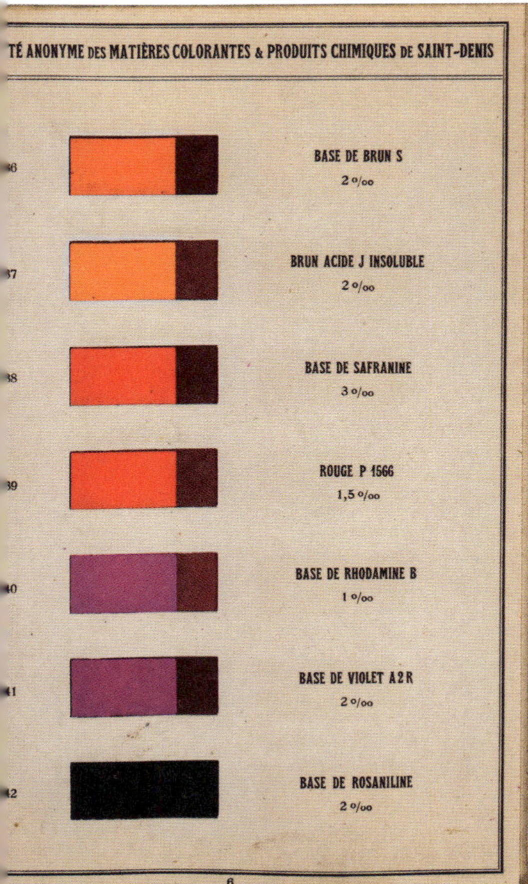
TÉ ANONYME DES MATIÈRES COLORANTES & PRODUITS CHIMIQUES DE SAINT-DENIS
BASE DE BRUN S 2 ‰
37 BRUN ACIDE J INSOLUBLE 2 ‰
BASE DE SAFRANINE 3 ‰
ROUGE P 1566 1,5 ‰
BASE DE RHODAMINE B 1 ‰
BASE DE VIOLET A2R 2 ‰
BASE DE ROSANILINE 2 ‰
6

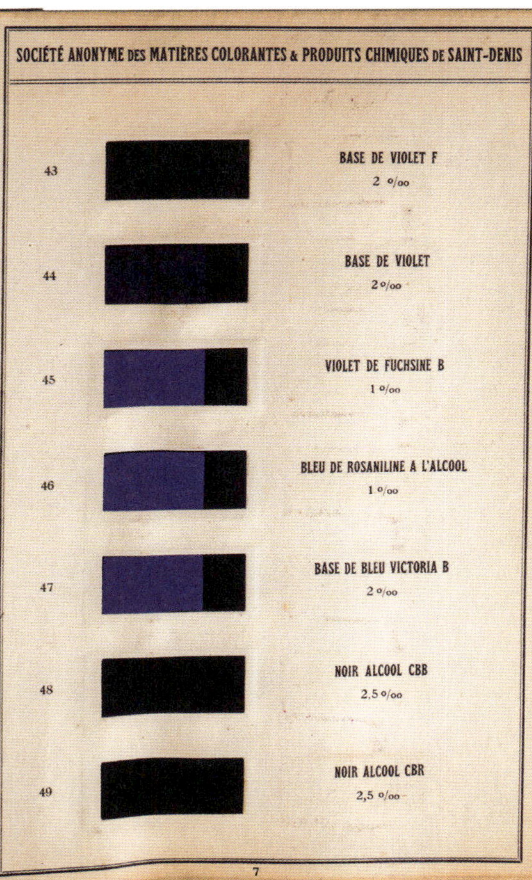
SOCIÉTÉ ANONYME DES MATIÈRES COLORANTES & PRODUITS CHIMIQUES DE SAINT-DENIS
43 BASE DE VIOLET F 2 ‰
44 BASE DE VIOLET 2 ‰
45 VIOLET DE FUCHSINE B 1 ‰
46 BLEU DE ROSANILINE A L'ALCOOL 1 ‰
47 BASE DE BLEU VICTORIA B 2 ‰
48 NOIR ALCOOL CBB 2,5 ‰
49 NOIR ALCOOL CBR 2,5 ‰
7

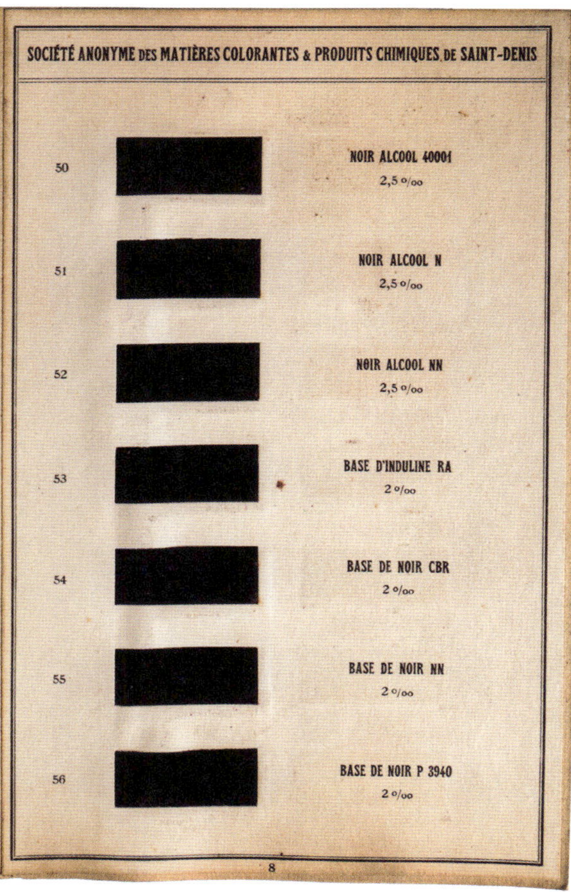
SOCIÉTÉ ANONYME DES MATIÈRES COLORANTES & PRODUITS CHIMIQUES DE SAINT-DENIS
50 NOIR ALCOOL 40001 2,5 ‰
51 NOIR ALCOOL N 2,5 ‰
52 NOIR ALCOOL NN 2,5 ‰
53 BASE D'INDULINE RA 2 ‰
54 BASE DE NOIR CBR 2 ‰
55 BASE DE NOIR NN 2 ‰
56 BASE DE NOIR P 3940 2 ‰
8

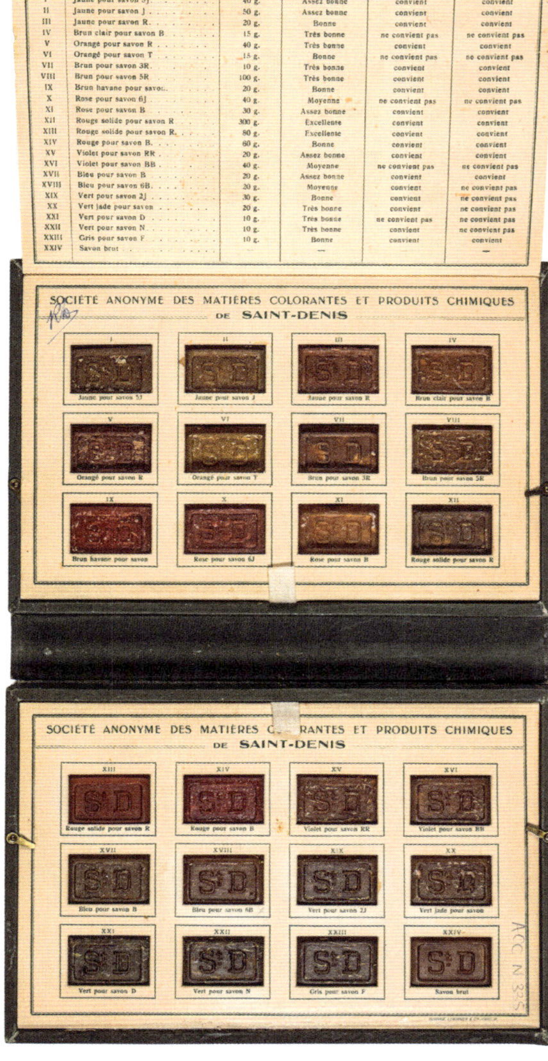

DÉSIGNATION DES COLORANTS		QUANTITÉS UTILISÉES pour la coloration des Échantillons	SOLIDITÉ A LA LUMIÈRE	SAPONIFICATION A FROID	SAPONIFICATION A CHAUD
		Pour 100 kg.			
I	Jaune pour savon 3J	40 g.	Assez bonne	convient	convient
II	Jaune pour savon J	50 g.	Assez bonne	convient	convient
III	Jaune pour savon R	20 g.	Bonne	convient	convient
IV	Brun clair pour savon B	15 g.	Très bonne	ne convient pas	ne convient pas
V	Orangé pour savon R	40 g.	Très bonne	convient	convient
VI	Orangé pour savon T	15 g.	Bonne	ne convient pas	ne convient pas
VII	Brun pour savon 3R	10 g.	Très bonne	convient	convient
VIII	Brun pour savon 5R	100 g.	Très bonne	convient	convient
IX	Brun havane pour savon	20 g.	Bonne	convient	convient
X	Rose pour savon 6J	40 g.	Moyenne	ne convient pas	ne convient pas
XI	Rose pour savon B	30 g.	Assez bonne	convient	convient
XII	Rouge solide pour savon R	300 g.	Excellente	convient	convient
XIII	Rouge solide pour savon R	80 g.	Excellente	convient	convient
XIV	Rouge pour savon B	60 g.	Bonne	convient	convient
XV	Violet pour savon RR	20 g.	Assez bonne	convient	convient
XVI	Violet pour savon BB	40 g.	Moyenne	ne convient pas	ne convient pas
XVII	Bleu pour savon B	20 g.	Assez bonne	convient	convient
XVIII	Bleu pour savon 6B	20 g.	Moyenne	convient	ne convient pas
XIX	Vert pour savon 2J	30 g.	Bonne	convient	ne convient pas
XX	Vert jade pour savon	20 g.	Très bonne	convient	ne convient pas
XXI	Vert pour savon D	10 g.	Très bonne	ne convient pas	ne convient pas
XXII	Vert pour savon N	10 g.	Très bonne	convient	ne convient pas
XXIII	Gris pour savon F	10 g.	Bonne	convient	convient
XXIV	Savon brut	—	—	—	—

ABOVE

Soap

The Société Anonyme des Matières Colorantes et Produits Chimiques de Saint-Denis produced a marketing tool showing dyes for saponification. The twenty-four samples, little bars of molded soap decorated with the company's initials, were carefully displayed in a cardboard box. The plates had cut-outs for accessing the products. Today they have the appearance of dull browns and reds, but their colors must have been brighter and more distinctive originally, as shown by the list of dyes: all tones were represented, and in several shades, with one sample left plain as a point of comparison. Information about the colors' resistance to light and their stability during the saponification process is carefully specified, together with the formula, which is given for 100 kg. However, there is no mention of the skin's tolerance for the dyes. This concern came later.

Dyes for Soap, nº 33, Société Anonyme des Matières Colorantes et Produits Chimiques de Saint-Denis, Saint-Denis, 1930, box, 14.5 × 22 × 4 cm, containing 2 plates, Albi Couleurs, Association Mémoire des Industries de la Couleur, Albi

OPPOSITE

Fluorescence

Fluorescence had been understood since the mid-nineteenth century, but it was not until 1929 that dyes with this property were industrially produced. It was then necessary to develop a color chart that could reproduce their particular characteristics. The Société Anonyme des Matières Colorantes et Produits Chimiques de Saint-Denis illustrated various applications in this color chart: the coloring of various textile fibers (the first two panels), the detection of manufacturing flaws in prints (panel 3), and then the dyeing of paper and even of ink, which could be used for printing documents such as checks. Finally, there are three small bags (one has disappeared) containing powders for makeup. The formula advises mixing them with purified water and starch and applying them onto skin to which petroleum jelly has been applied.

This color chart uses the same marketing approach (a collection of samples) as did the authors of the very first treatises on dyeing after the discovery of synthetic color.[19] With fluorescent salts, new horizons opened up for chemists' imagination. What applications could be found? Their field of choice would be the detergent and paper industries, for, by absorbing light in the ultraviolet range and re-emitting it in blue, the impression of whiteness in the products the dyes colored was accentuated.

Fluorescence, nº 88, Société Anonyme des Matières Colorantes et Produits Chimiques de Saint-Denis, Saint-Denis, 1938, leporello, 21.5 × 14.5 cm, 5 panels, Albi Couleurs, Association Mémoire des Industries de la Couleur, Albi

NEXT PAGE SPREAD

Infrared Index

War was on the horizon again, mobilizing the chemical field to move into military research. Here, raffia was colored with dyes that produced an infrared index identical to that of chlorophyll. A photograph intended for the Ministry of the Air Force was evidence of the camouflaging properties of products dyed these colors. The handwritten notes reveal the urgent atmosphere in which this color chart was developed. The description of the conditions in which the photograph was taken offers a poetic touch to an era that would end with darkness and barbarism: "5-second pause, partially cloudy sky, May 6, 1940 at 9:30 am."

Infrared Dye for Raffia, Société Anonyme des Matières Colorantes et Produits Chimiques de Saint-Denis, Saint-Denis, May 1940, leporello, 22 × 14.5 cm, 5 panels, Albi Couleurs, Association Mémoire des Industries de la Couleur, Albi

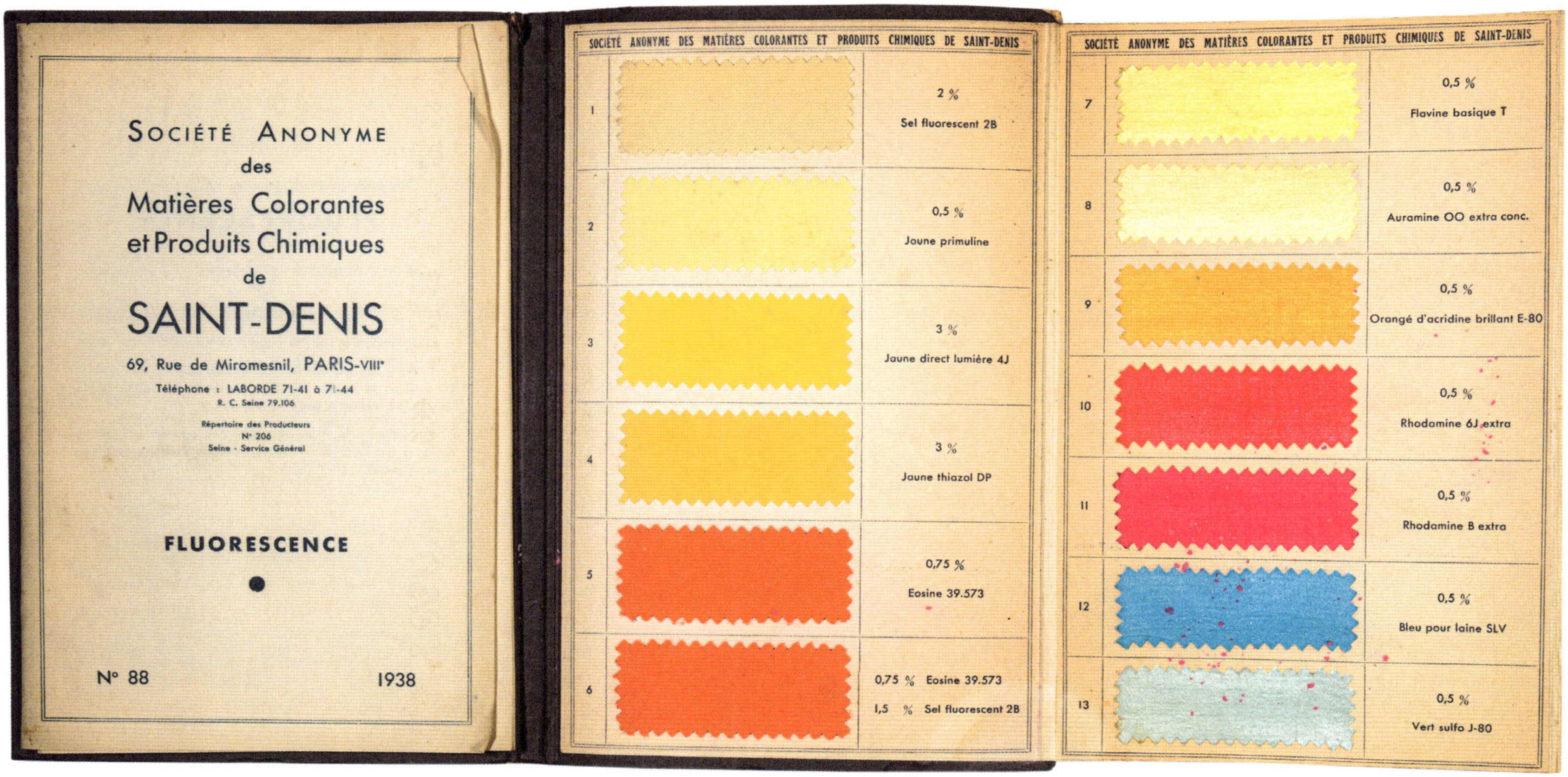

Société Anonyme
des
Matières Colorantes
et Produits Chimiques
de
SAINT-DENIS

69, Rue de Miromesnil, PARIS-VIIIe

Téléphone : LABORDE 71-41 à 71-44
R. C. Seine 79.106

Répertoire des Producteurs
N° 206
Seine - Service Général

FLUORESCENCE

N° 88 1938

SOCIÉTÉ ANONYME DES MATIÈRES COLORANTES ET PRODUITS CHIMIQUES DE SAINT-DENIS

1		2 % Sel fluorescent 2B
2		0,5 % Jaune primuline
3		3 % Jaune direct lumière 4J
4		3 % Jaune thiazol DP
5		0,75 % Eosine 39.573
6		0,75 % Eosine 39.573 1,5 % Sel fluorescent 2B

SOCIÉTÉ ANONYME DES MATIÈRES COLORANTES ET PRODUITS CHIMIQUES DE SAINT-DENIS

7		0,5 % Flavine basique T
8		0,5 % Auramine OO extra conc.
9		0,5 % Orangé d'acridine brillant E-80
10		0,5 % Rhodamine 6J extra
11		0,5 % Rhodamine B extra
12		0,5 % Bleu pour laine SLV
13		0,5 % Vert sulfo J-80

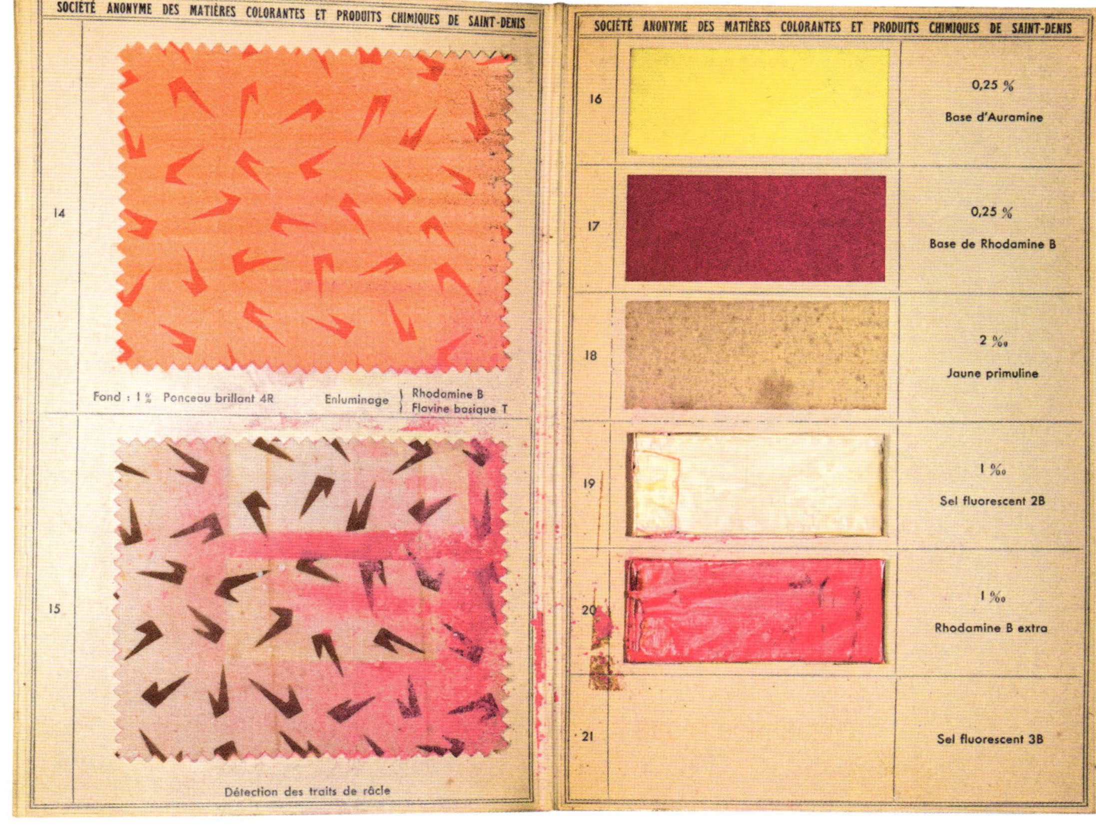

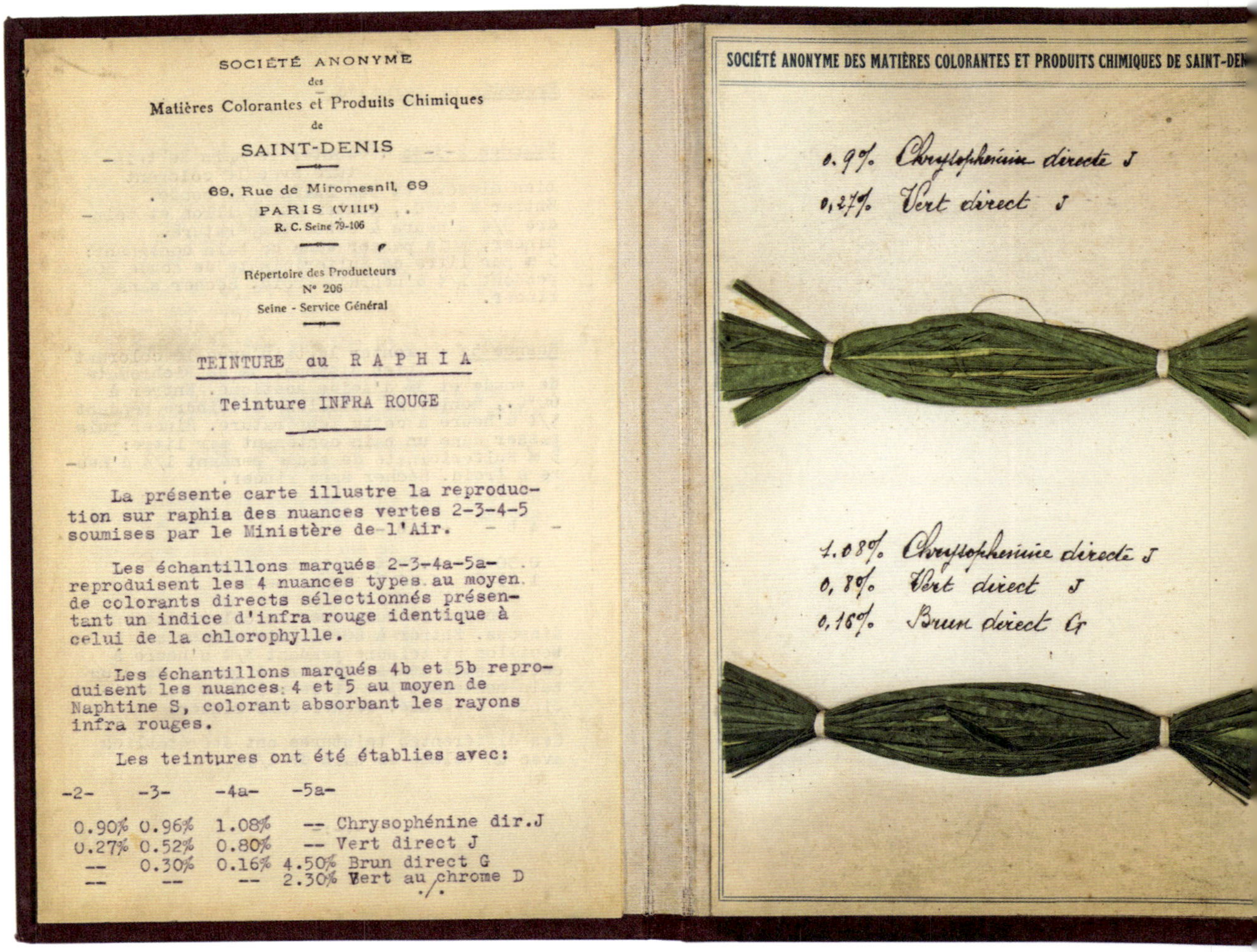

SOCIÉTÉ ANONYME
des
Matières Colorantes et Produits Chimiques
de
SAINT-DENIS

69, Rue de Miromesnil, 69
PARIS (VIIIe)
R. C. Seine 79-106

Répertoire des Producteurs
N° 206
Seine - Service Général

TEINTURE au R A P H I A

Teinture INFRA ROUGE

La présente carte illustre la reproduction sur raphia des nuances vertes 2-3-4-5 soumises par le Ministère de l'Air.

Les échantillons marqués 2-3-4a-5a-reproduisent les 4 nuances types au moyen de colorants directs sélectionnés présentant un indice d'infra rouge identique à celui de la chlorophylle.

Les échantillons marqués 4b et 5b reproduisent les nuances 4 et 5 au moyen de Naphtine S, colorant absorbant les rayons infra rouges.

Les teintures ont été établies avec:

-2-	-3-	-4a-	-5a-	
0.90%	0.96%	1.08%	--	Chrysophénine dir.J
0.27%	0.52%	0.80%	--	Vert direct J
--	0.30%	0.16%	4.50%	Brun direct G
--	--	--	2.30%	Vert au chrome D

./.

SOCIÉTÉ ANONYME DES MATIÈRES COLORANTES ET PRODUITS CHIMIQUES DE SAINT-DEN

0.9% Chrysophénine directe J
0,27% Vert direct J

1.08% Chrysophénine directe J
0,8% Vert direct J
0,16% Brun direct G

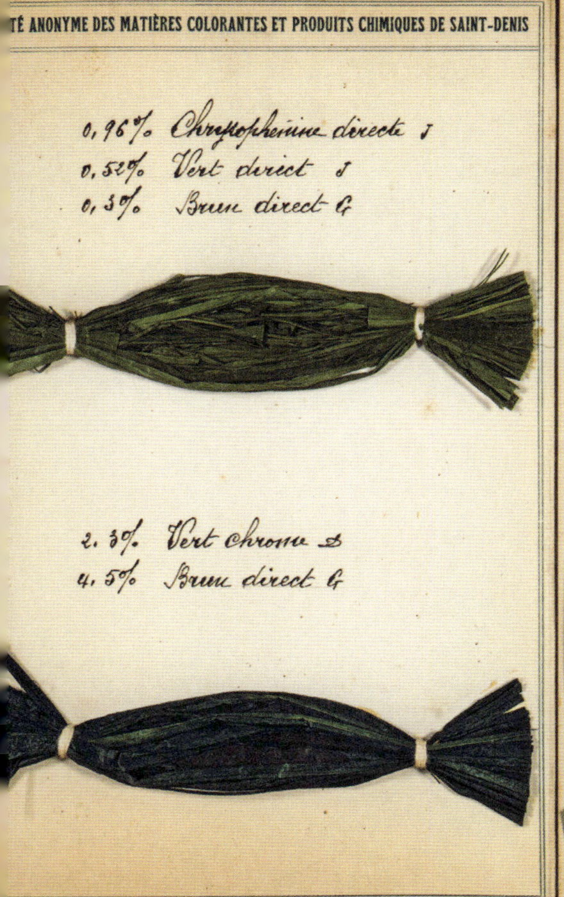
TÉ ANONYME DES MATIÈRES COLORANTES ET PRODUITS CHIMIQUES DE SAINT-DENIS
0,96% Chrysophénine directe J
0,52% Vert direct J
0,3% Brun direct G
2.3% Vert chrome S
4.5% Brun direct G

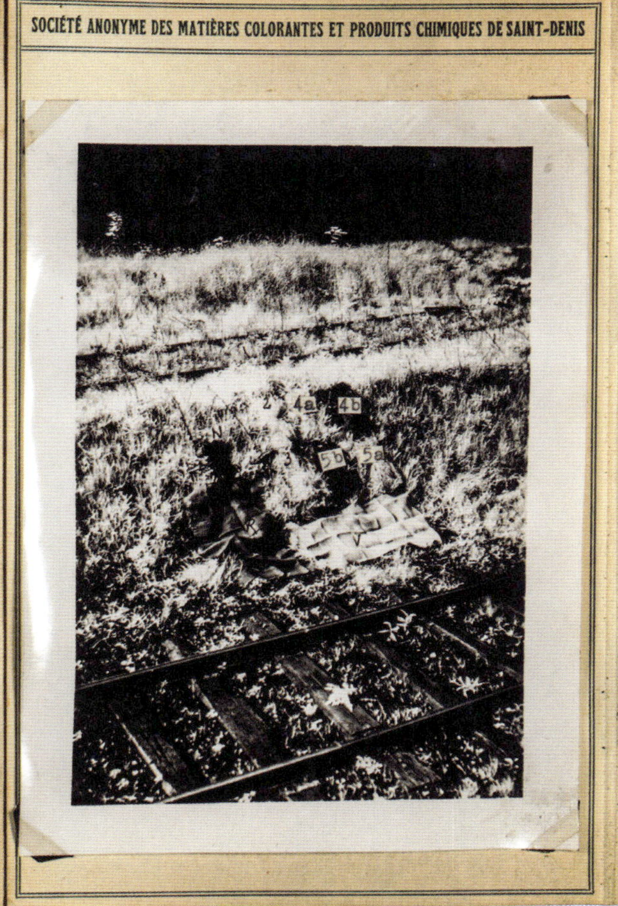
SOCIÉTÉ ANONYME DES MATIÈRES COLORANTES ET PRODUITS CHIMIQUES DE SAINT-DENIS

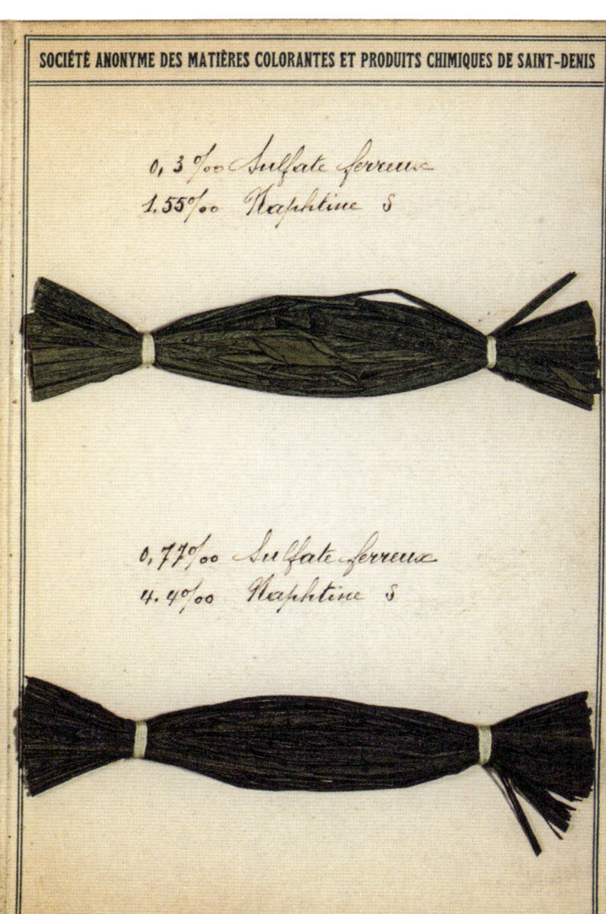
SOCIÉTÉ ANONYME DES MATIÈRES COLORANTES ET PRODUITS CHIMIQUES DE SAINT-DENIS
0,3‰ Sulfate ferreux
1.55‰ Naphtine S
0,77‰ Sulfate ferreux
4.4‰ Naphtine S

——— We do not know the companies for whom these color charts were created, or how many copies were circulated. While the history of the chemical industry's color charts still needs further study, these marketing tools express happiness, as if the joy that these scientists and manufacturers felt at the possibility of coloring the world has made its way across time to us. Joy is expressed in the perfect rows of fur pompoms, the shimmering feathers, the shiny disks of bone arranged in alternating patterns. It can be found in the kaleidoscopic list of materials to which chemists intended to give color. It emanates from the beauty and cheerfulness these tools contain and the care with which they were developed.

These color charts express confidence in progress. The instructions accompanying the samples are scientifically rigorous, without a superfluous word, while remaining easy to understand, even for a novice. Did their authors wish to target a clientele of beginner dyers? Or allow any enterprising person to explore the adventure of synthetic color? In any case, these color charts offered the means to do so. These marketing tools also show adaptability to change and a responsiveness to creating bespoke colors. Their formats varied according to the material to be dyed and the characteristics of the desired palette in the case of responses to client requests. As it pursued new markets, the chemical industry also stimulated new scientific and technical breakthroughs. Moreover, in its attempts to use color on dissimilar materials as displayed on color charts (apple-green leather, multicolor rubber, fluorescent makeup), the chemical industry inspired manufacturers and acted as a style catalyst.

These color charts from the interwar period are a sampling of the colors available. The profusion of colors may surprise us, for our memory of these years has taken on the shades of black and white of the photography and cinema of the period. However, many of these colors are found in textile color charts as well as color charts for household paints and artists' paints. Other uses would need to wait until society continued its process of mastering color, but these color charts foretold the color jubilation to come. It was born in the laboratory before spreading to the populace.

THE SEWING AND FASHION INDUSTRIES: GENERAL STABILITY AND A FEW INNOVATIONS

The chemical industry's zeal for color after World War I had reached the world of clothing slowly. Rationing of textile materials due to the war and the need to deal with overwhelming changes in daily life led to the adoption of functional clothing, in all social classes. After the war, haute couture companies multiplied, but for the middle classes, only a discreet elegance could be envisioned, even before the Great Depression devastated the fashion industry.[20] Prêt-à-porter, or ready-to-wear, which was initially mass-produced by the army as uniforms, was in its infancy until the 1930s. It was still the norm to make clothes at home or to hire a seamstress; this practice was encouraged by women's magazines, which published patterns and praised the Singer sewing machine.

Social constraints were still at work. For instance, bed linen had not changed since the mid-eighteenth century. During this era, snuggling into bed in sheets dyed with indigo or madder was inconceivable. By 1930, it would have been easy and inexpensive to dye bedsheets in the powerful reds or blues of fuchsin or methylene blue, but, just as in the eighteenth century, no one wanted to sleep on these, or could even imagine such a thing. That would come later.

In this rather dull context, the main development in color charts was the display of colors on new fibers, especially rayon and viscose.

Ribbon Color Charts: Unchanging, but Now Trend-Setting

The ribbon industry in Saint-Étienne recovered from the war due to massive mechanization. The founding of the haute couture houses brought new orders, and new export markets were opened: the United States, where demand for new ready-to-wear clothing lines was growing, and colonial markets. However, silk manufacturers rejected artificial fibers that would have allowed them to lower costs and reach a clientele of modest means. The stock market crash of 1929 deprived the ribbon makers of their American clientele, then their European one, and led the surviving companies to convert to synthetic fibers.

NEXT PAGE, TOP

Summer Shades from Flower and Feather Makers

The time when a name was given to each sample was over. Now, names designated groups of three to six shades, which, as before, were versions of a single tone and had names taken from the natural world. Here, names including *Hollyhock*, *Marmot*, *Green Gold*, *Reed*, *Lobelia*, *Girolle*, *Ablet*, *Nigella*, *Richelieu*, and *Langoustine* have been meticulously written by hand.

The trade associations of flower and feather makers had distributed these color charts since the end of the nineteenth century; this seems to have been one of the last. It is also shown here because of the wonderful traces it bears: as a work tool, it has been used and stained, for it was constantly consulted. Long after playing its temporary role showing the color range of a season's trends, it clearly served as a model in the feather makers' workshops for creating colors. It then became a valuable reference tool. This long-term aspect of the commercial color chart should not be neglected. Even if it was designed to accompany or stimulate the development of tastes at a particular moment in time, it remained relevant afterward for both inspiration and labor.

Colors Adopted by the Chambres Syndicales Réunies des Fleurs et des Plumes, summer season 1923, Chambre Syndicale des Fleurs et Plumes de Paris, Paris, 1923, leporello, 17 × 11.5 cm, 4 panels, Patrimoine Lemarié—Fonds Legeron, Paris

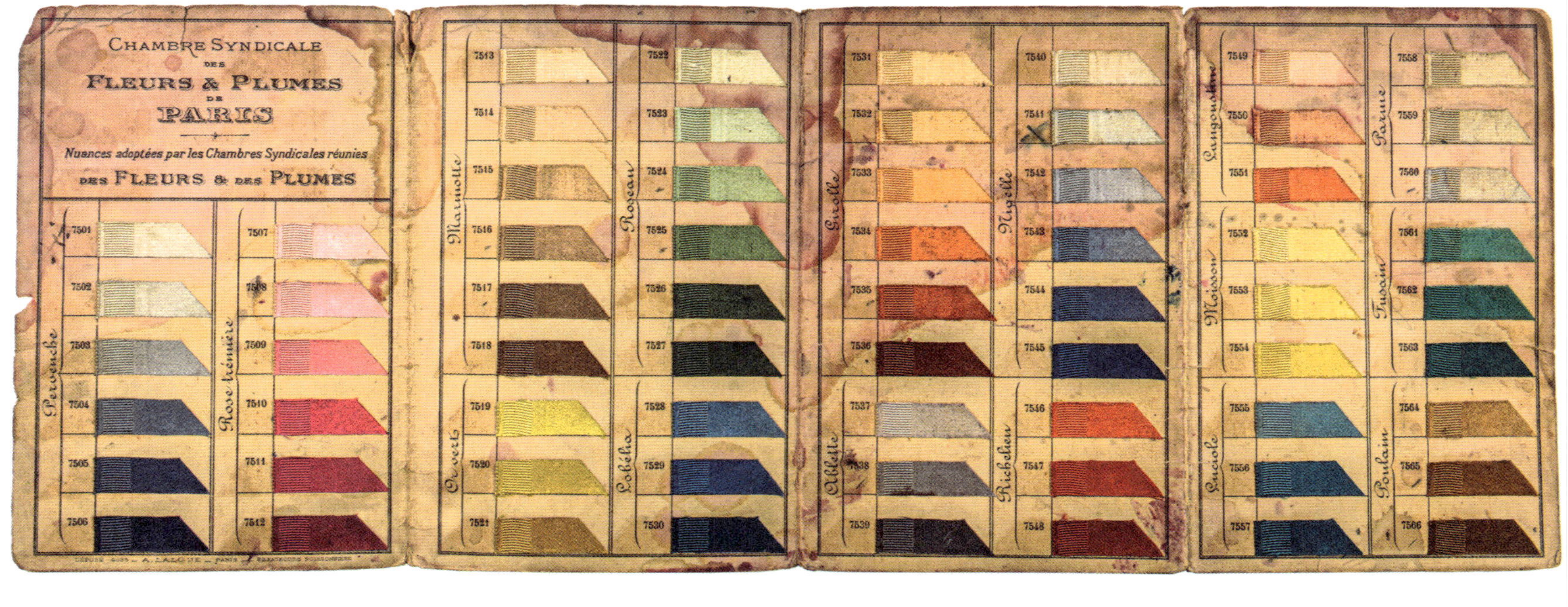
CHAMBRE SYNDICALE
DES
FLEURS & PLUMES
DE
PARIS
Nuances adoptées par les Chambres Syndicales réunies
DES FLEURS & DES PLUMES
Pervenche
Rose trémière
Marmotte
Roseau
Oeverl
Lobélia
Girolle
Nigelle
Œillette
Richelieu
Langouste
Parme
Moisson
Fusain
Luciole
Poulain
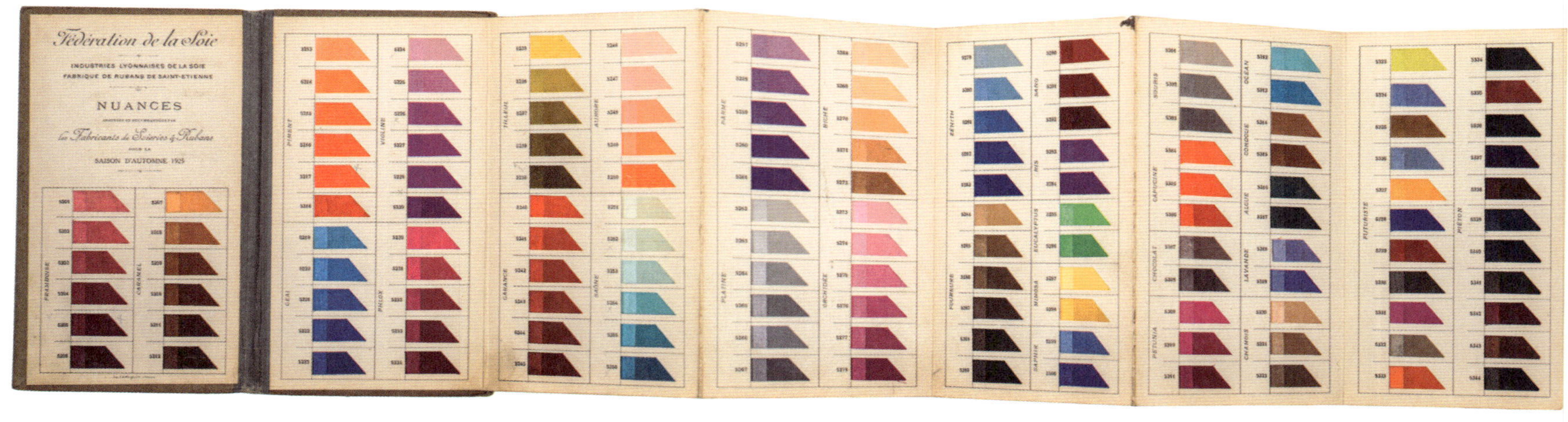
Fédération de la Soie
INDUSTRIES LYONNAISES DE LA SOIE
FABRIQUE DE RUBANS DE SAINT-ETIENNE
NUANCES
les Fabricants de Soieries & Rubans
POUR LA
SAISON D'AUTOMNE 1925
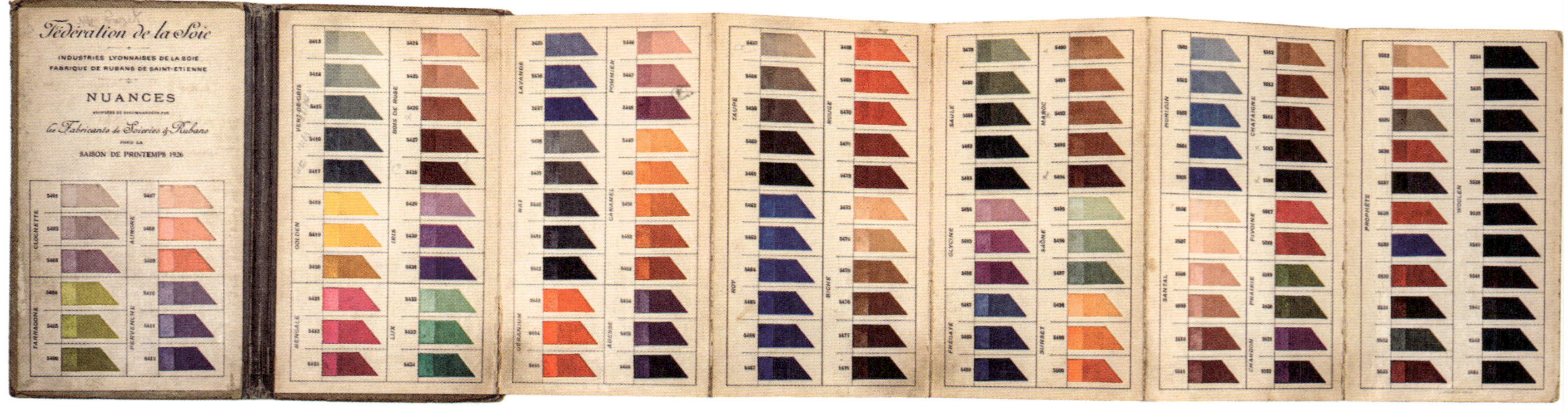
Fédération de la Soie
INDUSTRIES LYONNAISES DE LA SOIE
FABRIQUE DE RUBANS DE SAINT-ETIENNE
NUANCES
les Fabricants de Soieries & Rubans
POUR LA
SAISON DE PRINTEMPS 1926

OPPOSITE, BOTTOM

Fédération de la Soie Recommended Colors, Autumn 1925 and Spring 1926

Just after the end of the war, the Fédération de la Soie, which represented up to two hundred businesses in Lyon and Saint-Étienne, took over for the Union des Syndicats of Paris, Lyon, Saint-Étienne, and Calais. In these color charts, again a single name designated a set of colors, and the names were predominantly chosen from the natural world.

However, an important change had taken place. A new generation of leaders had taken the reins at the textile industries and revamped production: silk and ribbon manufacturers not only adopted colors; they recommended them. In the early 1920s, the Fédération de la Soie took on an advisory role, which the Société Anonyme des Matières Colorantes et Produits Chimiques would also do, but much later.[21]

In this way, the silk producers were among the first to guide their clients, both retailers and individuals, toward a recommended color range. Comparing the color charts from two consecutive seasons gives us a sense of the strategy. Colors that had already been selected (such as *Iris*, *Caramel*, *Doe*, *Saône*) were recommended the following year. The unsold items thus reappeared, while new ranges for each season could be tested as new shades were added to the old.

This advising undertaking the Fédération de la Soie took on is clear on the last panel of both color charts. For winter 1925, the silk producers offered two surprising ranges, *Futurists* and *Pedestrian*, and then, the following summer, *Prophet* and *Wooden*. These combinations of colors were taken from multiple hues to develop a unique range. This was a stylistic choice. The selection of tones to create a series of versions of a color was already a challenge, of course, but the exercise here was even more adventurous. There was no soothing effect of displaying a color in shades moving from light to dark, and any user of the chart may or may not be fond of the proposed combinations. The time would come when it would be enough to decree that a color is fashionable for society to adopt it, but already in the 1920s, this principle had been implemented, and the silk producers' color charts would apply it until the late 1930s.[22]

Colors Adopted and Recommended by Producers of Silk and Ribbons for the Fall Season 1925, Fédération de la Soie, Industries Lyonnaises de la Soie, Fabrique de Rubans de Saint-Étienne, Saint-Étienne, 1925, leporello, 20 × 10.5 cm, 7 panels, private collection, Paris

Colors Adopted and Recommended by Producers of Silk and Ribbons for the Spring Season 1926, Fédération de la Soie, Industries Lyonnaises de la Soie, Fabrique de Rubans de Saint-Étienne, Saint-Étienne, 1926, leporello, 20 × 10.5 cm, 7 panels, private collection, Paris

NEXT PAGE, TOP

Colors for Spring 1941

In 1941, restrictions World War II imposed obliged the Fédération de la Soie to break with the rule that had been followed since the 1920s of beginning its color charts with versions of colors from the same family. The first panel presents shades that are all pastel, but of different colors. The last panel also innovated by combining two distinct samples end to end. There was a need to offer color ranges with the resources available. The Fédération took advantage of this arrangement to make a political statement against the German army, which had been occupying northern France since June 1940: the single sample at the bottom is a bit larger than the others and combines *France* blue with *Coq* red (Coq [rooster] being the national symbol of France), with a white ribbon in the center. On June 17, 1940, Maréchal Pétain asked the Germans for an armistice. The defeat was hard to bear, and the Resistance began to organize itself. This color chart makes its own small statement on the hope of liberating the nation.

Colors Adopted and Recommended by Producers of Silk and Ribbons for the Spring Season 1941, Fédération de la Soie, Industries Lyonnaises de la Soie, Fabrique de Rubans de Saint-Étienne, Saint-Étienne, 1941, leporello, 20 × 10.5 cm, 7 panels, Anne Varichon collection, Sète

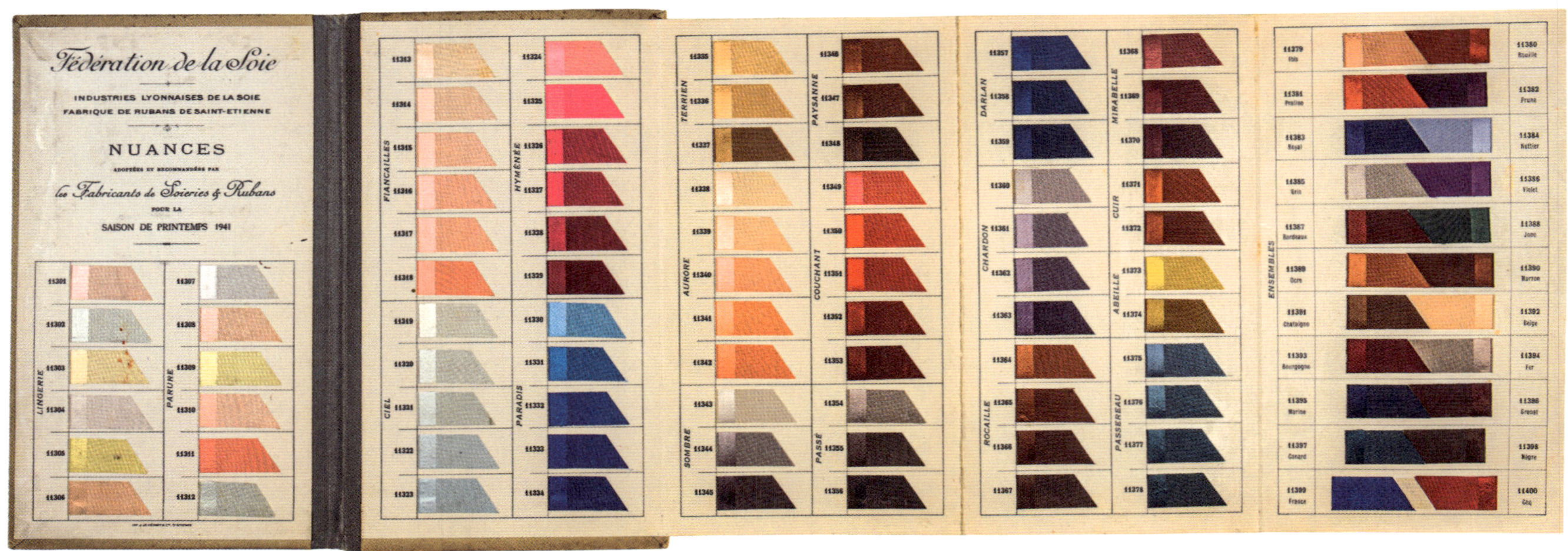
Fédération de la Soie
INDUSTRIES LYONNAISES DE LA SOIE
FABRIQUE DE RUBANS DE SAINT-ETIENNE
NUANCES
les Fabricants de Soieries & Rubans
POUR LA
SAISON DE PRINTEMPS 1941
LINGERIE
PARURE
FIANÇAILLES
HYMÉNÉE
CIEL
PARADIS
TERRIEN
PAYSANNE
AURORE
COUCHANT
SOMBRE
PASSÉ
DARLAN
MIRABELLE
CHARDON
CUIR
ABEILLE
ROCAILLE
PASSEREAU
ENSEMBLES

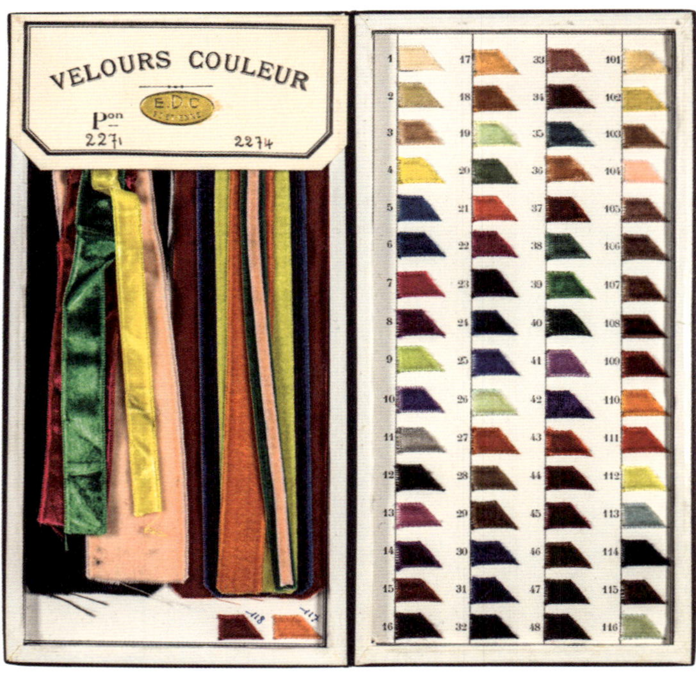
VELOURS COULEUR
E.D.C.
2271
2274

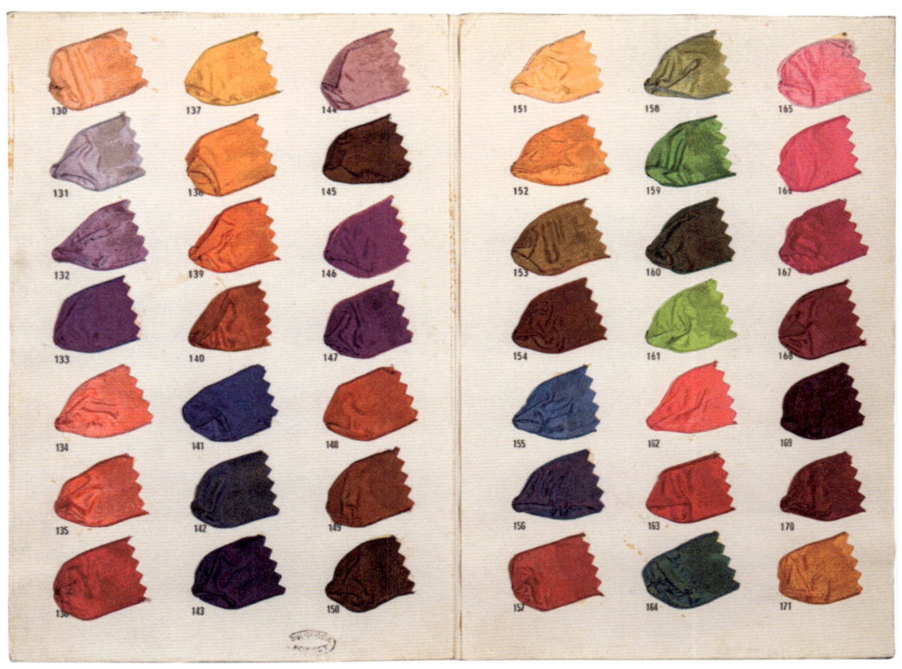

The word exotic is not the right word, not a true word, it's an approximation due to ignorance and paternalism. An exotic person is never intelligent. An exotic person is never a Nobel Prize winner. An exotic person is always kind of an idiot, who doesn't know how the world works, a gentle soul, a backward person.

Nathacha Appanah, *La Noce d'Anna*, 2009

NEXT PAGE SPREAD

Colors for Export

Another piece of historical evidence: this color chart is part of the industrialized nations' plan to sell their products to the colonies, which were viewed as a market to be conquered. Beginning in the mid-1920s, the European chemical industry had been exporting its synthetic dyes and pigments. In places such as Fez and Khartoum, dyers adopted these new synthetic dyes and pigments and gradually abandoned their vast knowledge and elaborate skill in natural dyes. Exporting consumer goods led to the same result, as industrially produced European goods slowly replaced local craftsmanship.

It seems unlikely that specific color charts were developed by the Fédération de la Soie for European or American clients. The phrase "for export" quite clearly means "for the colonies." This color chart may have met the double goal of reaching new markets while also finding an outlet for older stock. Indeed, several shades from color charts of the years 1925 to 1935 can be seen here. This was a selection of preexisting colors intended for both local populations and colonists. It is characterized by its abundance (219 samples), but there are few dark colors, which confirms that this selection is for locations where winters are nonexistent or at least milder than in France. No season is indicated, nor is a year given.

Since the late nineteenth century, color charts had drawn inspiration from Orientalist or Japonist movements. Conversely, color charts such as this one exported a Western aesthetic to countries it had not yet reached. In this way, these innocent little pieces of ribbon participated in a profound and lasting cultural transformation in many distant lands. Slowly but surely, by replacing Indigenous products, this transformation would lead to the extinction of most of the artisanal practices and traditional knowledge outside Europe, as was already happening within Europe itself.[23]

Colors Adopted and Recommended by Producers of Silk and Ribbons for Export, Fédération de la Soie, Industries Lyonnaises de la Soie, Fabrique de Rubans de Saint-Étienne, Saint-Étienne, 1930s, leporello, 20 × 10.5 cm, 10 panels, Bibliothèque Forney, Paris, call number RES ICO 7927

OPPOSITE, BOTTOM LEFT

E.D.C. Velvet Colors

The ribbon makers of Saint-Étienne perfected other types of color charts, such as these boxes for showcasing their velvet ribbons. The various available widths are illustrated by a series of eleven ribbons, with approximately 15 cm hanging loose, allowing clients to fully appreciate their shimmer, texture, and resistance, along with the quality of the edging. Very small samples (0.5 × 1.5 cm) display the 118 possible shades. In no apparent order, they are fully attached to the back of the right-hand panel, with two additional samples placed at the bottom of the left-hand panel.

The careful presentation enhances a valuable product whose dense thread count ensures a downy, high-quality surface. While touching the texture may have encouraged purchases, there was no attempt at poetic naming, as the ribbons were given only plain numbers.

Colored Velvet, E.D.C., Saint-Étienne, 1920s, box, 24 × 12 cm, France Lavergne-Cler collection, Paris

OPPOSITE, BOTTOM RIGHT

Small-scale Ribbons

The Bibliothèque Forney has an extensive archive of samples from creative industries; some of the color charts were produced on a small scale. The ribbon color chart of the Fédération de la Soie clearly inspired these modest, but nonetheless significant, marketing tools. Some use the same structure as larger color charts but are produced on humble sheets of school paper. They bring to mind the patient cutting and gluing of samples, the meticulous and almost meditative task of organizing colors into a harmonious whole, which may have been carried out by employees while business in a ribbon shop was slow. This color chart was produced in such a manner and features forty-two samples of ribbons (most likely made of artificial silk) that have been cut with pinking shears. One end was slid into a perforation on the card and the other was attached to the sheet of paper. Both ends were glued down on each side of the card.

Ribbon color chart, company unknown, France, 1920s, card, 25 × 16 cm, 1 fold, Bibliothèque Forney, Paris, call number RES ICO 7906 7

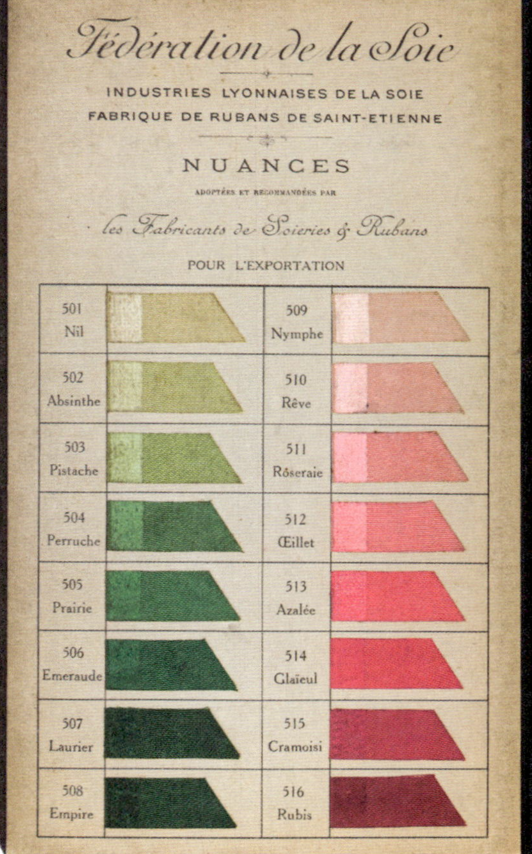

517 Porcelaine		529 Capucine	
518 Horizon		530 Feu	
519 Serbie		531 Etincelle	
520 Chasseur		532 Vésuve	
521 Toile		533 Orient	
522 Amiral		534 Rouge	
523 Roy		535 Cardinal	
524 Drapeau		536 Ecarlate	
525 France		537 Sultan	
526 Matelot		538 Acajou	
527 Geai		539 VieuxRouge	
528 Marine		540 Grenat	

Blanc	541		553 Jaune	
	542		554 Moisson	
	543		555 Pépite	
	544		556 Or	
Ivoire	545		557 Genêt	
	546		558 Ciel	
	547		559 Firmament	
Crème	548		560 Mexique	
	549		561 Caspienne	
	550 Paille		562 Mésange	
	551 Blé		563 Oriflamme	
	552 Maïs		564 Madone	

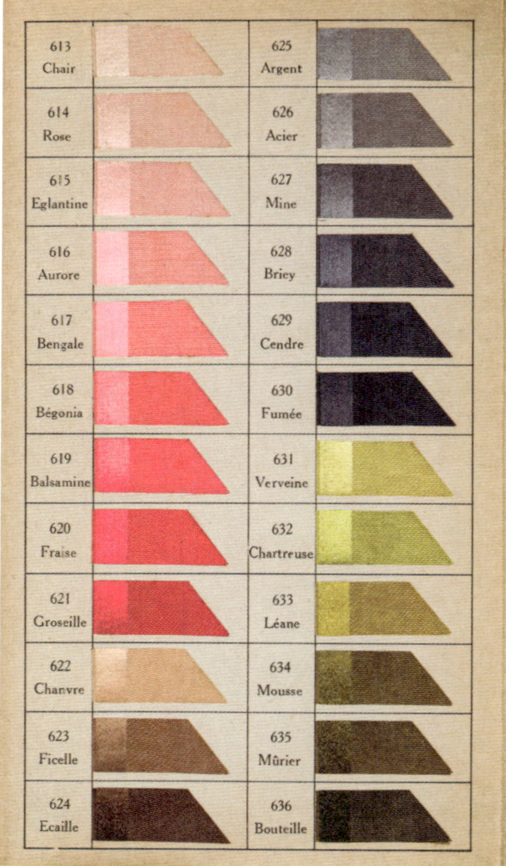

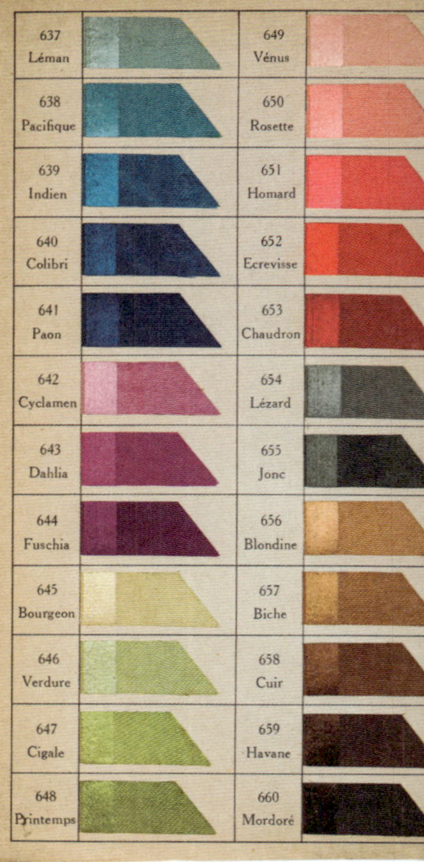

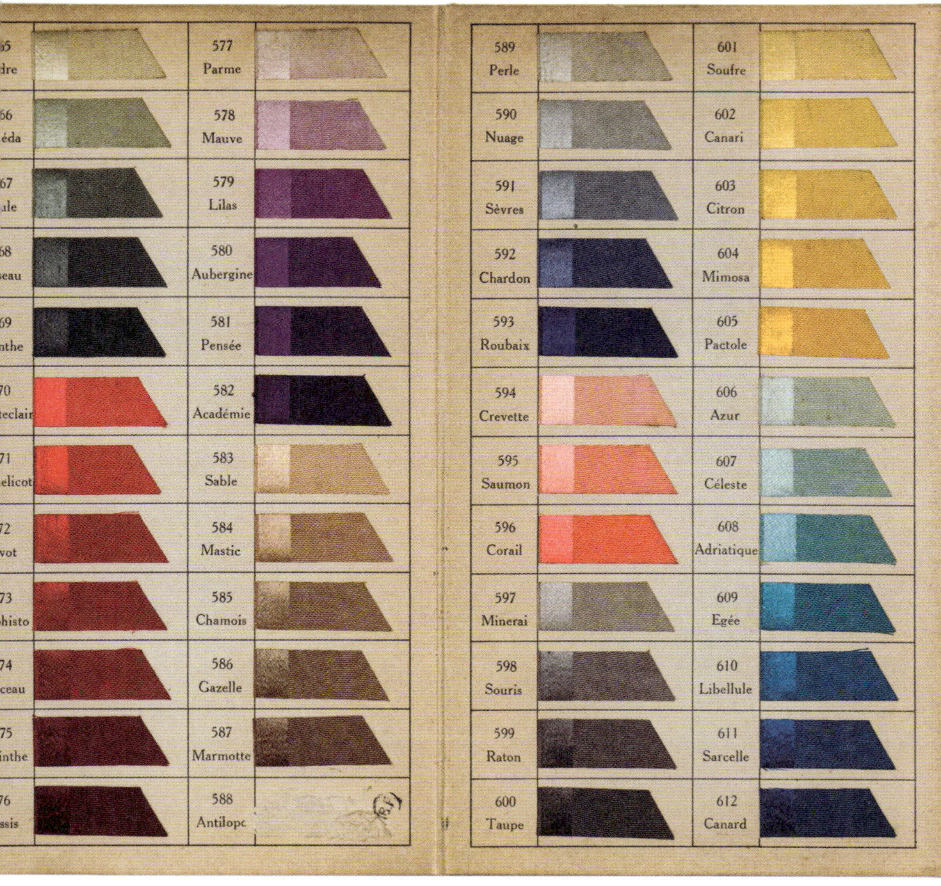
577 Parme
578 Mauve
579 Lilas
580 Aubergine
581 Pensée
582 Académie
583 Sable
584 Mastic
585 Chamois
586 Gazelle
587 Marmotte
588 Antilope
589 Perle
590 Nuage
591 Sèvres
592 Chardon
593 Roubaix
594 Crevette
595 Saumon
596 Corail
597 Minerai
598 Souris
599 Raton
600 Taupe
601 Soufre
602 Canari
603 Citron
604 Mimosa
605 Pactole
606 Azur
607 Céleste
608 Adriatique
609 Egée
610 Libellule
611 Sarcelle
612 Canard

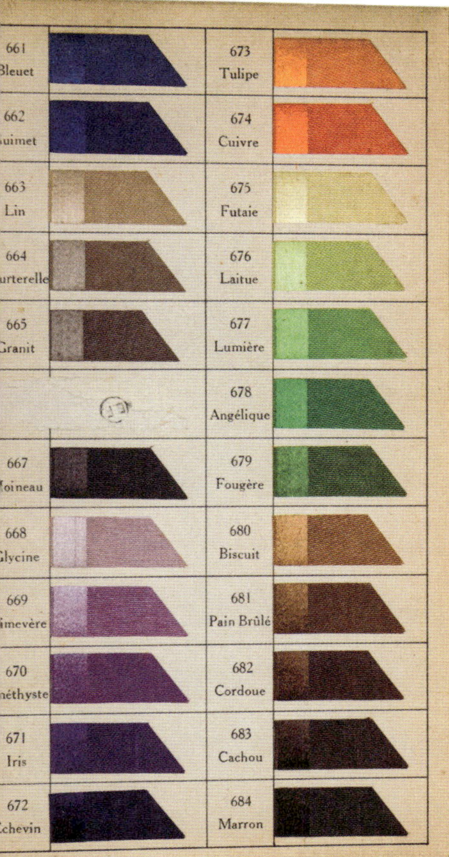
661
662
663 Lin
664
665
667
668
669
670
671 Iris
672
673 Tulipe
674 Cuivre
675 Futaie
676 Laitue
677 Lumière
678 Angélique
679 Fougère
680 Biscuit
681 Pain Brûlé
682 Cordoue
683 Cachou
684 Marron

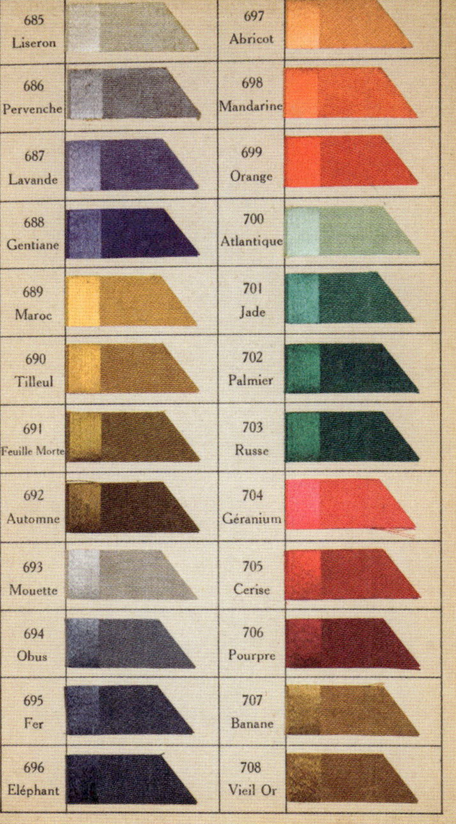
685 Liseron
686 Pervenche
687 Lavande
688 Gentiane
689 Maroc
690 Tilleul
691 Feuille Morte
692 Automne
693 Mouette
694 Obus
695 Fer
696 Eléphant
697 Abricot
698 Mandarine
699 Orange
700 Atlantique
701 Jade
702 Palmier
703 Russe
704 Géranium
705 Cerise
706 Pourpre
707 Banane
708 Vieil Or

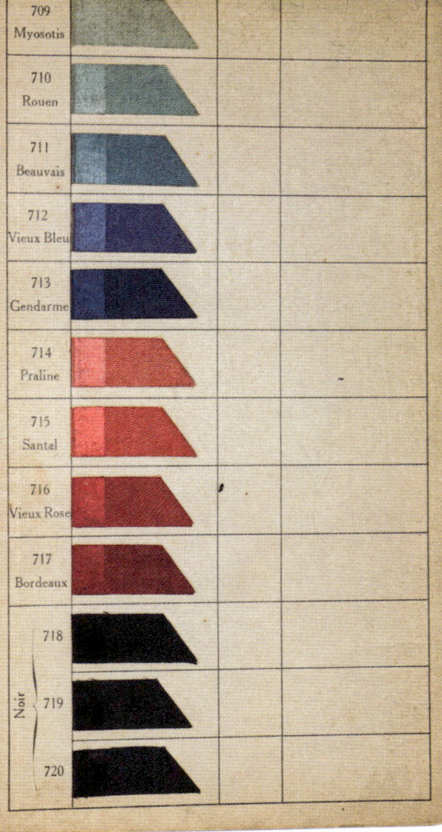
709 Myosotis
710 Rouen
711 Beauvais
712 Vieux Bleu
713 Gendarme
714 Praline
715 Santal
716 Vieux Rose
717 Bordeaux
718
Noir 719
720

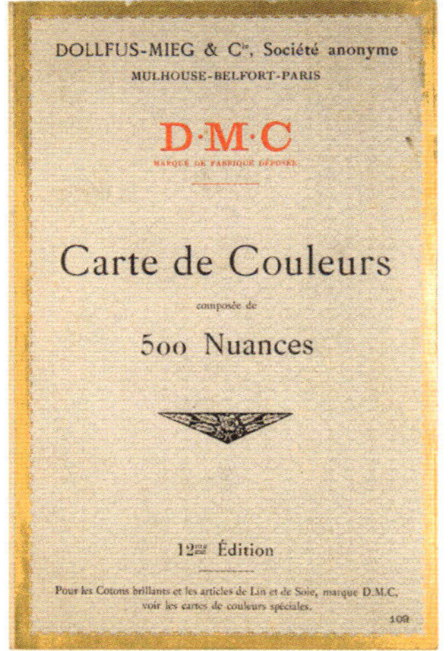

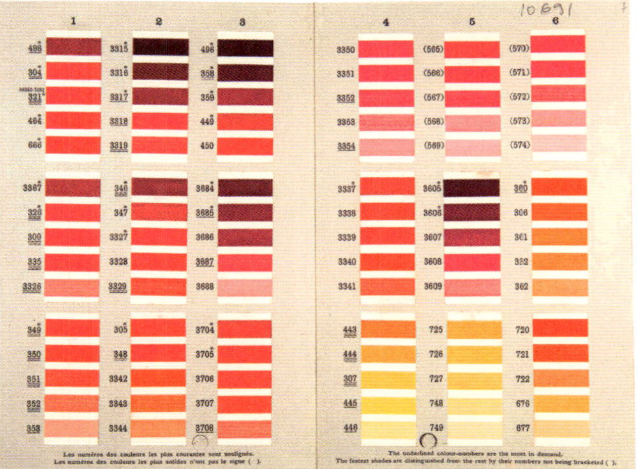

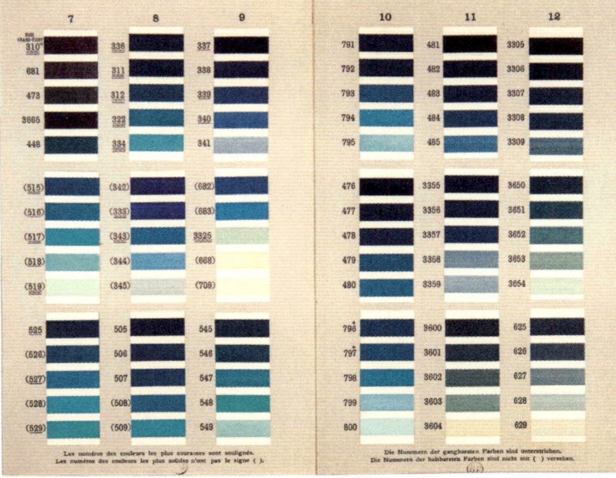

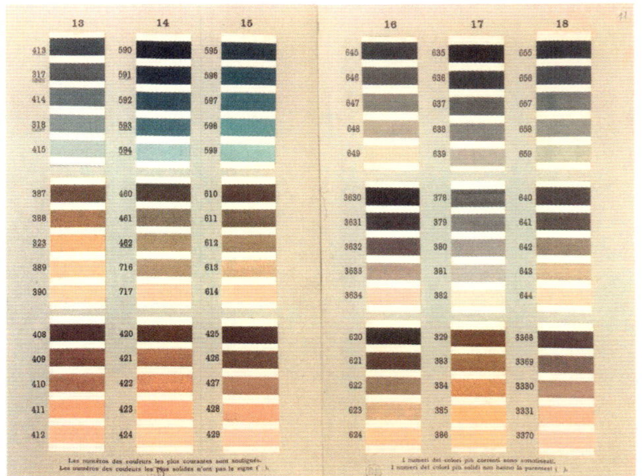

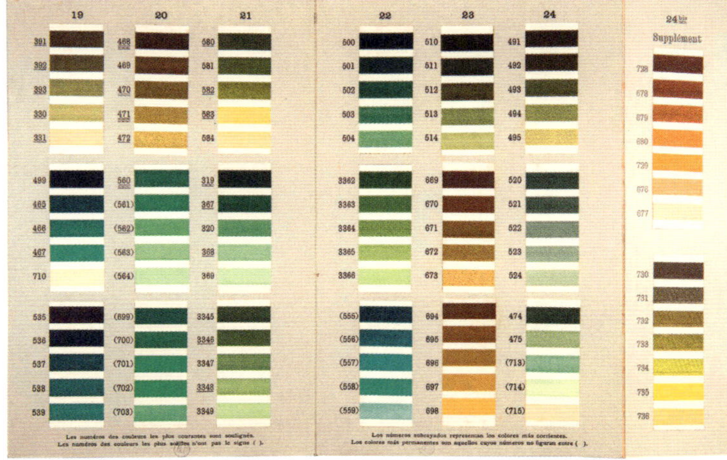

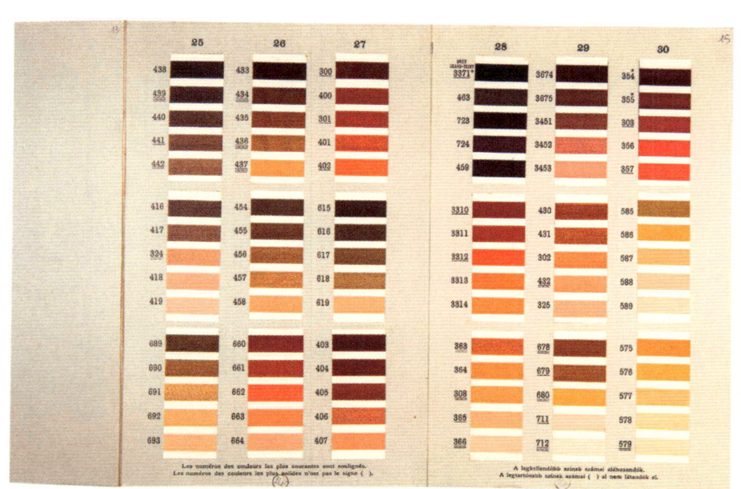

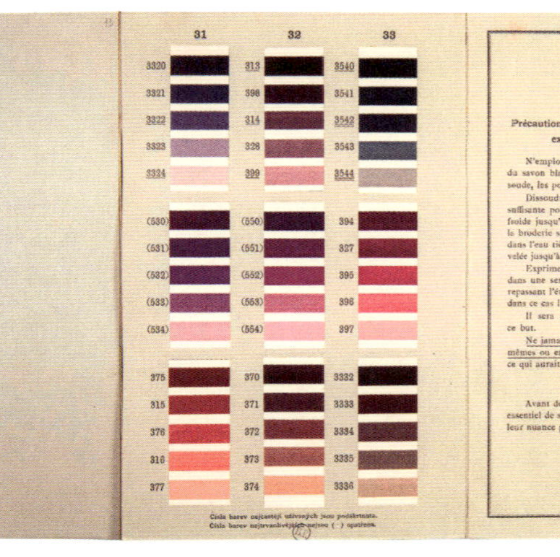

AVIS IMPORTANT

Précautions à prendre pour le lavage des broderies exécutées avec les fils de couleurs.

N'employer qu'un savon parfaitement neutre, de préférence du savon blanc de Marseille de 1re qualité; éviter surtout la soude, les poudres à lessiver et le chlore.

Dissoudre dans de l'eau bouillante une quantité de savon suffisante pour rendre l'eau bien mousseuse, ajouter de l'eau froide jusqu'à une température moyenne et laver rapidement la broderie sans trop la frotter. Rincer bien, une première fois dans l'eau tiède, puis dans de l'eau froide plusieurs fois renouvelée jusqu'à ce que le savon ait complètement disparu.

Exprimer à la main sans tordre, ou en roulant la pièce dans une serviette souple, et sécher rapidement à l'air ou en repassant l'étoffe à l'envers au moyen d'un fer pas trop chaud; dans ce cas l'étendre entre deux toiles, l'envers en-dessus.

Il sera toujours préférable d'employer la calandre dans ce but.

Ne jamais laisser les broderies mouillées repliées sur elles-mêmes ou entassées; ne jamais se servir d'un fer trop chaud, ce qui aurait pour résultat de ternir certaines couleurs.

Avant de commencer un ouvrage de longue haleine, il est essentiel de se procurer des quantités suffisantes de fournitures, leur nuance pouvant légèrement varier d'un achat à l'autre.

Displaying an Increasing Variety of Products with Color

The many colors the chemical industry developed found an outlet in a large number of items that could be produced at low cost due to ongoing advances in the mechanization of spinning and weaving.

OPPOSITE

DMC Color Card

Color charts of embroidery thread were some of the earliest to offer the individual consumer a significant number of samples. Additionally, they were so widely distributed that they are still iconic in memory today. They have become something like an archetype of the color chart. This is especially true for those produced by Dollfus-Mieg & Compagnie (DMC), founded by descendants of Alsatian manufacturers of *indienne* cloth. In the nineteenth century the company specialized in the production of mercerized thread. DMC supported a famous embroiderer, Thérèse de Dillmont, who founded a specialized school and wrote the 1886 work *Encyclopédie des ouvrages de dames* (Encyclopedia of Ladies' Needlework), which would be translated and sold in seventeen countries! This shows how central embroidery was for women in European culture, and this trend continued after the Great War.

Embroidery thread was a significant market, dominated by DMC. The company's greatest asset was the reliability of its color chart—an important quality, for embroidery is often a lengthy undertaking (for bridal trousseaux in particular), requiring meticulous attention to the thread colors, even if dyes continued to change constantly during this time of chemical innovations.

The first DMC color charts for thread, distributed at the very beginning of the twentieth century, already had almost four hundred colors, and more were added to each new edition every two or three years. The colors corresponded to the themes of needlepoint designs, for which the company also provided patterns. The company had international ambitions and featured text in eight languages in addition to French.[24]

The five hundred colors were printed rather than displayed as swatches. It is likely that this approach was selected to lower costs, as developing these marketing tools represented a significant expense. The colors are organized by tone, with each color represented by a set of five shades. Using the table provided, consumers could link the printed colors to their names. The possibility of custom dyeing was offered, with instructions specifying to "attach sample but not too small."

Later, DMC would bring back product samples. In the textile market, considering color without the sensory experience of feeling its material was found to be challenging. The names were as important as the texture. The embroidery color chart offered a narrative for women who engaged in needlepoint. From one generation to the next, the patterns that had actively circulated since the nineteenth century stimulated an imaginary world of various landscapes and scenes, which came to life in the embroidery threads and their names, such as *Dogwood Fruit Red* or *Scabiosa Violet*. The indication "twelfth edition" on this color chart and the following ones affirms the almost literary aspect of these elaborate maps of colors.

Color Chart of 500 Shades, DMC, Belfort-Mulhouse, 1920s, booklet, 22 × 14 cm, 37 pages, Bibliothèque Forney, Paris, call number RES ICO 8410

NEXT PAGE SPREAD

L. & C. Braids

Flat braids acquired a certain elasticity from the weaving process and were used in clothing design, hat making, and upholstery. While the column for "Greek braids" shows various colors, the repetition of shades in the "strong braids" column suggests that the initial colors have faded. The issue of color resistance to washing, wear, and UV light was a perpetual concern for manufacturers. Colors were sometimes unstable, and, in this case, the light shades we see today here are not what the manufacturer initially intended.

Color chart of woven braids, L. & C., France, 1930s, pamphlet, 27.5 × 14 cm, 5 folds, private collection, Paris

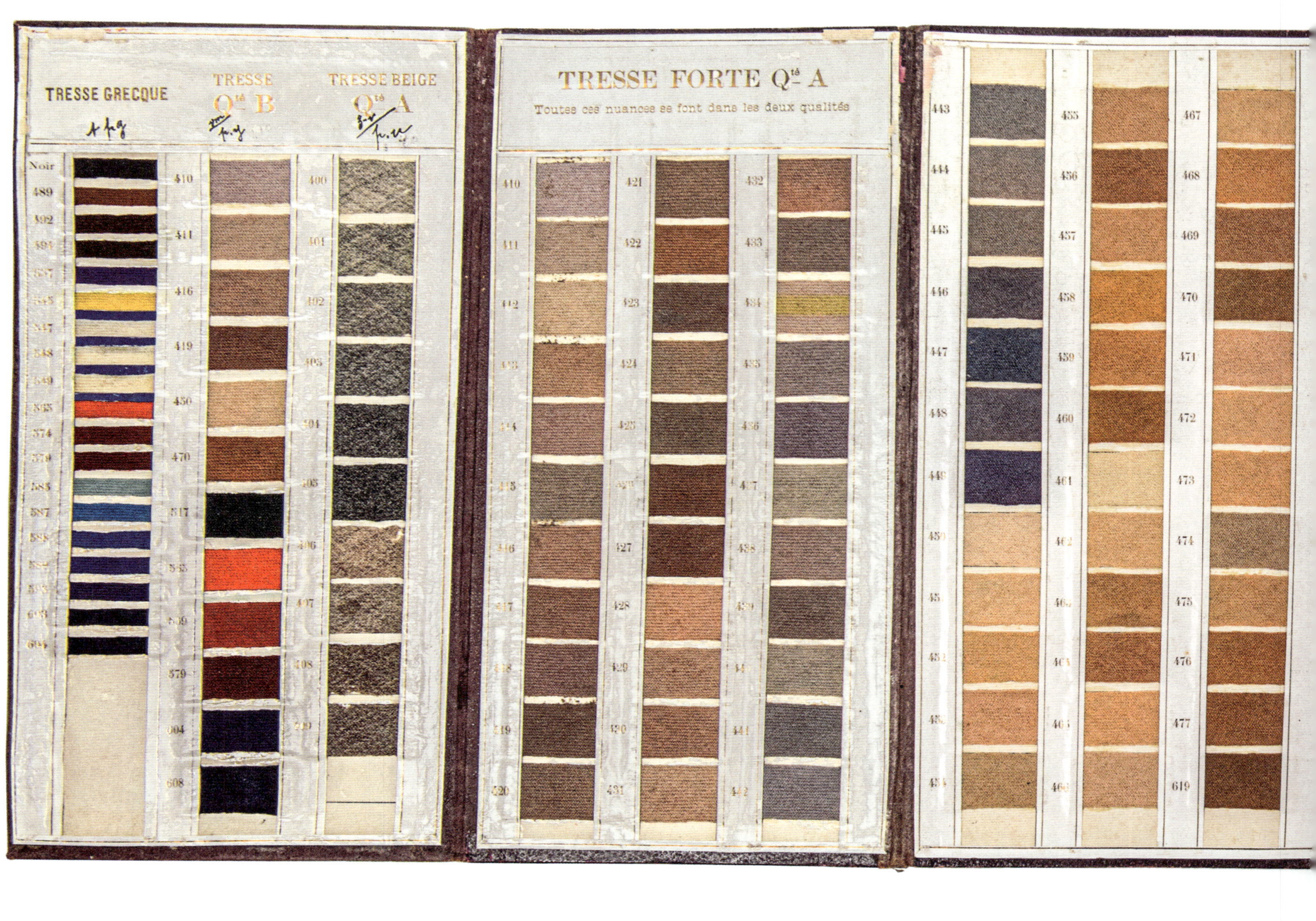
TRESSE GRECQUE
TRESSE Qté B
TRESSE BEIGE Qté A
TRESSE FORTE Qté A
Toutes ces nuances se font dans les deux qualités

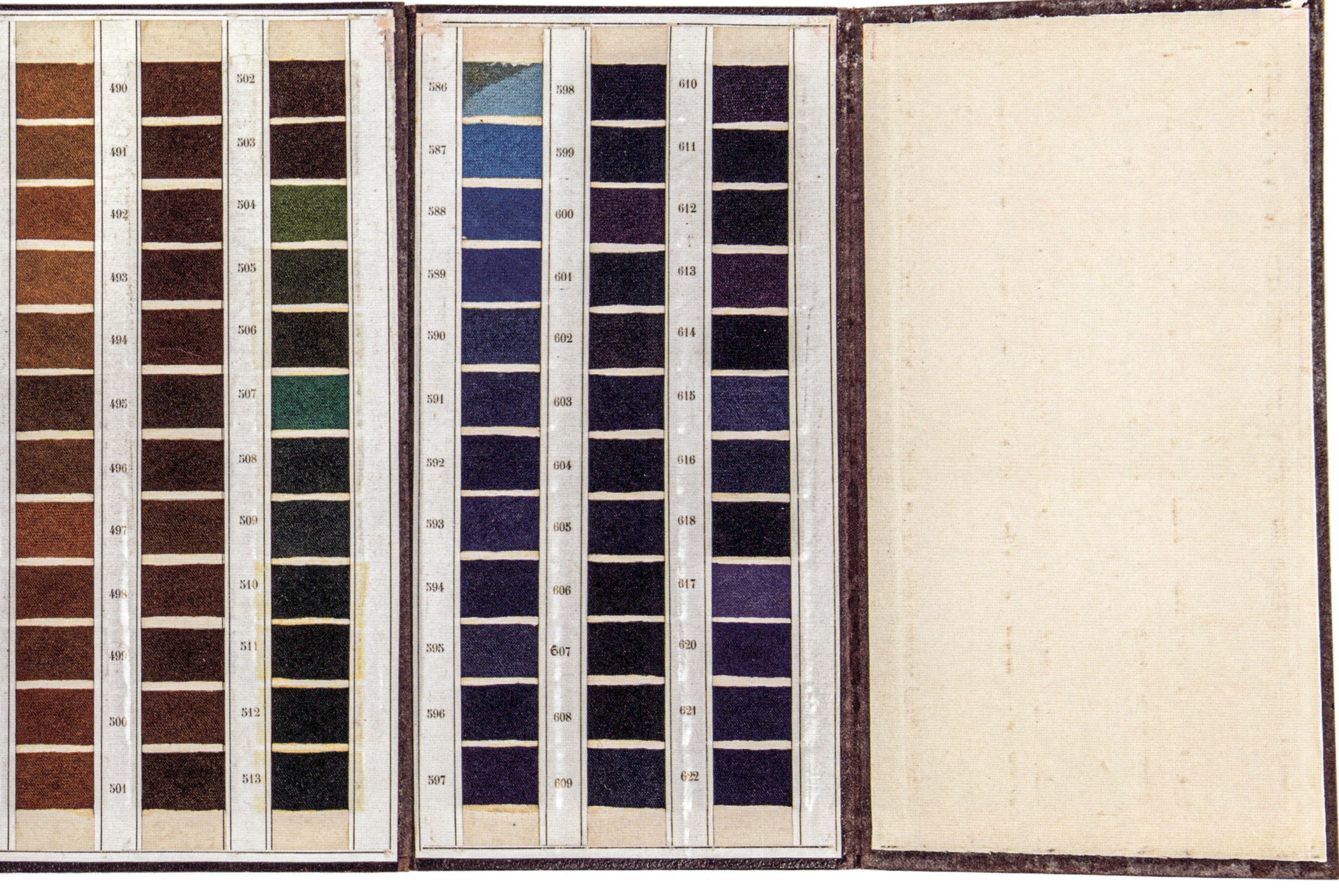
490
491
492
493
494
495
496
497
498
499
500
501
502
503
504
505
506
507
508
509
510
511
512
513
586
587
588
589
590
591
592
593
594
595
596
597
598
599
600
601
602
603
604
605
606
607
608
609
610
611
612
613
614
615
616
618
617
620
621
622

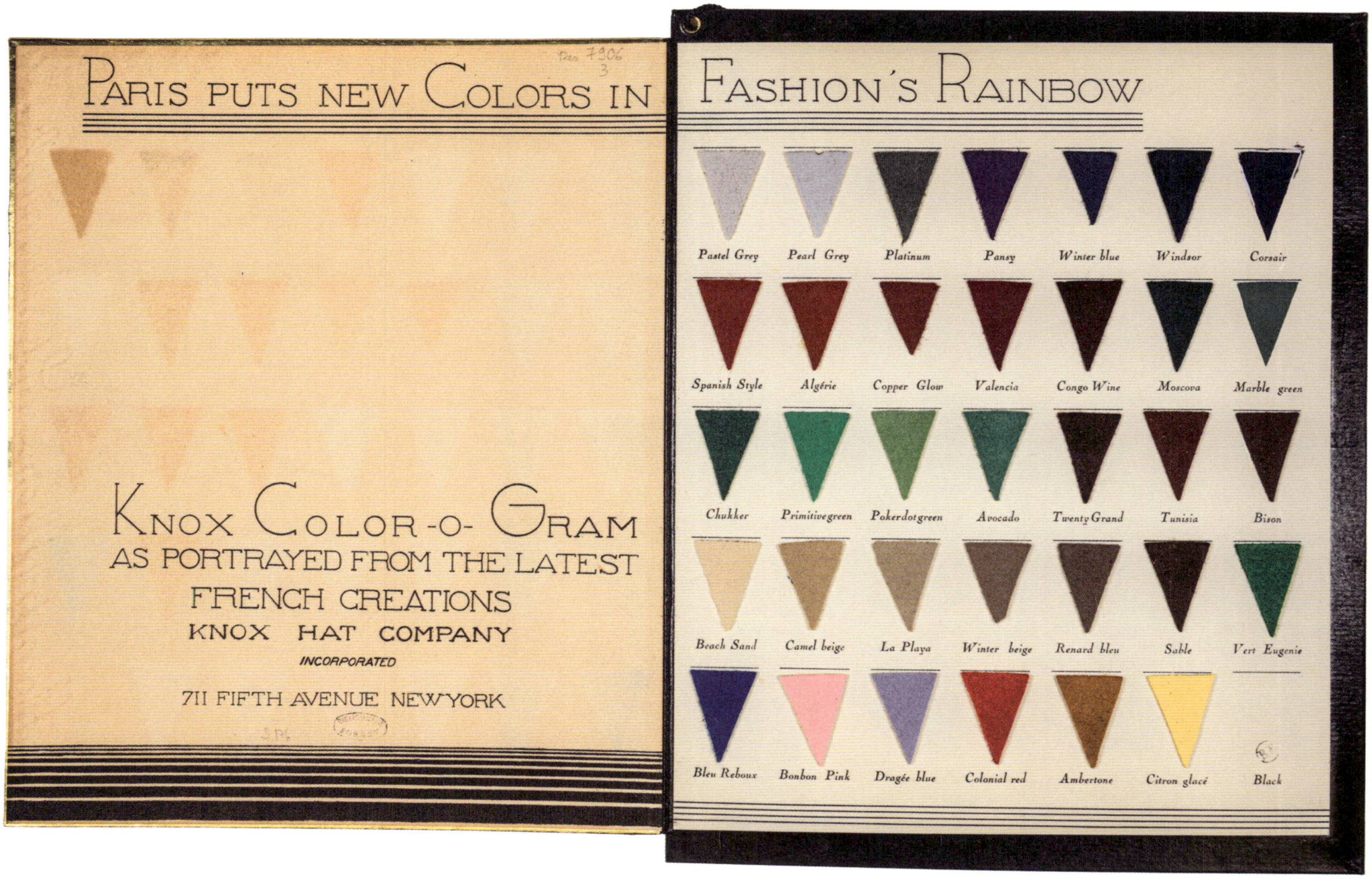

PARIS PUTS NEW COLORS IN FASHION'S RAINBOW

KNOX COLOR-O-GRAM
AS PORTRAYED FROM THE LATEST
FRENCH CREATIONS
KNOX HAT COMPANY
INCORPORATED
711 FIFTH AVENUE NEW YORK

Pastel Grey · Pearl Grey · Platinum · Pansy · Winter blue · Windsor · Corsair

Spanish Style · Algérie · Copper Glow · Valencia · Congo Wine · Moscova · Marble green

Chukker · Primitive green · Pokerdot green · Avocado · Twenty Grand · Tunisia · Bison

Beach Sand · Camel beige · La Playa · Winter beige · Renard bleu · Sable · Vert Eugenie

Bleu Reboux · Bonbon Pink · Dragée blue · Colonial red · Ambertone · Citron glacé · Black

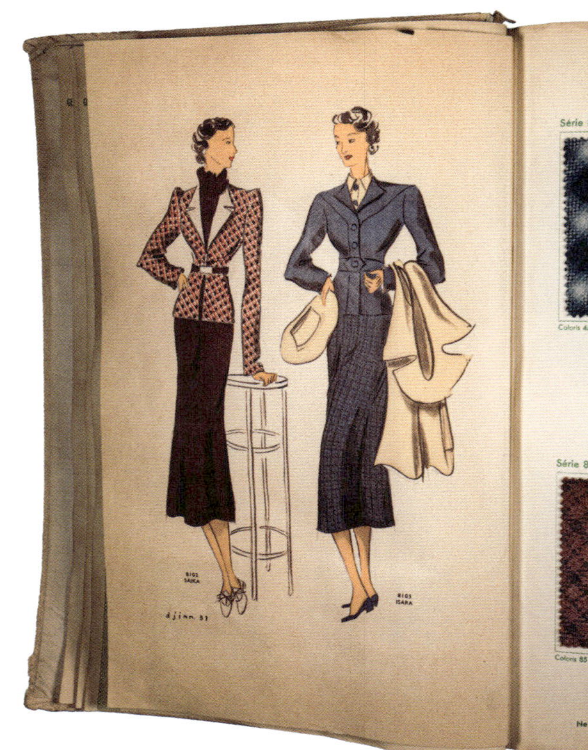

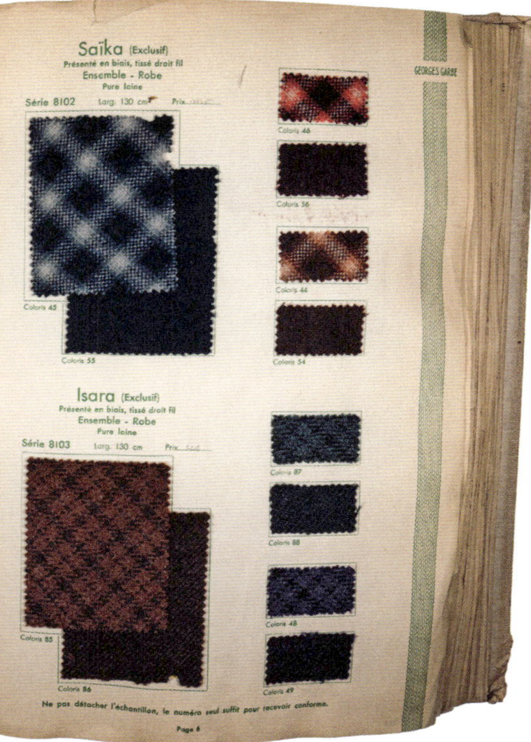

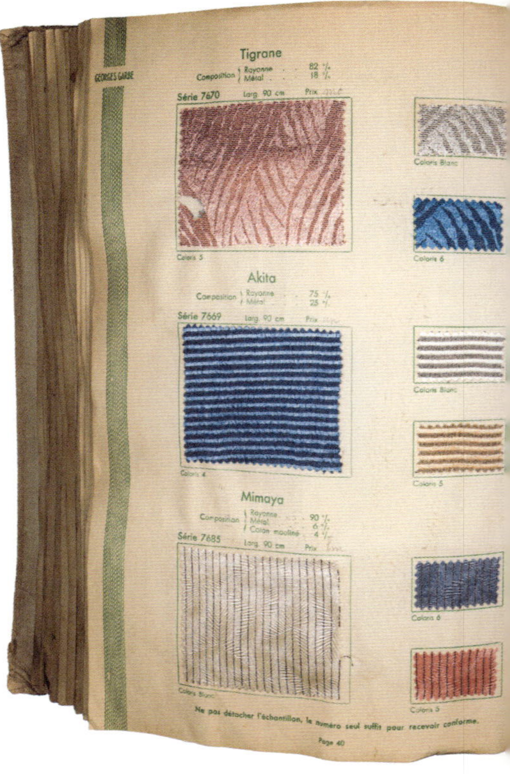

OPPOSITE, TOP

Knox Color-o-Gram

While the chemical industry had a bit of fun when presenting its *Acid Dyes for Felt Pile* in 1938 by shaping the samples into little fedoras, in this color chart by the Knox Hat Company, the samples of felt are cut into plain triangles.[25] However, they maintain a naming vocabulary related to travel and exoticism, at a time when poetic names in France tended to be replaced by numbers. The company combined names in English (*Spanish Style*, *Congo Wine*, *Colonial Red*) with French names (*Algérie*, *Camel beige*, *Renard bleu*, *Citron glacé* [Algeria, Beige Camel, Blue Fox, Iced Lemon]), in keeping with its slogan: "As portrayed from the latest French creations." Starting as a modest shop on Broadway in 1838, by the late 1920s, Knox had become a vast company selling its hats in over two thousand shops in the United States, and clearly aspired to be associated with the prestige of Parisian fashion, known for being the most trendy and the most colorful.

Knox Color-o-Gram, Knox Hat Company, New York, late 1920s–early 1930s, cardboard, 28 × 22 cm, 1 fold, Bibliothèque Forney, Paris, call number RES ICO 7906 3

OPPOSITE, BOTTOM, AND BELOW

Georges Garbe Catalog

By the late nineteenth century, department stores were already printing catalogs of designs for tailor-made clothing. Between the world wars, the design of the color chart began to be used for the presentation of clothing collections, like this catalog from designer Georges Garbe, who was active in Paris in the late 1930s. A two-page spread was reserved for one or two designs that were illustrated in ink and gouache. The drawings were accompanied by suggested fabrics, with a large sample of fabric (cut with pinking shears) indicating the pattern and other, smaller samples showing the available colors. The texture remains difficult to appreciate though, because the swatches are all glued down to the page. Customers must have tried to remove them, for there is a recurring warning: "Do not detach the sample; the number alone is sufficient to receive the identical item."

This is a winter wardrobe, and only after a few pages of evening gowns do lighter and brighter colors appear. However, the presentation of the coats and day dresses reveals an astonishing variety of shades of dark grays and browns, even of blacks, depending on the suggested materials and styles, including reversible designs.

New Items at Georges Garbe for Winter 1937–38, Georges Garbe, Paris, 1937, catalogue, 49 × 37 cm, 51 pages, Bibliothèque Forney, Paris, call number RES ICO 8232

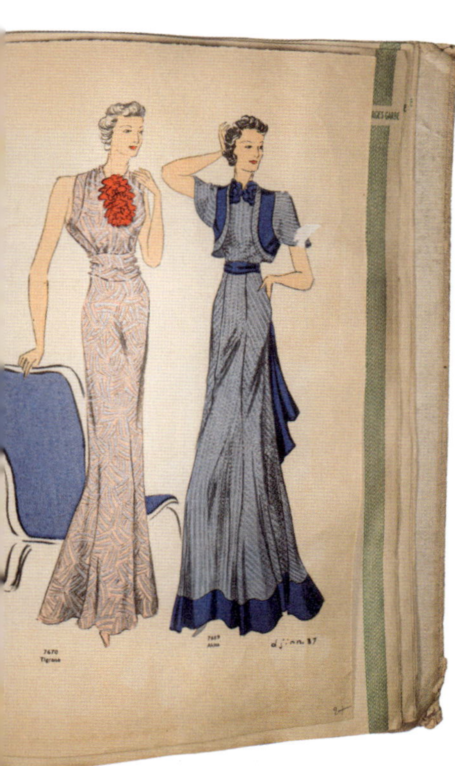

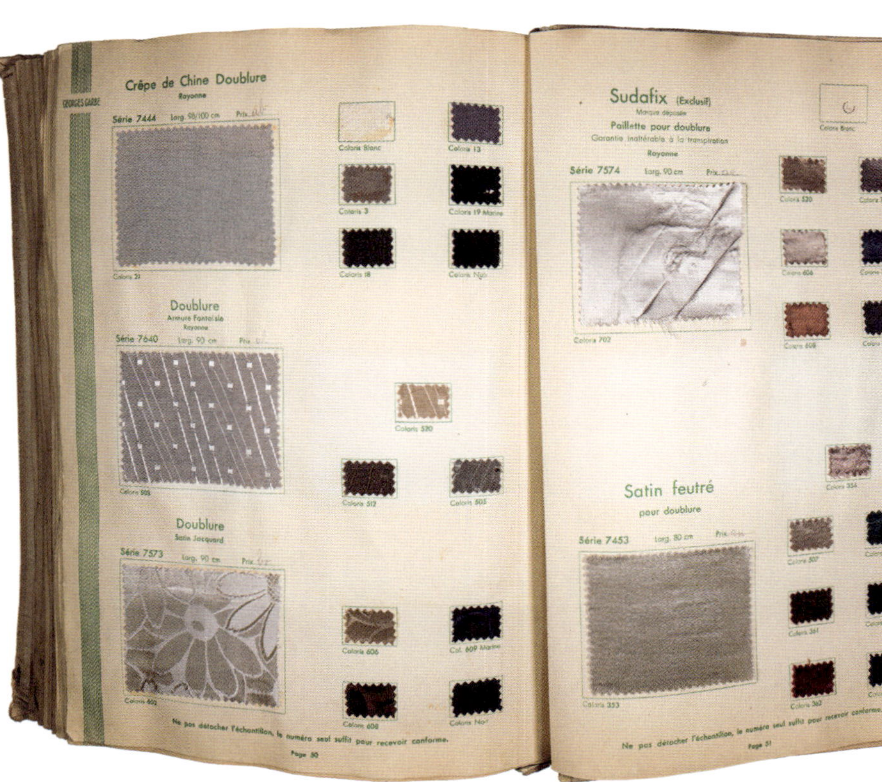

The Swan Song of the Feather Color Charts

The magnificent color charts developed by feather and flower makers before World War I were produced into the following decades.

"Oh, nonsense!
You've worn mourning long enough!
Plus, you have to think of the children."
"It's true! Just yesterday Prando said to me: 'Either you take off that black thing or I'm leaving.'"
The Art of Joy

OPPOSITE, TOP

Lemarié Feather Decorations

These decorations of goose and rooster feathers that have been dyed and cut (the black borders would indicate partridge feathers) apply the rules of geometry and symmetry and the typical colors of the art deco movement. They may have been used to decorate the center of the turbans that women wore beginning in the 1920s or the cloche hats that became fashionable in the following decade. Gradually, embroidered decorations or artificial flowers consigned these feather ornaments to oblivion.

Color chart of feather decorations, Maison Lemarié, Paris, 1920s, sheet of paper, 17 × 46 cm, Patrimoine Lemarié—Fonds Lemarié, Paris

OPPOSITE, BOTTOM

Legeron Petals

The Maison Lemarié has preserved plates and collections of petals that have been cut and dyed in a variety of ways. These archives are difficult to date, and it is not always easy to identify the flower reproduced. Some may be the products of the fertile imaginations of the craftspeople. This record book has approximately one hundred pages on which petals of various sizes, shapes, and fabrics have been glued; the fabrics include satin, cotton nainsook, and velvet. Several types of flowers can be recognized—roses, carnations, pansies, and hydrangeas. This is thus a kind of catalog of the skills of the Maison Legeron, to which new items were added as they were designed. This record book is also a set of distinct color charts illustrating the various color possibilities for a given shape of petal. Artisans referred to it when they wished to invent or change a design, and clients could make their choices from it.

On a few pages only, the samples have names similar to those of the color charts of artificial flowers from before the war. All the others are identified by numbers, which perhaps referred to dye record books where the formulas were located.

Color chart of fabric petals, Maison Legeron, Paris 1920s (?), record book, 33 × 24 cm, 50 sheets of white canvas, Patrimoine Lemarié—Fonds Legeron, Paris

NEXT PAGE SPREAD

Legeron Petal Groups

The samples, placed onto gridded paper, are formed by groups of petals of various colors arranged in a half corolla. Each set has a name, written in calligraphy, with most of them referring to exotic locales (*Egyptian*, *Indian*, *Sioux*, etc.). There is also a gray set called *Métro* (subway) and a yellow range called *Quarantine*. Yellow was very rarely seen in flower color charts, as it was perceived to be a difficult color to wear, and its name here does not help matters, as it refers to the yellow flag indicating an epidemic.[26] A few annotations served to record the ingredients of the dye used.

Color chart of fabric petals, Maison Legeron, Paris 1920s (?), record book, 27 × 34 cm, 3 plates on paper, Patrimoine Lemarié—Fonds Legeron, Paris

PAGE 170

Guillet Petals

In addition to displaying the available colors for these flower designs, these two color charts show the different dyeing techniques used in the artificial flower workshops.

The plate with fanned-out petals (*left*) features a dyeing process of soaking the raw fabric (no. 1) in solutions of dye of varying dilution for a uniform shade (no. 4). Applying these solutions with a large brush creates effects from light to saturated (including nos. 2, 10, 15) or combinations of colors (no. 16). On the plate of irises (?) (*right*), delicate gold veins have been applied with a fine brush.

Few feather and flower makers were able to survive when fashions changed after World War II, and especially when hats for women and men became passé after the 1950s. In 2002, Chanel began preserving ten exceptional workshops, their knowledge, and their archives under the designation "Maisons d'art." The archives of Maison Lemarié are among them, and thus these color charts were saved and can be studied today.

Color charts of fabric petals, Maison Guillet, Paris, 1930s (?), sheets of heavy-duty paper, 50 × 32 cm, Patrimoine Lemarié—Fonds Guillet, Paris

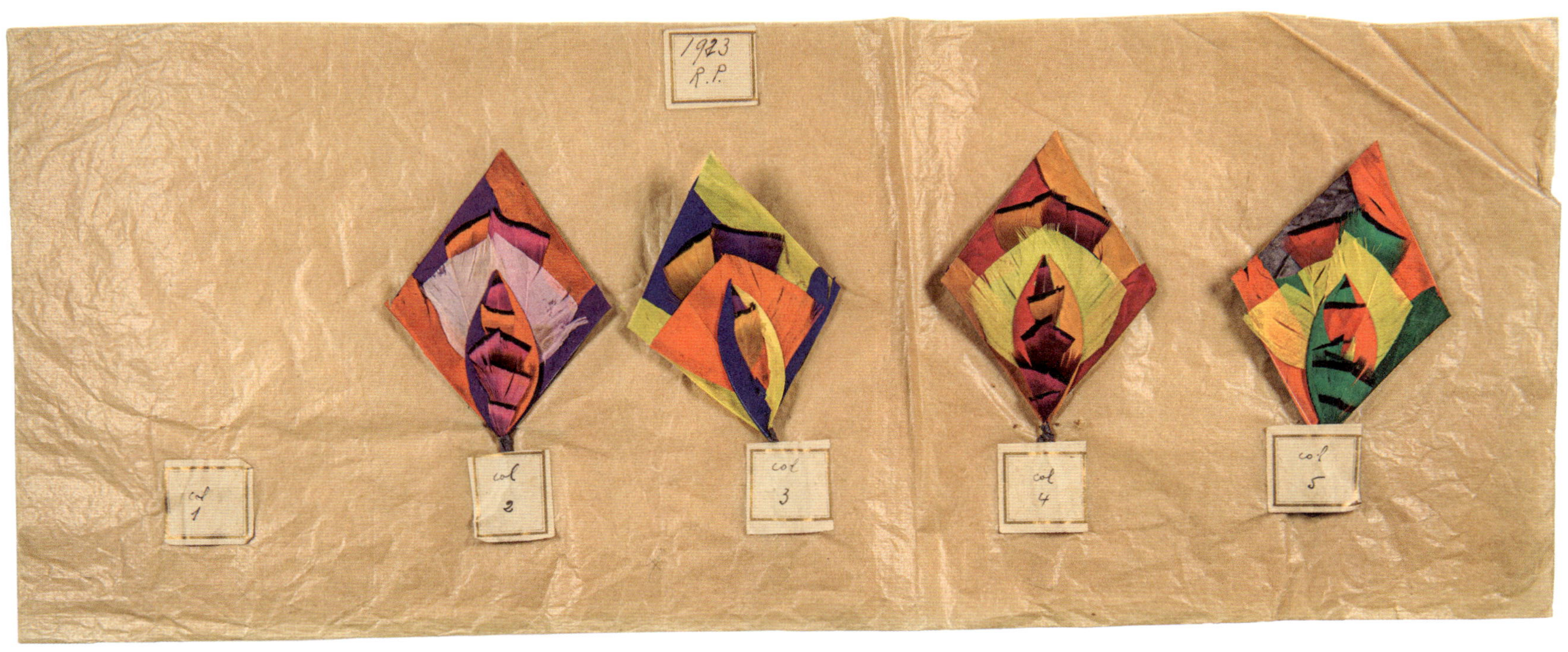
1923
R.P.
col 1
col 2
col 3
col 4
col 5

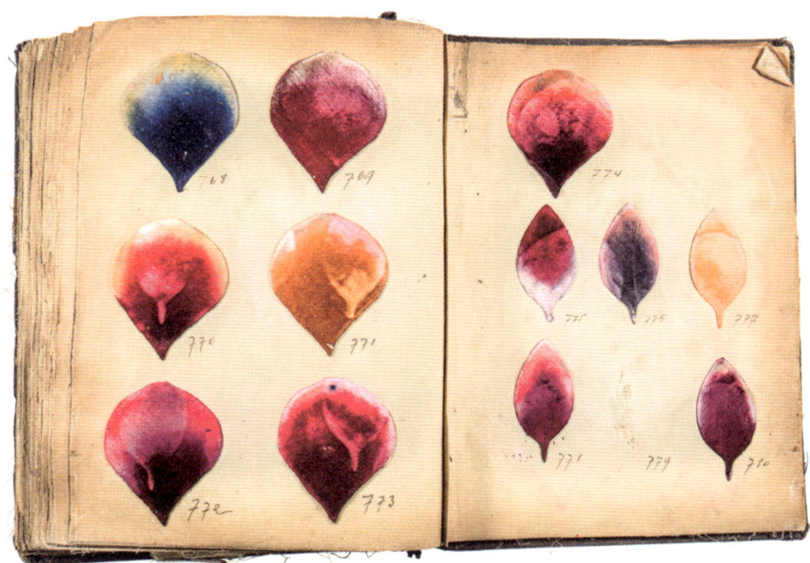

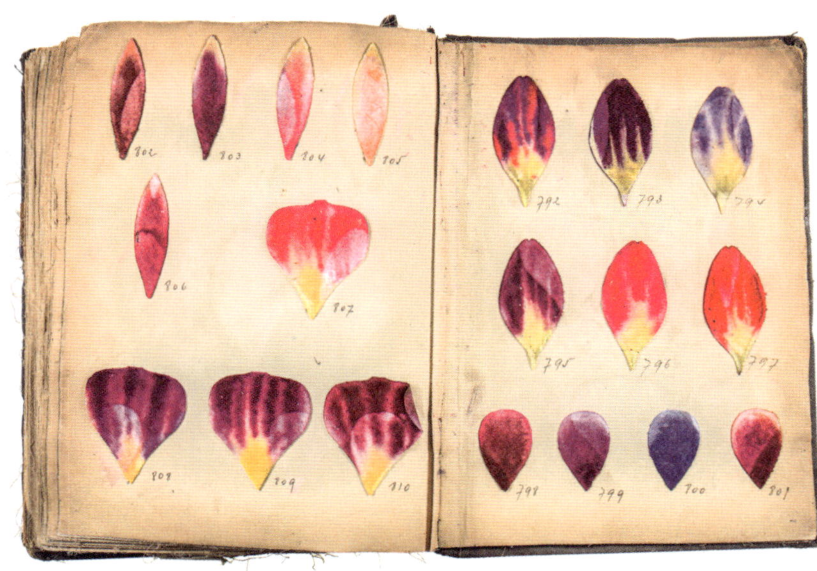

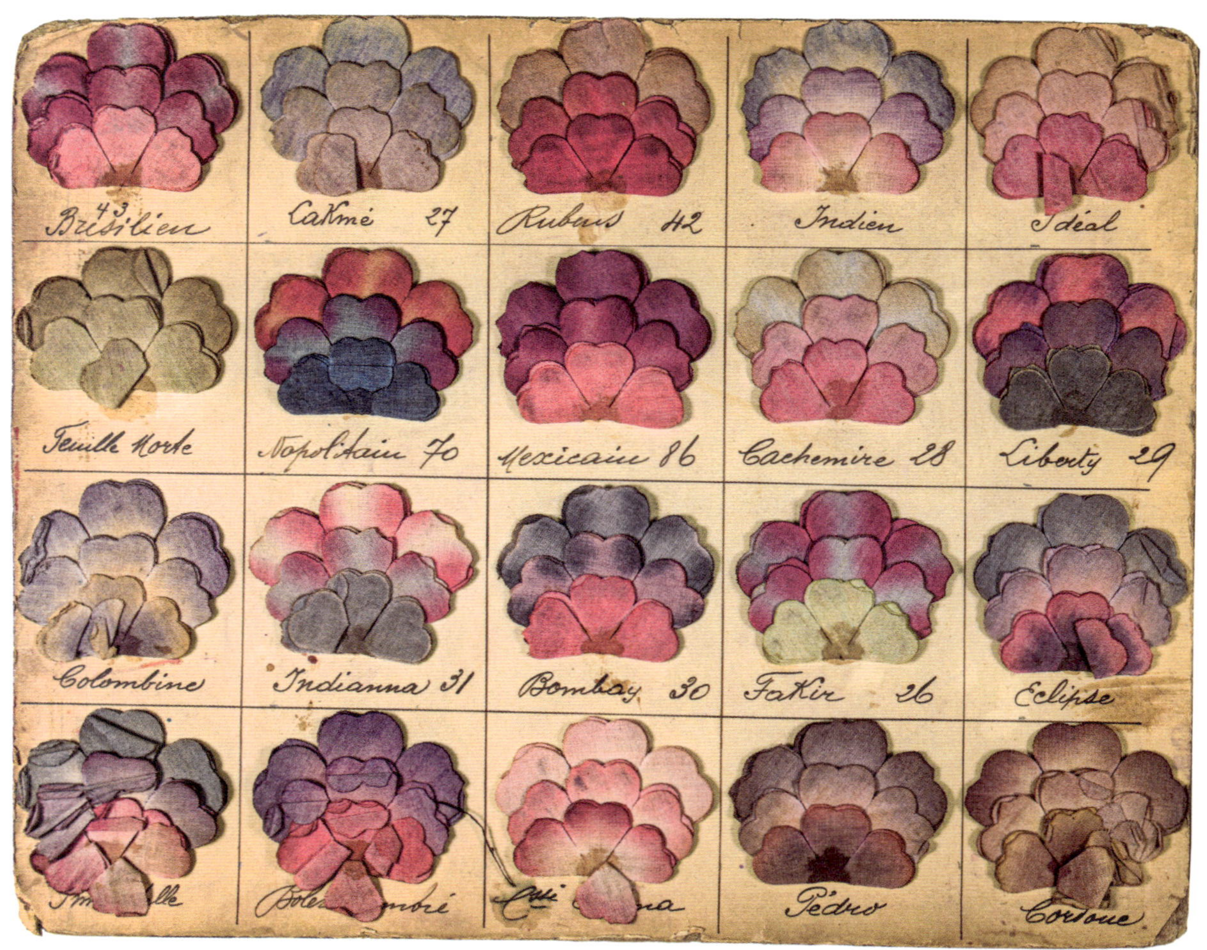

Brésilien 43
Carmé 27
Rubus 42
Indien
Idéal
Feuille Morte
Napolitain 70
Mexicain 86
Cachemire 28
Liberty 29
Colombine
Indianna 31
Bombay 30
Fakir 26
Eclipse
Pédro

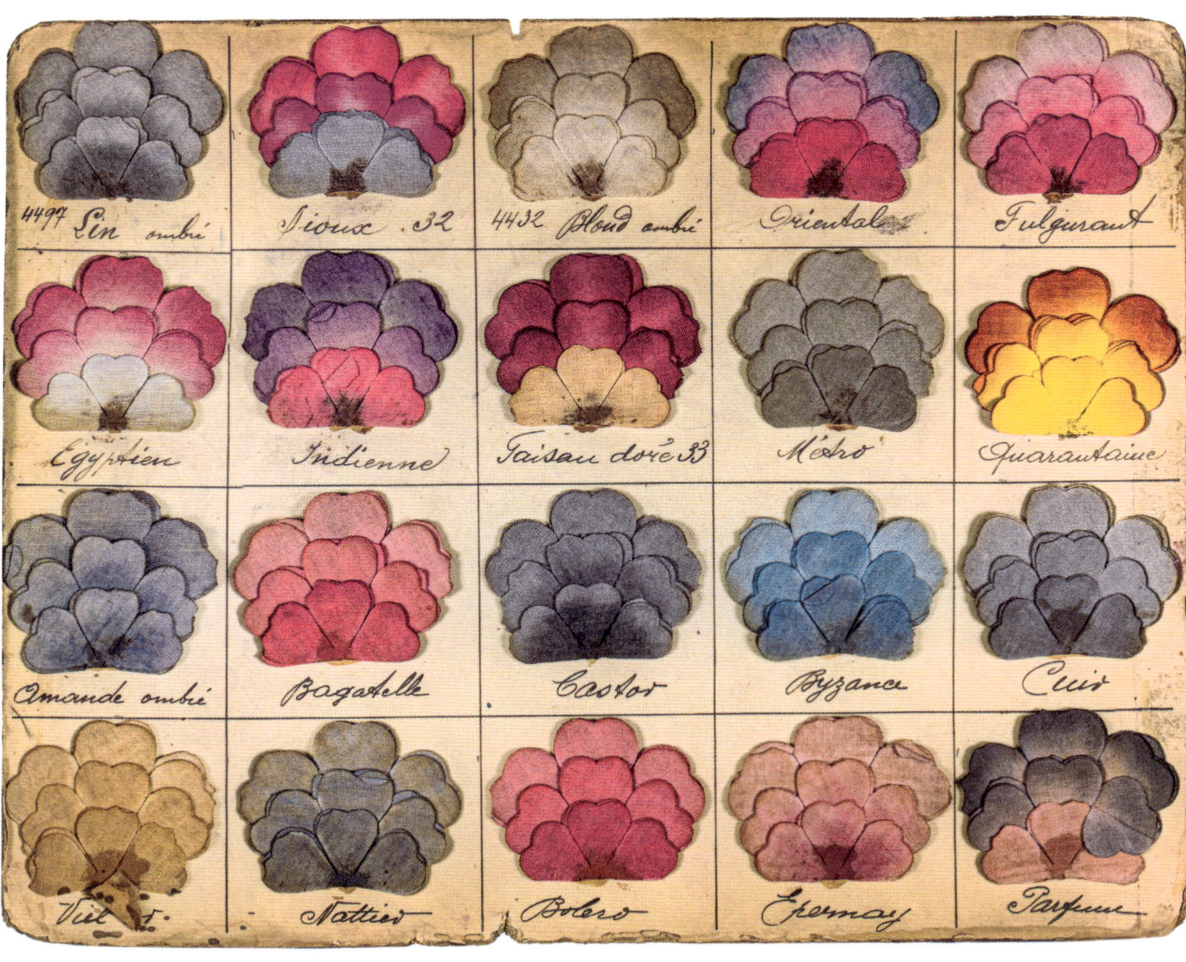
4497 Lin ombré
Sioux 32
4432 Blond ombré
Oriental
Fulgurant
Egyptien
Indienne
Faisan doré 33
Métro
Quarantaine
Amande ombré
Bagatelle
Castor
Byzance
Cuir
Nattier
Boléro
Epernay

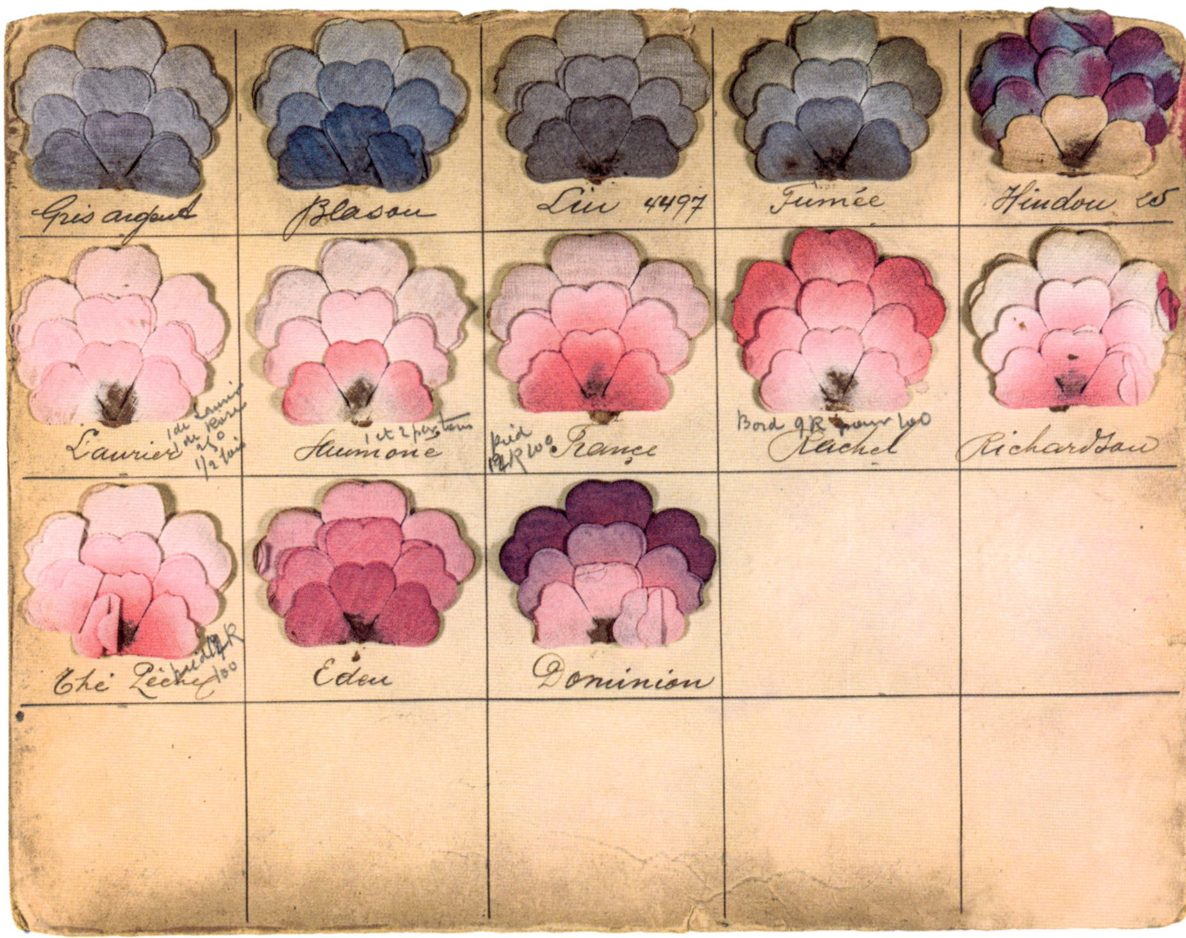
Gris argent
Blason
Lin 4497
Fumée
Laurier
France
Rachel
Eden
Dominion

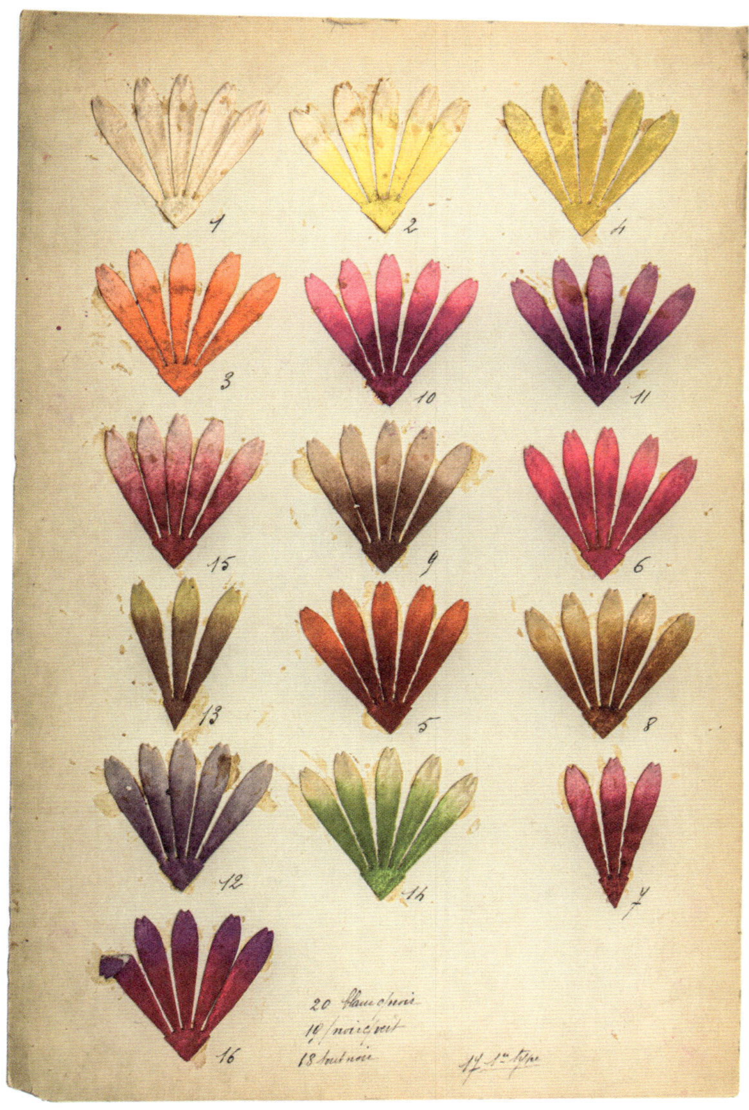

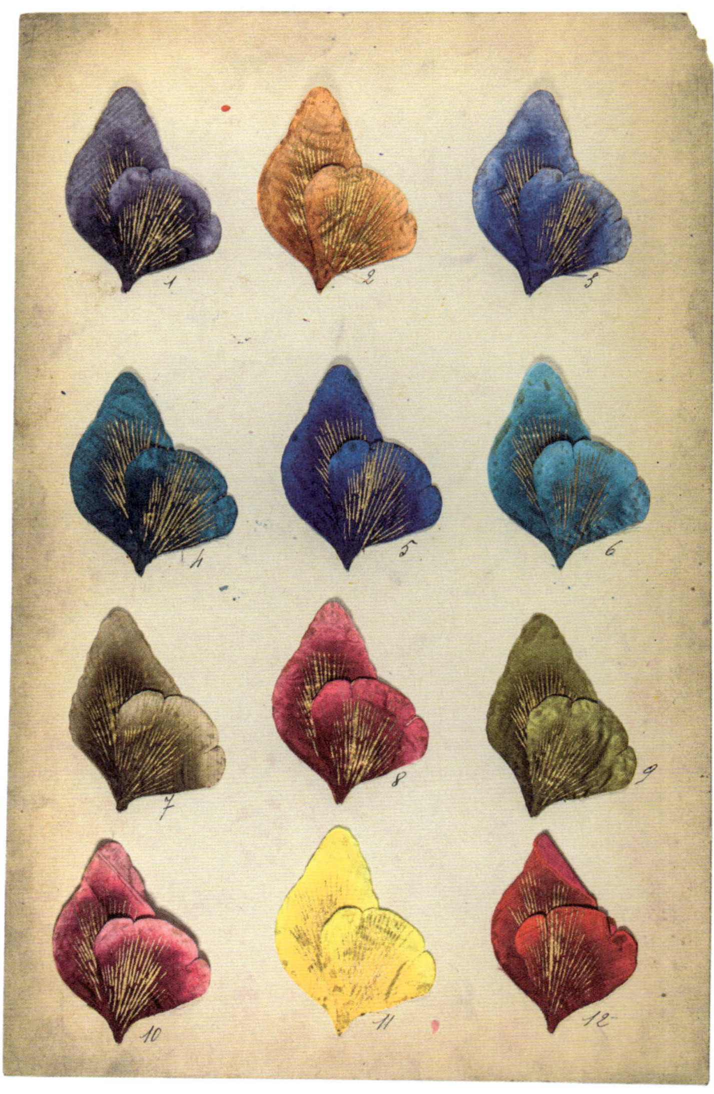

Artisanal workshops perpetuated the beauty of textile color charts, but they were either stagnant (the unchanging aesthetic of the ribbon color charts) or sterile (the DMC chart with reproductions). None reflected the opportunities for color display and the artistic creativity that the contemporary chemical industry demonstrated. In the world of clothing, the color charts of the Roaring Twenties are noticeably lacking in whimsy. Moreover, the tendency to convert the poetic names of yore into numbers began to flatten out the rich experience of color for the people who consulted these marketing tools. Fortunately, the prewar color charts had already established an evocative aesthetic and terminology that could stimulate the imagination, and the valuable product sample was still present.

THE PAINT COLOR CHART INTRODUCES USERS TO NEW PRODUCTS, CUSTOMS, AND PERCEPTIONS

——— In the color charts of the early twentieth century, decorative painters and their clients had discovered palettes that used innovative formulas and synthetic dyes. Between the world wars, the sector benefited from decisive advances made by chemistry in binding agents and pigments, particularly titanium white.[27]

In industrialized countries, attention was focused on the home: governments tried to prevent slums and encouraged construction; consumers discovered the first home decorating magazines and trade fairs devoted to interior design and household appliances.[28]

The color charts of the 1920s and 1930s reflect these developments. Manufacturers of specialized paints used color charts to inform customers about their new products. As for decorative paints, the color charts now were addressed less to professionals than to individuals, who were starting to take charge of maintaining and decorating the interiors of their homes. In this era, two major transformations took root: the first was replacing the product sample with sample colors reproduced by the printing process, and the second was standardizing shades.

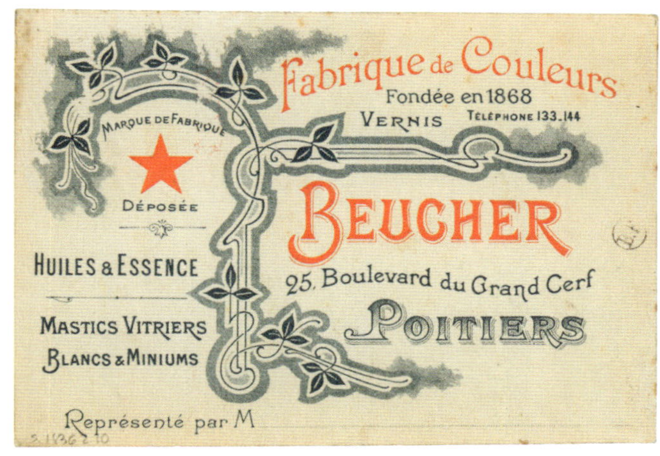

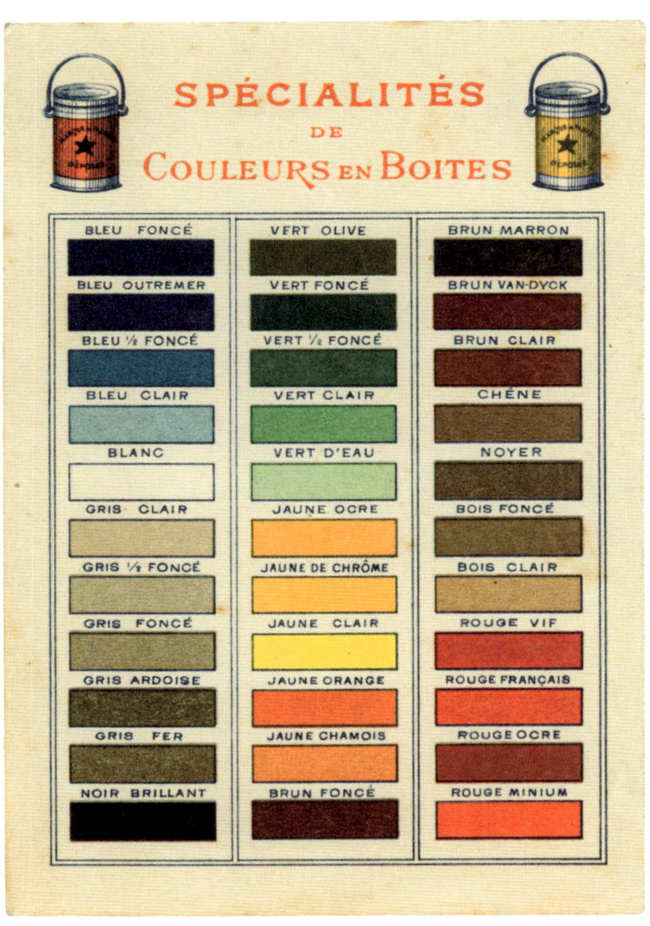

RIGHT

Beucher Business Card

At the same time, the color chart began to be reduced to an advertisement. This one served as a business card for the salespeople of the Beucher color factory in Poitiers. But these are not the company's colors or reproductions of its paint cans. This is simply a representation featuring an especially attractive image, one that was also used by other brands and was even published as a postcard.[29] The history of the color chart as icon was only beginning.

Business card color chart, Beucher, Poitiers, 1930s, card, approximately 15 × 10 cm, Bibliothèque Forney, Paris, call number RES ICO 8104

LE RIPOLIN remplace à la fois la peinture à l'huile et le vernis et donne aux objets l'aspect de la porcelaine.

LE RIPOLIN ne crevasse pas et résiste parfaitement aux intempéries.

LE RIPOLIN couvre, au kilogramme, une surface d'environ 8 mètres carrés, en une couche.

LE RIPOLIN est en vente en quatre-vingt-six nuances. Par le mélange des différentes teintes, on peut multiplier les tons à l'infini.

TOUT CE QUI NE PORTE PAS LE NOM ET LA MARQUE

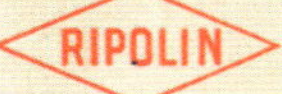

N'EST PAS DU "RIPOLIN"

MODE D'EMPLOI :

Bien remuer la couleur avec une spatule avant de s'en servir. Prendre un pinceau propre, ferme et flexible pour faire des couches minces. Le travail achevé ou interrompu, fermer la boîte et laver le pinceau dans l'essence de térébenthine.

Pour les objets poreux : le bois, le plâtre, la pierre, etc., il faudra au moins deux couches minces ; il est encore préférable d'appliquer d'abord quelques couches d'apprêt. Notre apprêt "FLETTO" est particulièrement recommandé pour cet usage. Avoir soin de bien laisser sécher la première couche avant d'appliquer la seconde. Avant de peindre, il faut, pour assurer un succès complet, un nettoyage radical enlevant la poussière, la rouille et les traces d'ancienne couleur n'adhérant pas suffisamment. La vieille peinture, bien adhérente, ne gêne pas. Du RIPOLIN devenu trop épais peut être rendu plus liquide par addition de quelques gouttes d'essence de térébenthine.

QUALITÉS SPÉCIALES

RIPOLIN	Spécial pour Radiateurs (mat et brillant)
RIPOLIN	Noir Spécial pour Tôlerie
RIPOLIN	Spécial pour Intérieur de Baignoires
RIPOLIN	Spécial p^r Planchers et Carrelages
RIPOLIN	Mat
RIPOLIN	p^r Carenes (parties immergées) pour Embarcations (parties non immergées)
RIPOLIN	Noir Spécial pour Tableaux d'Écoles
APPRÊT	Spécial pour Ciment Sec
APPRÊT	Spécial pour Murs Frais et Humides

SUR DEMANDE, QUALITÉS SPÉCIALES POUR TOUS BESOINS INDUSTRIELS.

N. B. -- Les prix et formats de boîtes de ces différentes qualités figurent sur le Tarif RIPOLIN.

R.C. Seine 58.105

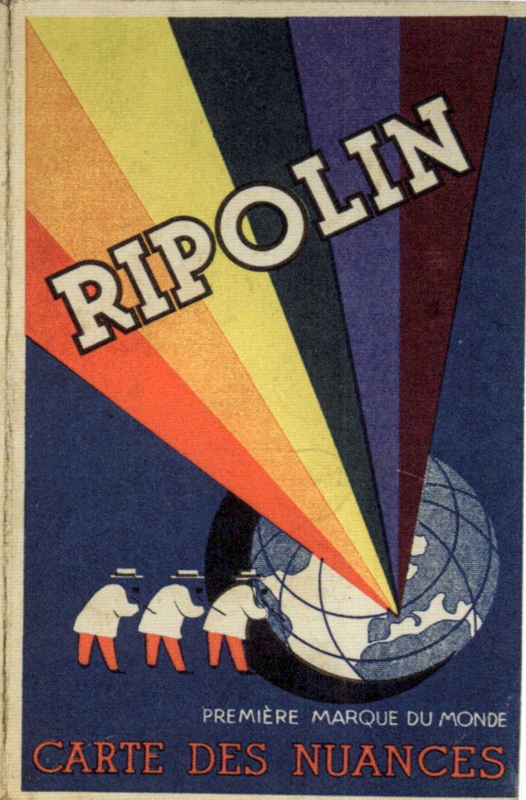

LES NUANCES 27, 78, 13, 54 NE SONT PAS RECOMMANDÉES POUR L'EXTÉRIEUR

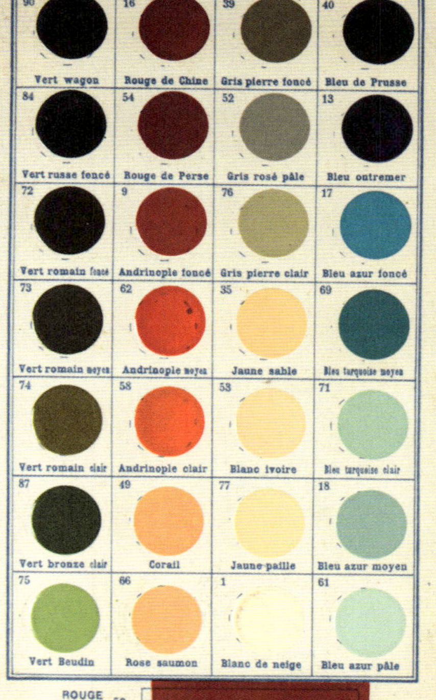

Bleus Fixes pour Extérieur : demander carte-nuances spéciale

55 Havane moyen	83 Vert bronze foncé	8 Vert jaune foncé	19 Mine orange
98 Havane foncé	88 Vert réséda foncé	80 Vert jaune clair	94 Jaune orangé
95 Bois (ton de)	68 Bleu turquoise foncé	92 Vert réséda clair	14 Jaune foncé
42 Havane clair	63 Violet bleu	7 Vert de mer foncé	4 Jaune clair
56 Ocre jaune	64 Violet rose	44 Vert de mer clair	46 Jaune soufre
70 Chamois foncé	67 Violet mauve	45 Vert d'eau pâle	2 Crème
31 Chamois clair	Or foncé	Argent	Or pâle

Nos petites pastilles étant faites avec le Ripolin même, les nuances sont donc identiques au produit livré. Cependant elles peuvent foncer légèrement sur une carte très ancienne ou conservée à l'obscurité.

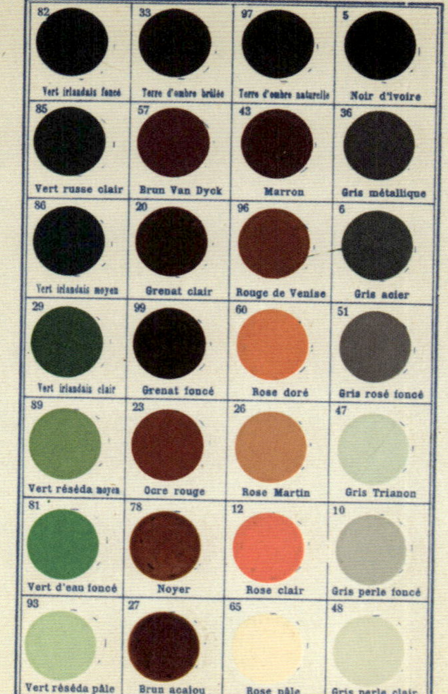

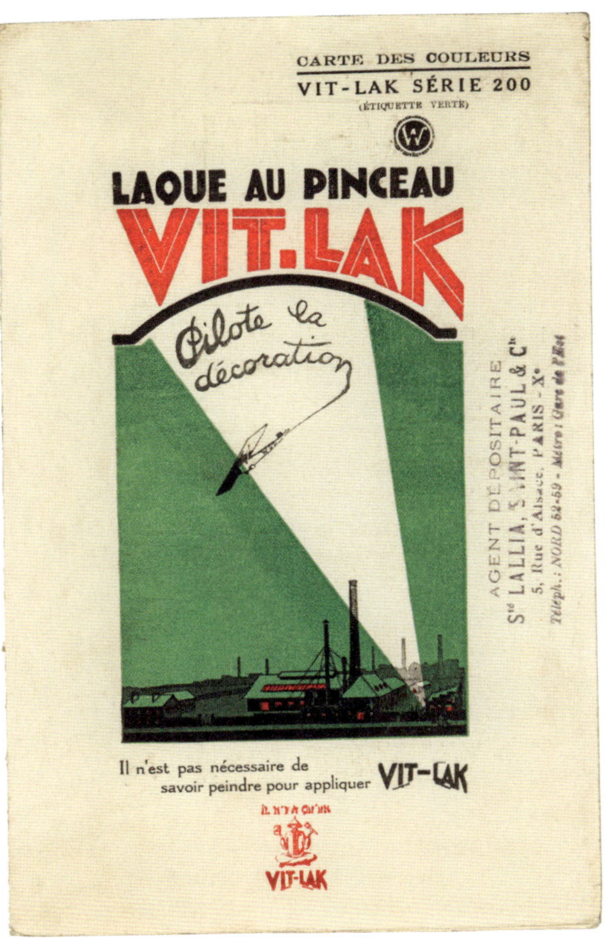

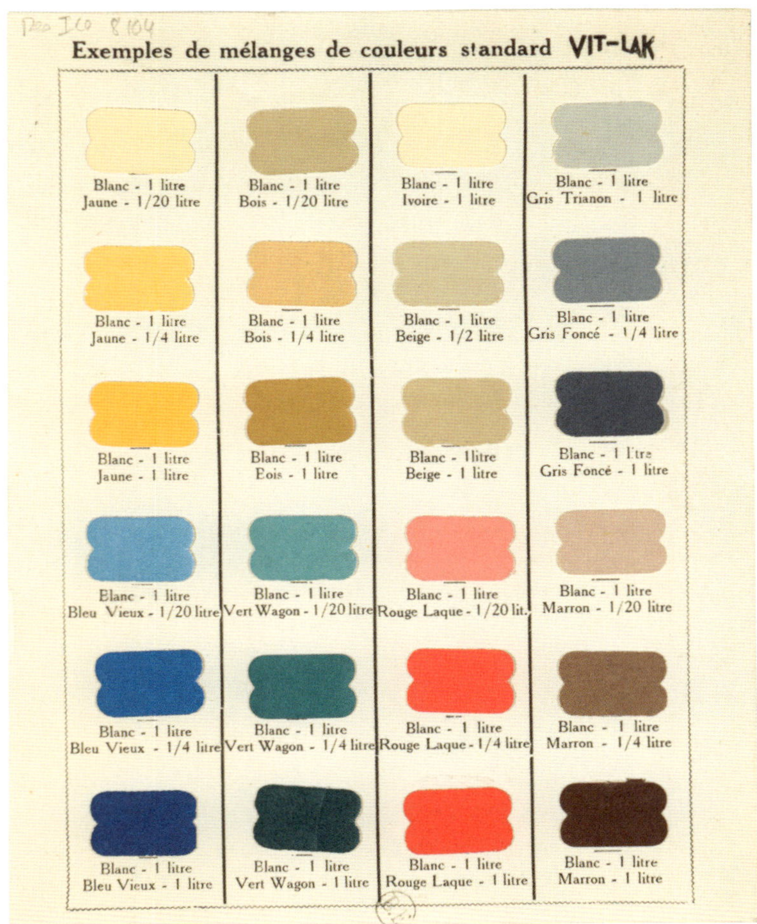

VIT-LAK SÉRIE 200 N° 011028
(Etiquette Verte)
AU PINCEAU

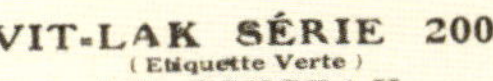

VIT-LAK

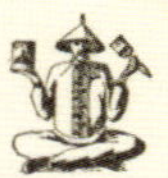

LAQUE-ÉMAIL NITROCELLULOSIQUE

VIT-LAK AU PINCEAU
(Etiquette verte) Série 200

N° 200	1/20 de litre	la boite frs	4.25
N° 201	1/10 »	» »	6.75
N° 203	1/4 »	» »	16.50
N° 205	1/2 litre	» »	30.»»
N° 206	1 litre	» »	58.»»

Bleu Marine, Bleu Vieux, Bleu Delft, Vert d'Eau, Vert Jardin, Vert Wagon, Bois, Marron, Orange, Jaune Maïs, Canari, Ivoire, Beige, Rouge Laque, Rouge Ancien, Grenat, Gris Clair, Gris Foncé, Gris Trianon Aubergine, Blanc, Noir.

Pour bois naturel
Transparent (Incolore, Acajou).

BOUCHE-PORES

Liquide au pinceau
pour BOIS à laquer avec "VIT-LAK"

N° 265	1/2 litre	frs	16.»»
N° 266	1 litre	»	30.»»

APPRET ISOLANT

au Pinceau pour "VIT-LAK"

N° 443	pour obtenir 1/4 de litre	fr.	11
N° 445	» » 1/2 litre	»	20
N° 446	» » 1 litre	»	37

Blanc, Jaune, Rouge, Gris Foncé, Gris Clair

Pour isoler les anciennes peintures avant l'applicationdu "Vit-Lak" au pistolet.

Une excellente sous-couche pour métal, bois, plâtre, fibro-ciment, etc...

DILUANT pour VIT-LAK

pour allonger "Vit-Lak" s'il devient trop épais et pour nettoyer les brosses ou pour décaper sur anciennes peintures.

N° 309	1/16 de litre	frs	3.75
N° 310	1/8 de litre	»	5.»»
N° 313	1/4 de litre	»	9.»»
N° 315	1/2 litre	»	16.»»
N° 316	1 litre	»	27.»»

Le Diluant pour "Vit-Lak" est spécialement étudié pour assurer un bon résultat. — Ne pas employer des Diluants ordinaires.

Contenances approximatives
Prix sans engagement.

PINCEAUX pour VIT-LAK

N° 1	larg. env.	15 m m	Pièce	2.25
N° 2	» »	25 »	»	5.50
N° 3	» »	35 »	»	8.50
N° 4	» »	45 »	»	13.50
N° 5	» »	55 »	»	21.50

TENILISSE

est employé pour lisser les surfaces Vit-Lakées et pour éliminer toutes défectuosités, traces, poussières, etc..., survenues pendant l'application du "Vit-Lak"

Son emploi sur "Vit-Lak" assure un beau fini velouté.

N° 271	petite boite	Frs :	9.»»
N° 273	moyenne	»	18.»»

TENILUSTRE

est employé pour polir et lustrer la surface préalablement lissée au Tenilisse donnant ainsi au "Vit-Lak" un brillant superbe.

N° 281	petite boite	Frs :	9.»»
N° 283	moyenne		18.»»

UNE NOUVEAUTÉ

Le Pulvériseur à main VIT-LAK a été créé par nous sur la demande d'une nombreuse clientèle pour accélérer l'application par pulvérisation de Vit-Lak sur toutes surfaces et spécialement sur les surfaces irrégulières comme meubles en osier, rotin, chaises cannées, radiateurs, paniers, objets moulés, grillages, etc....

Pulvériseur à main pour VIT-LAK

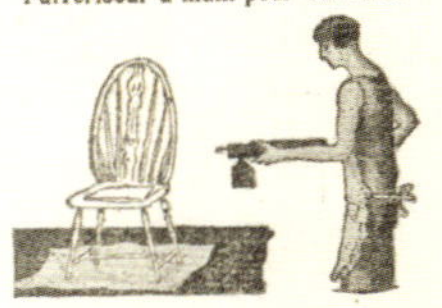

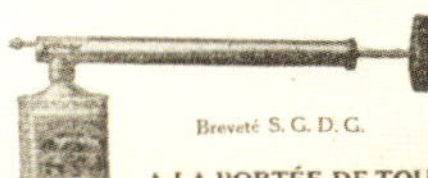

Breveté S. G. D. G.

A LA PORTÉE DE TOUS

N° 701	Pulvériseur complet	Frs	35.»»
N° 722	Godet de rechange.	»	4.50

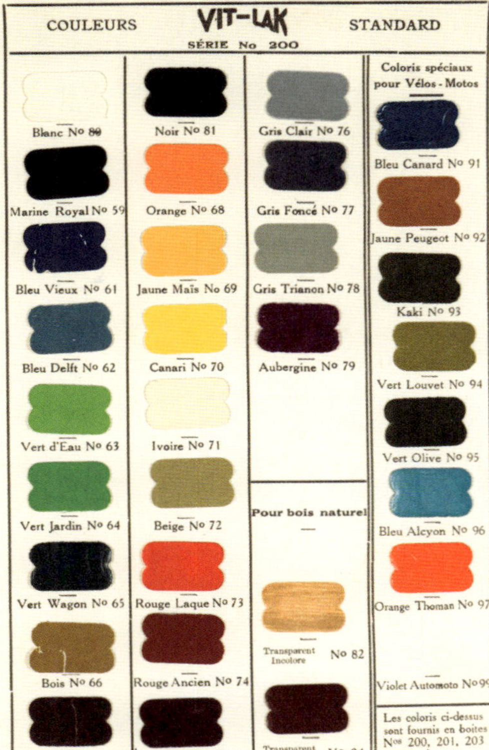

En mélangeant les coloris ci-dessus on peut multiplier à l'infini les couleurs désirées, en obtenant toujours des tons doux et agréables.

Les couleurs "Vit-Lak" se mélangent avec beaucoup plus de facilité que la peinture à l'huile.

K 501

Decorative Paint Color Charts Target the Individual—Especially Women

PREVIOUS PAGE SPREAD, LEFT

Ripolin Shades

The Ripolin color range had remained unchanged since its very first color charts in the early twentieth century, and they still featured this guarantee: "As these dots are made with a thin layer of Ripolin itself, the colors are therefore identical to the delivered product." However, the back of the printout now featured the logo with the famous trio of painters. The three are also seen hard at work in the list of nine specialized products.

The Ripolin color charts are a kind of recurring theme throughout the history of French society and color. With reassuring consistency, their palette and color names continued into the 1950s and rooted the association between a color and its name in consumers' memories, especially since these names were quite simple. Only a few of them puzzle us today: *Roman Green*, *Russian Green*, *Beudin Green* (once again), and *Réséda Green*.[30] And what shade is *Martin Pink*?

Color Card, Ripolin, Paris, 1920s, card, 10.5 × 17 cm, 2 folds, Bibliothèque Forney, Paris, call number RES ICO 8104

PREVIOUS PAGE SPREAD, RIGHT

Vit-lak

This color chart reflects several developments in the history of paints. Of course, the reference to Chinese lacquer existed before the war, even if the conjugation of the product's name is new: "Tout peut être vit-laké en quelques minutes" ("Everything can be vit-laked in a few minutes"), with the participle "vit-laké" pronounced like "quickly lacquered." Using paint as a tool to combat poor quality is also quite a common argument in color charts ("any object with an ugly appearance takes on value and beauty after one or two layers of Vit-lak") and, in fact, had long contributed to the distrust of color.[31] The samples always consisted of paint applied to paper that was glued to the backing, and enamel lacquers had been sold since the early twentieth century.

However, a new formula was now available: nitrocellulose paint. It was the result of recycling remaining stores of explosives from the war, with chemists taking advantage of the strong filmogenic powers of their components. And the image of a worker painting was replaced by an ordinary female consumer. In fact, the image of a woman was used several times, in connection with these phrases: "It's not necessary to know how to paint," "Everyone can do it," and "Easy for the whole family to use." As of the 1920s, color charts affirmed the independence of consumers. The territory had been prepared by an abundance of amateur how-to guides on maintaining and beautifying the home, which had been circulating since the previous century.[32] The goal of the how-to guides was to allow beginners to improve the cleanliness, comfort, and aesthetics of their living environment in an economic and creative way. They converted workers and farmers to a bourgeois lifestyle and spread the values promoted by this social class. And, most of all, by associating free time with the domestic space, they helped keep the working class away from the bars or—even worse!—workers' movements or union meetings.

The instructions available on color charts before the war prepared individuals for these practices, but these consumers still needed guidance. Thus, the printout also had another color chart showing examples of mixing colors to create new shades. In other words, anyone who decided to pick up a brush could mix their own paint. A new field of experiencing color was open to all.

Vit-lak Color Chart, 200 Series, Établissements Weeks, Paris, 1920s, cards, 22 × 14 cm, 1 fold, and 22 × 14 cm, Bibliothèque Forney, Paris, call number RES ICO 8104

Product Samples at Stake

OPPOSITE

Novémail

This color chart also reassures consumers of the ease of painting the interiors and furnishings of their homes. "Every day," it states, "thousands of people, most of them with no experience, beautify their interior with Novémail." Yet a new dimension has been added: "It's a pleasure to decorate your home yourself, to express your taste by the choice of colors." Illustrations give examples of colorful interiors and improved objects, including a refrigerator, radio, and sink.

However, the range has only twenty colors. And what about these colors? Very discreetly, a major transformation in the history of the color chart had taken place. The document stipulates in a very small font: "As the colors above were obtained with printing ink, there is no guarantee that they are strictly similar to Novémail colors." While cosmetics

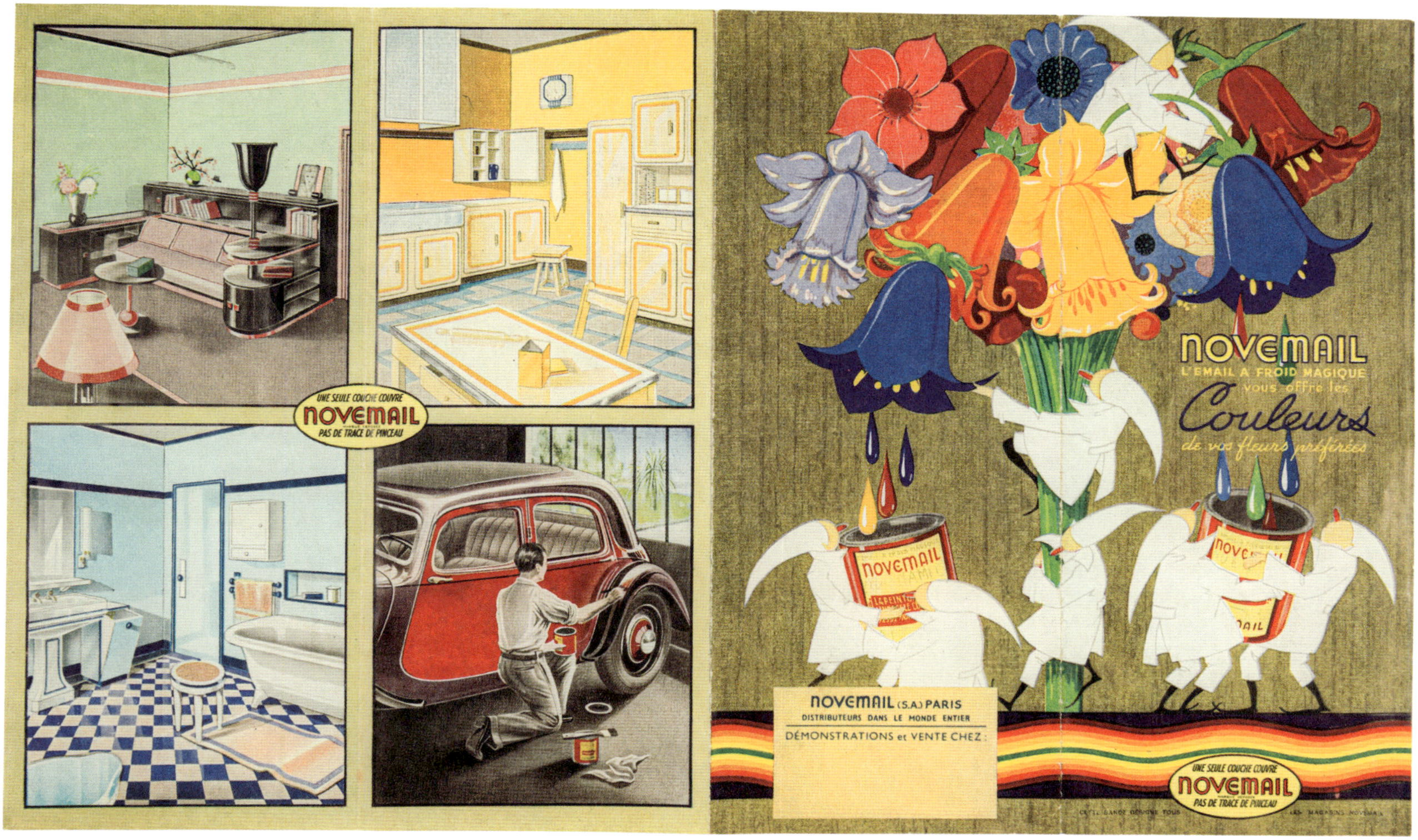

UNE SEULE COUCHE COUVRE
NOVEMAIL
PAS DE TRACE DE PINCEAU

NOVEMAIL
L'EMAIL A FROID MAGIQUE
vous offre les
Couleurs
de vos fleurs préférées

NOVEMAIL (S.A.) PARIS
DISTRIBUTEURS DANS LE MONDE ENTIER
DÉMONSTRATIONS et VENTE CHEZ :

UNE SEULE COUCHE COUVRE
NOVEMAIL
PAS DE TRACE DE PINCEAU

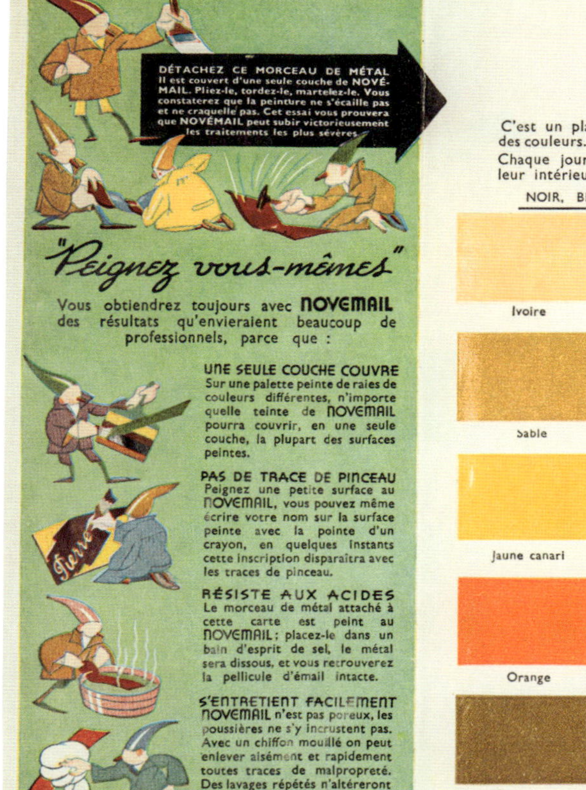

Entourez-vous de Couleurs Gaies

C'est un plaisir de décorer soi-même son intérieur et d'exprimer son goût par le choix des couleurs. Avec NOVEMAIL vous aurez la sensation de vivre au milieu de vos fleurs favorites. Chaque jour, des milliers de personnes, la plupart sans aucune expérience, embellissent leur intérieur avec NOVEMAIL ; vous le pouvez également : c'est étonnamment simple.

NOIR, BLANC, TRANSPARENT, ALUMINIUM ET DANS LES COULEURS SUIVANTES :

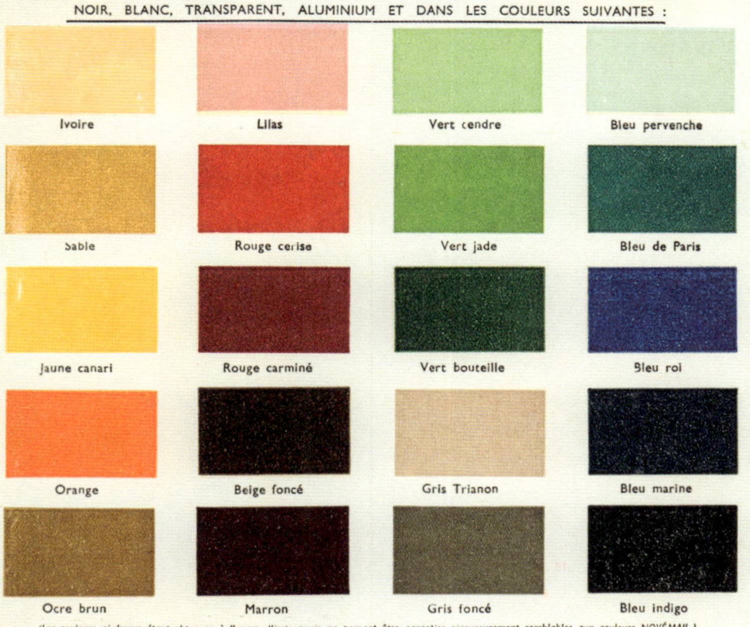

(Les couleurs ci-dessus étant obtenues à l'encre d'imprimerie ne peuvent être garanties rigoureusement semblables aux couleurs NOVÉMAIL.)

PRODUITS NOVÉMAIL EMPLOYÉS ET RECOMMANDÉS DANS LE MONDE ENTIER

NOVÉMAIL — INTÉRIEUR — EXTÉRIEUR — BLANC MAT — PARQUET — VERNIS (INCOLORE) — VERNIS (ACAJOU OU NOYER) — PINCEAUX (GARANTIS PURE SOIES) — ENDUIT (NOIR) — CHASSIS (NOIR) — DILUANT — MASTIC — PLATREINE — PAPIER ABRASIF — CHIFFONS — TIROT (RUBAN ADHÉSIF) — POLISH — COLLE — FILTRES

F 23 B 1000 M-6-37 R. C. Seine 261.682 B

NOTA. Les coloris Lilas, Bleu pervenche et Marron sont remplacés par Rose bébé, Bleu clair et Bordeaux.
Nouveau coloris : Gris clair. Juillet 1939

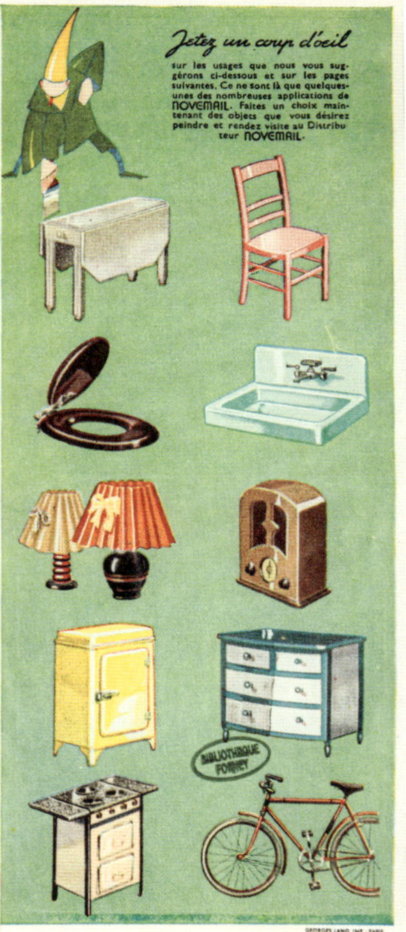

manufacturers were compelled to give up product samples, paint manufacturers had the option of keeping them. In other words, when they chose to reproduce colors instead of providing samples of actual paint, they accepted and approved the fact that the samples on their color charts were now only approximations of shades.

The major role of the color chart—presenting color—was losing its meaning. The shift was not immediate, for use of the product sample would continue for some time, but the movement was underway. Thanks to the color chart, society had discovered that all colors were now accessible. People had learned to extrapolate from a small sample the future color of a kitchen or a facade, but now they would need to become accustomed to imagining color on the basis of an inadequate sample.

Novémail, the Magic Cold Enamel, Offers You the Colors of Your Favorite Flowers, Novémail, Paris, 1939, card, 21.5 × 17.5 cm, 2 folds, Bibliothèque Forney, Paris, call number CC PEIN 1 Plano

Paints Become Specialized

OPPOSITE, TOP LEFT

Ripolin Car Glaze

Product samples continued in color charts whose products were intended for more specialized applications, like this glazing to cover up marks on the body of cars. In the 1920s, paint brands offered ranges of colors to maintain or change a vehicle's appearance.

Of the twenty-eight color samples, dark and unsaturated tones dominate, with occasional shades that are lighter and brighter, including two reds that are generically called "For Train" and "Automobile." Several are associated with a brand of car (Delahaye, Citroën, Renault), and the range is clearly adapted for the maintenance of these vehicles, which were often two- or three-tone.

An advertisement for a special tire paint completed the chart: "This product is used on the tires and running boards of cars, bicycles, etc. and on all rubber objects to which you would like to give a new appearance." We do not know if it was available in several colors, like the color chart for rubber produced by the Société Anonyme des Matières Colorantes et Produits Chimiques de Saint-Denis in 1928.[33] In any case, considering the elasticity of the material, the results must have been mixed.

Ripolin Glazing with Special Finish for Cars, Ripolin, Paris, 1920s, card, 10.5 × 16 cm, 1 fold, Bibliothèque Forney, Paris, call number RES ICO 8104

OPPOSITE, BOTTOM

Merville & Morgan Lacquers

This marketing tool for lacquers has an innovative system: thin disks of painted resin with labels on the back nestled into a box. The labels indicate that in this case some shades were developed for automobiles, such as *Rider Green* and *Light Torpedo Green*. Dark and/or unsaturated colors dominate, but it is possible that they have darkened over time. The set is compact, easy to transport in its solid container, and perfectly suited to comparing colors. The lacquered material can be examined at different angles and its opaqueness and polish can be evaluated. Experiencing color is complete and immediate.

Superlaque Color Chart, Merville & Morgan, Aubervilliers, 1920s, box, 6.5 × 12 × 6.5 cm, containing 80 resin disks, Albi Couleurs, Association Mémoire des Industries de la Couleur, Albi

OPPOSITE, TOP RIGHT

Fils Lévy-Finger Polilac

This marketing tool for lacquer has been less stable over time, as the paint was applied to a thin, supple medium that appears to be cellophane. On the back of the samples, the name of each color has been stamped (*Aurora Red no. 15*, *Green no. 28*), but it is difficult today to determine the formula that produced them. Indeed, the Fils Lévy-Finger company produced various products: colors in powder form, colors ground with essence and bone glue, and Rénéine (a resin) for car bodies.[34] Applying the lacquer to the backing must have been problematic because it is stipulated inside the box: "As these samples cannot be reproduced under identical conditions, our delivered products are as similar to them as possible."

Polilac Color Chart, S.A. Les Fils Lévy-Finger, Paris, 1921, box, 5 × 8 × 8 cm, containing approximately 200 sheets of painted cellophane (?), Albi Couleurs, Association Mémoire des Industries de la Couleur, Albi

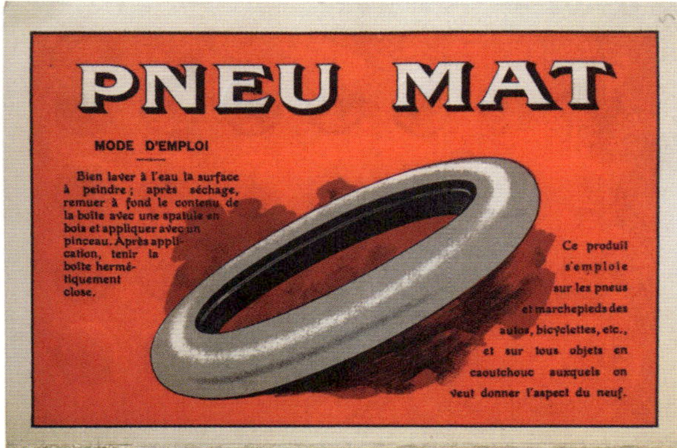

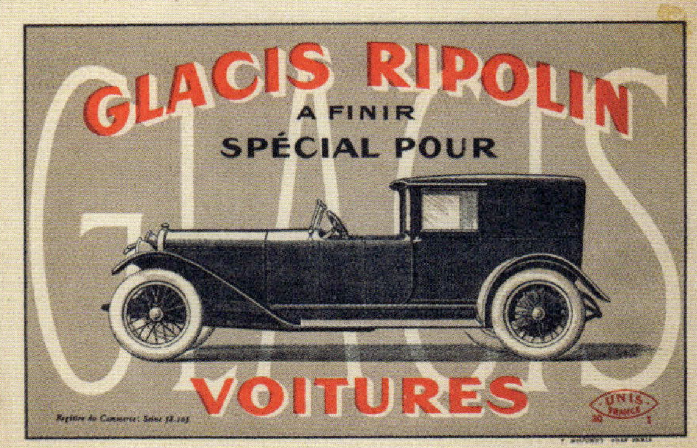

BIEN REMUER AVANT USAGE

MODE D'EMPLOI

Appliquer uniformément, grassement mais sans e[illegible] GLACIS RIPOLIN A FINIR sur l[illegible]face à couvrir en passant la brosse horizontalement et verticalement.

Décharger ensuite la brosse de l'excès de GLACIS, croiser à nouveau en terminant le travail de bas en haut.

RECOMMANDATION IMPORTANTE

Employer des brosses plates, fermes et flexibles dites "QUEUES DE MORUE"

Les qualités de notre **GLACIS**, *dont la durée et la beauté sont remarquables, en font un :: :: :: produit incomparable :: :: ::*

Tous les propriétaires de voitures pourront appliquer **eux-mêmes**, avec agrément, notre **GLACIS**, grâce à sa merveilleuse facilité d'emploi, qui le met à la portée des mains les moins expérimentées.

Son usage fait réaliser une économie considérable et peut rendre la voiture disponible en 48 heures.

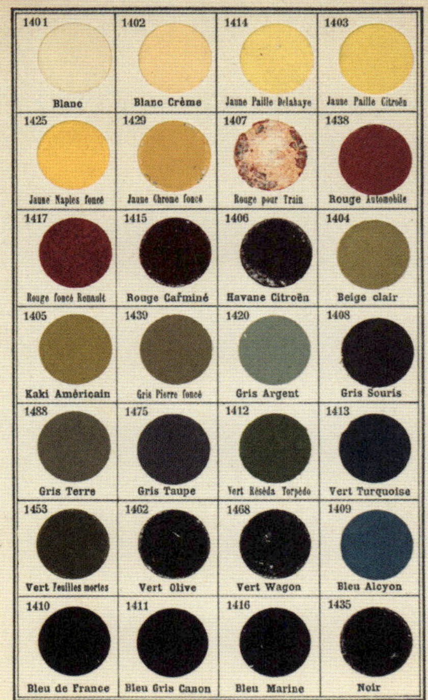

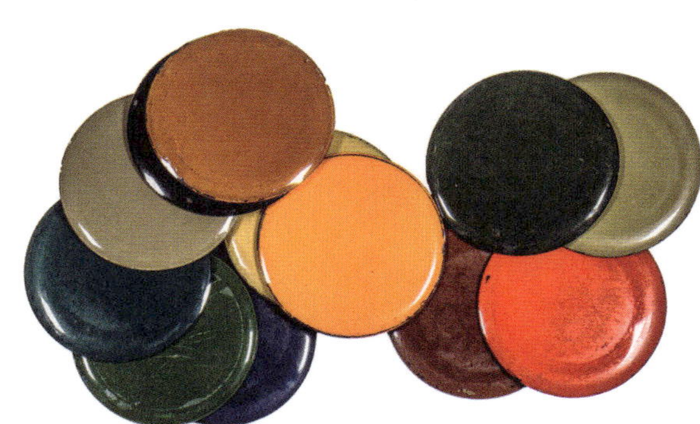

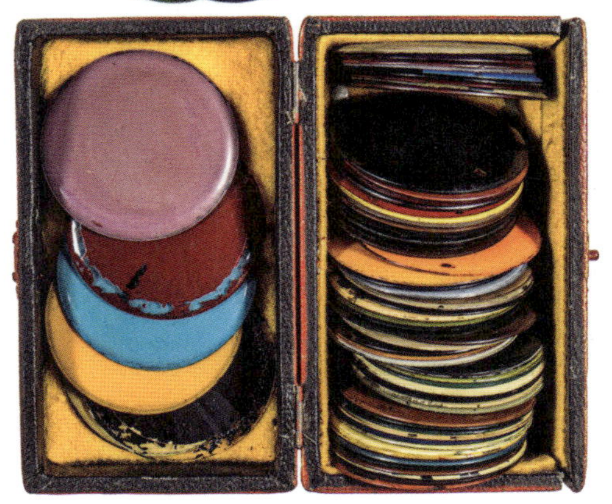

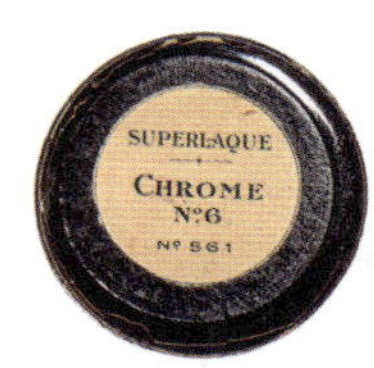

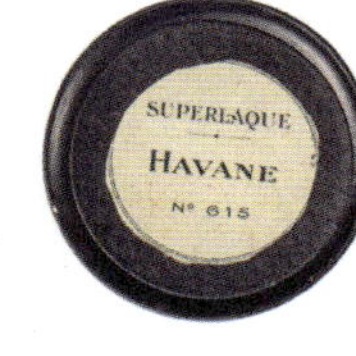

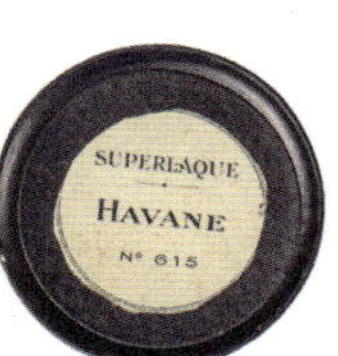

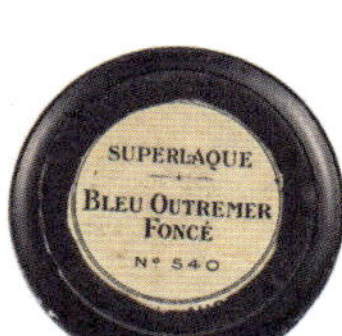

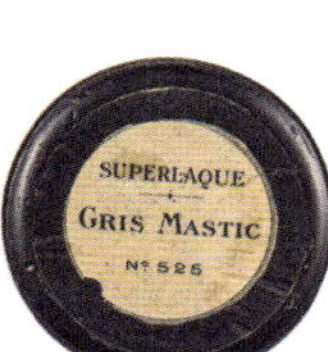

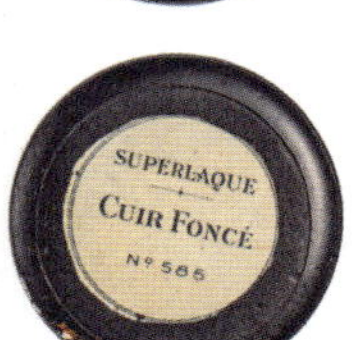

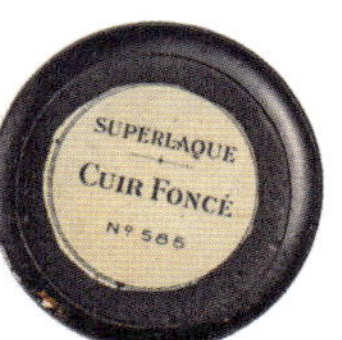

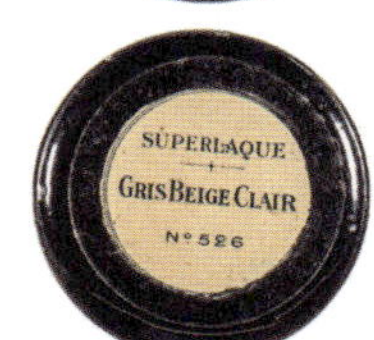

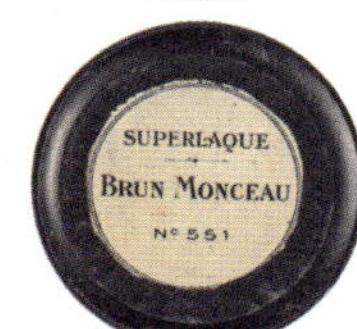

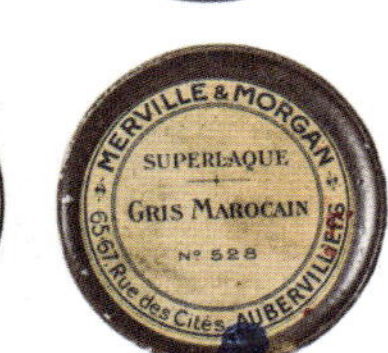

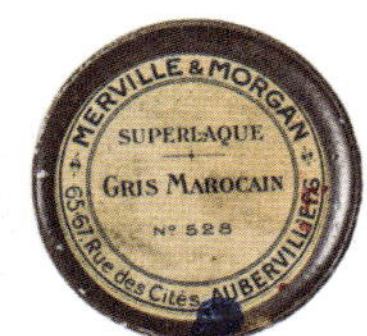

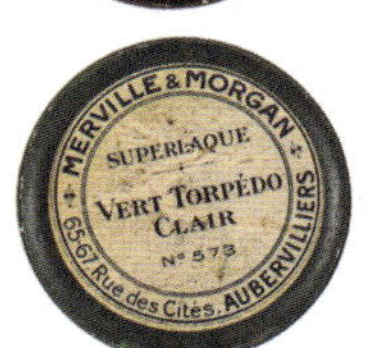

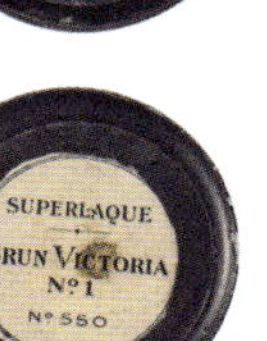

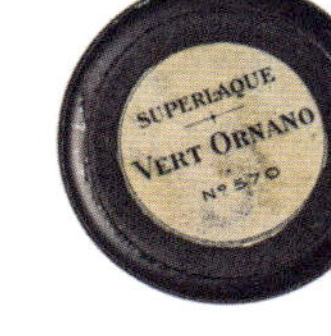

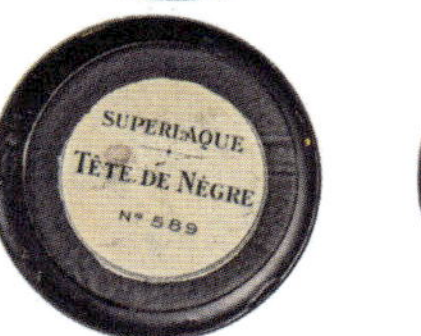

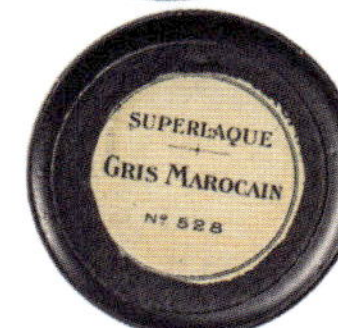

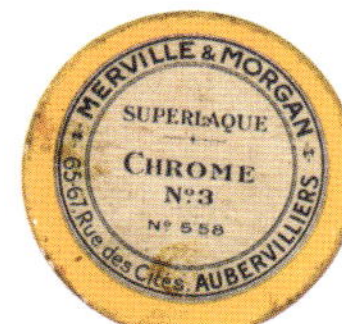

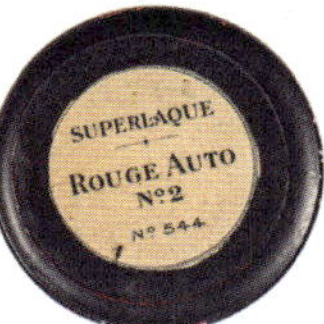

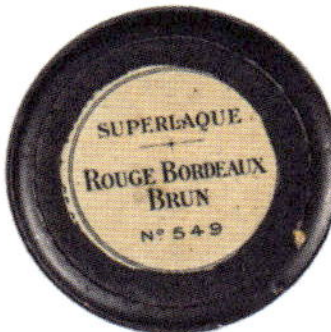

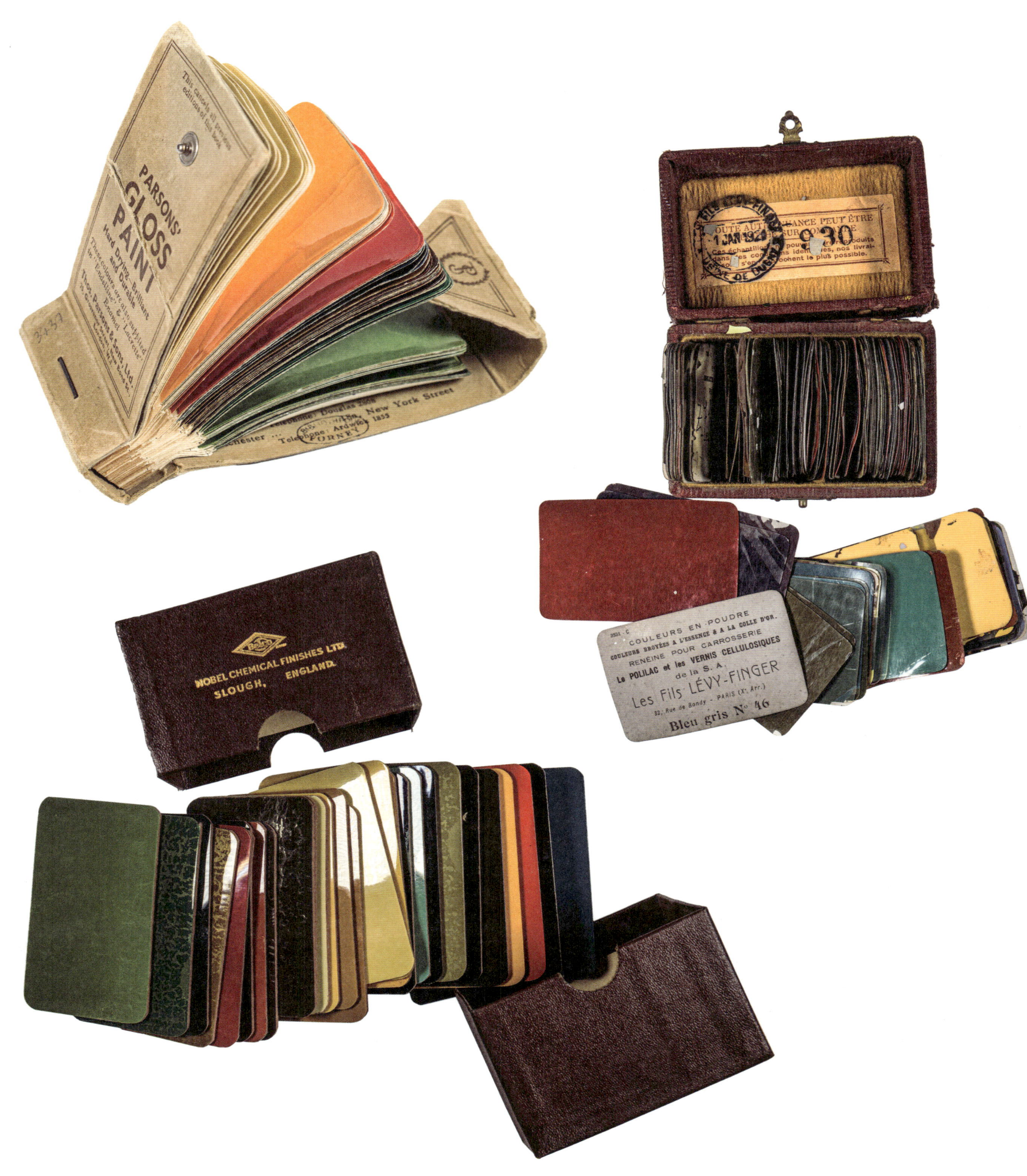
PARSONS' GLOSS PAINT
NOBEL CHEMICAL FINISHES LTD.
SLOUGH, ENGLAND.
COULEURS EN POUDRE
COULEURS BROYÉES A L'ESSENCE & A LA COLLE D'OR.
RENÉINE POUR CARROSSERIE
Le POLILAC et les VERNIS CELLULOSIQUES
de la S. A.
Les Fils LÉVY-FINGER
32, Rue de Bondy - PARIS (Xe Arr.)
Bleu gris N° 46

OPPOSITE BELOW

Belco Enamel

Nobel Chemical Finishes, a London company, specialized in the 1920s in selling paints and other finishing products for cars, like this line called Belco, a hard enamel that was first marketed in 1926. Each color sample is presented here applied to a felt plate, with the company's logo and address and the name and number of the color printed on the back. The range of bright, varied colors has been preserved in all its freshness. As with the Merville & Morgan color chart, this boxed set is perfectly functional as well as aesthetically pleasing.

Belco Color Chart for Coatings on Felt, Nobel Chemical Finishes, London, 1930s, box, 7 × 10 × 6.5 cm, containing 30 felt plates, Albi Couleurs, Association Mémoire des Industries de la Couleur, Albi

Standardization

OPPOSITE TOP LEFT

Parsons Gloss Paint

The quality of Thomas Parsons & Sons' varnishes and paint colors for car bodies, theaters, and manors was celebrated soon after the company's founding in London in 1802. The company endlessly innovated; it acquired a colorimeter in 1915 that allowed it to offer five hundred new shades. It also related the history and customs of decorative painting in various publications, including *A Few Suggestions for Ornamental Decoration*, *A Collection of Designs & Colour Schemes for Painters' & Decorators' Work*, and *A Tint Book of Historical Colours Suitable for Decorative Work* published in 1908 and 1934 with many illustrations and with color samples.[35] These books inspired the decoration of many buildings. They would also help instruct several generations of color experts in all the applied arts.

This marketing tool includes a statement indicating that the samples represent only the color, not the final appearance; this information refers to the way in which paint may change depending on the surface to which it is applied and its exposure to light, and is not a disclaimer regarding flawed samples. The range, with a variety of shades and degrees of saturation, is arranged in the order of a color wheel. This very small marketing tool prefigures the fan-shaped color charts that would soon appear. The tool is connected with a staple. Another innovation: it adapted the standards expressed in 1931 by the British Standards Institution, and its codes appear on the back of each sample. Gradually, standardization reached all colors used in industry and evolved toward the establishment of a universal color range.

Parsons' Gloss Paint, Hard Drying, Brilliant and Durable, Thos. Parsons & Sons, Ltd., London, 1930s, bundle, 11.5 × 6 cm, Bibliothèque Forney, Paris, call number CC 3737[1900] Plano—Thema PEIN

——— These color charts reflect a paint industry that could now be divided into two types.[36] For paints for industrial use, the color chart adopted new forms but continued its function of exemplifying color. For decorative paints, the ranges began to shrink while also becoming approximative as the reproduction replaced the product sample.

FINE ARTS COLOR CHARTS BECOME INCREASINGLY DECORATIVE

Pure color, blues, reds, and yellows,
escape from this painting and inscribe
themselves in posters, store windows,
along the roads, in signage.
Color had become free.

Fernand Léger, *The Functions of Painting*, 1946

——— Color charts for artists' supplies added new synthetic pigments, which were often more expensive but replaced the fragile lacquers from the first discoveries of chemistry. The relationship of artists and their suppliers was based on trust: the issue of stability, whether it meant resisting light or variations in temperature and humidity, was increasingly taken into account. Manufacturers conducted multiple tests and subjected their products to ever more rigorous standards.

Drawings appeared on the color charts, first outlines of the containers, and then true multicolored illustrations. The color card became more attractive. It was also now designed to win over and convince a clientele of amateur painters that continued to grow, including children. Specific products were also developed for a new market: advertising illustrators.

While the color charts reflect these developments, they also reveal that society's perception of color was becoming abstract.[37] The various strategies implemented by manufacturers to reestablish a close relationship between their products and those who use them can be read as symptoms of this distancing.

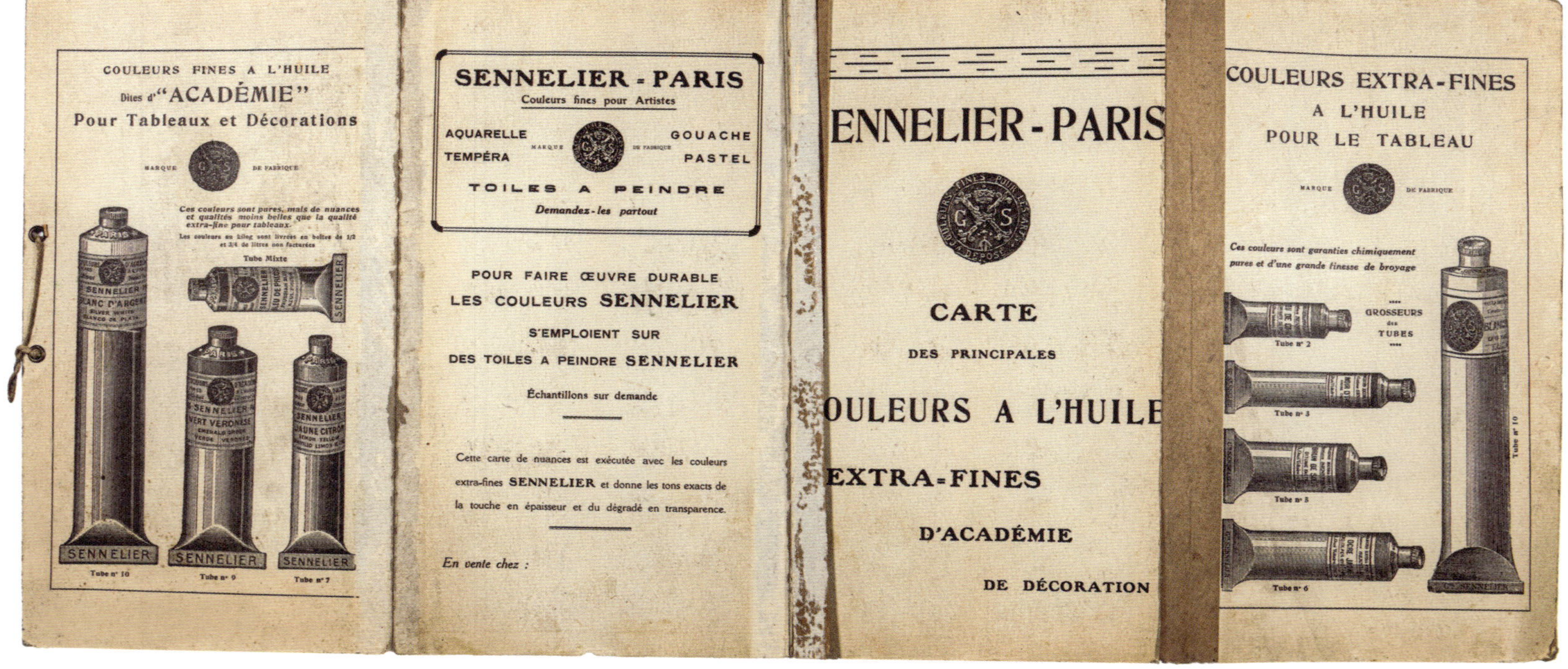

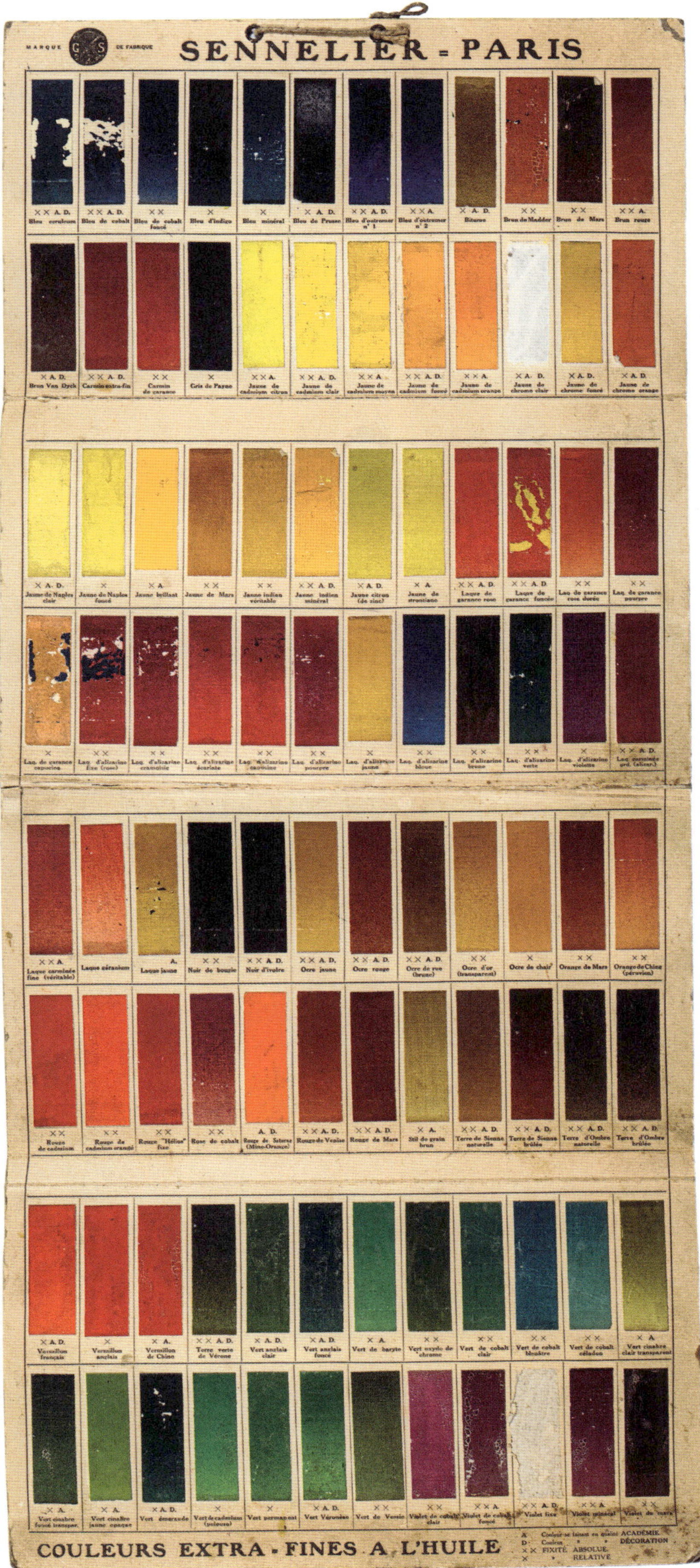

Bringing the Product Closer to Its User

OPPOSITE AND FACING PAGE

Sennelier Oils

Gustave Sennelier used a vertical format for this color chart. The ninety-six samples are gathered by tone, with the order interrupted by lacquers, grouped onto three lines. The stability of the colors is indicated by a cross, and some of these symbols were drawn by hand following artists' comments on the products. The color chart also states: "This color chart has been produced with extra-fine Sennelier colors and gives the exact tones of a thick application and lighter, more transparent shades." When Gustave Sennelier died in 1929, his son Henri took over the company; he gave the same attention to the quality of the paints as his father had. Henri Sennelier studied chemical engineering in Mulhouse, France; he created new product lines, including oil pastels that would set standards in the industry.

Extra-Fine Oil Colors, Sennelier, Paris, 1920s, pamphlet, 14.8 × 26 cm, 3 folds, Sennelier family collection, Paris

NEXT PAGE SPREAD

Girault Pastels

The production of color sticks by Maison Girault dates to the late eighteenth century, the golden age of pastel. As in the Macle color chart, the samples were produced by rubbing the color on rectangles of paper that were then glued to the backing, featuring versions of a single tone, from the darkest to the lightest shade.[38] Yet there are fewer of them here (526). However, the range has been divided into four categories according to the artistic project: Figure (generally a body or a face, hence an abundance of skin-toned colors), Landscape, Flowers and Fruits (the most multicolored plate), Mixed Colors, and Background Colors. Only numbers identify the shades, and if there was once a list of names, it has disappeared.

Pastel Color Chart, Girault, Montignac, 1920s, pamphlet, 32.3 × 23 cm, 3 folds, Sennelier family collection, Paris

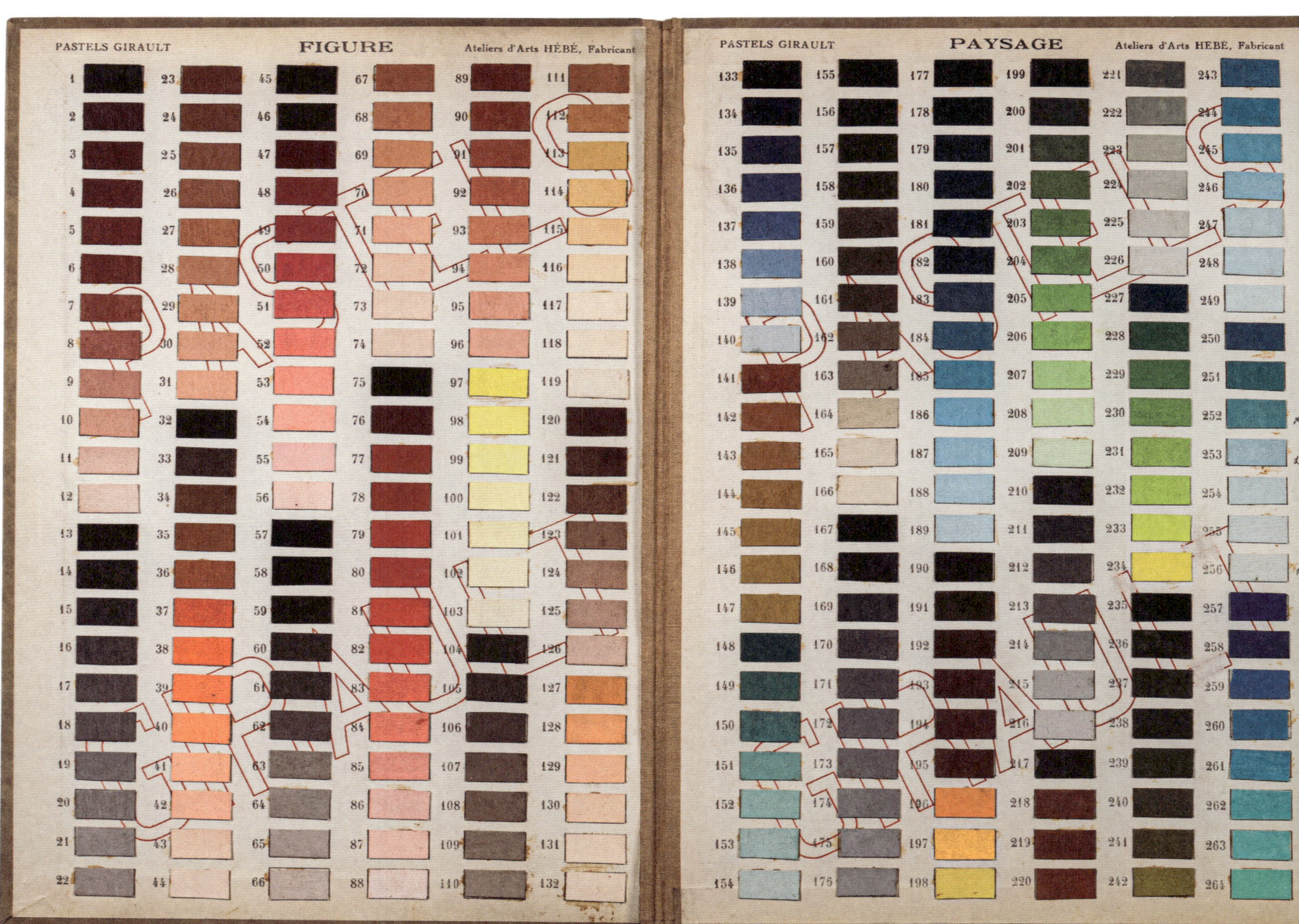

PASTELS GIRAULT
FIGURE
Ateliers d'Arts HÉBÉ, Fabricant
PASTELS GIRAULT
PAYSAGE
Ateliers d'Arts HÉBÉ, Fabricant

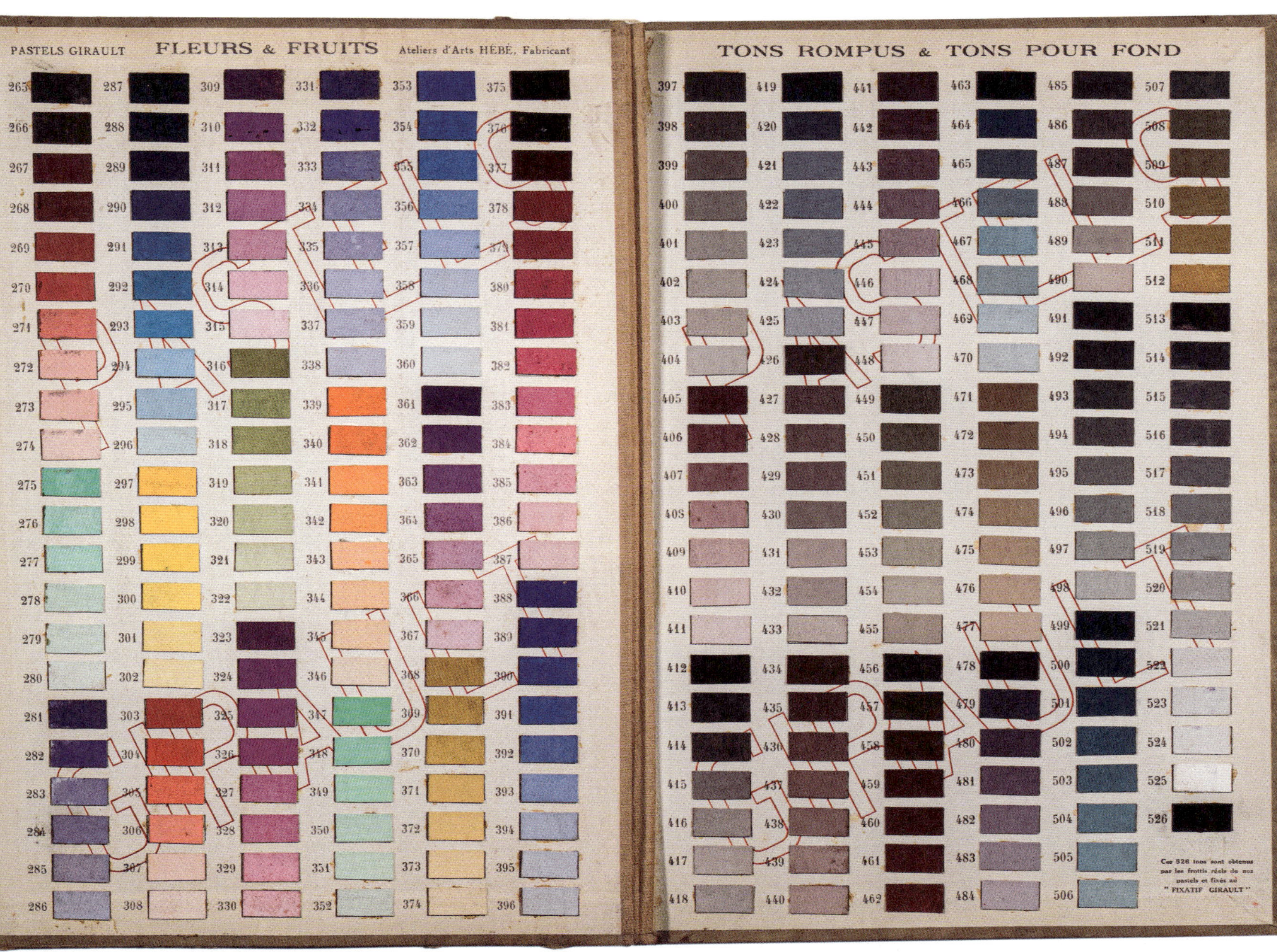
PASTELS GIRAULT
FLEURS & FRUITS
Ateliers d'Arts HÉBÉ, Fabricant
TONS ROMPUS & TONS POUR FOND
Ces 526 tons sont obtenus par les frottis réels de nos pastels et fixés au "FIXATIF GIRAULT"

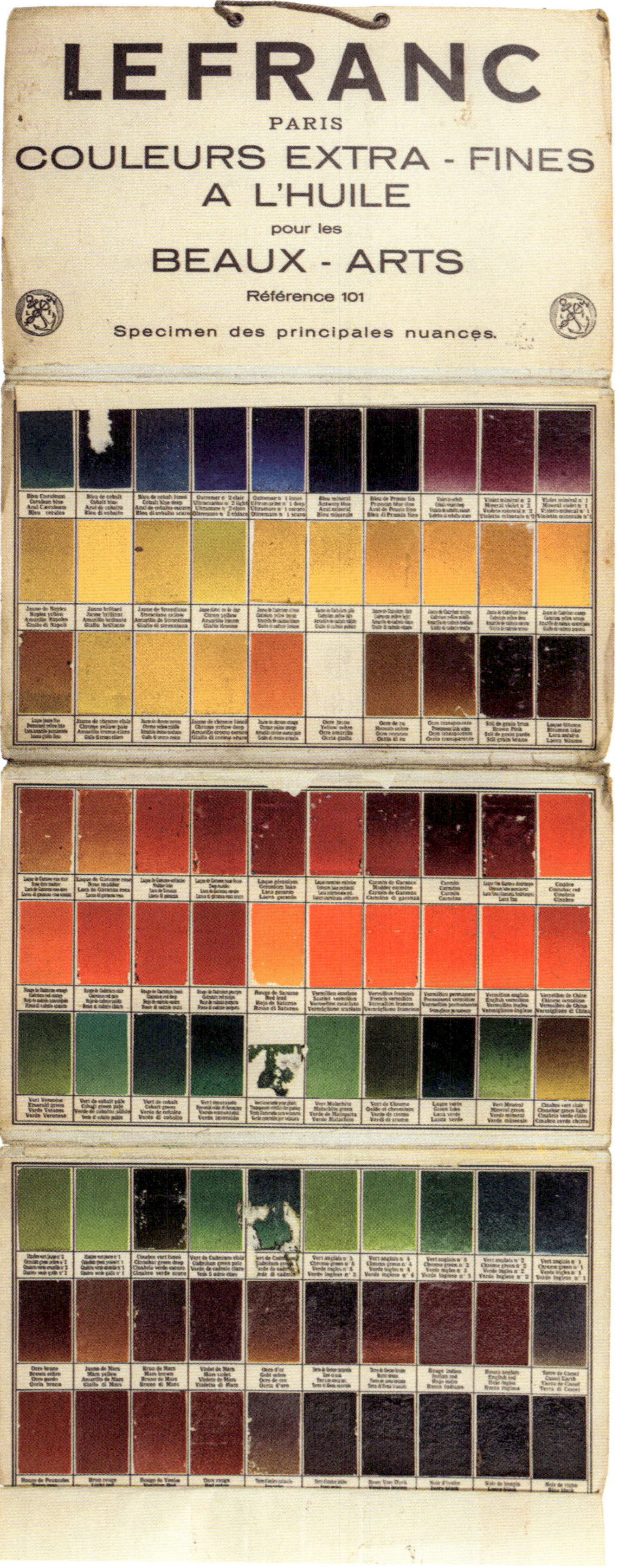

LEFT

Lefranc Oils

The type of color chart and the order of the colors are similar to the Sennelier chart above in this brochure from the Maison Lefranc, a venerable company established in Paris in 1720 by an apothecary. Fifty-five years later, Lefranc specialized in artists' supplies, and then, before the end of the nineteenth century, industrial production began and the firm opened branches in Italy, Belgium, and Germany. On this color chart, the names of the colors appear in French, English, Spanish, and Italian.

Lefranc also circulated a booklet of thirty-one pages, *Colors, Their Origin, Manufacture, and Use*, in the 1920s. It presents various products and mentions an interesting initiative: the opening of a museum of color on the company's premises in Paris. "We thought it would be interesting to bring together the various products used in the Fine Arts and to exhibit to public view . . . the materials passed down by previous generations [as well as those of] the fruitful research and scientific approach [of] chemists." The description of this museum mentions seven sections, most of which were devoted to contemporary materials, with one reserved for "colors used in the eighteenth and nineteenth centuries that have become obsolete" and another for "defective colors." There was even a panorama of raw materials for color. The booklet specifies that, "In many cases, this presentation offers no interest; concerning hydrazine dyes, for instance, which, by a series of numerous complex reactions, derive from phenols, which are produced by the distillation of coal."

Thus, starting in the 1920s, while color was reaching many products (due precisely to hydrazine dyes among others!) and began to finally be within reach for the masses, the intimate relationship with color was already perceived as so perilously thin that it became necessary to reconstruct it, to recall its memory.

Samples of the Principal Extra-Fine Oil Colors for the Fine Arts, Lefranc, Paris, 1920s, pamphlet, 16.2 × 25.6 cm, 3 folds, Sennelier family collection, Paris

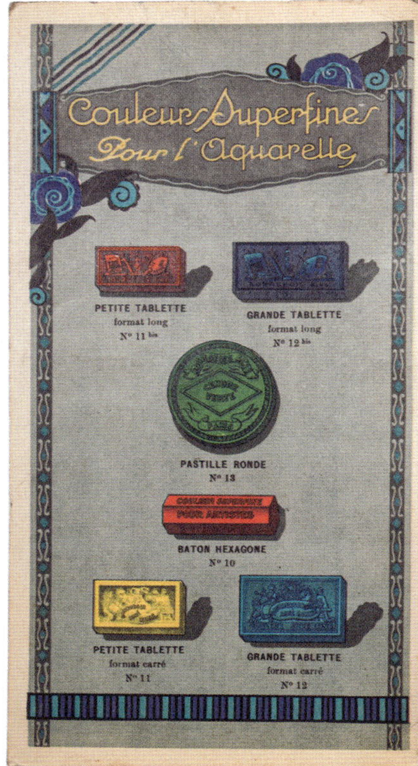

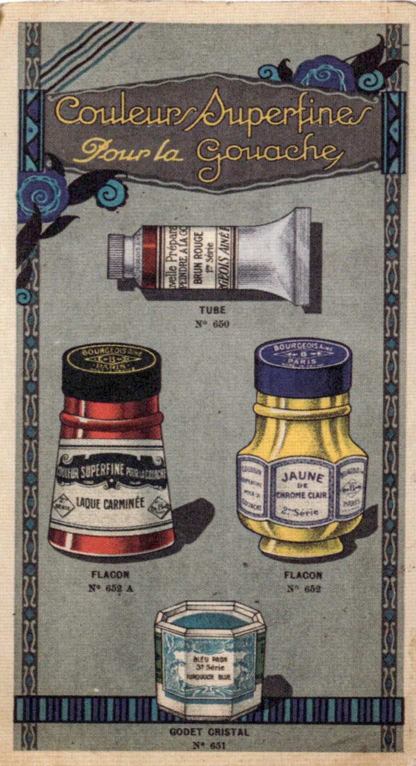

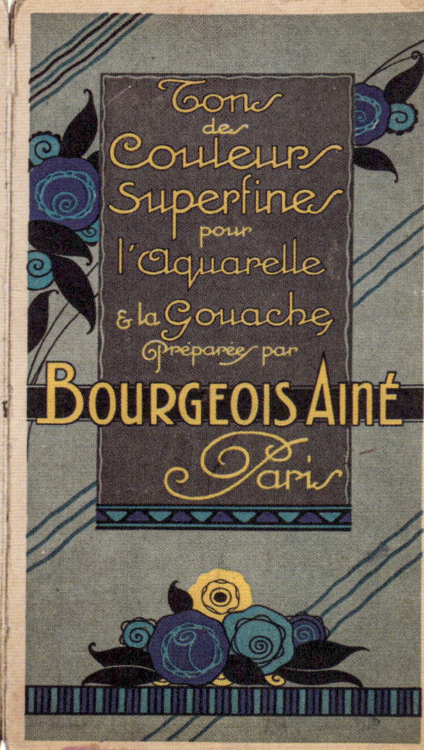

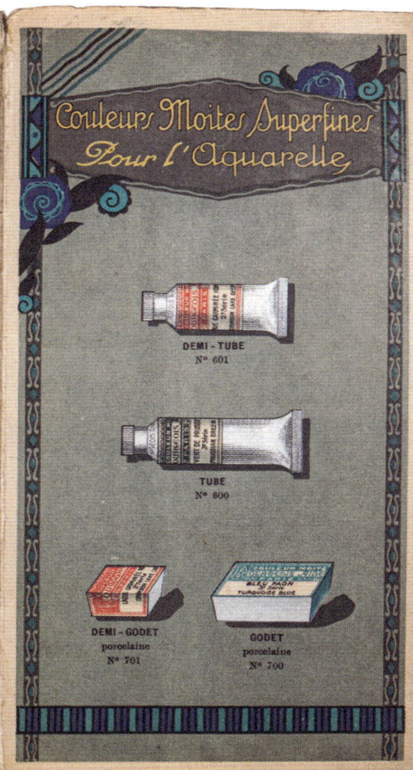

T.S. TRÈS SOLIDE.
A.S. ASSEZ SOLIDE.
P.S. PEU SOLIDE.

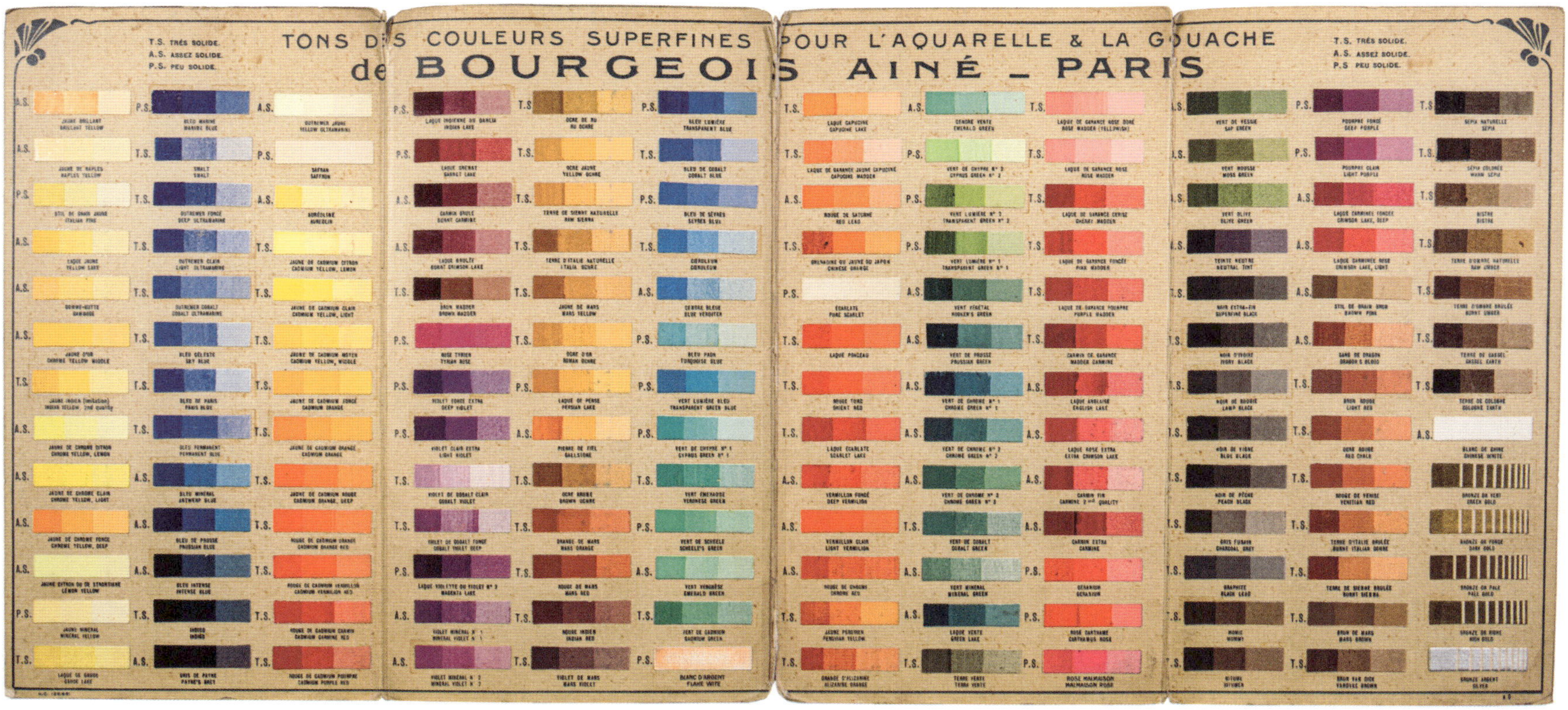

TONS DES COULEURS SUPERFINES POUR L'AQUARELLE & LA GOUACHE
de BOURGEOIS AINÉ – PARIS

DARSTELLUNG DER PELIKANFARBEN
IN NATÜRLICHER GRÖSSE.

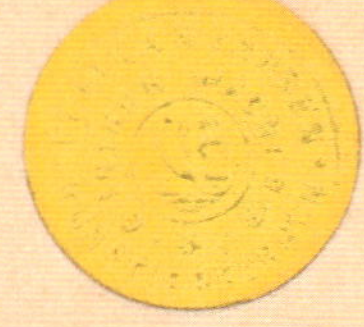

Sorte 0, runde Tafeln.

Sorte 1, ganze Tafeln.

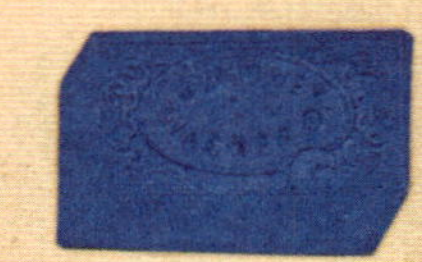

Sorte 2, halbe Tafeln.

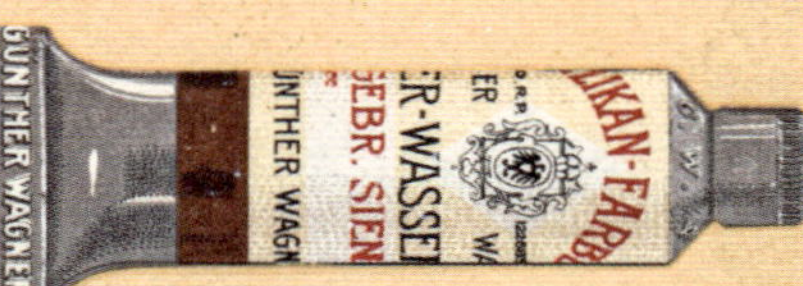

Sorte 20, ganze Tuben.

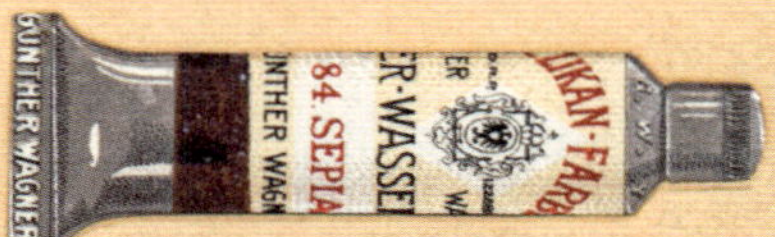

Sorte 21, dreiviertel Tuben.

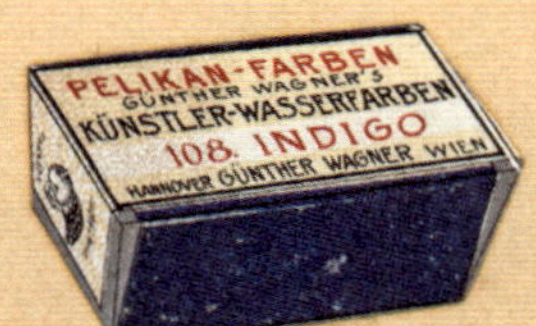

Sorte 22, ganze Näpfe.

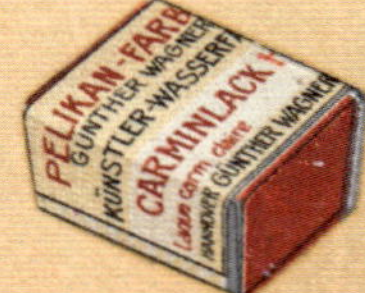

Sorte 23, halbe Näpfe.

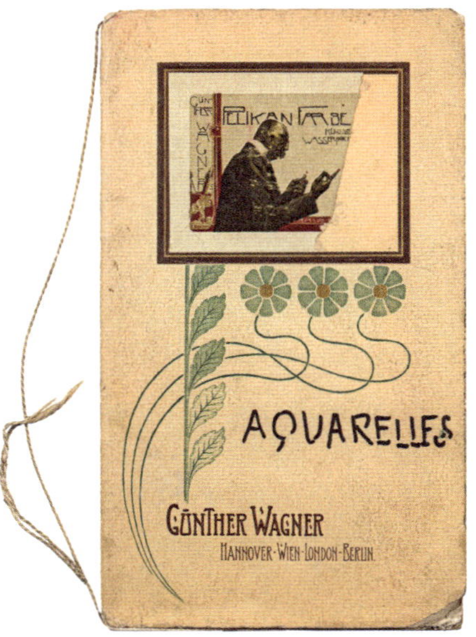

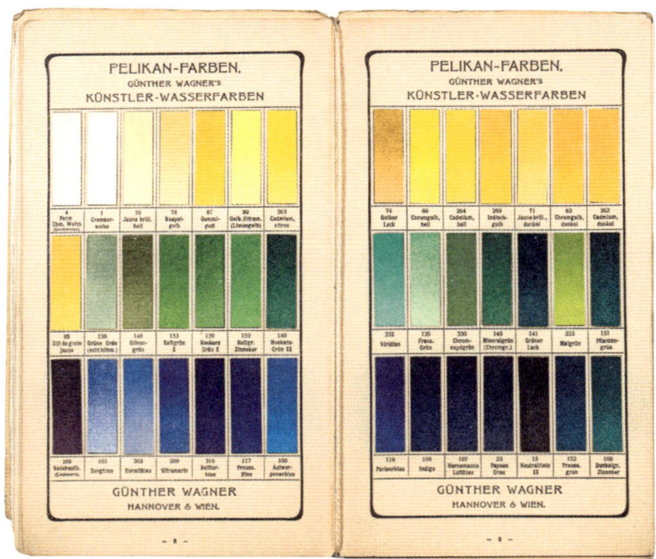

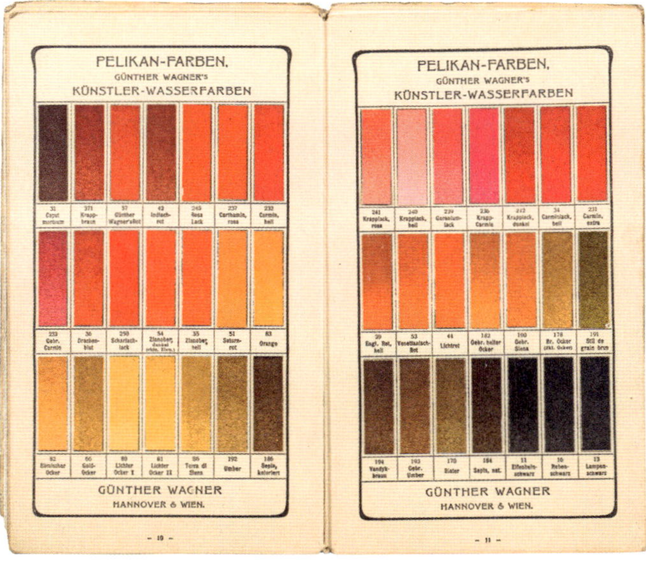

PAGE 185, OPPOSITE, AND LEFT

Bourgeois Aîné and Günther Wagner Paints

The clientele for artists' colors appreciated beautiful things, and manufacturers perfected arrangements and images to appeal to them, as perfumers had already done in the late nineteenth century when they designed meticulous color illustrations for powder boxes and bottles for their sales catalogs.[39]

The color chart by Bourgeois Aîné, a company founded in the mid-nineteenth century, presented a range that applied to both gouache and watercolor paints, with indications of their stability. The 156 shades appear in three degrees of concentration. Gouache was a different type of watercolor made more opaque by the addition of inert substances. The *couleurs moites* ("damp colors") were formulas with a creamier texture produced by the addition of honey or glycerin.

Günther Wagner had specialized since the late nineteenth century in various types of inks that he produced in Gdańsk, but he also sold watercolors. His color chart shows a range of eighty-four colors, with their names in German.

The products on these two color charts were presented in a sophisticated layout focused on primary colors. At Bourgeois Aîné, the various types of packaging were silkscreened with brightly colored inks, with the shadows creating a three-dimensional appearance.[40] The illustration was completed with geometrical and floral decorations, along with meticulous calligraphy. The same choice was made to illustrate the containers in realistic fashion under the title *Life-Sized Depiction of Pelikan Colors* in Günther Wagner's color chart, but these illustrations seem to be attached lithographs.

Superfine Color Tones for Watercolor and Gouache, Bourgeois Aîné, Paris, 1920s, pamphlet, 24.2 × 13.5 cm, 3 folds, Sennelier family collection, Paris

Watercolor color chart, Günther Wagner, Hanover–Vienna–London–Berlin, 1920s, notebook, 21 × 12.2 cm, 16 pages, Sennelier family collection, Paris

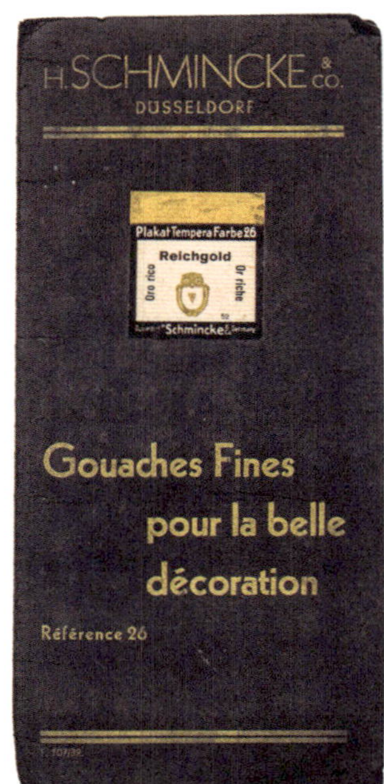
H. SCHMINCKE & Co.
DUSSELDORF
Plakat Tempera Farbe 26
Reichgold
Gouaches Fines
pour la belle
décoration
Référence 26

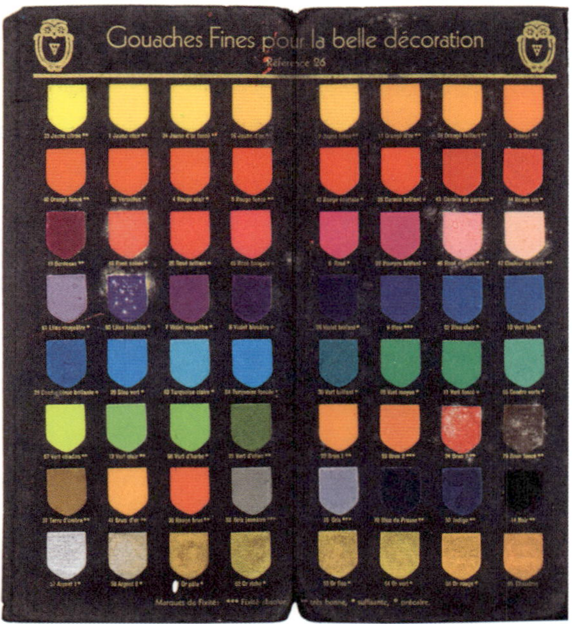
Gouaches Fines pour la belle décoration
Référence 26

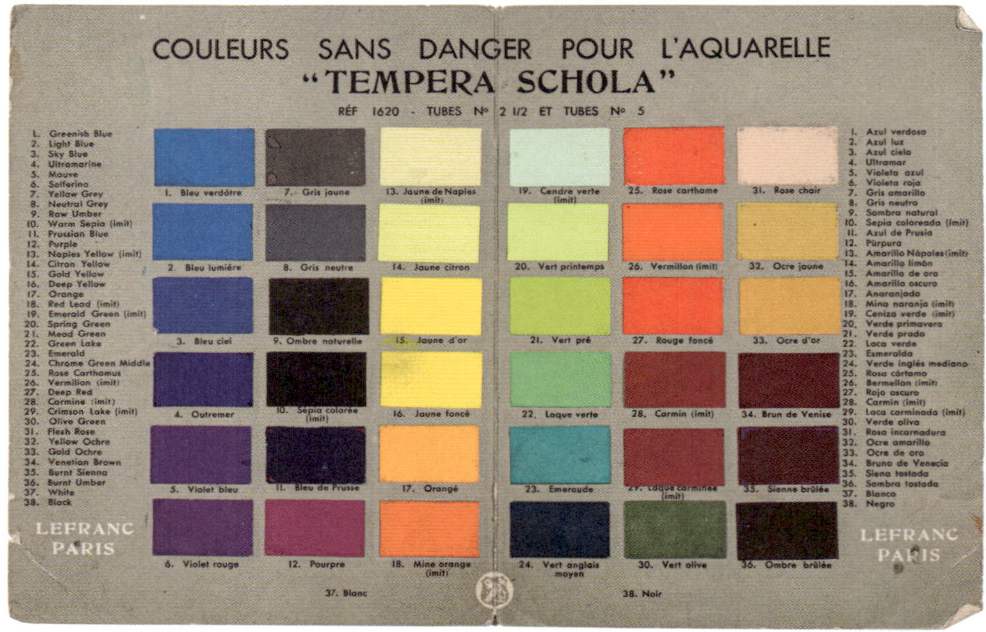
COULEURS SANS DANGER POUR L'AQUARELLE
"TEMPERA SCHOLA"
RÉF 1620 - TUBES N° 2 1/2 ET TUBES N° 5
LEFRANC
PARIS
LEFRANC
PARIS

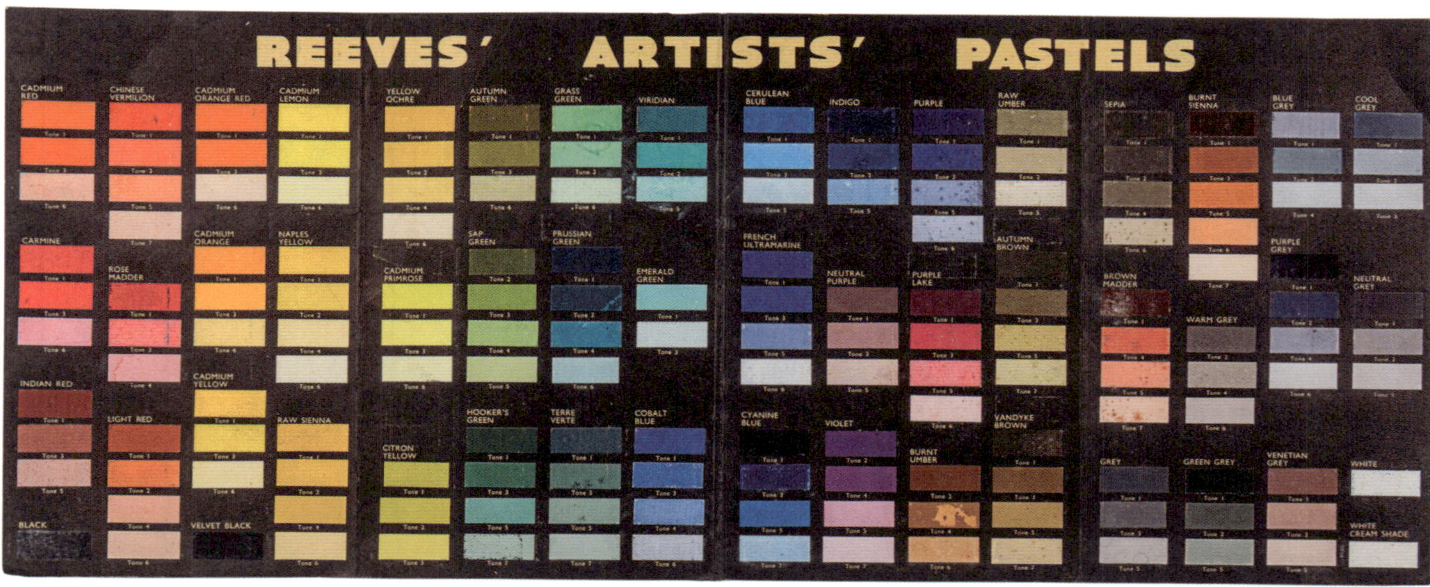
REEVES' ARTISTS' PASTELS

Presenting Color Ranges on a Black or Gray Background

In the 1930s, color charts on gray or black backgrounds appeared. As early as 1839, in his *Law of Simultaneous Contrasts*, Chevreul considered the relationship between the color of the backing materials and the colors applied to them. He even anticipated that decorative artists would develop this as a skill. A century later, significant advances had been made in paper dyeing and printing inks, and the color chart, having become a common commercial tool, applied Chevreul's teachings.

OPPOSITE

H. Schmincke & Co., Lefranc, and Reeves Paints

These three color charts highlight the international nature of the business in artists' supplies. During the same period, H. Schmincke & Co. in Germany, Lefranc in France, and Reeves in England all adopted dark neutral backgrounds for their color charts as they marketed specific products.

In the late nineteenth century, H. Schmincke & Co., a company founded by chemists, provided a majority of the paints for German artists, but also distributed its products in France. On this color chart, which seems to have been intended for the new market of advertising illustration, the sixty-four samples take the shape of shields, which we saw previously at the beginning of the century for decorative paints.[41]

Lefranc chose a gray background for its paints, *Colors without Danger for Schools*. During the nineteenth century, the teaching of art expanded, whether with utilitarian aims (training illustrators) or recreational purposes. By the end of the century, sets of paints for children were already available from many brands, and they contributed to the rise of a new generation of painters.

The Reeves company, founded by the London color merchant William Reeves in the mid-eighteenth century, became well known for its sets for adults containing everything needed for using watercolors outdoors. Reeves began selling them even before the century ended. In particular, the sets included watercolor in cubes that needed simply to be dampened before use, a very successful innovation.

Fine Gouache Paints for Beautiful Decoration, H. Schmincke & Co., Düsseldorf, 1930s, pamphlet, 21 × 11 cm, 2 folds, Sennelier family collection, Paris

Tempera Schola, Lefranc, Paris, late 1930s, pamphlet, 16.5 × 12.2 cm, 1 fold, Sennelier family collection, Paris

Reeves' Artists' Pastels, Reeves, London, 1940s, pamphlet, 20.5× 12.5 cm, 3 folds, Sennelier family collection, Paris

Paint Color Charts for Advertising

Europe's economic rise after the Great War was accompanied by a new awareness of marketing strategies.[42] Poster competitions had already been held in the last years of the nineteenth century, but it was not until the Exposition Internationale des Arts Décoratifs et Industriels Modernes in Paris in 1925 that a section was devoted to what was called advertising art. Business owners realized that this was an essential way to win business in national and international markets. At the Exposition Internationale des Arts et des Techniques in 1937, it was clear that advertising had arrived: advertising had its own pavilion with multiple objects and documents on display, and even featured an explanation of how an advertising campaign worked. Starting in the 1920s, paint manufacturers designed specific products and lines to produce illustrations and posters, even before the first advertising agencies appeared and the profession of poster artist was replaced by that of advertising executive in the late 1930s.

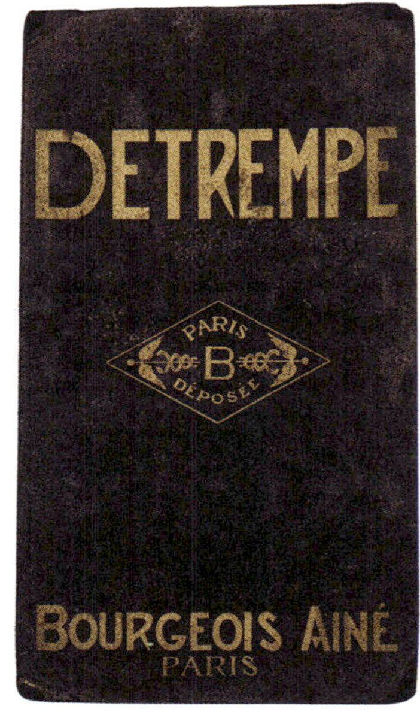
DETREMPE
PARIS
B
DÉPOSÉE
BOURGEOIS AINÉ
PARIS

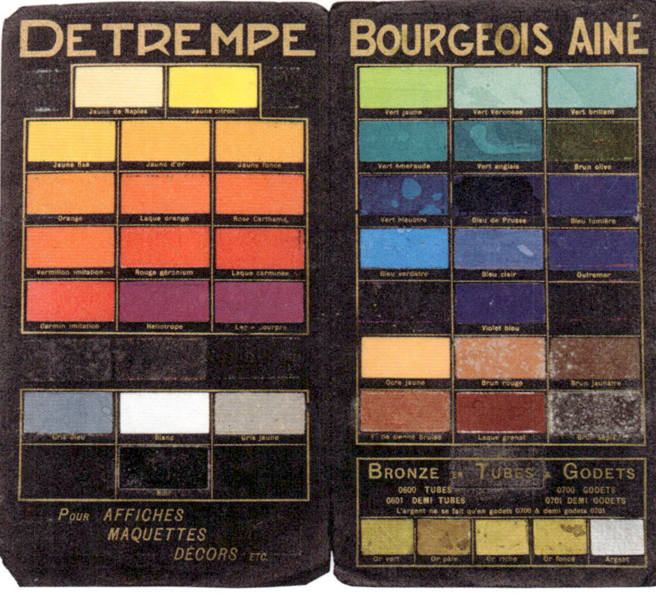
DETREMPE
BOURGEOIS AINÉ
Jaune de Naples
Jaune citron
Orange
Laque orange
Vermillon imitation
Rouge géranium
Carmin imitation
Héliotrope
Gris bleu
Blanc
Gris jaune
Pour AFFICHES
MAQUETTES
DÉCORS ETC.
Vert jaune
Vert Véronèse
Vert brillant
Vert anglais
Brun olive
Bleu de Prusse
Bleu clair
Outremer
Violet bleu
Ocre jaune
Brun rouge
Laque grenat
BRONZE EN TUBES & GODETS
0600 TUBES 0700 GODETS
0601 DEMI TUBES 0701 DEMI GODETS
Or vert
Or pâle
Or riche
Or foncé
Argent

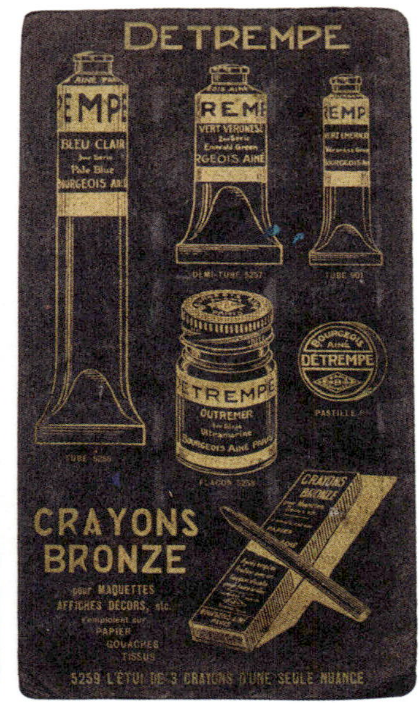
DETREMPE
CRAYONS
BRONZE
pour MAQUETTES
AFFICHES DÉCORS, etc.
5259 L'ETUI DE 3 CRAYONS D'UNE SEULE NUANCE

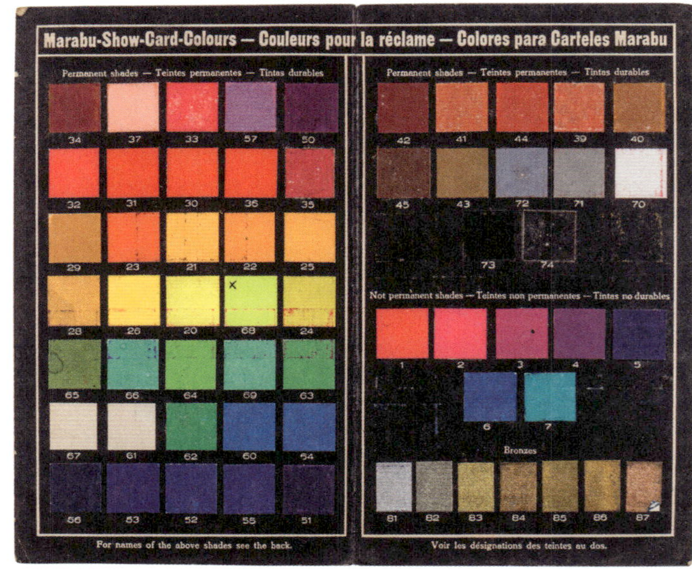
Marabu-Show-Card-Colours — Couleurs pour la réclame — Colores para Carteles Marabu
Permanent shades — Teintes permanentes — Tintes durables
34 37 33 57 50
32 31 30 36 35
29 23 21 22 25
28 26 20 68 24
65 66 64 69 63
67 61 62 60 54
56 53 52 55 51
For names of the above shades see the back.
Permanent shades — Teintes permanentes — Tintes durables
42 41 44 39 40
45 43 72 71 70
73 74
Not permanent shades — Teintes non permanentes — Tintes no durables
1 2 3 4 5
6 7
Bronzes
81 82 83 84 85 86 87
Voir les désignations des teintes au dos.

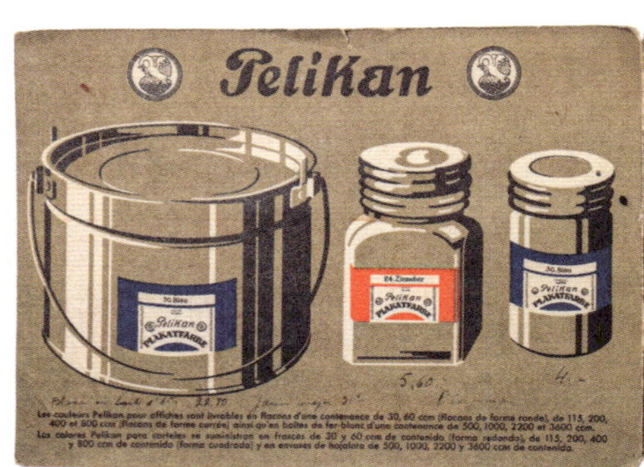
Pelikan

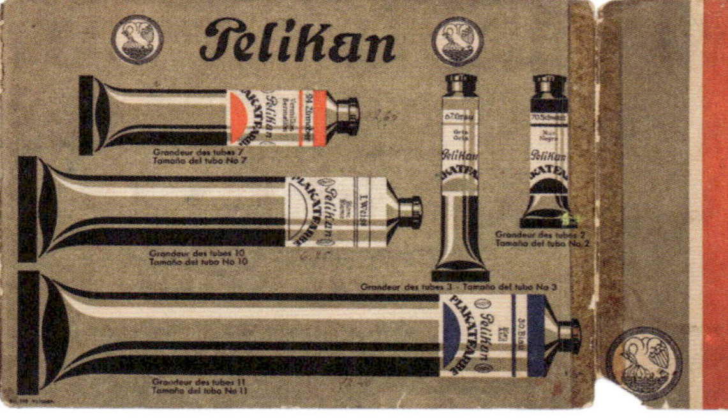
Pelikan

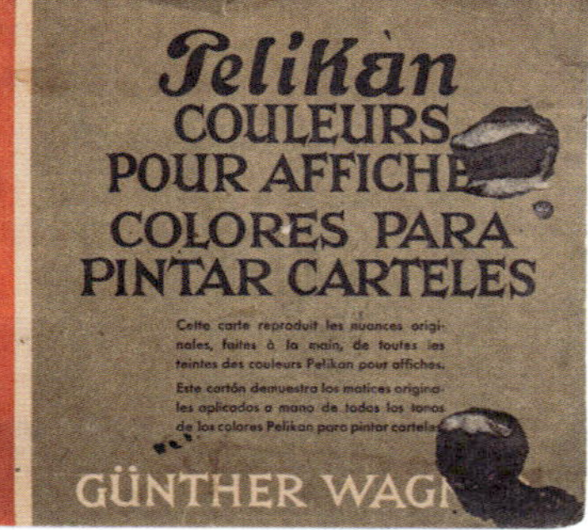
Pelikan
COULEURS
POUR AFFICHE
COLORES PARA
PINTAR CARTELES

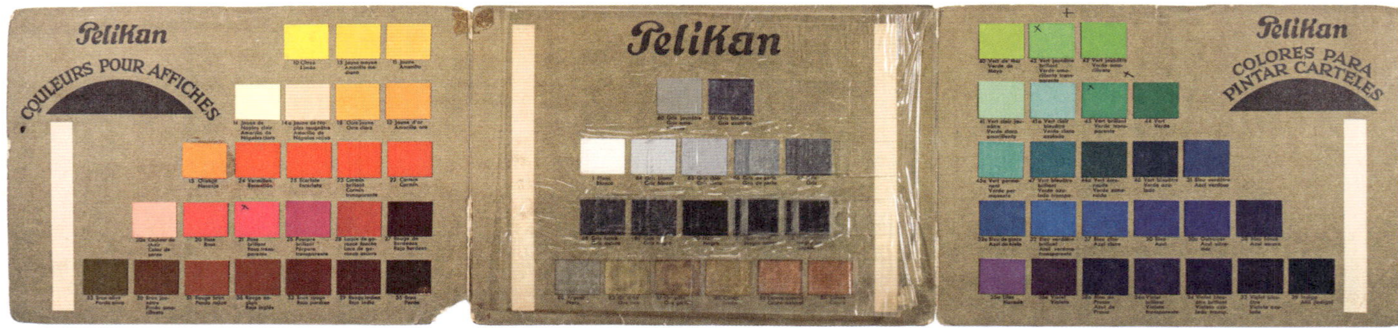
Pelikan
COULEURS POUR AFFICHES
Pelikan
Pelikan
COLORES PARA PINTAR CARTELES

OPPOSITE

Bourgeois Aîné, Marabu, and Pelikan–Günther Wagner Tempera Paints

Between the world wars, paints for advertising art were formulated without an oily binder; this facilitated easier use, rapid drying, and lower cost. The reduced ranges emphasized bright, metallic colors that were clearly visible. The names of the colors were simplified compared to those of products intended for the fine arts, and the terminology approached that used for decorative paints. But, unlike decorative paint color charts, the product sample was maintained.

Bourgeois Aîné sold a range of tempera paints (which were water-based) for producing "posters, models, sets, etc." and took the same care in producing this color chart as when producing the previous color chart of superfine colors for artists. However, the range featured only thirty-six colors, with the addition of five metallic colors, also available in crayon form.

In 1920, Marabu (a German company founded in 1859) marketed a specialized paint for illustrators called Plakattempera. It had a casein base and was very luminous, as well as resistant enough to be used on outdoor posters. The range shown on its color chart was similar to that on the Bourgeois Aîné chart, and the company's international marketing aims were clear, with text in English, French, and Spanish; the list of eighty-seven shades appeared on the back of the chart.

The same marketing approach for foreign markets can be seen on the Pelikan color chart. This company was founded in 1838 by a chemist near Hanover to compete with paints and inks imported from France or England.[43] This color chart displays many gray tones (twelve distinct shades), which may have been in response to the rise of political posters using three colors (white, red, and black) in Europe in the mid-1930s.

Tempera, Bourgeois Aîné, Paris, 1930s, pamphlet, 25.5 × 14.2 cm, 1 fold, Sennelier family collection, Paris

Show Card Colours, Couleurs pour la réclame, Colores para Carteles, Marabu, Würtemberg, Germany, 1930s, pamphlet, 19.7 × 11.5 cm, 1 fold, Sennelier family collection, Paris

Couleurs pour affiches, Colores para pintar carteles [Colors for Posters], Pelikan–Günther Wagner, Germany (?), late 1930s, pamphlet, 14.8 × 21 cm, 2 folds, Sennelier family collection, Paris

NEXT PAGE SPREAD

Dambremé Printing Inks

The industry developed ranges of printing inks that fulfilled the new needs of print advertising. The Dambremé company offered a sizable range (204 shades) of colors that were almost all saturated. As with the color charts for poster paints, the colors are designated by simple terms (*Dark Red*, *Dark Yellow*, *Extra Pink*, *American Green*, *Swallow Blue*, and so forth), only occasionally mentioning a pigment (such as *Chromium Yellow* or *Sienna Earth*). However, indications of the stability of the colors, which had disappeared on previous color charts, appear here.

Printing Inks, E. Dambremé, Brussels, Belgium, late 1930s, leporello, 16 × 25 cm, Bibliothèque Forney, Paris, call number RES ICO 8377

——— Like manufacturers of decorative paints, companies producing artists' supplies began during the interwar period to attract new clients with elaborately designed covers, but, unlike the contemporary cosmetics color charts, the drawings or references to the containers, tubes of paint, or cubes of watercolor did not bring a user closer to a product that was absent. Color charts for artists' supplies maintained the product sample. Yet they also soon made way for reproductions. Whether for artists' colors or paints for home decor, the image of the color chart had become an advertisement in and of itself, as seen in this postcard promoting products by Lefranc.

BELOW

Lefranc postcard, Draeger Printing, Paris, 1932, card, approximately 15 × 9 cm, Albi Couleurs, Association Mémoire des Industries de la Couleur, Albi

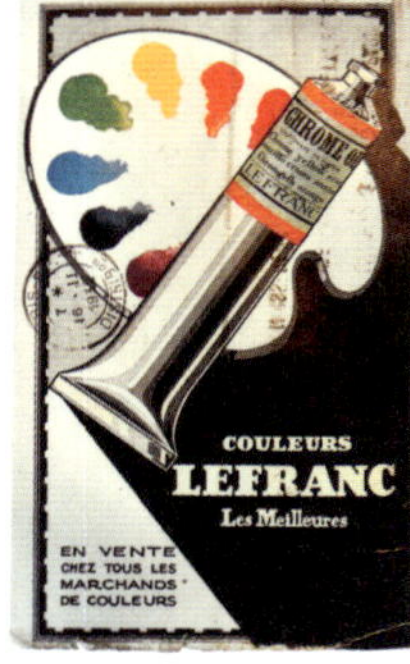

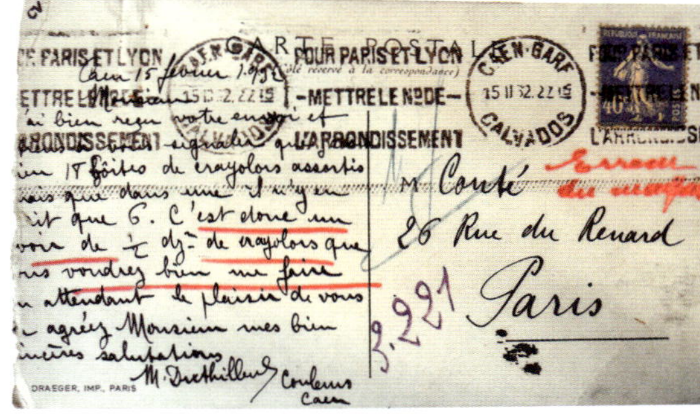

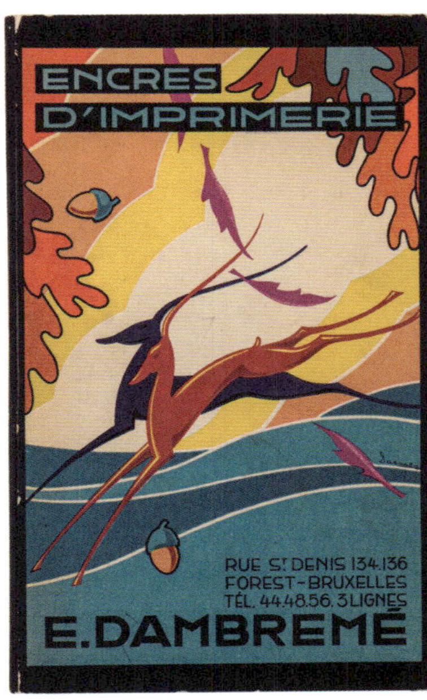
ENCRES
D'IMPRIMERIE
RUE St DENIS 134.136
FOREST-BRUXELLES
TÉL. 44.48.56. 3 LIGNES
E.DAMBREMÉ

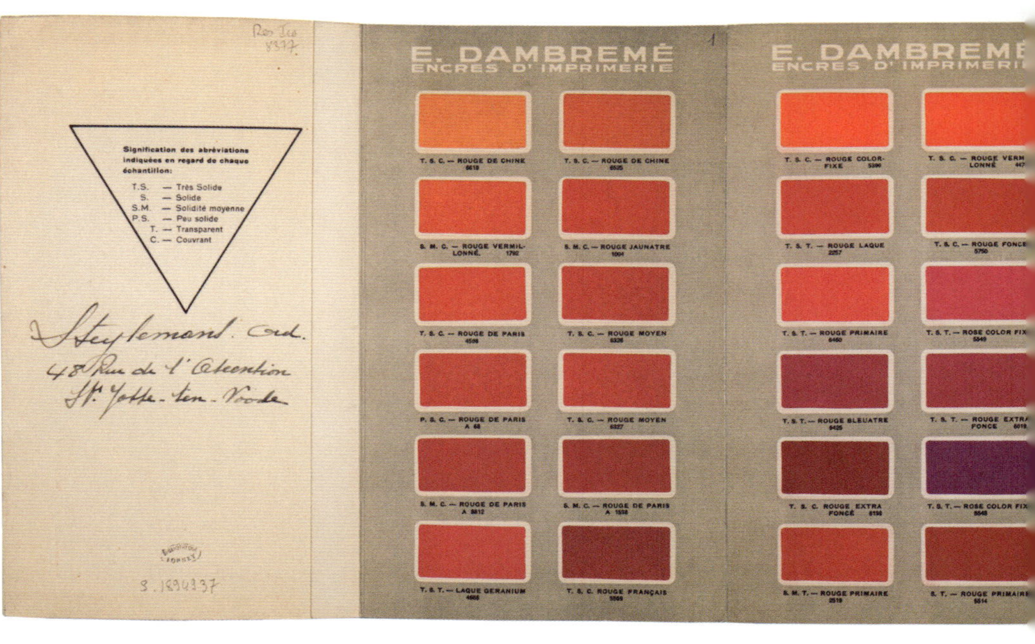
Signification des abréviations indiquées en regard de chaque échantillon:
T.S. — Très Solide
S. — Solide
S.M. — Solidité moyenne
P.S. — Peu solide
T. — Transparent
C. — Couvrant
E. DAMBREMÉ
ENCRES D' IMPRIMERIE

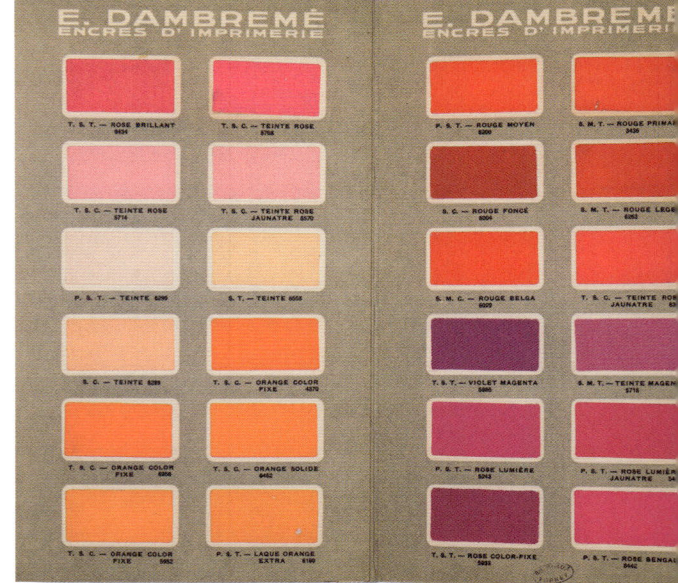
E. DAMBREMÉ
ENCRES D' IMPRIMERIE

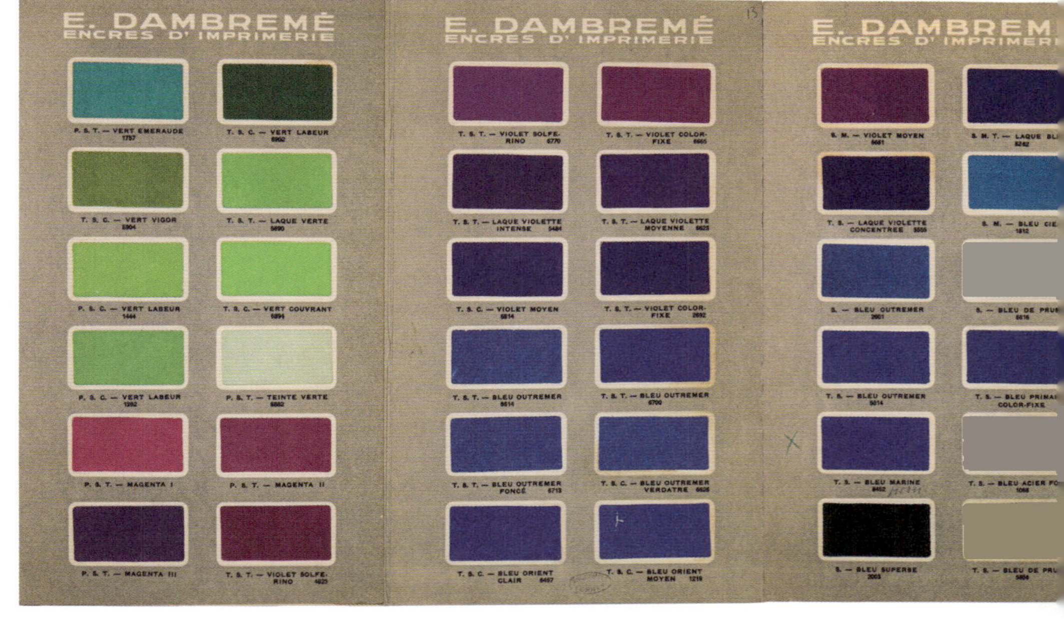
E. DAMBREMÉ
ENCRES D' IMPRIMERIE

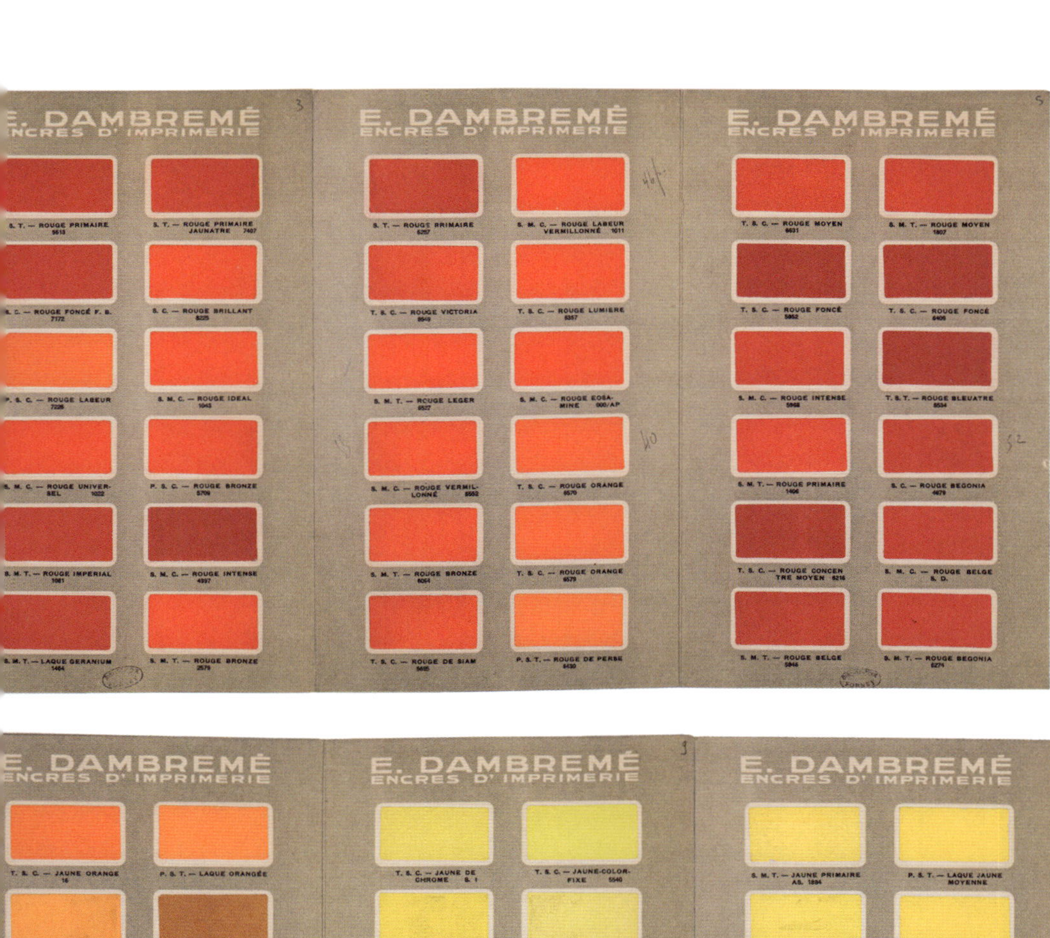
E. DAMBREMÉ
ENCRES D' IMPRIMERIE
E. DAMBREMÉ
ENCRES D' IMPRIMERIE
E. DAMBREMÉ
ENCRES D' IMPRIMERIE

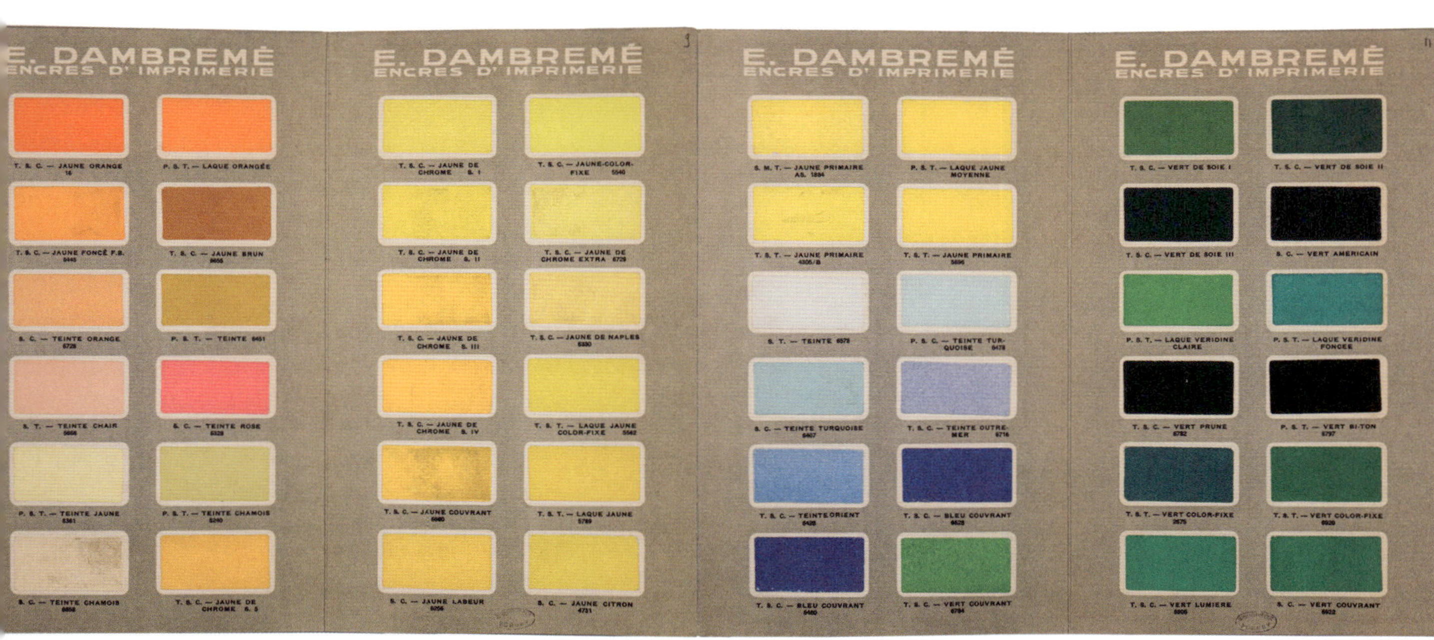
E. DAMBREMÉ
ENCRES D' IMPRIMERIE
E. DAMBREMÉ
ENCRES D' IMPRIMERIE
E. DAMBREMÉ
ENCRES D' IMPRIMERIE
E. DAMBREMÉ
ENCRES D' IMPRIMERIE

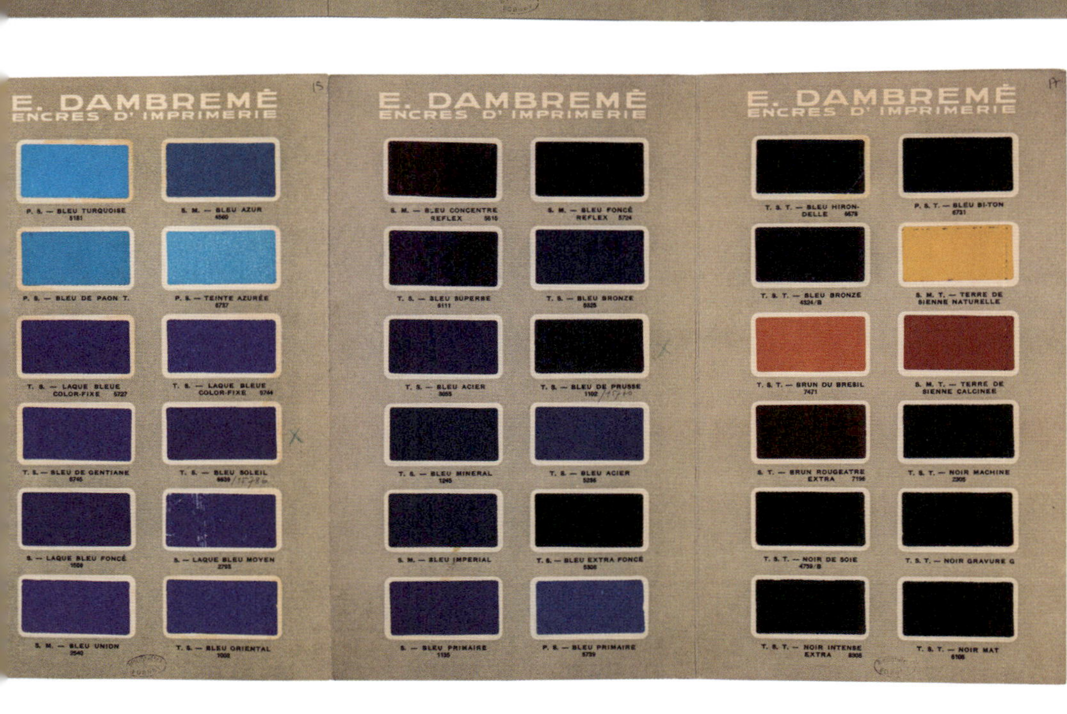
E. DAMBREMÉ
ENCRES D' IMPRIMERIE
E. DAMBREMÉ
ENCRES D' IMPRIMERIE
E. DAMBREMÉ
ENCRES D' IMPRIMERIE

COSMETICS COLOR CHARTS REFLECT AN ARTISTIC APPROACH TO REPRODUCTIONS

Wishing to be in love,
I shove a strawberry
into my mouth
Haiku by **Masajo Suzuki**[44]

——— With the rise of the "flapper," women began to liberate themselves from social conventions.[45] Between the world wars, it was common for women to draw attention to their mouths and eyes, and the first beauty magazines appeared. French perfumers, who were pioneers in the cosmetics field, for a long time had offered different shades for the same product.[46] They knew that the color chart could be an asset for increasing sales, but the oily, sticky texture of makeup and the loose particles of powder were not suited for sampling. Manufacturers had to rely on reproductions.

For two centuries, in their development of organized systems and color reference guides, naturalists had reproduced a wide range of colors—including skin tones.[47] In fact, reproduced color had already been used in the sales materials of some perfumers in the late nineteenth century. It embellished the depictions of makeup boxes while also giving an idea of the product. Expressing a creamy or powdery substance on a dry, smooth, permanent surface was possible, and printing made including cosmetics on the color chart a reality. But printing eliminated the ability to feel the original product's texture, to discern whether the product was matte or brilliant, and also to smell its fragrance—features that were independent of color, but extremely important when choosing makeup to be applied to the skin. Cosmetic products could not be reduced to their color alone. Moreover, the first reproductions were made with inks or paints that had not yet been perfected for this type of use: the colors of the samples were unreliable, and they looked either hard and glassy or heavy and opaque. This was almost anti-advertising.

During the 1920s, the cosmetics color chart emerged in a paradoxical situation: clients had to deduce the real textures and colors of very personal products from flawed imitations. And this was at a time when, except for the few users of color references or those who consulted theoretical color systems, no one was familiar with reproduced colors! It is important to emphasize this, for it is easy to err by viewing the past through the lens of the present when studying color. Of course, the printing industry had circulated chromolithographs and many multicolored reproductions, but no one expected the same exemplification from a landscape or a religious image that was expected of a color chart whose very raison d'être was to indicate color. The color chart induces a series of mental operations involving a process of familiarization.[48] This had indeed been occurring since the turn of the century thanks to commercial color charts, but the reproduction clearly came into effect too soon in the context of cosmetics. However, these color charts would mark the beginning of a new stage in the history of color sampling.

After the war, perfume and cosmetics companies, most of which were still small operations, refined their sales strategies and innovated by finding attractive communication methods and structured arrangements of samples. These methods encouraged the acceptance of reproductions. These methods were also valuable for manufacturers, for the need to separate blush, powders, and other types of makeup resulted in the printing of several color charts within the same marketing tool. While the range of shades was limited, the variety of makeup products made some cosmetics color charts quite complex.

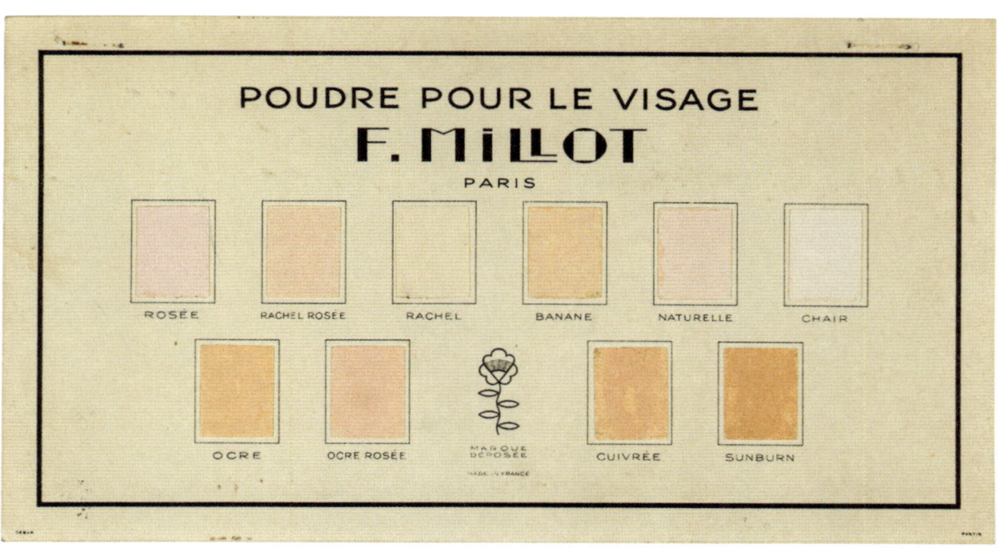
POUDRE POUR LE VISAGE
F. MILLOT
PARIS
ROSÉE
RACHEL ROSÉE
RACHEL
BANANE
NATURELLE
CHAIR
OCRE
OCRE ROSÉE
MARQUE DÉPOSÉE
CUIVRÉE
SUNBURN

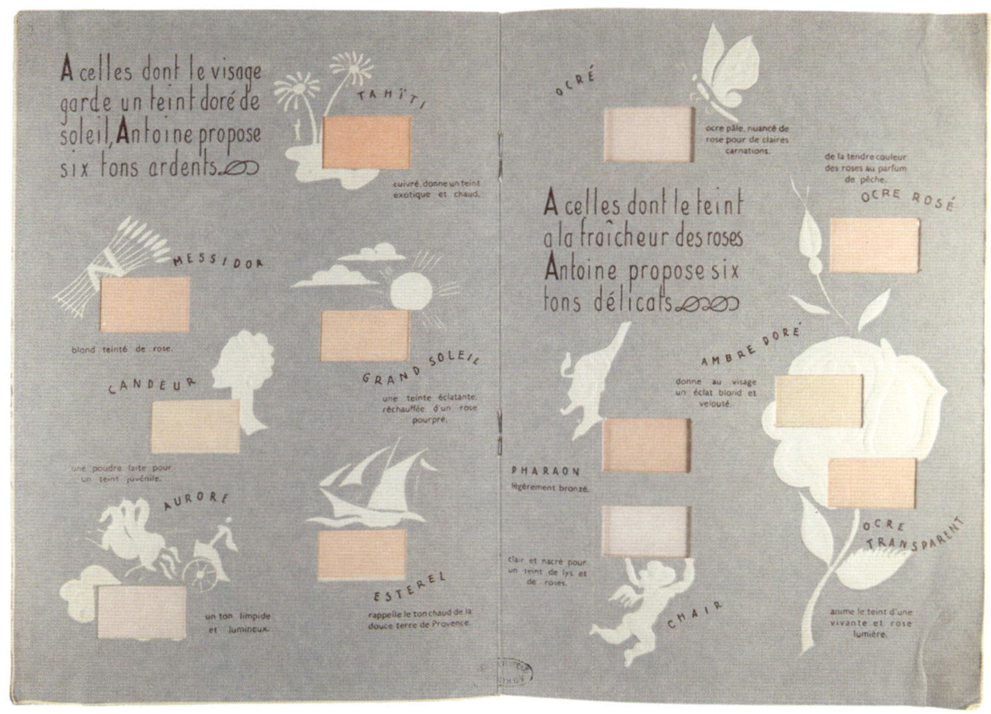
A celles dont le visage garde un teint doré de soleil, Antoine propose six tons ardents.
TAHÏTI
cuivré, donne un teint exotique et chaud.
MESSIDOR
blond teinté de rose.
GRAND SOLEIL
une teinte éclatante, réchauffée d'un rose pourpré.
CANDEUR
une poudre faite pour un teint juvénile.
AURORE
un ton limpide et lumineux.
ESTEREL
rappelle le ton chaud de la douce terre de Provence.
OCRÉ
ocre pâle, nuancé de rose pour de claires carnations.
A celles dont le teint a la fraîcheur des roses Antoine propose six tons délicats
de la tendre couleur des roses au parfum de pêche.
OCRE ROSÉ
AMBRE DORÉ
donne au visage un éclat blond et velouté.
PHARAON
légèrement bronzé.
clair et nacré pour un teint de lys et de roses.
CHAIR
OCRE TRANSPARENT
anime le teint d'une vivante et rose lumière.

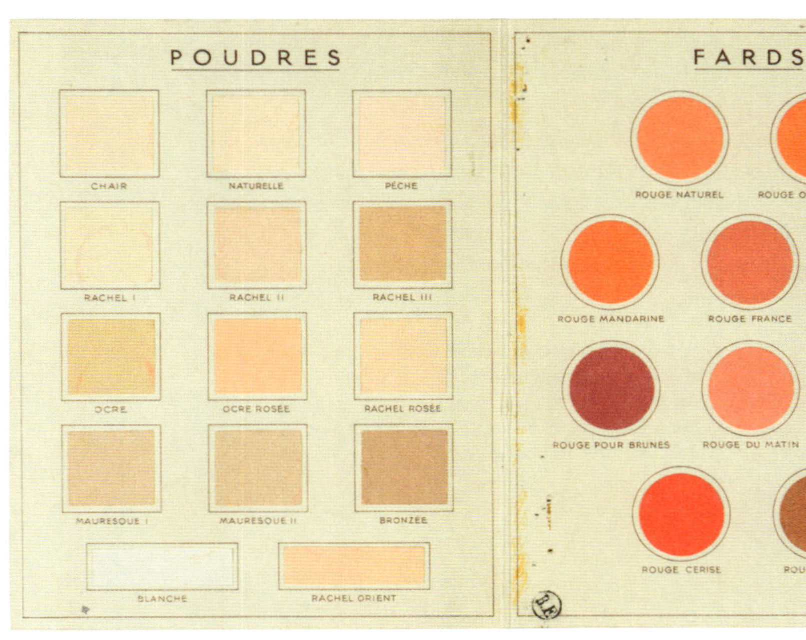
POUDRES
CHAIR
NATURELLE
PÊCHE
RACHEL I
RACHEL II
RACHEL III
OCRE
OCRE ROSÉE
RACHEL ROSÉE
MAURESQUE I
MAURESQUE II
BRONZÉE
BLANCHE
RACHEL ORIENT
FARDS
ROUGE NATUREL
ROUGE ORANGE CLAIR
ROUGE MANDARINE
ROUGE FRANCE
ROUGE VELOUTÉ
ROUGE POUR BRUNES
ROUGE DU MATIN
ROUGE INCARNAT
ROUGE CERISE
ROUGE TAHÏTI

Helping the Customer to Choose a Color

Your shiny or reddish skin will be graced with ideal matte-ness and incomparable velvetiness, without which no elegance is possible.
Advertisement for Velouty powder by Dixor from the press of the 1920s.

PREVIOUS PAGE

Millot, Antoine, and Lenthéric Powders

The oldest powder color charts we have today offered approximately ten shades,[49] to which a similar number of shades of rouge were added in the 1930s. The samples, cut from painted strips of paper and then glued to the backing, do not inspire a great deal of confidence. Moreover, on the Antoine color chart, the particular layout of windows with openings adds a sheet of transparent cellophane, giving the powder color samples a shiny appearance, although they are intended to look matte. Faced with these shortcomings, manufacturers immediately established strategies to help their clients become familiar with these marketing tools.[50]

The first such strategy was to give the samples a shape similar to the boxes in which the products were sold: rectangular or square for powder and round for rouge.[51] The second was to choose descriptive or poetic names, as was done in color charts for decorative paints or ribbons in the late nineteenth century. The name *Rachel*, which was already present in the Bourjois color chart of 1898, was repeated and featured various sub-shades.[52] The approach was still quite Orientalist: in addition to five shades of *Rachel*, Lenthéric offered two shades called *Moorish*.

The color chart for Antoine powders innovated by dividing its shades into *Freshness of Roses* or *Fiery Tones*, with the latter having exotic names (such as *Pharaoh*, *Tahiti*) or sentimental (*Innocence*). Note that Millot has a shade called *Sunburn*, which reflects a new attraction to tanned skin.[53]

Perfumers also wrote attractive and informative marketing materials: starting in the 1930s, Antoine described the beautiful effects of powder, and, like Lenthéric, recommended shades based on skin tone or hair color. Antoine also decorated its color chart with silhouette-like figures.

Powder for the Face, F. Millot, Paris, 1920s, card, 10 × 21 cm, Bibliothèque Forney, Paris, call number RES ICO 8108–2

Antoine Powders, Antoine, Paris, 1930s, notebook, 22 × 15 cm, 4 pages, Bibliothèque Forney, Paris, call number RES ICO 8108–2

Lenthéric's Powders and Makeup to Make Your Face Velvety without Masking It, Lenthéric, Paris, late 1930s, card, 15 × 11.5 cm, 1 fold, Bibliothèque Forney, Paris, call number RES ICO 8108–2

BELOW

Emdé Lipstick Shades

In the United States, lipstick use became widespread in the 1910s. Its use even became a symbol of women's rights when Elizabeth Arden offered it to suffragettes protesting in New York in 1912. During the following decade, when the first lipsticks made their appearance in Europe, sticks inside cardboard cases were available, but most were still offered in liquid or creamy form in vials and applied with a brush. In print advertisements from the 1920s, lipsticks in stick form were already present, but if samples were shown, they appeared as on this color chart in a round shape, most likely because the product was still too new for a specific form to have been invented. The shape associated with rouge was used since the colors were similar.

The range shown here is very saturated, and it would remain so for a long time under the influence of silent films, where the mouths were heavily emphasized in order to facilitate lip-reading of dialogue. Three of the five samples on this color chart were indicated by numbers, which may represent an American influence.

The Range of Shades by Rougix, Brilliant Lips, Emdé, Paris, late 1920s, card, 12 × 10 cm, Bibliothèque Forney, Paris, call number RES ICO 8108–1

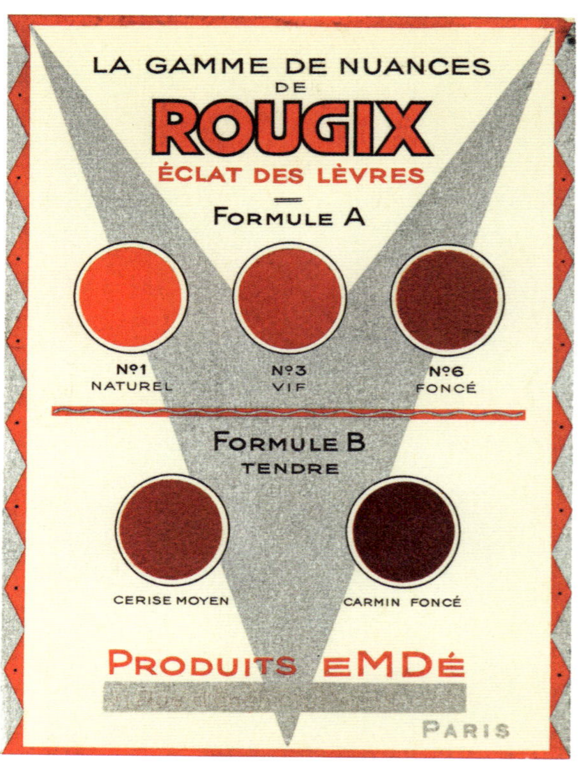

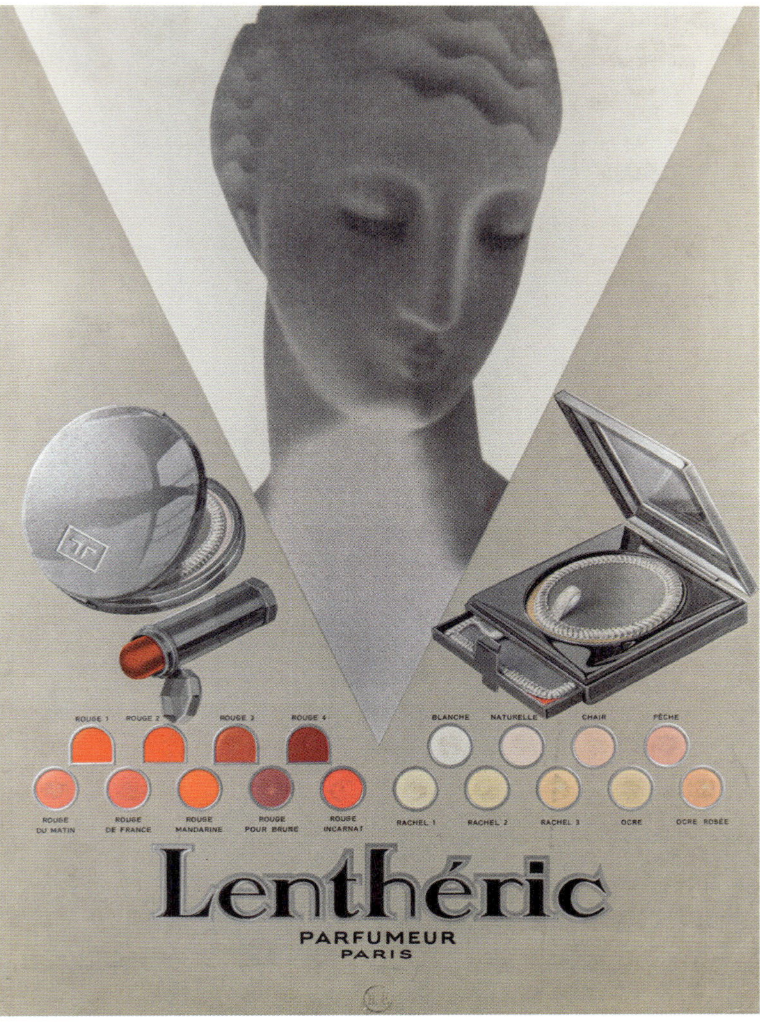

Illustrators Take Charge of the Color Chart

ABOVE

Lenthéric Makeup Shades

This composition (signed Siégel?) offers many enchanting elements: a beautiful woman's face, art deco cases, and meticulous samples, all in subtle relief and outlined with metal. In the late 1910s, thanks to industrial and technological advances, pressed powder in compacts appeared and made it easy to apply makeup on the go.

There were few changes in the color ranges and names (*Rachel* was still there), but the lipstick samples now had their own shape. However, they were designated with numbers.

Color chart for powders, rouges, and lipsticks, Lenthéric, Paris, 1930s, card, 27.5 × 20 cm, Bibliothèque Forney, Paris, call number RES ICO 8108–2

NEXT PAGE SPREAD

Rival Lipstick Shades

The forms of samples specifically for lipstick became varied in the late 1930s. This color chart, planned for eight shades with the names of flowers, fruits, and the cigarette brand Craven (!), highlights the way in which the color was here directly applied to the paper, most likely silkscreened. Immediately identifiable, the shape of the lips made it unnecessary to mention the product. The illustration made sense and would pave the way for samples simulating fullness that would appear after World War II.

For the first time, the term nuancier (color chart) appeared on the presentation of a color range. According to the Trésor de la Langue Française, the word nuancier is not attested until 1953 in the newspaper *Combat* to describe a "fabric display rack." This color chart and one of the two following charts show that it was used in the cosmetics field approximately fifteen years earlier.

Pre-printed sheet for color chart, Rival, 1930s (?), Paris, sheet of paper, 4 × 11 cm, 4 folds, Bibliothèque Forney, Paris, call number RES ICO 8108–2

NEXT PAGE SPREAD

Rival Cosmetics Shades

These two color charts indicate that sales and marketing techniques similar to those already used in many industrial sectors were becoming established in the cosmetics field.[54] In the late nineteenth century, perfumers had already turned to ornamentalists to decorate their advertising materials.[55] Now, illustrators created the color charts and were credited for their work. The lipstick color chart is signed by Paulin—perhaps Maurice Paulin who became known for illustrating the covers of the *Bibliothèque Rose* and the *Bibliothèque Verte* (series of children's books). The color chart of powders and rouges with the mythological atmosphere bears the name of Henri Biais, an illustrator who was active in the late 1930s.

The nine shades of lipstick and rouge share poetic names borrowed mainly from the plant world and are arranged near each other for ease of matching the colors for cheeks and lips, which was still an unbreakable rule. Rouges and powders are elaborately highlighted in the second color chart. The seven shades of powders, which are hard to see, reveal on fluttering white ribbons a series of unusual names: *AOF Powder*,[56] *Summer Beauty*, *Zanzibar*, *Fashion*, *Blonde Lady*, *Garden Burnet*, *18 Years Old*.

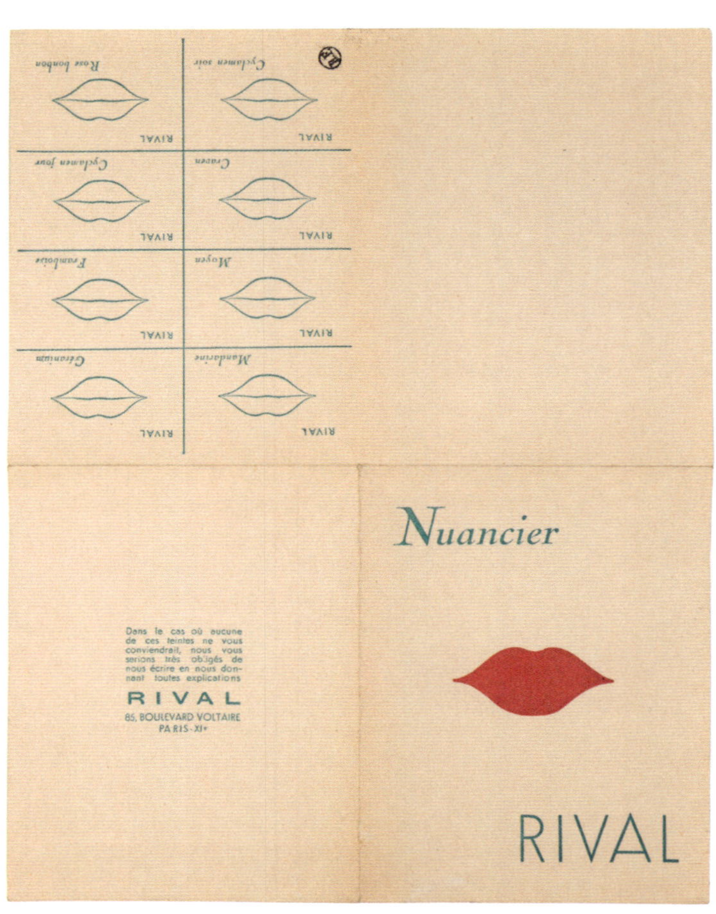

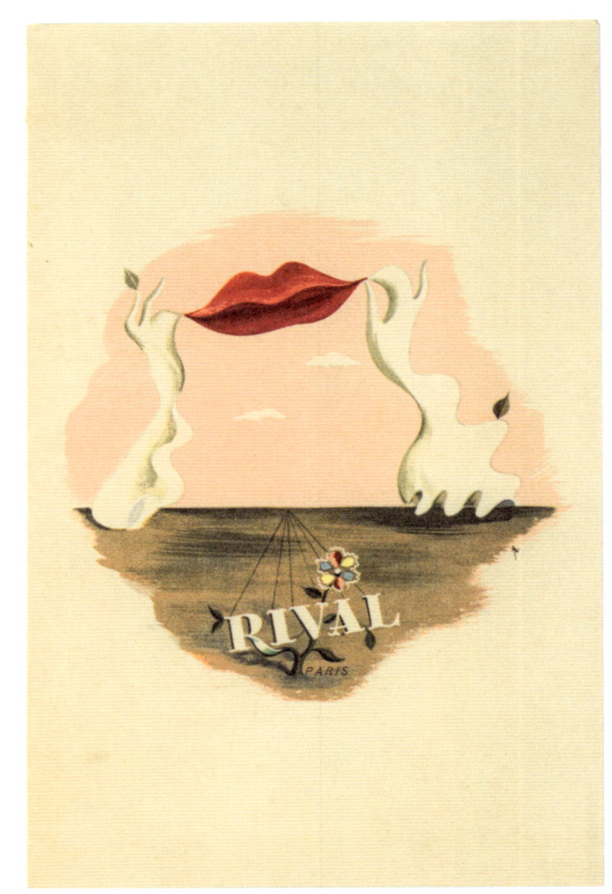

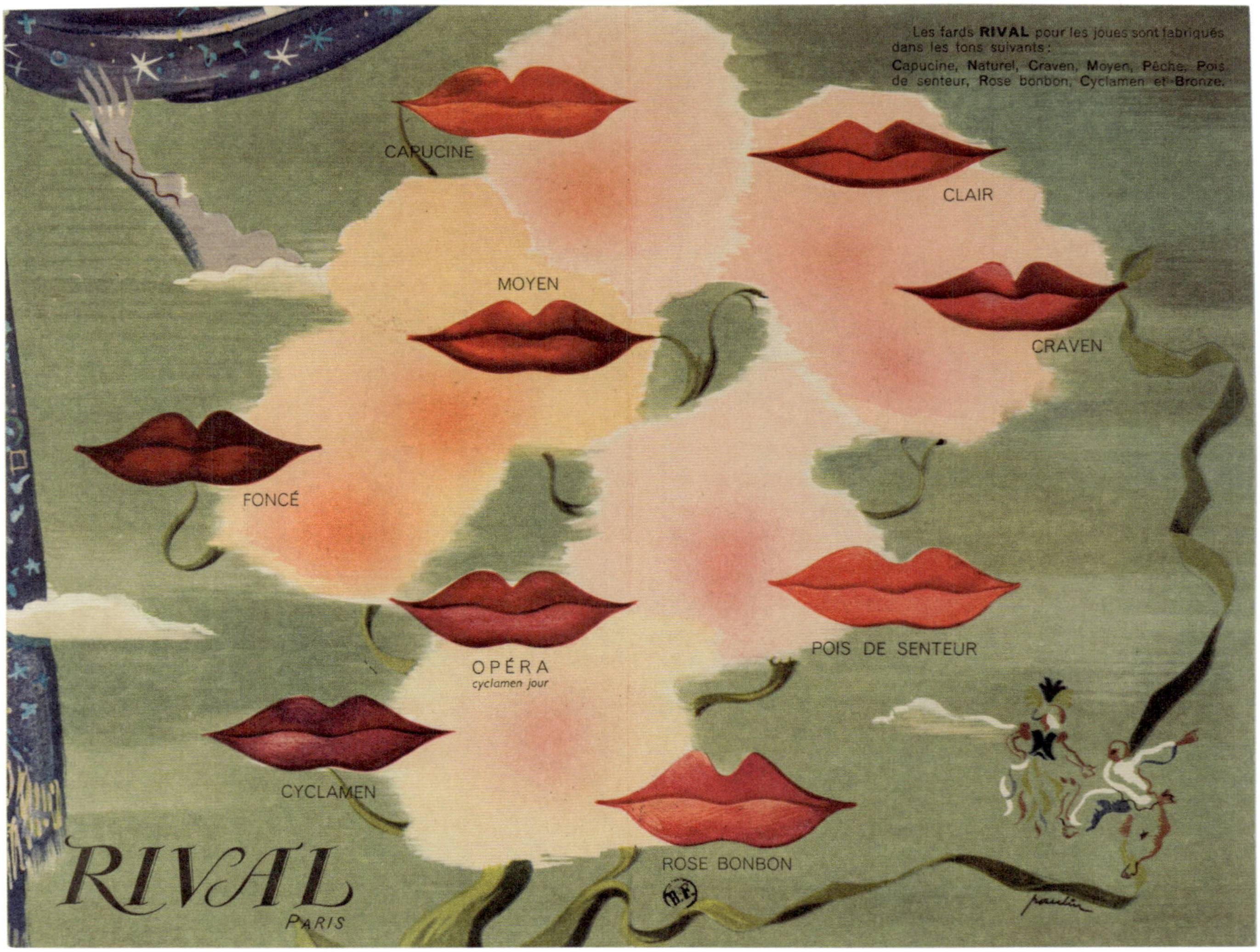

Les fards **RIVAL** pour les joues sont fabriqués dans les tons suivants:
Capucine, Naturel, Craven, Moyen, Pêche, Pois de senteur, Rose bonbon, Cyclamen et Bronze.

CAPUCINE
CLAIR
MOYEN
CRAVEN
FONCÉ
OPÉRA
cyclamen jour
POIS DE SENTEUR
CYCLAMEN
ROSE BONBON
RIVAL
PARIS

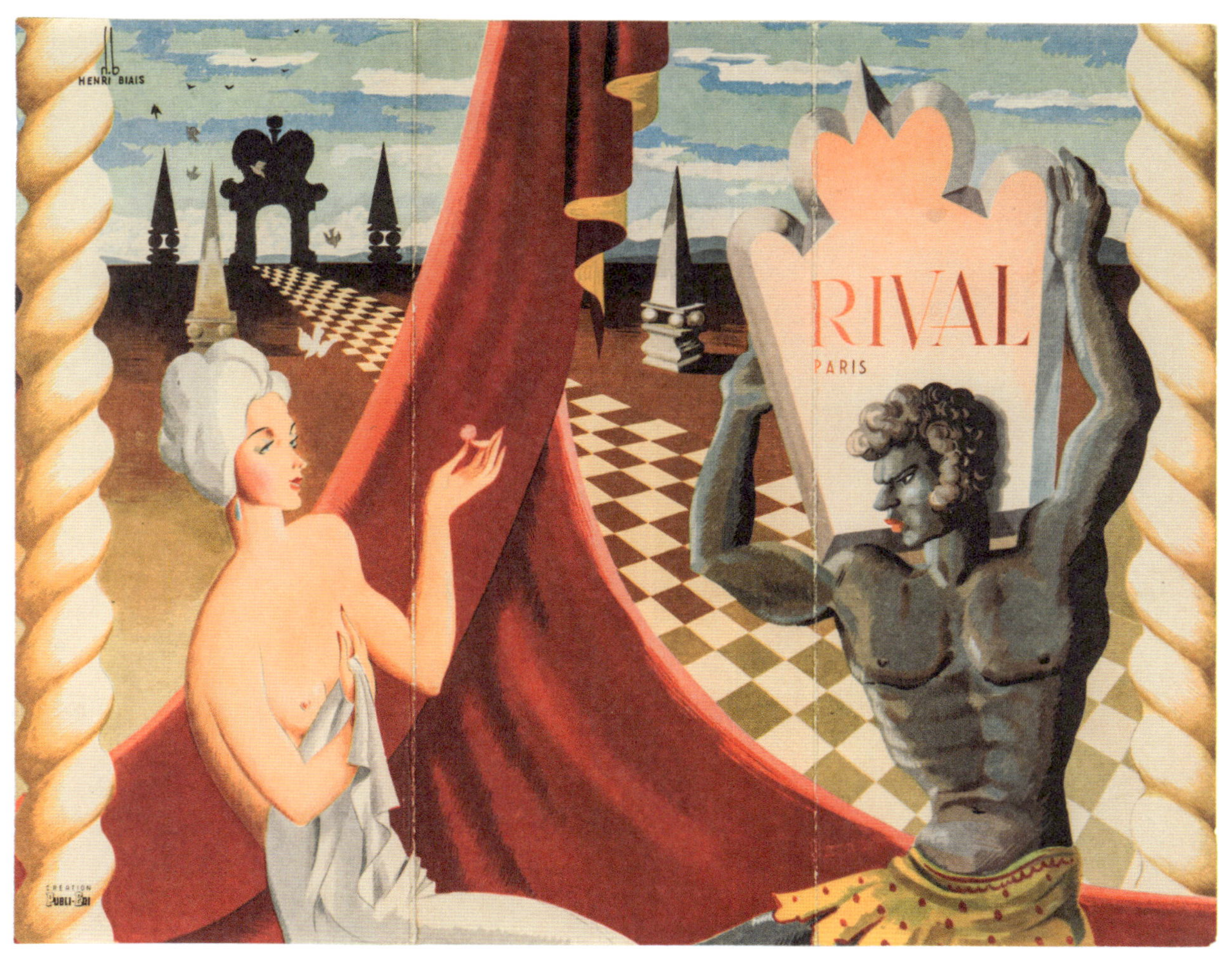
HENRI BIAIS
RIVAL
PARIS
CRÉATION
PUBLI-BRI

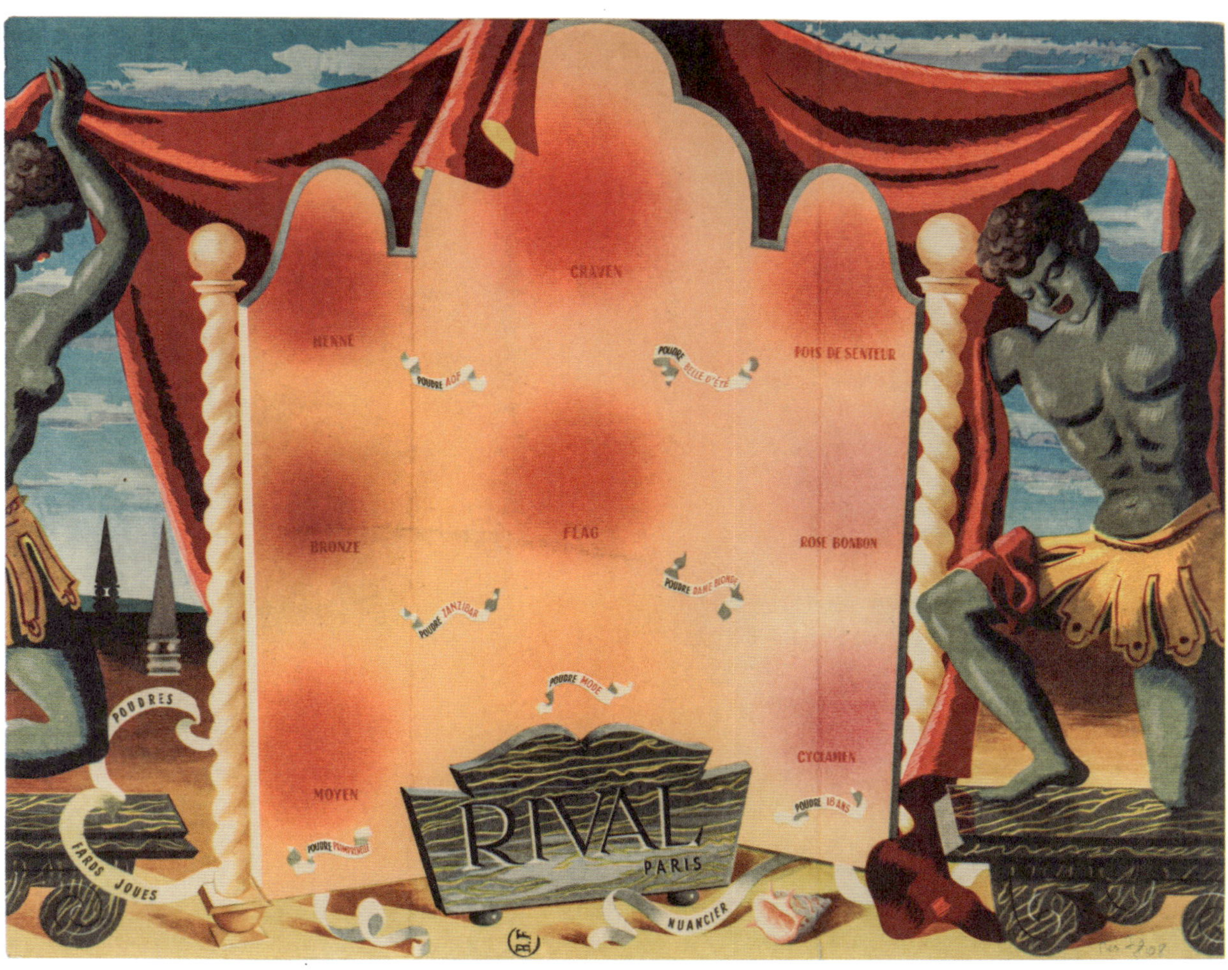
CRAVEN
HENNÉ
POUDRE AOF
POUDRE BELLE D'ÉTÉ
POIS DE SENTEUR
BRONZE
FLAG
ROSE BONBON
POUDRE DAME BLONDE
POUDRE ZANZIBAR
POUDRE MODE
POUDRES
CYCLAMEN
MOYEN
POUDRE 18 ANS
POUDRE POIMPRENELLE
RIVAL
PARIS
FARDS JOUES
NUANCIER

Despite its beautiful color charts, the Rival company seems to have had a fleeting existence, in business just before and after World War II only.

Lipstick and rouge color chart, Rival, Paris, late 1930s–early 1940s, card, 21 × 13.5 cm, 1 fold, Bibliothèque Forney, Paris, call number RES ICO 8108–2

Color Chart, Rival, Paris, late 1930s–early 1940s, card, 22 × 7 cm, 2 folds, Bibliothèque Forney, Paris, call number RES ICO 8108–2

OPPOSITE

Phebel Makeup Shades

These marketing tools reveal how cosmetics color charts were developed between the world wars.

The history of the Phebel company is emblematic of the rise of the beauty industry in the 1920s and 1930s, when many women established beauty companies, salons, and schools in Europe and the United States. Phebel was started by Marceline Sebalt, a young woman studying pharmacy and herbal medicine who opened a laboratory after the war where she developed cosmetic creams using plant extracts.[57] She founded her brand in 1925, exported her products in Europe, and became one of the pioneering figures of beautician training.

For these color charts, Marceline Sebalt called on Alfred Tolmer, who had founded an advertising and design agency in 1910.[58] He had a printing and packaging workshop where he developed this display device, which, when closed, featured metallic panels and three-dimensional decorations.

On these mock-ups, we can see lines traced in pencil to position the drawings and texts (written by hand), as well as the samples. Careful attention has been paid to the reproduction of the colors, which are depicted in gouache on paper that has been cut out and glued to the backing. The lipsticks are depicted in stick form, and there is a striking innovation: eyeshadow is present with several different shades, although almost exclusively in blue tones.

These color charts are original even in their naming of the colors. We can see that Marceline Sebalt was drawn to names from the plant world (such as *Strawberry Heart*, *Hollyhock*, *Red Currant*), although the names did not necessarily correspond to the color (the strawberry is not ripe, and the raspberry is quite pale). The evocative power of words was invoked in the naming of the eyeshadows, which included *Tender Evening*, *Golden Symphony*, *Glimmers of the Nile*, and *Virginal*.

Because these documents were preserved, we have a behind-the-scenes look at an advertising agency producing work of rare quality in technique and graphic design.

Mock-ups for a powder color chart and a display of color charts for Phebel powders, blushes and rouges, eyeshadows, and lipsticks, Marceline Sebalt, Alfred Tolmer, Paris, 1930s, card, approximately 20 × 8 cm, 1 fold, and cardboard display, approximately 30 × 10 cm, 2 folds, Bibliothèque Forney, Paris, call number RES ICO 5600 5 Fol

NEXT PAGE

Gemey Powders and Lipsticks

These Gemey color charts show other attractive innovations in the presentation of cosmetics. The box and the sleeve held the samples that promoted the company's powders and lipsticks. The writing is addressed directly to the consumer ("Samples chosen for you"). The tone is reassuring ("completely harmless") and scientific ("formula studied by renowned experts who have combined Science with Beauty"). The colors are even described as "synthochrome," a term that seems to have been invented by the brand to indicate compatibility between the shade and the complexion. Tests invite the customer to evaluate the softness and matte-ness of the powder. Finally, powder/eye/hair/complexion combinations are recommended. However, the names of the lipsticks and powders are quite classic (there are three powders called *Rachel*). There are instructions for applying lipstick, and the shades could be tested using the six cardboard sticks holding the samples.

Founded in the United States in 1923, Gemey soon began exporting its products to Europe and its colonies and protectorates, while introducing American marketing methods such as those behind these inventive and instructive folding color charts.

Gemey Powder and *Gemey Lipstick*, Richard Hudnut, Paris—New York, c. 1936, thin cardboard box, 5 × 5 cm, and thin cardboard sleeve, 5 × 8 cm, Bibliothèque Forney, Paris, call number RES ICO 8108–1

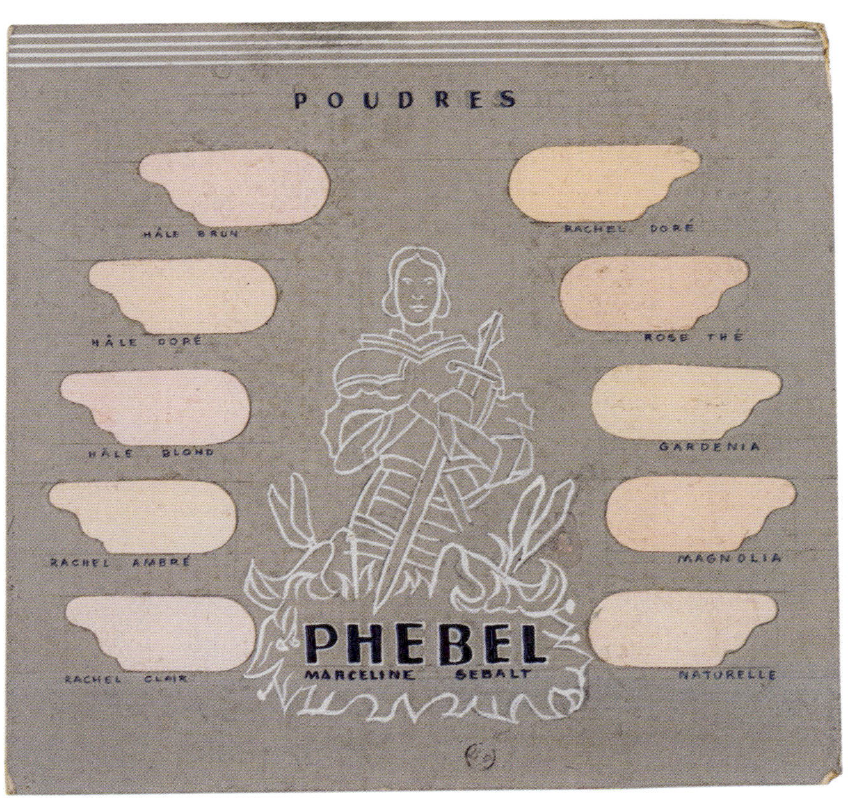
POUDRES
HÂLE BRUN
RACHEL DORÉ
HÂLE DORÉ
ROSE THÉ
HÂLE BLOND
GARDENIA
RACHEL AMBRÉ
MAGNOLIA
RACHEL CLAIR
NATURELLE
PHEBEL
MARCELINE SEBALT

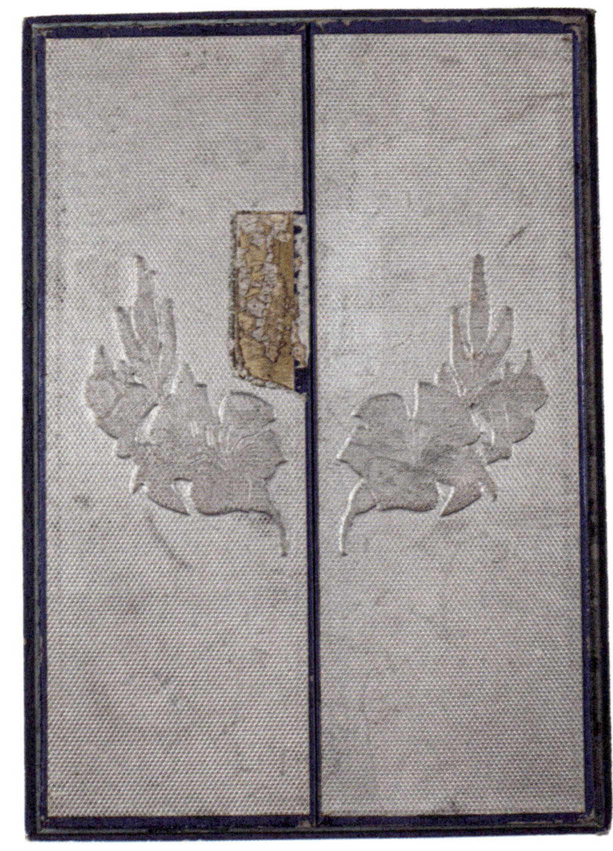

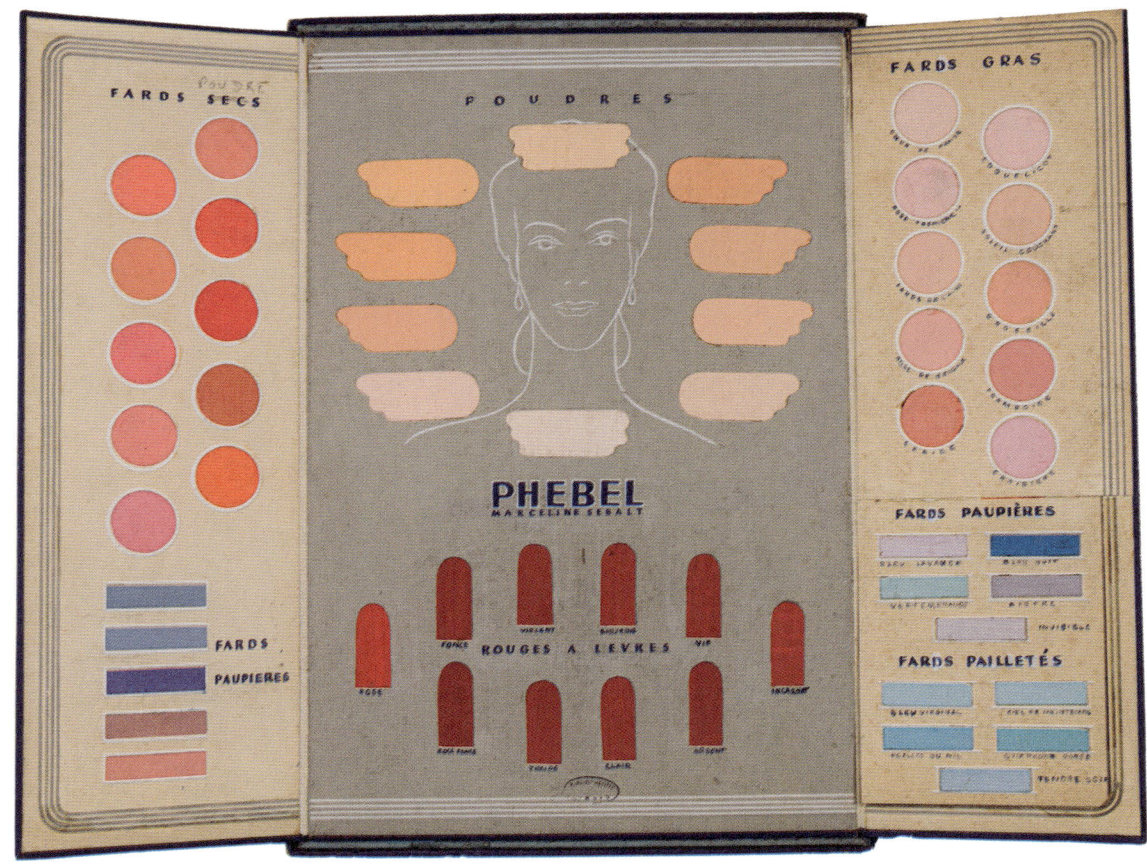
FARDS SECS
POUDRES
PHEBEL
MARCELINE SEBALT
FARDS
PAUPIERES
ROUGES A LEVRES
FARDS GRAS
FARDS PAUPIÈRES
FARDS PAILLETÉS

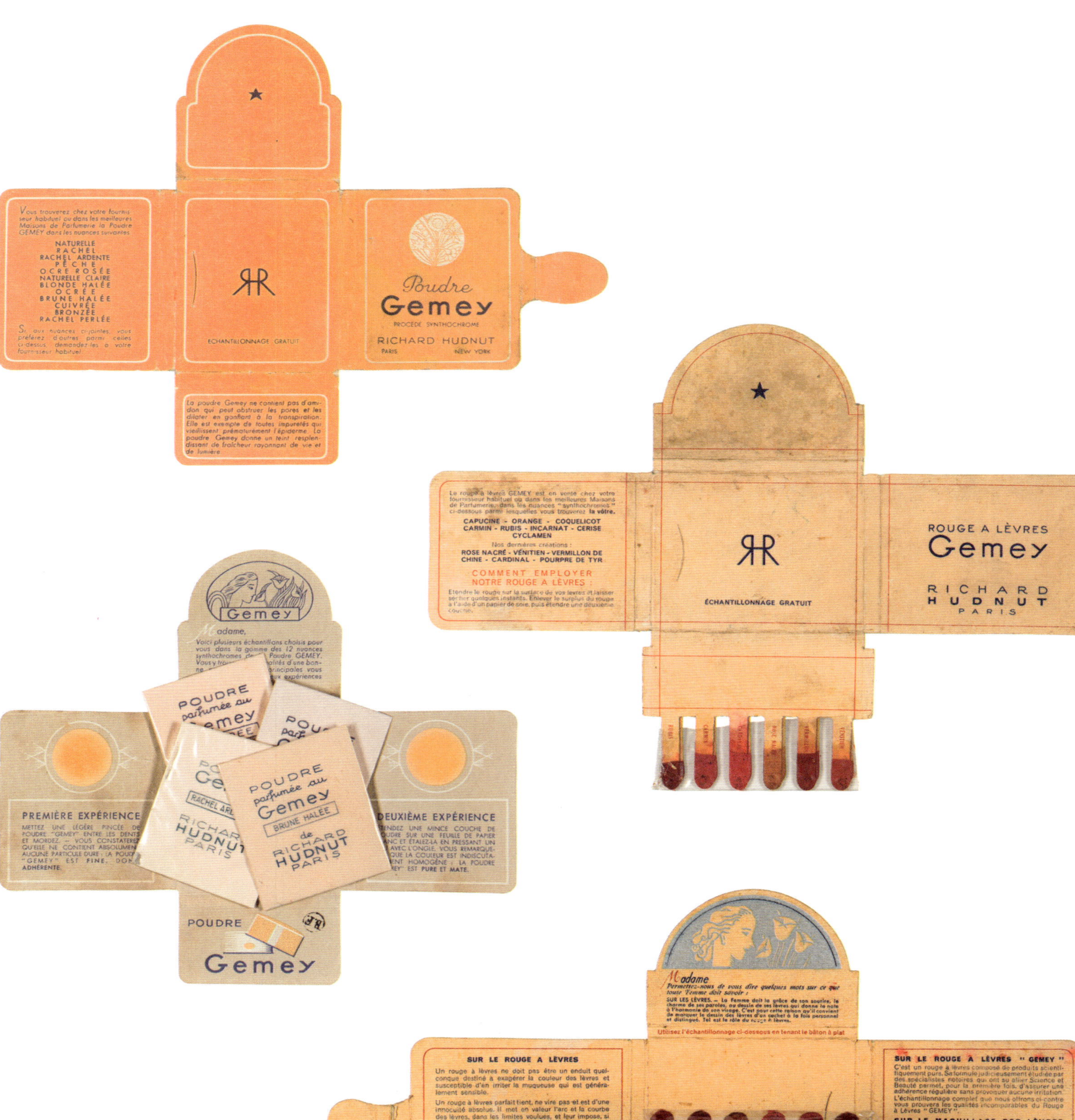

Poudre
Gemey
PROCÉDÉ SYNTHOCHROME
RICHARD HUDNUT
PARIS NEW YORK
ÉCHANTILLONNAGE GRATUIT
NATURELLE
RACHEL
RACHEL ARDENTE
PÊCHE
OCRE ROSÉE
NATURELLE CLAIRE
BLONDE HALÉE
OCRÉE
BRUNE HALÉE
CUIVRÉE
BRONZÉE
RACHEL PERLÉE
ROUGE A LÈVRES
Gemey
RICHARD
HUDNUT
PARIS
ÉCHANTILLONNAGE GRATUIT
CAPUCINE - ORANGE - COQUELICOT
CARMIN - RUBIS - INCARNAT - CERISE
CYCLAMEN
ROSE NACRÉ - VÉNITIEN - VERMILLON DE
CHINE - CARDINAL - POURPRE DE TYR
COMMENT EMPLOYER
NOTRE ROUGE A LÈVRES :
Gemey
Madame,
PREMIÈRE EXPÉRIENCE
DEUXIÈME EXPÉRIENCE
POUDRE
parfumée au
Gemey
BRUNE HALÉE
de
RICHARD
HUDNUT
PARIS
RACHEL
POUDRE
Gemey
Madame
SUR LE ROUGE A LÈVRES
LE ROUGE A LÈVRES GEMEY
SUR LE ROUGE A LÈVRES "GEMEY"
SUR LE MAQUILLAGE DES LÈVRES

In the 1920s and 1930s, the problems posed by the material aspect of cosmetic products led to use of color reproductions, although this approach was clearly premature. A woman choosing her makeup on the basis of a color chart has very few elements to connect her to a known, tangible reality: limited experience with recently developed products, samples with textures and colors that are only approximate, and a few words describing the colors. Women could not be expected to embrace the cosmetics color chart without help. Strategies of structure, design, and language attempted to compensate as color moved from a product sample to a reproduction. Thus, the names of the samples (which used a particular vocabulary marked by the recurrence of terms such as "natural") and the drawings of lips or sticks of lip color made connections so that the mind could become gradually familiar with the delicate transfers that reproduced color required. In this way, even before World War II, skills had been developed to perceive a product based on hints that were increasingly tenuous, as a result of a familiarization process in which the color chart played a major role.

COLOR CHARTS APPEAR THROUGHOUT THE HOUSEHOLD

During the 1920s and 1930s, scientific and industrial advances led to a large number of items that brought color, and also the color chart, into homes. There, the color chart would continue the familiarization process that had begun in retail stores: teaching a color vocabulary when the names of colors were not replaced by numbers, but, above all, bringing color within reach, allowing consumers to immerse themselves—for hours at a time if they wished—in the dream that color expressed.

Paper Color Charts

The chemical industry had managed to bring every possible color to paper, and it was now concerned with encouraging manufacturers to purchase the synthetic dyes and pigments that it produced. It was up to these manufacturers to use the dyes to produce products, and then to convince customers that they needed the products. The profusion of colors helped considerably with this undertaking, because needs became obsolete once desire was present. And color provoked desire.

NEXT PAGE

Papeterie de la Bourse Catalog

The Papeterie de la Bourse in Paris printed its own catalog to showcase the variety of its papers. Paper products had multiplied since the beginning of the twentieth century, particularly dyed sheets of paper intended for artists or merchants of office supplies. Paper was available in many shades and patterns, which were regularly updated, as shown by the frequent indication of "New Colors." Fashion had reached paper products, and their distributors wanted to spread the word with these little catalogs, even if their design was a bit careless.

Paper color chart, Papeterie de la Bourse, France, 1930s, sheet of paper, 15 × 23 1 fold, Bibliothèque Forney, Paris, call number RES ICO 8767

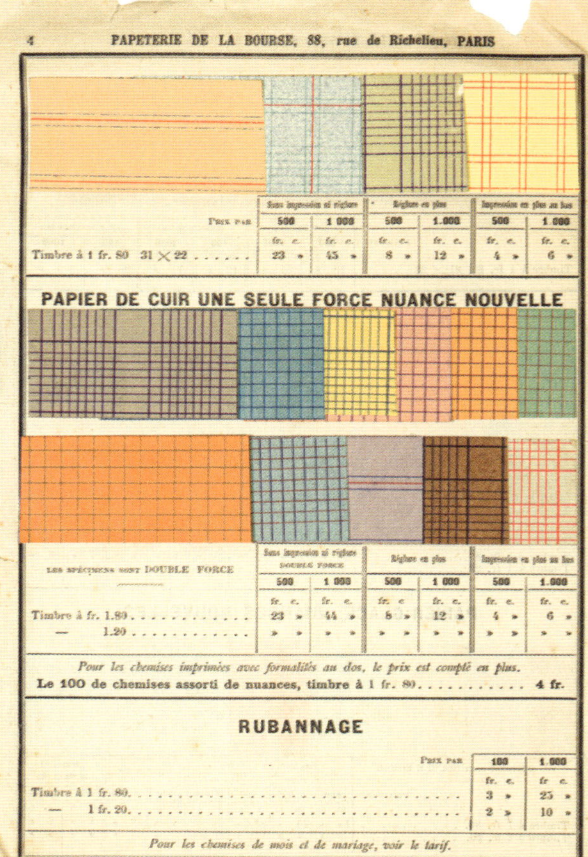

4 PAPETERIE DE LA BOURSE, 88, rue de Richelieu, PARIS

Prix par	Sans impression ni réglure		Réglure en plus		Impression en plus au bas	
	500	1 000	500	1.000	500	1.000
	fr. c.	fr. c.	fr. c.	fr. c.	fr. c.	fr. c.
Timbre à 1 fr. 80 31 × 22	23 »	45 »	8 »	12 »	4 »	6 »

PAPIER DE CUIR UNE SEULE FORCE NUANCE NOUVELLE

Les spécimens sont DOUBLE FORCE	Sans impression ni réglure DOUBLE FORCE		Réglure en plus		Impression en plus au bas	
	500	1 000	500	1 000	500	1.000
	fr. c.	fr. c.	fr. c.	fr. c.	fr. c.	fr. c.
Timbre à fr. 1.80	23 »	44 »	8 »	12 »	4 »	6 »
— 1.20	» »	» »	» »	» »	» »	» »

Pour les chemises imprimées avec formalités au dos, le prix est compté en plus.

Le 100 de chemises assorti de nuances, timbre à 1 fr. 80 . . . . 4 fr.

RUBANNAGE

Prix par	100	1.000
	fr. c.	fr. c.
Timbre à 1 fr. 80.	3 »	25 »
— 1 fr. 20.	2 »	10 »

Pour les chemises de mois et de mariage, voir le tarif.

Papeterie de la Bourse, 88, rue Richelieu, Paris.

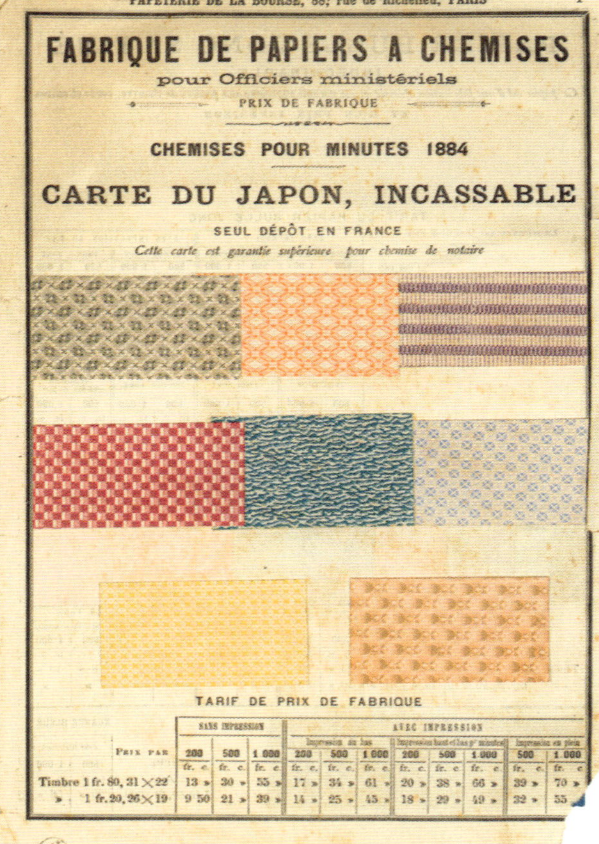

PAPETERIE DE LA BOURSE, 88, rue de Richelieu, PARIS 1

FABRIQUE DE PAPIERS A CHEMISES

pour Officiers ministériels

PRIX DE FABRIQUE

CHEMISES POUR MINUTES 1884

CARTE DU JAPON, INCASSABLE

SEUL DÉPÔT EN FRANCE

Cette carte est garantie supérieure pour chemise de notaire

TARIF DE PRIX DE FABRIQUE

Prix par	Sans impression			Avec impression: Impression au bas			Impression haut et bas pr minutes			Impression en plein	
	200	500	1.000	200	500	1.000	200	500	1.000	500	1.000
	fr. c.	fr. c.	fr. c.	fr. c.	fr. c.	fr. c.	fr. c.	fr. c.	fr. c.	fr. c.	fr. c.
Timbre 1 fr. 80, 31×22	13 »	30 »	55 »	17 »	34 »	61 »	20 »	38 »	66 »	39 »	70 »
» 1 fr. 20, 26×19	9 50	21 »	39 »	14 »	25 »	45 »	18 »	29 »	49 »	32 »	55

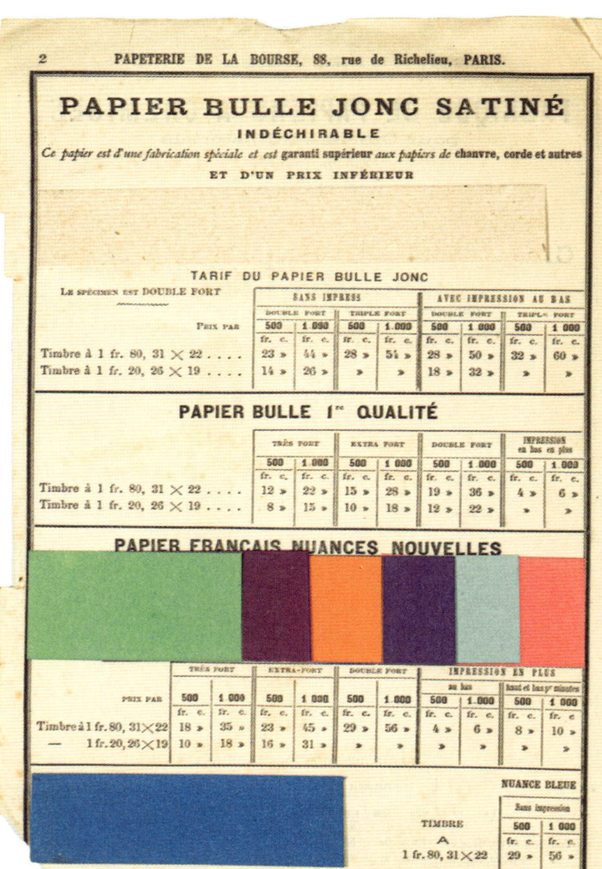

2 PAPETERIE DE LA BOURSE, 88, rue de Richelieu, PARIS.

PAPIER BULLE JONC SATINÉ

INDÉCHIRABLE

Ce papier est d'une fabrication spéciale et est **garanti supérieur** *aux papiers de* **chanvre, corde et autres**

ET D'UN PRIX INFÉRIEUR

TARIF DU PAPIER BULLE JONC

Le spécimen est DOUBLE FORT — Prix par	Sans impress. Double fort		Triple fort		Avec impression au bas. Double fort		Triple fort	
	500	1.000	500	1.000	500	1 000	500	1 000
	fr. c.	fr. c.	fr. c.	fr. c.	fr. c.	fr. c.	fr. c.	fr. c.
Timbre à 1 fr. 80, 31 × 22	23 »	44 »	28 »	54 »	28 »	50 »	32 »	60 »
Timbre à 1 fr. 20, 26 × 19	14 »	26 »	»	»	18 »	32 »	»	»

PAPIER BULLE 1re QUALITÉ

	Très fort		Extra fort		Double fort		Impression en bas en plus	
	500	1.000	500	1 000	500	1.000	500	1.000
	fr. c.	fr. c.	fr. c.	fr. c.	fr. c.	fr. c.	fr. c.	fr. c.
Timbre à 1 fr. 80, 31 × 22	12 »	22 »	15 »	28 »	19 »	36 »	4 »	6 »
Timbre à 1 fr. 20, 26 × 19	8 »	15 »	10 »	18 »	12 »	22 »	»	»

PAPIER FRANCAIS NUANCES NOUVELLES

Prix par	Très fort		Extra-fort		Double fort		Impression en plus: au bas		haut et bas pr minutes	
	500	1 000	500	1 000	500	1.000	500	1.000	500	1 000
	fr. c.	fr. c.	fr. c.	fr. c.	fr. c.	fr. c.	fr. c.	fr. c.	fr. c.	fr. c.
Timbre à 1 fr. 80, 31×22	18 »	35 »	23 »	45 »	29 »	56 »	4 »	6 »	8 »	10 »
— 1 fr. 20, 26×19	10 »	18 »	16 »	31 »	»	»	»	»	»	»

NUANCE BLEUE

Timbre à	Sans impression 500	1 000
	fr. c.	fr. c.
1 fr. 80, 31×22	29 »	56 »

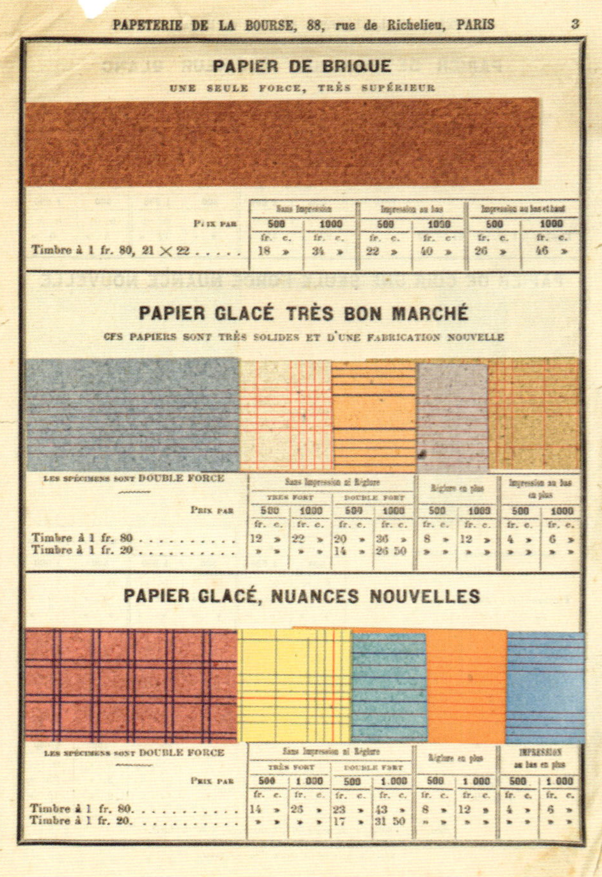

PAPETERIE DE LA BOURSE, 88, rue de Richelieu, PARIS 3

PAPIER DE BRIQUE

UNE SEULE FORCE, TRÈS SUPÉRIEUR

Prix par	Sans Impression		Impression au bas		Impression au bas et haut	
	500	1000	500	1000	500	1000
	fr. c.	fr. c.	fr. c.	fr. c.	fr. c.	fr. c.
Timbre à 1 fr. 80, 21 × 22	18 »	34 »	22 »	40 »	26 »	46 »

PAPIER GLACÉ TRÈS BON MARCHÉ

CES PAPIERS SONT TRÈS SOLIDES ET D'UNE FABRICATION NOUVELLE

Les spécimens sont DOUBLE FORCE — Prix par	Sans Impression ni Réglure: Très fort		Double fort		Réglure en plus		Impression au bas en plus	
	500	1000	500	1000	500	1000	500	1000
	fr. c.	fr. c.	fr. c.	fr. c.	fr. c.	fr. c.	fr. c.	fr. c.
Timbre à 1 fr. 80	12 »	22 »	20 »	36 »	8 »	12 »	4 »	6 »
Timbre à 1 fr. 20	» »	» »	14 »	26 50	» »	» »	» »	» »

PAPIER GLACÉ, NUANCES NOUVELLES

Les spécimens sont DOUBLE FORCE — Prix par	Sans Impression ni Réglure: Très fort		Double fort		Réglure en plus		Impression au bas en plus	
	500	1.000	500	1.000	500	1.000	500	1.000
	fr. c.	fr. c.	fr. c.	fr. c.	fr. c.	fr. c.	fr. c.	fr. c.
Timbre à 1 fr. 80.	14 »	26 »	23 »	43 »	8 »	12 »	4 »	6 »
Timbre à 1 fr. 20.	» »	» »	17 »	31 50	» »	» »	» »	» »

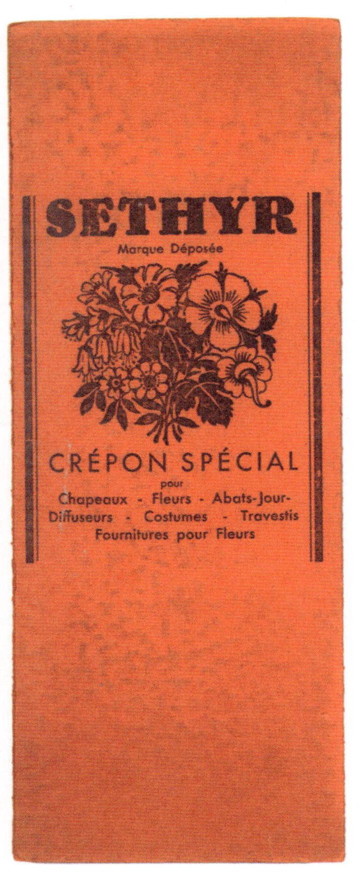
SETHYR
Marque Déposée
CRÉPON SPÉCIAL
pour
Chapeaux - Fleurs - Abats-Jour-
Diffuseurs - Costumes - Travestis
Fournitures pour Fleurs

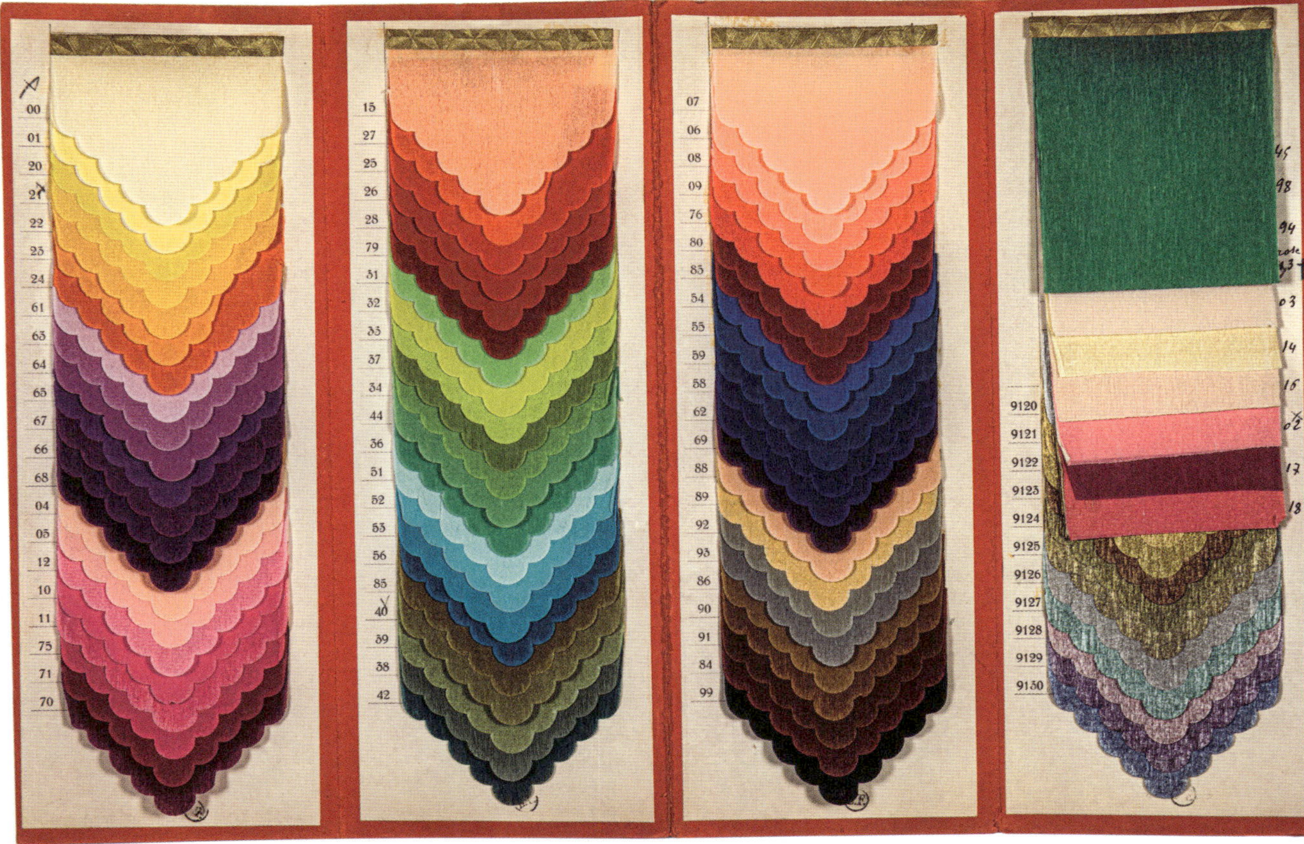
9120
9121
9122
9123
9124
9125
9126
9127
9128
9129
9130

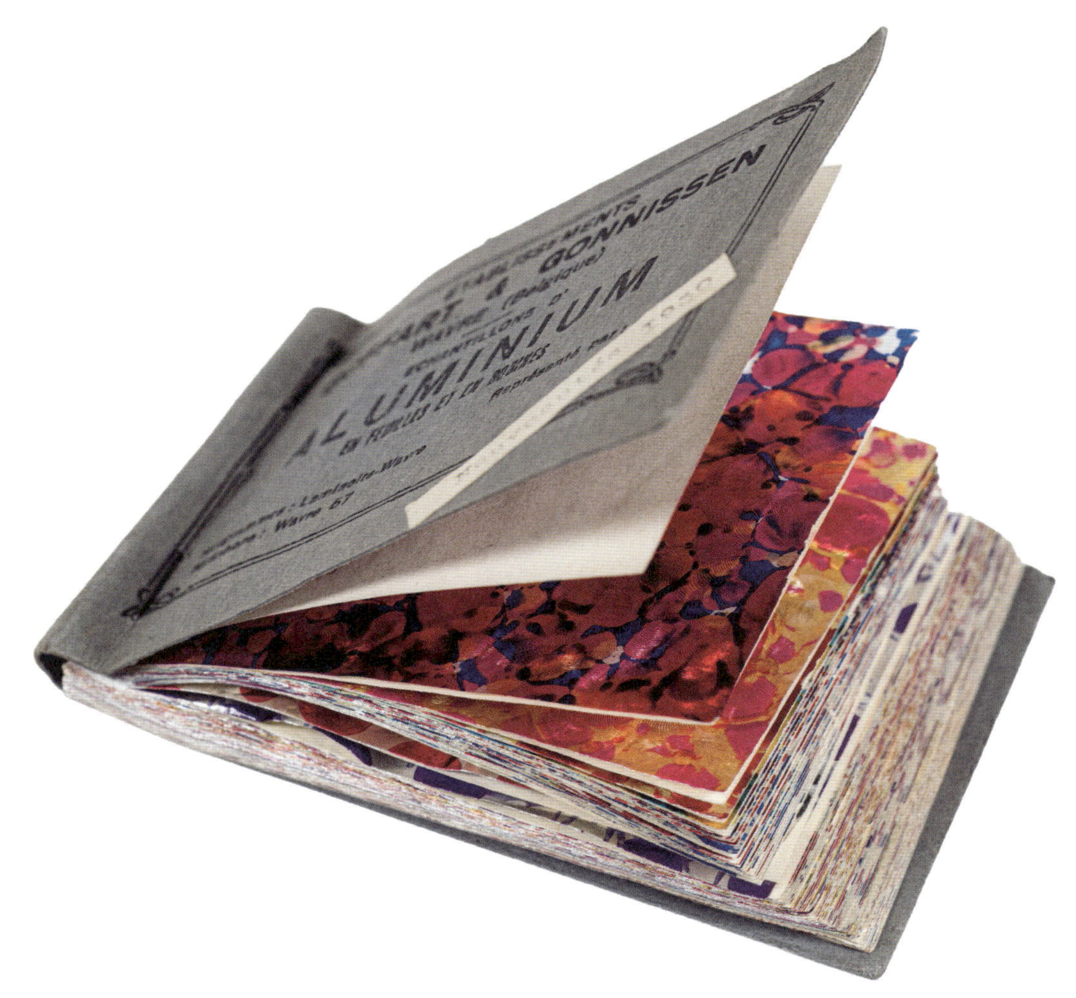
GONNISSEN
ALUMINIUM

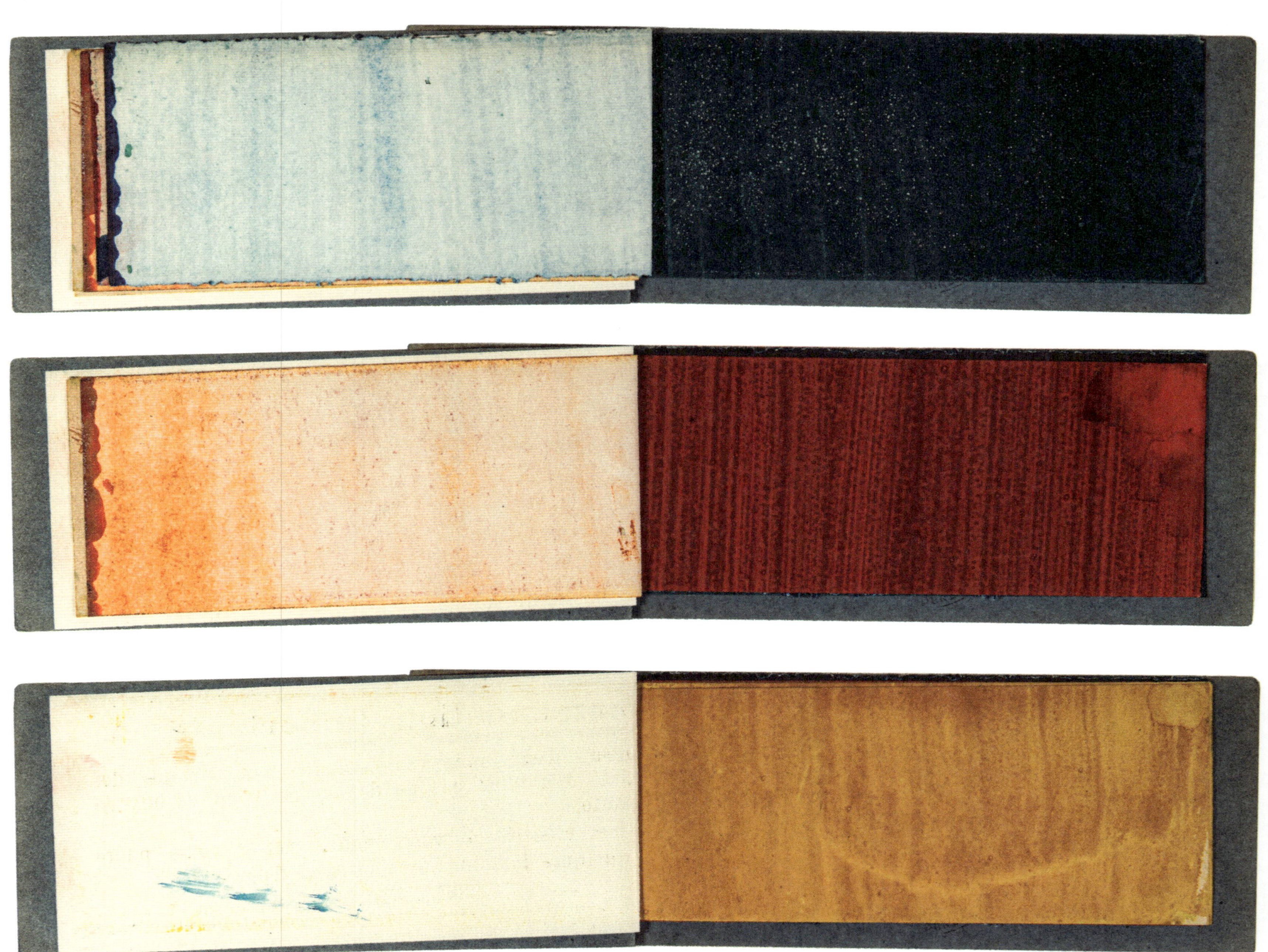

PREVIOUS PAGE, TOP

Séthyr Crepe Paper

Bright colors were particularly appropriate in this color chart of crepe paper for decorations and ornamentation. The choice of colors is abundant (eighty-seven) and the range includes delicate, bright, and metallic shades, and even the new fluorescent tones that the chemical industry had just developed.

Special Crepe Paper for Hats, Flowers, Lampshades, Diffusers, Traditional Costumes, Fancy-Dress Costumes, Supplies for Flowers, Séthyr, France (?), 1930s, card, 22 × 9.5 cm, 3 folds, Bibliothèque Forney, Paris, call number RES 7874

PREVIOUS PAGE, BOTTOM

Goffart & Gonnissen Aluminum Sheets

This notebook presents a hundred very thin sheets of aluminum foil paper offering a series of patterns in many different colors. This type of paper was used for packaging candy, but the indication "New Items 1930" confirms that the fashion phenomenon was now established for many different products featuring color.

Samples of Aluminum in Sheets and on Reels, Goffart & Gonnissen, Wavre, Belgium, 1930, notebook with approximately 100 sheets, 8 × 10 cm, Bibliothèque Forney, Paris, call number RES 5238

OPPOSITE

L.D. Photo-Color Palette

To improve black-and-white photos, various colorization techniques had been developed since the 1880s: photo-miniature, photo-painting, photo-watercolor.[59] But these techniques were delicate. A much simpler solution consisted in dipping a wet brush into the transparent ink on one of the pages of this album, which was both a palette and a color chart, and applying it to the light areas of the photographic print. It was even possible to correct mistakes by immersing the photo in salted water for a few moments.

Photo-Color Palette, L.D., Seine department, France, 1943 (?), album, 6 × 21 cm, 6 pages, Bibliothèque Forney, Paris, call number Res. ICO 8104

Color in Household Dyeing

——— With dye, consumers could alter their clothing for mourning or give a fresh look to worn, faded garments. This custom was already in use when it was still necessary to extract color from plants. Synthetic chemistry offered consumers dyes that were easier to use.

NEXT PAGE, TOP

L'Alsacienne Dyes

This color chart used the design codes of decorative paint color charts, with strips of colored paper glued under a sheet with openings. Light colors were rare because it was easier to move from light to dark than from dark to light, which required the preliminary step of bleaching (a process that could also weaken the fabric).

Card of Dyes, L'Alsacienne, Belgium, 1930s, card, 16 × 11.5 cm, Bibliothèque Forney, Paris, call number RES ICO 8104

NEXT PAGE, BOTTOM

Kabiline Dyes

Was the name Kabiline intended to appeal to European customers by its exoticism, or was it chosen to facilitate the export of these dyes to the Maghreb? Dyes were some of the principal products that industrialized nations sold to the colonies. This color chart was carefully developed, with strips of two types of fabric, thin and thick, illustrating each sample. It also showed that the Legris company was in touch with the times: the fabrics mentioned included rayon as well as nylon, which had just started to become available. Six of the seventy shades on this chart were developed specifically to dye stockings.

Kabiline Color Card, Établissements Legris, Versailles, late 1930s, card, 26 × 12.5 cm, Anne Varichon collection, Sète

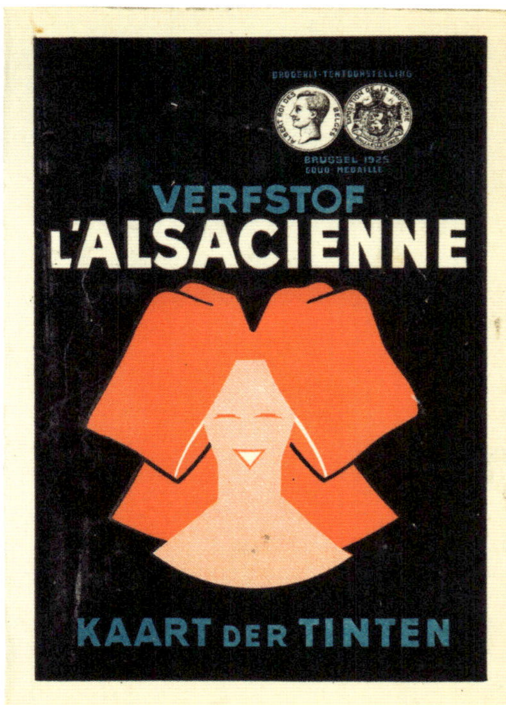
BRUSSEL 1925
VERFSTOF
L'ALSACIENNE
KAART DER TINTEN

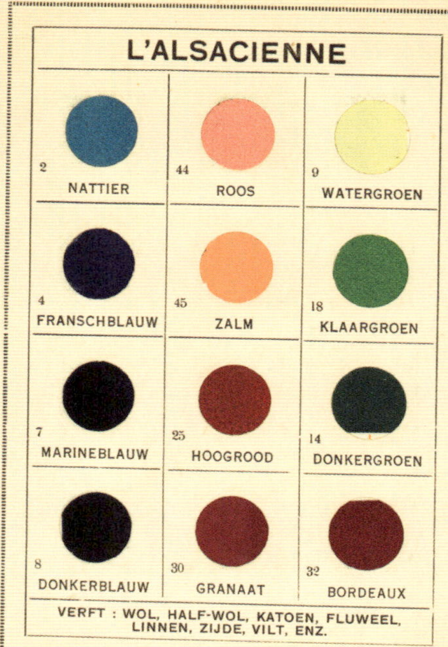
L'ALSACIENNE
2 NATTIER
44 ROOS
9 WATERGROEN
4 FRANSCHBLAUW
45 ZALM
18 KLAARGROEN
7 MARINEBLAUW
25 HOOGROOD
14 DONKERGROEN
8 DONKERBLAUW
30 GRANAAT
32 BORDEAUX
VERFT : WOL, HALF-WOL, KATOEN, FLUWEEL, LINNEN, ZIJDE, VILT, ENZ.

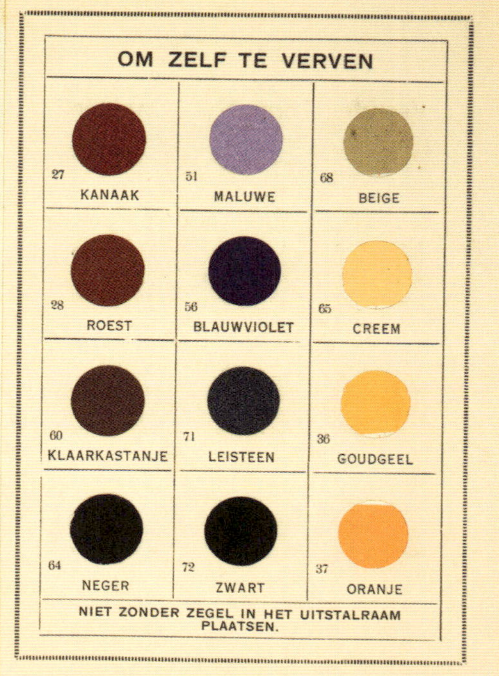
OM ZELF TE VERVEN
27 KANAAK
51 MALUWE
68 BEIGE
28 ROEST
56 BLAUWVIOLET
65 CREEM
60 KLAARKASTANJE
71 LEISTEEN
36 GOUDGEEL
64 NEGER
72 ZWART
37 ORANJE
NIET ZONDER ZEGEL IN HET UITSTALRAAM PLAATSEN.

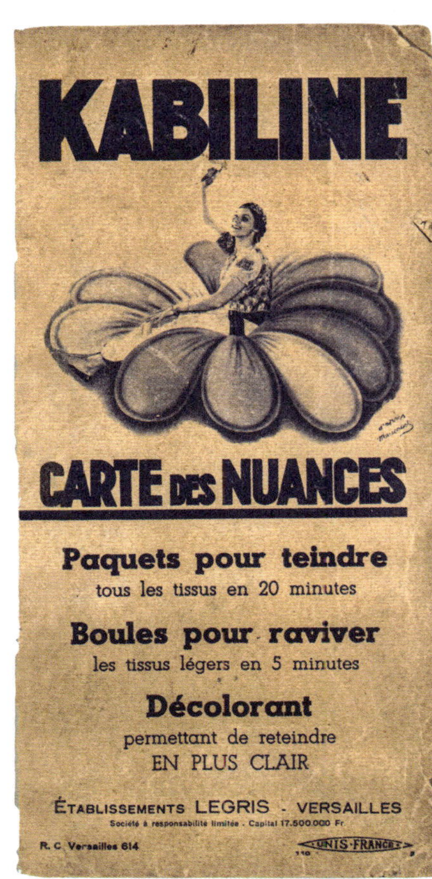
KABILINE
CARTE DES NUANCES
Paquets pour teindre
tous les tissus en 20 minutes
Boules pour raviver
les tissus légers en 5 minutes
Décolorant
permettant de reteindre
EN PLUS CLAIR
ÉTABLISSEMENTS LEGRIS - VERSAILLES
R. C. Versailles 614
UNIS-FRANCE

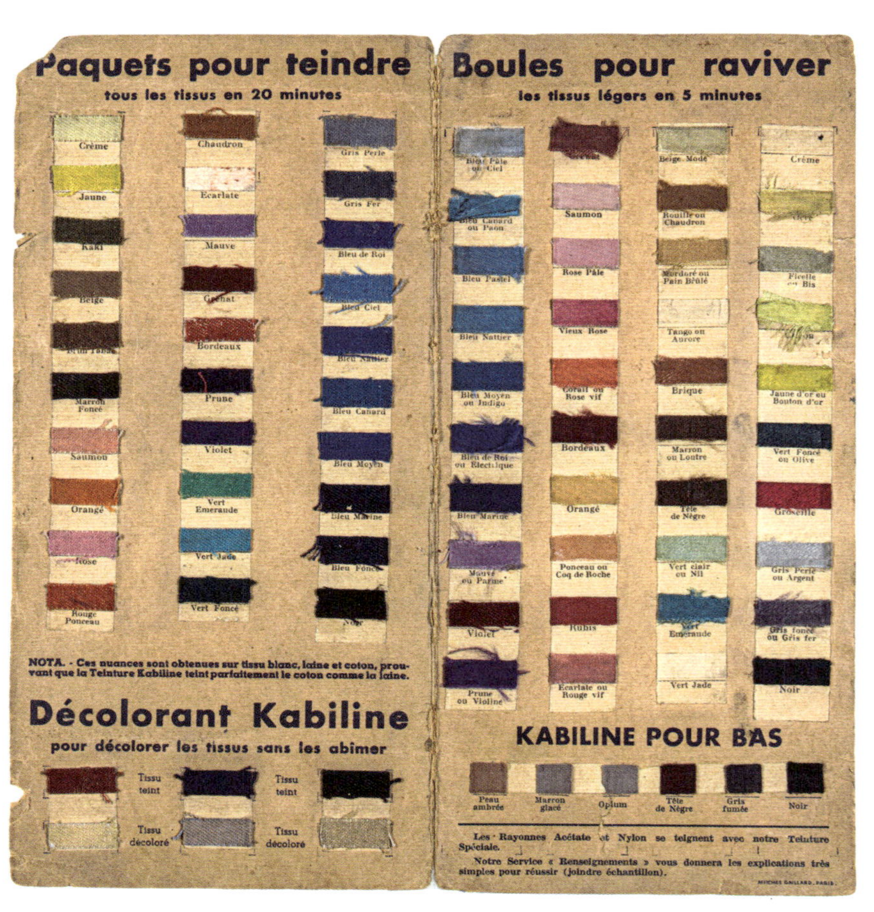
Paquets pour teindre
tous les tissus en 20 minutes
Boules pour raviver
les tissus légers en 5 minutes
NOTA. - Ces nuances sont obtenues sur tissu blanc, laine et coton, prouvant que la Teinture Kabiline teint parfaitement le coton comme la laine.
Décolorant Kabiline
pour décolorer les tissus sans les abimer
Tissu teint
Tissu décoloré
KABILINE POUR BAS
Peau ambrée
Marron glacé
Opium
Tête de Nègre
Gris fumée
Noir
Les Rayonnes Acétate et Nylon se teignent avec notre Teinture Spéciale.
Notre Service « Renseignements » vous donnera les explications très simples pour réussir (joindre échantillon).

NEXT PAGE SPREAD

Twink

The sampling on this color chart is less elaborate, as the colors are simply applications of ink, but the clever layout creates a convincing illusion of volume. New marketing strategies were beginning to transform packaging into an art. The color charts of the Trente Glorieuses, the postwar period, would offer wonderful examples of this.

Twink Color Card, Société Anonyme des Savonneries Lever, Haubourdin-lez-Lille, late 1930s, card with shaped edges, 13 × 10 cm, 1 fold, Bibliothèque Forney, Paris, call number RES ICO 8104

Color Charts and Mail Order

RIGHT

La Redoute Catalog

Launched in 1928, the mail-order catalog La Redoute originally had only sixteen pages, all about knitting, the company's specialty. It soon expanded its offerings, and its color charts of multicolored wool appeared in countless households. These catalogs were often kept and studied, even if the wool was no longer available and even if there was no knitting going on![60] Once again, the color chart was an invitation to daydream—inspired by its textures or the names of its colors (which appeared across from each yarn sample on a small ruler that has disappeared from this example). This ability to launch an imaginary journey is intrinsic to the color chart.

Catalog, La Redoute, Roubaix, 1936, catalogue, 37 × 25 cm, 75 pages, Bibliothèque Forney, Paris, call number CC 1560"1936"sept Plano

In the history of the color chart, the period between the two world wars was a magnificent era. Color abounded, its display was intensely creative, color vocabularies were still being enlarged, and the product sample still powerfully affected the relationship to color through its sensory nature. While social restrictions were still at work, imposing a list of forbidden or permissible shades in various contexts, the most beautiful and most stable colors were no longer reserved for the elite. The egalitarianism of color had occurred. The color chart was its instrument and its emblem. It stimulated an appetite for color, legitimized it, and satisfied it. Color was becoming a right, and it was exercised using the color chart.

The color chart also took on new functions. It guided the user more and more closely in the application of products that were constantly becoming more complex. It also took on an educational role in mixing colors or creating harmonies that would reflect the aesthetic criteria of the moment. Above all, and especially through the cosmetics color chart, it accustomed Western society to being able to consider color separately from its material. But the color chart's new missions were not layered over its old ones. They replaced them, for, as it developed, the color chart gradually abandoned the exemplification of color that had once been its kingdom. ●

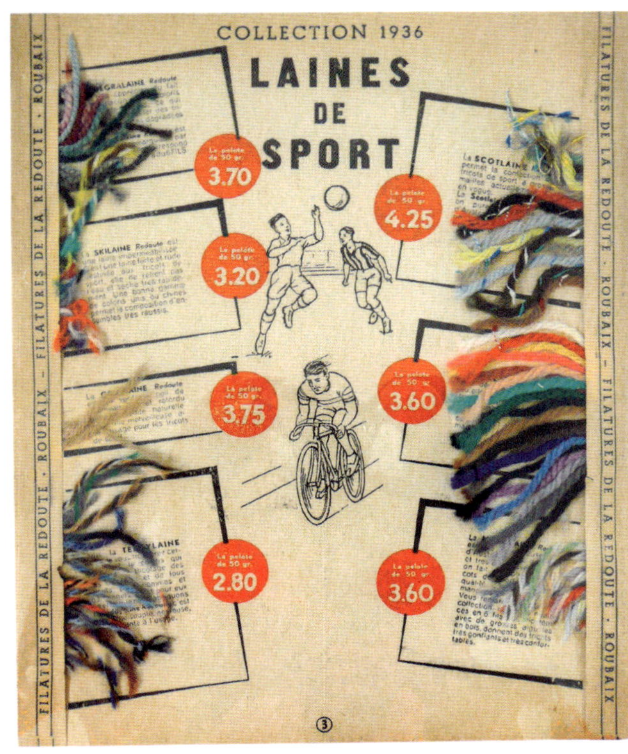

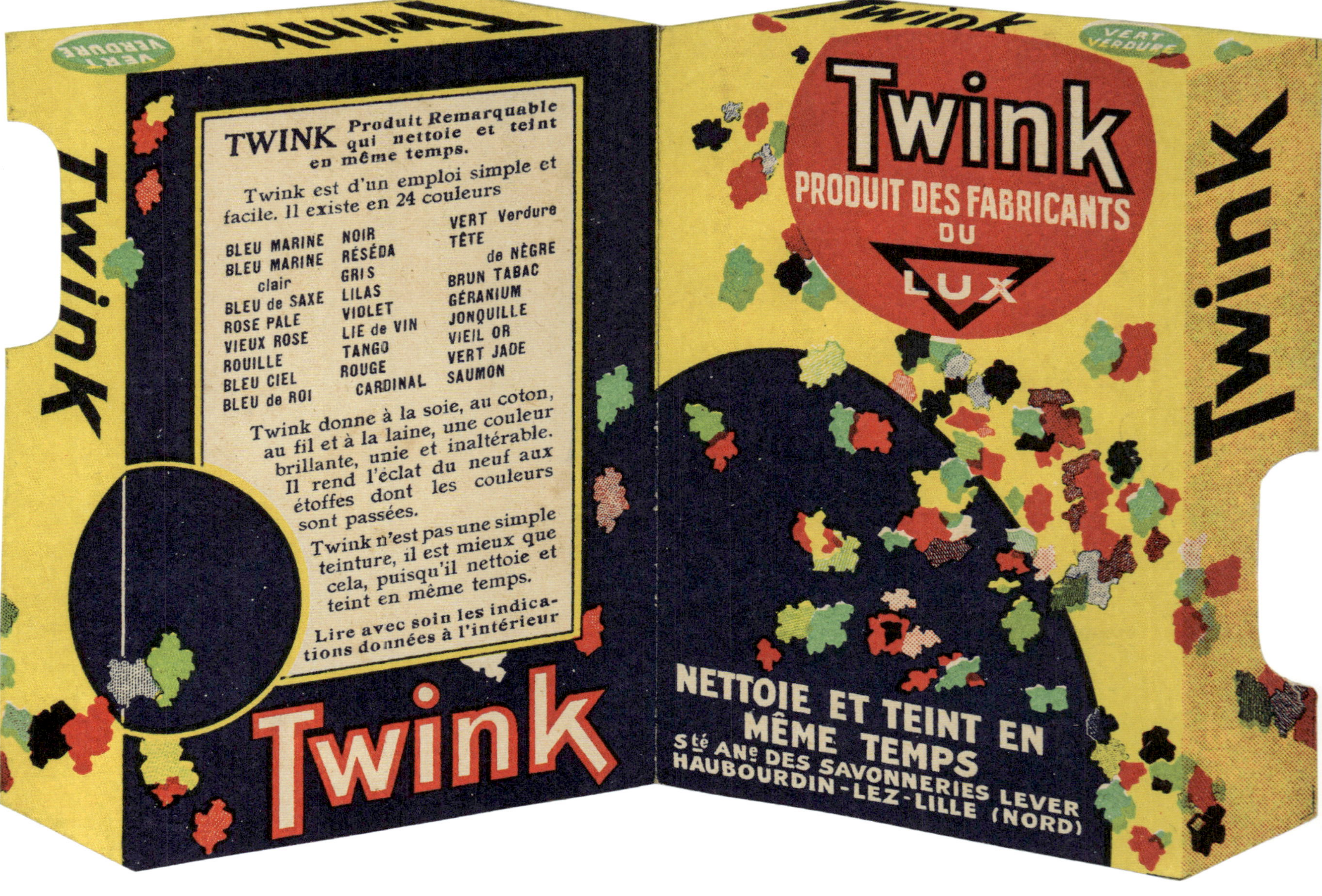
Twink
VERT VERDURE
Twink
TWINK Produit Remarquable qui nettoie et teint en même temps.
Twink est d'un emploi simple et facile. Il existe en 24 couleurs
BLEU MARINE
BLEU MARINE clair
BLEU de SAXE
ROSE PALE
VIEUX ROSE
ROUILLE
BLEU CIEL
BLEU de ROI
NOIR
RÉSÉDA
GRIS
LILAS
VIOLET
LIE de VIN
TANGO
ROUGE CARDINAL
VERT Verdure
TÊTE de NÈGRE
BRUN TABAC
GÉRANIUM
JONQUILLE
VIEIL OR
VERT JADE
SAUMON
Twink donne à la soie, au coton, au fil et à la laine, une couleur brillante, unie et inaltérable. Il rend l'éclat du neuf aux étoffes dont les couleurs sont passées.
Twink n'est pas une simple teinture, il est mieux que cela, puisqu'il nettoie et teint en même temps.
Lire avec soin les indications données à l'intérieur
Twink
Twink
VERT VERDURE
Twink
PRODUIT DES FABRICANTS DU
LUX
Twink
NETTOIE ET TEINT EN MÊME TEMPS
Sté Ane DES SAVONNERIES LEVER
HAUBOURDIN-LEZ-LILLE (NORD)

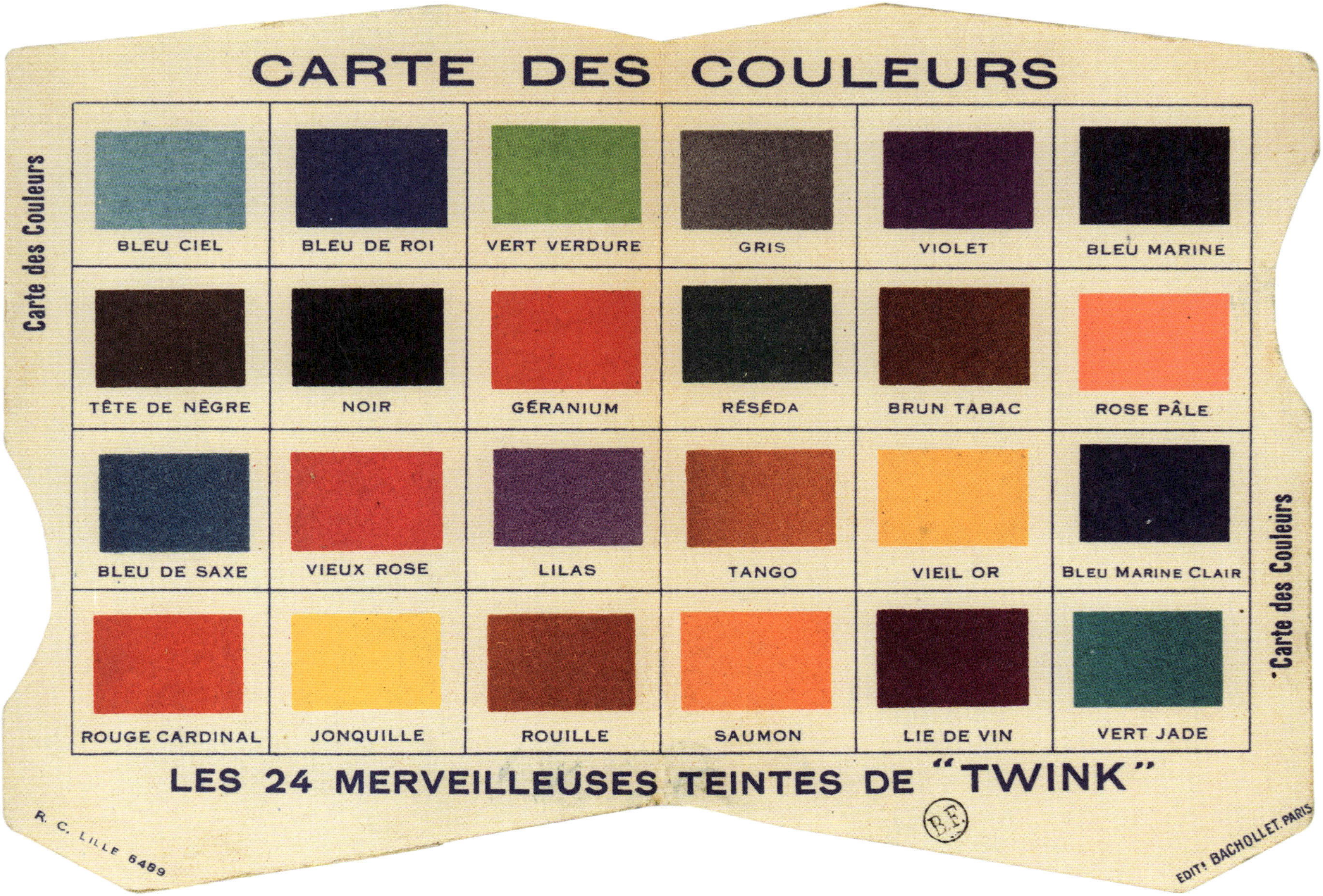

CARTE DES COULEURS

Carte des Couleurs

BLEU CIEL	BLEU DE ROI	VERT VERDURE	GRIS	VIOLET	BLEU MARINE
TÊTE DE NÈGRE	NOIR	GÉRANIUM	RÉSÉDA	BRUN TABAC	ROSE PÂLE
BLEU DE SAXE	VIEUX ROSE	LILAS	TANGO	VIEIL OR	BLEU MARINE CLAIR
ROUGE CARDINAL	JONQUILLE	ROUILLE	SAUMON	LIE DE VIN	VERT JADE

Carte des Couleurs

LES 24 MERVEILLEUSES TEINTES DE "TWINK"

R. C. LILLE 6489

B.F.

EDIT. BACHOLLET. PARIS

SCARLET

JUBILATION OF COLOR

1950s–1980s

—————— Thirty years after consumer society emerged in the United States, it came to Europe and grew strong, hardly slowing down when the oil crisis struck in the 1970s. Industry stimulated consumer society with myriad products, which sported every color possible thanks to the petrochemical industry. Colors were increasingly standardized and were no longer determined by custom but by the shifting demands of fashion. Industrialized countries had entered a period of colorful jubilation.

The color chart reflected this jubilation. Offset printing made it cheaper and faster to print in color. Thus all new products tended to have their own color chart, distributed in large numbers. Faced with this wave, manufacturers vied to stand out from the crowd. Color charts had to be attractive, creative, or educational. Many of them included information about color harmonies inspired by the work of Ignace Meyerson, Anni and Josef Albers, André and Monique Lemonnier, Jacques Fillacier, and others.[1]

Mirroring this richly dense chromatic world that was more deeply explored every day, the color chart did not truly embody color anymore, for the product sample was becoming a thing of the past. Inks could now be formulated with pearly or sparkly effects, but they had no texture. Above all, the colors themselves could fluctuate, and two copies of the same color chart could display noticeable differences. Manufacturers confirmed and acknowledged that the samples on their color charts were only approximate indications. After the interwar period when the sensory sample was gradually neglected and then wiped out, a new end was on the horizon: the color chart could no longer even claim to reproduce shades correctly.

THE COLOR CHART IN THE CHEMICAL INDUSTRY OF THE TRENTE GLORIEUSES

—————— After World War II, the chemical industry was reconfigured. The manufacturer IG Farben, which had been complicit in Nazi crimes, was dismantled by the Allies and split into several different companies.[2] In France, the company Francolor, placed under German authority during the war, absorbed the Compagnie Française des Matières Colorantes.[3] The United States, which had taken a decisive lead in the chemical industry, was followed by Great Britain, which was now the leader of the European chemical industry with I.C.I.

The production of pigments and dyes benefited from new technologies and the significant rise of the petrochemical industry beginning in the 1950s. Titanium oxide became a major element of the pigment titanium white, used in many applications, particularly in dyeing plastic, which was a key material from 1950 to 1980.

In this environment of competitive markets and ongoing innovation, the color chart remained the perfect tool to inform manufacturers about products. But, starting in the 1960s, the field's specialization led to extremely technical color charts. Humor had disappeared, and now the focus was on the molecular structure of dyes and the product to be colored; the layperson was shut out. Therefore, we will only cover a few color charts here whose applications still have meaning for a nonspecialist reader.

Conquering New Territory

——— As seen in postwar color charts, the chemical industry pursued the goal of selling its products outside Europe and, when new materials became available, it developed dyes that were suitable for them as quickly as possible.

OPPOSITE, TOP

Dyes for Raffia

The fact that the instructions specify that the formula should be adapted "to local work conditions" implies that these dyes for raffia, a fiber used for making hats and furnishings, were intended for export, which is confirmed by the name given to them: they are all called "Algerian" (*Algerian Pure Yellow*, *Algerian Dark Red*, and such) except for one, *Moroccan Red*.

Already before the war, the Société Anonyme des Matières Colorants et Produits Chimiques de Saint-Denis had printed labels with references to colonial territories (exotic peoples, desert animals, and such), which were as exaggerated as the reconstructions of villages displayed in the universal expositions of the second half of the nineteenth century.[4] They also displayed vats, tools, and activities of the artisanal dyeing methods specific to those regions, even as European countries were beginning to sabotage these skills by distributing replacement products developed by their dominant chemical industry.

Dyes for Raffia, Compagnie Française des Matières Colorantes Francolor, Seine-Saint-Denis, France, 1950s, pamphlet, 21.5 × 15.5 cm, 2 folds, Albi Couleurs, Association Mémoire des Industries de la Couleur, Albi

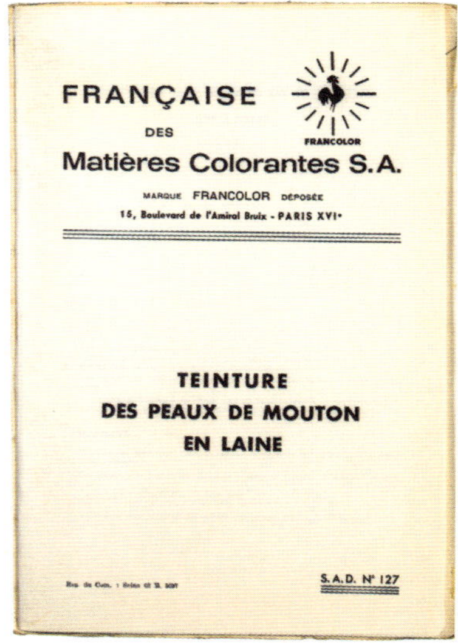

ABOVE AND FOLLOWING PAGE SPREAD

Dyes for Sheepskin

Winter sports, which became popular after the first Winter Olympics in 1924 in Chamonix, led in the 1950s to the dyeing of a very old material: sheepskin. The sports equipment industry needed sheepskin to produce clothing suitable for the cold. Francolor published this color chart to display the various combinations that its dyes could produce: dyeing the leather thoroughly but adding little color to the wool (samples 1 to 17), dyeing the leather and wool to match (samples 18 to 23), or dyeing them in two contrasting colors (no. 24).

Dyes for Sheepskin, Compagnie Française des Matières Colorantes Francolor, Paris, c. 1951, leporello, 24 × 17 cm, 5 panels, Albi Couleurs, Association Mémoire des Industries de la Couleur, Albi

OPPOSITE, BOTTOM

Dyes for Nylon Stockings

Nylon had just been invented by the American company DuPont de Nemours (1935). This lightweight, supple fiber, which had excellent resistance and was cheaper than silk, immediately generated a great deal of excitement. In the late 1930s, it was already used for women's lingerie in the United States before being requisitioned to produce parachutes and tires for bombers. When peace returned, European women were won over like their American counterparts by what were then called "synthetic silk stockings," which were resistant to runs although they were very delicate. Francolor rushed to develop dyes that could color them and even offered a new color range that was varied and bright (samples 1 to 8). This showed a keen development strategy but one that seems to have been premature. In Europe, multicolored stockings would not be worn until the 1960s, and by then were pantyhose, which were better suited for the shorter skirts that were in fashion.

Dyes for Nylon Stockings, no. 4, Société Anonyme de Matières Colorantes et Produits Chimiques Francolor, Paris, late 1940s, pamphlet, 21.5 × 15 cm, 2 folds, Albi Couleurs, Association Mémoire des Industries de la Couleur, Albi

Procédés d'application

PRÉPARATION A LA TEINTURE

Afin de faciliter l'unisson et la pénétration des colorants, il est recommandé de faire subir au raphia un mouillage d'une demi-heure à 1 heure dans un bain d'eau chaude, éventuellement additionné de :
1 *g* de Coptal BNA poudre par litre de bain.

TEINTURE

Procédé A.

Garnir le bain avec de l'eau tiède, ajouter le colorant dissous auparavant avec de l'eau bouillante et :
3 *cm*³ d'acide formique 80 % par litre de bain.

Entrer dans le bain de teinture le raphia préalablement mouillé, puis chauffer progressivement jusqu'au bouillon ; continuer la teinture à cette température pendant environ 1 heure, enlever et rincer.

Procédé B.

Garnir le bain de teinture avec de l'eau froide contenant, par litre :
2 *cm*³ d'acide acétique 6° Bé.

Ajouter à ce bain le colorant dissous séparément avec de l'eau chaude, puis entrer la marchandise et la manœuvrer assez rapidement.

Après 20 minutes de teinture effectuée sans chauffage, élever progressivement la température du bain jusqu'à 70° C environ, puis arrêter le chauffage et teindre pendant 15 à 20 minutes en bain refroidissant.

N.-B. — Le procédé de teinture à utiliser pour chacun des colorants illustrés dans cette carte est mentionné en face des illustrations.

Les renseignements contenus dans la présente carte ne sont donnés qu'à titre indicatif et sans engagement de notre part. Nous recommandons de les adapter aux conditions locales de travail et à la marchandise utilisée.

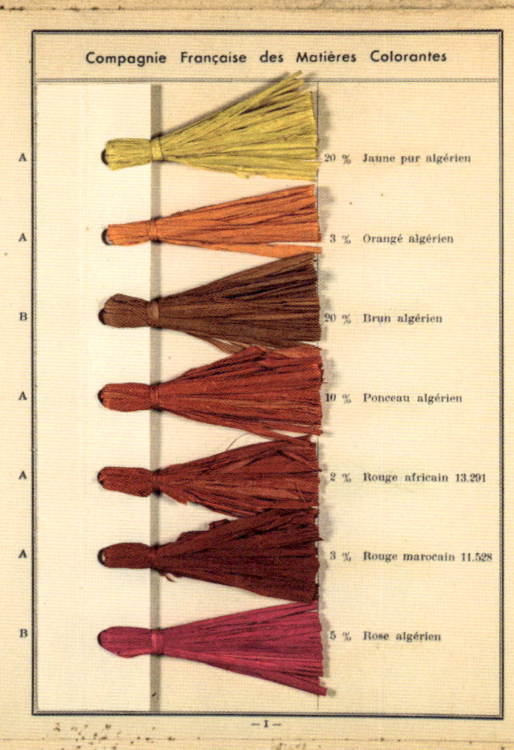

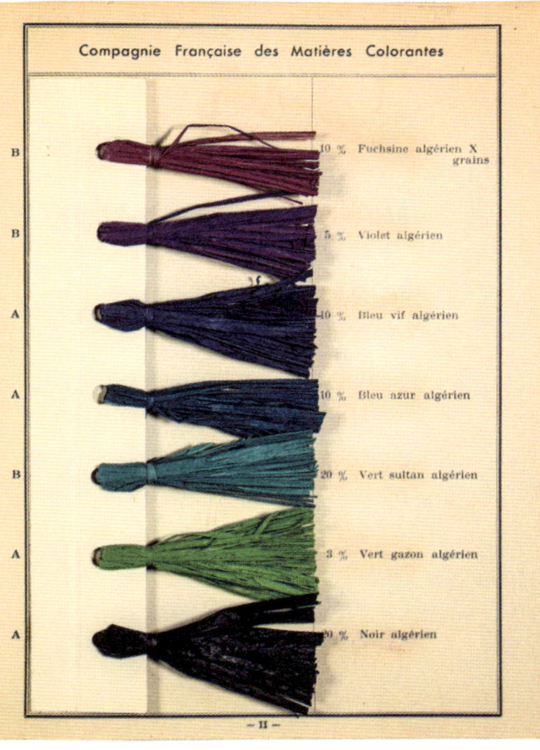

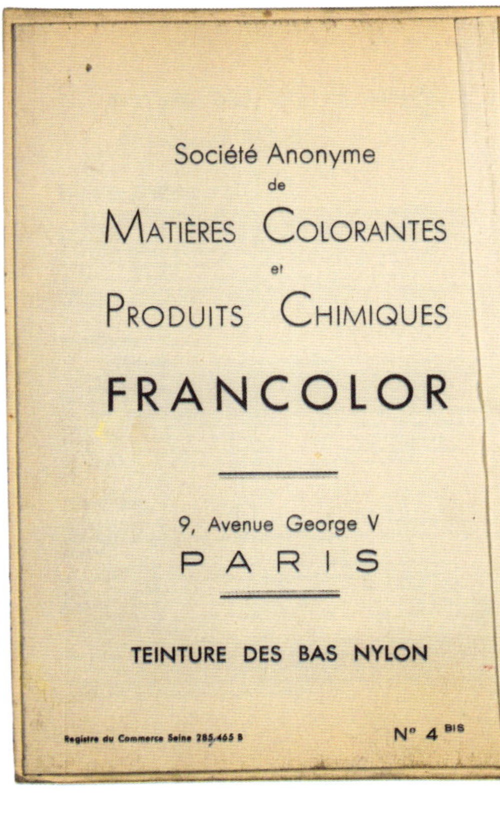

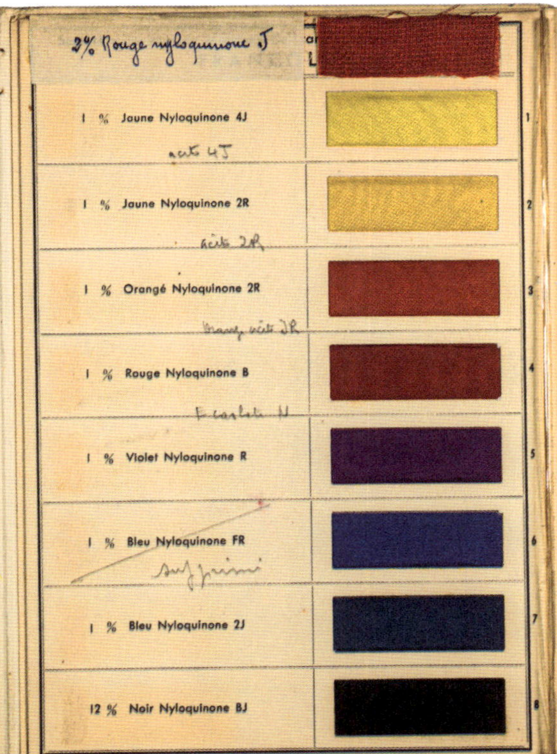

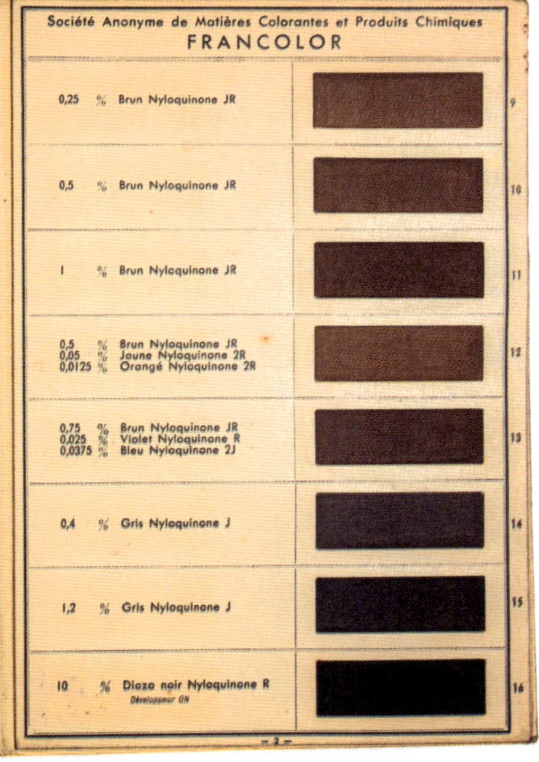

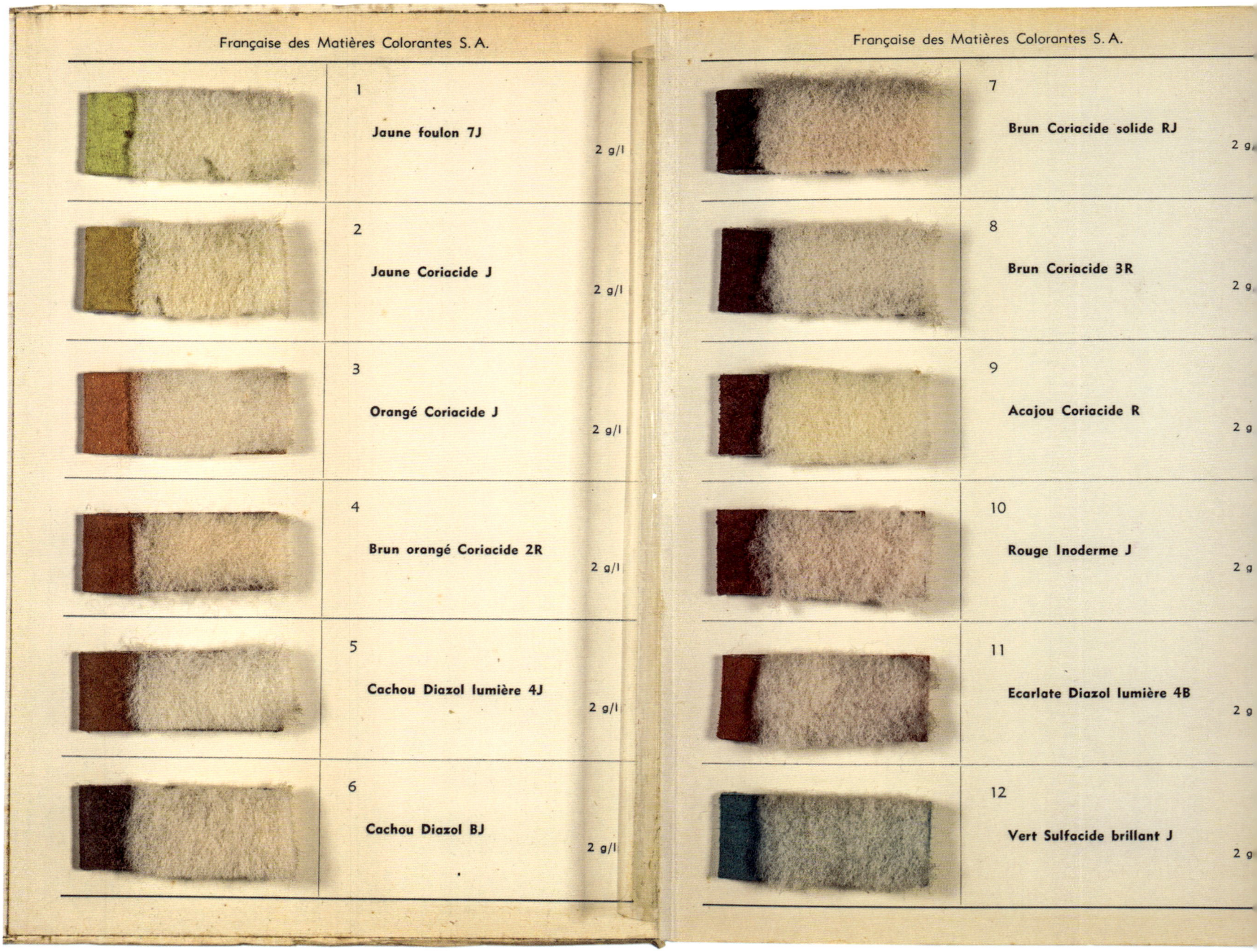

Française des Matières Colorantes S. A.

1	Jaune foulon 7J	2 g/l
2	Jaune Coriacide J	2 g/l
3	Orangé Coriacide J	2 g/l
4	Brun orangé Coriacide 2R	2 g/l
5	Cachou Diazol lumière 4J	2 g/l
6	Cachou Diazol BJ	2 g/l

Française des Matières Colorantes S. A.

7	Brun Coriacide solide RJ	2 g
8	Brun Coriacide 3R	2 g
9	Acajou Coriacide R	2 g
10	Rouge Inoderme J	2 g
11	Ecarlate Diazol lumière 4B	2 g
12	Vert Sulfacide brillant J	2 g

13

Vert Inoderme B 2 g/l

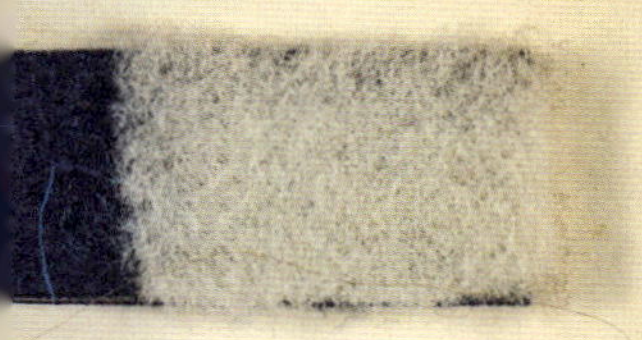

14

Bleu pur Diazol 6B 2 g/l

15

Bleu Diazol lumière R extra 2 g/l

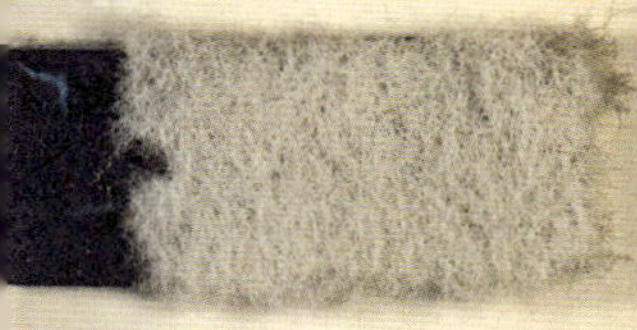

16

Gris Inoderme N 2 g/l

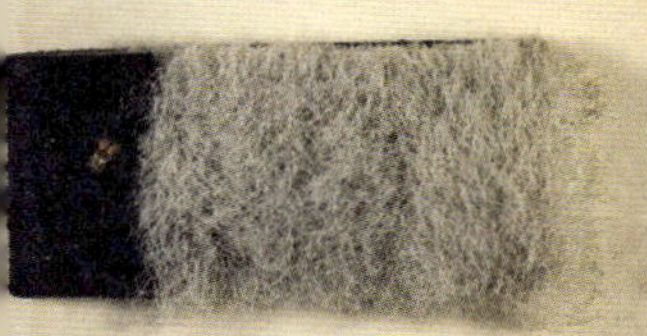

17

Noir Dimacide lumière JB double 2 g/l

18

Fouramine NZ	0,6	g/l
Brun foncé Coriacide RB	1	

Française des Matières Colorantes S. A.

19

Bleu Sulfacide lumière 2RL	0,1	g/l
Orangé Sulfacide JR extra	0,02	
Jaune Sulfacide lumière JL extra	0,125	
Brun foncé Coriacide VR	0,1	
Bronze Coriacide N	0,1	

20

Bleu Dimacide lumière JL	0,075	g/l
Ecarlate Dimacide lumière R	0,075	
Jaune Dimacide lumière N-5RL	0,225	
Brun foncé Coriacide R	0,5	

21

Brun Amichrome lumière RJLL	0,125	g/l
Noir Amichrome lumière RBLL	0,125	
Brun foncé Coriacide RB	0,5	

22

Noir Neutrichrome BRLL 0,75 g/l

23

Bleu Dimacide lumière JL	0,5	g/l
Orangé Sulfacide JR extra	0,2	
Jaune Sulfacide lumière 5RL	0,2	
Bleu Coriacide 2R	0,1	

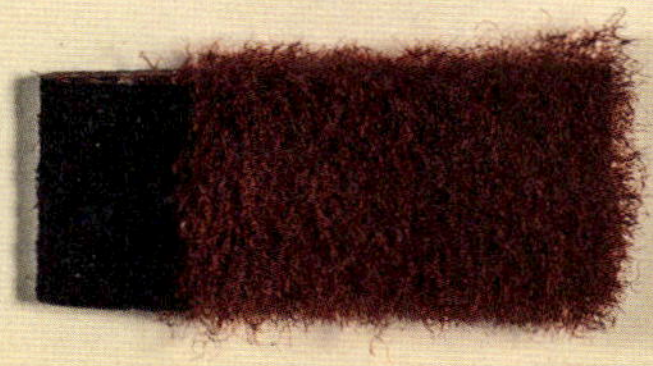

24

Jaune Sulfacide lumière JL extra	0,05	g/l
Rouge Acétacide R2B	0,35	
Bleu Diazol lumière R extra	0,3	
Jaune Coriacide J	0,25	

OPPOSITE, TOP

Food Coloring

Coloring food and drink is an age-old practice.[5] Naturally, the opportunities synthetic color offered were quickly seized on by the food processing industries that took off in the last quarter of the nineteenth century. Very soon, the issue of toxicity was raised, and the first lists of prohibited dyes were established by the early twentieth century. But the movement had been launched, and dyes were applied to a wide range of food items after World War II. The 117 samples on the color chart cover the full visible spectrum. Yellows, reds, and browns are particularly well-represented, for these shades reinforced the natural color of many foods. The blues and the artificial shades of greens that appear on this page could be used for candy or drinks.

Special Dyes for Foodstuffs, nº 13, Société Anonyme de Matières Colorantes et Produits Chimiques Francolor, Paris, 1948, booklet, 21.5 × 14 cm, 18 plates, Albi Couleurs, Association Mémoire des Industries de la Couleur, Albi, plates 12 and 13

Setting Trends in Fashion

——— In the late 1930s, the Société Anonyme des Matières Colorantes et Produits Chimiques de Saint-Denis already offered clothing manufacturers seasonal color ranges.[6] Francolor continued this trend, and, during the 1960s, distributed its "colors of Paris fashion" twice a year; the range of shades offered would be a reference for the Comité de Coordination des Industries de la Mode.

BELOW AND OPPOSITE, BOTTOM

Paris Fashion, Spring-Summer 1962

The formulas for dyes producing the selected colors are given in French, German, and English in a book that is attached to the color chart. But on the chart itself, the shades are designated by color names (*Pink Flamingo*, *Hummingbird*, and such) that are adapted to the world of fashion design. However, these book and charts would be supplanted by trend books from trend forecasters. The field of trend forecasting appeared in France in the late 1960s particularly through the influence of Maïmé Arnodin, the founder of the MAFIA agency. Trend forecasting became the standard for defining marketing strategies. First the fashion industry turned to trend forecasters for guidance, followed by interior design and, finally, all consumer sectors.

Colors of Paris Fashion, spring-summer 1962, Compagnie Française des Matières Colorantes Francolor, Paris, 1962, brochure, 25 × 17.5 cm, 14 pages, 2 plates, Albi Couleurs, Association Mémoire des Industries de la Couleur, Albi

——— Chemical manufacturers who marketed the raw materials for color still maintained product samples on their color charts, as these were at the heart of their profession, but their brochures would never again have the poetry of the color charts of the interwar period. However, ongoing advances in dyeing made by the chemical industry would allow contemporary manufacturers, especially those of cosmetics, to develop varied and attractive color charts.

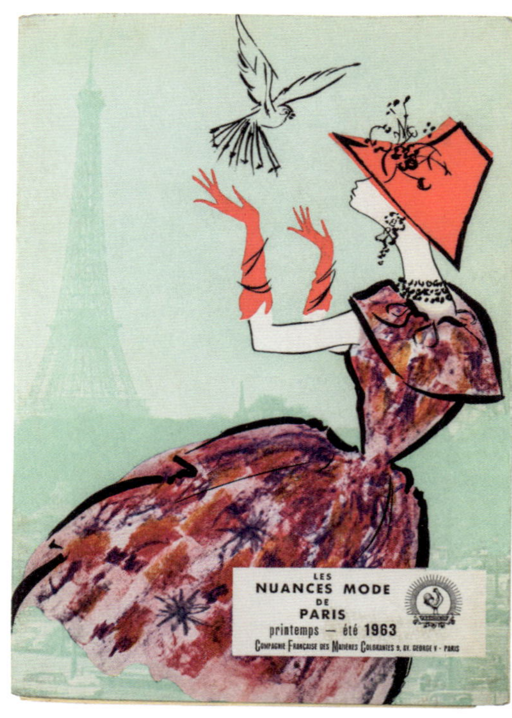

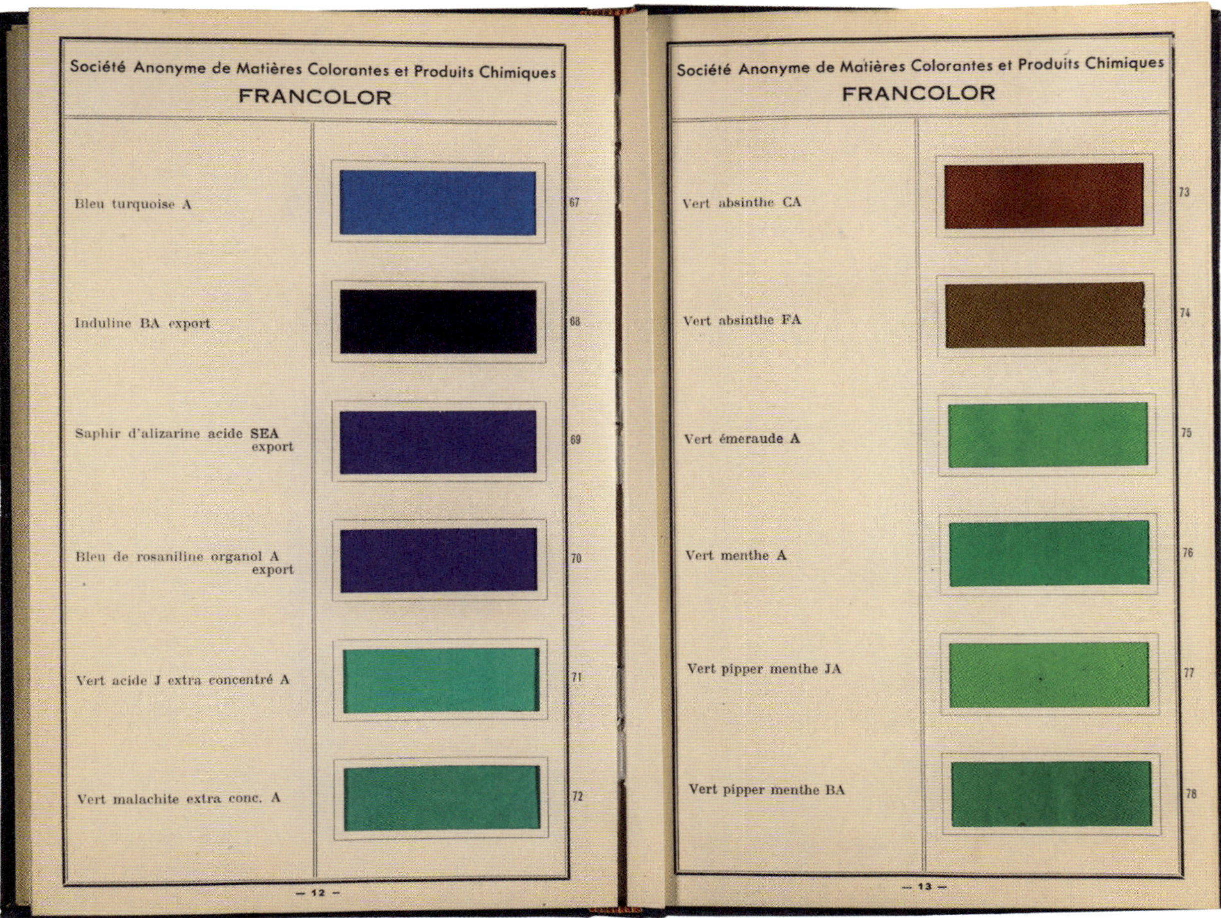
Société Anonyme de Matières Colorantes et Produits Chimiques
FRANCOLOR
Bleu turquoise A 67
Induline BA export 68
Saphir d'alizarine acide SEA export 69
Bleu de rosaniline organol A export 70
Vert acide J extra concentré A 71
Vert malachite extra conc. A 72
— 12 —
Société Anonyme de Matières Colorantes et Produits Chimiques
FRANCOLOR
Vert absinthe CA 73
Vert absinthe FA 74
Vert émeraude A 75
Vert menthe A 76
Vert pipper menthe JA 77
Vert pipper menthe BA 78
— 13 —

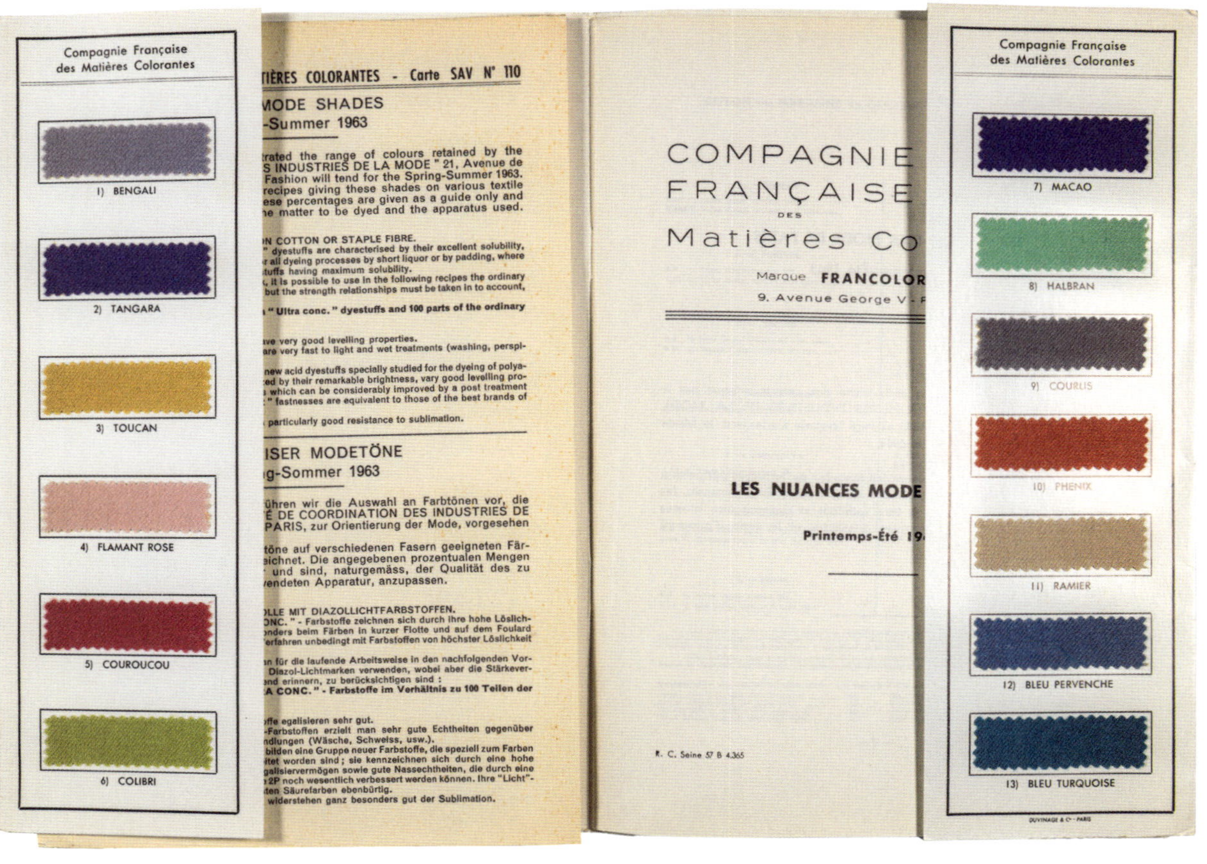
Compagnie Française des Matières Colorantes
1) BENGALI
2) TANGARA
3) TOUCAN
4) FLAMANT ROSE
5) COUROUCOU
6) COLIBRI
TIÈRES COLORANTES - Carte SAV N° 110
MODE SHADES
-Summer 1963
ISER MODETÖNE
g-Sommer 1963
COMPAGNIE
FRANÇAISE
DES
Matières Co
Marque FRANCOLOR
9, Avenue George V
LES NUANCES MODE
Printemps-Été 19
R. C. Seine 57 B 4.365
Compagnie Française des Matières Colorantes
7) MACAO
8) HALBRAN
9) COURLIS
10) PHENIX
11) RAMIER
12) BLEU PERVENCHE
13) BLEU TURQUOISE

COLOR CHARTS FOR CLOTHING THAT BECAME MORE COLORFUL

——— Items for haberdashery or sewing were less necessary after World War II as prêt-à-porter or ready-to-wear appeared in the mid-1950s and became widespread. This was a great relief to women, especially as more of them combined raising a family with working outside the home. In the 1970s, color charts for materials for making clothes were strictly for those who pursued this as a hobby.

Playing with the Arrangement of the Color Chart

NEXT PAGE SPREAD

A.G.P. 1952 Summer Catalog

AGP, a Paris fabric wholesaler, produced a catalog for summer 1952 with hundreds of fabrics available in several colors. It seems that the company's goal was that no two pages would look the same. There was also a significant effort made to identify each sample with the name of a color—a practice that had almost become a thing of the past. Five hundred terms were selected from various areas: the plant world (*Almond*, *Walnut*, *Geranium*, *Dead Rose*), literature (*Dante*), exoticism (*Malacca*, *Hispano*), and even astronomy (*Saturn*). On a few pages devoted to prints, there are gouache drawings of clothing styles. They are accompanied by a reproduction of the pattern on a larger sheet of paper. Since the beginning of the century, color charts had played many roles in educating all of society about color. They were also fertile ground for the kind of graphic design experiments that gave rise to this album.

Summer 1952, A.G.P., Paris, 1952, album, 40 × 28 cm, 160 pages, Bibliothèque Forney, Paris, call number RES ICO 8228

Changeless Ribbons

——— Ribbon color charts, discussed early in this book, have been one of the common threads here, for they continued without significant changes into the 1970s.

OPPOSITE, TOP

Silk Federation Shades, Spring-Summer 1951

However, this color chart for spring-summer 1951 is atypical. Of a large size but with only four panels, it seems to have been developed specifically to display the Silk Federation's products at an international textile exhibition that took place in Lille that year. Titled *Study Card*, it contains eighty-eight samples. On the last panel, the entire visible spectrum is recreated in a perfect rainbow.

The Silk Federation stopped distributing color charts after fall-winter 1976–77. The last sample was numbered 18100. For almost one hundred years of ribbon production, color charts had been produced for ribbons. Preserved in various collections and institutions, these color charts serve to reconstruct almost all the color ranges offered twice a year since 1884. However, their history, and the history of their vocabulary, remains to be written.

Colors Adopted and Recommended by Producers of Silk and Ribbons for the Spring-Summer Seasons 1951, Fédération de la Soie, Industries Lyonnaises de la Soie, Fabrique de Rubans de Saint-Étienne, Saint-Étienne, France, 1951, pamphlet, 31 × 21 cm, 4 panels, private collection, Paris

Haberdashery Items Move to Numbers

OPPOSITE, BOTTOM

Zwicky Thread

In the 1920s, the DMC's attempt to publish a color chart of reproduced colors did not convince its clientele, and when the Swiss mill Zwicky, which sold various types of silk thread, presented its products' colors in the 1950s, it used product samples. The colors are grouped fairly strictly in tones ranging from light to dark to encourage comparison. The presentation is elegant, but the poetic names have been replaced by numbers in order to facilitate exports. This would now be the case for most color charts for sewing materials.

Trim for Buttonholes, n° 83, Zwicky, Wallisellen, Switzerland, 1950s, pamphlet, 18 × 11 cm, 4 panels, Bibliothèque Forney, Paris, call number RES 5844

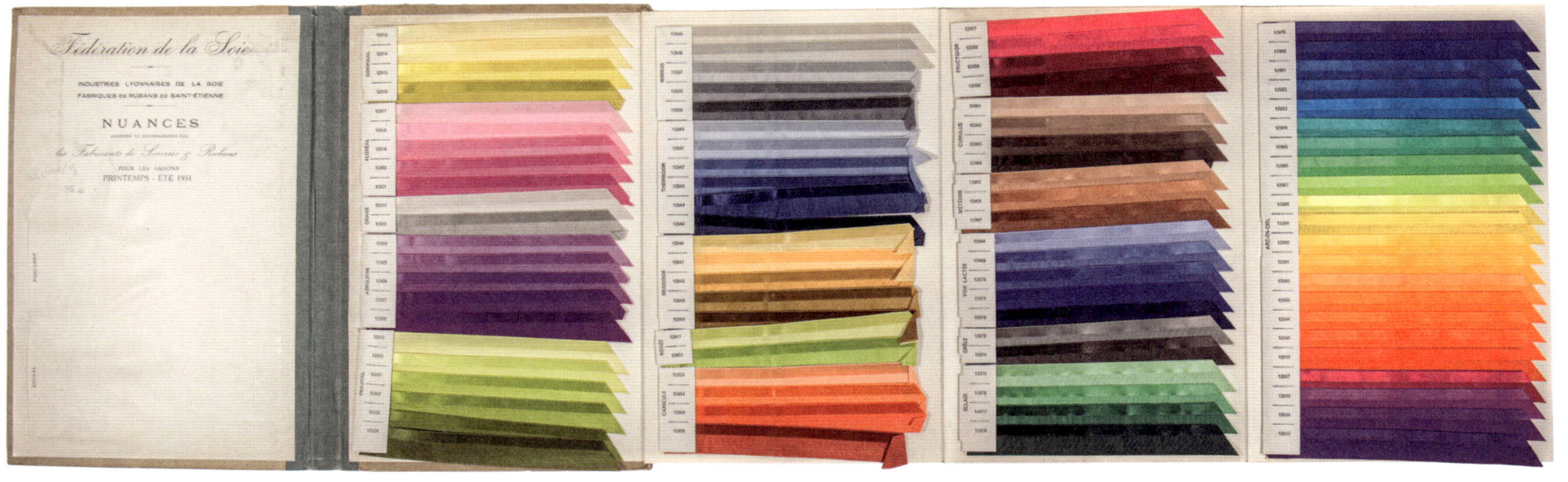

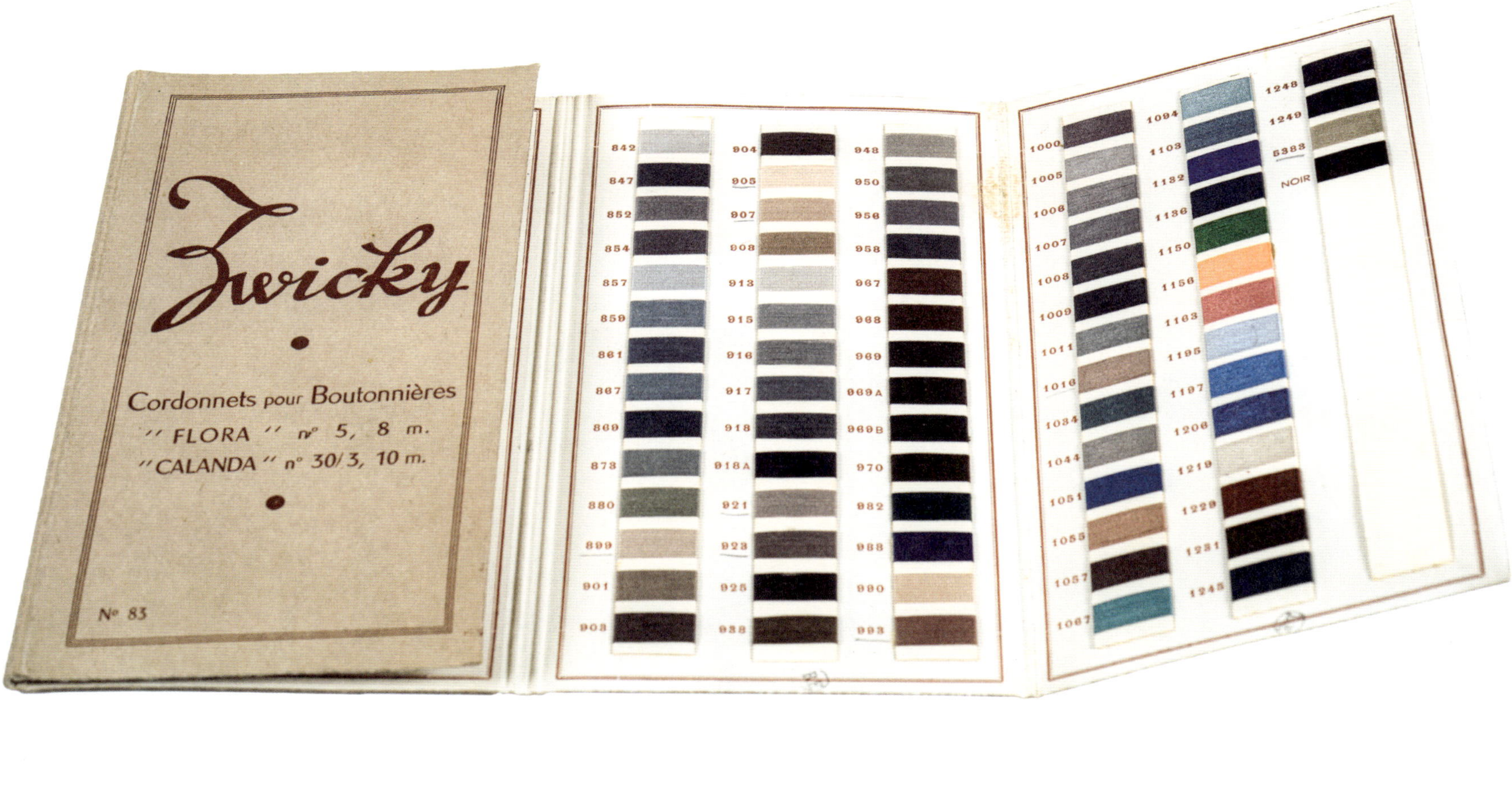

Zwicky
Cordonnets pour Boutonnières
" FLORA " nº 5, 8 m.
" CALANDA " nº 30/3, 10 m.
Nº 83

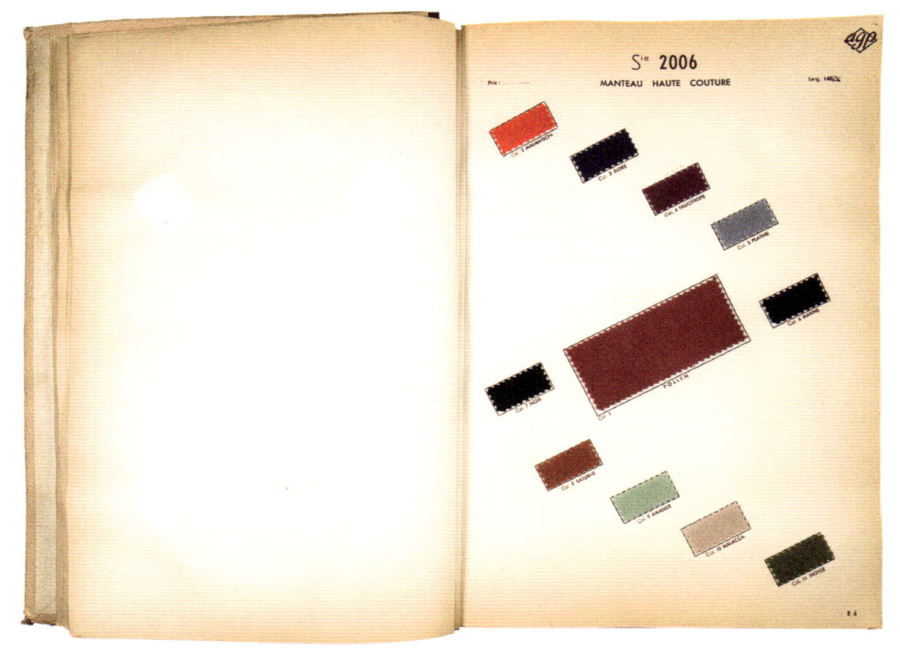

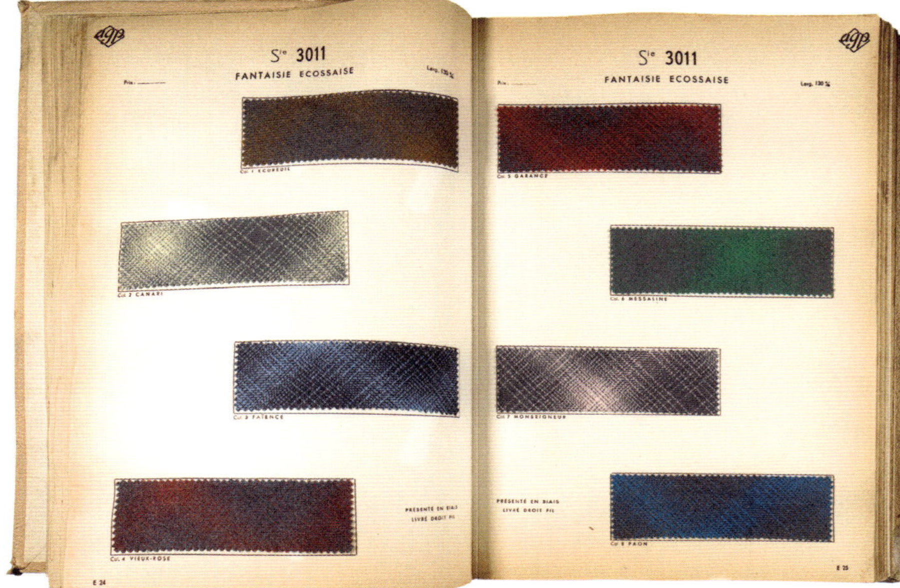

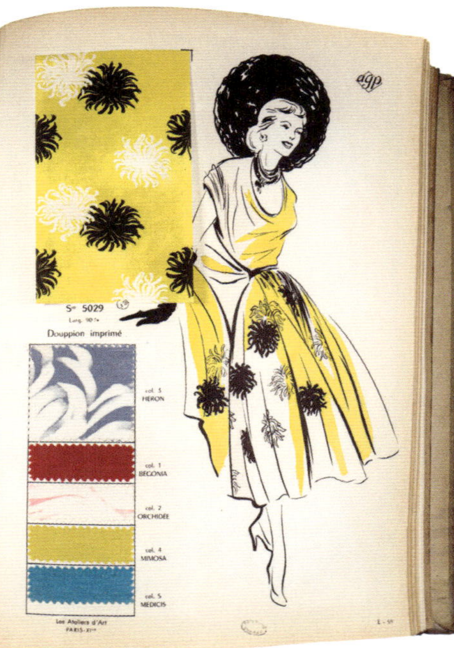
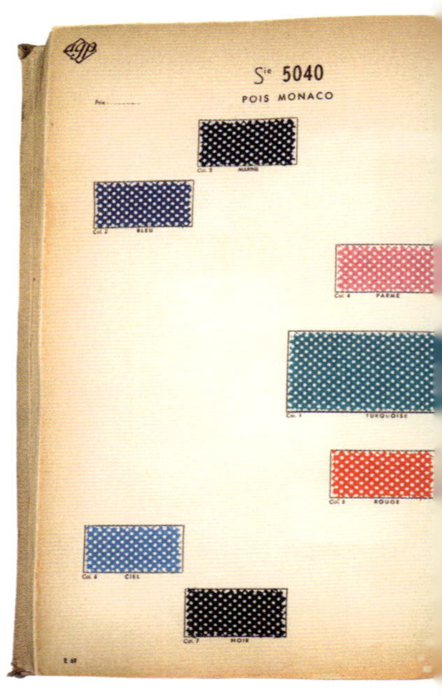

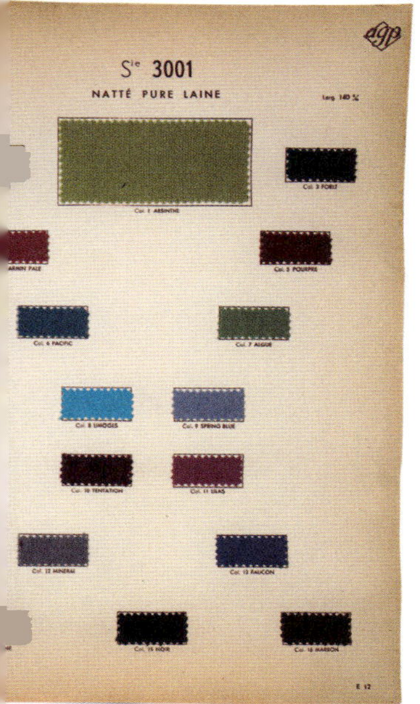
Ste 3001
NATTÉ PURE LAINE

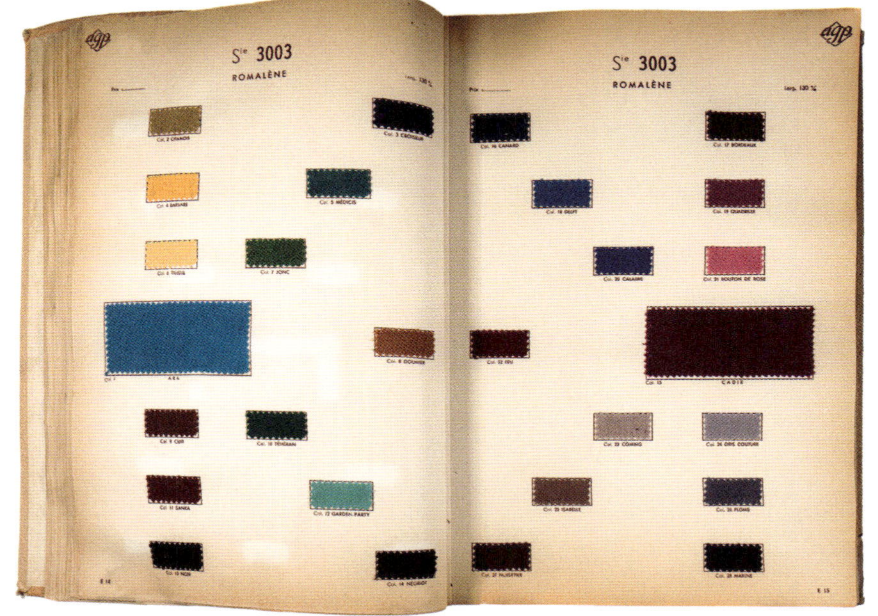
Ste 3003
ROMALÈNE
Ste 3003
ROMALÈNE

Ste 4001
GABARDINE IMPERMÉABILISÉE

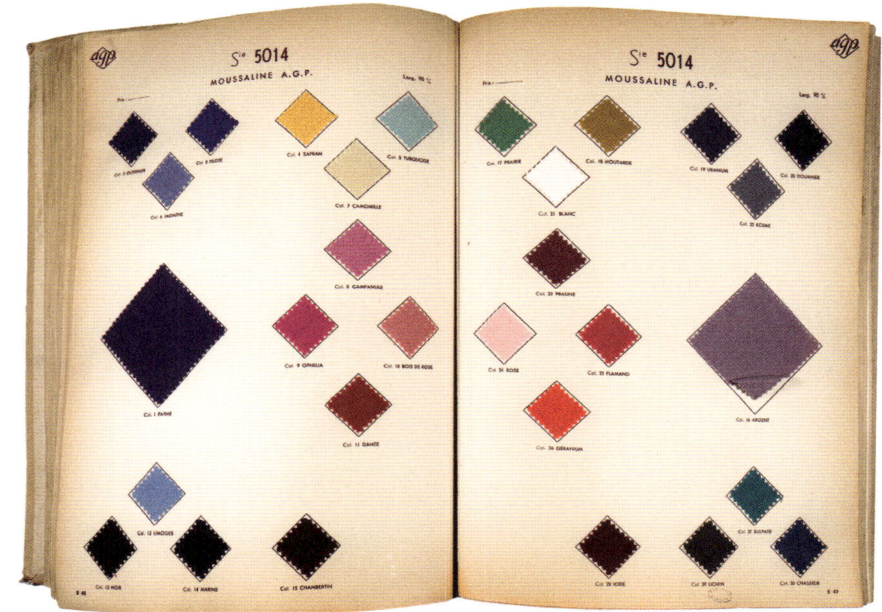
Ste 5014
MOUSSALINE A.G.P.
Ste 5014
MOUSSALINE A.G.P.

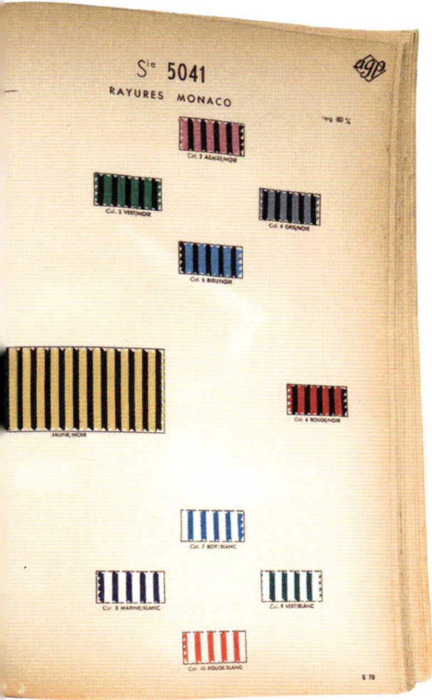
Ste 5041
RAYURES MONACO

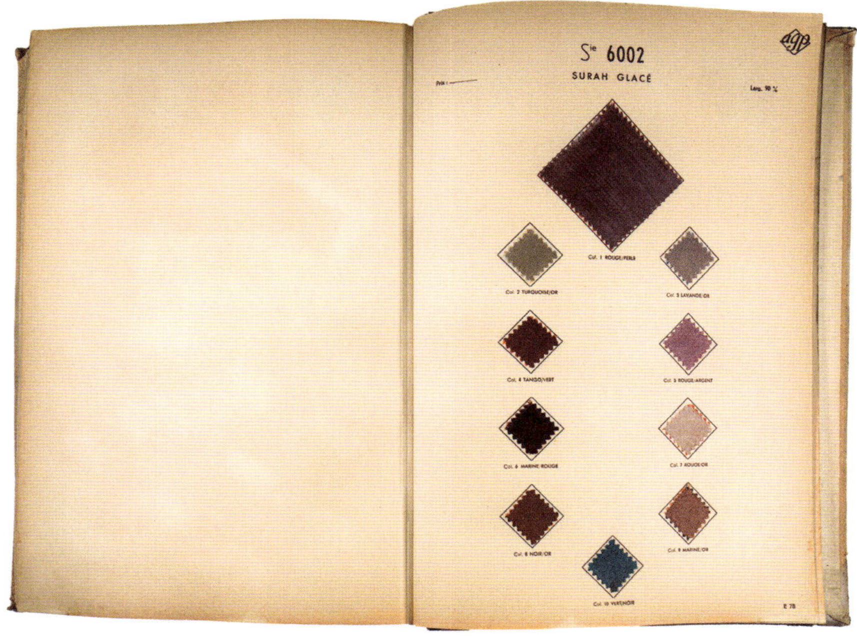
Ste 6002
SURAH GLACÉ

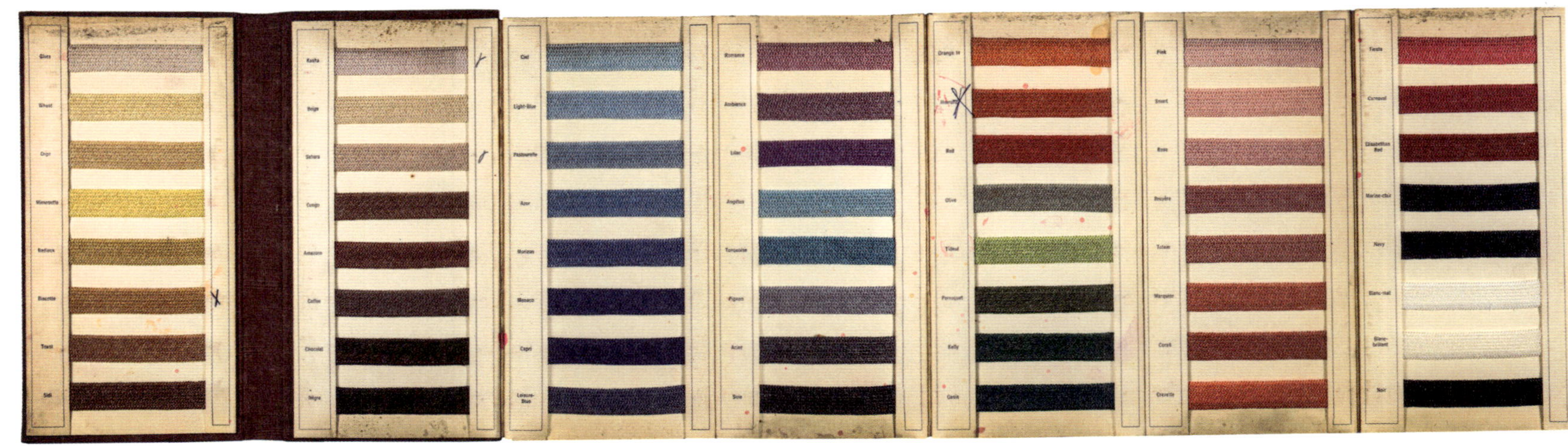

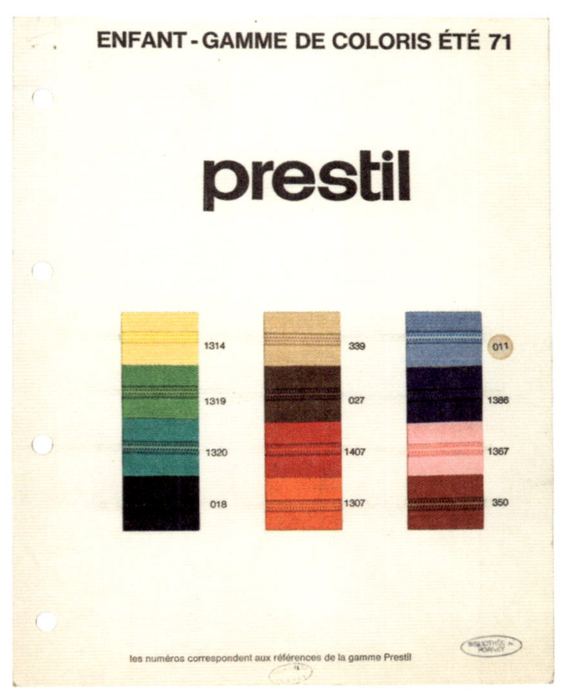

ENFANT - GAMME DE COLORIS ÉTÉ 71
prestil
1314
1319
1320
018
339
027
1407
1307
011
1386
1367
350
les numéros correspondent aux références de la gamme Prestil

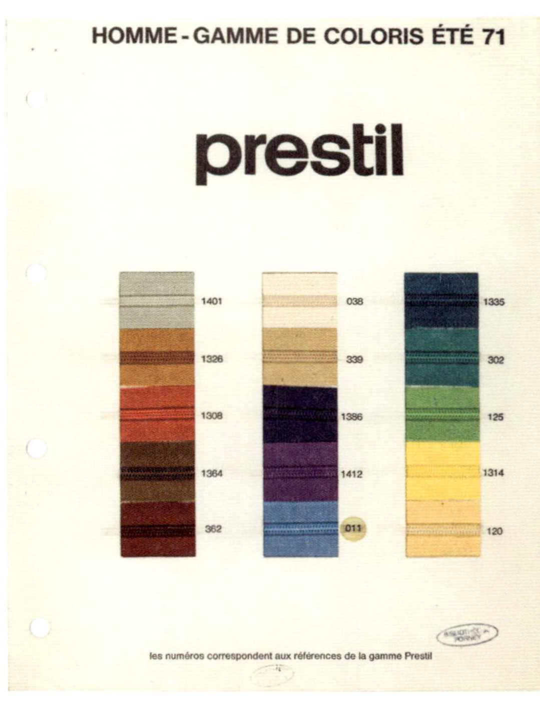

HOMME - GAMME DE COLORIS ÉTÉ 71
prestil
1401
1326
1308
1364
362
038
339
1386
1412
011
1335
302
125
1314
120
les numéros correspondent aux références de la gamme Prestil

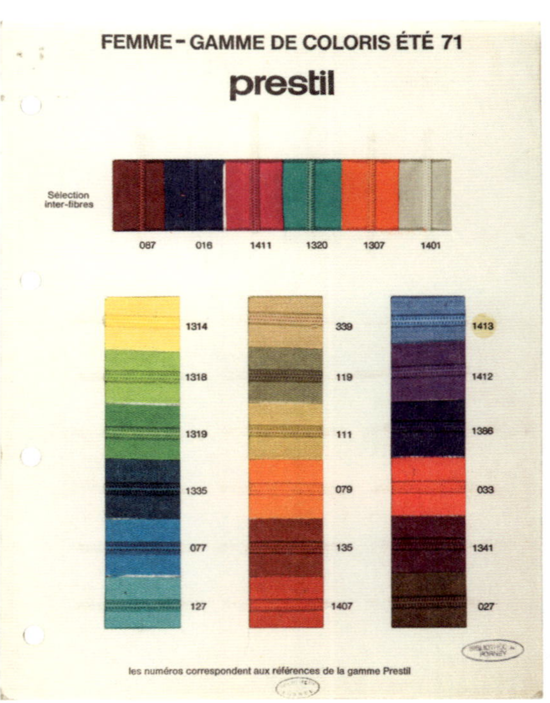

FEMME - GAMME DE COLORIS ÉTÉ 71
prestil
Sélection inter-fibres
067
016
1411
1320
1307
1401
1314
1318
1319
1335
077
127
339
119
111
079
135
1407
1413
1412
1386
033
1341
027
les numéros correspondent aux références de la gamme Prestil

OPPOSITE, TOP

Georges Meyer & Co Braids

These braids for hat making are also from a Swiss mill, but this time, evocative names have been maintained, with the clever addition of some terms in English (*Elisabethan Red, Navy, Smart, Lilac*) among the French ones (*Perroquet* [Parrot] *Homard* [Lobster] *Olive, Angélus* [Angelus]).

1957 Color Card, Georges Meyer & Co Ltd, Wohlen, Switzerland, 1957, pamphlet, 23 × 11 cm, 7 panels, Patrimoine Lemarié—Fonds Legeron, Paris

OPPOSITE, BOTTOM

Prestil Zippers

The French company Prestil registered the trademark "Éclair" (for *fermeture éclair* or zipper) in 1924 even though this fastener was still unreliable and thus rarely used.[7] The firm then developed a nylon model, patenting it in 1958. A few years later, zippers were already available in twenty-seven shades, with color ranges offered for men, women, and children. The color chart mentions that the Prestil company developed these shades based on information from several international fashion trend analysts and fashion designers. Interestingly, while the men's range is certainly less extensive than that for women, it is almost as bright and varied. It omits only pink, orange, and turquoise. As for the children's range, it is halfway in between these two, and except for soft pink, remains unisex.

Times were changing and fashion had become more liberated since the early 1960s with designers such as Courrèges, Mary Quant, Ungaro, Yves Saint Laurent and his Mondrian dress, and Kenzo Takada. Their influence permitted all kinds of new boldness in clothing styles. Above all, color combinations that were once thought of as ugly or inappropriate were now permissible thanks to these designers. This was a significant transformation. The color chart, which for almost half a century had presented a wide number of shades, whether for paint, buttons, or embroidery thread, clearly participated subtly but actively in this delicate introduction to new color harmonies.

Color Chart for Zippers, Colors for Summer 1971, Prestil, Paris, 1971, 4 plates, 27 × 21 cm, Bibliothèque Forney, Paris, call number RES ICO 8254

Dye Color Charts Follow Fashion

The Fascists had disappeared. You couldn't see any black shirts in the streets. They'd all be dyed grey, the colour nuncepenzammocchiù — we're not going to think about that anymore. Around here, we tend to forget the bad as soon as a bit of good comes our way.

Erri De Luca, *The Day Before Happiness*, 2010

——— The practice of home dyeing continued, encouraged by the textile shortages that followed the war, and persisted for long time afterward, adapting to new customs. The practice would be updated for the Flower Power era and the Do It Yourself movement that were imported from the United States.

NEXT PAGE

Solicolor Dyes

Solitaire dyes, which seem to have existed already before World War II, adopted in the 1950s the drawn or embossed image of the dancer whose dress features the reproduced color of the available dyes. They are designated by names, including *Tête de nègre* (Negro's head), a name that had frequently appeared on color charts since the late nineteenth century, along with *Nègre*. They would not really become controversial until the 2000s.

Deluxe Household Dye with Solicolor Ultra-Pigments, Solitaire, Levallois-Perret, France, 1950s, card, 26 × 35 cm, Bibliothèque Forney, Paris, call number RES ICO 8104

——— In the textile world, the product sample persisted, for the material lent itself easily to cutting swatches, and fabric was an especially tactile item. However, the very imaginative and pretty names that appeared on the haberdashery color charts were beginning to disappear. Perhaps they were no longer necessary. A color lexicon with its references to shades had entered consumers' vocabulary in the period between the world wars, essentially due to decorative paint color charts. Remaining very stable since that time (*Train Car Green*, *Ultramarine Blue*, and such), many of them had been passed down to the next generation and could now be mentioned in various contexts.

SOLICOLOR

TEINTURE MÉNAGÈRE DE LUXE AUX ULTRA-COLORANTS

26 COLORIS PRÉPARÉS PAR SOLITAIRE

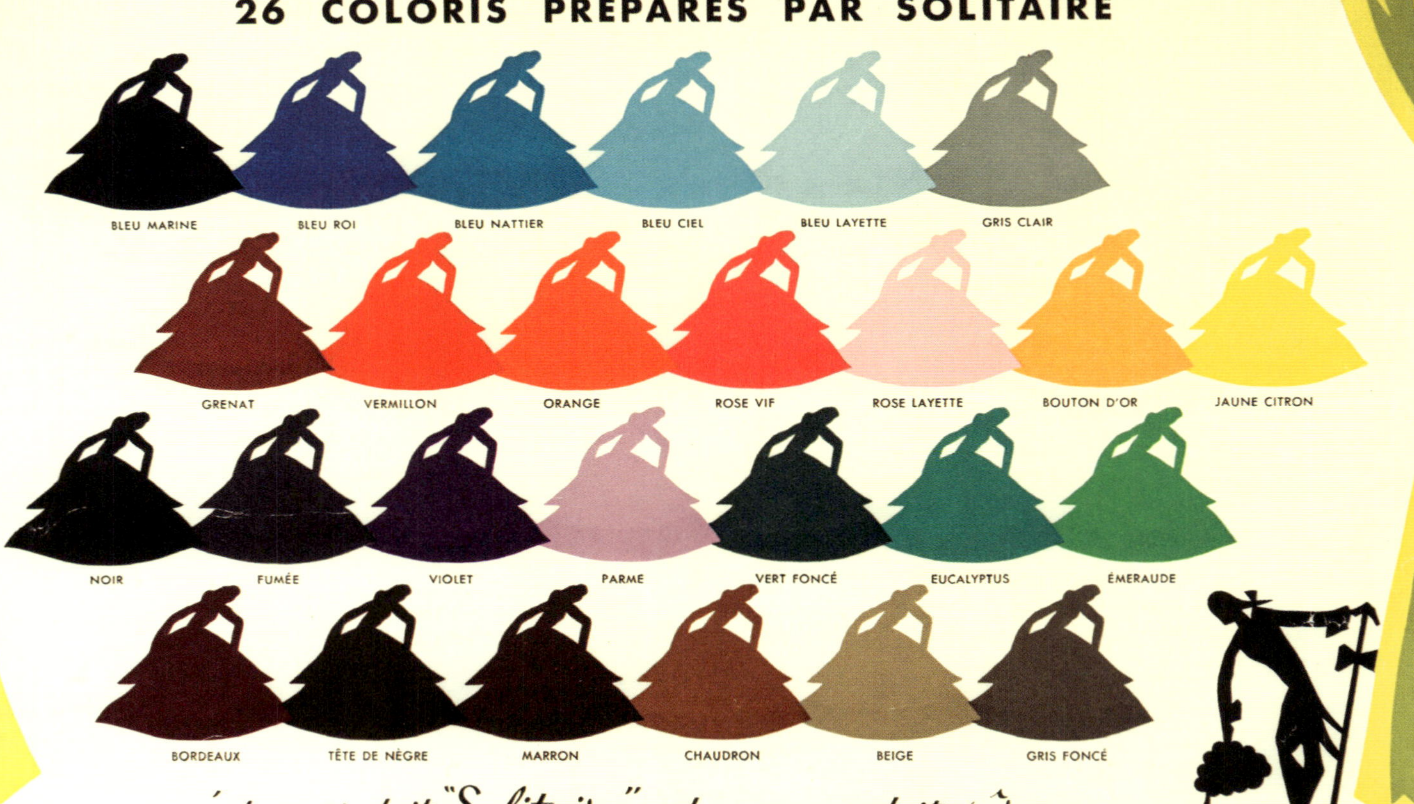

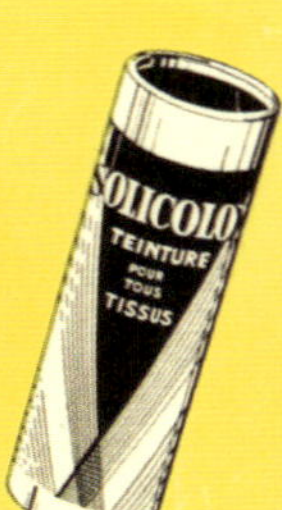

c'est un produit "Solitaire"..... donc un produit sûr

LES CINQ AVANTAGES EXCLUSIFS DE SOLICOLOR

1. SOLICOLOR se conserve indéfiniment dans son étui-cartouche. — 2. SOLICOLOR donne des teintes franches qui résistent au soleil et au lavage. — 3. SOLICOLOR teint parfaitement et uniformément les tissus de laine, de coton, de soie ou de rayonne. — 4. SOLICOLOR ne " brûle " pas les tissus fragiles et ne provoque ni rétrécissement ni relâchement du tissage. — 5. SOLICOLOR est très économique à l'emploi; une seule cartouche suffit pour teindre 300 grs de tissus, même s'il s'agit d'un tissu clair. Il n'est pas nécessaire de découdre une robe avant de la teindre.

CONSEILS CONCERNANT LE CHOIX DES COLORIS

TISSUS BLANCS. Ils peuvent être teints dans tous les coloris, la couleur obtenue est celle indiquée sur la présente carte de coloris. **TISSUS IMPRIMÉS OU CHINÉS.** Ces tissus, même reteints en nuances foncées, ne donnent pas des nuances unies. **TEINTURE EN NOIR.** Tous les tissus blancs ou de couleur peuvent être teints en noir. **TISSUS DE COULEUR.** Ils peuvent être teints : 1° Dans une couleur plus foncée, en restant dans leur propre gamme de coloris; par exemple on peut passer du rose au rouge, du rouge au grenat, du grenat au bordeaux, etc. 2° Dans une couleur appartenant à une autre gamme de coloris, pourvu que la couleur initiale du tissu soit très claire et que celle cherchée soit beaucoup plus foncée; par exemple, on peut passer du beige clair au vert foncé, du vert clair au tête de nègre. Certaines combinaisons sont cependant impossibles. On ne peut pas teindre : en mauve ou violet un tissu jaune; en bleu un tissu jaune ou orange; en vert un tissu orange ou rouge. Les combinaisons inverses sont également impossibles; par exemple, on ne peut teindre : en jaune un tissu mauve ou violet; en orange ou rouge un tissu vert, etc.

Mercadé

DRAEGER, IMP.

IN INTERIOR DESIGN, COLOR CHARTS FOR INCREASINGLY VARIED APPLICATIONS

The color charts of paints for the home did not move abruptly after the war from a sample out of the can to offset printing but went through an intermediate phase, the application of color, where a product formulated specifically for the color chart provided the characteristics of the product sold without being exactly the same.

Two new developments occurred: instead of presenting an exhaustive selection, the goal was to organize the samples into a range that would be attractive to the eye, and the targeted purchasers were primarily nonprofessionals.

The Introduction of the Fan Color Chart

The 1930s had seen the appearance of color charts with the samples attached to a card by a staple at one end.[8] Its replacement by a rivet improved the tool. While still maintaining protection from UV light, it offered a much easier and flexible way of comparing all the samples or merely a few. It became easy to try out all the possible combinations. However, the fan offered less room than other devices for featuring instructions or other product information.

NEXT PAGE SPREAD, TOP LEFT

Lesoufaché Shades

This color chart was doubly innovative. It used a fan format and offered a selection of colors from the work of Joseph Lesoufaché (1804–1887), who built elegant homes in Paris. The connection between the architect and this range of paints, which is difficult to trace today, may relate to the collection of works on interior design and architecture that he authored. In any case, about thirty years after the *Tint Book of Historical Colours* by Thomas Parsons, but well before contemporary brands revived the shades of the past, Marcolac paid homage to the color work of an architect.[9]

Lesoufaché Colors, Société des Peintures et Vernis Marcolac, Paris, 1950s, fan, approximately 11 × 6 cm, approximately 20 samples, Albi Couleurs, Association Mémoire des Industries de la Couleur, Albi

NEXT PAGE SPREAD, RIGHT

Valentine Hammered Paints

Hammered paints, used to simulate metal, are paint coatings with a metallic finish containing lamellar aluminum pigments. Very resistant, they were extensively used in furnishings for schools in the 1960s and 1970s. Early on, the Valentine company, which was founded in the United States in the late eighteenth century, specialized in varnishes and paints for vehicles, and then expanded into decorative paints after setting up shop in France in the 1920s. There is no technical reason for such a limited color range. It does include a bright red (*Rouge Estérel*), which could have been combined with other strong colors, like the bright ranges that were beginning to be used in the home. It must have been too soon; Hammered Valdur's only objective was to imitate metal.

Hammered Valdur, Valentine, Gennevilliers, France, 1950s, fan, 9 × 4 cm, 10 samples, Albi Couleurs, Association Mémoire des Industries de la Couleur, Albi

NEXT PAGE SPREAD, BOTTOM LEFT

Astroni Lacquers(?)

The company Pieter Schoen & Zoon N.V. dates to the early eighteenth century. It was then one of many Dutch mills that crushed pigments to develop paints for artists. With advances in mechanization and the rise of chemistry, the company began to sell decorative paints in the early twentieth century, and then, after World War II, distributed its products all over the world and advertised them on packets of powdered sugar! The bright range of these lacquers showed that strong colors may already have been used in homes in northern Europe in the 1960s, especially in the Netherlands, thanks to the prestige of Dutch lacquers.[10] But the company also marketed its products in France, as shown by the translation of the instructions on the back of each sample.

Lacquer color chart (?) Astroni, Pieter Schoen & Zoon N.V. Verfchemie, Zaandam, Holland, 1970s, fan, 7 × 2 cm, 40 samples, Bibliothèque Forney, Paris, call number RES ICO 7208 Plano

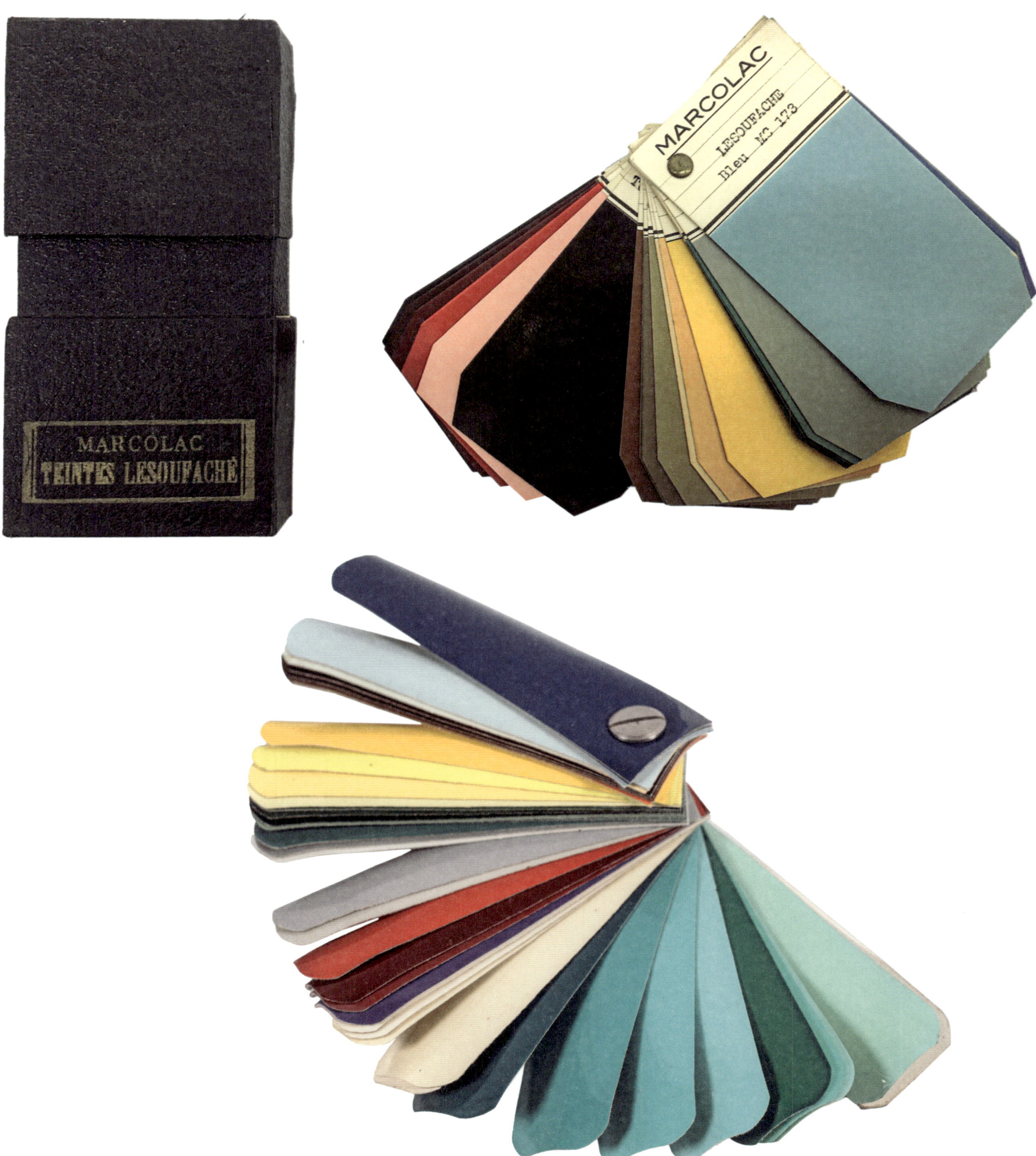
MARCOLAC
TEINTES LESOUFACHÉ
MARCOLAC
LESOUFACHE
Bleu MC 173

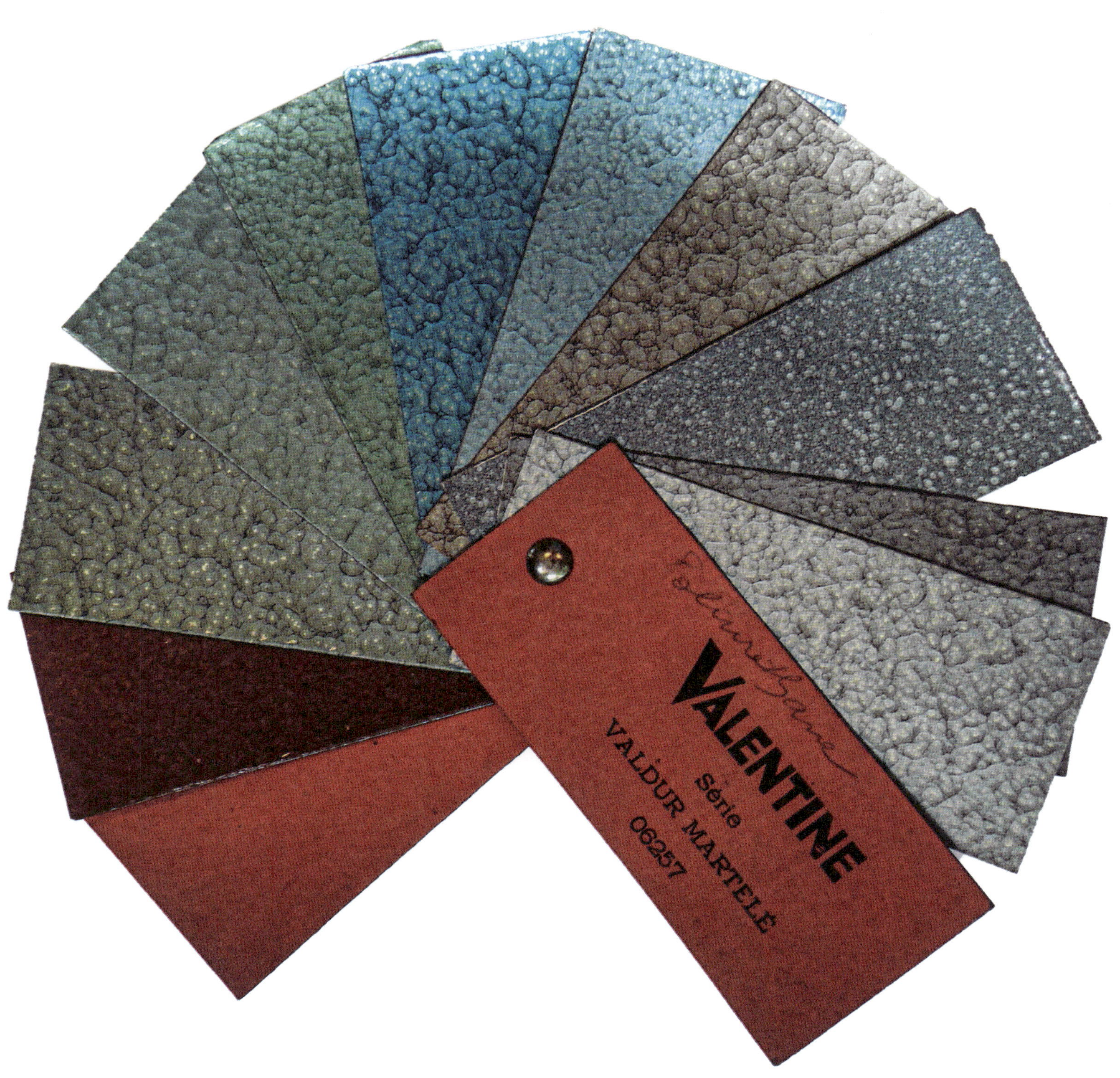
VALENTINE
Série
VALDUR MARTELÉ
06257

"The Creative Activity of the Practitioners of the Ordinary"

——— These words are taken from a book that the philosopher Michel de Certeau wrote in 1980 on the practice of everyday life, the "art of doing" that individuals perform, including consumerism.[11] Even before the emergence of big-box hardware stores in the 1970s, many products were designed for nonprofessionals, and one of the primary ways they learned how to use them was through the instructions on prewar color charts.

OPPOSITE, TOP

Renaulac Synthetic Enamel

Renaulac, a long-established French paint company (founded in 1827), distributed this color chart illustrated with female figures and including the following information: "Beautify your interior yourself—you will enjoy expressing your taste by choosing fresh, cheerful colors." Homemakers are invited to paint a bathtub, a cradle, a rowboat, or a car! They can rest assured that using this enamel while the weather is cold "presents no problems," and the need for maintenance "is nonexistent." The twenty-eight colors are printed in the shape of brushstrokes, a clever idea that would become common in order to restore a bit of sensory impression to samples that no longer had physical presence.

Renaulac Synthetic Enamel, Renaulac, France, 1960s, card, 11 × 12 cm, 4 folds, Bibliothèque Forney, Paris, call number RES ICO 8104

OPPOSITE, BOTTOM

Ripolin Developments

The Ripolin color chart, which had been remarkably consistent since the late nineteenth century, profoundly changed after World War II. It began using printed color samples in the shape of diamonds; it organized its color range, which had been noticeably reduced, into pastel and bright colors; and it changed its descriptive language (*Cinderella*, *Dream Blue*). This development was not due only to the specific formulation of the product, which in this case had a latex base. Ripolin was embracing the new styles of marketing.

Spred Liquid Rubber, Ripolin, France, card, approximately 13 × 10 cm, 1 fold, late 1950s, Bibliothèque Forney, Paris, inv. RES ICO 8104

A Color Chart for the Workplace

NEXT PAGE SPREAD

Sherwoods Paints Ltd. Workplace Colors

During the 1950s, thanks to the work of Munsell and Faber Birren in particular, there was interest in "functional colors" used in workplaces.[12] Following this movement, Sherwoods Paints Ltd., an English paint company, published a color chart with a detailed brochure intended to display and illustrate the best approach to using color in industrial work spaces "in the interest of British production." For the colors of machines, it was recommended to proceed "exactly contrary to camouflage" and to opt for a less depressing color than gray ("in order to reduce absenteeism"). A light-colored ceiling "will avoid the feeling of spending the day inside a tunnel," while distinguishing the palette of the cafeteria from that of the workshop or office "will encourage relaxation during mealtime and aid digestion." These recommendations were intended to establish "an atmosphere of cheerful efficiency" and were accompanied by attention paid to the colors of signs; in order to avoid accidents, sign colors were analyzed and signs created accordingly (they even took color-blindness into account). The color chart presents shades that have been carefully selected according to their use. While the names given to the shades for walls and door and window frames borrowed the lingo of interior decor, those for machines or signage clearly announced their specific purpose: *Machine Fawn*, *Machine Stone*, etc., and *Indicator Yellow*, *Indicator Orange*, etc. This carefully designed marketing tool eloquently traces the organization of factory work in the 1950s.

Colour Art Work, Sherwoods Paints Ltd., Barking, England, c. 1950, booklet, 28 × 22 cm, 11 pages, Bibliothèque Forney, Paris, call number CC 3734 [1960] Plano—Thema PLEIN

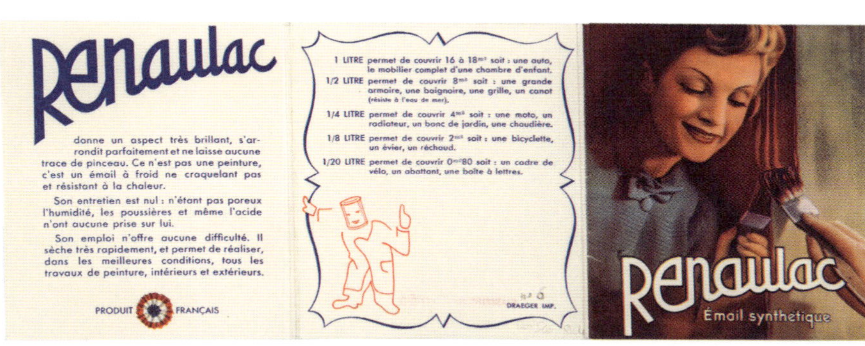
Renaulac
donne un aspect très brillant, s'arrondit parfaitement et ne laisse aucune trace de pinceau. Ce n'est pas une peinture, c'est un émail à froid ne craquelant pas et résistant à la chaleur.
Son entretien est nul : n'étant pas poreux l'humidité, les poussières et même l'acide n'ont aucune prise sur lui.
Son emploi n'offre aucune difficulté. Il sèche très rapidement, et permet de réaliser, dans les meilleures conditions, tous les travaux de peinture, intérieurs et extérieurs.
PRODUIT FRANÇAIS
1 LITRE permet de couvrir 16 à 18m² soit : une auto, le mobilier complet d'une chambre d'enfant.
1/2 LITRE permet de couvrir 8m² soit : une grande armoire, une baignoire, une grille, un canot (résiste à l'eau de mer).
1/4 LITRE permet de couvrir 4m² soit : une moto, un radiateur, un banc de jardin, une chaudière.
1/8 LITRE permet de couvrir 2m² soit : une bicyclette, un évier, un réchaud.
1/20 LITRE permet de couvrir 0m²80 soit : un cadre de vélo, un abattant, une boîte à lettres.
DRAEGER IMP.
Renaulac
Émail synthétique

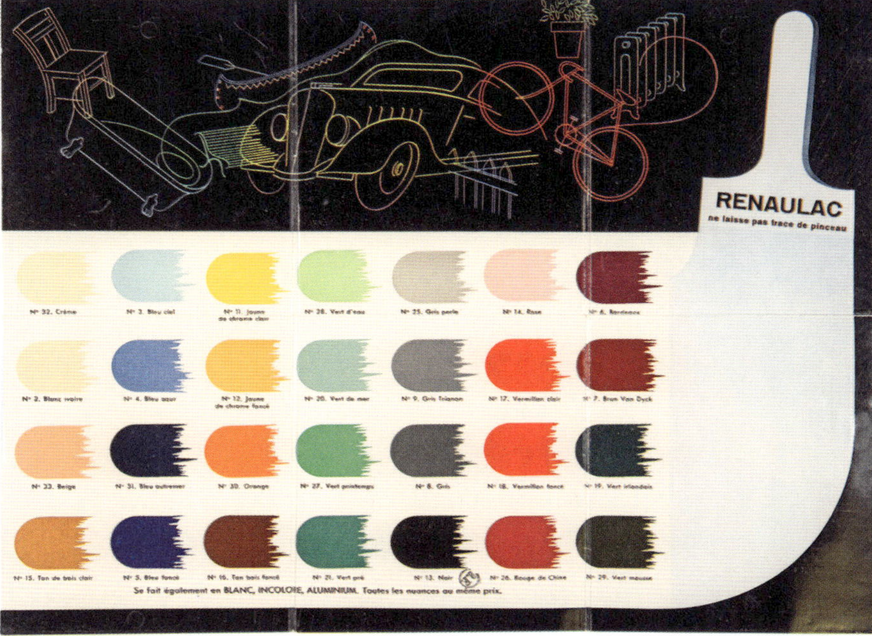
RENAULAC
ne laisse pas trace de pinceau
N° 32. Crème
N° 3. Bleu ciel
N° 11. Jaune de chrome clair
N° 28. Vert d'eau
N° 25. Gris perle
N° 14. Rose
N° 6. Bordeaux
N° 2. Blanc ivoire
N° 4. Bleu azur
N° 12. Jaune de chrome foncé
N° 20. Vert de mer
N° 9. Gris Trianon
N° 17. Vermillon clair
N° 7. Brun Van Dyck
N° 33. Beige
N° 31. Bleu outremer
N° 30. Orange
N° 27. Vert printemps
N° 8. Gris
N° 18. Vermillon foncé
N° 19. Vert irlandais
N° 15. Ton de bois clair
N° 5. Bleu foncé
N° 16. Ton bois foncé
N° 21. Vert pré
N° 13. Noir
N° 26. Rouge de Chine
N° 29. Vert mousse
Se fait également en BLANC, INCOLORE, ALUMINIUM. Toutes les nuances au même prix.

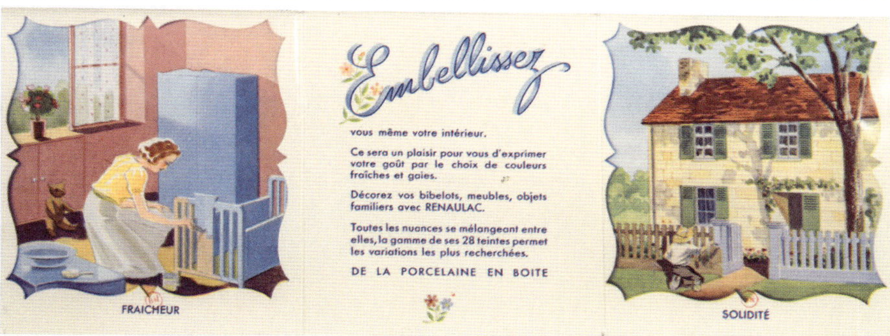
Embellissez
vous même votre intérieur.
Ce sera un plaisir pour vous d'exprimer votre goût par le choix de couleurs fraîches et gaies.
Décorez vos bibelots, meubles, objets familiers avec RENAULAC.
Toutes les nuances se mélangeant entre elles, la gamme de ses 28 teintes permet les variations les plus recherchées.
DE LA PORCELAINE EN BOITE
FRAICHEUR
SOLIDITÉ

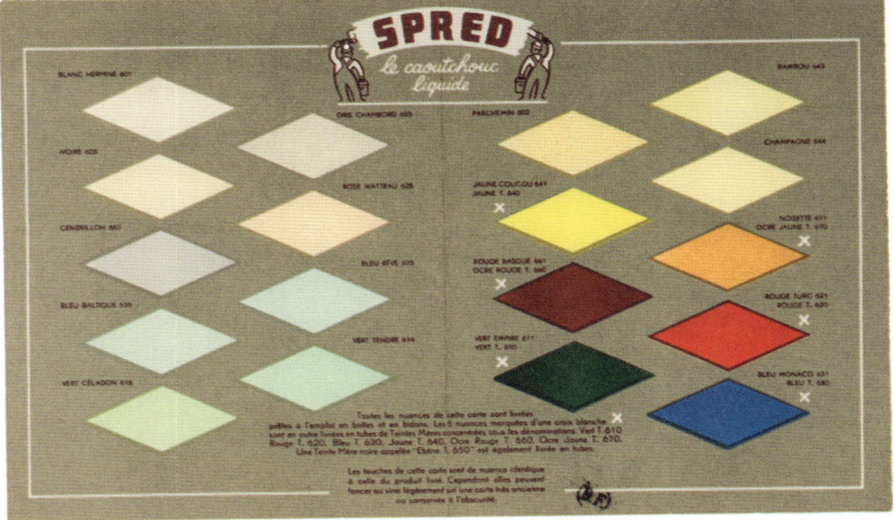
SPRED
le caoutchouc liquide

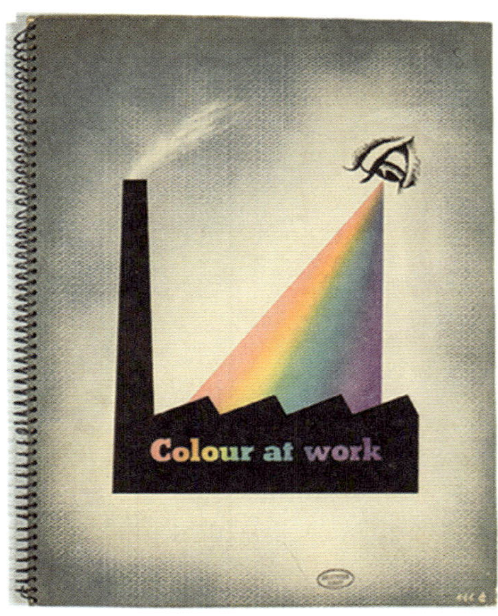
Colour at work

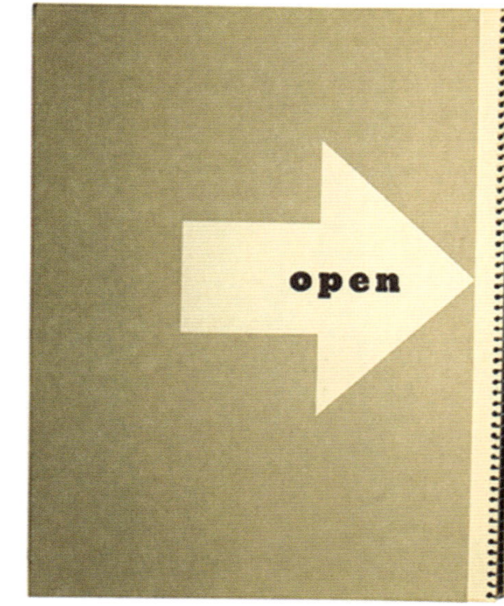
open

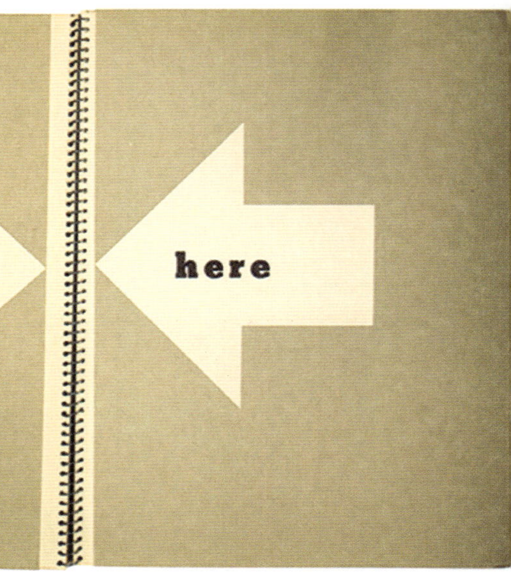
here

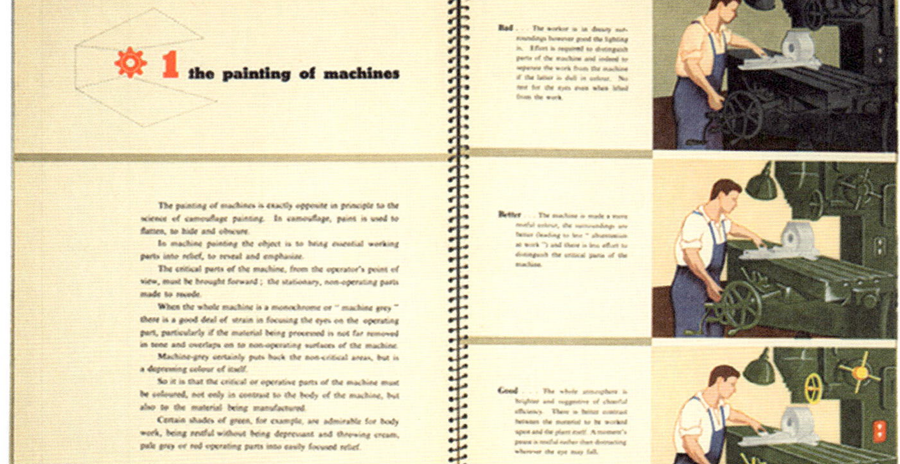
1 the painting of machines
Bad
Better
Good

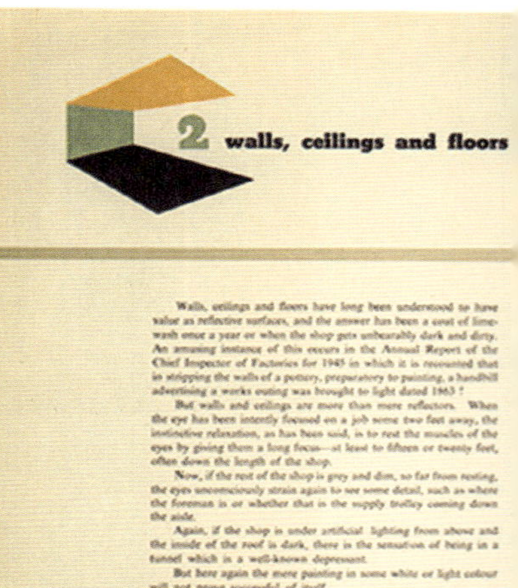
2 walls, ceilings and floors

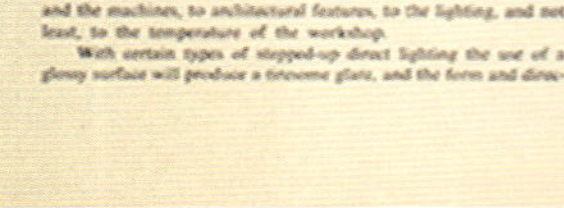

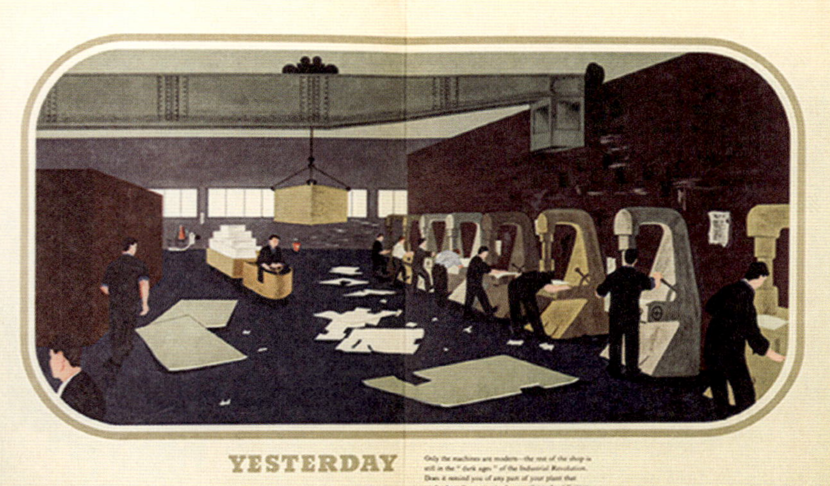

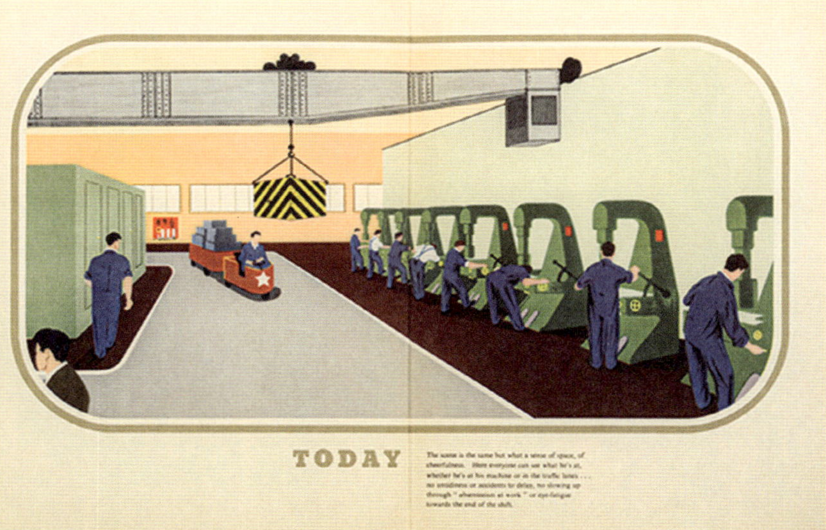

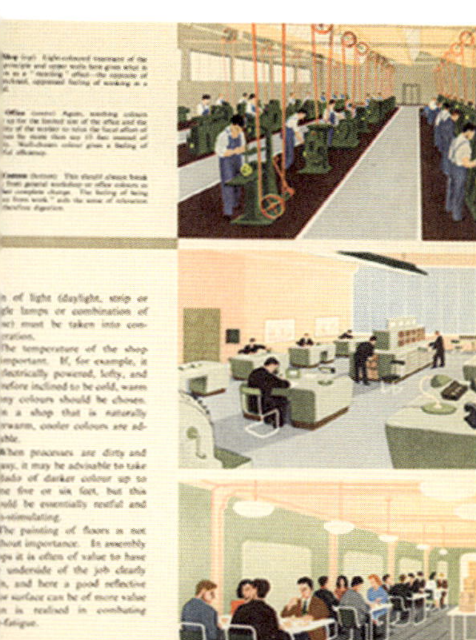

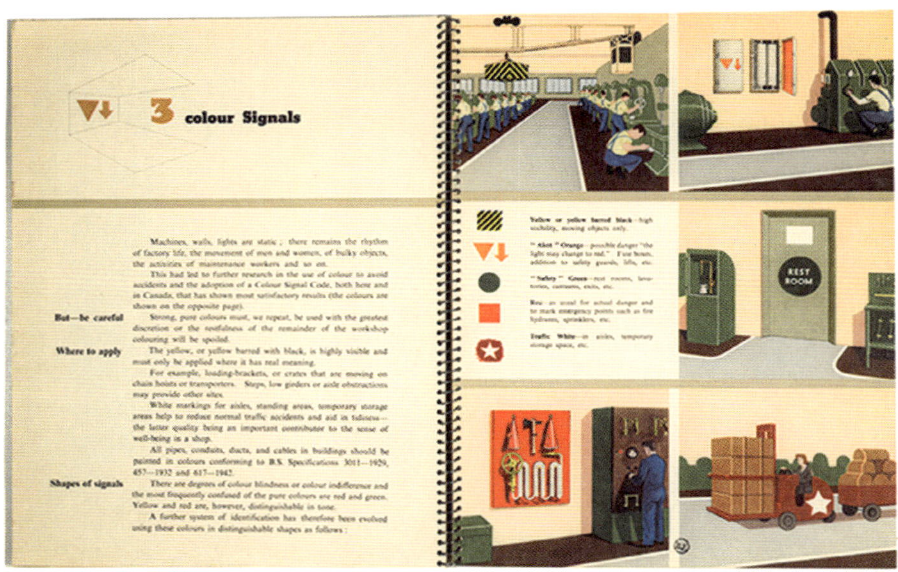

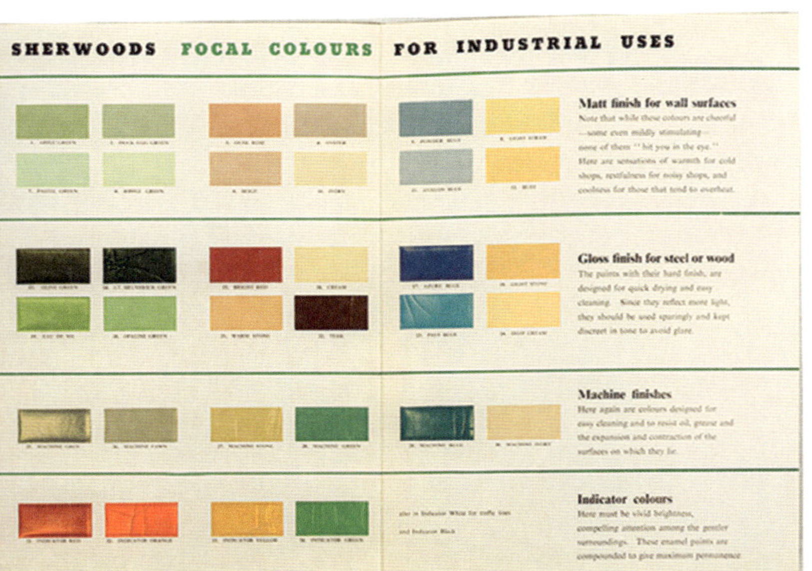

SHERWOODS
EST. 1777
PAINTS LTD

Pockets of Resistance

OPPOSITE, AND FOLLOWING PAGE SPREAD

Sarlino Linoleum

While product samples were increasingly rejected for decorative paints, they were still used when the material of the product to be sampled was significant. Since 1927, the Société Anonyme Rémoise du Linoléum (or Sarlino) had produced flooring made of oxidized linseed oil and cork powder applied to canvas. Linoleum, which was easy to dye and could also feature patterns, changed according to fashion trends and led to a series of collections. The 1966–67 collection was showcased in a heavy binder with a color chart of sixty-seven small samples organized according to type of pattern (marbled, solid, mottled, iridescent, and such). Larger samples, organized by tones, are glued to half-pages of heavy cardboard. This system allowed for evaluating the appearance and texture of the linoleum; it was also easy to remove a page from the binder to compare colors or try out combinations. Moreover, two ingenious printed diagrams offered a comprehensive view of the range of grays and beiges and the various other shades. The twelve orbits (*top*) correspond to degrees of increasing lightness, with the different tones near each other in the same area. Thus, it was easy to make a choice, either according to the color, or according to the desired lightness of shade. Finally, a color photo depicted four other floorings, which are apparently the first PVC linoleum tiles, which were thin, smooth, and cold, the very same ones that would replace the original variety in the 1970s. From that time on, clever color charts with product samples on display, such as this one, would have no more raison d'être.

Linoleum Collection 1966–1967, Sarlino, Reims, France, 1966, binder, 36 × 30 cm, 14 pages, Bibliothèque Forney, Paris, call number CC RES ICO 8330

——— The first paint color charts specified in about 1900 that: "As these dots are made with a thin layer of Ripolin itself, the colors are therefore identical to the delivered product." Similar specifications appeared on the color charts of other brands. This guarantee of conformity evolved over the twentieth century and starting in the 1960s became an expression of protection against possible claims. A study of how this statement changed, with examples from the corpus of color charts used for this book, is enlightening:

- 1920s: "These dots were painted with our 'Fresca' paint" (on a color chart by Badigeons Français Girard & Cie)
- c. 1945: "The samples on this card are identical to the delivered product" (on a color chart by Ripolin)
- 1950s: "Despite all the attention applied to producing our color cards, we cannot guarantee absolute similarity with our delivered products" (on a color chart by Glasso et Siccolac)
- 1950s–1960s: "The indicated colors may not be the exact reproduction of the real colors" (on a color chart by Lavenne Dour)
- 1960s: "The process used to print our color cards and our lids reproduces the colors of Avi paint only approximately"

From the 1950s to the 1980s, color charts for paint for the home moved toward the printed reproduction of color while quietly beginning a shift that would lead the consumer gradually to associate the act of choosing with the act of creating, to the point where the two merged.

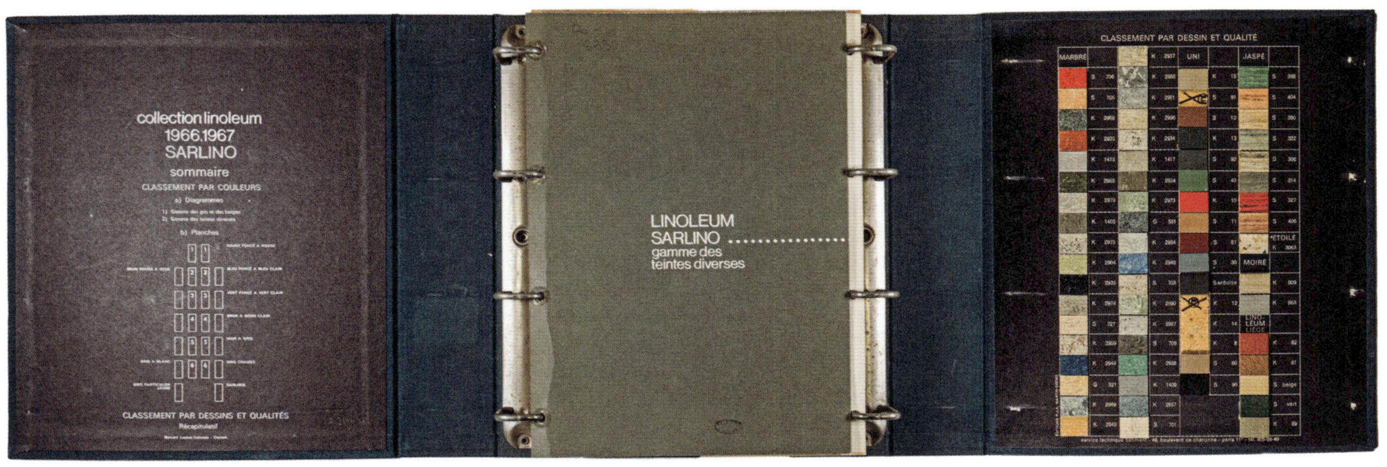
collection linoleum
1966.1967
SARLINO
sommaire
CLASSEMENT PAR COULEURS
CLASSEMENT PAR DESSINS ET QUALITÉS
LINOLEUM
SARLINO
gamme des
teintes diverses
CLASSEMENT PAR DESSIN ET QUALITÉ
MARBRE
UNI
JASPÉ
ÉTOILE
MOIRÉ
LINO-LEUM LIÈGE

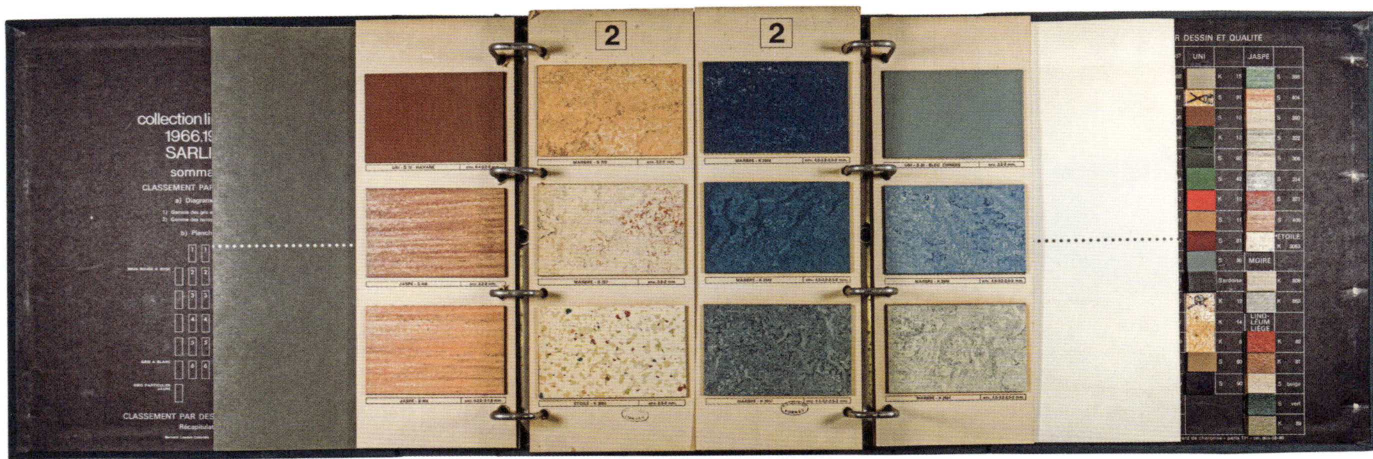
2
2

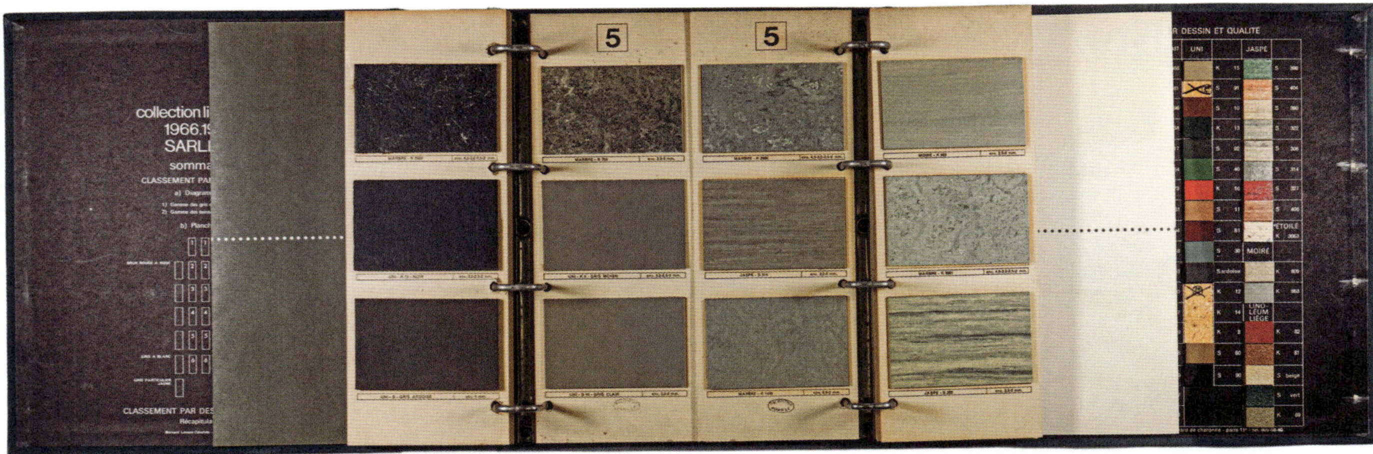
5
5

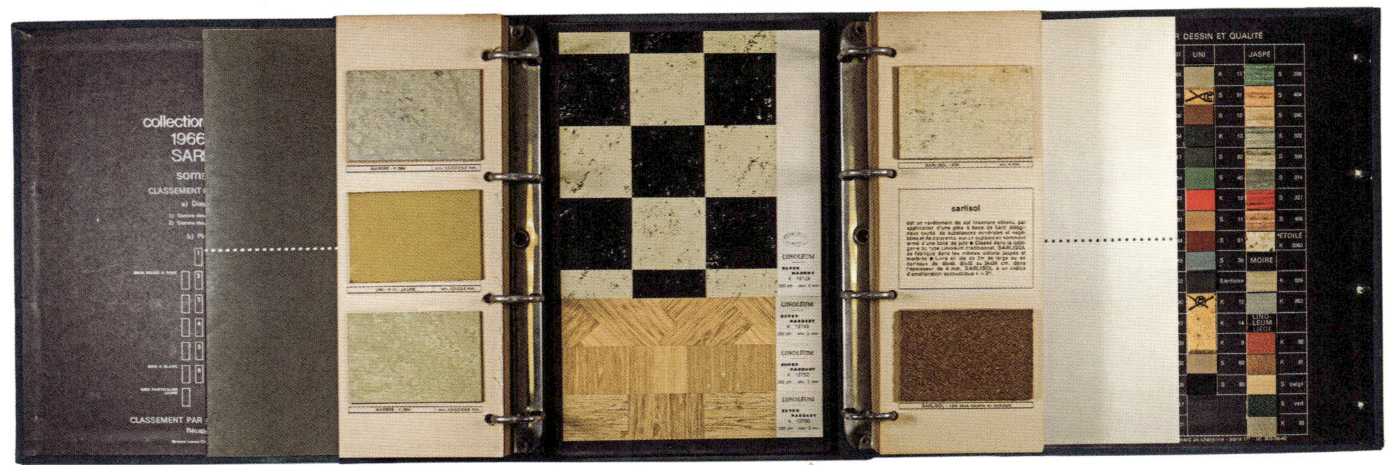
sarlisol

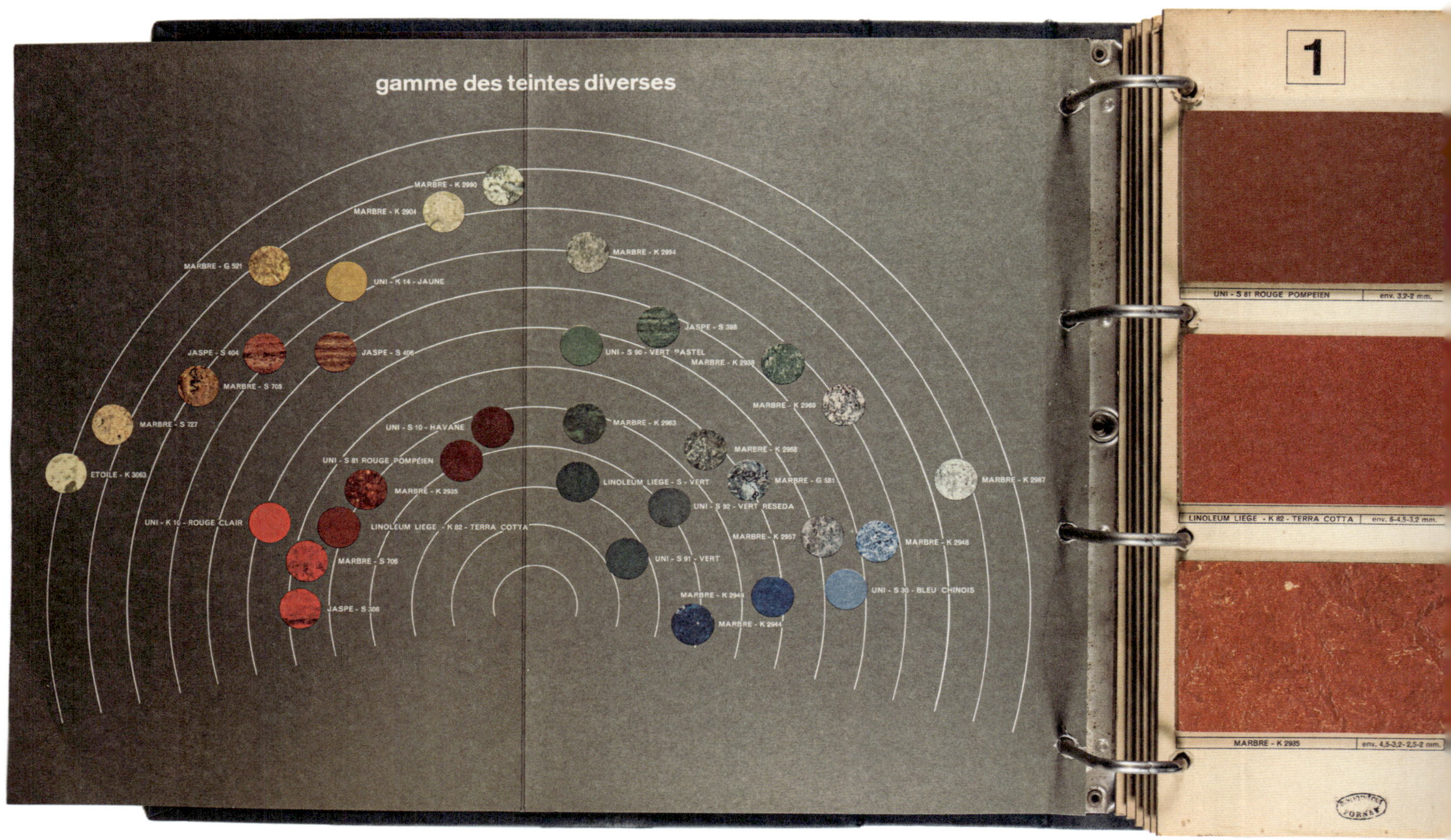
gamme des teintes diverses
MARBRE - K 2990
MARBRE - K 2904
MARBRE - G 521
UNI - K 14 - JAUNE
MARBRE - K 2954
JASPE - S 398
JASPE - S 404
JASPE - S 406
UNI - S 90 - VERT PASTEL
MARBRE - K 2938
MARBRE - S 705
MARBRE - K 2969
MARBRE - S 727
UNI - S 10 - HAVANE
MARBRE - K 2963
MARBRE - K 2968
UNI - S 81 ROUGE POMPÉIEN
ETOILE - K 3063
MARBRE - K 2935
LINOLEUM LIEGE - S - VERT
MARBRE - G 581
MARBRE - K 2987
UNI - S 92 - VERT RESEDA
UNI - K 10 - ROUGE CLAIR
LINOLEUM LIEGE - K 82 - TERRA COTTA
MARBRE - K 2957
MARBRE - K 2948
MARBRE - S 706
UNI - S 91 - VERT
UNI - S 30 - BLEU CHINOIS
MARBRE - K 2949
JASPE - S 306
MARBRE - K 2944
1
UNI - S 81 ROUGE POMPEIEN
env. 3,2-2 mm.
LINOLEUM LIEGE - K 82 - TERRA COTTA
env. 6-4,5-3,2 mm.
MARBRE - K 2935
env. 4,5-3,2- 2,5-2 mm.

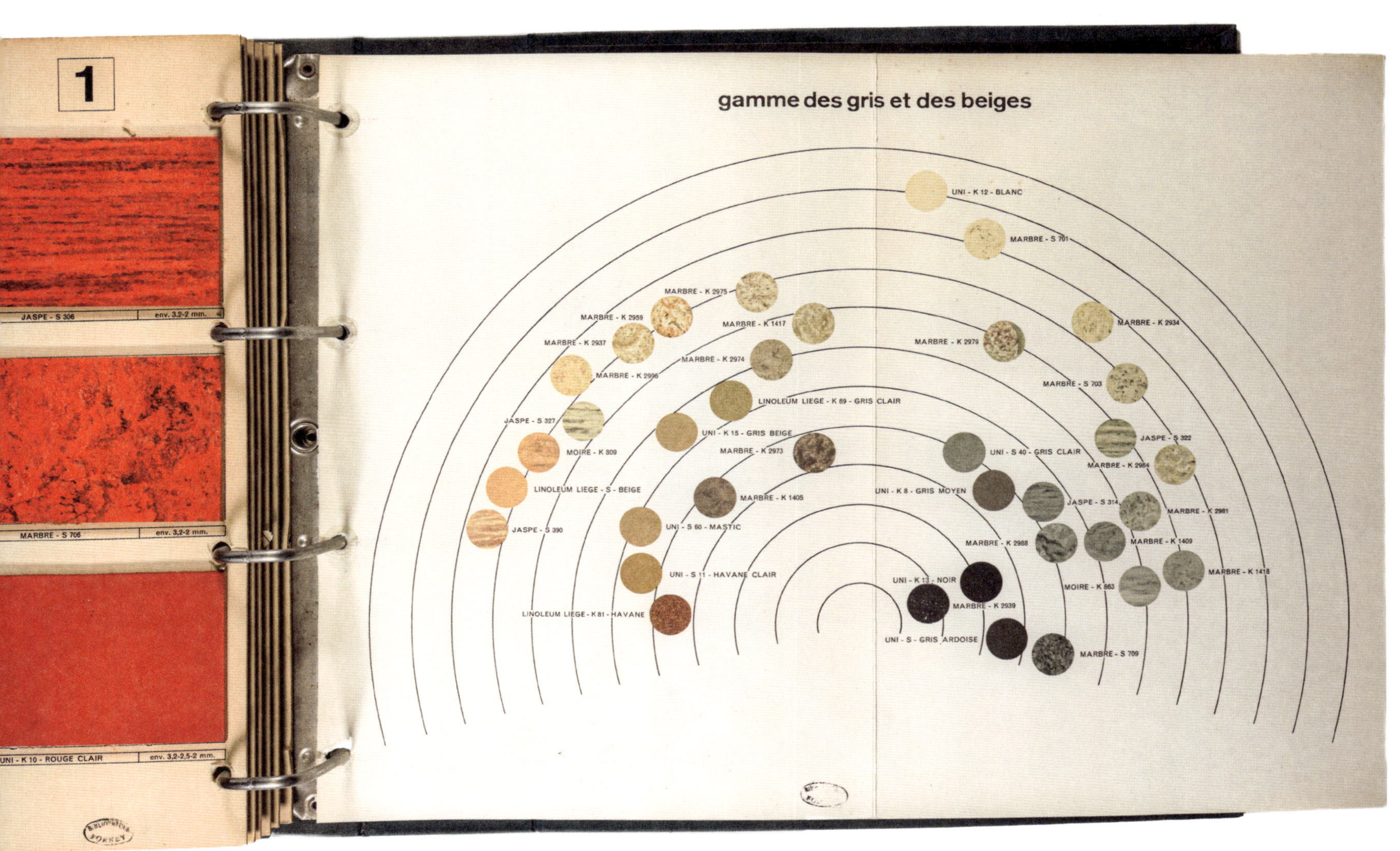
1
JASPE - S 306
env. 3,2-2 mm.
MARBRE - S 706
env. 3,2-2 mm.
UNI - K 10 - ROUGE CLAIR
env. 3,2-2,5-2 mm.
gamme des gris et des beiges
UNI - K 12 - BLANC
MARBRE - S 701
MARBRE - K 2975
MARBRE - K 2959
MARBRE - K 1417
MARBRE - K 2934
MARBRE - K 2937
MARBRE - K 2979
MARBRE - K 2974
MARBRE - K 2996
MARBRE - S 703
LINOLEUM LIEGE - K 89 - GRIS CLAIR
JASPE - S 327
UNI - K 15 - GRIS BEIGE
JASPE - S 322
MARBRE - K 2973
UNI - S 40 - GRIS CLAIR
MOIRE - K 809
MARBRE - K 2984
LINOLEUM LIEGE - S - BEIGE
UNI - K 8 - GRIS MOYEN
MARBRE - K 1405
JASPE - S 314
MARBRE - K 2981
JASPE - S 390
UNI - S 60 - MASTIC
MARBRE - K 2988
MARBRE - K 1409
UNI - S 11 - HAVANE CLAIR
MARBRE - K 1418
UNI - K 13 - NOIR
MOIRE - K 863
LINOLEUM LIEGE - K 81 - HAVANE
MARBRE - K 2939
UNI - S - GRIS ARDOISE
MARBRE - S 709

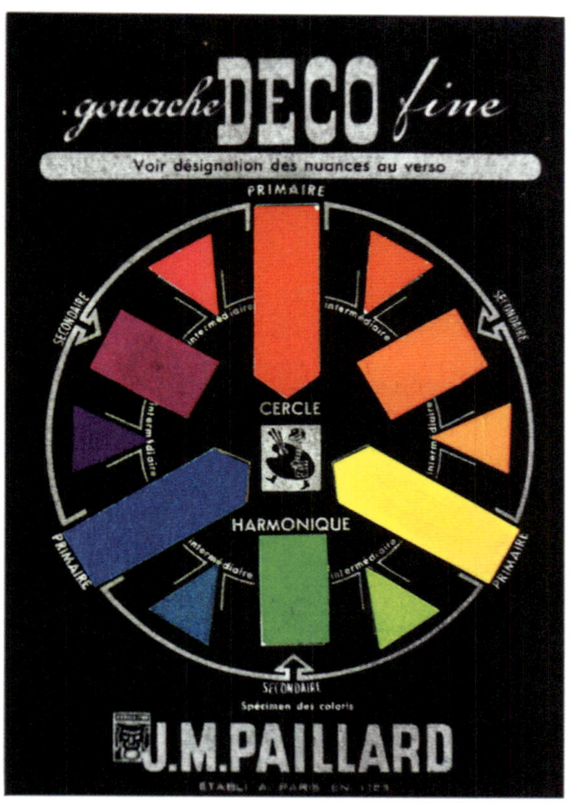

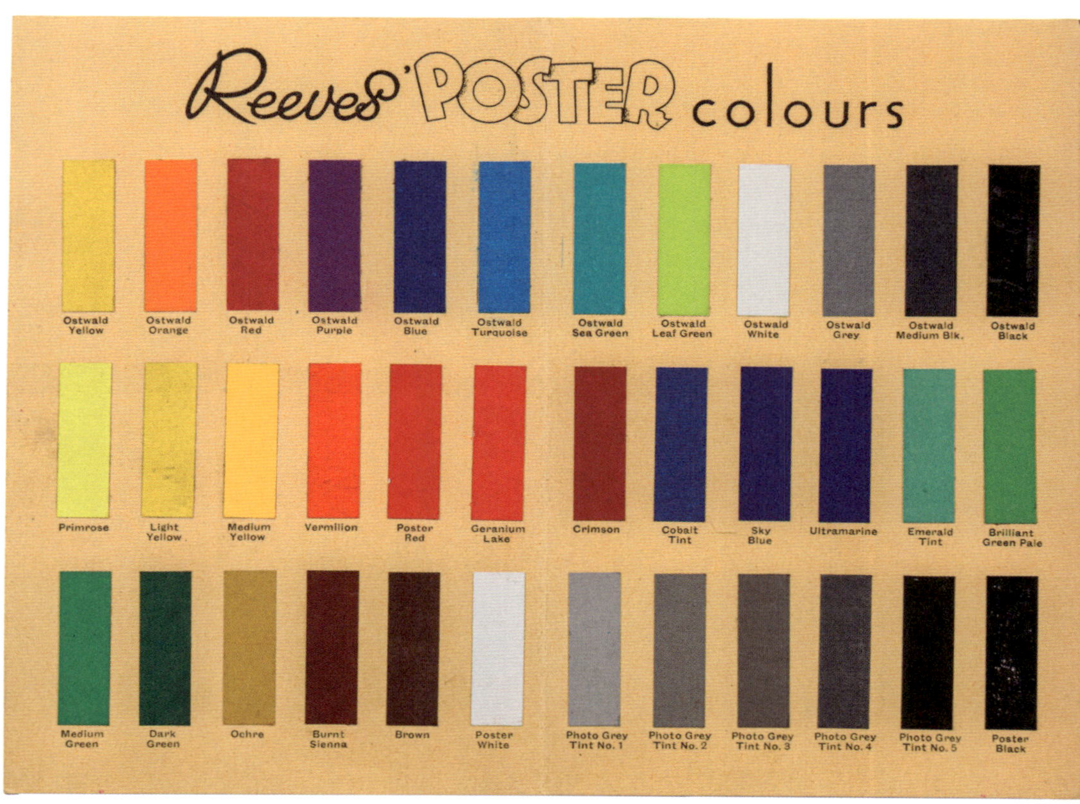

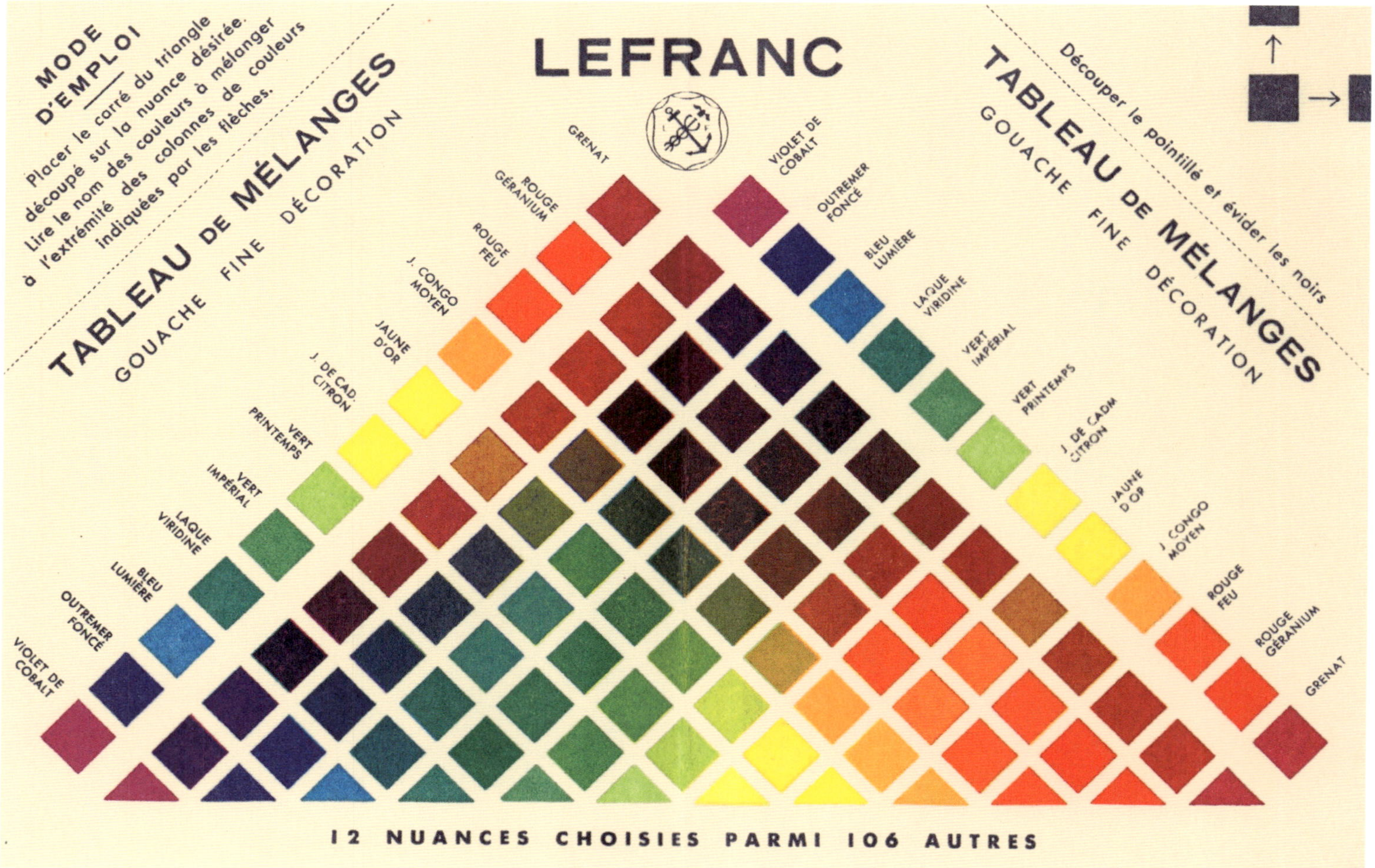

MODE D'EMPLOI

Placer le carré du triangle découpé sur la nuance désirée. Lire le nom des couleurs à mélanger à l'extrémité des colonnes de couleurs indiquées par les flèches.

TABLEAU DE MÉLANGES

GOUACHE FINE DÉCORATION

LEFRANC

TABLEAU DE MÉLANGES

GOUACHE FINE DÉCORATION

Découper le pointillé et évider les noirs

GRENAT
ROUGE GÉRANIUM
ROUGE FEU
J. CONGO MOYEN
JAUNE D'OR
J. DE CAD. CITRON
VERT PRINTEMPS
VERT IMPÉRIAL
LAQUE VIRIDINE
BLEU LUMIÈRE
OUTREMER FONCE
VIOLET DE COBALT

VIOLET DE COBALT
OUTREMER FONCE
BLEU LUMIÈRE
LAQUE VIRIDINE
VERT IMPÉRIAL
VERT PRINTEMPS
J. DE CADM CITRON
JAUNE D'OR
J. CONGO MOYEN
ROUGE FEU
ROUGE GÉRANIUM
GRENAT

12 NUANCES CHOISIES PARMI 106 AUTRES

COLOR CHARTS FOR ARTISTS' SUPPLIES: TEACHING AND DISTANCING

——— From 1950 to 1980, color charts for artists' supplies reflect the variety of materials available. New products were marketed for artists and for students and hobbyists.[13] The color ranges proposed for these increasingly specialized activities gave rise to many color charts.

Teaching Mixing

——— After World War II, manufacturers enhanced their color charts with figures, diagrams, or information geared toward teaching about color.

OPPOSITE, TOP LEFT

Paillard Gouaches

The manufacturer Paillard promoted its gouaches for "advertising, illustration, decorative composition, studies of flowers, landscapes, etc." with a circle displaying samples of three. It showed how by mixing them one could obtain three secondary shades as well as three shades called intermediary, resulting from the mixture of a primary shade and the secondary shade that follows it. The diagram is clear and features product samples.

Fine Deco Gouache, Harmonic Circle, Specimens of Colors, J. M. Paillard, Paris, 1950s, card, 17.5 × 12 cm, Albi Couleurs, Association Mémoire des Industries de la Couleur, Albi

OPPOSITE, BOTTOM

Lefranc Color Mixtures

During the same period, Lefranc also distributed an educational tool but without explicitly connecting it to one of its products. This display is therefore not a color chart, even if it is contemporary with the company's fine decorative gouache paints, mentions them, and uses the names of their colors. The diagram, simple in appearance, did however require the use of the provided cover sheet. What was important was to give the impression that everyone can master color and obtain all its shades. It thus inspired the desire to take action, which was the goal.

Table of Color Mixtures, Lefranc, Paris, 1960s, card, 14.5 × 11 cm, 1 fold, Anne Varichon collection, Sète

Referring to Standardized Systems

OPPOSITE, TOP RIGHT

Reeves Watercolors

The samples on the first line of this color chart all include "Ostwald" in their names (*Ostwald Yellow*, *Ostwald Orange*, and so on). They refer to the study of colors published in 1914 by a German chemist, Wilhelm Ostwald, at the request of the Deutscher Werkbund, an association of artists, artisans, architects, and manufacturers dedicated to the promotion of innovation in the applied arts. Ostwald, who knew Munsell's work, published an atlas of standardized colors in 1917, which was used for the creation and identification of colors in many fields and inspired artists including Piet Mondrian. Although Reeves had two centuries of expertise, the company chose to give a prominent place to the shades developed by Ostwald in his effort to systematize the study of color. This is evidence of the industry's emphasis on the need to standardize colors.[14]

Poster Colours, Specimen Washes, Reeves, England, late 1940s, card, 17 × 11.3 cm, 1 fold, Sennelier family collection, Paris

From the Brushstroke to the Printed Box

NEXT PAGE, TOP

Sennelier Gouaches

The Sennelier company continued to produce the same meticulous color charts as it did before the war; it constantly added to its color ranges and changed the formulation of its shades when necessary.

Card of Fine Gouache Colors, Sennelier, Paris, 1950s, card, 21 × 15.6 cm, 2 folds, Sennelier family collection, Paris

NEXT PAGE, BOTTOM

Flash Inks

Milori used a fan system for its "Flash" line to display approximately forty shades, which were either vivid or pale depending on the density of the application. Founded in 1827 in Montreuil, just outside Paris, by the early twentieth century the company produced over two million kilograms of colors per year for the construction industry, wallpaper, artificial flowers, car bodies, artists, and such, and had given its name to several shades, including *Milori Blue* and *Milori Green*. This color wheel demonstrates the ongoing advances achieved in formulating color inks. They allowed artists and printers to have access to more extensive ranges.

"Flash" Inks, Milori, Paris, 1960s, fan, 17 × 8.5 cm, approximately 40 samples, Bibliothèque Forney, Paris, call number RES ICO 7208 Plano

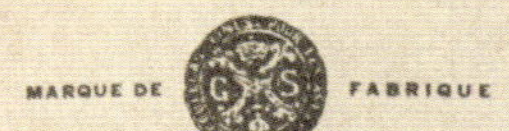

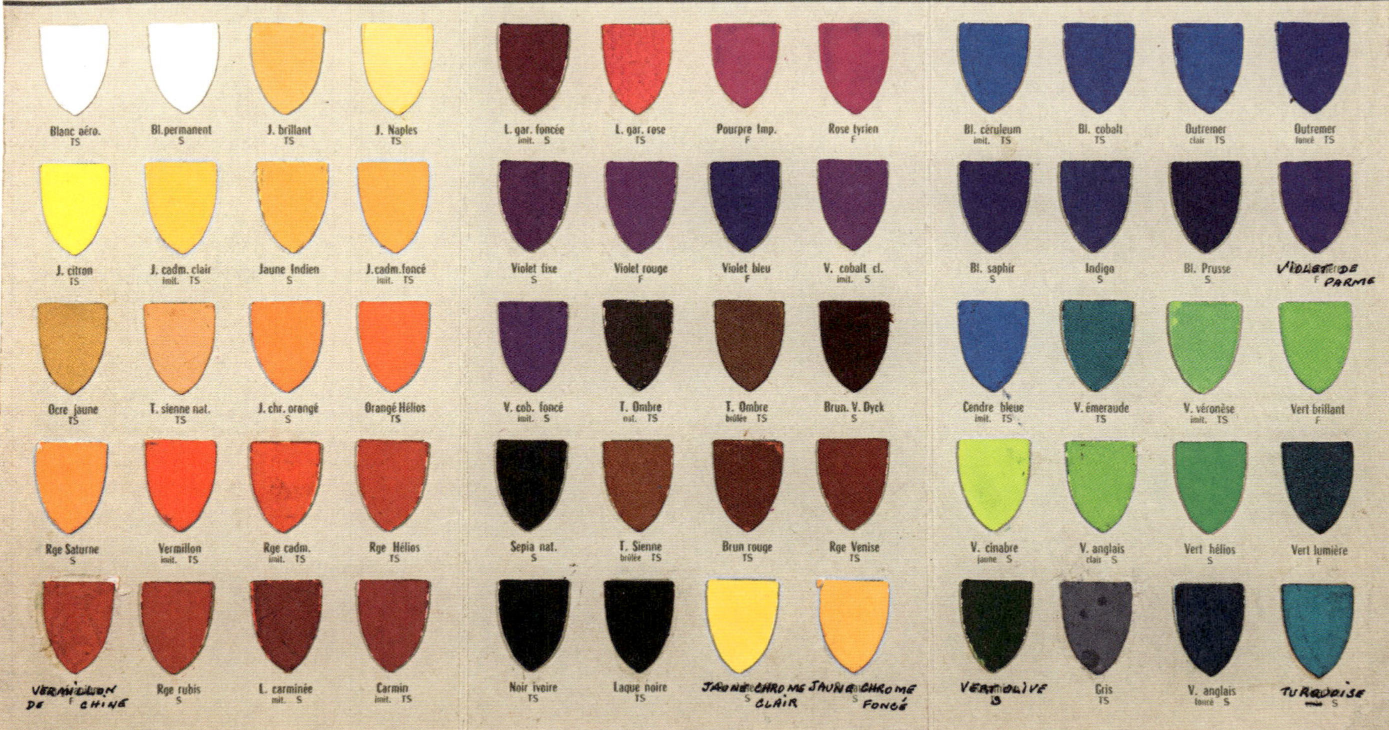

MARQUE DE FABRIQUE
SENNELIER FRÈRES
Gouaches Fines
TUBES — FLACONS — AU POIDS A PARTIR DE 0 K. 500
SOLIDITÉ A LA LUMIÈRE
TS très solide
S solide
F fragile
Blanc aéro. TS
Bl. permanent S
J. brillant TS
J. Naples TS
L. gar. foncée imit. S
L. gar. rose TS
Pourpre Imp. F
Rose tyrien F
Bl. céruleum imit. TS
Bl. cobalt TS
Outremer clair TS
Outremer foncé TS
J. citron TS
J. cadm. clair imit. TS
Jaune Indien S
J. cadm. foncé imit. TS
Violet fixe S
Violet rouge F
Violet bleu F
V. cobalt cl. imit. S
Bl. saphir S
Indigo S
Bl. Prusse S
VIOLET DE PARME F
Ocre jaune TS
T. sienne nat. TS
J. chr. orangé S
Orangé Hélios TS
V. cob. foncé imit. S
T. Ombre nat. TS
T. Ombre brûlée TS
Brun. V. Dyck S
Cendre bleue imit. TS
V. émeraude TS
V. véronèse imit. TS
Vert brillant F
Rge Saturne S
Vermillon imit. TS
Rge cadm. imit. TS
Rge Hélios TS
Sepia nat. S
T. Sienne brûlée TS
Brun rouge TS
Rge Venise TS
V. cinabre jaune S
V. anglais clair S
Vert hélios S
Vert lumière F
VERMILLON DE CHINE F
Rge rubis S
L. carminée imit. S
Carmin imit. TS
Noir ivoire TS
Laque noire TS
JAUNE CHROME CLAIR S
JAUNE CHROME FONCÉ S
VERT OLIVE S
Gris TS
V. anglais foncé S
TURQUOISE S

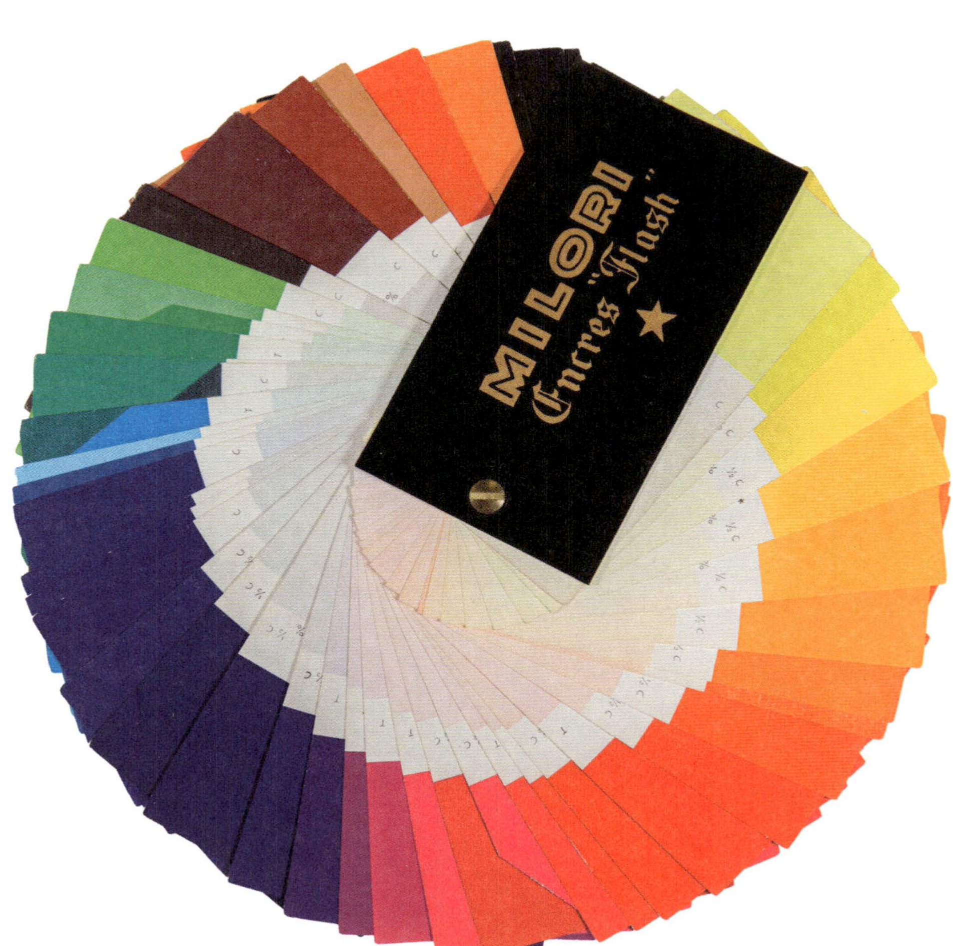

MILORI
Encres "Flash"

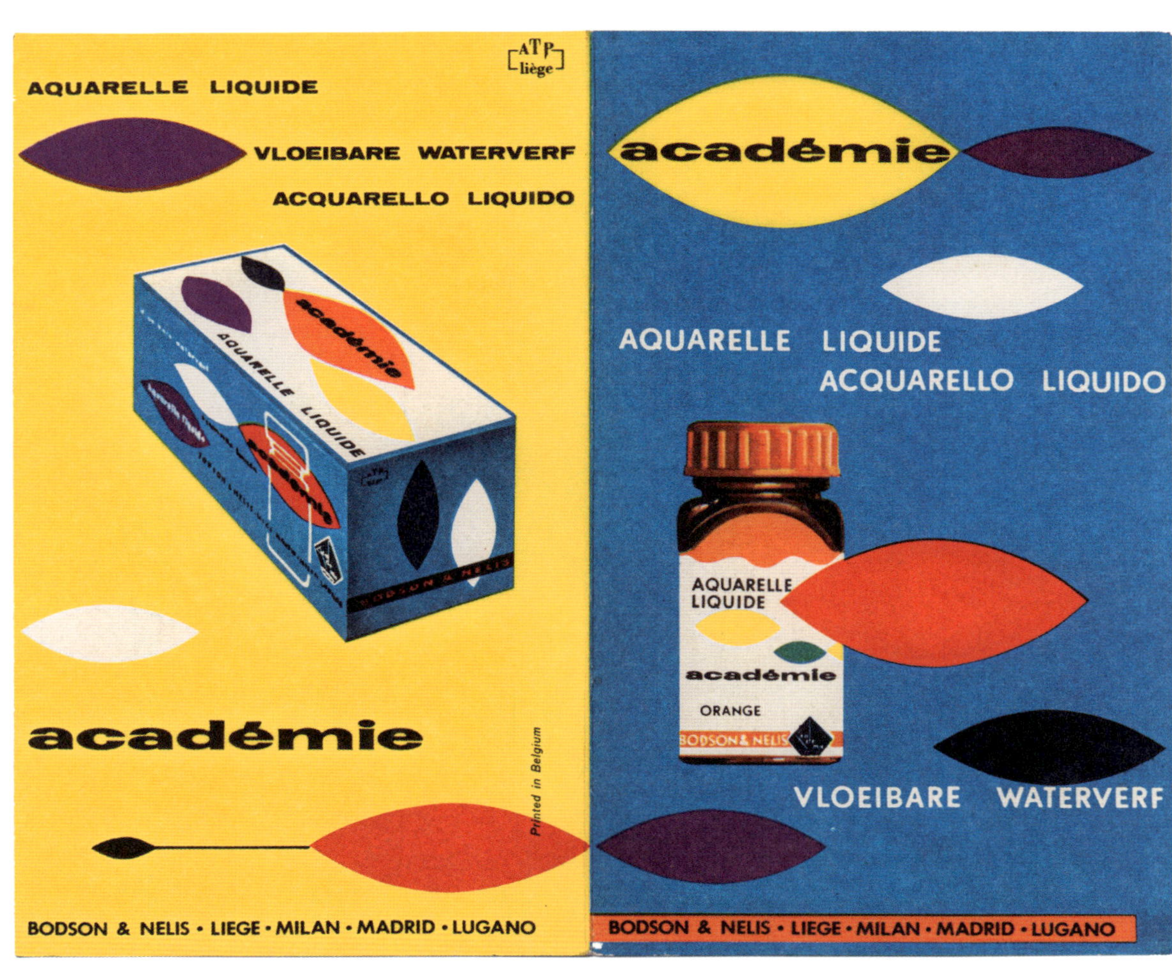
AQUARELLE LIQUIDE
VLOEIBARE WATERVERF
ACQUARELLO LIQUIDO
académie
Printed in Belgium
BODSON & NELIS • LIEGE • MILAN • MADRID • LUGANO
académie
AQUARELLE LIQUIDE
ACQUARELLO LIQUIDO
AQUARELLE LIQUIDE
académie
ORANGE
BODSON & NELIS
VLOEIBARE WATERVERF
BODSON & NELIS • LIEGE • MILAN • MADRID • LUGANO

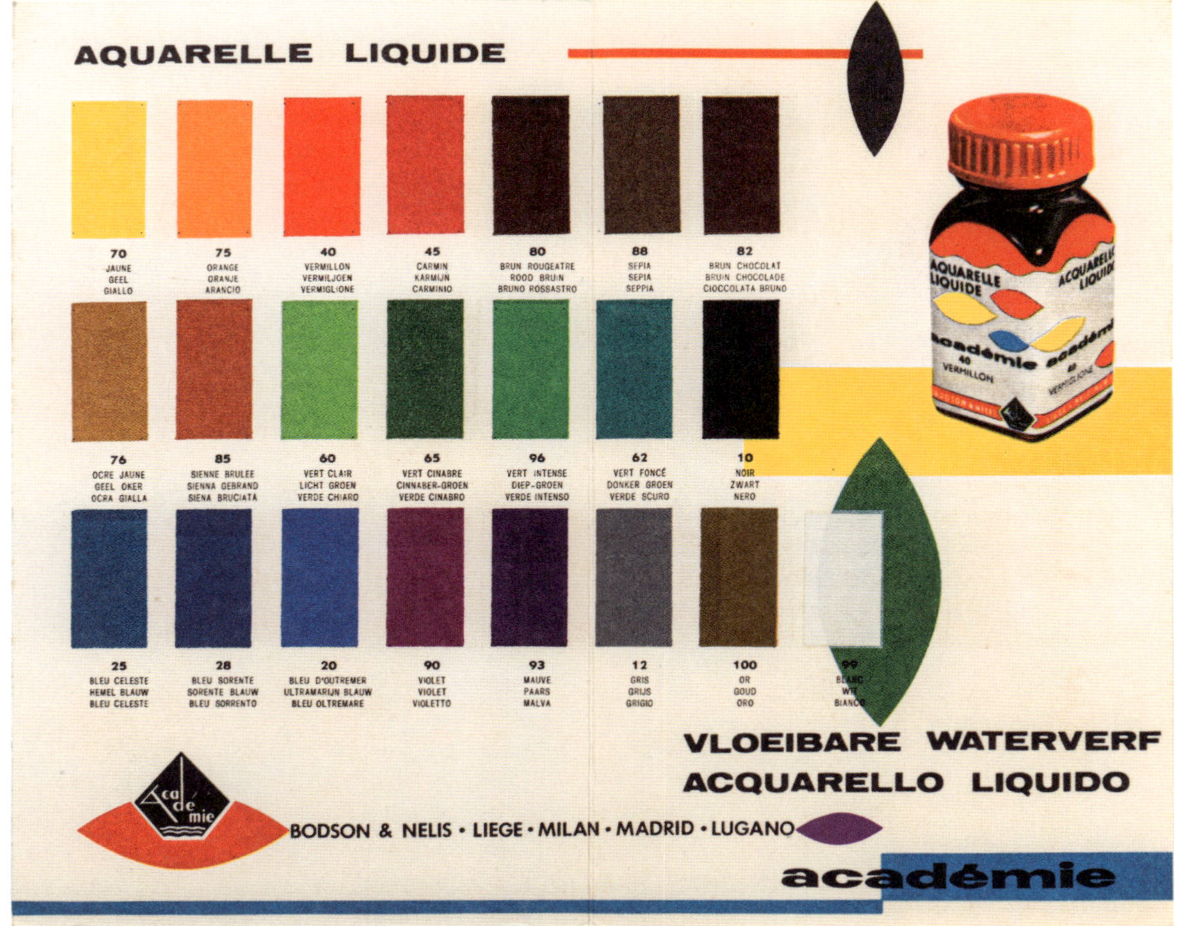
AQUARELLE LIQUIDE
70 JAUNE GEEL GIALLO
75 ORANGE ORANJE ARANCIO
40 VERMILLON VERMILJOEN VERMIGLIONE
45 CARMIN KARMIJN CARMINIO
80 BRUN ROUGEATRE ROOD BRUIN BRUNO ROSSASTRO
88 SEPIA SEPIA SEPPIA
82 BRUN CHOCOLAT BRUIN CHOCOLADE CIOCCOLATA BRUNO
76 OCRE JAUNE GEEL OKER OCRA GIALLA
85 SIENNE BRULEE SIENNA GEBRAND SIENA BRUCIATA
60 VERT CLAIR LICHT GROEN VERDE CHIARO
65 VERT CINABRE CINNABER-GROEN VERDE CINABRO
96 VERT INTENSE DIEP-GROEN VERDE INTENSO
62 VERT FONCÉ DONKER GROEN VERDE SCURO
10 NOIR ZWART NERO
25 BLEU CELESTE HEMEL BLAUW BLEU CELESTE
28 BLEU SORENTE SORENTE BLAUW BLEU SORRENTO
20 BLEU D'OUTREMER ULTRAMARIJN BLAUW BLEU OLTREMARE
90 VIOLET VIOLET VIOLETTO
93 MAUVE PAARS MALVA
12 GRIS GRIJS GRIGIO
100 OR GOUD ORO
99
AQUARELLE LIQUIDE
académie
40 VERMILLON
BODSON & NELIS
VLOEIBARE WATERVERF
ACQUARELLO LIQUIDO
BODSON & NELIS • LIEGE • MILAN • MADRID • LUGANO
académie

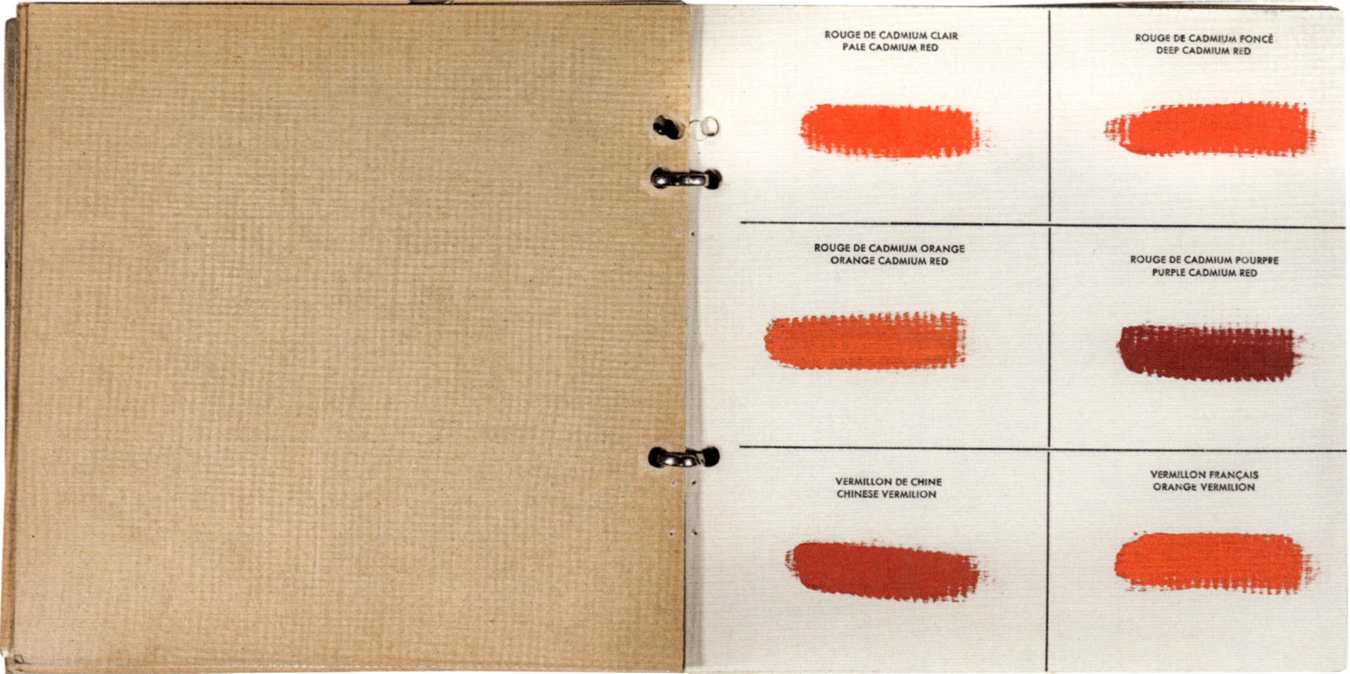

PREVIOUS PAGE

Académie Watercolors

Color charts for artists' supplies now included illustrations. These printed charts emphasized primary colors, as many artists from the Bauhaus or De Stijl movements did.[15] Liquid watercolor was an earlier form of the medium that had generally been replaced by watercolor in solid cubes. But liquid watercolor returned in the 1960s in a reduced color range, as can be seen in the twenty-two shades printed on this color chart.

Académie Liquid Watercolor, Bodson & Nelis, Liège, Belgium, 1960s, card, 18 × 11 cm, 1 fold, Sennelier family collection, Paris

ABOVE

Leroux Oils

At a time when color charts for artists' supplies were printed, manufacturers began to feel the need to reincorporate the product sample into their marketing tools. This was the case with Manufacture Leroux, which was founded in Burgundy in 1910, and which originally produced oil paints for buildings and then, after World War I, fine oil colors for artists. There must have been only a few copies of this hand-made color chart, but it represented the quality of the sixty shades that it displayed by a simple stroke onto a sheet of card stock.

Extra-Fine Colors Ground with Oil, M. Leroux, Haumont, France, 1970s, binder, 16.5 × 16.2 cm, 10 pages, Sennelier family collection, Paris

——— The use of printed color in artists' color charts came about quite slowly because artists were very demanding and selective about the paint they used. The disappearance of the product sample was surely easier to accept in paints for children or decorative paints, and the shift took place in those applications first. When, later, the printing process took over all their color charts, the manufacturers of artists' supplies attempted to compensate just as the cosmetics manufacturers had done between the two world wars. They would print samples in the shape of brushstrokes, or would try to reproduce a dab of paint with printing techniques.

COSMETICS COLOR CHARTS EVOKE ENTHUSIASM

The cosmetics industry went through several changes. American companies exported their products to Europe and beyond while starting new makeup trends. The color charts of the Trente Glorieuses demonstrate this expansion through new types of makeup and an explosion of colors. They used materials developed by the petrochemical industry, plastics, and inks of all types that could enhance transparency, matte-ness, and shininess as well as create pearly effects. While many color charts continued to present samples as had been done before World War II, others reflected creative approaches.

Color Charts That Were Always Inspired

NEXT PAGE SPREAD

Antoine Cosmetics

This color chart, one of the last made by the perfumer Antoine, presented its latest types of makeup by using meticulous design. The panels of the leporello were designed in different widths so that no samples needed to be folded. The chart was still produced with paper that was painted and then cut out and glued to the backing. Eyeshadows, mascaras, and some nail polish shades were added to the traditional types of makeup. The colors are varied, saturated, and even daring at times (such as the very dark *Lilac* nail polish, or the bright blue and mauve eyeshadows). Alongside a docile femininity (with names like *Sweet* and *Innocence*), a new and bolder version was emerging (see colors called *Adventurous*, *Dazzling*, or *Triumph*). *Pharaoh* replaced the earlier name *Moorish* that predated World War II.

Color Chart, Antoine, Paris, late 1940s, leporello, 15.5 × 7 to 11 cm, 5 panels in a case, Bibliothèque Forney, Paris, call number RES ICO 8108–1

PAGE 248, TOP

Tho-Radia Lipstick

Seeking to capitalize on the discovery of radioactivity by Marie and Pierre Curie and the hopes raised by radiation therapy, by the 1910s several companies had begun to market cosmetics containing radioactive elements. In 1932, the French pharmaceutical company Tho-Radia, founded by a pharmacist and a doctor, began advertising creams, toothpastes, powders, and soaps containing radium or thorium.[16] But in 1937 new regulations required indicating "Poison" or "Toxic" on such products, and Tho-Radia removed these suspect ingredients and focused on making lipsticks. In the 1940s, lipsticks were packaged in cases shaped like balls. The 1301 line, launched in March 1951, adopted a design that may have been inspired by Hemingway's *Death in the Afternoon*. The line drawings of a matador evoke a dance, with the choreographic theme emphasized by the samples in the shape of capes; the names of the lipsticks refer to the calm world of flowers and to luxury tourism.

Tho-Radia 1301 Lipstick, Tho-Radia, Paris, c. 1950, card, approximately 8 × 20 cm, Bibliothèque Forney, Paris, call number RES ICO oblong 8865

PAGE 248, BOTTOM

Max Factor Lipstick

After World War II, Max Factor, like other giants of the American cosmetics industry such as Revlon and Elizabeth Arden, began selling its products on the European market. Pearly surfaces, which were already present in nail polish, were now used on lipsticks, embracing a glamorous style embodied by stars such as Elizabeth Taylor in *Cat on a Hot Tin Roof* and Marilyn Monroe in *The Seven-Year Itch*. The pearly lipsticks inspired this color chart, with the oyster suggesting the fascinating creation of pearls as well as festive holiday meals. The colors of these ten lipsticks were printed and then a special varnish was applied to represent their sheen. The names all used terms such as *pearl*, *frost*, or *mother-of-pearl*.

Sparkling Lipstick, Max Factor, Paris, 1960s, card, 21 × 17 cm, 1 fold, Bibliothèque Forney, Paris, call number RES ICO oblong 8865

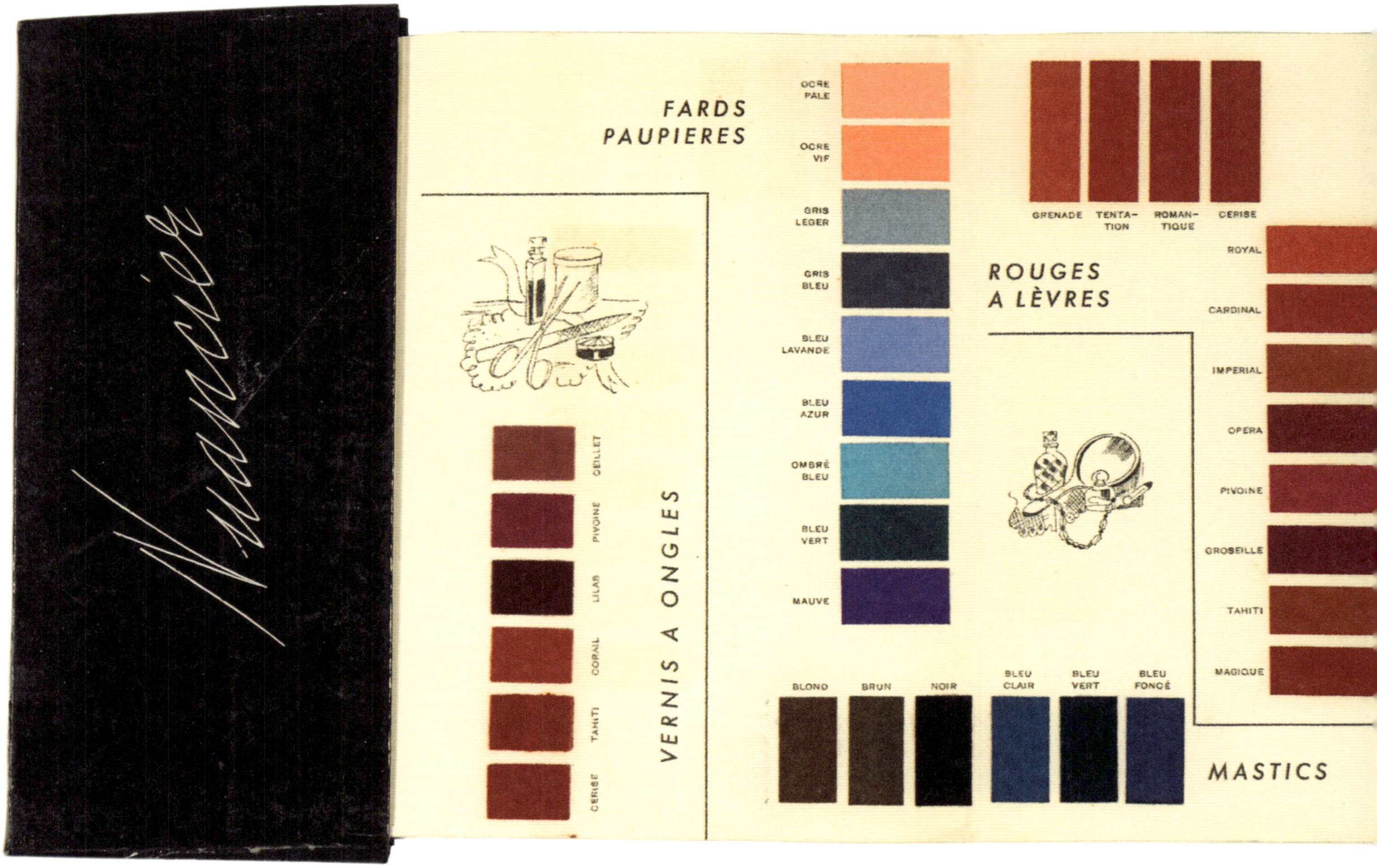

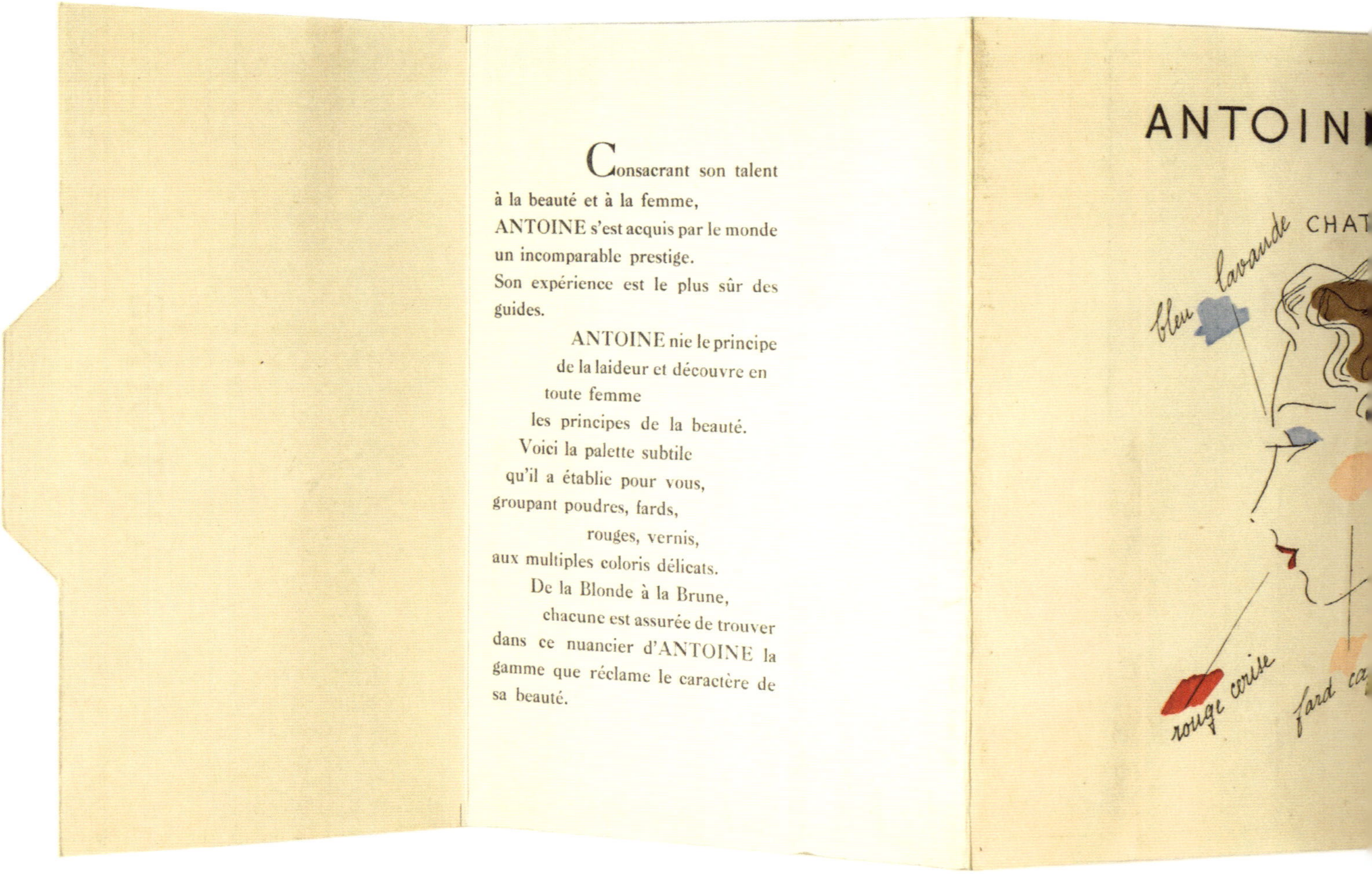

Nuancier

FARDS PAUPIERES

OCRE PALE
OCRE VIF
GRIS LEGER
GRIS BLEU
BLEU LAVANDE
BLEU AZUR
OMBRÉ BLEU
BLEU VERT
MAUVE

VERNIS A ONGLES

OEILLET
PIVOINE
LILAS
CORAIL
TAHITI
CERISE

ROUGES A LÈVRES

GRENADE
TENTA-TION
ROMAN-TIQUE
CERISE
ROYAL
CARDINAL
IMPERIAL
OPERA
PIVOINE
GROSEILLE
TAHITI
MAGIQUE

MASTICS

BLOND
BRUN
NOIR
BLEU CLAIR
BLEU VERT
BLEU FONCÉ

Consacrant son talent
à la beauté et à la femme,
ANTOINE s'est acquis par le monde
un incomparable prestige.
Son expérience est le plus sûr des
guides.
ANTOINE nie le principe
de la laideur et découvre en
toute femme
les principes de la beauté.
Voici la palette subtile
qu'il a établie pour vous,
groupant poudres, fards,
rouges, vernis,
aux multiples coloris délicats.
De la Blonde à la Brune,
chacune est assurée de trouver
dans ce nuancier d'ANTOINE la
gamme que réclame le caractère de
sa beauté.

ANTOIN

bleu lavande CHAT

rouge cerise

fard ca

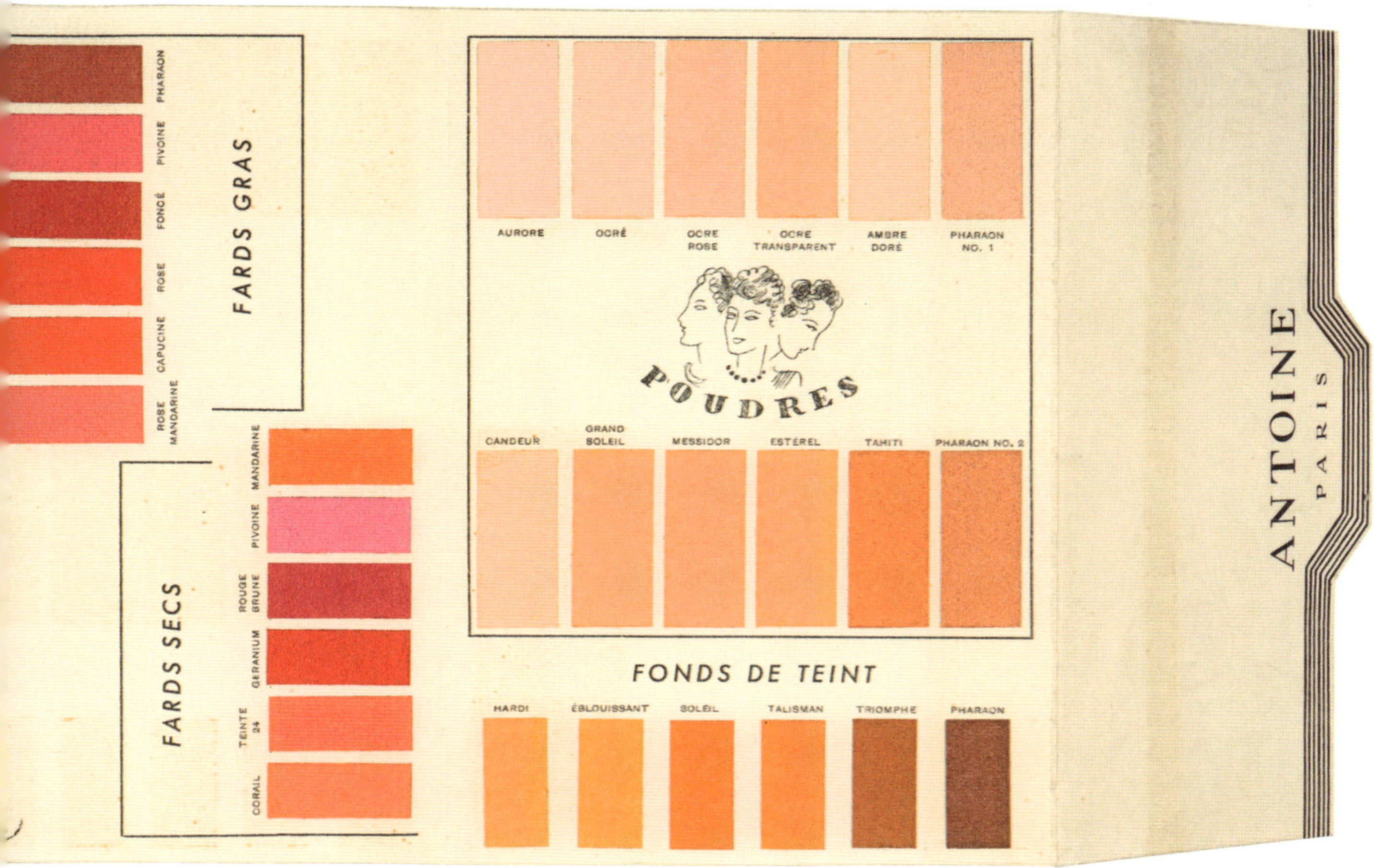

PHARAON
PIVOINE
FONCÉ
ROSE
CAPUCINE
ROSE MANDARINE

FARDS GRAS

AURORE
OCRÉ
OCRE ROSE
OCRE TRANSPARENT
AMBRE DORÉ
PHARAON NO. 1

POUDRES

CANDEUR
GRAND SOLEIL
MESSIDOR
ESTÉREL
TAHITI
PHARAON NO. 2

ANTOINE
PARIS

FARDS SECS

MANDARINE
PIVOINE
ROUGE BRUNE
GERANIUM
TEINTE 24
CORAIL

FONDS DE TEINT

HARDI
ÉBLOUISSANT
SOLEIL
TALISMAN
TRIOMPHE
PHARAON

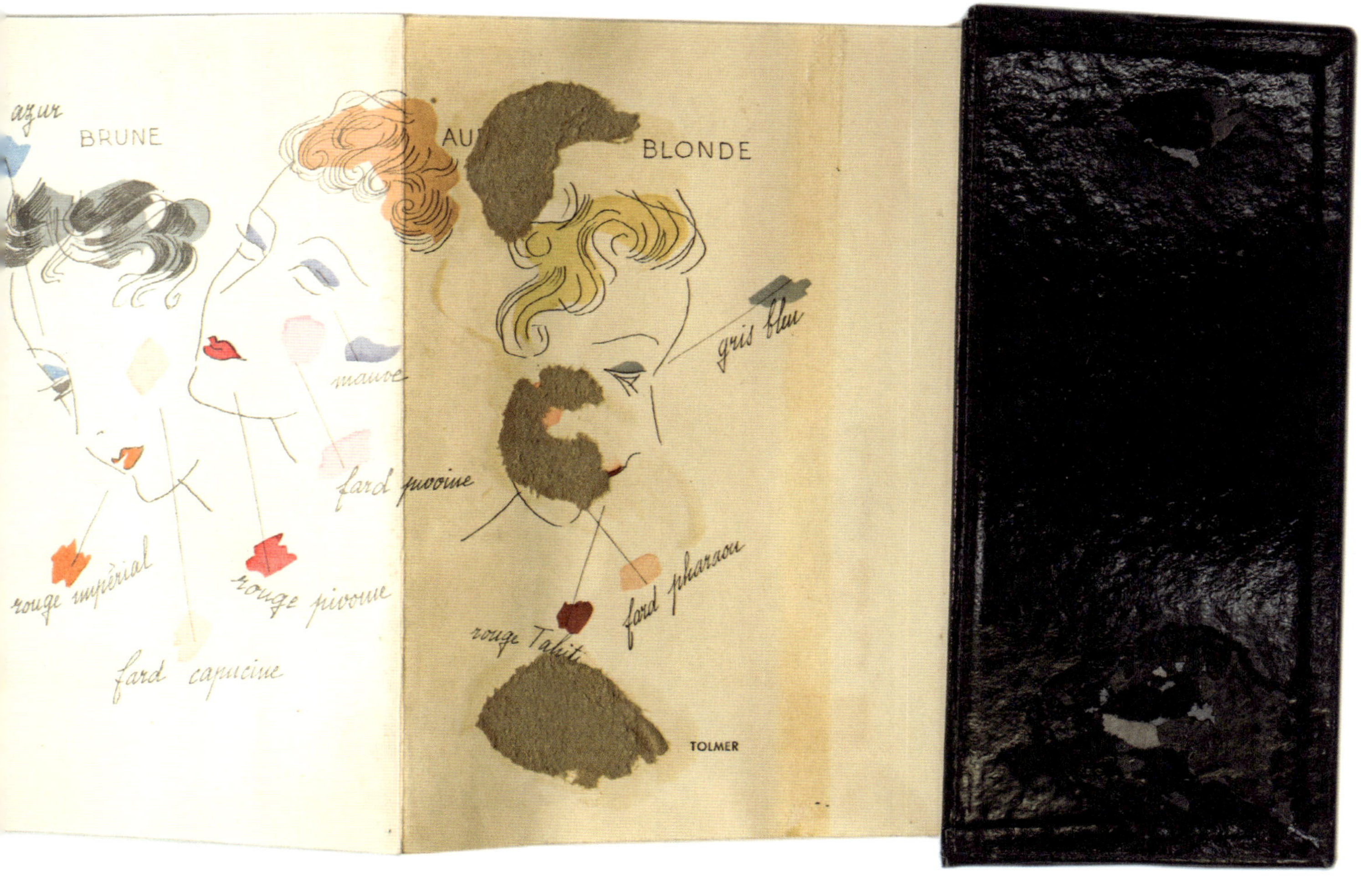

azur
BRUNE
AU
BLONDE
gris bleu
mauve
fard pivoine
rouge impérial
rouge pivoine
fard pharaon
rouge Tahiti
fard capucine
TOLMER

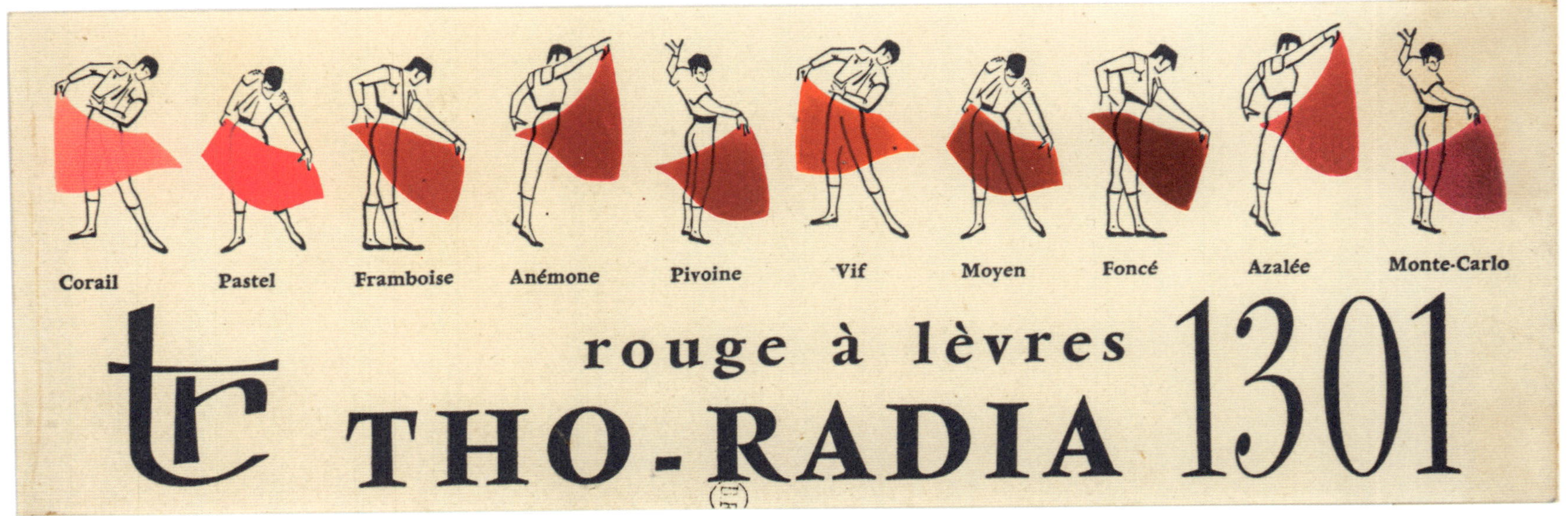
Corail
Pastel
Framboise
Anémone
Pivoine
Vif
Moyen
Foncé
Azalée
Monte-Carlo
tr
rouge à lèvres
THO-RADIA
1301

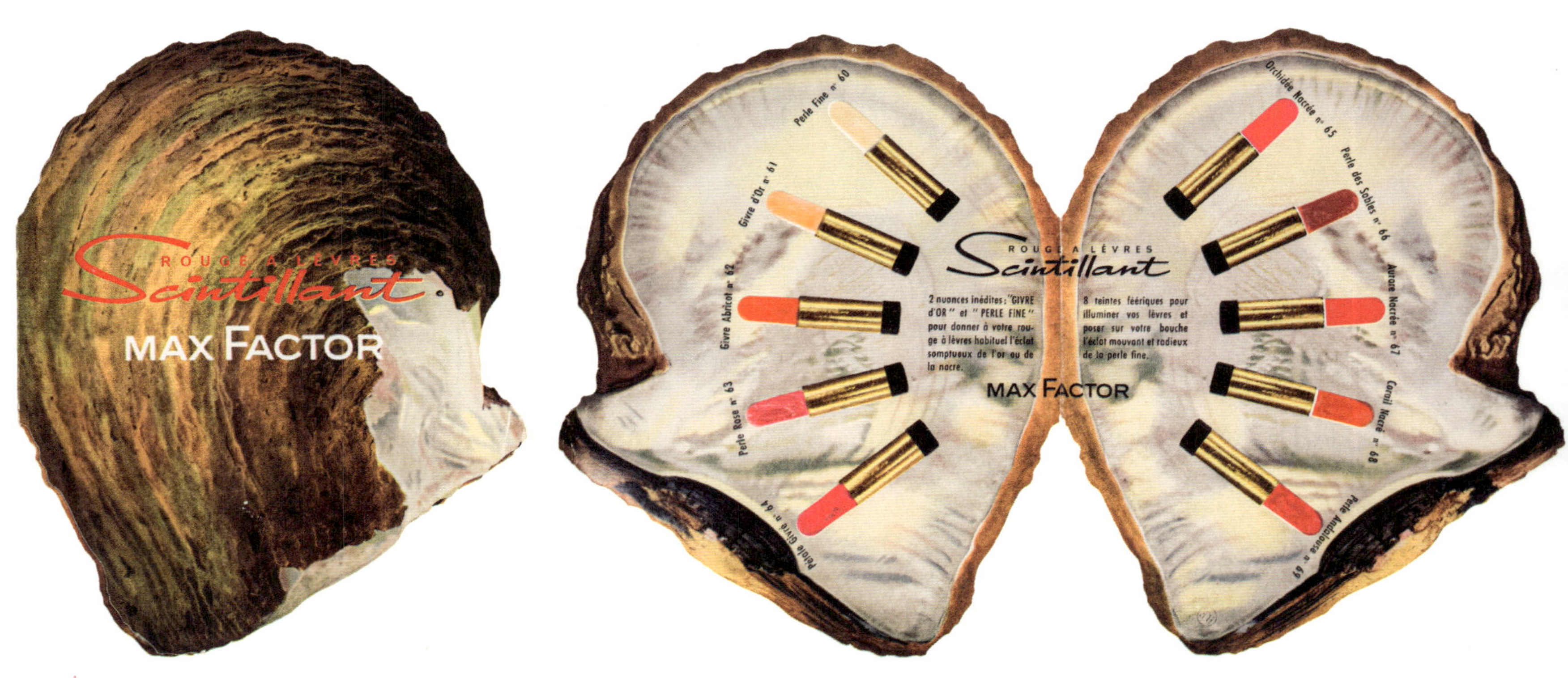
ROUGE À LÈVRES
Scintillant
MAX FACTOR
Perle Fine n° 60
Givre d'Or n° 61
Givre Abricot n° 62
Perle Rose n° 63
Pétale Givre n° 64
ROUGE À LÈVRES
Scintillant
2 nuances inédites : "GIVRE D'OR" et "PERLE FINE" pour donner à votre rouge à lèvres habituel l'éclat somptueux de l'or ou de la nacre.
8 teintes féériques pour illuminer vos lèvres et poser sur votre bouche l'éclat mouvant et radieux de la perle fine.
MAX FACTOR
Orchidée Nacrée n° 65
Perle des Sables n° 66
Aurore Nacrée n° 67
Corail Nacré n° 68
Perle Andalouse n° 69

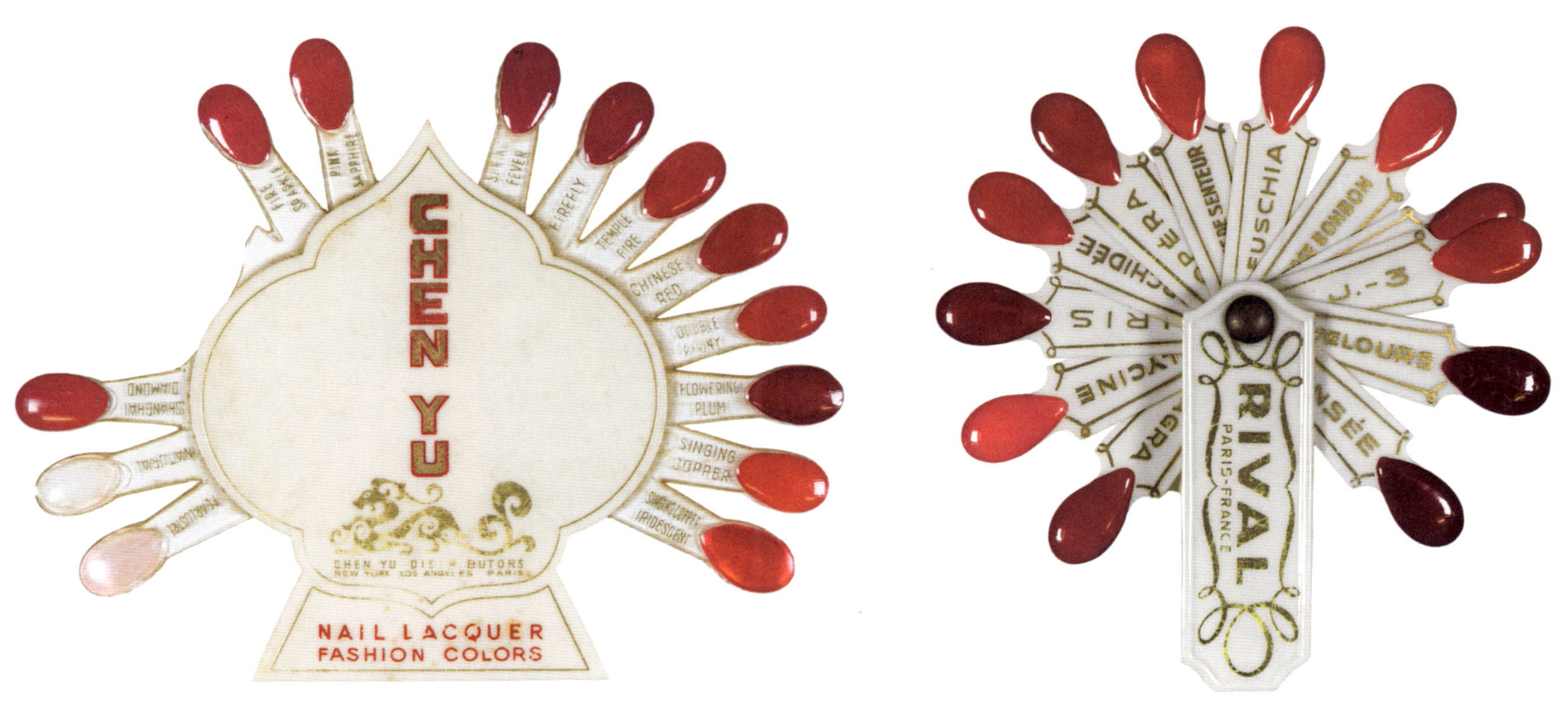

CHEN YU
PINK SAPPHIRE
FIREFLY
TEMPLE FIRE
CHINESE RED
FLOWERING PLUM
SINGING COPPER
DIAMOND
CHEN YU DISTRIBUTORS
NEW YORK LOS ANGELES PARIS
NAIL LACQUER
FASHION COLORS
RIVAL
PARIS-FRANCE
ORCHIDÉE
OPÉRA
FUSCHIA
BONBON
VELOURS
IRIS
GLYCINE

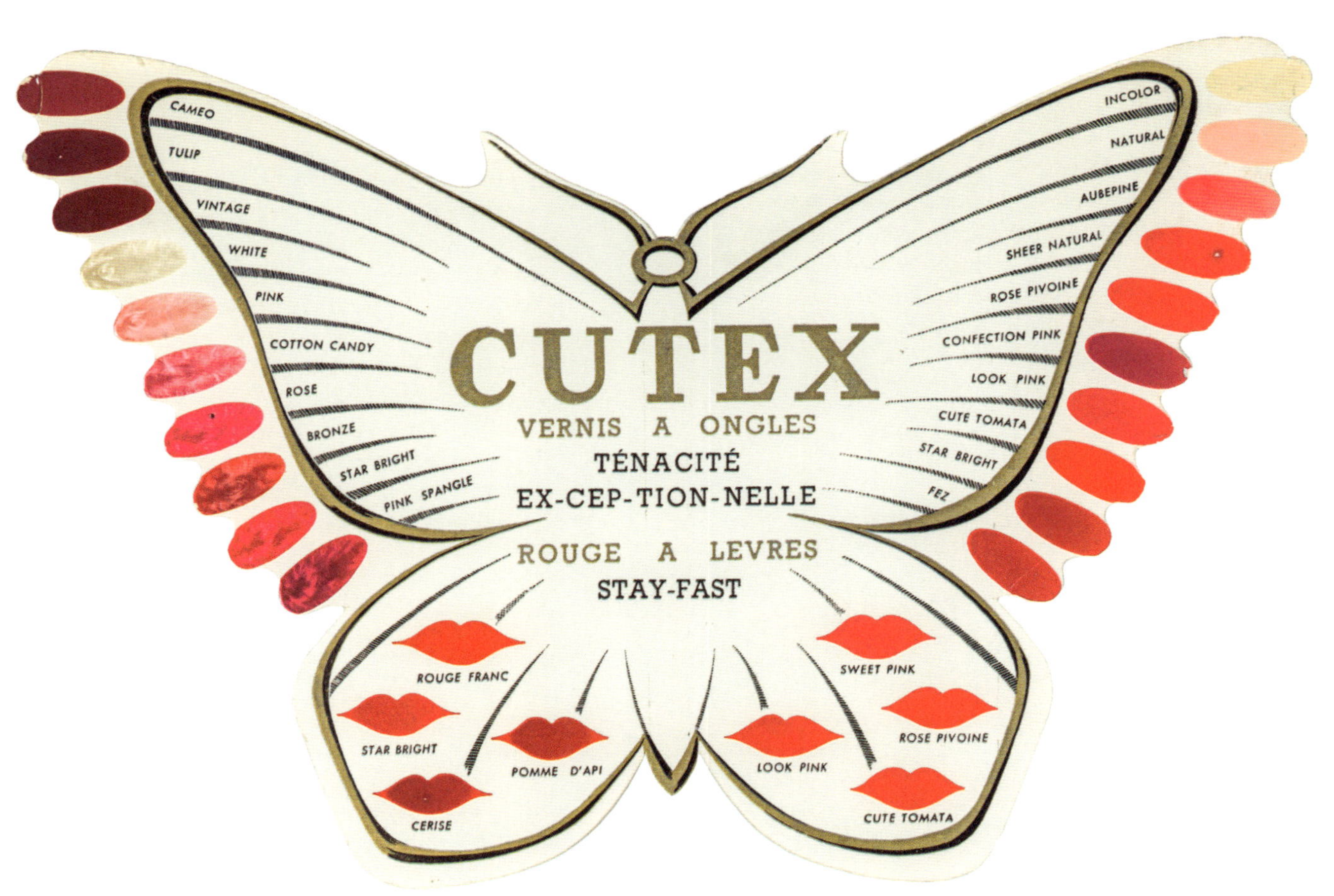

CAMEO
TULIP
VINTAGE
WHITE
PINK
COTTON CANDY
ROSE
BRONZE
STAR BRIGHT
PINK SPANGLE
INCOLOR
NATURAL
AUBEPINE
SHEER NATURAL
ROSE PIVOINE
CONFECTION PINK
LOOK PINK
CUTE TOMATA
STAR BRIGHT
FEZ
CUTEX
VERNIS A ONGLES
TÉNACITÉ
EX-CEP-TION-NELLE
ROUGE A LEVRES
STAY-FAST
ROUGE FRANC
STAR BRIGHT
POMME D'API
CERISE
SWEET PINK
ROSE PIVOINE
LOOK PINK
CUTE TOMATA

The Delights of Varnish and Plastic

In the 1920s, cellulose varnishes were developed from supplies of gunpowder left over from World War I, and advances in automobile paint allowed for the development of lacquers that formed a resistant film after the solvents evaporated. The American cosmetics industry took hold of varnishes and lacquers, especially Revlon, to create the first nail polish. It arrived in Europe following Liberation. The many shades in which they were available and the new plastic materials inspired unique designs for presenting the color ranges. On the back there is often a list of lipsticks with which the nail polishes should be matched in order to avoid a major fashion faux pas.

PREVIOUS PAGE, TOP

Chen Yu and Rival Nail Polish

The American brand Chen Yu drew on the fascination with the East to appeal to its clients in the United States and Europe. It had sixteen shades arranged in fanned plastic rods imitating ivory with fingernail shapes at the end. The names evoked Asian references, such as *Shanghai Diamond*, *Rose of China*, *Peking Pink*, and *Chinese Red*. The same type of display was used by Rival, but the Parisian company continued the traditional names for cosmetics colors, while naming one shade *J-3*, a mysterious designation that harmonizes with a French spirit of seduction.

Nail Lacquer Fashion Colors, Chen Yu, New York–Los Angeles–Paris, late 1940s, fan, 17 × 16 cm, plastic, Bibliothèque Forney, Paris, inv. RES ICO 8108–1

Nail polish color chart, Rival, Paris, late 1940s, hinged fan, 10 × 11.5 cm, plastic, Bibliothèque Forney, Paris, inv. RES ICO 8108–2

PREVIOUS PAGE, BOTTOM

Cutex Nail Polish and Lipstick

Another American brand, Cutex, offered only a very subtle pale pink in the 1920s. It soon became emboldened and in the 1950s exported to the European market ranges of nail polishes that were much more extensive, combining them with lipsticks. They were accompanied by detailed instructions, evidence that for many women makeup was something new. For instance, women are advised to wait two minutes after applying lipstick ("above all do not wipe") and to apply nail polish at night "before going to bed." Lipstick was still packaged in cases that were activated by "pushing the stick with the head of a pin through the hole in the base." The names were only rarely translated from English, but, as with contemporary French makeup, they were related to the plant world or exotic locales. It should also be noted that there is already a shade called *Vintage* in nail polish.

Ex-cep-tion-al Hold Nail Polish, Stay-Fast Lipstick, Cutex, New York, early 1950s, card, 18 × 26 cm, Bibliothèque Forney, Paris, call number RES ICO 8108–1

Color Charts for New Markets

OPPOSITE, TOP

Viz Zande Lipstick

Viz Zande, another American company, specialized in the late 1940s in exporting cosmetics to Iran and the Arab world. Despite the presence of phrases in Persian evoking makeup "that gives your lips the freshness of flowers and the scent of hyacinth," these were products developed in the United States and exported as is, with the same saturated color range that was typical of Western lipsticks of the 1940s and 1950s. Easy to print and ship around the world, these color cards transmitted a Western aesthetic and began to participate in a standardization of the conception of female beauty.

Lipstick color chart, Viz Zande, New York, 1950s, card, 11 × 17.5 cm, Bibliothèque Forney, Paris, call number RES ICO 8108–2

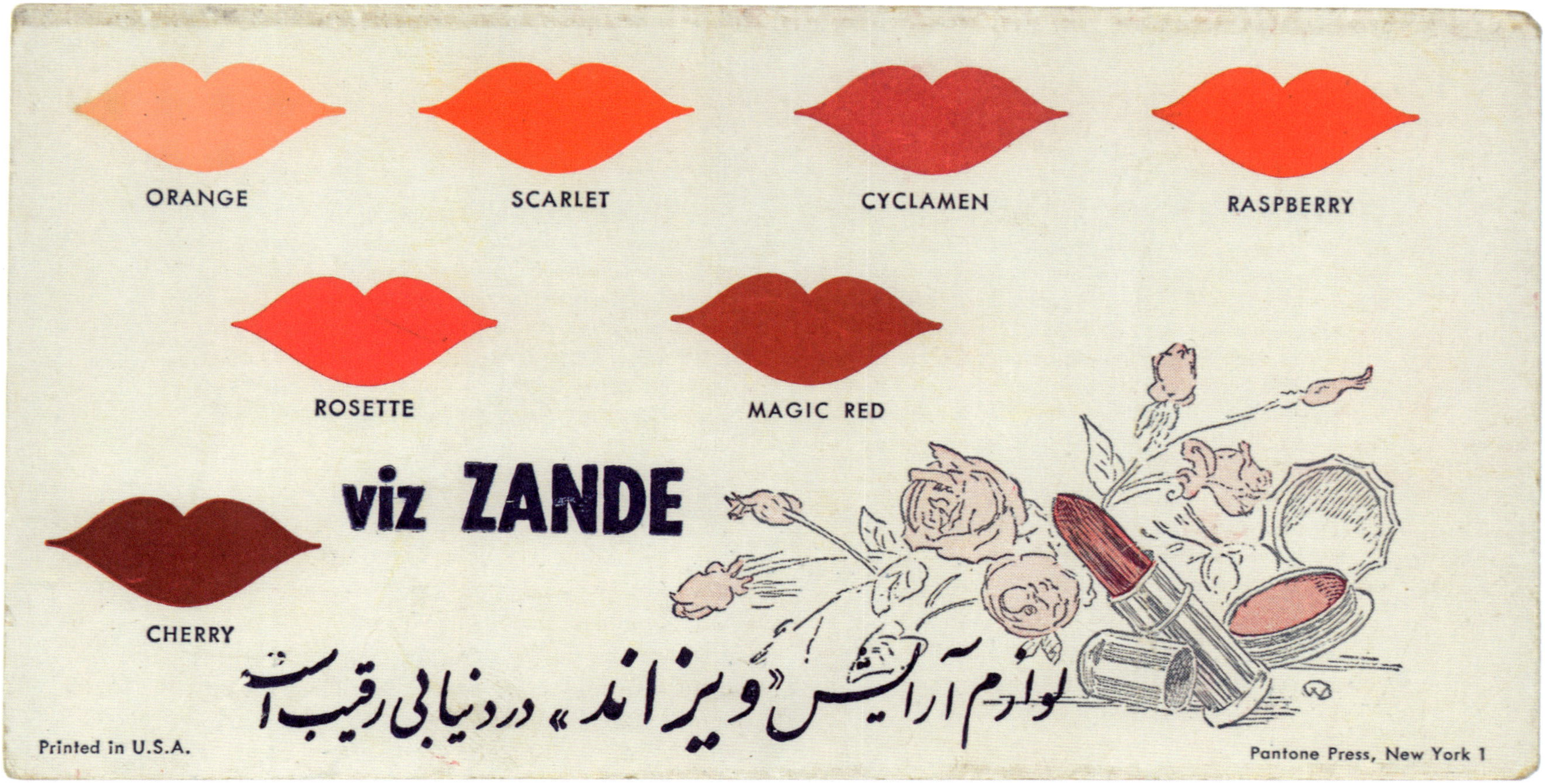

ORANGE
SCARLET
CYCLAMEN
RASPBERRY
ROSETTE
MAGIC RED
CHERRY

viz ZANDE

لوازم آرایش «ویزاند» در دنیا بی رقیب است

Printed in U.S.A.

Pantone Press, New York 1

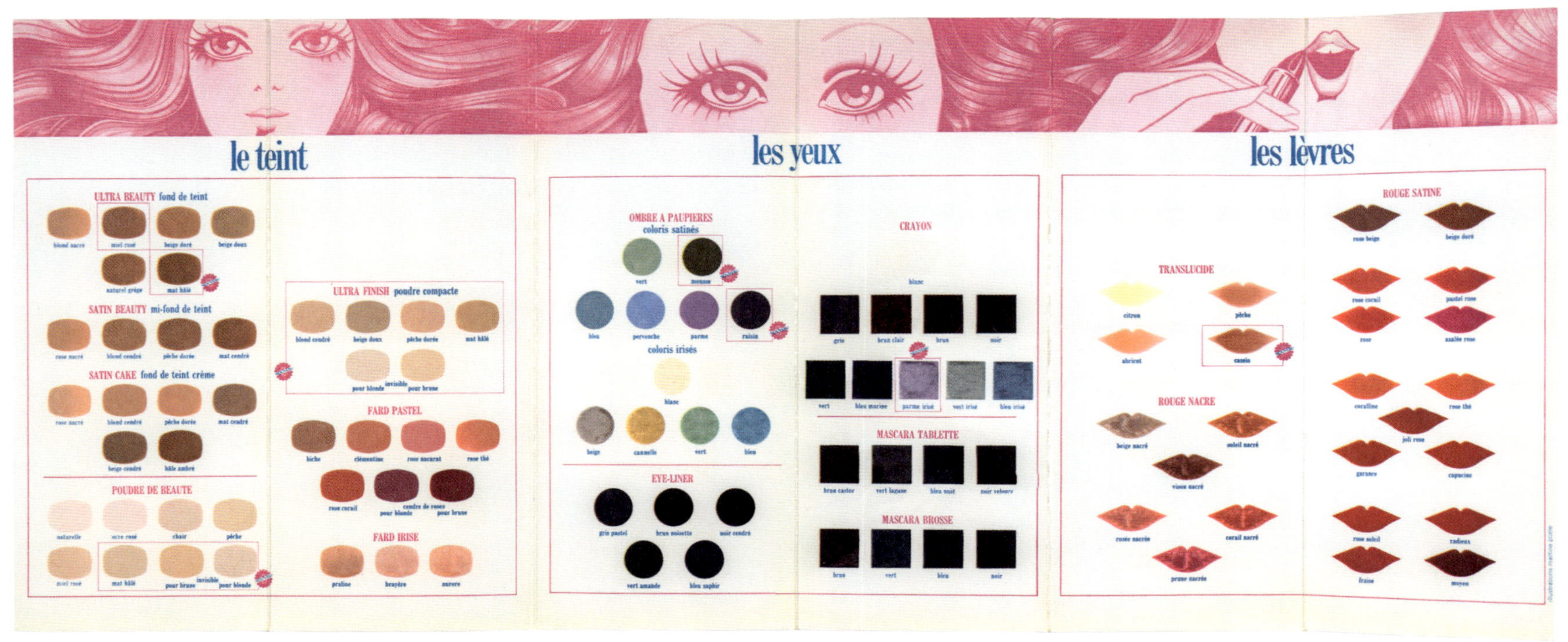

PREVIOUS PAGE, BOTTOM

Bourjois Makeup

With the "teenager" becoming a new marketing target in the 1950s, and with the demands for freedom that young people were expressing, many companies saw a new marketing opportunity. Bourjois offered this youthful market an extensive range of ninety-eight colors for makeup as soon as authorization was issued for girls to wear makeup in French high schools in 1968. Information guided them to a selection of face makeup that was suitable for their skin tone and hair color; combinations of foundations and powders were also recommended. The presence of dark foundation shades shows that companies were already aware that French society contained a variety of different skin colors.

Bourjois Makeup Color Chart, Bourjois, Paris, early 1970s, pamphlet, 24 × 10 cm, 5 folds, Patrimoine de Chanel collection, Paris

Finding Solutions to Abundance

OPPOSITE, LEFT

Pinaud Eye Makeup

By the 1960s, cosmetics firms had added so many new kinds of makeup that were available in such numerous shades that new presentation formats had to be developed. Pinaud, a company founded in Paris in 1830, used a binder to display the sixty-three colors of its eye cosmetics line, which included makeup for eyelids, eyelashes, and eyebrows. This color chart did not establish harmonies between the various types of makeup, but the samples were large enough to be easily perceived. Above all, it aroused desires for creativity that were in sync with the countercultural impulses of Western youth. Young women could color their eyebrows green, make up their eyelids with *Whisky* pink, and then add a stroke of gold or silver or draw a line of navy blue eyeliner.

Pinaud 612 Color Chart, Pinaud, Paris, early 1960s, binder, 21 × 12 cm, 8 pages, Bibliothèque Forney, Paris, call number RES ICO 8108–2

OPPOSITE, RIGHT

Gemey Cosmetics

For cosmetics companies, displaying all their colors was a complicated challenge. Gemey found a clever solution in the mid-1980s by featuring its fifteen makeup color ranges (or 120 shades) on a plastic disk, with colors for nails, skin, and lips on one side and those for the eyes on the other. The shades are still recognizable, but soon, as the profusion of colors required the sample size to be shrunk even further, it would no longer be possible to get an exact idea of the color.

Makeup Color Chart, Gemey, Paris, 1986, disk, 23 cm in diameter, plastic, Bibliothèque Forney, Paris, call number RES ICO 8108–2

——— From the 1950s to the 1980s, cosmetic manufacturers focused on the need to organize an exuberant abundance of products on a color chart. Obtaining formulas for reproductions that could express different textures for the samples was not a priority. The color of a pink loose powder is thus represented with exactly the same type of ink as a creamy coral eyeshadow: they have the same appearance. What would the role of the sample be from this point on?

——— Concluding a development that had begun after World War II, the goal of manufacturers using color charts had changed: it was now enough to give merely a cursory idea of the available color ranges, to offer harmonies, and to explain how to obtain them.

However, in color charts intended to provide a color standard, it was quite clear that the veracity of the samples had to be maintained.

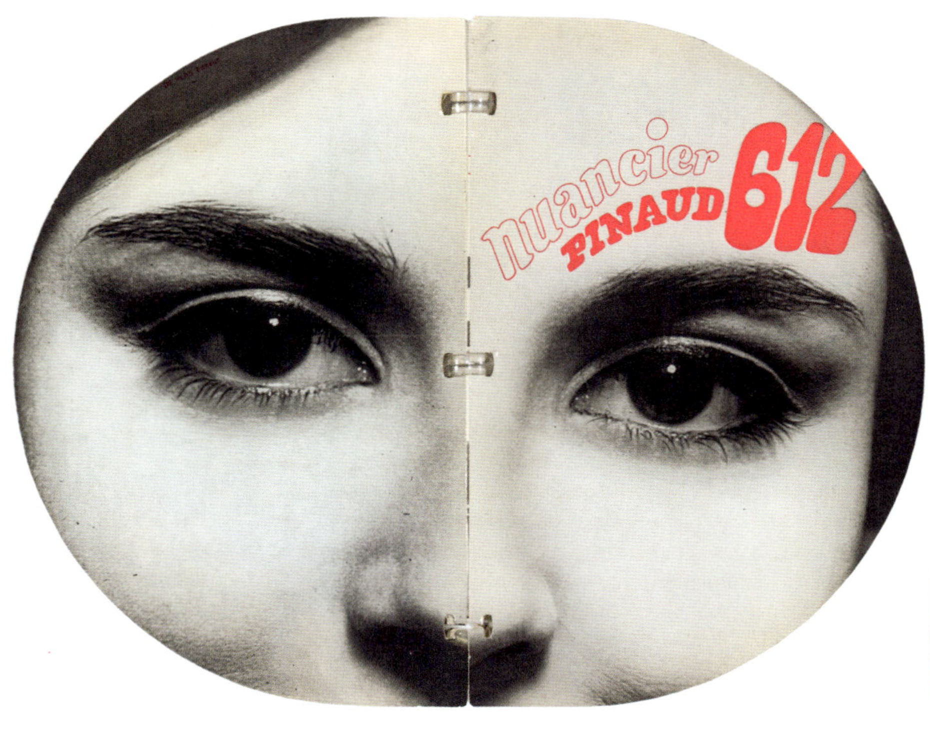

nuancier
PINAUD
612

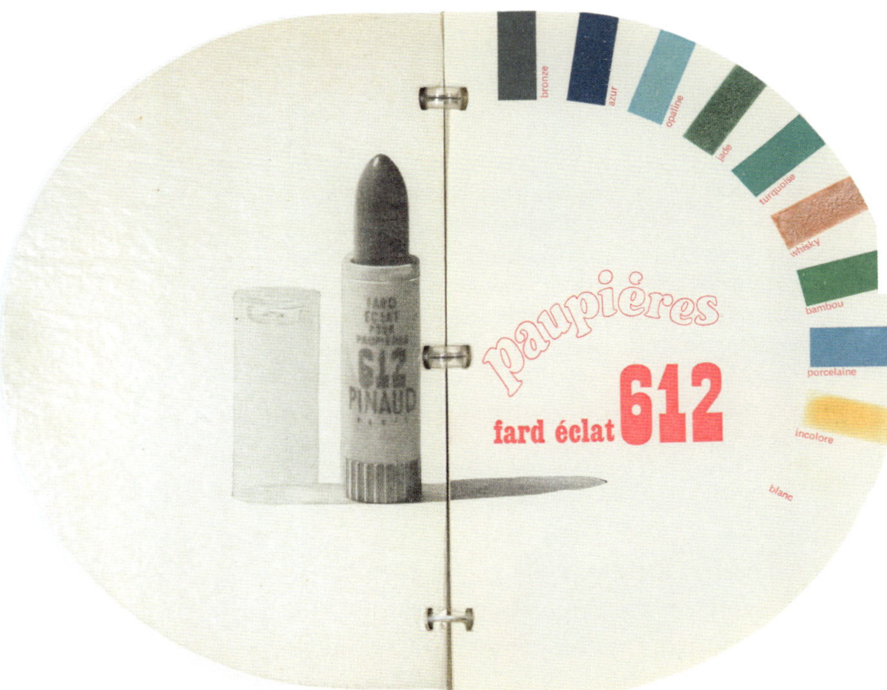

FARD
ÉCLAT
POUR
PAUPIÈRES
612
PINAUD
paupières
fard éclat 612
bronze
azur
opaline
jade
turquoise
whisky
bambou
porcelaine
incolore
blanc

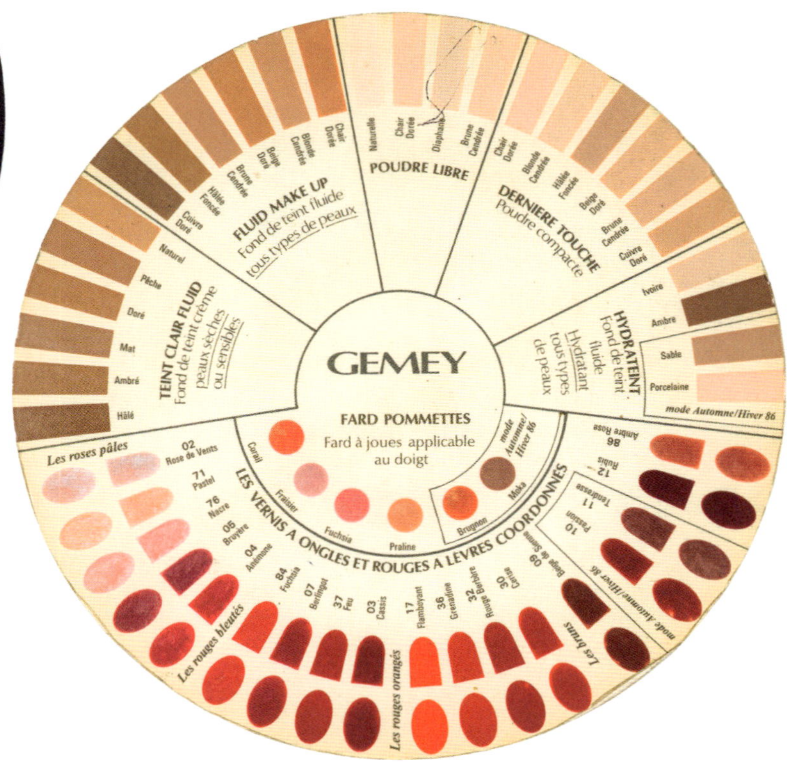

GEMEY
POUDRE LIBRE
FLUID MAKE UP
Fond de teint fluide
tous types de peaux
DERNIERE TOUCHE
Poudre compacte
TEINT CLAIR FLUID
Fond de teint crème
peaux sèches
ou sensibles
HYDRATEINT
Fond de teint
fluide
Hydratant
tous types
de peaux
Naturel
Pêche
Doré
Mat
Ambré
Hâlé
Ivoire
Ambre
Sable
Porcelaine
mode Automne/Hiver 86
FARD POMMETTES
Fard à joues applicable
au doigt
LES VERNIS A ONGLES ET ROUGES A LEVRES COORDONNES
Les roses pâles
Les rouges bleutés
Les rouges orangés
Les bruns

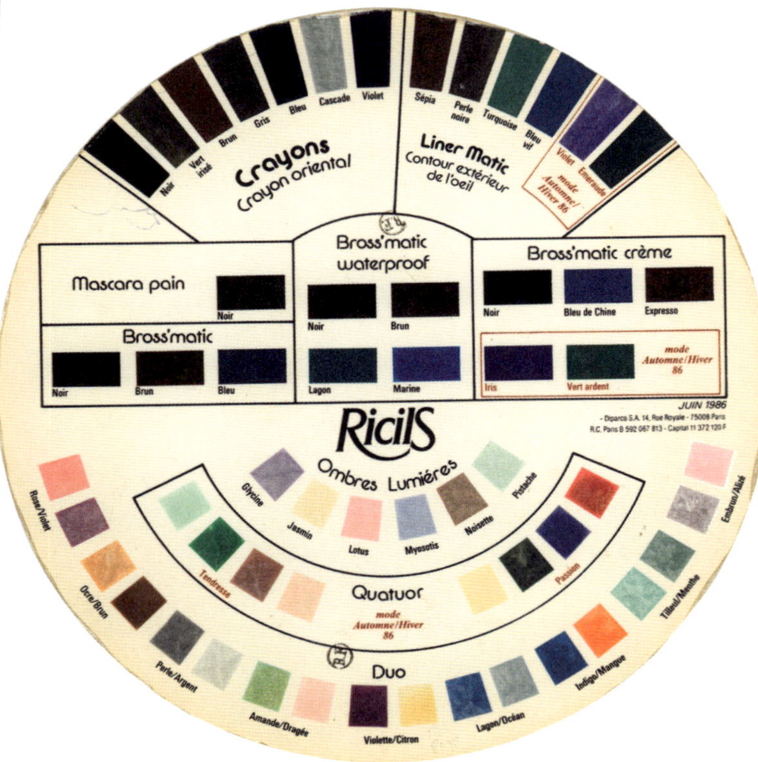

Noir
Vert irisé
Brun
Gris
Bleu
Cascade
Violet
Sépia
Perle noire
Turquoise
Bleu vif
Violet
Emeraude
Crayons
Crayon oriental
Liner Matic
Contour extérieur
de l'oeil
mode Automne/Hiver 86
Bross'matic waterproof
Bross'matic crème
Mascara pain
Noir
Bross'matic
Noir
Brun
Bleu
Noir
Brun
Lagon
Marine
Noir
Bleu de Chine
Expresso
Iris
Vert ardent
mode Automne/Hiver 86
JUIN 1986
Ricils
Ombres Lumières
Glycine
Jasmin
Lotus
Myosotis
Noisette
Pistache
Tendresse
Passion
Quatuor
mode Automne/Hiver 86
Duo
Rose/Violet
Ocre/Brun
Perle/Argent
Amande/Dragée
Violette/Citron
Lagon/Océan
Indigo/Mangue
Tilleul/Menthe
Embrun/Aloé

OPPOSITE, TOP LEFT

U.S. Military Colors

In the military world, standardization of colors had been imposed since the early twentieth century. Standardization guaranteed order and efficiency and, through the uniform, helped create the collective spirit necessary to the army.

Book of Colors of U.S. Munitions, P. Hautducoeur Printing, Paris, April 1954, fan, approximately 11 × 6 cm, Albi Couleurs, Association Mémoire des Industries de la Couleur, Albi

BELOW

Vitapan-System Tooth Colors

Standardization also allowed for rigorous definition of products where the slightest difference in color was significant. After World War II, synthetic resins and dyes were used to produce artificial teeth and bridges with subtle differences in shades so that they would match the natural teeth. In French, there is a specific term for a dentistry color chart, a *teintier*. As this was a sensitive subject, the samples were for a long time shaped like incisors (even if the tooth to be replaced could be a molar), although technically a rectangular sample would have sufficed.

Vitapan-System Tooth Color Chart, Vita Zahnfabrik, Säckingen, Germany, 1950s, plastic box, 5 × 15 cm, Anne Varichon collection, Sète, gift of Arnaud Cadenes

——— Standardization also played a major role in the food-processing industry and began to individualize the client as food products increased in number.

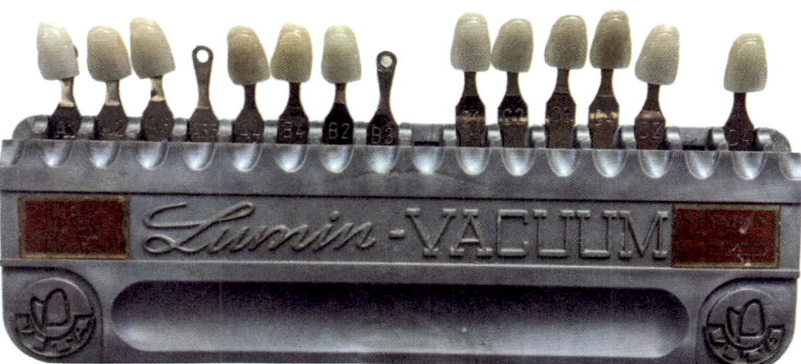

OPPOSITE, TOP RIGHT

Veal Identification

Color has always been a decisive factor for food (identifying ripe vegetables, detecting rotten grain, and so on). In the 1970s, color charts for categorizing the colors of foods multiplied, especially to organize the picking of fruit. The color chart above responded to the Confédération de la Viande's need to provide its wholesalers with a tool for identifying veal that had been milk-fed, fed milk and grass, or fed only grass, and to detect any possible fraud (as the price of milk-fed veal was higher than that of other veal). Chemist Jacques Roire used plastisols to give this color chart not only the required colors but also an appearance similar to that of meat in terms of its size, sheen, irregular surface, and cool, smooth feel.

Color chart to describe veal, produced by Jacques Roire for EREC, illustration from the article "Le jugement de la couleur de veau" ["Judging the Color of Veal"], *Couleurs*, no. 100, 3rd quarter 1978, Albi Couleurs, Association Mémoire des Industries de la Couleur, Albi

OPPOSITE, BOTTOM

Stockings Card

By the 1960s, manufacturers' efforts to anticipate their clients' needs generated tools designed to determine exactly which color worked best, like this card that let users identify how tan their legs were, with the recommended shades for stockings listed on the back. The company also recommended keeping the card: "It will be useful to you again two or three months from now when your tan has faded." The color chart for products for the body also incorporated marketing strategies.

Tanning Card for Stockings, Bel, France, 1960s, card, 10 × 15 cm, Bibliothèque Forney, Paris, call number RES ICO 8108-1

——— The color charts of the Trente Glorieuses period highlight the fact that these were not simply samples; the perception of color itself was being transformed. Reproductions reduced the tangible aspect of color; the lexicon became impoverished; and standardization diminished the variety of shades. Sensory experience, poetry, and variety were gradually disappearing from consumers' relationship to color. ●

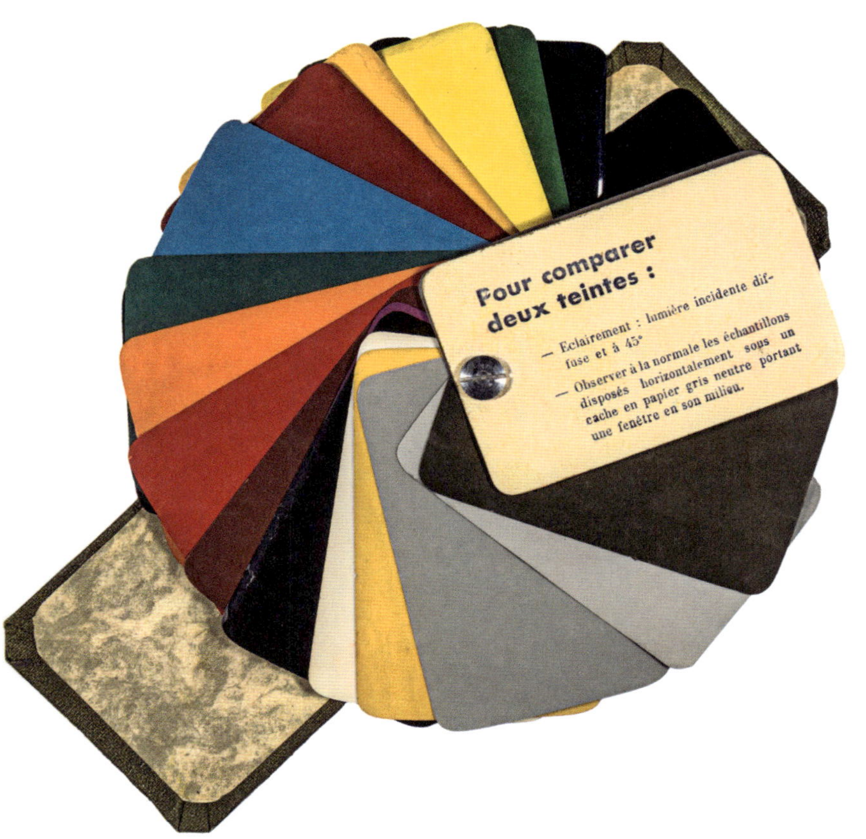
Pour comparer deux teintes :
— Eclairement : lumière incidente diffuse et à 45°
— Observer à la normale les échantillons disposés horizontalement sous un cache en papier gris neutre portant une fenêtre en son milieu.

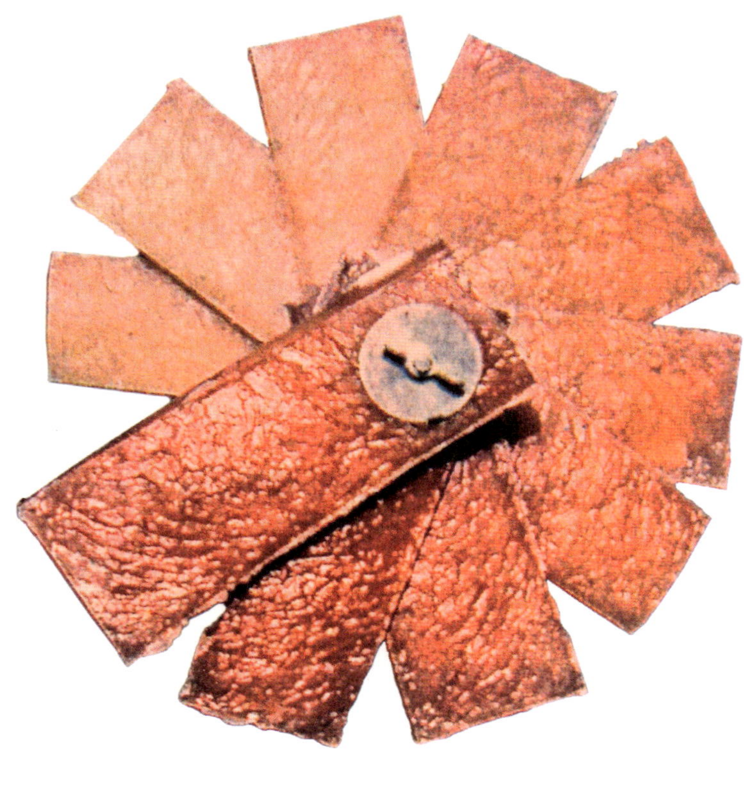

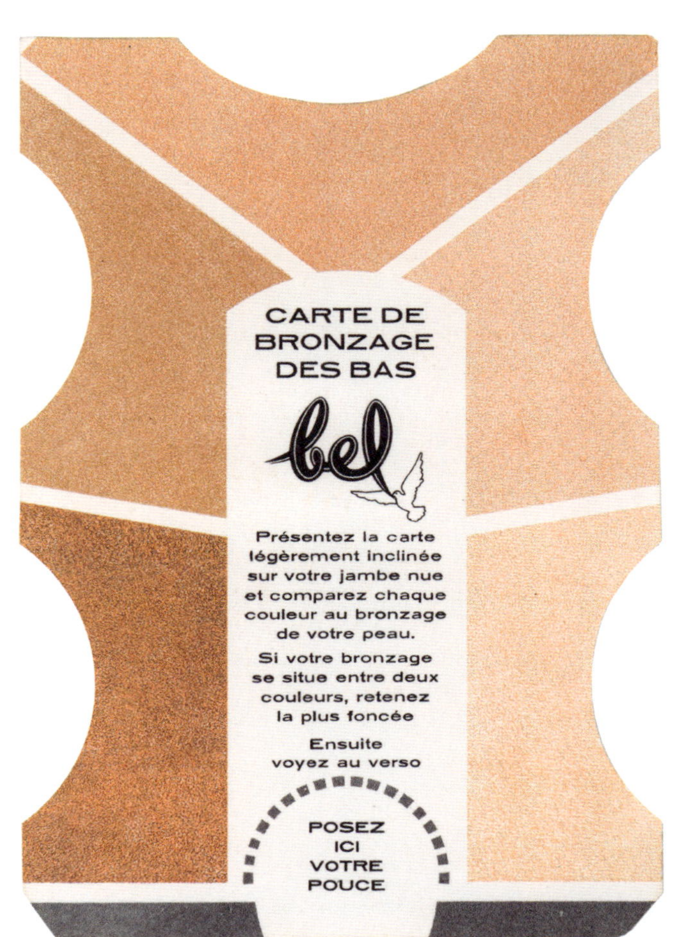
CARTE DE BRONZAGE DES BAS
bel
Présentez la carte légèrement inclinée sur votre jambe nue et comparez chaque couleur au bronzage de votre peau.
Si votre bronzage se situe entre deux couleurs, retenez la plus foncée
Ensuite voyez au verso
POSEZ ICI VOTRE POUCE

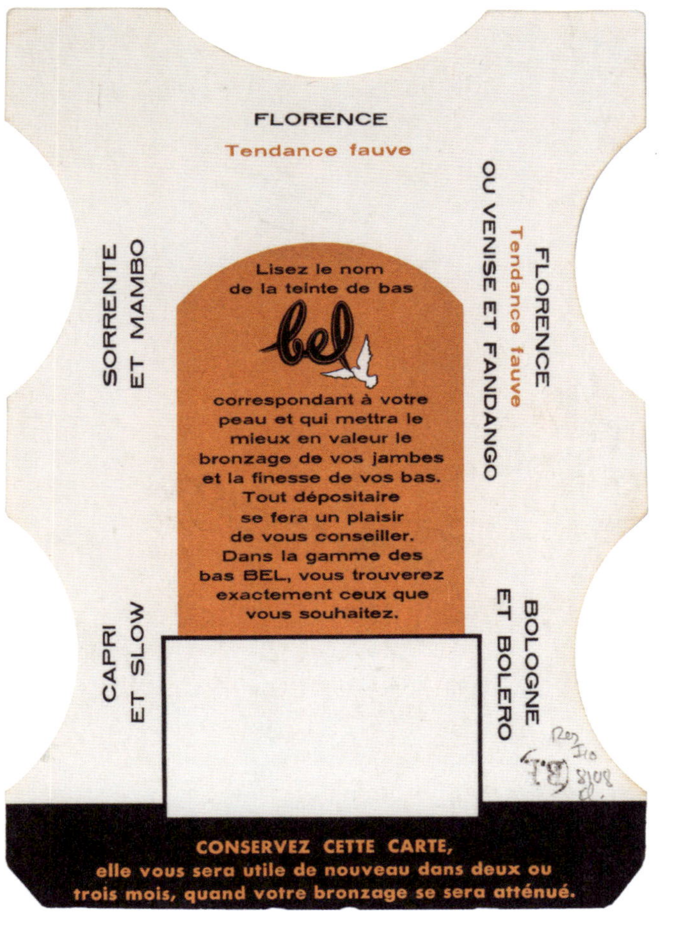
FLORENCE
Tendance fauve
FLORENCE
Tendance fauve
OU VENISE ET FANDANGO
SORRENTE ET MAMBO
Lisez le nom de la teinte de bas
bel
correspondant à votre peau et qui mettra le mieux en valeur le bronzage de vos jambes et la finesse de vos bas. Tout dépositaire se fera un plaisir de vous conseiller. Dans la gamme des bas BEL, vous trouverez exactement ceux que vous souhaitez.
CAPRI ET SLOW
BOLOGNE ET BOLERO
CONSERVEZ CETTE CARTE,
elle vous sera utile de nouveau dans deux ou trois mois, quand votre bronzage se sera atténué.

280

THE COLOR CHART

MULTITUDE, ICON, IDOL, 1990s TO THE PRESENT

—————— By the late 1980s, the color chart, solidly established in the individual and collective imagination, had become the symbol of the very chromatic euphoria that it had helped to create. Everything was in place for it to permeate an expanding world: a profusion of consumer products that were available in many colors, as exponentially reflected in printed color charts.

ORDINARY AND EXTRAORDINARY COLOR CHARTS

—————— From its origins, color sampling had given rise to different but simultaneous tools, and this coexistence continues today.

The proliferation of color charts that had begun in the 1960s increased and, starting in the 1990s, most items put on the market were accompanied by charts of their available colors, which were circulated in large numbers in the press or as flyers made available to customers. Of course, a code or a name individualized the samples and clever graphic design attempted to compensate for their deficiencies in terms of the reproduction of the colors (matte-printed samples simulating reflectiveness to evoke shiny paint, for example). Advice on the selection and use of products, suggestions for colorful decor, or storytelling strategies could also support these inadequate color charts. But it was no longer really about the colors, and the poor quality reduced these marketing tools to a single function: showing a glimpse of the color choices for a given product. This situation, in which it is in fact impossible to make an informed choice, nevertheless became common.

However, color sampling was not entirely diminished. Exact colors represented by product samples continued in color sample books for fabrics where texture was important and that were designed for long use and were costly: upholstery, wall coverings, carpeting, and such. When it was a question of changing the color of one's hair, the specificity of shades and the tactile nature of the sample were necessities. Until recently, color charts for hair color featured strands of synthetic hair dyed the specific shade.[1]

Some companies stand out from the competition with color charts best described as aristocratic. The sample shows the end product (for instance, a color chart of cashmere yarns, or applications of paint for high-end paint brands), and the backing, the finishes, and the design of the samples show great care. The sampling of the colors is exact and reveals aspects

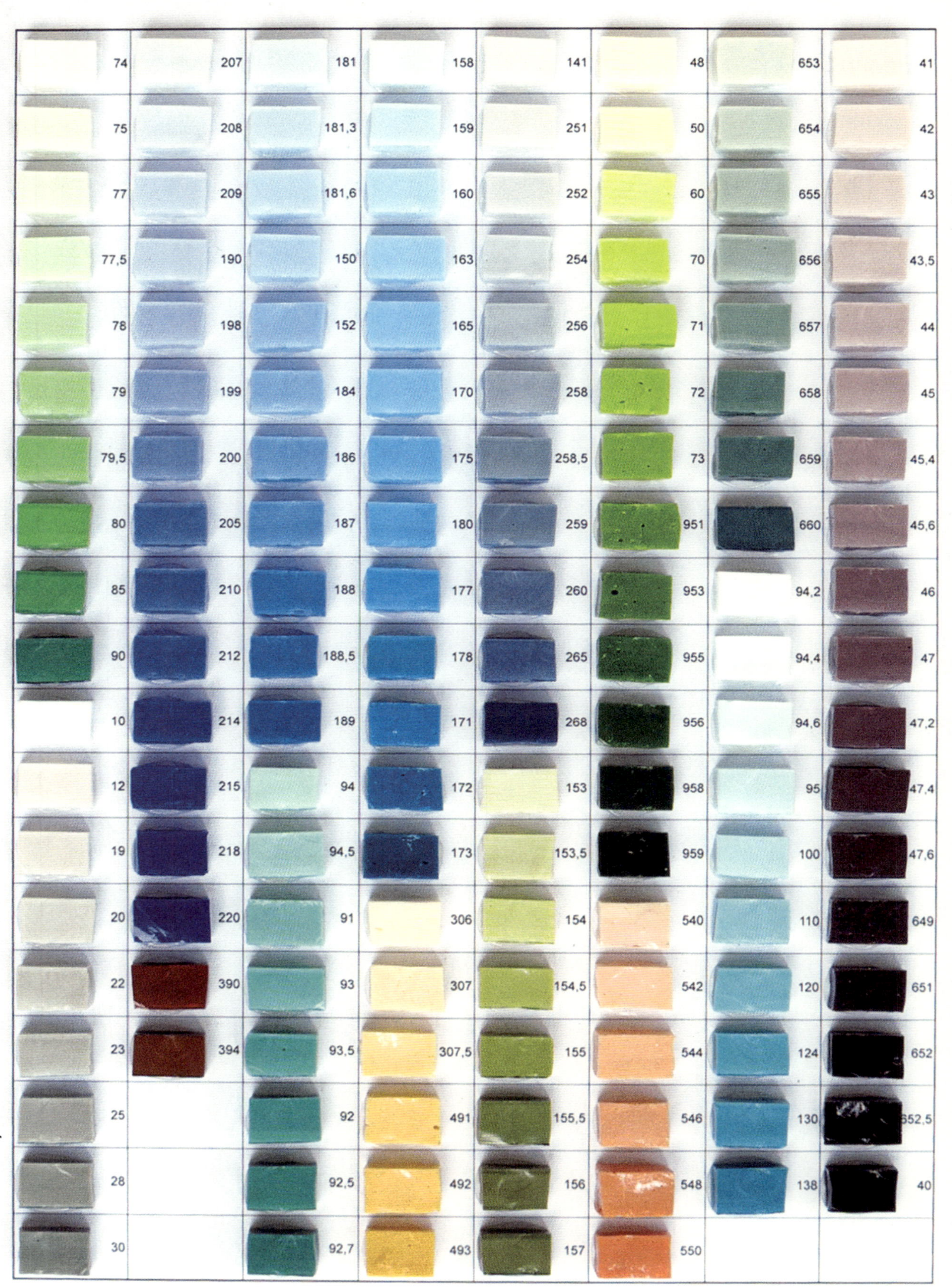

MOSAICI DONA' MURANO

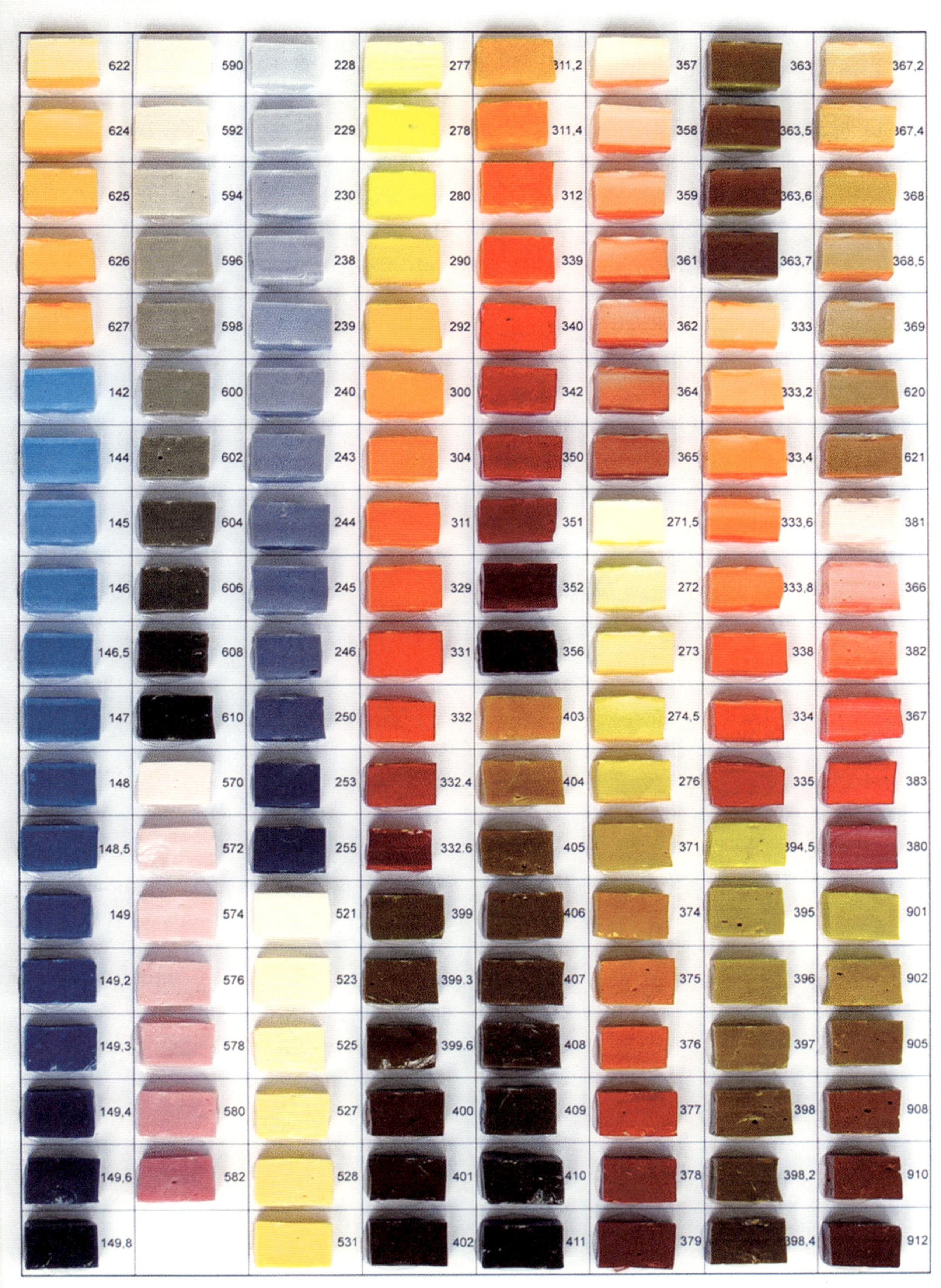

MOSAICI DONA' MURANO

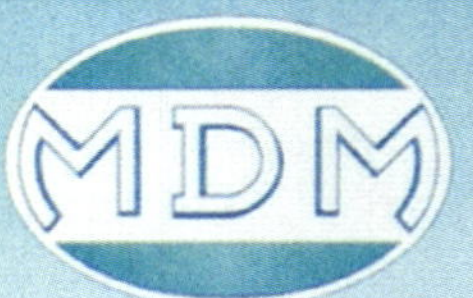

- Glass Factory -

MOSAICI DONA' MURANO

di Donà Stefano

- Produzione smalti ed ori per mosaici
- Produzione vetri trasparenti
- Composizione musiva artistica
- Smalti filati
- Attrezzature per mosaicisti
- Millefiori e filigrana
- Oggettistica in micromosaico

48 ORI

LISCIO Fondo verde 5 mm		ONDULATO Fondo verde 5 mm		ANTICO Fondo verde 6 mm	
1	Bianco	26	Bianco	19	Bianco
1.5	Limone chiaro 1	26.5	Limone chiaro 1	19.5	Limone chiaro 1
2	Limone chiaro 2	27	Limone chiaro 2	20	Limone chiaro 2
2.5	Limone chiaro 3	27.5	Limone chiaro 3	20.5	Limone chiaro 3
3	Limone medio 1	28	Limone medio 1	21	Limone medio 1
3.3	Limone medio 2	28.3	Limone medio 2	21.3	Limone medio 2
3.6	Limone medio 3	28.6	Limone medio 3	21.6	Limone medio 3
4	Limone scuro 1	29	Limone scuro 1	22	Limone scuro 1
4.3	Limone scuro 2	29.3	Limone scuro 2	22.3	Limone scuro 2
5	Naturale	30	Naturale	23	Naturale
6	Gaggia chiaro	30.1	Gaggia chiaro	24	Gaggia chiaro
7	Gaggia scuro	30.3	Gaggia scuro	25	Gaggia scuro
8	Ramino chiaro 2	30.5	Ramino chiaro 2	25.5	Ramino chiaro 2
9	Ramino scuro 1	30.7	Ramino scuro 1	25.7	Ramino scuro 1

LISCIO Fondo cristallo 5 mm	
10	Bianco
11	Naturale

ONDULATO Fondo cristallo 5 mm	
31	Bianco
32	Naturale

DOPPIO cristallo 10 mm	
33	Bianco
34	Naturale

www. mosaicidonamurano.com

MOSAICI DONA' MURANO

of the surface, so that distinctions can be made. For these companies, the quality and beauty of the color chart reflect those of their products themselves. They thus reactivate the role of color as a social marker, with only the elite having access to certain colors.

PREVIOUS PAGE SPREAD AND OPPOSITE

Glass mosaics, Mosaici Dona' Murano, Murano, Italy, 2014, 3 boards, 32 x 23 cm, Anne Varichon collection, Sète. Copyright © Philippe Durand Gerzaguet

A WIDE RANGE OF CHOICES

The market ideal of Choice by an autonomous Self seems to act as a kind of narcotic that makes the displacing of embodied agency go smoothly, or precludes the development of such agency by providing easier satisfactions.
Matthew B. Crawford, *Shop Class as Soulcraft*, 2009

——— When the color chart no longer presents a product sample, when its samples are too small or too poorly reproduced to express color precisely, it is reduced to an image, that of an abundant selection, although it does not become an inert figure.

Indeed, color charts continue to reveal aspects of our societies. For instance, when cosmetics companies include colors formulated for dark skin in their range of foundations, they confirm the existence of a variety of human characteristics. Additionally, for the women whose skin tones are represented in these color charts, the range indicates that they are finally taken into consideration. Here the important aspect is not to perceive a color, but to observe that one of the available colors is right for us, that we have our place in the world just as the color of our skin has its place in the color chart.

The color chart thus becomes a space where, through choice, everyone can affirm their identity. In the moment preceding the selection of a certain item or a certain color for a particular surface, the vaster the range, the more intense the excitement. The color chart leads to a purchase, and thus satisfies our desire. But once the moment of choosing has passed, the color chart maintains its wholeness. It offers the possibility of continuing to look at all the colors, to keep on envisioning every possibility. The color chart reconciles reality and fantasy.

Since the 2000s, the attraction of this powerful combination of "satisfied urge/continued desire" has been strengthened through digital tools and the widespread use of color charts on screens. The circulation of images has become intense and results in multiple aesthetics that intersect and overlap. The hybridization of color preferences generated by globalization has shaken up preexisting codes. It is now necessary to offer colors that can appeal to various cultures. The stakes are even higher as consumer needs reach their limit in households that are already well furnished and equipped: color is invoked even more often to create a desire and lead to a nonessential purchase. In e-commerce, the color chart is now associated with the mind-boggling speed and the ubiquity of smartphones, as consumers scroll through seemingly endless combinations of models, materials, and colors. It leads to the narcissistic delights of complete power and custom-made solutions. These pleasures can be so thrilling that they make the acquisition of the colored object superfluous. It does not matter then whether the color characteristics are displayed exactly or imprecisely—the color chart responds only to the single desire of defining oneself, signifying oneself by clicking on one of a myriad of colors. The color chart becomes a mirror in which we can all contemplate our own image ad infinitum.

The paint-mixing machines at big-box hardware stores may be representative in this regard. They allow individuals to use color charts to produce paint in the desired shade, but the approach turns into a kind of ritual. Customers are flooded with opportunities:

the digital color chart with its branching paths leading to formulations for floor/iron/wood, qualities of matte/satin/brilliant, color ranges that are hot/cold, various atmospheres and harmonies, and so on. Faced with each set of choices, consumers must take a position, affirming their desires. They are thus led to believe that they have manufactured "their" color. In fact, they have merely circulated in a maze of overlaid color charts of standardized products.

In a few decades, the color chart evolved from a tool for a limited industrial selection into the sign of an overabundant supply, where an individual can satisfy a desire: a color chart that guides you. It has now become a strategy where everything is arranged so that the item will correspond perfectly and intimately to your unique desire as an individual: a color chart that belongs to you.

IN THE 2000S, THE COLOR CHART MOVES FROM ICON TO IDOL

——— The color chart has gradually been emptied of the substance that created it; the form has devoured the content. But because it carries meaning that goes far beyond the exemplification of color, a function that has ultimately become secondary, it can now fully express its properties as a symbol.[2] Free of the dust of the workshops, exempt from its function as a tool, but maintaining its evocative power, the color chart can become a stereotype, an icon, or even an idol.

When we look at advertising campaigns since the 2000s, the slippage from the color chart's function as a tool to its role as an icon clearly appears: decorative paint brands thus display the color chart as a work of art, framed like a painting or highlighted on a piece of furniture, like a valuable sculpture.[3]

OPPOSITE

Arrangement of bottles of rosé wines in a color chart, Vidauban, 2009 © Fourmy/Andia

Mamie Nova advertising campaign, 2012 © Grandma Nova

It can also be used to signify the richness of the aromas of a wine-growing region or a coffee brand. In this type of visual, the information that is specific to the color chart is wiped out, as it would be in a blurry image: we recognize the form, and it is possible to connect it to functions, but its use turns out to be illusory. It is simply no longer made to be used.

When the color chart functions simply as a symbol of order, harmony, and abundance, it can be used in campaigns that no longer have any direct relationship to color, to promote travel or financial products, for instance.[4]

A bank uses an image of a color chart to encourage consumers to take out a car loan or purchase auto insurance; the message is: the institution will spare us the tedious part (the paperwork) and leave us only the pleasure (the selection, represented here by a color chart).

It is indeed because the image of the color chart now refers to something other than color, that society can appropriate it and play with it in different fields. The image of the color chart had to become a stereotype in order for LICRA (Ligue Internationale Contre le Racisme et l'Antisémitisme) to use it to illustrate the struggle against discrimination based on skin color.

It even appears that the color chart can produce a kind of worship, like the worship of an idol. This seems to be the case with the rise of collections of color charts or objects derived from them, like those made by Pantone: it becomes possible to possess a color accompanied by its exact reference, to collect samples of certainty.[5] Wild color, domesticated in the eighteenth century, and then conquered down to its most intimate particles after the mid-nineteenth century, can now be the property of anyone, in a little individual cage.

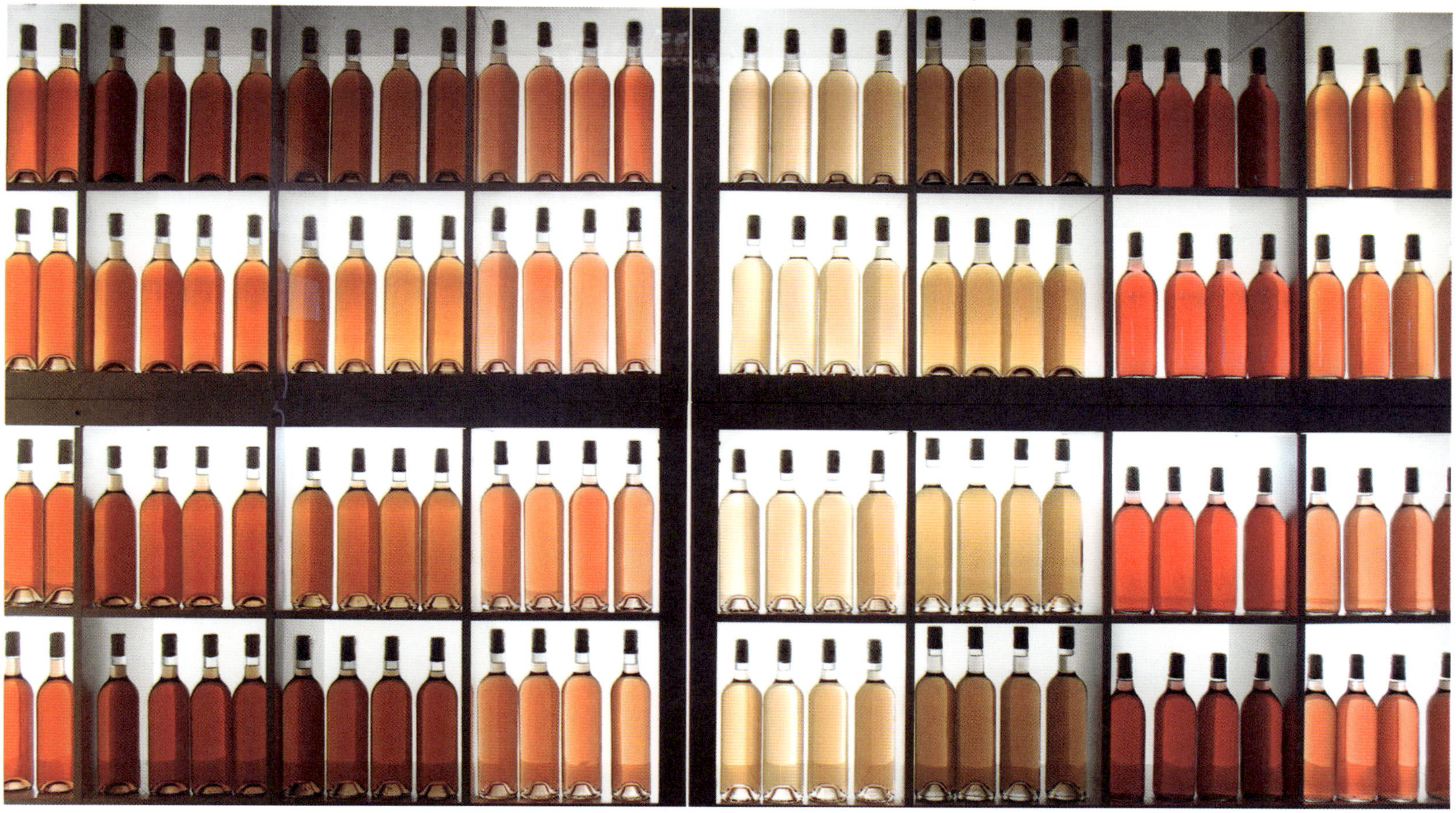

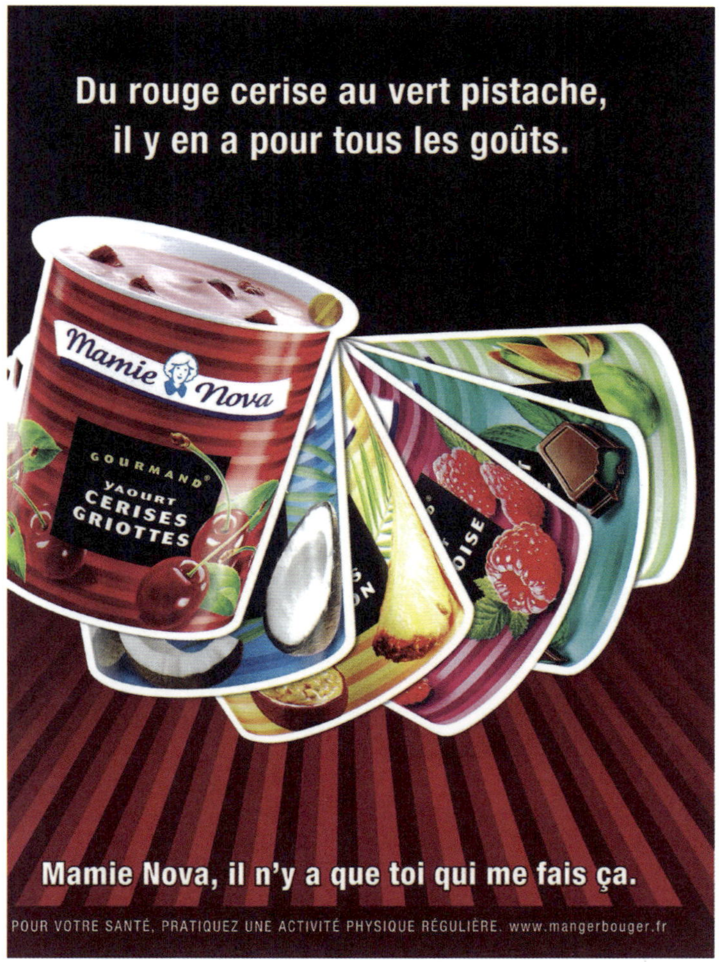
Du rouge cerise au vert pistache,
il y en a pour tous les goûts.
Mamie Nova
GOURMAND
YAOURT
CERISES
GRIOTTES
Mamie Nova, il n'y a que toi qui me fais ça.
POUR VOTRE SANTÉ, PRATIQUEZ UNE ACTIVITÉ PHYSIQUE RÉGULIÈRE. www.mangerbouger.fr

This movement of idolatry is regularly played with, often with a great deal of humor, by graphic designers or illustrators. Such items include a fan color chart of the official outfits of the Queen of England[6] and the girls drawn by Soledad who use color charts to evaluate their tans.[7] The color chart has also inspired designers to create many elegant or dazzling items.

OPPOSITE

Color chart of German Chancellor Angela Merkel's outfits, 2012, Noortje van Eekelen © Noortje van Eekelen

COLOR CHARTS AND ARTISTS

For a long time now, the omnipresence of the color chart in daily life and its roots and ramifications in the imagination have produced many artistic interpretations.[8]

As early as the 1880s, as part of the "Exhibition for People Who Cannot Draw," Alphonse Allais, a member of the group Arts Incohérents, showed single-color samples that had titles such as "First Communion of Chlorotic Young Girls in the Snow." Since then, many artists have used the color chart (Herman de Vries, Simon Hantaï, Kôichi Kurita, and others) to reflect on the world or to explore transformations that deeply affect societies today. One very interesting example is the work of Pierre David in the exhibition *Nuancier* (Color Chart) at the Museu de Arte Moderna, in Salvador da Bahia, Brazil, from 2008 to 2009.[9]

The artist photographed the skin of the backs of forty employees at the museum and developed a fan color chart of the shades. Then, with the help of Sikkens/AkzoNobel, a manufacturer of industrial paints, he formulated paints corresponding to these shades, put them into cans, and used them to paint the rooms of the museum. When the color chart is used to emphasize how much the human and the living in general can be absorbed and wiped out in efforts of classification, which are always suspect, we can conclude that the color chart has not entirely lost its raison d'être.

BELOW

Nuancier, Pierre David, exhibition at the Museu de Arte Moderna da Bahia, Brazil, 2009

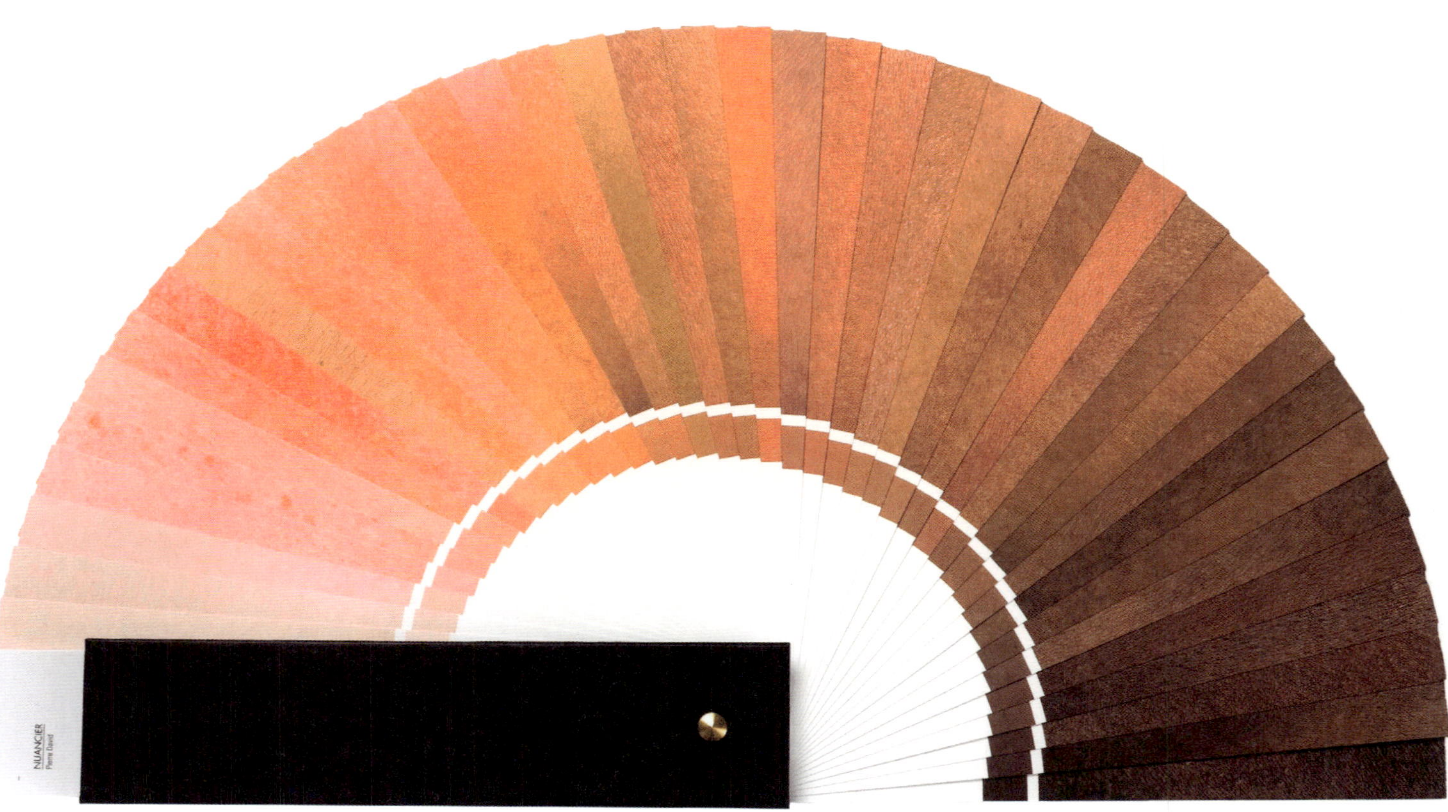

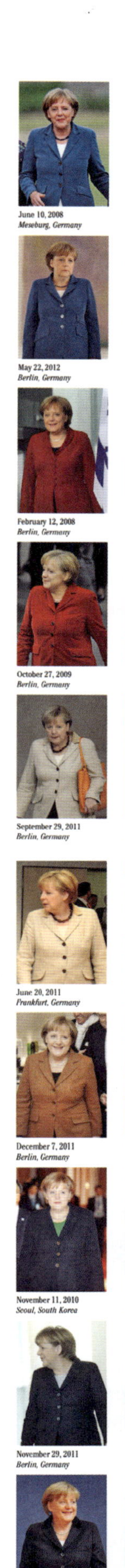
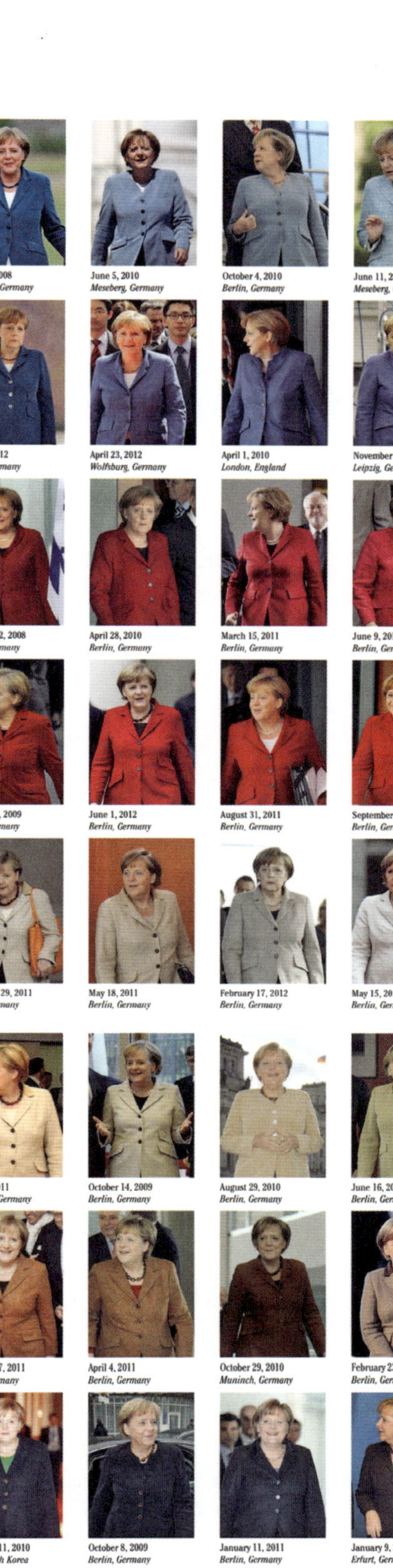
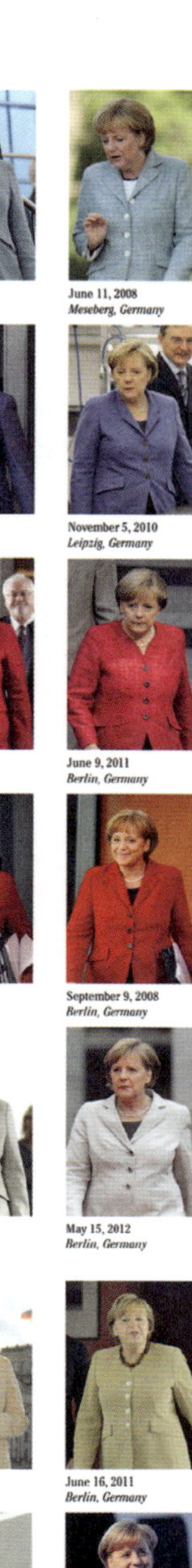
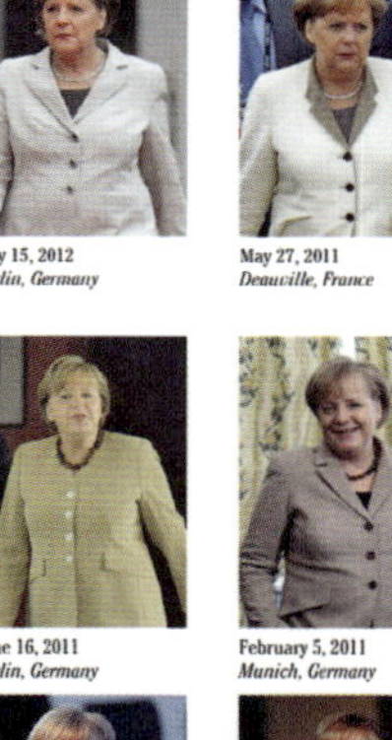
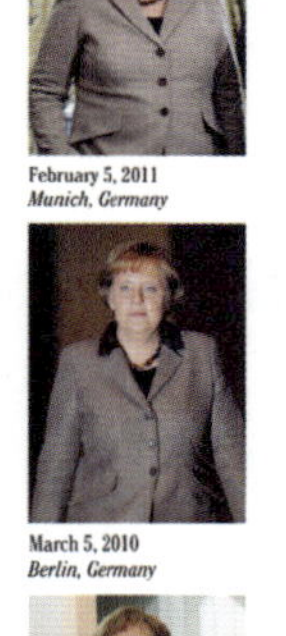
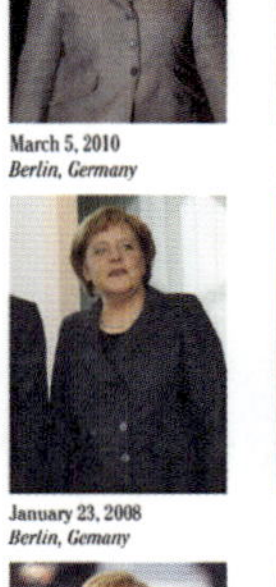
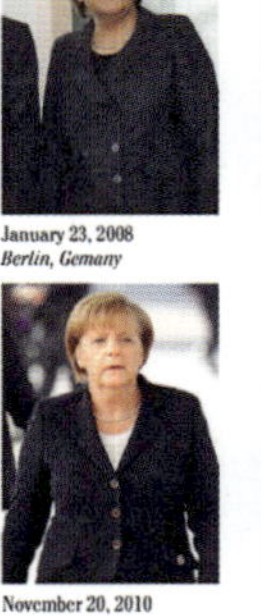
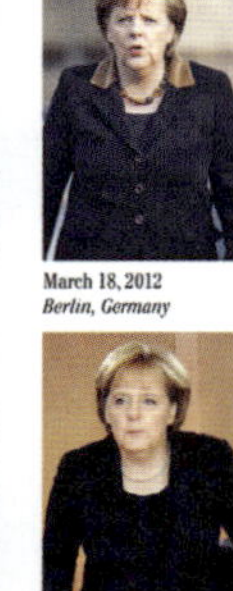
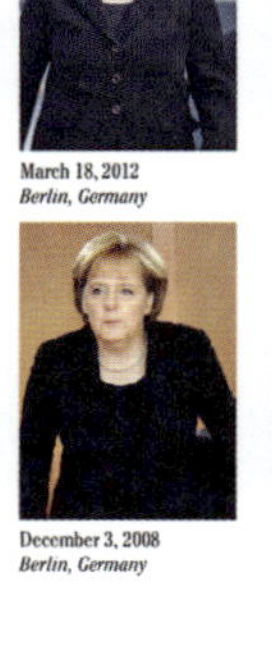
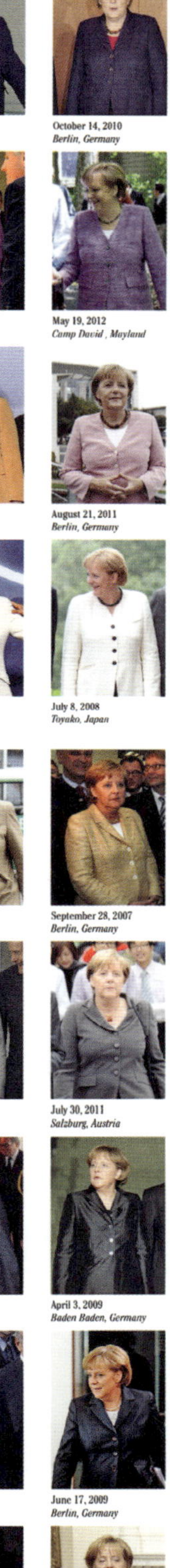
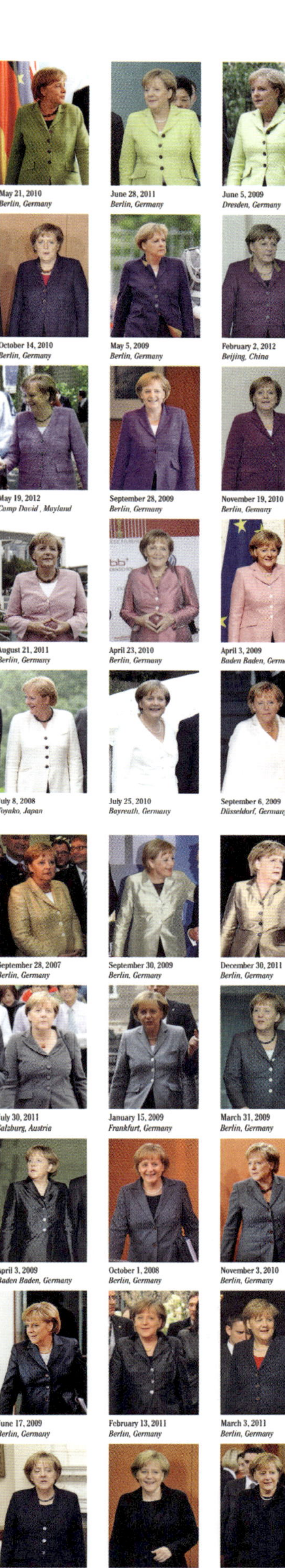
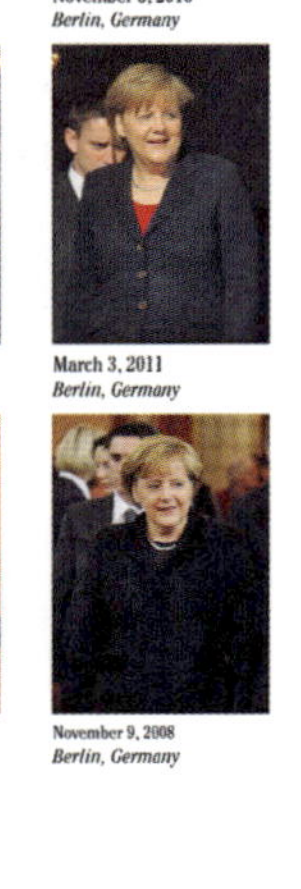

June 10, 2008 *Meseburg, Germany*
June 5, 2010 *Meseberg, Germany*
October 4, 2010 *Berlin, Germany*
June 11, 2008 *Meseberg, Germany*
July 24, 2008 *Berlin, Germany*
August 25, 2010 *Berlin, Germany*
August 26, 2009 *Berlin, Germany*
May 21, 2010 *Berlin, Germany*
June 28, 2011 *Berlin, Germany*
June 5, 2009 *Dresden, Germany*

May 22, 2012 *Berlin, Germany*
April 23, 2012 *Wolfsburg, Germany*
April 1, 2010 *London, England*
November 5, 2010 *Leipzig, Germany*
July 8, 2009 *l'Aquila, Italy*
January 9, 2012 *Berlin, Germany*
July 15, 2008 *Berlin, Germany*
October 14, 2010 *Berlin, Germany*
May 5, 2009 *Berlin, Germany*
February 2, 2012 *Beijing, China*

February 12, 2008 *Berlin, Germany*
April 28, 2010 *Berlin, Germany*
March 15, 2011 *Berlin, Germany*
June 9, 2011 *Berlin, Germany*
July 25, 2011 *Bayreuth, Germany*
February 9, 2009 *Berlin, Germany*
June 25, 2009 *Washington, DC*
May 19, 2012 *Camp David , Mayland*
September 28, 2009 *Berlin, Germany*
November 19, 2010 *Berlin, Gemany*

October 27, 2009 *Berlin, Germany*
June 1, 2012 *Berlin, Germany*
August 31, 2011 *Berlin, Germany*
September 9, 2008 *Berlin, Germany*
June 17, 2011 *Berlin, Germany*
July 18, 2008 *Nuremberg, Germany*
May 20, 2012 *Chicago, Illinois*
August 21, 2011 *Berlin, Germany*
April 23, 2010 *Berlin, Germany*
April 3, 2009 *Baden Baden, Germany*

September 29, 2011 *Berlin, Germany*
May 18, 2011 *Berlin, Germany*
February 17, 2012 *Berlin, Germany*
May 15, 2012 *Berlin, Germany*
May 27, 2011 *Deauville, France*
September 27, 2011 *Berlin, Germany*
April 12, 2010 *Washington, DC*
July 8, 2008 *Toyako, Japan*
July 25, 2010 *Bayreuth, Germany*
September 6, 2009 *Düsseldorf, Germany*

June 20, 2011 *Frankfurt, Germany*
October 14, 2009 *Berlin, Germany*
August 29, 2010 *Berlin, Germany*
June 16, 2011 *Berlin, Germany*
February 5, 2011 *Munich, Germany*
April 23, 2009 *Berlin, Germany*
October 22, 2009 *Berlin, Germany*
September 28, 2007 *Berlin, Germany*
September 30, 2009 *Berlin, Germany*
December 30, 2011 *Berlin, Germany*

December 7, 2011 *Berlin, Germany*
April 4, 2011 *Berlin, Germany*
October 29, 2010 *Muninch, Germany*
February 23, 2011 *Berlin, Germany*
March 5, 2010 *Berlin, Germany*
September 22, 2010 *Berlin, Germany*
July 4, 2008 *Berlin, Germany*
July 30, 2011 *Salzburg, Austria*
January 15, 2009 *Frankfurt, Germany*
March 31, 2009 *Berlin, Germany*

November 11, 2010 *Seoul, South Korea*
October 8, 2009 *Berlin, Germany*
January 11, 2011 *Berlin, Germany*
January 9, 2009 *Erfurt, Germany*
January 23, 2008 *Berlin, Gemany*
June 1, 2008 *Berlin, Germany*
November 2, 2010 *Brussels, Belgium*
April 3, 2009 *Baden Baden, Germany*
October 1, 2008 *Berlin, Germany*
November 3, 2010 *Berlin, Germany*

November 29, 2011 *Berlin, Germany*
September 7, 2011 *Berlin, Germany*
June 12, 2010 *Sassnitz, Germany*
November 18, 2011 *Berlin, Germany*
November 20, 2010 *Lisbon, Portugal*
March 18, 2012 *Berlin, Germany*
March 16, 2008 *Ben Gurion, Israel*
June 17, 2009 *Berlin, Germany*
February 13, 2011 *Berlin, Germany*
March 3, 2011 *Berlin, Germany*

November 14, 2011 *Leipzig, Germany*
October 9, 2008 *Berlin, Germany*
October 13, 2008 *Berlin, Germany*
December 5, 2011 *Paris, France*
January 5, 2009 *Berlin, Germany*
December 3, 2008 *Berlin, Germany*
February 23, 2012 *Berlin, Germany*
October 30, 2008 *London, England*
November 17, 2008 *Berlin, Germany*
November 9, 2008 *Berlin, Germany*

ELEGY OR EPILOGUE?

——— The end of the twentieth century has confirmed the disappearance of glorious color sampling. The color chart is perhaps envisioned now only as a measureless field of opportunities. It was always this, by its very essence. But it did not always give a mere glimpse of possible color abundance; it once embodied this abundance.

Our relationship to color has profoundly changed since the 1950s, when industrial production began to take charge of, monopolize, and conceal its manufacturing materials and processes. Purchasing color has been depersonalized, the experience of its sensory nature has become standardized, and its uniqueness has been abolished by mass production. The evolution of color charts as seen in this book is evidence of these transformations. In this regard, each document is itself a sample of the larger whole that is the broad history of Western societies' relationship to color.

Today, there is a plethora of standardized products, multiplied identically and infinitely, and often produced at low cost, whose colors are dictated on a global scale by trend forecasters and influencers. We are inundated with an unsightly monotony that we now find normal. At the same time, backlit computer screens obliterate the reflections and delicate shimmers of surfaces that were part of the subtlety of color, gradually reducing our ability to perceive exquisite shades. We even reach the point of clamoring for colors that are ever more blinding, ever more inert.

Everyone has learned how to use color charts, to juggle their codes and numbers, but full, fleshy, juicy color has now become an endangered species. Except for a privileged few who have access to luxury products with color charts displaying their exceptional materials in shades reflecting pioneering creativity, we can only observe the decline of delectable color.

But this beautiful tool has perhaps not yet said its final word.

Even if many color charts today seem bland, the arrangement of colors in space that they offer is preserved. The rules of order and harmony that were already perceptible in the fifteenth century and that have dominated since the late nineteenth century are respected, as is the uniform format of the samples. This appealing structure, where abundance is combined with serenity, may mean that color can still spark fantasy in contemporary society. Because it is no longer physical, because it is no longer a painstaking part of production, since its roots with the material have been broken, all the power of color has found refuge and been concentrated in the image of the color chart.[10] This image, like the color charts themselves, may turn out to be a rare site for sensing the ghostly presence of something missing, a diminished history.

Aside from its references for evaluating color and despite its flaws, the color chart endures by its ability to open up the imagination—the very ability that allowed it to travel down such a long path. Extrapolating a dress from a piece of fabric, projecting a drawing from a dab of vermilion watercolor, polishing desire by languidly painting one's fingernails . . . the color chart has always been calibrated to humans and their emotions, and it remains a source of contemplation, a space where it is possible to keep time at bay and allow the mind to absorb the rays that are necessary for well-being.

Fatigue from sterile overconsumption in wealthy nations, the welcome demands of sustainable development, and an increasingly intense quest for unique and meaningful objects are modifying our relationship to the world and will perhaps help reinvent color charts to lead us to the next metamorphosis in the concept of color.

Will the color chart of tomorrow achieve a reconciliation between the sensory experience of materials and the rediscovered delicacy of its shades? ●

NOTES

GRASPING COLOR

1 • Precious silk fabric.
2 • Cardon 1994, p. 18.
3 • Cardon 1994, p. 19.
4 • Le Breton 2006, p. 95.
5 • The French word *échantillon* was used from the thirteenth to the fifteenth centuries to indicate a standard (of measures, weights, or coins). In the fifteenth century, it took on the modern sense of "a small quantity of a commodity that is shown to make known the quality of the whole" (Rey 2006, p. 1161).
6 • Cardon 1994, pp. 17–26.
7 • Gage 2008, p. 129.
8 • Goodman 2006, p. 97.
9 • Mollard-Desfour 1998 to 2015.
10 • Moulinier-Brogi 2016.
11 • They are thus color reference systems (Karliczek 2013). John Gage links these urine wheels to Robert Fludd's color wheel in the 1620s (Gage 2008, p. 162, 171).
12 • Pastoureau 2019, fig. 107.
13 • Fischer and Silvestrini 1996, pp. 19–22.
14 • Dagognet 1970.
15 • Including the manual by Valentin Boltz von Ruffach published in 1549 (Nickelsen 2005).
16 • Parmentier 2016 and 2017 and Karliczek and Schwarz 2016.
17 • These pigments, from the mineral, plant, and animal kingdoms (in particular, cochineal from the animal kingdom), already appeared in the fifteenth century in the work of the painter Cennino Cennini, the *Libro delle Arte*.
18 • I would like to express my thanks to Erma Hermens and to Sylvie Constantin, who carried out an initial study of the manuscript with the medievalist Erik Kwakkel.
19 • It seems that it was not until the fourth edition of *The Art of Painting* by John Smith in 1705 that a color chart was attached to a manual (Baty 2017).
20 • Van Zuylen 1994.
21 • Eco 2009, pp. 9–18.

AN IDEAL SYSTEM

1 • Until Newton's *Opticks* (1704), color was essentially considered according to lightness or darkness on a linear scale from black to white. With its seven colors placed on a continuum, Newton's color wheel opened up vast fields of research that would be explored by his successors. On this, see Fischer and Silvestrini 1996, pp. 39–44.
2 • Lowengard 2006.
3 • Lehman 2012 and, concerning the F / 12 collection of the French National Archives, Raimondo 2020.
4 • Maruzuka 2021.
5 • In the Getty Foundation collection, there is a manuscript of dye formulas written in German circa 1680 that contains approximately five hundred samples of fibers and textiles (see Leonhard and Brafman 2015). For manuscript books including samples dating from 1716 to 1744 from the John Crutchley wool fabric dyeing company located in London, see Quye, Cardon, and Balfour Paul 2020.
6 • Miller 2014.
7 • As per the *Anecdotes de notre Temps* found in the library of the Duc de Richelieu (Weigert 1964).
8 • Cardon 1999; Cardon 2019; Cardon and Brémaud 2020.
9 • Cardon 2019 and Cardon and Brémaud 2020.
10 • Bacteria perform the slow, essential task of digesting components that release the dyeing capacity of their seed pods.
11 • One of these was Jean Hellot (Lowengard 2006; Delamare and Guineau 1999, p. 92; Cardon 2019, p. 73).
12 • Beginning with another master of colors from the region, who wrote another major document that was also discovered and analyzed by Dominique Cardon (Cardon 2013 and Cardon and Brémaud 2022).
13 • See the color assortment cards sent to buyers in the port cities of the Levant beginning in the late 1720s and the ranges of blues that dyers in the south of France were already producing (Cardon 1999, p. 171).
14 • Nougarède 1989 and 2006.
15 • Karliczek and Schwarz 2016; Simonini 2018.
16 • Werner differs in this from Linnaeus, who considered color to be an unconvincing distinguishing feature and who was skeptical of contemporary attempts to reproduce the colors of nature.
17 • Seven whites, six grays, four blacks, six blues, six greens, nine yellows, ten reds, six browns.
18 • Fischer and Silvestrini 1996, pp. 45–58.
19 • See the anonymous catalog *Wiener Farbenkabinet* published in 1794 using the 4,608 colors collected in 1782 by Christian Friedrich Prange (see Karliczek and Schwarz 2016; Simonini 2018).
20 • On the practical side, the paints were not always properly formulated, and their application to the pages of the book compromised their preservation. From a methodological point of view, the color selection was not varied enough.
21 • Whites, grays, blacks, blues, purples, greens, yellows, oranges, reds, browns (the 1821 edition has 110 colors).
22 • The absence of equivalents for the plant world is particularly noticeable, which is surprising considering it was a domain familiar to Patrick Syme.
23 • Bertrand 2019, pp. 127–130.
24 • This reproduction was carried out by Reverend Leonard Jenyns.
25 • The naturalists of the early nineteenth century had already realized that they would never know everything about the world.
26 • Henri Dauthenay would also do this one hundred years later. See pp. 117–120.
27 • Lehman 2012.
28 • During long and delicate operations, the madder dye had to interact with fatty substances and feces, ox blood, and alum.
29 • Leprun 1990.
30 • Jacqué 1995; Batella and Dieu 1995, pp. 126–127; Cardon 2003, p. 103.
31 • The MISE museum preserves the laboratory journals of Léonard Schwartz dated from 1833 to 1842. On this subject, see Sarda, Lescuyer, and Raimondo 2020.
32 • Leprun 1990.
33 • Mordants are treatments applied to the fiber in order to form a solid complex with the dye so that it will be permanent.
34 • Eco 2009, pp. 9–18.
35 • Like his colleagues, Léonard Schwartz filed patents. The laboratory notes were part of a new configuration where science was at the service of trade, while commerce funded scientific progress (Leprun 1990).
36 • Page 691.
37 • 37th lesson, "Immediate dyeing principles."
38 • In the *Theoretical and Practical Treatise on Fabric Printing* by Jean Persoz (1846), in particular.
39 • These formulas have a color name that, with the number assigned to it, identifies the sample and are followed by the dyeing process.
40 • In the state of raw fiber, not yet spun.
41 • Single, binary, or mixed colors.
42 • It is interesting to note in this regard that according to the *Trésor de la Langue Française*, when added to the word "nuance" (color), the suffix "ier" indicates the case where the derived word "designates an object whose function involves a set of other objects."
43 • Foucault 1996, p. 9.

THE CHAOS OF SYNTHETIC COLOR

1 • Nature-based colors are the result of the synergy between several components and not of any single one.
2 • In the 1770s, an exceptional master dyer, Antoine Quemizet, experimented with rational color organization systems. He brought to these experiments an exceptional combination of expertise, a history of in-depth investigations carried out in various dyeing workshops, and the results of constant experiments. He tirelessly read the scientific literature of the time. On this subject, see Belhoste 2015.
3 • Fischer and Silvestrini 1996, pp. 64–68 and pp. 78–82. Regarding Goethe, see also Karliczek and Schwarz 2016, and regarding Chevreul, see Roque, Bodo, and Viénot 1997.
4 • The *Treatise of Colorants* published by Marcel-Paul Schützenberger in 1867 is an example of this, as is the work *Bleaching and Primers, Dyeing and Printing, Colorants*, published in 1895 by Charles-Ernest Guignet, Fernand Dommer, and Eugène Grandmougin.
5 • Piéquet provided the list of establishments that had offered him the most interesting choice of dyes: Poirrier and Durand and Huguenin, BASF, Bayer and Co.
6 • For example, Robert Ridgway and his *Nomenclature of Colors for Naturalists* published in 1886 (see Baty 2017, p. 244, and Karliczek and Schwarz 2016).
7 • The discipline of physical anthropology studies the human species from a physical and biological point of view. See Dias 1999; Wartelle 2004; and Boëtsch, Hervé, and Rozenberg 2007.
8 • Dias 1999.
9 • Karliczek and Schwarz 2016, pp. 13–62.
10 • Following Chevreul, who would inspire authors including Albert Henry Munsell (*A Colour Notation*, 1905) and then the work of Oswald.
11 • Guichard's list includes artists, students of the decorative arts, decorative painters, wallpaper manufacturers, painters-glaziers, and even "Ladies who occupy themselves by doing upholstery."
12 • Da Silveira 1995 and 1997; Bruna and Demey 2018.
13 • Zola 1977, pp. 276, 344, and 457. See also his *Carnets d'enquêtes* (research notebooks) where the author notes that 150 women worked in the sampling department (Zola 1986).

A REVOLUTION IN COLOR

1 • *L'Art et la mode*, *Les Modes*, *Femina*, *Le Figaro-Modes*, etc.
2 • Batchelor 2001.
3 • The major companies at this time were, in Germany, Bayer, BASF, Meister, Licius and Bruning; in France, Établissements Kuhlmann, Maison Dalsace, and Manufacture Lyonnaise de Matières Colorantes; in Switzerland, the Gesellschaft für Chemische Industrie Basel (Ciba).
4 • In just a few years, the production of alizarin caused the ruin of the madder producers in southern France and Holland.

5 • The traditional fibers of wool and silk were now joined by cotton, which since the 1880s had played an important role in the textile industry. Cotton's rising popularity was due to the aniline dyes that gave it radiance, beauty, and delicate color.
6 • Like *nouet*, the term *mouchet*, although it is frequently used by collectors of color charts, is not listed in dictionaries, even specialized textile dictionaries.
7 • Glazes are vitrifiable coatings (also called enamel) at a low or high temperature placed on ceramics to make them impermeable and give them color using metallic oxides.
8 • Lajoix 1992.
9 • Particularly the range of greens, due to chromium. On this subject and on the crucial role of Alexandre Brongniart at the Manufacture de Sèvres, see Dargaud 2017.
10 • Knott 2021.
11 • Many works on color printing were published, including *La Reproduction des Couleurs par la Superposition des Trois Couleurs Simples* by the printer Robert Steinheil, which appeared in 1896.
12 • This blue was named for a Parisian color manufacturer, A. Milori Cie.
13 • The last color was probably intended for colorizing black-and-white photographs.
14 • In the collection of the Mobilier National, the *Register of Experiments and Trials no.1 of the Dyeing Laboratory of Les Gobelins* was written from 1890 to 1902 by Th. Valette and É. Gerspach and had a large number of samples to support its comparisons of various types of dyes.
15 • Clerget 1925, pp. 56–58.
16 • See pp. 66–70.
17 • Delobre 2018.
18 • "La Grande Fabrique" was the organization of all the crafts connected to silk production (Meunier 2018).
19 • Gras 1906.
20 • In Lyon, the Musée Historique des Tissus, which opened in 1864, was designed to inspire and educate designers with a collection of fabrics and samples, including many foreign silks. The museum also saved part of the archives of the major silk manufacturers when they began to close their doors in the late nineteenth century.
21 • Comparison with a color chart by Rolland & Cie, autumn 1900, private collection, Paris.
22 • The name *Mousmé* or *Mousmée*, a corruption of the Japanese term *musume*, is related to the Japonism movement that had a strong influence on European art and literature from the 1860s until the end of the century.
23 • See pp. 84–86.
24 • For instance, the term *Mousmé* is associated here with a series of pale pinks, but in a ribbon color chart from 1904, it is used for a bright yellow.
25 • In Belgium, particularly in Comines-Warneton, and in Normandy, in the Lieuvin region.
26 • Lemercier 2006.
27 • These were very staid names compared to those that still flourished in the late eighteenth century, such as *Indiscreet Tears*, *Smothered Sighs*, *Paris Mud*, *Common Ham*, *Chimney Sweep*, *Poisoned Monkey*, etc. (Gay 1887, Franklin 1896).
28 • Some of the sentimental names on the card of *Colors Adopted for the Summer Season 1905* were *Frisson*, *Innocent*, *Mischievous*, and *Cuddly*.
29 • Lemercier 2006; Monjaret 2008.
30 • Monjaret 2008.
31 • *Encyclopédie*, Diderot, D'Alembert, and Jaucourt (1751–1772), "Feather Maker" ("*Plumassier*").
32 • See pp. 137–139.
33 • Monjaret 2008.
34 • Anne Monjaret points out that the term *marabou* was given to turkey or stork feathers, and the term *swan* was applied to goose feathers.
35 • On this subject, see the delightful silent instructional film produced by the ministry of agriculture in 1912 that is in the collection of the Institut National de l'Audiovisuel (INA), *La Fleur Artificielle*, intended to give young women an introduction to the tasks performed by female workers at home.
36 • It included three light yellows with similar tones (a greenish cream called *Lemon Yellow*, another cream described as *Ordinary*, and a color named *Corn Yellow Ivory*). The other colors were ocher, pink (*Rosa*), and dark purple (called *Ecru*).
37 • A phenomenon known as *metamerism* (Sève, Indergand, and Lanthony 2007, p. 142).
38 • Particularly cellulose paint and zinc oxide paint (Baty 2017).
39 • American companies seem to have been the first to distribute paint color charts: Harrison Brothers and Company; Moore, Kellogg Oil, Paint & Varnish Co. of Buffalo; Averill Chemical Paint Company; Wadsworth, Martinez and Longman Pure Prepared Paints of New York; and the Alabastine Company.
40 • This shared lexicon can be connected to the common roots of manufacturers and sellers of these products: the color merchant or hardware dealer who preceded them before professions became specialized.
41 • See pp. 160–161.
42 • La Pastorine was one of many factories that were established along the Canal Saint-Denis as of the 1850s (Katz 2003).
43 • Lead white, obtained by the oxidization of strips of lead by acetic acid vapors, had been produced continually ever since ancient times for making paint and cosmetics (Varichon 2005, p. 36).
44 • Bengaline clearly evokes Bengal, and in the late nineteenth century, the term also designated a fabric imported from that region.
45 • Strictly speaking, distemper is a mixture of pigments, water, and a non-oily binder (Perego 2005, p. 258–259).
46 • Petit, Roire, and Valot 2005, p. 314.
47 • See Grasping Color chapter.
48 • Roque 1994 and Gage 2008, pp. 177–190.
49 • See pp. 35–38.
50 • See Lowengard 2006 for the color referencing of Auguste Louis Pfannenschmidt (1788); for the first scientific study on pigments by George Field (1835) and the standardization of the reproduction of colors by Robert Ridgway (1886), see Karliczek and Schwarz 2016 and Simonini 2018.
51 • Grinding pigments in a mill developed in the 1740s, but it was not until the late eighteenth century that media that were ready for use could be more widely distributed (Baty 2017).
52 • Renoir would have preferred to master mixing his own colors, but without an apprentice and preferring painting over grinding, he purchased ready-made colors (Indergand 1994).
53 • Including greens and purples that no longer required prior mixing.
54 • Especially since poppy seed oil led to a uniform consistency that could not be obtained when paints were ground by hand (Delamare and Guineau 1999, pp. 110–115).
55 • Sofio 2017.
56 • In the 1850s, the Belgian painter Jozef Laurent Dyckmans was said to have age-tested over 150 pigments (MacEvoy 2015).
57 • A lacquer is a pigment obtained by using an organic dye to color an inert mineral material that is generally white (Petit, Roire, and Valot 1999, p. 66).
58 • Many synthetic dyes for textiles would be tested to develop paints for artists (Delamare and Guineau 1999, p. 113).
59 • The packaging of watercolors, first in half-shell format and then in little metal pots, dates to the 1760s and is said to be the result of the initiative of the English color merchant William Reeves.
60 • In 1884, the American Society for Testing and Materials (ASTM) defined minimal standards to be met by the paint industry.
61 • In the late 1880s, Van Gogh was still using a geranium lacquer whose bright pinks changed to pale blue in several of his paintings, as also occurred in the works of Gauguin (Blockx 1881).
62 • It should be noted that while there is still a color called *Geranium Lacquer*, it is specified that it is made from aniline and not the unstable eosine.
63 • It was made from toluidine, a by-product of coal.
64 • This vocabulary is to a large extent still in use today.
65 • A few years later, the Société Anonyme des Matières Colorantes et Produits Chimiques de Saint-Denis distributed charts of dyes for paper with over 200 shades (see pp. 132–135). But in 1912, regulations were issued restricting the dyes for food packaging.
66 • Starting in the second half of the nineteenth century, due especially to synthetic dyes and pigments and other industrial components and processes, many French companies began selling hygiene products and cosmetics. See Jones 2014.
67 • See Collectif 2021.
68 • This was the name of the famous tragedienne Rachel (1821–1858), who used a somewhat yellow powder in harmony with her olive complexion. Her name would be used for a long time to indicate a makeup shade.
69 • Tornay 1978, pp. IX–LI, Varichon 2011, pp. 117–118, 183, 206, 219–220, Lecerf 2012, Karliczek and Schwarz 2016.
70 • Lecerf 2012.
71 • Henri Dauthenay thus repeated the Newtonian order of Chevreul's disks but created series that were suitable for horticultural uses, especially for shades of pink, violet, and blue and darker shades, which are very frequent in his corpus.
72 • The terms used in the textile industry were too arbitrary and ephemeral (*Dawn*, *Sunset*, *Talisman Yellow*, *Graziella*, *Misanthropic Violet*), while the names of inks did not mean anything to the public or were too imprecise.
73 • Such as *Parrot Green* or *Bishop Violet*.
74 • It would inspire the British 2 volume *Horticultural Colour Chart* published in 1939–1942 (Paclt 1983).
75 • Varichon 2005.

BRINGING COLOR TO THE MASSES

1 • Drawing on the previous work of Rood, Maxwell, and Chevreul, Albert H. Munsell created an orderly and pragmatic system of colors that was rapidly circulated and used in the sciences and then for many other applications. By finally offering a common standard, it created the possibility of developing ranges of shared trends for fashion, decor, and consumer goods (Paclt 1983; Fischer and Silvestrini 1996, pp. 134–37).
2 • In 1931, the British Colour Council was founded with the mission of establishing color standards and publishing dictionaries of the selected colors. In France, these standardization efforts were led by AFNOR (Association Française de Normalisation).
3 • See Eiseman and Recker 2011, pp. 44–80.
4 • In 1914, German dye production represented 88 percent of the value of the global market.
5 • Joly 2009; Emptoz, Fauque, and Breysse 2018; Deplaute 2020; Gannon 2021.

6 • In France, Kuhlmann and the Compagnie Nationale des Matières Colorantes; in England, Imperial Chemical Industries Ltd. (ICI); in Germany, IG Farben, which would once again dominate the global chemical market in 1939.
7 • Its origin is said to date to the mid-nineteenth century. In 1925, 1,600 worked there, including fifty chemical engineers. Later, when the German cartel IG Farben took charge of it in 1941, it would be called Francolor (Kartz 2003).
8 • Only a few color charts from Bayer and IG Farben dating to the period from 1918 to 1939 could be identified.
9 • The association Mémoire des Industries de la Couleur (MIC), founded in 1987 by Albert Corduant, Louis Deleschaud, Jacques Roire, Bertrand Tézenas du Montcel, and Jacques Thérond, had the goal of preserving the history of manufacturers of paints, fine colors, and inks and professions in related industries. Annik Chauvel also played an important role.
10 • See pp. 70–71.
11 • See pp. 70–73.
12 • *Marianne*, July 11, 1934, p. 6.
13 • Viscose was developed from cellulose in 1884 by the French chemists Auguste Delubac and Hilaire de Chardonnet. In French it is sometimes called "soie de Chardonnet" ("Chardonnet silk").
14 • See pp. 87–93.
15 • From its start as a small dyeing company founded by a Frenchman in Basel, the Gesellschaft für Chemische Industrie grew rapidly and changed its name to Ciba (Chemische Industrie Basel).
16 • See pp. 79–86.
17 • Varichon and Roccella 2006.
18 • Cocylima 1999; Simonin 2000; Mariot Leduc 2013; and the website of Ôkhra, https://okhra.com.
19 • See in particular the book by Oscar Piéquet, pp. 50–51.
20 • These haute couture designers included Jeanne Lanvin, Paul Poiret, Madeleine Vionnet, Coco Chanel, and Elsa Schiaparelli.
21 • See pp. 131–132.
22 • Cuvellier 2008.
23 • On this subject, see Collectif 2008.
24 • The other languages included Dutch, Hungarian, Czech, Russian, and Danish.
25 • See pp. 131–132.
26 • Mollard-Desfour 2017 and Pastoureau 2019.
27 • Luminous and intensely opaque, titanium white was also used as a clear, colorless base for pigments.
28 • Paris hosted the first Salon des Appareils Ménagers (Household Appliance Fair) in 1923, and the first Salon des Arts Ménagers (Interior Design Fair) in 1926.
29 • See p. 191.
30 • Mollard-Desfour 2012.
31 • This aspect is present even in the etymology of the term "couleur," because it is "from Latin *color*, a word connected to the group of *celare*, 'to hide,' according to the idea that color is what covers and hides the surface of a thing, . . . conceals the nudity, the truth of the thing" (*Trésor de la Langue Française*, article "Couleur," vol. 6, 1978).
32 • Le Thomas 2008.
33 • See pp. 144–145.
34 • The indication *colle d'or* ("gold glue," rather than *colle d'os*, "bone glue") on the card inside the sample box must be a typo.
35 • Baty 2017.
36 • The quality and the lower cost of these paints meant that many artists preferred them to fine arts colors. On this subject, see the international colloquium *From Can to Canvas* that took place in Marseille and Antibes in 2011, https://www.artic.edu/articles/373/art-scene-investigation-from-can-to-canvas.
37 • On this subject, see Indergand 1994.
38 • See pp. 111–113.
39 • See pp. 116–117.
40 • Watercolor bars, disks, and sticks; "damp colors" in tubes, half tubes, pots and half pots; and gouache paints in tubes, bottles, and glass pots.
41 • See pp. 100–101.
42 • On this subject, see the exhibition *De la Réclame à la Publicité: Collections du Musée de la Publicité, 1920–1950*, which took place at the Musée des Arts Décoratifs in 2003 (https://madparis.fr/de-la-reclame-a-la-publicite). See also Tsikounas 2010.
43 • In 1871, Pelikan was absorbed by Günther Wagner, which began using its logo of a bird "with a stomach pouch under its beak," as it would be described later by Gotlib.
44 • *Anthologie du rouge aux lèvres* (Lipstick Anthology) (Chipot and Kemmoku 2008, p. 97).
45 • We should recall that the French verb *maquiller* (to apply makeup) comes from the Picard verb *maquier*: to do and to feign (Rey 2006, p. 2130).
46 • In the early twentieth century, powders were presented in glass tubes (Collectif 2021, p. 58).
47 • Such as Christian Friedrich Prange, who, in 1782, illustrated thirty-three colors called "flesh" in his *Color Lexicon* (Paclt 1983; Karliczek and Schwarz 2016).
48 • The first step is to imagine the sample spread out over a much larger surface (a face, body, or wall) and/or with more significant volume (a cheekbone or a duvet). Next, the customer must consider how this mental projection will fit into her personal world. To really take possession of this extrapolation, it must be associated with several parameters, either consciously or unconsciously: Who will wear this dress? What will these curtains look like if the weather is overcast? How will I look if I powder my face with the shade called *Banana*?
49 • "According to *Vogue*, Mediterraneans prefer white powder, the British and Northern Europeans, the shade called Rachel, and Americans, pink." *Brunette* brown was to be avoided, "a dirty, pink-brown yellow, like the coat of an Irish pony" (Collectif 2021, pp. 37–38).
50 • The perfumer Millot opened his first shop in the 1860s. Lenthéric was a brand that had existed since the last years of the nineteenth century. Antoine was active from the early 1930s to the late 1940s.
51 • This was a stylistic decision for color chart design, since contemporary powder containers could also be round. See Collectif 2021.
52 • See pp. 116–117.
53 • Starting in the 1920s, tanned skin no longer signified working in the fields but began to be associated with outdoor sports and the seaside. Powders attempted to reproduce the tanned look extolled by Gabrielle Chanel and Jean Patou.
54 • Remaury 2009.
55 • Collectif 2021.
56 • Perhaps for Afrique-Occidentale Française? (French West Africa).
57 • *L'Officiel de la Mode*, no. 175, 1936, pp. 118–19, cited by Couteau and Coiffard 2015. See also Jones 2014.
58 • The Bibliothèque Forney collected a significant portion of his archives.
59 • Viraben 2021.
60 • Fagot 2004.

JUBILATION OF COLOR

1 • Meyerson 1957; Albers 1963; Lemonnier 1975; Fillacier 1986.
2 • Including Bayer, BASF, Hoechst, and Agfa, but IG Farben was not really liquidated until 2003.
3 • The Francolor company had been founded in 1941 by the Vichy regime (Furio 2020).
4 • Collectif 2004, 136–37.
5 • Blin Barrois 2003.
6 • See pp. 144–145.
7 • Baum and Boyeldieu 2006, 253.
8 • See pp. 178–179.
9 • For example, the brands Farrow & Ball, 1825 Théodore Collection, Mériguet-Carrère, and others.
10 • Lenclos 1999, 145–57.
11 • Certeau 1990. On this subject, see also Crawford 2010 and Crawford 2016.
12 • American color consultant (1900–1988).
13 • The appearance of acrylic paint especially in the 1950s.
14 • Other color charts from the same era also refer to Ostwald's system, including those of the Bodson & Nelis company.
15 • See also *I colori* published by the Italian artist Luigi Veronesi in 1945.
16 • Collectif 2021, 37–38. See also Lefebvre and Raynal 2002.

MULTITUDE, ICON, IDOL

1 • In stores, hair dye color charts have been replaced with a simple photo of the expected result on the box. At hair salons, however, color charts with strands of synthetic hair are still available.
2 • Varichon 2013.
3 • Ressource (2012) and Little Greene (2013) ad campaigns.
4 • Passion des Îles (2015) and Société Générale (2012) ad campaigns.
5 • In the 2010s, Pantone began selling colorful objects (mugs, notebooks, boxes, bikes, chairs, lighters, umbrellas, etc.) featuring the corresponding Pantone reference number.
6 • This color chart was designed in 2012 by the London advertising agency Leo Burnett in collaboration with Pantone to celebrate the sixtieth anniversary of the reign of Elizabeth II.
7 • In *Elle* magazine in the early 2010s.
8 • Temkin 2008.
9 • See the artist's website: www.pierredavid.net/projets/nuancier/.
10 • Products increasingly imitate other products and express the illusion in their color charts, such as paint that can make any type of wall look like cement.

GLOSSARY

Color Reference Guide

A set of color samples, generally reproductions, developed with a scientific objective in order to identify, characterize, and express the color characteristics of a specific collection as exactly and exhaustively as possible.

Color Scale

A short series of examples of colors, often reproductions. They can also be used to identify a stage in the development of a given product, such as absorption or removal of dye or the ripening of a fruit.

Organized System

A vast set, intended to be universal, of samples of reproduced colors that differ only by their shade. Its goal is to represent all possible colors in an organized and regular manner. It is thus designed to be able to incorporate new references indefinitely. Starting in the twentieth century, the naming of each shade indicates its characteristics in terms of tone, lightness, and saturation.

Sample

In French, the word *échantillon* (English sample) was used from the thirteenth to the fourteenth centuries to indicate a standard (of measures, weights, or coins). In the fifteenth century, it took on the modern sense of "a small quantity of a commodity that is shown to make known the quality of the whole" (Rey 2006, p. 1161). In this book, the term sample indicates any element that is naturally colored, or has been dyed, or whose color has been removed, whether through an artisanal or industrial process, with the function of exemplifying color, whether it embodies color in a particular material (a scientific specimen or product sample) or evokes it through printing or digital processes (reproduction).

Sample Collection

A set of samples that is distinguished by characteristics other than color or shade of color (for instance, various origins, multiple shapes, or individual patterns).

BIBLIOGRAPHY

Albers 1963
Josef Albers, *L'Interaction des couleurs*. Vanves: Hazan, 1963.

Appanah 2009
Nathacha Appanah, *La Noce d'Anna*. Paris: Gallimard, 2009.

Arendt 1981
Hannah Arendt, *The Life of the Mind*, chapter 1.2, "Appearance," section 2: "(True) Being and (Mere) Appearance." New York: Harcourt, 1978, 24.

Batchelor 2001
David Batchelor, *La Peur de la couleur*. Paris: Éditions Autrement, 2001.

Baty 2017
Patrick Baty, *The Anatomy of Colour*. London: Thames & Hudson, 2017. See also http://patrickbaty.co.uk.

Batella and Dieu 1995
Nadine Batella and Valérie Dieu, "Analyse des brouillons de laboratoire," in *Andrinople, le rouge magnifique. De la teinture à l'impression, une cotonnade à la conquête du monde*. Paris: La Martinière; Mulhouse: Musée d'Impression sur Étoffes, 1995, 124–135.

Baum and Boyeldieu 2006
Maggy Baum and Chantal Boyeldieu, *Dictionnaire des textiles*. Lille: Les Éditions du Paillié, 2006.

Belhoste 2015
Bruno Belhoste, "Dyeing at the Gobelins in the Eighteenth Century. The Challenge of Quémizet," in Magdalena Bushart and Friedrich Steinle, *Colour Histories*. Berlin; Boston: De Gruyter, 2015, 67–91.

Bennett 2009–2021
James Bennett, *Cosmetics and Skin*, http://www.cosmeticsandskin.com/bcb/greasepaint.php.

Bernus-Taylor 1989
Marthe Bernus-Taylor, "La nature, objet d'étude scientifique," in *Arabesques et jardins du paradis*. Paris: Editions de la Reunion Des Musées Nationaux (RMN), 1989.

Bertrand 2019
Romain Bertrand, *Le Détail du monde, l'art perdu de la description de la nature*. Paris: Seuil, 2019.

Blin Barrois (ed.) 2003
Barbara Blin Barrois (ed.), *Couleurs à boire, couleurs à manger*. Les Livrets du conservatoire, no. 2. Aix-en-Provence: Edisud, 2003.

Blockx 1881
Jacques Blockx, *Compendium à l'usage des artistes peintres. Peinture à l'huile, matériaux, définition des couleurs fixes et conseils pratiques sur l'ambre dissous*. Vanderhaeghen, 1881.

Boëtsch, Hervé et Rozenberg (ed.) 2007
Gilles Boëtsch, Christian Hervé, and Jacques Rozenberg (ed.), *Corps normalisé, corps stigmatisé, corps racialisé*. Paris: De Boeck Supérieur, 2007.

Bruna and Demey (ed.) 2018
Denis Bruna and Chloé Demey (ed.), *Histoire des modes et du vêtement du Moyen Âge au XXIe siècle*. Paris: Textuel, 2018.

Cardon 1994
Dominique Cardon, "Sensibilité aux couleurs des teinturiers d'autrefois: Manifestations, implications techniques et scientifiques," in *La Couleur, Regards croisés sur la couleur du Moyen Âge au XXe siècle*. Paris: Cahiers du Léopard d'Or, no 4, 1994, 17–26.

Cardon 1999
Dominique Cardon, "Quand la réalité est plus belle que les mythes" ["When reality is more beautiful than myths"] and "Antoine Janot, Mémoire," in *Teinture précieuses de la Méditerranée*. Carcassonne: Musée des Beaux-arts de Carcassonne, Centre de Documentació i Museu Tèxtil, 1999, 10–21 and 73–74.

Cardon 2003
Dominique Cardon, *Le Monde des teintures naturelles*. Paris: Belin, 2003.

Cardon 2013
Dominique Cardon, *Mémoire de teinture, voyage dans le temps chez un maître des couleurs*. Paris: CNRS Éditions, 2013.

Cardon 2019
Dominique Cardon, *Des couleurs pour les lumières, Antoine Janot, teinturier occitan, 1700–1778*. Paris: CNRS Éditions, 2019.

Cardon and Brémaud 2020
Dominique Cardon and Iris Brémaud, *Le Cahier de couleurs d'Antoine Janot / Workbook, Antoine Janot's colours*. Paris: CNRS Éditions, 2020.

Cardon and Brémaud 2022
Dominique Cardon and Iris Brémaud, *Les 157 Couleurs de Paul Gout / Paul Gout's 157 Colours*. Paris: Ulmer [Mérinchal], 2022.

Cennini 1998
Cennino Cennini, *Il libro dell'arte*, Colette Déroche (trans.). Paris: Éditions Berger-Levrault, 1998.

Chauvel 2001
Annik Chauvel, *Petit Dictionnaire des couleurs et des matières colorantes*. Puteaux, France: EREC, 2001.

Chaveau 2003
Robert Chaveau, *Des couleurs plein la tête*. Marseille: Jeanne Laffitte, 2003.

Chipot and Kemmoku 2008
Dominique Chipot and Makoto Kemmoku (trans.), *Du rouge aux lèvres, Haïjins japonaises*. Paris: La Table Ronde, 2003.

Clerget 1925
Pierre Clerget, *Les Industries de la soie en France*. Paris: Armand Colin, 1925.

Cocylima 1999
Callixte Cocylima and Régis Ferré (illus.), *Petite Anthologie de l'ocre, Barbentane*. Équinoxe, 1999.

Cousin 2008
Françoise Cousin (ed.), *Chemins de couleurs: Teintures et motifs du monde*. Paris: Quai Branly, 2004.

Couteau and Coiffard 2015
Céline Couteau and Laurence Coiffard, *Beauté mon beau souci*. Paris: Edilivre, 2015.

Crawford 2009
Matthew B. Crawford, *Shop Class as Soulcraft: An Inquiry into the Value of Work*. New York: Penguin, 2009, 70–71, https://archive.org/details/shop-class-as-soulcraft/page/n7/mode/2up.

Crawford 2010
Matthew Crawford, *Éloge du carburateur, essai sur le sens et la valeur du travail*. Paris: La Découverte, 2010.

Crawford 2016
Matthew Crawford, *Contact*. Paris: La Découverte, 2016.

Cuvillier 2008
Dominique Cuvillier, *Comprendre les tendances*. Paris: Chêne, 2008.

Dagognet 1970
François Dagognet, *Le Catalogue de la vie*. Paris: Presses Universitaires de France, 1970.

Dallet 2007
Sylvie Dallet, "Gazette des atours de Marie-Antoinette," *Annales historiques de la Révolution française*. Paris: Armand Colin, 2007.

Dargaud 2017
Olivier Dargaud, "Du blanc de Vincennes aux mille couleurs de la manufacture de Sèvres," in *L'Expérience de la couleur*. Exhibition catalogue. Sèvres: Cité de la céramique, and Paris: Lienart Éditions, 2017, 18–35.

Da Silveira 1995
Piedade da Silveira, *Les Grands Magasins du Louvre au XIXe siècle*. Paris: Caisse de retraite des entreprises à commerces multiples (CCM), 1995.

Da Silveira 1997
Piedade da Silveira, *Au pauvre diable et Au coin de la rue*. Paris: Caisse de retraite des entreprises à commerces multiples (CCM), 1997.

Davidson and Dixon 2020
Peter Davidson and Joyce Dixon, "From Minerals to Pigments, and Saxony to Scotland: The Creation of Werner's Nomenclature of Colors (1814)," in *Ordering Colors in 18th and Early 19th Century*. New York: Columbia University, Center of Science and Society, 2020.

De Certeau Michel 1990
Michel de Certeau, *L'Invention du quotidien. Arts de faire* [1980]. Paris: Gallimard, 1990.

Delamare and Guineau 1999
François Delamare and Bernard Guineau, *Les Matériaux de la couleur*. Paris: Découvertes Gallimard, 1999.

Delobre 2018
Marie-Josée Delobre, "Une Fabrique de l'innovation: la saga des colorants à Lyon au 19e siècle," *L'Influx*. Lyon, July 2018, http://www.linflux.com/lyon-et-region/une-fabrique-de-linnovation-la-saga-des-colorants-a-lyon-au-19e-siecle/#chapitre1.

De Luca 2010
Erri De Luca, *The Day Before Happiness*. New York: Other Press, 2011, 29, https://archive.org/details/daybeforehappine0000delu_e2q5/page/n3/mode/2up?view=theater.

Déplaude 2020
Marc-Olivier Déplaude, "La couleur des aliments: une histoire des colorants alimentaires aux États-Unis," *Transhumances*, February 7, 2020, https://rithme.hyspotheses.org/11825.

De Thoisy-Dallem et al. 2021
Anne de Thoisy-Dallem, Catherine Lanoë, Dominique Paquet, Grégory Couderc, Ève Duperray, Cindy Levinspuhl, and Béatrice Cornet, *Le Siècle des poudriers (1880–1980), la poudre et ses écrins, autour de la collection d'Anne de Thoisy-Dallerm*. Paris: Éditions Faton, 2021.

Dias 1999
Nélia Dias, "La fiabilité de l'œil," *Terrain, revue d'ethnologie de l'Europe, no. 33*, September 1999. Paris: Ministère de la culture, ARCHETIS-DAPA, http://terrain.revues.org/2674.

Eco 2009
Umberto Eco, *Vertige de la liste*, Myriem Bouzaher (trans.). Paris: Flammarion, 2009. Umberto Eco, *The Infinity of Lists*, Alastair McEwen (trans.). New York: Rizzoli, 2009. Internet Archive accessed 15 May 2023, https://archive.org/details/infinityoflists0000ecou/page/14/mode/2up?view=theater.

Eiseman and Recker 2011
Leatrice Eiseman and Keith Recker, *Pantone, le XXe siècle en couleurs*. Paris: Huginn & Muninn, 2011.

Emptoz, Fauque, and Breysse 2018
Gérard Emptoz, Danielle Fauque, Jacques Breysse (eds.), *Entre reconstruction et mutations: les industries de la chimie entre les deux guerres*. Les Ulis: EDP Sciences, 2018, https://www.edp-open.org/images/stories/books/fulldl/Entre_reconstruction_et_mutations_les_industries_de_la_chimie_entre_les_deux_guerres.pdf.

Fagot 2004
Philippe Fagot, "Rêver la couleur sans la toucher, mise en scène de la chromaticité dans les catalogues de vente par correspondance," in *Couleurs, travail et société du Moyen Âge à nos jours*. Paris: Somogy, 2004, 74–81.

Fillacier 1986
Jacques Fillacier, *La Pratique de la couleur*. Malakoff: Dunod, 1986.

Fischer and Silvestrini 1996
Ernst Peter Fischer and Narciso Silvestrini, *Les Systèmes de couleurs dans l'art et les sciences*. Cologne, Germany: Dumont/Farbe, 1996.

Foucault 1996
Michel Foucault, *The Order of Things: An Archaeology of the Human Sciences*, Alan Sheridan (trans.). New York: Vintage Books, 1994, xvii–xviii.

Franklin 1896
Alfred Franklin, *La Vie privée d'autrefois, arts et métiers, modes, mœurs, usages des Parisiens du XIIe au XVIIIe siècle*. Paris: Plon, Nourrit, 1896.

Furio 2020
Antoine Furio, "Francolor, Compagnie française des matières colorantes, Ugine-Kuhlmann," *Atlas de l'architecture et du patrimoine Seine-Saint-Denis*, 2020, https://patrimoine.seinesaintdenis.fr/Laboratoire-de-chimie-de-la-societe-Francolor-puis-de-la-Compagnie-francaise.

Gage 2008
John Gage, *Couleur and Culture*, Ann Béchard-Léauté and Sophie Schvalberg (trans.), London: Thames & Hudson, 2008.

Gannon 2021
Frédéric Gannon, "La refondation de l'industrie chimique française de l'azote au lendemain du traité de Versailles à travers le parcours de l'un de ses protagonistes: Georges Partart," *Revue de l'ORCE*, 171 (January 2021), https://www.ofce.sciences-po.fr/pdf/revue/10-171OFCE.pdf.

Gay 1887
Victor Gay, *Glossaire archéologique du Moyen Âge et de la Renaissance*. Paris: Librairie de la Société bibliographique, 1887.

Girard 1994
L. Giard, "Des moments et des lieux" préface à M. de Certeau et al., *Les Arts de faire*, L'invention du quotidien III, habiter, cuisiner. Paris: Gallimard, "Folio," 1994, ii.

Girard 1998
Luce Giard, "Times and Places," preface to *The Practice of Everyday Life: Volume 2: Living and Cooking*, by Michel de Certeau, Luce Giard, Pierre Mayol. Timothy J. Tomasik (trans.). Minneapolis: University of Minnesota Press, 1998, xxxv. https://monoskop.org/images/b/be/De_Certeau_Giard_Mayol_The_Practice_of_Everyday_Life_Vol_2_Living_and_Cooking.pdf.

Goodman 2006
Nelson Goodman, "When Is Art?" in *Ways of Worldmaking*, by Nelson Goodman. Indianapolis, Indiana: Hackett Publishing, 1978, 57–70.

Gras 1906
Louis Joseph Gras, *Histoire de la rubanerie et des industries de la soie à Saint-Étienne et dans la région stéphanoise*. Saint-Étienne, 1906, https://archive.org/details/HistoireDeLaRubanerieEtDesIndustri/page/n10/mode/1up.

Indergand 1994
Michel Indergand, "De l'expérience matérielle à l'expérience immatérielle de la couleur. Manière d'agir, manière de penser, évolutions et ruptures . . . ," in *La Couleur, Regards croisés sur la couleur du Moyen Âge au XXe siècle*. Paris: Cahiers du Léopard d'Or, no. 4, Éditions du Léopard d'Or, 1994, 7–15.

Jacqué 1995
Jacqueline Jacqué, "Le Rôle déterminant de Mulhouse au XIXe siècle," in *Andrinople, le rouge magnifique*. Paris: La Martinière; Mulhouse: Musée d'Impression sur Étoffes, 1995.

Joly 2009
Hervé Joly, *Les Relations entre les entreprises françaises et allemandes dans l'industrie chimique des colorants des années 1920 aux années 1950, entre Occupation, concurrence, collaboration et coopération*. Vincennes: Institut de la gestion publique et du développement économique, 2009, https://books.openedition.org/igpde/4433?lang=fr#text.

Jones 2014
Geoffrey Jones, "Firmes mondialisées et imaginaire de la beauté," *Relations internationales*, 157, no. 1 (2014): 131–146, https://doi.org/10.3917/ri.157.0131, https://www.cairn.info/revue-relations-internationales-2014-1-page-131.htm.

Karliczek 2013
André Karliczek, "Vom Phänomen zum Merkmal: Farben in der Naturgeschichte um 1800," in *Erkenntniswert Farbe*, Ernst-Haeckel-Haus, https://www.researchgate.net/publication/282327141_Vom_Phanomen_zum_Merkmal_Farben_in_der_Naturgeschichte_um_1800.

Karliczek and Schwarz (ed.) 2016
André Karliczek and Andreas Schwarz (ed.), *Farre. Farbstandards in den frühen Wissenschaften*. Jena, Germany: Ernst Haeckel Haus, 2016.

Katz 2003
Cécile Katz, *Seine-Saint-Denis, Territoire d'usines*. Grâne: Créaphis, 2003.

Knott 2021
Stephen Knott, "Gestes d'amateurs: la décoration de céramique à la fin du XIXe siècle," presented at the conference, in *Visu: Gestes d'images*, for the session, "Colorier, décorer" (USR 3103 CNRS-INHA, session: 4 March 2021), http://b-a-t-o-n-s.fr/gestesdimages/pages/intervention1/1.html.

Lajoix 1992
Anne Lajoix, "La palette aveugle du céramiste," *La Revue du musée des Arts et Métiers*, 1 (September 1992): 57–62.

Le Breton 2006
David Le Breton, *La Saveur du monde*. Paris: Métailié, 2006.

Lecerf 2012
Guy Lecerf, "Le répertoire de couleur d'Henri Dauthenay: mémoire et imagination à l'œuvre," in *Primaires*. Paris: Centre français de la couleur, 2012, 44–49.

Lefebvre and Raynal 2002
Thierry Lefebvre and Cécile Raynal, "De l'Institut Pasteur à Radio Luxembourg. L'histoire étonnante du Tho-Radia," *Revue d'histoire de la pharmacie*, 90, no. 335 (2002): 461–480, www.persee.fr/doc/pharm_0035-2349_2002_num_90_335_5401.

Léger 1973
Fernand Léger, "Modern Architecture and Color" [1946], George L. K. Morris (trans.). In *Functions of Painting*, Alexandra Anderson (trans.), Edward F. Fry (ed.). New York: Viking, 1973. Digitized by the Internet Archive in 2010, https://archive.org/details/functionsofpaint00lg/page/150/mode/2up?q=free.

Léger 1997
Fernand Léger, *Fonctions de la peinture* [1946]. Paris: Folio Essais, 1997.

Lehman 2012
Christine Lehman, "L'art de la teinture à l'Académie royale des sciences au xviiie siècle," *Methodos*, published online March 19, 2012, http://journals.openedition.org/methodos/2874, https://doi.org/10.4000/methodos.2874.

Lemercier 2006
Claire Lemercier, "Articles de Paris, fabrique et institutions économiques à Paris au xixe siècle," 2006, https://halshs.archives-ouvertes.fr/halshs-00106161.

Lemonnier 1974
André and Monique Lemonnier, *Couleur. Échelles et schémas, André Lemonnier*. Paris: Éditions du Centre Georges Pompidou, 1974.

Lenclos 1999
Jean-Philippe et Dominique Lenclos, *Couleurs du monde*. Paris: Le Moniteur, 1999.

Leonhard and Brafman 2015
Karin Leonhard and David Brafman, "Dyeing Wool in Seventeenth-Century Germany," *Hypotheses, The Recipes Project*, published online July 30, 2013, https://recipes.hypotheses.org/1726.

Leprun 1990
Sylviane Leprun, *Du maître teinturier au coloriste, les savoir-faire de la couleur*. Report by the Toucouleur Association, Heritage Department, Ethnological Heritage Mission, Ministry of Culture, Communication and Major Works. Montreuil : Association Toucouleur, 1990, https://www.qwant.com/?q=Sylviane+Leprun+Laboratoires&t=web.

Le Thomas 2008
Claire Le Thomas, "Une littérature du foyer: les livres de travaux manuels amateurs," *Voix plurielles*, 5, no. 1 (May 2008).

Lowengard 2006
Sarah Lowengard, *The Creation of Color in Eighteenth-Century Europe*. New York: Columbia University Press, 2006, www.gutenberg-e.org/lowengard.

Mariot Leduc 2013
Sophie Mariot Leduc, *Ocres*. Aix-en-Provence : Édisud, Eyrolles, 2013.

MacEvoy 2015
Bruce MacEvoy, "Labeling, Lightfastness, and Toxicity," January 2015, http://www.handprint.com/HP/WCL/pigmt6.html.

Maruzuka 2021
Kanako Maruzuka, "A Study of Color Sample Books from the Late Edo to Meiji Periods," *Bulletin of the Faculty of Home Economics Kyoritsu Women's University*, 67 (January 2021): 15–27, https://cir.nii.ac.jp/crid/1050283688738068992 (in Japanese).

Meunier 2018
Lucie Meunier, "La fabrique du Musée, le musée de la Fabrique," *L'Influx*. Lyon, 2018, https://www.linflux.com/lyon-et-region/la-fabrique-du-musee-le-musee-de-la-fabrique/.

Meyerson 1957
Ignace Meyerson, *Problèmes de la couleur*. Paris: S.E.V.P.E.N., 1957.

Miller 2014
Lesley Ellis Miller, *Soieries, le livre d'échantillons d'un marchand français au siècle des lumières*. Lausanne: La Bibliothèque des arts, 2014.

Mollard-Desfour 1998–2015
Annie Mollard-Desfour, *Dictionnaire des mots et expressions de couleur du xxe siècle*. Paris: CNRS Éditions: Le Bleu, 1998, 2004 and 2013; Le Rouge, 2000 and 2009; Le Rose, 2002; Le Noir, 2005; Le Blanc, 2008; Le Vert, 2012; Le Gris, 2015.

Mollard-Desfour 2017
Annie Mollard-Desfour, "La haute note jaune. Identité chromatique du Midi," in *Oh couleurs! Le design au prisme de la couleur*. Exhibition catalogue. Bordeaux: Musée des arts décoratifs et du design de Bordeaux, 2017.

Monjaret 2008
Anne Monjaret, "Plume et mode à la Belle Époque," *Techniques & Culture*, 50 (2008): 228–255.

Moulinier-Brogi 2016
Laurence Moulinier-Brogi, "L'examen des urines dans la médecine médiévale en terre d'Islam et en Occident. Un aperçu," *Médiévales*, 70 (Spring 2016): 25–41, published online June 15, 2018, https://doi.org/10.4000/medievales.7707, http://journals.openedition.org/medievales/7707.

Nickelsen 2005
Kärin Nickelsen, "The Challenge of Colour: Eighteenth-Century Botanists and the Hand-colouring of Illustrations," *Annals of Science*, 63, no. 1 (2005): 3–23.

Nord Archives and Archives Nationales 2004
Nord Archives départementales, Archives nationales du monde du travail France, *Couleur, travail et société du Moyen Âge à nos jours*. Paris: Somogy, 2004.

Nougarède 1989
Martine Nougarède, *Rouge, Bleu, Blanc, teintures à Nîmes*. Nîmes: Musée du Vieux-Nîmes, 1989.

Nougarède 2006
Martine Nougarède, *Petits bouts d'étoffe, petits bouts d'histoire*. Nîmes: Musée du Vieux-Nîmes, 1989.

Paclt 1983
Jiřic Paclt, "A Chronology of Color Charts and Color Terminology for Naturalists," *Taxon* 32, no. 3 (August 1983): 393–405, https://doi.org/10.2307/1221496.

Parmentier 2016
Cécile Parmentier, "À la (re)découverte du Sloane Ms 2052 de la British Library (Londres)," *Groupe de recherche en histoire de l'art moderne* [Research group on the history of modern art], (May 2016), https://grham.hypotheses.org/2295.

Parmentier 2017
Cécile Parmentier, "Le réseau au cœur de la méthodologie de Théodore de Mayerne," in Arnaud Hurel (ed.), *La France savante*, digital edition of CTHS (proceedings of the 140th Congrès national des sociétés historiques et scientifiques held in Reims, 2015), http://books.openedition.org/cths/2721.

Pastoureau 2019
Michel Pastoureau, *Jaune, histoire d'une couleur*. Paris: Seuil, 2019.

Perego 2005
François Perego, *Dictionnaire des matériaux du peintre*. Paris: Belin, 2005.

Petit, Roire, and Valot 1999, 2001, and 2005
Jean Petit, Jacques Roire, and Henri Valot, *Encyclopédie de la peinture; formuler, fabriquer, appliquer*, 3 vols. Puteaux, France: EREC, 1999, 2001, and 2005.

Quye, Cardon, and Balfour Paul 2020
Anita Quye, Dominique Cardon, and Jenny Balfour Paul, "The Crutchley Archive: Red Colours on Wool Fabrics from Master Dyers, London 1716–1744," *Textile History*, 51, no. 2 (2020): 119–166.

Raimondo 2020
Alexia Raimondo, "Color in the Archives or Color Archives," in *Book of Abstracts of the International Colour Association (AIC)*, Symposium Natural Colours—Digital Colours (20, 26–28 November 2020), 22.

Remaury 2009
Bruno Remaury, "Le big bang de la cosmétique," in Élizabeth Azoulay (ed.), *100 000 ans de beauté*, vol. 4. Paris: Gallimard, 2009, 37–39.

Rey (ed.) 2006
Alain Rey (ed.), *Dictionnaire historique de la langue française* [1992, 1998]. Paris: Dictionnaires Le Robert, reprinted in 3 volumes, 2006.

Roque 1994
Georges Roque, "Les couleurs complémentaires: un nouveau paradigme," in *Revue d'histoire des sciences*, 47, no. 3–4, (January 1994): 405–434. Paris: Armand Colin.

Roque, Bodo, and Viénot 1997
Georges Roque, Bernard Bodo, and Françoise Viénot, *Un savant des couleurs*. Paris: Éditions du Muséum national d'histoire naturelle, 1997.

Sapienza 2005
Goliarda Sapienza, *L'Art de la joie*. Paris: Viviane Hamy, 2005.
Goliarda Sapienza, *The Art of Joy*. New York: Farrar, Straus and Giroux, 2013, 366, https://archive.org/details/artofjoy0000sapi_k6q9/page/366/mode/1up?view=theater.

Rouanet 2010
Marie Rouanet, *Tout jardin est Eden*. Paris: Albin Michel, 2010.

Sarda, Lescuyer, and Raimondo 2020
Marie-Anne Sarda, Clémence Lescuyer, and Alexia Raimondo, "À la recherche des sources techniques de la teinture," in *Book of Abstracts of the International Colour Association* (AIC), Symposium Natural Colours—Digital Colours (20, 26–28 November 2020) 37.

Sève, Indergand, and Lanthony 2007
Robert Sève, Michel Indergand, and Philippe Lanthony, *Dictionnaire des termes de la couleur*. Paris: Editions Sepia—Terra Rossa, 2007.

Simonin 2000
Francine Simonin, *Les Ocres, de la belle marchandise. . . .* Roussillon, France: Ôkhra, 2000.

Simonini 2018
Giulia Simonini, "Organising Colours: Patrick Syme's Colour Chart and Nomenclature for Scientific Purposes," 75 (2018): xvii–xviii, published online December 31, 2018, http://journals.openedition.org/1718/1327.

Sofio 2017
Séverine Sofio, "Les marchands de couleurs au XIXe siècle, artisans ou experts (Paris-Tours)," *Ethnologie française*, 47, no. 1 (2017): 75–86. Paris: Presses Universitaires de France, https://www.cairn.info/revue-ethnologie-francaise-2017-1-page-75.htm.

Suzuki 2000
Masajo Suzuki, *Love Haiku–Masajo Suzuki's Lifetime of Love*, Lee Gurga and Emiko Miyashita (trans.). Illinois: Brooks Books, 2000. Cited in: Charles Trumbull, "Between Basho and Ban'ya (bypassing Barthes): A New Brand of Haiku?" presentation at the fourth Cradle of American Haiku Festival, 2014. published online, A Hundred Gourds, 4:3 (June 2015), http://ahundredgourds.com/ahg43/feature05.html.

Syme 1821
Patrick Syme, title page to Werner's *Nomenclature of Colours, Adapted to Zoology, Botany, Chemistry, Mineralogy, Anatomy, and the Arts*, 2nd ed. Edinburgh: Printed for William Blackwood, Edinburgh, and T. Cadell, Strand, London. 1821, https://archive.org/details/gri_c00033125012743312/page/n5/mode/2up.

Temkin 2008
Ann Temkin, *Color Chart: Reinventing Color, 1950 to Today*. New York: The Museum of Modern Art, 2008.

Tornay 1978
Serge Tornay, introduction to *Voir et nommer les couleurs, ix–li*. Nanterre: Laboratoire d'ethnologie et de sociologie comparative de Nanterre, 1978.

Tsikounas 2010
Myriam Tsikounas, "La publicité, une histoire, des pratiques," *Sociétés & Représentations*, 30 (December 2010): 195–209, https://doi.org/10.3917/sr.030.0195, https://www.cairn.info/revue-societes-et-representations-2010-2-page-195.htm.

Van Zuylen 1994
Gabrielle Van Zuylen, *Tous les jardins du monde*. Paris: Découvertes Gallimard, 1994.

Varichon 2005
Anne Varichon, *Couleurs, pigments et teintures dans les mains des peuples*. Paris: Seuil, 2005.

Varichon 2011
Anne Varichon, *Couleur et nuancier, territoires et fonctions, analyse poïétique de l'échantillonnage de la couleur par les manufactures, l'industrie et le commerce*. Doctoral dissertation in applied arts, Université Toulouse Le Mirail, 2011.

Varichon 2013
Anne Varichon, "Le nuancier, de l'outil pratique de communication de gammes colorées à la palette de signifiés," From the international conference proceedings ORC-IARSIC- ESSACHESS, *Communication du symbolisme et symbolique de la communication dans les sociétés modernes et postmodernes*, 6, no. 1 (2013): 69–87.

Varichon and Roccella 2006
Anne Varichon and Carlo Roccella, *Être Caoutchouc*. Paris: Seuil, 2006.

Viraben 2021
Hadrien Viraben, "Colorier, embellir et s'approprier : un geste d'amateur." Presented at the conference, In Visu: *Gestes d'images*, for the session, "Colorier, décorer" (USR 3103 CNRS-INHA, session: 4 March 2021), http://b-a-t-o-n-s.fr/gestesdimages/pages/intervention1/1.html.

Wartelle 2004
Jean-Claude Wartelle, "La Société d'anthropologie de Paris de 1859 à 1920," *Revue d'histoire des sciences humaines*. Paris: Éditions de la Sorbonne, 10, no. 1 (2004): 125–171.

Weigert 1964
Roger-Armand Weigert, *Textiles en Europe sous Louis XV. Les plus beaux spécimens de la collection Richelieu*, Fribourg, Switzerland: Office du Livre, 1964.

White 1995
Kenneth White, *L'Atelier du Héron, Groupe de géopoétique*, 1 (Fall 1995): 67.

Zola 1977
Zola, Émile. *The Ladies' Paradise*, Brian Nelson (trans.). Oxford: Oxford University Press, 1998, 294. Accessed from Internet Archive, https://archive.org/details/ladiesparadise00zola/page/293/mode/1up?q=%22Not+so+loud%2C+please%21%22.

Zola 1986
Émile Zola, *Carnets d'enquêtes, une ethnographie inédite de la France*, texts compiled/collected and introduced by Henri Mitterrand. Paris: Plon, 1986.

CONTENTS

CREDITS

The titles that appear in italics in the captions of the book are those present on the objects. Those in roman are given by the author.

Albi Couleurs, Association Mémoire des Industries de la Couleur, Albi: pages 58, 71, 72 (bottom), 107 (left), 122 (detail), 130, 131, 133, 136, 138–139, 140 (middle and bottom), 142–143, 145, 148, 149, 150–151, 177 (bottom), 178 (top right and bottom), 191, 216–219, 220–221, 230 (top), 231, 240 (top left), 255 (top).

Anne Varichon collection, Sète: pages 118–119, 128–129, 156 (top), 208 (bottom), 240 (bottom), 254, 256 (detail), 260–262.

Archives of the Hérault department, Montpellier: page 33.

Bibliothèque Forney, Paris: pages 60–61, 67–69, 74, 79, 88–89, 94–95, 96, 98–99, 101, 102, 103, 104, 107 (right), 115, 134–135, 140 (top), 156 (bottom right), 158–159, 160, 164 (top), 164–165, 171, 172, 173, 175, 177 (top), 178 (top left), 192–193, 195, 196, 197, 198, 199, 201, 202, 204, 205, 206, 208 (top), 209, 210–211, 212 (detail), 223 (bottom), 224–225, 226 (bottom), 228, 230 (bottom), 233, 234–235, 237–239, 242 (bottom), 246–247, 248, 249, 251 (top), 253, 255 (bottom).

Bibliothèque Méjanes, Aix-en-Provence: pages 12 (detail), 21–23.

Bibliothèque Nationale de France, Paris: pages 17, 45, 56.

British Library, London © Bridgeman Images: page 19.

© Fourmy/Andia: page 265 (top).

France Lavergne-Cler Collection, Paris: page 156 (bottom left).

Getty Research Institute, Los Angeles: pages 36–37.

Mamie Nova: page 265 (bottom).

Musée de l'Impression sur Étoffes, Mulhouse: page 40.

Musée du Vieux Nîmes, Nîmes: pages 28 (detail), 33, 34, 54–55, 76–77, and cover visual.

© Noortje van Eckelen: page 267.

Ôkhra-Ecomuseum of Ocher, Roussillon: pages 42, 51.

Patrimoine Chanel, Paris: pages 116, 251 (bottom).

Patrimoine Lemarié, Paris: pages 62 (detail), 90, 92–93, 154 (top), 167–170, 226 (top).

Pierre David © Thierry Chassepoux: page 266.

Private collection, Paris: pages 46 (detail), 52–53, 72 (top), 80–81, 83, 85, 154 (middle and bottom), 162–163, 223 (top).

Sennelier family collection, Paris: pages 108, 110, 111, 112–113, 146–147, 180–181, 182–183, 184, 185, 186–187, 188, 190, 240 (top right), 242 (top), 243, 244.

Smithsonian Libraries and Archives, Washington DC: pages 24–25.

ACKNOWLEDGMENTS

I'd like to express my deep gratitude to those who gave me access to their collections, without which I could not have written this book.

Armelle and Dominique Sennelier,
Sylvie Johnson,
France Lavergne-Cler,
Carole Loo and her team, Bibliothèque Forney,
Nadia Rouquette, the members of the association Albi Couleurs and the archives of the Tarn department, also in memory of Annik Chauvel and Jacques Roire, Association Mémoire des Industries de la Couleur,
Élise Giansily, Patrimoine Lemarié,
Mathieu Barrois and the team at Ôkhra, Ecomuseum of Ocher,
Julie Deydier, Patrimoine Chanel,
Aurélie Bosc, Bibliothèque Méjanes,
Sylvie Desachy, archives of the Hérault department, and Dominique Cardon, historian specializing in the history and archeology of textile technologies and organic natural dyes (CNRS),
Lisa Laborie-Barrière and her team, Musée du Vieux Nîmes,
Aziza Gril-Mariotte and Mathilde Humbert, Musée de l'Impression sur Étoffes,
As well as the collectors who wished to remain anonymous.

Many thanks to Philippe Durand Gerzaguet, who agreed to lend his photography skills to this adventure.

Thanks also to all those who, since 2007, have helped with my research by translating texts, contributing information, or directing me to other individuals and resources as I dug deeper.

Shigefumi Akagi,
Mylène Beaufils,
Bruno Belhoste,
Christine Bento,
Alice Besnard,
Dominique Billard,
Barbara Blin-Barrois,
Maxime Bonnike,
Abol Bolour Froushan,
Inge Bösken-Kanold,
Hélène Bras,
Jean-Pierre Brazs,
Françoise Caugan,
Gérard Cazé,
Marion Chataing,
Hélène de Clermont-Gallerande
Elisabeth Condemine,
Sylvie Constantin,
Amandine Corvaisier,
Eva Davidson,
Bertrand Dumas,
Caroline Eude,
Nicolas Flamant,
Anne Galloyer,
Alexandre Godin,
Sylvie Granier,
Brigitte Guillet,
Volkhard Hente,
Erma Hermens,
Michel Indergand,
Jean-Philippe Lenclos,
Marianne Magnin,
Lucie Meunier,
Annie Mollard-Desfour,
Christiane Naffah Bayle,
Jean-Michel Petit,
Elena Phipps,
Florence Quignard-Debuisson,
Doriane Robert,
Carlo Roccella,
Mikuko Sasaki,
Marie-Anne Sarda,
Delphine Terrasson,
Monsieur Toupie,
Bénédicte Van Campen,
François Viol,
Aya Yoda,
Libero Zuppiroli.

A precious color chart of intelligence and goodwill . . .

Finally, thank you to the one who is by my side.

Beyond its functionality, the structure of the color chart produces a captivating feeling of calm.
On its small surface, a memory or an idea can burst forth, and multiple emotions can unfold, from aversion to fascination.
With its variety nicely framed in little boxes, it offers abundance without chaos and peacefully fulfills our aspirations for opulence, while its silent simplicity enables all kinds of wanderings.
It seems able to include everything and creates the illusion of never taking sides.
There is no wildness in this place; even strangeness is identified, channeled, domesticated, and falls in line.
It's an aesthetic and emotional world that is serene, diverse, enclosed, self-sufficient.
Perhaps even the perfect artistic embodiment of fascination and delight.

Image Processing: Chromostyle